INTRODUCTION TO BUSINESS

Fifth Edition

JOSEPH T. STRAUB
Valencia Community College

RAYMOND F. ATTNER
Brookhaven Community College

Wadsworth Publishing Company
Belmont, California
A Division of Wadsworth, Inc.

To Pat and Stacey (J.S.)
and
To Deborah—
my wife, my friend,
my support, my partner (R.A.)

Business Editor: Larry Alexander
Assistant Editor: Karen Mandel
Editorial Assistant: Joan Paterson
Production: Del Mar Associates
Print Buyer: Randy Hurst
Permissions Editor: Judith Gimple
Text and Cover Designer: John Odam
Design Coordinator: Jonathan Parker
Copy Editor: Jackie Estrada
Photo Researcher: Gail Meese
Technical Illustrators: John Odam and Cher Threinen
Digital Typography: John Odam Design Associates
 and Del Mar Associates
Color Separator: Digital Output
Printer: R. R. Donnelley & Sons, Inc.

I(T)P™

International Thomson Publishing
The trademark ITP is used under license

Printed in the United States of America

2 3 4 5 6 7 8 9 10—98 97 96 95 94

Library of Congress Cataloging-in-Publication Data
Straub, Joseph T.
  Introduction to business / Joseph T. Straub, Raymond F. Attner. —
5th ed.
    p. cm.
  ISBN 0-534-21330-8
  1. Industrial management. 2. Business. I. Attner, Raymond F.
II. Title.
HD31.S6965 1994
658—dc20   93-34878
                                                    CIP

CONTENTS

CHAPTER 3
THE UNINCORPORATED BUSINESS: SOLE PROPRIETORSHIPS AND PARTNERSHIPS 67

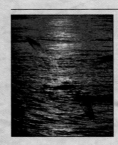

CHAPTER 4
THE MODERN CORPORATION 89

CHAPTER 5
THE SMALL BUSINESS AND FRANCHISING 117

PART TWO
**THE HUMAN
SIDE OF
BUSINESS 151**

CHAPTER 6
**MANAGING
BUSINESS
OGANIZATIONS 153**

CHAPTER 9
MANAGING PEOPLE: MOTIVATION AND LEADERSHIP 257

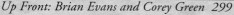

PART THREE
**PRODUCTION
& MARKETING
ACTIVITIES 335**

CHAPTER 11
**PRODUCING THE
PRODUCT 337**

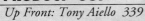

PART FOUR
FINANCE &
MANAGEMENT
INFORMATION
469

CHAPTER 15
MONEY AND FINANCIAL INSTITUTIONS 471

CHAPTER 16
FINANCING FOR PROFITS 497

CHAPTER 17
RISK AND INSURANCE 539

PART FIVE
SPECIAL CHALLENGES & ISSUES 645

CHAPTER 20
BUSINESS LAW AND THE LEGAL ENVIRONMENT OF BUSINESS 647

CHAPTER 21
INTERNATIONAL BUSINESS 675

PREFACE

Basic Intent

Introduction to Business is *not* business as usual. It has been written by authors with a total of forty-seven years of hands-on classroom experience teaching the introductory business course. Our classroom expertise, combined with our grasp of what students and professors need in an introductory business textbook, is apparent in the caliber of the book itself and its supporting teaching/learning materials: student study guide, instructor's manual, test bank, and color overhead transparencies.

Colleagues agree that the introductory business course is the keystone of college-level business programs, and our textbook rises to this challenge:

- *Introduction to Business* gives students a macro view of business that is essential to such advanced and specialized courses as finance, marketing, management, and human relations.
- *Introduction to Business* provides students with meaningful, real-world-oriented information that can play a key role in their success both within and beyond the classroom.
- *Introduction to Business* is specifically designed to give students an integrated view of the dynamic and exciting world of business.

By placing business in perspective and surveying the topic comprehensively, the fifth edition of *Introduction to Business* gives business majors a solid foundation for success in advanced business courses. In addition, the many nonbusiness majors who take the introductory business course as an elective will applaud our thorough and vivid coverage of a subject that touches many aspects of their daily lives. Our text prepares these students to make well-informed consumer decisions and to understand the significant role that business plays in today's national and global society.

Organization

Our decisions about how to organize the sequence of parts and chapters were based on an extensive market survey of professors who teach the introduction to business course. The organization we selected reflects their consensus about how the course and text should be structured.

Part One, The Business Setting, guides students into the course by examining the role of business in our economy, the ethical and social concerns of business, unincorporated and incorporated forms of business organization, and small business and franchising.

Part Two, The Human Side of Business, discusses the importance of and need for management, the functions that managers perform, the roles they play, and the skills they need to do their jobs effectively. This part also addresses the processes, concepts, and alternative designs that managers may choose in order to create a business organization. Following this, we explore the principles and processes managers use to plan for, recruit, select, orient, train, appraise, and compensate their organizations' human resources. This leads to a chapter on the importance of and approaches to working with human resources by building an organizational climate, creating the opportunity for motivation, and providing leadership. Part Two ends with a chapter on labor relations, including exceptional coverage of the principles and objectives of unions, labor history and legislation, the reasons employees join unions, labor and management tactics, the collective bargaining process, the grievance procedure, and mediation and arbitration processes.

Part Three, Production and Marketing Activities, examines and illustrates current production principles and techniques and investigates marketing principles and the elements of product, promotion, distribution, and pricing strategies.

Part Four, Finance and Management Information,

contains chapters on money and financial institutions, finance, risk and insurance, data gathering and processing, and accounting. Our accounting chapter is purposely preceded by one on gathering and processing data so that students will better appreciate the widespread impact of computers on business operations and on the lifestyles of individuals who own, or who plan to purchase, a personal computer. Moreover, we cover the subject of accounting clearly and understandably but without oversimplifying or distorting this complex topic.

Part Five, Special Challenges and Issues, investigates the areas of business law and international business.

Learning Aids

As dedicated classroom teachers, we have invested a great deal of time and effort to create pedagogical devices that help students maximize the return on their investment in our text. The array of learning aids that supplement the fifth edition of *Introduction to Business* set a new standard for business texts.

CHAPTER OUTLINE Each chapter opens with an outline of the topics that will be covered. This outline provides students with a framework for discussion and an overview of the chapter's contents.

CHAPTER OBJECTIVES Chapter Objectives establish benchmarks by which students can measure their success. Organized according to the sequence of chapter topics, they clarify what students should be able to do in order to master the chapter's material.

CHAPTER QUOTATION Each chapter opens with a thought-provoking quotation relating to one or more areas of discussion. This is an upbeat way to launch each new topic.

UP FRONT As business practices often reflect individual attitudes, efforts, and personalities, this edition continues the tradition of preceding editions by presenting Up Front personality profiles for each chapter. These profiles (all new in this edition) feature business leaders whose careers reflect concepts discussed in the chapters.

Our Up Front business personalities provide positive role models for students of all ages and backgrounds. In addition, our Up Fronts personalize the chapter material, giving it a real-world orientation that is essential to an introductory business text.

GLOBAL PERSPECTIVE New to the fifth edition, a Global Perspective box appears in each chapter to acknowledge and showcase the unmistakable trend toward multinational business operations. Each Global Perspective positions a selected aspect of the chapter in an international framework and helps students see that today's successful companies recognize few national boundaries.

YOU DECIDE The You Decide feature, which appears at two strategic points in each chapter, poses thought-provoking questions that students may answer by referring to material just read or to personal experience. The questions encourage introspection and critical thinking while providing a study break.

MANAGER'S NOTEBOOK The Manager's Notebook feature complements each chapter's Up Front by presenting a profile of a company or a contemporary business issue that is linked to chapter concepts or principles. Like the Up Fronts, the Manager's Notebooks give the text real-world focus and credibility. Students come to realize how the material they learn is applied in the world beyond the classroom. All of our Manager's Notebook features, like our Up Front personality profiles, are new to the fifth edition.

SUMMARY Each chapter closes with a concise narrative summary. Students may use the summary as a general review and for placing chapter material in perspective.

KEY TERMS Key terms follow each chapter summary so that students can find the entire chapter's terms in one location. Terms are alphabetized and are followed by the page number where they first appear. And for easy review, all definitions appear in the margin near where terms are first introduced.

REVIEW AND DISCUSSION QUESTIONS We supply a generous number of review and discussion questions that require students to apply the material they have learned and to study and comprehend the vocabulary and concepts presented in the chapter. Our review and discussion questions are thoroughly coordinated with the objectives at the beginning of the chapter. Mastery of these review and discussion questions will ensure that students accomplish the chapter objectives.

CASES All cases in the fifth edition, like the Up Front personality profiles and the Manager's Notebook features, are new. Each chapter contains two cases that encourage students to explore, reflect on, and relate to actual business situations while synthesizing and applying the concepts learned in the chapter. Cases complement the role of the Up Fronts and the Manager's Notebooks by blending theory with practice. They are excellent devices for generating classroom discussion and independent, analytical thought.

Careers

Students are eager to learn about how they can prepare for careers in certain business areas. To meet their expectations, we provide two valuable types of learning aids.

The first, Career Capsules, appear at the end of each of the five parts of the text. They describe the qualifications, training, career opportunities, and challenges associated with jobs at such companies as General Mills, R. R. Donnelley, Agway, Texaco, and General Electric. The Career Capsules expand the text's real-world orientation by giving students a glimpse into career opportunities and challenges offered by businesses whose names are household words.

The second career-oriented learning aid is the Appendix, The Business of Getting a Job. Here we examine in detail how to choose a career (including selecting a major in college), prepare a résumé, locate job openings, and interact with company recruiting activities (including successful interviewing and job offer evaluation). This outstanding feature of the text can be blended with classroom discussion or reading assignments.

Vocabulary

Command of business vocabulary is an integral goal of any introduction to business course, and our text ensures understanding through several techniques. Each key term is printed in boldface and defined in italics where it first appears in the chapter. It is also printed and defined in the margin to draw students' attention to it during chapter review. And, as previously mentioned, key chapter terms, along with their page numbers, are conveniently grouped at the end of each chapter. Finally, every key term and its definition is repeated in a comprehensive glossary at the end of the book. Our reviewers confirm that no other introduction to business text goes to such lengths to help students gain a firm command of the language of business.

Graphics and Photographs

Significant chapter information and relationships are presented effectively and impressively through the use of accent colors and color graphics combined with highly informative tables and figures. Full-color photographs in each chapter, an improvement over the previous edition, give our text striking visual appeal and enhance the impact of chapter topics and learning aids.

A Commitment to Credibility

The fifth edition of *Introduction to Business* was developed through the insightful comments and recommendations of an outstanding team of colleagues who teach the introductory business course at both the community college and university levels. We solicited their input and incorporated their suggestions into every facet of this edition, from the content and sequence of the chapters to the design and layout of the book.

This new edition reflects both our expertise in and dedication to our chosen profession. We share a commitment to translate decades of classroom teaching experience into what we believe will become the new standard of excellence in introduction to business textbooks. We share our commitment to excellence with our publisher, reviewers, adopting professors, and students. Their success is truly a reflection of our own.

Supplemental Items

We realize that many professors place great value on the supplemental items that accompany a text. With the help of our publisher and team of reviewers, we proudly offer the following array of supplements to make teaching and learning about business an exciting and rewarding experience for professors and students alike.

STUDENT STUDY GUIDE Authored by Nancy Carr of the Community College of Philadelphia, the self-paced study guide contains questions in several formats that promote thorough vocabulary mastery and command of chapter concepts.

INSTRUCTOR'S MANUAL The fifth edition of *Introduction to Business* offers a state-of-the-art instructor's manual second to none. It contains:

- Detailed lecture outlines for each chapter
- Suggested course outlines

- Suggested references, including business periodicals, films, and sources of guest speakers
- Course-building activities that will help you gather material to supplement and enhance classroom discussion
- Answers to all the questions and case problems contained in the textbook and the study guide

MORE THAN 100 MULTICOLORED ACETATE TRANSPARENCIES Transparencies are keyed to the text chapters, and many of them present information that does not appear in the text. They may be used in conjunction with the Instructor's Manual's detailed lecture outlines to illustrate various chapter concepts, promote class discussion, and supplement the instructor's personal file of transparencies.

TEST BANK The comprehensive Test Bank containing over 2,100 questions is provided to adopters of *Introduction to Business,* fifth edition. The Test Bank, which has been extensively revised for this edition, contains a balanced mix of true/false and multiple-choice questions for each chapter, further categorized by chapter objective. Codes for each question indicate the type of question (either fact recall or application), the correct answer, and the page in the text on which the answer can be found. These codes are found in the margin and can easily be blocked out if the instructor wishes to photocopy pages for use in class testing.

Highlights of This Edition

We have already stated that numerous chapter elements, including Up Fronts, Manager's Notebooks, and cases, have been completely replaced in the fifth edition. We also want to emphasize that the statistics cited in chapter body material have been thoroughly updated. Data in charts, graphs, and tables that illustrate and enrich chapter discussions have been updated to reflect changes in the business environment. Following are chapter highlights for this edition.

Part 1—The Business Setting

Chapter 1 *The Role of Business in Our Economic Setting*

New discussion of the functions and activities inherent in all businesses.

Expanded discussion of socialism and communism as economic systems.

Expanded discussion of evaluating the performance of economic systems featuring gross domestic product (GDP).

New discussion of the trends and challenges facing today's businesses.

New discussion of the keys to being successful in business.

Chapter 2 *The Social and Ethical Environment of Business*

New discussion of the stakeholders of business.

New discussion of the three approaches to social responsibility: resistant, reactive, and proactive.

Revised and expanded discussion of the areas a company may pursue for social responsibility.

Updated and expanded discussion of environmental responsibility.

Updated and expanded discussion of consumer protection.

Revised and expanded discussion of top management's commitment to social responsibility.

New discussion of unethical business practices.

New discussion of causes of unethical practices.

New discussion of how to encourage ethical behavior.

Chapter 3 *The Unincorporated Business: Sole Proprietorships and Partnerships*

New discussion of deciding which legal form of business is best.

Revised and expanded discussion of the advantages and disadvantages of the sole proprietorship.

Revised and expanded discussion of the advantages and disadvantages of partnerships.

Updated discussion of joint ventures.

New discussion of how to make a partnership work.

Chapter 4 *The Modern Corporation*

Updated information on mergers and acquisitions, including recent examples of horizontal and conglomerate mergers.

New discussion of professional corporations (also known as professional associations, or PAs).

Chapter 5 *The Small Business and Franchising*

Expanded discussion of the significant role that small businesses play in creating new jobs.

New discussion of the roles and contents of a business plan.

New discussion of business format franchises and product or trade name franchises.

New discussion of major areas that should be investigated before signing a franchise contract.

New discussion of the traits of a successful franchisee.

Revised and expanded discussion of how Federal Trade Commission regulations may help prospective franchisees decide whether or not to purchase a franchise.

Career Capsule 1—
Career Opportunities at General Mills

Part 2—The Human Side of Business

Chapter 6 *Managing Business Organizations*

New discussion of the manager's environment.

New discussion of the myths and realities of a manager's job.

New discussion of the areas of management.

Revised and expanded discussion of management roles.

New discussion of total quality management (TQM).

Chapter 7 *Designing an Organization Structure*

New discussion of downsizing an organization.

New discussion of power and the sources of power.

Revised, expanded, and updated discussion of contemporary organizational structures, including team and network designs.

Revised and expanded discussion of the informal organization.

Chapter 8 *Human Resources Management*

Updated discussion of the legal environment of human resources.

New discussion of sexual harassment, cultural diversity, glass ceilings and glass walls, AIDS, and drug testing.

Revised discussion of the employee selection process.

Updated and expanded discussion of compensation factors and compensation types.

New discussion of the Americans with Disabilities Act.

Chapter 9 *Managing People: Motivation and Leadership*

New discussion of developing a positive work environment, quality of work life (QWL), and morale.

New discussion of developing management expectations: the self-fulfilling prophecy.

New discussion of providing support in the work environment and recognizing cultural diversity.

New discussion of Vroom's expectancy theory of motivation.

New discussion of leadership traits.

New discussion of management versus leadership.

Revised and expanded discussion of leadership styles.

New discussion of empowering employees.

New discussion of developing self-directed work teams.

New discussion of providing an effective reward system.

Revised and expanded discussion of redesigning jobs.

New discussion of promoting intrapreneurship.

Chapter 10 *Labor-Management Relations*

Revised and expanded discussion of the history of labor unions.

New discussion of labor and the law.

Updated union membership statistics.

Updated discussion of problems facing unions.

Updated and expanded future trends and directions of the unions.

New discussion of the steps in the union organizing process.

Revised, updated, and expanded discussion of management and labor bargaining issues.

Updated discussion of management and labor negotiating tools.

Career Capsule 2—
Career Opportunities at R. R. Donnelley

Part 3—Production and Marketing Activities

Chapter 11 *Producing the Product*

Updated examples illustrating the assembly, continuous, and intermittent production processes.

New discussion of computer-aided design (CAD),

computer-aided manufacturing (CAM), and computer-integrated manufacturing (CIM).

Updated information on the use of robotics.

Updated examples of make-or-buy decisions.

New discussion of single-source versus multisource buying.

New discussion of just-in-time (JIT) inventory systems.

New discussion of the role of quality engineers in improving product quality.

New discussion of total quality management (TQM).

Chapter 12 *Marketing and Product Strategy*

New discussion of the value of marketing.

Expanded discussion of implementing the marketing concept.

Updated and revised discussion of the process for developing a marketing strategy.

Updated and revised discussion of industrial products.

Revised and updated discussion of brand strategy.

Updated and expanded discussion of the product life cycle.

New discussion of new product development.

Chapter 13 *Marketing Promotional Strategy*

Revised discussion of consumer buying motives and industrial buying motives.

New discussion of advertising media.

Updated discussion of truth in advertising.

Expanded discussion of the nature of publicity.

Revised and expanded discussion of promoting to final consumers.

Revised and expanded discussion of promoting to middlemen.

Chapter 14 *Distribution and Pricing Strategy*

Revised and expanded discussion of the criteria for selecting a distribution channel.

Revised, updated, and expanded discussion of retailing middlemen.

New discussion of off-price retailers and warehouse clubs.

Updated and expanded discussion of out-of-store retailing.

Revised and expanded discussion of the physical distribution system.

New discussion of the modes of transportation.

Revised and expanded discussion of pricing strategies.

New discussion of power retailers in the marketplace.

Career Capsule 3—
Management Opportunities at Agway, Inc.

Part 4—Finance and Management Information

Chapter 15 *Money and Financial Institutions*

New discussion of techniques used to deter counterfeiting.

Additional information on the purchase and sale of Treasury bills.

Expanded discussion of the impact of changes in the discount rate.

New discussion of the role of bankers and their responses to the Federal Deposit Insurance Corporation Improvement Act (FDICIA).

Updated discussion of the current status of commercial bank failures and interstate banking.

Updated discussion of the status of the savings and loan bailout and the work of the Resolution Trust Corporation.

New discussion of savings banks.

Chapter 16 *Financing for Profits*

New discussion of how the Securities and Exchange Commission's disclosure requirements affect information provided on proxy forms.

New discussion of the Investment Company Act and the Investment Advisers Act.

New discussion of how stock splits and stock dividends affect the number and value of an investor's shares.

New discussion of mutual funds, including front-end load, back-end load, and no-load funds.

Chapter 17 *Risk and Insurance*

New discussion of the steps some corporations have taken to protect key executives from being kidnapped.

New discussion of how consumers can investigate an insurance company's financial condition and ability to pay policyholders' claims.

Updated discussion of the status of Lloyd's of London.

New discussion of the impact of Hurricane Andrew on insurance claims and premiums.

Chapter 18 *Managing Information*

New discussion of speech-recognition programs.

New discussion of computer networking, including local area networks and wide area networks.

New discussion of the current and potential applications of virtual reality.

Chapter 19 *Accounting for Profits*

Updated discussion of the audit function's role in ensuring that a company's financial statements fairly represent its financial condition.

New discussion of the role and importance of a cash flow statement.

New discussion of the impact that the Financial Accounting Standards Board's Standard 106 (reporting the cost of retirees' health care benefits) has made on companies' financial performance.

Career Capsule 4—
Career Opportunities with Texaco

Part 5—Special Challenges and Issues

Chapter 20 *Business Law and the Legal Environment of Business*

New discussion of the number of U.S. patents granted by nationality of the inventor.

New discussion of how patents may be awarded to co-inventors.

New discussion of the impact that an expiring patent has on a company's sales and profits.

New discussion of commercial use as a prerequisite to maintaining the rights to a registered trademark.

Updated information on bankruptcies.

Chapter 21 *International Business*

Revised and updated discussion of the scope and importance of international trade.

Revised and updated discussion of United States importing and exporting.

Updated statistics on the scope of international trade.

Updated statistics on companies engaged in international trade.

Expanded discussion of the concepts associated with international trade.

Revised discussion of absolute and comparative advantage.

New discussion of why businesses go international.

Revised and expanded discussion of alternative approaches in international business.

Updated and revised discussion of barriers to international trade.

Revised and updated discussion of aids to international trade.

Updated discussion of the European Community (EC).

New discussion of a company's strategy for globalization.

Career Capsule 5—
Career Opportunities with General Electric

Appendix—The Business of Getting a Job

Acknowledgments

We would like to thank the following reviewers whose comments and suggestions for this edition of *Introduction to Business* were invaluable: Bert T. Adkins, Eastern Kentucky University; Jose Duran, Riverside Community College; Gene Hastings, Portland Community College–Sylvania; Gary Selk, University of Alaska; George Tanner, Colorado Mountain College; and J. Robert Ulbrich, Parkland College.

Joseph T. Straub   *Raymond F. Attner*

A STRATEGIC PLAN FOR LEARNING

with *Straub & Attner's* *Introduction to Business,* *Fifth Edition*

- **Establish goals**
- **Organize to accomplish those goals**
- **Apply the organization effectively**
- **Analyze effectiveness in terms of goal achievement**

Successful business operations depend on these elements. So does this text. You can use the same strategic planning to master the material presented in *Introduction to Business.*

The **goal** of this text is the same as the goal of the course you are taking: to introduce you to the role business plays and how it functions on individual, national, and global levels.

The **organization** of the book is logical, building on a five-part framework that considers—in order—the business setting, the human side of business, production and marketing activities, finance and management information, and legal and international issues.

Within this structure, individual chapters use a number of devices consistently: **applications** features that provide a real-world perspective on theory and **analysis** features that aid learning.

In *Introduction to Business,* all of these elements work together for effective learning. On the following pages, you will find specific examples of ways to use its carefully crafted design to fully understand the principles that govern successful business operations today.

A STRATEGIC STUDY PLAN

To help you organize your study effectively, every chapter follows this consistent format:

Chapter outlines. The first page of each chapter presents an overview of the topics covered that you can use as a framework for study.

We will never give up the principle of decentralization, which is to give our operating executives ownership of a business. They are ultimately accountable.

RALPH LARSEN
CEO, Johnson & Johnson

CHAPTER OBJECTIVES

After studying this chapter, you should be able to:

1. Explain the importance of the organizing process.
2. List and describe the five steps in the organizing process.
3. Identify the four forms of departmentalization and the situations in which each would be appropriate.
4. Define authority, and explain the differences among line, staff, and functional authority.
5. Explain the concept of power and its sources.
6. Relate the concepts of delegation of authority, responsibility, and accountability.
7. Explain the organizational concepts of span of control and centralization and decentralization.
8. Differentiate among line, line-and-staff, matrix, team, and network organization structures.
9. Explain the nature of the informal organization.

Chapter objectives, listed in the same order that topics are covered, establish goals for learning before you start the chapter. Refer back to these objectives to check your progress and identify areas that require further study.

A summary at the end of each chapter offers a capsule version of main points that you can use as a convenient way to review.

Key terms, with page references to definitions, provide a quick guide to reviewing vocabulary introduced in the chapter.

"For Review and Discussion" activities coordinated with each chapter's objectives allow you to test your understanding of concepts and your ability to analyze and apply those concepts to actual business situations.

SUMMARY

Today's business firms operate in an environment of interdependence with society and government. Out of this interdependence has come the realization that they must pursue their overriding goal of profit within a social and political framework. Business decisions must be made while evaluating their total effects on business's stakeholders: investors, employees, consumers, suppliers, and the community.

This in turn has led to an emphasis on social responsibility—the belief that business decisions should be made within the confines of both social and economic considerations.

Businesses can adopt one of three approaches to the demands made on them by social responsibility: to resist, to react, or to be proactive.

Many businesses have taken a proactive approach in the community. Companies have approached social responsibility from multiple directions, including community involvement, small-business investment, and urban renewal. Many business leaders have also made commitments to education. Recognizing that the future of their corporations, their communities, and their country is directly linked to the opportunities for and quality of education and job training, corporations have provided funds, personnel, and equipment.

In the area of employment policies and programs, businesses are addressing wide-ranging areas of concern, including employment opportunities for minorities and women, employing the disabled, employee health, and family-friendly programs.

Although a long way from perfection, businesses have been addressing environmental concerns. They have focused attention on disposal of hazardous and solid wastes and maintenance of air, land, and water resources. Business has also initiated programs to support energy conservation. Not only has business attempted alternative sources of energy, but it has initiated programs to reduce energy consumption through improved operations and van pooling.

Consumerism—consumer protection—has been a major concern for business. Companies have concentrated on improving product safety, providing consumer information, offering consumers a choice of products in the marketplace, and providing means for consumers to be heard.

Ethics are the standards that govern moral conduct. They are important because they affect all business transactions. The problem in the business environment is that ethics have been modified by changing situations. The factors that influence ethics include the competitive business environment, the organizational climate, and individual personal values. Business ethics depend on each employee's code of ethics and on the development and reinforcement of a company code of ethics.

KEY TERMS

FOR REVIEW AND DISCUSSION

1. Explain in your own words what is meant by social responsibility.
2. Why do you think companies have become socially responsive? Do you believe their actions have been voluntary or involuntary? Why?

3. Distinguish between the three approaches a company can take toward social responsibility. For each approach write one sentence that describes management's operating philosophy on social responsibility.

Case studies blend reality with theory. They present real, contemporary business problems and ask you to apply the chapter's concepts to their solution. Two of these interesting cases appear at the end of each chapter; their questions encourage you to analyze the issues critically on your own.

References to up-to-date sources guide you to additional information for independent study or research papers that may be assigned in your course.

Case 4.2: Strategic Alliances Make Strange Bedfellows

The computer industry, like many other high tech trades, was once a ground for astonishingly high-profit startups and equally quick failures. Multibillion-dollar companies such as Apple Computer and Microsoft, started on shoestrings, gained incredible prominence through excellent engineering or simple luck.

Today the industry is more mature and startups are less frequently successful. In fact, even major corporations have found it necessary to form strategic alliances in order to stay competitive. Computer companies in particular have found themselves constantly making and breaking alliances in order to gain market share.

An example of the constantly shifting alliances between computer giants is the relationship between IBM and Microsoft. Strong business partners in the early 1980s, the two companies had a falling out over a jointly developed product. Microsoft developed an operating system for IBM called OS/2, then later came out with a competing product named Windows NT. IBM retaliated by forming counter-alliances with other computer companies such as Apple. The ties between the companies were not severed, however, and when IBM was searching for a new CEO, the founder of Microsoft, Bill Gates, was informally consulted. The man who was chosen, Louis Gerstner, has met with Bill Gates and there has been a warming of relationships. This trend of improving relationships has not eliminated the competition between the companies, however. IBM has continued to position OS/2 as a competing product to Windows NT. With various divisions of IBM producing software that will compete with Microsoft and yet other divisions making products that will be sold with bundled Microsoft's Windows NT, it is clear that a great amount of alliance shifting will be going on in the future.

Strategic alliances are becoming prevalent in other high tech fields. New technologies, new standards, and new markets all cause major corporations to seek alliances with each other in order to share technology, resources, and clout as well as to become more competitive with Japanese firms. Other industries where alliances have become common are video and telecommunications. American A/V manufacturers have worked together to create technologies for the new high-definition television (HDTV) standard, while both telephone and cable companies are trying to dominate the emerging market for interactive television services.

Questions

1. How do alliances between corporations fit into the model of corporations presented in the chapter?

2. What disadvantages are brought about by the alliance/counteralliance business climate?

3. Does the business climate caused by alliances result in more competitive business or merely more complicated business?

4. What other major U.S. industries could use cooperative efforts to improve their performance against foreign competitors?

5. Should the government oversee or facilitate cooperative ventures? Why or why not?

For more information, see G. Pascal Zachary, "Chiefs of IBM, Microsoft Corp. Plan to Meet," *The Wall Street Journal*, May 10, 1993, p. A3.

REFERENCES

1. "Merrill Lynch Business Brokerage and Valuation Says Number of Mergers and Acquisitions Announced in 1992 Were the Highest in Six Years." (Press release issued by Doremus & Company, January 25, 1993)

2. Rita Koselka, "Candy Wars," *Forbes*, August 17, 1992, p. 76.

3. Seth Lubove, "How to Grow Big Yet Stay Small," *Forbes*, December 7, 1992, p. 64.

4. Rick Tetzeli, "Johnson Controls: Mining Money in Mature Markets," *Fortune*, March 22, 1993, p. 77.

---

affirmative action
Requiring employers to make an extra effort to hire and promote members of protected groups.

AFFIRMATIVE ACTION Some laws go beyond prohibiting discrimination. Laws that mandate **affirmative action** *require employers to make an extra effort to hire and promote members of protected groups.* Affirmative action laws apply to employers that have, in the past, practiced discrimination or failed to develop a work force that is representative of the whole population of their community. (Under current laws, affirmative action is not required with regard to disabled Americans.) The fact that an organization has an affirmative action plan does not necessarily mean that the organization practiced unfair employment practices in the past, however. Managers of many organizations choose to develop affirmative action plans even when the law does not require them to do so. Affirmative action plans must identify how the organization plans to take aggressive or affirmative steps in recruiting, hiring, developing, and promoting, and ultimately how it will achieve greater representation of and equity for protected groups.

YOU DECIDE

Why do you think discrimination in employment occurs? If you were discriminated against, what would you do? Why?

sexual harassment
Unwelcome sexual advances, requests for sexual favors, or verbal or physical conduct of a sexual nature on the job.

SEXUAL HARASSMENT Title VII of the Civil Rights Act and guidelines established by the EEOC prohibit sexual harassment.[3] **Sexual harassment** includes *unwelcome sexual advances, requests for sexual favors, and other verbal or physical conduct of a sexual nature on the job* when

- Submission to such conduct is an explicit or implicit term or condition of employment.
- Submission to or rejection of such conduct is used as a basis for any employment decision.
- Such conduct has the purpose of unreasonably interfering with the individual's work performance or creating an intimidating, hostile, or offensive working environment.

This issue exploded into the national spotlight in 1991 when hearings of the Senate Judiciary Committee were broadcast on television. The hearings concerned allegations of sexual harassment made by Anita Hill, a University of Oklahoma law professor, about her ex-boss, Clarence Thomas, who was then a nominee for the Supreme Court. The hearings produced a renewed focus on the importance and consequences of sexual harassment. Managers in every industry should work to prevent harassment and establish procedures for dealing with it properly when it does occur. Sexual harassment can severely damage morale and undermine productivity and quality.

Violations of sexual harassment laws can be expensive. Settlements have been as large as $500,000. Louis W. Brydges, Jr., a management-labor attorney in Chicago, urges companies to create a policy statement telling everyone in the workplace that sexual harassment will not be tolerated and that those engaging in it will be disciplined.[4]

Key terms, essential to your business vocabulary, are highlighted in boldface type and defined in italic type within the text where they are first used and are placed in the margin as well for easy review. (They are also listed at the end of each chapter and defined in the Glossary at the end of the book.)

"You Decide" boxes (two per chapter) purposely interrupt the text at strategic points. They are designed to make you think critically about material you have just read and apply the concepts, often in terms of your own experience.

APPLICATIONS FOR UNDER- STANDING

Translating abstract ideas into practical, real-world examples, these special elements appear in every chapter to illustrate how business actually works:

"Up Front" profiles show how men and women can achieve rewarding careers in the dynamic world of business. These contemporary success stories personalize the concepts presented in the chapter and serve as role models for your own career planning.

"Global Perspective" boxes place chapter material in a multinational context. They expand your horizons and help you grasp the international impact of today's business environment.

UP FRONT

Brian Evans and Corey Green illustrate a redefinition of how employers and employees, management and labor, can work together in contemporary America. They are work unit module managers at Saturn, the GM auto company that was designed from scratch—from management to labor relations, from design to manufacturing—to address "the sins of the fathers" and become the American automaker of the future. If sales are any indication of success, we can note that Saturn is only the second automaker in U.S. history for which each of its dealers each sold over 1,000 cars in one year.

Although Evans and Green share the title of work unit module adviser, they represent two sides of the management-union coin. Evans is responsible for long-range planning and short-term problem solving, managing people, and addressing issues of product quality. Green represents the United Auto Workers and the plant workers, providing support and resources for people with concerns and needs. "We value people here," says Green, "and try to involve the union worker more in the processes of the auto business than has ever been done at any other company."

Each work unit module at Saturn is made up of several work teams. Each team, usually consisting of six to thirteen members, is represented by a work unit counselor (WUC). The WUC is elected by the team to represent them and is a counselor to the union. The WUCs report to the work unit module advisers (WUMAs), in

this case Green and Evans, who are WUMAs in the final process area, the last stops for Saturn autos on the assembly line.

Green worked his way through General Motors at the Delco-Remy division, as a team leader, as an auditor, and in customer supplier relations. At Saturn he was a charter team member, the first person in one of Saturn's teams. He was a WUC before becoming a WUMA.

Evans came to Saturn from a college work-study program, first working in human relations to help hire the first Saturn employees and administer salary programs. He became an Equal Employment Opportunity counselor and helped administer the work-study program before asking for responsibility on the shop floor. "I didn't know a lot about building cars, so I got a job in the doors module," he says. Later, he was promoted to his current WUMA position in the final process work unit.

Brian Evans and Corey Green share an office, "where sometimes our distinct duties overlap, but all in all we try to keep a shared vision of our work," says Corey. "We beat up on ourselves daily, and sometimes we agree to disagree, but we get the issues out on the table and we deal with them," adds Brian. They work with their work teams to ensure that Saturn's goals are being met.

BRIAN EVANS AND COREY GREEN

WORK UNIT MODULE MANAGERS, SATURN CORPORATION

GLOBAL PERSPECTIVE

Multinational manufacturing has become a way of life. American manufacturers routinely make parts and assemble final products in other countries, while their foreign competitors set up shop in the United States. For example:

- General Motors employs approximately 68,000 people in Mexico to build vehicles and assemble components such as electrical wiring harnesses from parts manufactured in the United States.
- Rubbermaid planned to invest between $1.3 million and $1.5 million in 1993 to upgrade its plastics and rubber molding plants in Mexico. The plants make approximately 120 products from trash cans to tool boxes.
- Levi Strauss & Co. has eighty-two production, finishing, and customer service facilities in twenty-three countries and usually manufactures clothing in the countries or regions where they will be sold.
- There are more than 1,500 Japanese-affiliated factories in the United States. Most of them are entirely owned by a Japanese firm. Honda now has more than 25 percent of its manufacturing capacity in the United States. The company has invested $3 billion in the United

States and $230 million in Canada to build research and development, tool-making, engine production, and vehicle assembly facilities.
- More than 200 German companies, including such giants as BMW and Siemens, have spent $4 billion to build plants in North and South Carolina.

These examples imply at least one thing: manufacturers who compete in the global business arena tend to ignore artificial and geographic boundaries when they establish or expand production facilities. Building component or final-assembly plants in other countries often enables firms to take advantage of lower labor and real estate costs and to minimize the shipping expense to get their finished products to a major market.

Manufacturing: A Transnational Activity

[For more on foreign companies in the United States and vice versa, see Mike Allen and Jim Dunn, "America Goes International," *Popular Mechanics*, October 1992, p. 37; Bill Bregar, "Rubbermaid Upgrading Mexican Plant," *Plastics News*, February 22, 1993, p. 1; "Japan's U.S. Plants Up 9% in 1991," *Fortune*, April 20, 1992, p. 16; and Robert M. Ady, "Why BMW Cruised Into Spartanburg," *The Wall Street Journal*, July 6, 1992, p. 10.]

Loctite Corporation, which makes a variety of adhesives and sealants including the popular Super Glue, recently built a plant in Ireland to manufacture adhesives for many of the eighty-odd countries in which the company's products are sold. (Different languages pose no problem; a computerized system prints labels in the language of the country where the product is being shipped.[1])

MANAGER'S NOTEBOOK

A not-so-quiet revolution is under way in organizations throughout the United States. This revolution focuses on the need to improve quality—quality as a gateway to survival, competitiveness, long-range productivity, and profitability.

For years managers gave quality a nod and then went about the business of the business—developing or delivering a product, process, or service. But, that product, process, or service did not necessarily contain the overall features and characteristics that truly satisfied the stated (or implied) requirements of either the producers or the users.

Today managers at all levels in an organization are becoming engulfed in the business of quality. This quality focus, called *total quality management (TQM)*, involves much more than an individual manager's efforts. Rather, it is a company-wide effort to ensure that quality is an integral part of an organization's culture and operation. Companies such as Motorola, Hewlett-Packard, Ford, Texas Instruments, and Xerox have made the commitment to TQM.

In general, TQM embraces four essential elements:

1. Intense efforts to satisfy customers.
2. Accurate standards of measurement of every critical operation. These standards help identify problems and eliminate their causes.
3. Work relationships based on trust and teamwork. Central to TQM is *empowerment*—managers giving employees autonomy and support and motivating them to give their best. TQM must be a part of suppliers' culture and activities as well.
4. Continual improvement of processes, products, and services.

To be successful, TQM requires 100 percent commitment from everyone. Past efforts by companies to improve quality did not work because they were too dependent on a few people and not company-wide, committed efforts. Specifically:

Total Quality Means Total Commitment

- Top management must show a personal commitment to TQM. This commitment is expressed in actively discussing the need for quality improvement; developing written mission statements, value statements, and policies focusing on quality; removing fear from the workplace; and living the values of TQM.
- Middle managers must be active participants in planning for quality and quality control. They must have the authority and responsibility to execute plans and deal with problems. Middle management needs to develop systems that encourage and ensure cooperation and communication. Specific actions that can be taken include creating cross-functional teams, rearranging work flow and reassigning tasks, developing incentives and rewards to encourage cooperation, and creating accountability for internal customers.
- First-line management, team leaders, and employees must have a say in planning and in executing plans. First-line managers need to involve employees in decision making, to remove the fear of failure and blame for making mistakes, and to give workers the authority, training, and incentives to promote quality.

Total quality management is everyone's concern. To be successful, it requires total commitment at all levels.

(For more about total quality management, see Michael Barrier, "Putting Quality First," *Nation's Business*, May 1993, pp. 55–59.)

"Manager's Notebook" features link each chapter's topics to a contemporary business issue or company profile. In common with the "Up Front" personality profiles, these vignettes illustrate how material in the text applies to the real world you will find outside the classroom.

CAREER CAPSULE 1

Career Opportunities at General Mills

Echoing the slogan of its popular Wheaties breakfast cereal, General Mills calls itself "The Company of Champions." This global corporation recruits innovative, aggressive college graduates who thrive on challenge, relish competition, and pursue unlimited opportunity.

With annual sales of more than $7.1 billion, General Mills enjoys an enviable reputation not only in the packaged food industry but also as a restaurateur through its popular Red Lobster and Olive Garden restaurant chains. It's no surprise, then, that General Mills offers exceptional career opportunities for men and women in many fields. The company promotes from within; management assures employees that outstanding performance will be rewarded with advancement and incentives.

What's it like to work for General Mills? Here are profiles of several areas.

- Employees who work in *marketing management* have the opportunity to become involved with a broad range of products. They're challenged to be creative, decisive, and analytical and to work successfully with a broad range of people. The projects and products to which they're assigned provide a wealth of team-oriented general management experience that includes setting strategic sales and market-share goals; helping to develop and evaluate advertising campaigns; making plans for product promotional activities; and dealing with the production and distribution decisions required to bring General Mills's products to market. Such activities prepare them to reach their full potential during their career with the company.

- Employees who work in *finance* are responsible for improving the company's financial position and keeping production costs to a minimum. This requires a blend of analytical, managerial, and interpersonal skills, backed by a degree in business administration, accounting, finance, economics, or liberal arts. Graduates with bachelor's degrees begin work as financial associates, cost accountants, or financial auditors. They're responsible for financial analysis and for reporting information about ongoing company operations. Graduates with M.B.A. (master of business administration) degrees are immediately involved in evaluating and analyzing various projects and operations from a financial perspective.
- Employees in *human resources management* have often done graduate-level work in human resources, industrial relations, or business administration. After joining the company, they may be responsible for such activities as recruitment, hiring and placement, orientation, wage and salary administration, training, and labor relations. Human resources management employees may work in various plants or subsidiary companies or in divisions at General Mills's corporate headquarters in Minneapolis.
- Employees who work in *information systems* are exposed to every aspect of the business. After identifying key information that employees in other divisions need in order to make timely decisions, they design data processing systems to gather, summarize, and deliver that information quickly and accurately to colleagues throughout the company, who will use it to keep the business competitive and productive.

"Career Capsules"—at the end of each part of the text—describe opportunities and challenges you will encounter in typical business organizations. They help you succeed in your choice of a future business career.

UNDERSTANDING— BY DESIGN

Written text and graphics work together in this book. All of the design elements are carefully integrated with the written matter to emphasize, personalize, and organize important information. Colorful photographs, charts, and diagrams—like the ones shown here—appear on practically every page. These strategically placed graphics do much more than make the book attractive: they help you grasp, retain, and apply concepts and theories.

Figure 3.3
The most popular sole proprietorships.

Source: U.S. Bureau of the Census, *Statistical Abstract of the United States, 1992*, 112th ed. (Washington, D.C.: U.S. Government Printing Office, 1992), p. 519.

- *Freedom in decision making.* As the owner and the boss, the sole proprietor enjoys freedom and flexibility in decision making. Decisions can be made promptly, without consulting others. This freedom and control also allows the sole proprietor to react quickly to changes in business conditions—without having to discuss the reasons why.
- *Personal satisfaction.* Sole proprietors enjoy the satisfaction that comes from personal achievement. Entrepreneurs who form sole proprietorships are highly motivated to achieve, desire independence, and place success or failure solely within their abilities. As a result of their actions, they personally can enjoy the rewards.

Most local retail stores and services are sole proprietorships.

FORM OF OWNERSHIP	ADVANTAGES	DISADVANTAGES
Sole proprietorship	Easy to establish.	Owner has unlimited liability.
	Owner retains all profits.	Funds for expansion may be difficult to obtain.
	Owner enjoys relative freedom and flexibility in decision making.	Owner's lack of business skills may impede success.
	Owner gets satisfaction and independence.	Employee lack opportunities.
	Easy to dissolve.	Business lacks continuity; it dies when owner dies.
General partnership	Individuals with diverse talents can pool knowledge and skills.	Partners may have conflicting personalities, ideas, and interests.
	More funds may be more easily available than for sole proprietorship.	Business lacks permanence.
	There is the potential for a better credit rating than sole proprietorship can obtain.	General partners have unlimited liability.
		Investments are frozen.
		Value of partners' claims may be disputed.
	Valuable employees can be retained by allowing them to become partners.	
Corporation	Owners have limited liability.	More expensive and complicated to organize.
	Easy to expand.	Taxes are frequently higher.
	Easy to transfer ownership.	Government restrictions and reporting requirements can be costly and time consuming.
	Business can have relatively long life.	Employees may lack identification with and commitment to corporate goals.
	First-rate, specialized managers can be hired and kept more easily.	

income (regardless of whether the amount was actually paid to them), and it is taxed at their personal income tax rate. This may be a clear advantage, because the maximum personal income tax rate is now 28 percent, while the maximum corporate rate is 34 percent.

Table 4.3
Advantages and disadvantages of the three forms of business ownership.

The Subchapter S Revision Act of 1982 made several significant changes in the conditions and qualifications that apply to S (formerly called Subchapter S) corporations. Major conditions are:

1. The firm must be chartered in the United States.
2. Only one class of stock may exist.
3. A maximum of thirty-five stockholders is allowed.
4. Shareholders must be individuals or estates.

The steps in a grievance procedure are not standardized in all labor-management contracts, but a typical sequence of events, as shown in Figure 10.4, is as follows:

union steward
An employee who has been elected by fellow union members to serve as their representative.

Step 1. An employee with a grievance takes his or her complaint to a **union steward**—*an employee who has been elected by fellow union members to serve as their representative.* Both the shop steward and the employee present the grievance to the employee's supervisor. Normally both the grievance and the supervisor's response are put in writing.
Step 2. If the union steward and the supervisor cannot reach agreement, the matter will be forwarded to the chief union steward and the supervisor's boss. The supervisor, union steward, and employee participate.

Figure 10.4
Steps in a grievance procedure.

Part One
The Business Setting

1

THE ROLE OF BUSINESS IN OUR ECONOMIC SETTING

*W*e Russians do have the spirit of entrepreneurship. Hey, we are better *than Germans or Frenchmen or Americans. If these bureaucrats would leave us alone, we could do wonders here.*

VERA PAVLOVA
*Co-manager, Dmitrieve Cheese Shop
Nizhny Novgorod, Russia*

CHAPTER OBJECTIVES
After studying this chapter, you should be able to:

1. Describe the types of business firms that compose the American business system.
2. Identify and explain the four factors of production.
3. Distinguish among the economic systems of capitalism, socialism, and communism.
4. Describe the principles or rights of the private enterprise system.
5. Explain the evolution of the American business system.
6. Identify and discuss the challenges that business will face in the future.
7. Identify four reasons for studying business.

UP FRONT

If anyone had told Eliot Weinstock when he graduated from Brooklyn College with a degree in psychology that one day he would preside over an empire of twenty optometry boutiques, he would have thought it was a joke. At that time he was headed for teaching high school. There he found out that many students had learning problems. "Many of these problems were really vision problems," he recalls, "which led to my desire to help correct those problems with proper eye care. I left teaching to attend the Massachusetts College of Optometry, and after graduating I joined with another optometrist and opened a practice near Harvard Square."

This was the first office of Cambridge Eye, where Weinstock was one of the first optometrists in the country to offer affordable eye care. Day after day, patients would sit in the tiny waiting room while he and his partner conducted eye exams in the adjacent office. "There were four factors that made us successful," he says. "One was that soft contact lenses were just becoming popular, and everyone wanted them. Unfortunately, the price most charged for them was around $300. Another factor was the baby boom, so we had lots of customers. The Federal Trade Commission had recently allowed professionals to advertise, so we could publicly offer an eye exam and soft contacts for $99. The last was that our offices had been a storage closet for a real estate company. In other words, we had very low rent."

Yet another factor played an important role in Eliot Weinstock's success: his personal values system. "What you do has a lot to do with who you are, as a person. I wasn't into people telling me what to do, so it was good for me, being in business for myself. I wasn't really into earning a lot of money, but I wanted people to have good eye care at a reasonable price. These were things that were part of my personal philosophy then. Now I guess it's called a marketing philosophy."

Whatever the philosophy, Eliot Weinstock created an innovation he calls *integrated eye care*, in which the client is examined by an optometrist and then fitted with glasses or contact lenses by a dispensing optician, both at the same premises. "I believed there should be some rapport between the doctor and the optician, to help select the proper eyewear for the patient, and that wasn't happening the old way. Cambridge Eye provided the same high-quality eye exam with a high level of service in fitting and dispensing the eyewear. We offered a wide variety of quality frames and contacts at affordable prices."

It was a winning idea, and soon Weinstock decided to try it at a second location, in Brockton, Massachusetts. He hired an O.D. and an optician/manager, who would be in charge of the business side of things—appointments, finances, orders. In a short time, the Brockton location had two optometrists and three optician assistants. The company continued to grow, becoming a privately held corporation; later, Weinstock's partner died of cancer, leaving

ELIOT WEINSTOCK

PRESIDENT, CAMBRIDGE EYE DOCTORS

him at the helm. Today, with its own fabrication laboratory in Holliston and twenty Cambridge Eye Doctors locations across the state, it's common for an office to have two optometrists, a manager, and three to five assistants for fittings and orders.

Cambridge Eye hires and trains its people carefully. Most promotions are from within the company, with employees working their way up into positions of responsibility. "I believe our people should be one hundred percent knowledgeable about eye care, because we are always striving for higher levels of service," says Weinstock. Cambridge Eye Doctors also publishes a quarterly newsletter that is mailed to its customers, announcing new eye-care products and services and offering coupons for discounts and special offers, such as prescription sunglasses. Says Weinstock, "Anybody can sell you a pair of glasses for $20 less than we do, but customers want to know that you care about them, and they want their questions and concerns addressed. To my mind, integrated eye care means we are all working toward the same goal, to fit our patients with the best optical care based on their individual lifestyle and personal needs. You know, it's not uncommon for this to be a less than pleasant experience. I want each of our customers to recommend us to ten other people!"

To paraphrase an old song, "Business makes the world go 'round." Businesses and business activities are everywhere in our daily lives, from the time we get up in the morning until we go to sleep at night. The radio alarm that wakes you with your favorite music, the orange juice you gulp down going out the door, the car you drive, the sandwich you eat for lunch, and the groceries you buy on the way home are all produced, distributed, and sold by businesses. And, more than likely, the money spent to buy these products was earned working at a business.

Right now, this description may apply to business as you have experienced it, but it does not explain the *nature* of business—what a business is, what it does, or how it does it—and, more specifically, what the American business system is all about. In this chapter we will explore all these topics, as well as provide a review of America's business history and reasons for studying our business system.

The Business of Business

When you think of "business," what picture do you have in your mind? Is it corporations like Xerox, Procter & Gamble, Home Depot? If so, you're right, but there is more to business than these large corporations. It's Tony's Family Cafe, Venturi's Beauty Shop, Carla's Pizza, and Sartor's Appliance Service. It also includes Consolidated Freightways, which hauls your goods, your local newspaper, and the "mom-and-pop store" just around the corner.

business
An organization engaged in producing and selling, at a profit, goods and services that consumers want.

Businesses come in all shapes and sizes, but, despite the variations in size and activity, each is what we call a **business** because each is *an organization engaged in producing and selling, at a profit, goods and services that consumers want.* This definition focuses on some key points about businesses. All businesses:

A business can be many things, from a small operation (such as a local brewery) to a large international corporation (such as Anheuser-Busch).

Busch Corporate Center

- Produce either goods or services
- Seek profit
- Try to satisfy consumer wants

Goods- and Services-Producing Firms

All businesses are either goods-producing or services-producing firms. Goods-producing firms, such as Toyota, Chapparel Steel, and Endicott Mining Corporation, all produce tangible products or **goods**—*items that have a physical presence.* On the other hand, services-producing firms provide **services**—*activities that benefit consumers or other businesses.* Delta Airlines, Prudential Insurance Company, Supercuts, and Stadium Dry Cleaners are all examples of services-producing businesses.

goods
Items that have a physical presence.

services
Activities that benefit consumers or other businesses.

Regardless of the type of business, all businesses:

- Require the same functions or activities to be performed to operate the business
- Use the same inputs to produce the final goods or services

IDENTICAL FUNCTIONS AND ACTIVITIES Each business—large or small, goods-producing or services-producing—must perform the same functions and activities:

- Create a product or service
- Market the product or service to the consumer
- Account for the financial transactions
- Hire, train, and evaluate employees
- Acquire financing
- Process information

In addition, each business must perform the same management functions:

- Plan what it wants to accomplish
- Organize its resources
- Acquire the people to operate the business
- Guide the people to operate the business
- Monitor progress

The only differences in these functions and activities in various businesses are in the degree of sophistication involved; in some small businesses the owner may do it all, while in large businesses specialists are available to accomplish these tasks.

factors of production
Inputs or resources used to produce goods and services.

land
The natural resources that can be used to produce goods and services.

labor
The total human resources required to turn raw material into goods and services.

capital
The total of tools, equipment, machinery, and buildings used to produce goods and services.

INPUTS All businesses use the same **factors of production:** *inputs or resources used to produce goods and services.* The four resources—land, labor, capital, and entrepreneurship—are blended to create a business good or service as shown in Figure 1.1. Let's examine each.

- **Land** is *the natural resources that can be used to produce goods and services.* Natural resources are all resources growing on and under the earth's surface, such as trees, minerals, oil, and gas.
- **Labor** is *the total human resources required to turn raw materials into goods and services.* It includes all employees of a business, from top management through the entire organization structure.
- **Capital** is *the total of tools, equipment, machinery, and buildings used to produce goods and services.* In this case capital does not refer simply to money. Money by itself is not productive, but when it purchases drills,

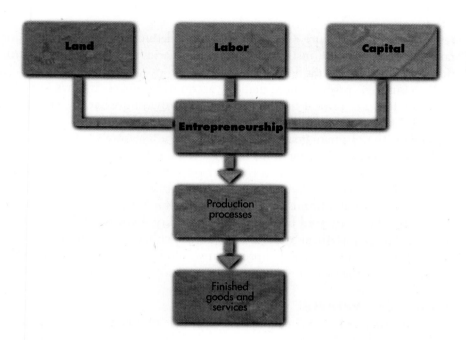

Figure 1.1
The four factors of production blended to produce goods and services.

typewriters, forklifts, and the building to place them in, it becomes productive.

- **Entrepreneurship** is *the skills and risk taking needed to combine the other three factors of production to produce goods and services.* Entrepreneurship is the catalyst—like heat to a fire. It is supplied by an **entrepreneur,** *an individual who is willing to take risks in return for profits.*

entrepreneurship
The skills and risk taking needed to combine with the other three factors of production to produce goods and services.

A good example of how a business uses the basic resources to produce its services is TME of Houston, Texas. Entrepreneur Cherrill Farnsworth founded TME when she saw that hospitals couldn't afford to spend $1.5 to $2 million to buy their own magnetic resonance imaging (MRI) equipment. Farnsworth's solution was to provide the MRI services for the hospitals. As the hospitals became convinced that the service would meet their needs, she convinced Toshiba America Medical Supplies and Paine Webber to invest in TME, hired a start-up staff of six, and acquired state-of-the-art equipment. Today the company operates twenty imaging centers in nine states, serving thirty-six hospitals and five universities. TME employs 164 people and is adding about 18 a year. Revenues—about $28 million annually—are reinvested to help the company grow.[1]

entrepreneur
An individual who is willing to take risks in return for profit.

Profit: The Reward

Regardless of whether a business produces a good or provides a service, the common ingredient is profit. **Profit** is *the amount of money remaining from a firm's sales revenues after it deducts its total expenses*—production costs, operating costs, and taxes. For example, TME of Houston had $28 million of sales

profit
The amount of money remaining from a firm's sales revenue after it deducts its total expenses.

revenue. From that figure, Cherrill Farnsworth deducts the expenses of maintaining the equipment, insurance costs, rent, salaries of employees, and utilities to arrive at her profit figure.

To a business, profit is more than the accounting process that we just went through. It is the reward to the business for providing what the consumers want and for satisfying their needs.

Profit is the ultimate goal of business. It is the measure of success for the businessperson and the reward for taking a chance. Each person who operates a business is risking money, as is each person who invests in a business—and profit is the payback. When Cherrill Farnsworth started TME, she did not know that hospital administrators would buy the MRI services, but money had already been invested based on the possibility. Farnsworth's investors—Toshiba America Medical Systems and Paine Webber—were taking a chance, a risk. If there were no potential profits, it would not be worthwhile for either investor to risk the capital.

Economic Systems

Cherrill Farnsworth and Paine Webber were able to invest money and receive a profit from TME because of the type of economic system found in America. This same option might not have been available in another country with a different economic system.

economic system
The method a society uses to allocate its resources and meet its needs for goods and services.

An **economic system** is *the method a society uses to allocate its resources—*land, labor, capital, and entrepreneurship—*and meet its needs for goods and services.* The economic system, chosen by a society, provides the answers to the following questions:

- What goods and services will be produced?
- How much of each good or service will be produced?
- Who will produce the goods and services?
- Who will receive the goods and services?

In the modern world there are three primary types of economic systems: capitalism, socialism, and communism. What distinguishes one economic system from another is the control of the factors of production and the interactions of business, government, and consumers.

capitalism
An economic system in which both the factors of production and businesses are owned by private individuals.

private enterprise system
An economic system in which businesses or enterprises are privately owned.

Capitalism

The economic system in the United States is **capitalism**. It is *an economic system in which both the factors of production and the businesses are owned by private individuals*—not by the government. To businesspersons, this system is referred to as the **private enterprise system,** *an economic system in which businesses or enterprises are privately owned.*

This system of private enterprise is built on four principles or rights: private ownership of property, freedom of choice, competition, and profits, as shown in Figure 1.2.

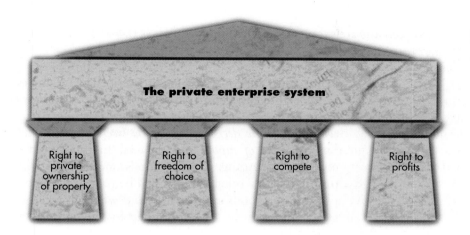

The private enterprise system

Right to private ownership of property

Right to freedom of choice

Right to compete

Right to profits

Figure 1.2
The rights of the private enterprise system.

1. *The right to private ownership of property.* In the private enterprise system, private individuals—you, your friends, your family, Tony of Tony's Cafe, Cherrill Farnsworth of TME—have the right to own property. This right of ownership means that the factors of production—land, buildings, capital equipment—are owned by private individuals. These individuals can buy, sell, or use the property as they see fit.

   For example, you personally own some or all of the factors of production and make decisions about them. As *labor,* you decide to sell your skills to a company. If you have money (*capital*) you can invest in a company or even start one. And if you do start a business—crafts, child care, yard service—you are deciding to be an entrepreneur and are supplying entrepreneurship in return for profits.

2. *The right of freedom of choice.* The private enterprise system also provides the right of freedom of choice—the right to decide what type of work to do, where to work, and how and where money is to be spent. This means that people can work for others or work for themselves if they so choose. It also means that a person is free to change jobs and work to improve his or her economic position in life.

3. *The right to compete.* Under the private enterprise system, businesses have the freedom to compete with others. Competition, along with profit, is the cornerstone of the private enterprise system. Competition pits one company against another in the struggle to attract and retain the customer. Companies compete by developing better products, altering prices, developing unique advertising programs, and having the product or service where and when the consumer wants it. The benefit to the consumer is that competition makes for better products and responsiveness to consumer needs.

4. *The right to profits.* In the private enterprise system, the person who takes the chance of starting a business is guaranteed the right to all profits. This right is what attracts people to begin businesses, and it is the ultimate goal of business. Inherent in starting a business is the freedom to fail. Not all

entrepreneurs are successful, but the opportunity is there to start a business and reap the rewards.

pure capitalism
An economic system in which economic decisions are made freely according to the market forces of supply and demand.

laissez-faire or hands-off approach
Government does not interfere in the economic system.

PURE CAPITALISM As originally described by Adam Smith in his eighteenth-century book, *Wealth of Nations,* **pure capitalism,** or a *market economy,* is *an economic system in which economic decisions are made freely according to the market forces of supply and demand.* In this system the economic questions of what goods and services will be produced, how much of each will be produced, who will produce the goods and services, and who will receive the goods and services are determined by the consumers in the marketplace.

In pure capitalism, *the government* takes a **laissez-faire,** *or* **hands-off, approach** and *does not interfere in the economic system.* Producers and consumers pursue their own self-interests. Producers make as much as they can sell, and consumers buy as much as they can afford.

In this interaction, consumers demand more of a product as its price decreases. This follows the commonsense notion that people are more willing to purchase something if it costs less. On the other hand, producers are more willing to supply a product that can be sold for a higher price. Being motivated by profit, they expect to earn more profit when they supply more.

Eventually, the two factors of supply and demand will balance each other out in such a way that some middle ground, called an equilibrium price, will be achieved. Producers will make as many units of a product as consumers are willing to buy at the price producers must charge to make a reasonable profit.

In this system each person behaves in the best interests of society, as if guided by an "invisible hand." The marketplace is regulated by the interaction of the buyers and producers. If a company produces a defective product or charges too much for the product, it is rejected by consumers. As a result, the producer has to improve the quality of the product or reduce the price to make any sales. The marketplace, in essence the invisible hand, regulates economic conduct. Government does not have to do any regulating.

PRODUCING GOODS AND SERVICES Just how goods and services are provided in this system can be seen in Figure 1.3. Remember that in capitalism the factors of production are owned by individuals—you and your friends—who live in households. (A *household,* in economic terms, is any person or group of people living under the same roof and functioning as an economic unit.) For businesses to produce any goods and services, they must acquire the factors of production from individuals in the households. This triggers a series of actions:

1. Businesses acquire the factors of production by providing household members with various types of income—rent, wages, interest, profit—in return

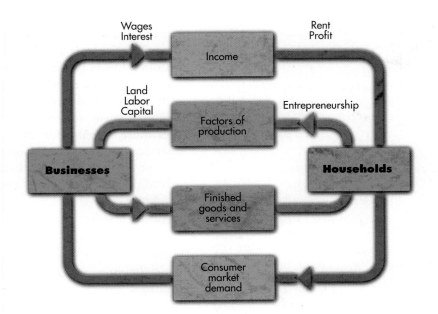

Figure 1.3
The circular flow of pure capitalism.

for the factors. The type of income exchanged depends on the factor of production needed, as shown in Table 1.1. For example, Chrysler needs to hire two employees. The factor of production, labor, is acquired by offering an agreed-upon wage.

2. The business—Chrysler—then combines the labor of employees with the other factors of production—capital, natural resources, and entrepreneurial skills—to produce goods and services: a Chrysler LeBaron automobile.

3. The individuals in the households, acting as consumers, need or want (market demand) the goods produced by the business (a new LeBaron).

4. Using the income received as wages, the individuals go to the marketplace—a Chrysler dealership—and purchase the goods and services produced by the company.

5. The business then takes the money received from the sale of the goods and services and uses it to purchase more factors of production.

This all happened as the result of the interaction of individuals (consumers) and businesses—with no government involvement. The invisible hand, the marketplace, regulates all the economic activity.

MIXED CAPITALISM Over time the United States has evolved to a system of **mixed capitalism,** which is *an economic system based on a market economy with limited government involvement.* Government has abandoned the principle of the invisible hand in favor of a more visible involvement in economic life.

In mixed capitalism government has two primary economic tools: the

FACTOR OF PRODUCTION	INCOME RECEIVED
Land	Rent
Labor	Wages or salaries
Capital	Interest
Entrepreneurship	Profit

Table 1.1
Income received for the factors of production.

mixed capitalism
An economic system based on a market economy with limited government involvement.

AREA	GOVERNMENT AUTHORITY
Employment practices	Equal Employment Opportunity Commission
Safety in the workplace	Occupational Safety and Health Administration
Food and drug quality	Food and Drug Administration
Compensation practices	Department of Labor
Product safety	Consumer Product Safety Commission
Management and labor relations	National Labor Relations Board
Employee retirement	Department of Labor
Business financing	Securities and Exchange Commission
Competitive practices	Federal Trade Commission
Interstate transporation	Interstate Commerce Commission
Communications	Federal Communications Commission
Waste disposal	Environmental Protection Agency

Table 1.2
Government involvement in business activities.

power to tax and the power to spend. By taxing individuals and businesses, it acquires funds to provide public programs: defense, education, transportation, and social services. In turn, the money spent for these services creates more demand for the goods and services produced by businesses.

The government has also become involved in the economic system through:

- Government-owned entities such as the Tennessee Valley Authority, which provides power to rural communities
- Government agencies that regulate the activities of some businesses, as when the Food and Drug Administration prevents a pharmaceutical company from selling a new medicine until tests have been done
- Government involvement in employer-employee relations, such as setting a minimum wage and initiating programs to create jobs for the unemployed

In addition to these examples, government has become involved in most facets of business operations. Table 1.2 provides a summary of the areas of government involvement in business activities. Keep in mind that government regulation also occurs at the state and local levels.

communism
An economic system in which the government controls the factors of production.

Communism

Another economic system is **communism,** *in which the government controls the factors of production.* Land, labor, and capital are under the control of the government, and entrepreneurship is supplied by the government. As a result, all decisions about production, distribution, consumption, and property ownership are made by the government. It decides what will be produced, who will produce it, how many units will be made, and who will receive it. Supply and demand and competition have no influence in this system. Central government planners make all the decisions about production and resource allocation. Cuba, North Vietnam, and the People's Republic of China still operate with this type of economic system.

Socialism

Socialism is *an economic system in which the government controls the operation and direction of basic industries but private ownership also exists.* The government control and direction are based on the belief that certain essential products and services need to be controlled so that all people will have them—not just those who have enough money. The industries normally under control of the government include mining, steel production, transportation, communication, health care, and auto manufacturing. In Sweden, for example, the government owns the transportation network, communications, the banks, and the mining, steel, and chemical industries.

Depending on the specific country—such as Denmark, Great Britain, Spain, France, India—there are varying degrees of ownership of private property and business. For example, in Denmark, where the majority of the population is sustained by government welfare programs, most businesses are privately owned and operated.

In a socialist economy, the economic decisions—what to produce, how to produce, and who will produce it—are determined by national government goals for those industries under government control. The same is true about the distribution of goods and services that are state-owned. For businesses not controlled by the state, the economic decisions are made as in capitalism.

Mixed Economic Systems

If you examine the economic systems in the world today, you will discover that no examples of pure capitalism or pure communism exist. Most economies are grouped in the center of a continuum that stretches from the complete private ownership and market economy of pure capitalism to the total public ownership of communism. This continuum, with some modern examples, is shown in Figure 1.4.

What this continuum shows is that most countries can be described as operating with **mixed economies**—*economies in which there is both private and government ownership and production of goods and services.* In essence there is more than one economic system at work in the country.

Another point of major importance is that economic systems are not static—they are constantly changing the mixture of the various economic alternatives. As a result, the countries on the continuum move a little in one direction or another as their society changes. This point is supported by the following examples:

socialism
An economic system in which the government controls the operation and direction of basic industries, but there is also private ownership.

mixed economies
Economies in which there is both private and government ownership and production of goods and services.

Figure 1.4
Selected countries on continuum from pure communism to pure capitalism.

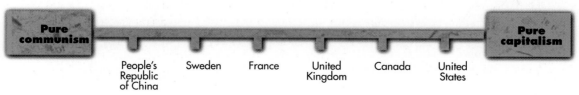

- Hungary, Poland, Czechoslovakia, and Russia (as described in this chapter's Global Perspective) are embracing capitalism after years of operating under communism. Each is struggling to make the huge transition from total government control to a market-driven system.[2]
- The People's Republic of China is beginning to embrace some of capitalism's concepts, as American and Western European businesses gain more access to China.[3]
- Spain, which has a predominantly socialist economic system, is pushing itself toward free-market economic reforms.[4]
- Sweden, long regarded as the model of socialism, is cutting back on generous state-financed benefits by reducing unemployment benefits. In

GLOBAL PERSPECTIVE

Russia: Caught in Transition

Americans take telephones and telephone service for granted. Everyone has a private line, and a call across the street or across the country is completed instantly. But the same can't be said for the telephone system in Russia.

Russia has only 12 telephone lines per 100 people, compared with 43 per 100 in Western Europe. Russian citizens are on a thirty-two-year waiting list for new telephone lines. Some 360,000 villages are without any telephone service at all. And the sole international telephone switch in Russia's public network can handle only 124 simultaneous calls between Russia and the United States.

From the sounds of the situation it would seem to be an ideal market opportunity for U.S. communication giants AT&T, GTE, and U.S. West—and it is. The three companies are licking their lips at the opportunities. But, like many other companies attempting to invest in Russia, they are caught in the transition between the old centralized command system and the market-driven decentralized one.

In a country once famous for its centralized five-year plans, there is no overall Russia-wide strategy to guide East-West partnerships. Bureaucrats enforce operating licenses inconsistently. Technical standards set in Moscow are often ignored by regional authorities. And there are still few incentives to lure U.S. investors to pump money into projects that will benefit the nation as a whole—as opposed to quick-fix projects, such as hooking hotels or oil rigs to the outside world via satellite.

How bad is it? The system is so bad that a number of U.S. companies find themselves yearning for good old central planning. "Decentralization helps in striking deals, but it also hurts because there's no grand plan," states Erik Jennes, AT&T's general manager in Russia.

(For more on Russia's telephone woes, see Deborah Stead, "Why Ivan Can't Place a Call," *Business Week*, June 4, 1993, pp. 92–93.)

addition, it is directing money into the private school system in order to provide competition for the state-controlled school system.[5]

- South Korea, a country working to become the model of socialism, has moved to eliminate controls and let free-market operations begin. Interest rates will no longer be set by the government, and foreigners will own business property outright.[6]

The Performance of Economic Systems

Various methods can be used to measure how well an economic system is performing. These measures include the gross national product, the gross domestic product, the standard of living, and productivity.

GROSS NATIONAL AND GROSS DOMESTIC PRODUCT One yardstick for measuring the performance of an economy has been *the total market value of all goods and services that a country produces in one year,* termed the **gross national product (GNP).** The GNP accounts for all goods and services a country produces—no matter where they were produced. For example, if Ford Motor Company has plants that manufacture cars in Ireland, this has been counted in the U.S. GNP. But now the GNP is being replaced by the **gross domestic product (GDP)**—*the total market value of all goods and services that a country produces in a year within its national boundaries.* This modification in accounting practices means that the United States—or any country—can only claim credit for goods produced inside its country and not in countries where its companies may be located. Table 1.3 shows the comparative GDPs of selected countries. Using this measure, the United States and Japan far outdistance all other countries in output, while Germany, France, Italy, and Great Britain are clustered together, and Canada is far behind.

STANDARD OF LIVING Another measure of economic performance is the **standard of living**—*the degree of material wealth in a country.* It shows just how well an individual is doing to satisfy his or her needs for goods and services. A country's standard of living is determined by dividing total GDP by the country's population, which produces a figure called *GDP per capita* (literally, "per head"), or GDP per person. A look at Table 1.4 shows that the United States has the highest standard of living for its citizens. Japan, second in GDP, follows Switzerland, Canada, and Germany in world-wide rankings.

PRODUCTIVITY A final measure of economic performance is productivity. Basically, **productivity** is *the amount of output for a given amount of input.* In the case of a country's economic performance, it is the output of goods and services per worker. It shows just how efficient an economic system is at producing goods and services.

gross national product (GNP) The total market value of all goods and services that a country produces in one year.

gross domestic product (GDP) The total market value of all goods and services that a country produces in one year within its national boundaries.

standard of living The degree of material wealth in a country.

productivity The amount of output for a given amount of input.

Table 1.3
GDP for selected countries.

COUNTRY	GDP (IN BILLIONS OF U.S. DOLLARS)
United States	$5,954.0
Japan	3,674.3
Germany	1,928.1
France	1,336.8
Italy	1,237.7
Great Britain	1,051.3
Canada	568.1

Source: Data from The WEFA Group.

COUNTRY	PER CAPITA GDP IN U.S. DOLLARS
United States	$21,571
Switzerland	20,893
Canada	20,694
Germany	18,122
Japan	17,792
Sweden	17,320
Australia	17,144

Source: Data from The WEFA Group.

Table 1.4
Standard of living around the world.

U.S. productivity has been a major concern in recent years. Although American workers produce more total goods and services than workers in any other country, the rate of growth of production has been in a period of decline. From 1982 to 1988 productivity increased at an average of 1.3 percent, but from 1989 to 1991 it grew by less than 1 percent. The latest figures have productivity increasing at about 2 percent each year. This performance has placed the United States in a position where its rate of productivity growth has been exceeded by those of Japan, Germany, and other European countries.

Up to this point we have taken an in-depth look at our business system and how it operates compared with other systems. But what are the "roots" of the system? Let's take a look at the historical development of American business.

A Brief History of American Business

The American business system is far different from what it was fifty or one hundred years ago. Over the course of time it has undergone a number of significant changes.

The Colonial Era

The American business system in the colonial era (before 1800) was agriculturally based: society depended on the production of agricultural products as the basis of commerce. In addition, the economy was closely tied to that of England. In exchange for raw materials and precious metals, England exchanged finished goods and provided financing.

During this time the most common form of industry was provided by the cottage system, in which workers were contracted by merchants to produce goods at home. The workers were in essence independent, highly skilled subcontractors who became specialists in producing certain goods. These goods were in turn sold by merchants in their stores.

The Industrial Revolution

The Industrial Revolution, which began in the mid-1700s, dramatically changed the American business system. The implementation of both power-driven machinery and new production methods changed the manufacturing processes. Instead of skilled craftspeople hand-producing products in cottages, factories were built and the goods were mass produced. The skilled workers left their homes and became employees in the factories.

Other ingredients further directed the march toward industrialization. With the invention of the reaper, agriculture became more mechanized; labor flooded American shores as a result of political and economic problems in Europe; communication was revolutionized by the telegraph; and the railroads pushed the boundaries of the United States to the Pacific Ocean.

The industrialization of America was in full swing by the turn of the century.

Growth of Modern Industry

Beginning in the second half of the nineteenth century, America became transformed into an industrial nation. A number of developments contributed to that evolution.

For the first time all the factors of production were abundantly available within national boundaries. Americans were no longer dependent on European countries. Reliance on foreign capital was removed with the development of a national treasury and the establishment of a better banking system. Technology supplied the telephone to improve communications. Entrepreneurs such as John D. Rockefeller and Andrew Carnegie were able to mesh the factors of production.

Toward the end of this era America survived the Great Depression. During this later period the concept of pure capitalism and the market economy was greatly modified by the government. The invisible hand in the marketplace was replaced by the government through such measures as Social Security, regulation of securities, and bank insurance.

An International Industrial Power

Since the end of World War II the United States has been the world's leading industrial power. Combining the immense production capabilities of its manufacturing facilities with managerial talent and financial resources has enabled America to provide the best standard of living for its citizens and to assist the economic development of other nations. The country has evolved from the ability simply to produce goods, even if demand exceeded supply, to the adoption of marketing based on identified consumer needs. These developments, together with the growth in the standard of living and evolving technology, have gradually resulted in a movement of the United States toward a service-oriented economy.

Business Today and Tomorrow

One conclusion that can be reached from this review of the American business system is that change is a way of life for businesses. The key to success is to be alert for change by being aware of and studying technology, trends, and major problems. Each is an indicator that some degree of change is coming. Successful businesses and businesspersons respond well to change. Ones who do not may not be in a position to take advantage of the opportunity or may even fail. Three examples from the immediate past that emphasize this point:

- When the television was invented, few could anticipate the effect it would have on American life and American business. Something that was only a novelty in the 1940s became widespread in the 1950s, and today almost every home has a television—many have more than one. Each set gives its owners access to information and entertainment. Each set also provides something for business: a huge audience, millions of people reachable by advertising. Television is a direct communication link to a company's products and services.
- A single event changed the way American consumers think and reshaped an entire industry. When the Organization of Petroleum Exporting Countries (OPEC) raised oil prices during the 1970s, American consumers began turning away from the larger American cars in favor of fuel-efficient foreign cars. The American automobile industry did not respond to the change. As a result, today more than a third of the cars bought in the United States are of foreign manufacture—a fact that threatens the future of the American automobile industry and the industries that support it.
- The solution to a problem revolutionized the way Americans transfer and process information. Specifically, although mechanical data processing first began late in the nineteenth century, it was not until the 1960s and 1970s that computers became available for widespread use. Today computers are revolutionizing business by helping small-business owners figure out their accounts, giant insurance companies handle their massive record-keeping chores, and manufacturers design new products.

Although many more examples could be cited, these three serve the purpose of emphasizing the importance of being alert to signs of change, studying the signs, and responding accordingly. With this in mind, there are a number of trends and challenges for businesses to be aware of:

- *Environmental protection.* The public's concern for protecting and preserving the environment is now a major business issue. Companies will have to make environmental considerations a part of strategic decision making—not because it is a law or some group wants it, but because it is the right thing to do.
- *International interdependence.* No nation is independent anymore. Coun-

tries have become interdependent, driven primarily by trade and economics. More and more countries depend on one another's products for business or personal use. And, the economic success (of Pacific Rim countries, for example) or failure of a country or region is felt in economies throughout the world. Businesses need to monitor the global economy.

- *International business competition.* Businesses now compete globally as well as locally. Competition takes on a new dimension when the entire world enters the game. Decision making for businesses will become more complex and time driven.

- *Quality.* The key word in business operations—whether it is manufacturing or service—has become "quality." Consumers want more of it, and companies must develop and implement total quality management to compete.

- *Family and work.* The changing composition and values of the work force will continue to force businesses to rethink policies and programs. The number of single parents and working mothers in the work force, coupled with the increased importance of family, challenges the core value of placing work before family. New and better answers are needed.

- *Cultural diversity.* The diversity represented by growing numbers of His-

Can you guess where this photo was taken? The international interdependence of business becomes evident when you see street scenes like this one in Guatemala.

panic, Asián, and African American members of the work force will require new leadership approaches and team-building programs.

- *Technological change.* Industries are in the midst of a technological revolution. Computer technology is evolving at breakneck speed; robotics and laser technology are also making their presence felt in the workplace. Heavy industries such as steel and automaking will have to update their facilities with new technology if they are to compete.
- *Productivity.* Managerial talent will have to focus on the productivity dilemma: American output per worker is not keeping stride with that of the rest of the world. Answers are needed to maintain U.S. production capabilities.
- *Social responsibility.* More demands will be placed on the business sector to accomplish the dual objectives of profitability and social responsiveness.

Some businesses will see these trends and respond, as in the past; those will be the businesses that survive. The firms that cannot adapt will fail. The excitement of business is that it allows people to observe their environment and respond creatively to it. People receive much satisfaction and can find great rewards in creating solutions to problems, and business provides them with the opportunities to do so.

Why Study Business?

People study business for many reasons. Some are preparing to pursue careers in one of the major fields of business. Others want to become better-informed consumers, understand their rights, and avoid costly mistakes. Here are some of the reasons that people study business:

- *The impact of business.* Business is a major force in American life. It affects our daily activities. It is always present—in newspaper stories or on television and radio broadcasts. Business provides most of the jobs that enable people to earn money, and it offers the goods and services that people spend that money on. As a result of the dominant role business plays in their lives, people have a natural curiosity to learn more about it. They take up the pursuit of business to be able to understand the hows and whys more thoroughly.
- *Career choice.* Studying business can help in selecting a career. Too often job selection is by accident and is not well designed. By becoming knowledgeable about the areas involved in business and business practices, one can make a better-quality decision. To aid you in making a career choice, review the Career Capsule at the end of each section of this text. Then read "The Business of Getting a Job" in the appendix, which outlines the steps to follow in choosing a career and getting a job in your chosen field.
- *Business ownership.* Owning a business is the goal of many individuals. If a person wants to increase his or her chances for success, one approach is to study business operations. A knowledge of accounting, management, mar-

MANAGER'S NOTEBOOK

The Keys to Success

There are no "quick fixes" in business, but there *are* keys to success. Entrepreneurs who have lived the great adventure of starting their own companies and guiding them to success have learned the hard way—by trial and error. The lessons they have learned are critical for anyone who wants to be successful in a business. Based on the experiences of entrepreneurs there are ten keys to success:

1. *Know how to manage and operate a business.* Having creativity or technical skills is not enough. Entrepreneurs need to develop managerial skills—particularly in cash management. The greatest advice for any entrepreneur is to recognize that something needs to be learned and then to go learn it.

2. *Have adequate financial resources.* Regardless of whether it is a startup operation or an ongoing business, adequate financial resources are a necessity. If a company has poor cash flow, lack of financial savvy, underfinancing, or poor money management, the result is the same thing—inadequate resources.

3. *Control the growth of the company.* Everyone wants to grow, but growing too fast means spinning out of control. Planning and controlling the growth of the company ensures that the quality of the good or service is consistently provided.

4. *Develop and maintain good interpersonal relationships.* Entrepreneurs must have a reasonably good relationship with the people they interact with on a day-to-day basis, whether it is customers, business associates, or employees.

5. *Work at strategic planning.* Many entrepreneurs, as well as other businesspeople, resist strategic planning because they think they don't know how to do it, can't afford it, or don't have the time. Actually, strategic planning puts a business in a position to compete effectively and to manage change.

6. *Innovate—never be complacent.* The accomplishment of goals should lead entrepreneurs to new and higher goals. Resting on one's laurels often means dousing the fires of creativity.

7. *Build a team.* Unsuccessful businesspeople most often prefer to do everything themselves. Successful businesspeople learn to gather associates who complement and contribute to each other's skills.

8. *Work at communicating.* To enlist the commitment of others, entrepreneurs must be able to share their vision. They need to sell goods, services, and ideas to customers. They need to hear the opinions of employees and understand what employees are thinking and feeling.

9. *Recognize strengths and weaknesses.* An entrepreneur needs to be able to identify both personal and organizational strengths and weaknesses. In the first situation, an entrepreneur should find people who complement and support his or her own skills. In the second area, the need is for a realistic assessment and action, rather than trying to cover up.

10. *Seek and respond to feedback.* To keep on track, entrepreneurs need honest, candid, straightforward feedback. For an objective perspective they can turn to old friends who care enough to tell the truth, consultants, and peers.

(For more on keys to success, see Charles Burck, "The Real World of the Entrepreneur," *Fortune*, April 15, 1993, pp. 62–65; and Sharon Nelton, "Ten Keys to Success," *Nation's Business*, June 1992, pp. 18–25.)

keting, risk management, and finance is a necessity for a small business as well as for a large one. The difference is that as a small-business owner a person must be knowledgeable in all these areas.

- *More knowledgeable consumer.* One role everyone plays in relationship to business is that of consumer. When you respond to an ad for a product, are told that the last one has just been sold, but learn that, conveniently, a more expensive model is available, what should you do? When a contractor does not meet specifications on remodeling a room, what options are available? Everyone has a need to improve his or her consumer skills. Studying business can provide some of the information to be a better-informed consumer.

Text Overview

Your journey into and through the world of business has just begun. To meet your goals and to get the most from your investment, approach the text chapters as if you were going into business and needed to understand the whys and hows of becoming a successful entrepreneur. Your study of business will follow this sequence:

- Chapter 2 discusses the social and ethical concerns and responsibility of business as it functions in the private enterprise system.
- Chapters 3 and 4 examine the legal forms that business can take: sole proprietorships, partnerships, and corporations.
- Chapter 5 explores the realities of owning and operating a small business or a franchise.
- Chapters 6, 7, 8, 9, and 10 examine the "people" side of business: how to manage, how to organize a business, how to hire and train employees, how to lead and motivate employees, and how to achieve good labor relations.
- Chapters 11, 12, 13, and 14 discuss the major activities of a business in manufacturing and marketing its goods or services: production, marketing, promotion, distribution, and pricing.
- Chapters 15, 16, 17, 18, and 19 examine the support systems that businesses need to conduct business profitably: the banking system, financing, insurance, gathering and processing data, and accounting.
- Chapters 20 and 21 discuss issues that confront American business: the legal setting of business and competition in an international environment.

SUMMARY

A business is an organization engaged in producing and selling, at a profit, goods and services that consumers want. Although businesses come in all sizes, shapes, and varieties, they are divided into goods-producing and services-producing firms. Regardless of type, all businesses require the same function or activi-

ties to be performed and all businesses use the same inputs—the factors of production (land, labor, capital, and entrepreneurship)—to produce goods and services.

An economic system is the method a society uses to allocate its resources and meet its needs for goods and services. In the modern world there are three types of economic systems: capitalism, socialism, and communism.

The economic system in the United States is capitalism. Also known as the private enterprise system, in it both the factors of production and the businesses are owned by private individuals—not by the government. This system is based on the right to private property, the right to freedom of choice, the right to profit, and the right to compete.

America's original economic system was pure capitalism (no government interference), but it has evolved to mixed capitalism, in which the government plays an active role.

In capitalism, to produce goods and services, the four factors of production are obtained from the individuals who own them in exchange for income. Once the factors of production are combined, they are sold to individual consumers. The consumers purchase these goods with the money obtained by selling the factors of production.

Communism is an economic system under which the government controls the factors of production. Supply, demand, and competition have no influence. Central government planners make all the economic decisions about production and resource allocation.

Socialism is an economic system in which the government controls the operation and direction of basic industries but there is also private ownership. The control is based on the belief that there are certain products and services everyone should have and that obtaining them should not depend on whether a person has money.

Most nations have mixed economies in which there is both private and public ownership. There are no examples of pure capitalism or pure communism.

Various methods can be used to measure how well an economic system is performing. Among them are the gross national product, gross domestic product, standard of living, and productivity.

The American business system today has undergone significant changes as it has evolved from the colonial period through the Industrial Revolution to become a national and international industrial power. More recently, because of the increased standard of living and growth in technology, the country has evolved to a service-oriented economy.

One of the lessons that the evolution of business in America has taught us is that change is constant and that survival depends on being able to recognize and adapt to change. The challenge is to recognize the signs of change—trends, problems, events—and study them. In today's world, business must study the following trends: environmental protection, international interdependence, international business competition, quality, family and work, cultural diversity, technological change, productivity, and social responsibility.

People undertake the study of business for different reasons. The most common are to understand the overall impact of business, to assist in selecting a career, to prepare for business ownership, and to become a more knowledgeable consumer.

KEY TERMS

business p. 8
capital p. 10
capitalism p. 12
communism p. 16
economic system p. 12
entrepreneur p. 11
entrepreneurship p. 11
factors of production p. 10
goods p. 9
gross domestic product (GDP) p. 19
gross national product (GNP) p. 19
labor p. 10

laissez-faire *or* hands-off approach p. 14
land p. 10
mixed capitalism p. 15
mixed economies p. 17
private enterprise system p. 12
productivity p. 19
profit p. 11
pure capitalism p. 14
services p. 9
socialism p. 17
standard of living p. 19

FOR REVIEW AND DISCUSSION

1. Distinguish between a goods-producing and a services-producing business.
2. "Regardless of whether a business produces goods or services, the same functions or activities must take place." Discuss this statement.
3. What are the four factors of production? Give an example of each.
4. Describe the importance of profits to a business-person. How is profit determined?
5. List and describe the four rights, or principles, of the private enterprise system.
6. What is the concept of the "invisible hand"?
7. Explain the interactions of businesses and households (individuals) in capitalism.
8. Distinguish between pure capitalism and mixed capitalism.
9. Who controls the factors of production in communism? How are the economic decisions made?
10. Describe the basic belief underlying socialism.
11. Distinguish between socialism and communism.
12. What is a mixed economy?
13. Explain each of four measures of the performance of an economic system.
14. What effect did the Industrial Revolution have on the production processes in the United States?
15. What challenges and trends face business in the future?
16. List and explain the reasons people study business.

APPLICATIONS

Case 1.1: International Business Accord

The Czech Republic is a country with severe economic problems. Like most East European countries, it is in the process of changing from a communist economy to capitalism. Most of the country's businesses were controlled by their biggest customer—the government. Now, the companies are making efforts to find the kind of entrepreneurship and leadership that can revitalize them.

In an arrangement that Czech Premier Vaclav Klaws calls "the first of its kind," the Tatra truck company has lured three successful American managers to help reform the company. Gerald Greenwald, who leads the team, was once on the fast track to succeed Lee Iacocca at Chrysler. Greenwald is supported by David Shelby and Jack Rutherford, who worked together at both International Harvester and Ford. Together, the hope is that these three businessmen have the right mix of industry experience and knowledge of how to run a for-profit business that will not only turn Tatra around, but will also be a model for other Czech companies to follow.

But, in the face of this optimism are the realities awaiting the American triad. The typical Czech employee has been conditioned by generations under the communistic economic system to follow orders—exactly as given. The result is an employee who works the *required* number of hours doing the job *as required,* with no emotional or intellectual involvement. Above the workers in the organization structure are managers—and in some cases layers of managers—

who have no training in business techniques and who also have waited to be told what to do, when to do it, and how to do it. As if these obstacles were not large enough, Greewald and company have inherited out-of-date technology and facilities with which to produce trucks that will be competitive in the marketplace.

The American managers must face one more overruling reality: While everyone in the Czech Republic wants capitalism, few know how it works. Profit is a tremendoul incentive, but to overcome generations of centralized control requires a basic understanding of how capitalisms's market economy works. Greenwald, Shelby, and Rutherford have a lot of work to do.

Questions

1. Which of the realities cited—employees, managers, equipment, and facilities—present the greatest obstacle to the American triad? Explain your answer.

2. If you were Greenwald, which obstacle would you try to overcome first? Why?

3. How would you change the attitude of employees and managers?

4. Why do you believe Greenwald, Shelby, and Rutherford accepted this task? What might their rewards be?

For more information, see Neil King, Jr., "Three Americans Try to Work Miracles at Czech Republic's Tatra Truck Plant," *The Wall Streeet Journal,* July 7, 1993, p. A7.

Case 1.2: Banking on Competition

In a free enterprise system, the companies that thrive and succeed are those that remain adaptable and responsive to consumer needs. The nature of society, business, markets, and people demands that businesses keep their eye on the ball—or fail. Banking is a business that for many years thought of itself as one that customers conformed to, not the other way around. Banks had something people wanted—money—and felt they could dictate the terms.

But the boom in finance and investment during the 1980s produced new notions about the business of banking. The old notion of low returns on passbook savings accounts—which were pretty much the only place people without great means could invest—was overturned by the emergence of money funds and mutual funds that allowed investors in for as little as a few hundred dollars. In addition, these funds paid a higher interest rate than passbook savings. Another notion that was overturned was the idea that credit cards came only from banks. Most people obtained a Visa or MasterCard through a bank, but suddenly one could be obtained from American Telephone and Telegraph, General Motors, American Airlines, and other nonbanking entities. And the terms and interest were often lower. Meanwhile, banks wanted even less direct contact with customers and were installing automated teller machines (ATMs) that many people did not prefer to use. Many customers wanted to entrust their money to a person, not a green, blinking screen.

In short, banking was thrown into formidable competition. Suddenly, bankers had to learn to understand customers and develop ways to keep them. While the government has regulated banks to protect both the economy and the consumer, during the 1980s certain regulations were eased and changed to permit banks to compete more freely. As a result, banks have had to learn business skills they previously lacked. And they've had to proceed cautiously, having seen what happened to the savings and loan industry.

Two banks that are leading the way in offering a smorgasbord of financial services to consumers are First Union Bank and NationsBank, both of Charlotte, North Carolina. In addition to all the regular banking services, they offer consumers stocks, mutual funds, and financial planning and are adding personalized finance and banking services that are entirely new to the industry. Edward Crutchfield, chairman and chief executive of First Union, says, "We'll live or die on our customer service." The banks are also offering a wider array of personalized banking and investment services to corporate customers; bank officers, who seem a great deal like salespeople, are out calling on current and prospective customers. Says Hugh L. McColl, Jr., head of NationsBank, "We found ourselves with a huge franchise of corporate customers. We had to decide whether to abandon this market or try to make lemonade out of what people call a lemon."

Questions

1. How does the free enterprise system keep companies competitive?

2. Why do businesses have to remain flexible and responsive to customer needs and demands? What are the consequences if they do not?

3. What specific changes by consumers and by the environment have caused banks to change the way they do business?

For more information, see Saul Hansell, "Taking On the Behemoths of Finance," *The New York Times,* July 18, 1993, Section 3, p. 1; Martha Brannigan and Eleena deLisser, "Two Rival Banks in Southeast Take On New-Age Competitors," *The Wall Street Journal,* July 8, 1993, p. 1.

REFERENCES

1. Charles Burck, "The Real World of the Entrepreneur," *Fortune,* April 5, 1993, pp. 64–65.
2. Richard Alm, "Capitalism's New Frontier," *Dallas Morning News,* March 21, 1993, pp. 1H–2H.
3. Bo Burlingham, "China, Inc.," *Inc.,* December 1992, pp. 111–121.
4. Gary Abramson, "Why Socialist Spain Will Move Toward the Middle," *Business Week,* June 21, 1993, p. 60.
5. Richard Alm, "Sweden, Korea Struggle to Remodel Economies," *Dallas Morning News,* May 24, 1993, pp. 1D, 4D.
6. Ibid.

2

THE SOCIAL AND ETHICAL ENVIRONMENT OF BUSINESS

ur business won't be healthy unless our community is healthy. I spend 40 percent of my time in community projects—I see that as part of my job description.

BILL SERETTA
President, Harper/Connecting Point Computer Center

CHAPTER OBJECTIVES
After studying this chapter, you should be able to:

1. Define the concept of social responsibility.
2. Explain the three alternative approaches to social responsibility available to an organization.
3. Describe the reasons for and the socially responsible actions taken by businesses in community involvement, education, employment policies and programs, environmental responsibility, energy, and consumer protection.
4. Discuss the role of top management in a company's social responsibility.
5. Define the concept of ethics.
6. Identify three influences on ethical behavior.
7. Discuss the importance of a personal code of conduct and a company's code of conduct in developing ethical behavior in a business.

UP FRONT

"Service to people has always been my main interest," says Kenneth Kunkel. That interest has taken him along several interesting paths in his life since graduating from St. John's University in Minnesota with a degree in philosophy. The first path was to a Catholic monastery and training for the priesthood, culminating in Kunkel's ordination and ministry in Peru, Illinois. His care and concern for people reached into activism during the turbulent 1960s. He demonstrated for civil rights and against the Vietnam war, and he was outspoken on certain issues within the Church, which culminated in his requesting a dispensation from his vows.

During his ministry, Kunkel continued his studies in education and counseling, leading to working as an employment counselor for the city of Chicago. Then the Veterans Administration hired him to train supervisors for one of its Illinois operations. He subsequently became involved in personnel management and civil rights issues, including those for people with disabilities. His work led to a promotion to the VA offices in Washington, D.C.

Kunkel was made manager of two programs: one for people with disabilities, the other for disabled veterans. "The programs really dovetailed," he explains. The program for disabled veterans is overseen by the Office of Personnel Management, while the one for people with disabilities is overseen by the U.S. Equal Employment Opportunity Commission (EEOC). The EEOC has targeted nine severe disabilities, including blindness, deafness, missing extremities, mental retardation, and epilepsy,

for special focus. There are approximately 43 million disabled Americans; of those, about 13 million are willing and able to work.

Today, Kunkel has the responsibility for improving employment opportunities for people with disabilities within the VA. In 1993 Congress passed legislation requiring federal agencies to take special steps for increasing employment opportunities for people with disabilities, as well as removing the word "handicapped" from usage. (In 1974 Congress had passed similar legislation for disabled veterans.) "The word 'handicapped' is often associated with a cap-in-hand mentality," says Kunkel, "or those who beg for a living. That word is part of the discrimination, and the federal government has replaced it with 'people with disabilities.' Most people with disabilities do not wish to be considered any differently than others. And, given the opportunity, they have as good a chance to do a job as anyone else."

The federal government spends $200 billion a year to *care* for disabled people and loses $100 billion in taxes that these people could have paid had they been employed. "The goal is to empower these people so they can be independent and employed, free to be capable to do whatever they want to do," says Kunkel.

In 1990, when then President George Bush signed the Americans with Disabilities Act, people with disabilities represented

KENNETH KUNKEL

NATIONAL MANAGER, PEOPLE WITH DISABILITIES PROGRAM, U. S. DEPARTMENT OF VETERANS AFFAIRS

6.9 percent of the U.S. government work force but only 3.9 percent of the civilian work force. Bush said, "As a nation, we face a shortage of qualified workers in the coming years. The federal government must be a model for the rest of the country to ensure that people with disabilities are afforded opportunities to become full participants in our society."

The VA sets annual goals for hiring people with disabilities, consistent with federal affirmative action programs. Overall, the U.S. government's goal is 6 percent representation of its work force by disabled workers. Of the VA's 227,613 permanent workers, 20,647, or about 9 percent, have a disability.

There are two principal barriers to hiring workers with disabilities. One is people's attitudes toward those with disabilities; the other is physical barriers, such as access to buildings, transportation, or communication. The government spends millions each year to renovate its premises for the disabled. "All too often, we either pity people with disabilities or we make superheroes of them," says Kunkel. "We must move from the extreme to the mainstream."

Kunkel points out that many American companies have actively recruited people with disabilities, with great success. "Du Pont studies show that the work habits and attendance records of the disabled workers are just as good if not better than those of others. And at McDonald's, the 'McJobs' program has been extremely successful. The American attitude toward disabled people is compassion and sympathy. But what they really want is employment, opportunity, and independence," Kunkel concludes.

Today's news is filled with reports of business and corporate wrongdoing—of companies polluting the air, land, and water, of fraudulent savings and loan practices costing Americans an estimated $500+ billion, of Dow Corning selling breast implants even though "its executives had for years ignored memos showing that it had known silicone could and did leak from the implants."[1] Though few industries would openly endorse such actions, the reality is that people and companies do these things every day for reasons society does not accept or condone.

Society is demanding and should expect socially responsible and ethical conduct from businesses. Many individuals and companies consistently conduct themselves with honesty and integrity and act in a socially responsible way. Many companies—Southern California Edison, Johnson & Johnson, Hewlett-Packard, Motorola, 3M, Disney, McDonald's—prosper while cultivating the right conduct, equity, and enlightened respect for the community and environment. Unfortunately, there are other companies that do not maintain such standards.

Demands for Socially Responsible and Ethical Conduct

stakeholders
Those people who have an interest in or are affected by how a business conducts its operations.

Business does not operate in a vacuum, nor can business decisions be made without evaluating the total effect of those decisions on the business's **stakeholders**—*those people who have an interest in or who are affected by how a* *business conducts its operations.* The stakeholders of most businesses include investors, employees, customers, suppliers, and communities. Each has a specific focus and influence on management's decision making:

- *Investors.* The owners and stockholders expect assets to be used effectively and efficiently to maximize profits and return on investments. Owners also have the right to expect ethical, legal, and moral conduct from employees.
- *Employees.* Employees expect to be treated fairly and equitably in hiring, promotion, and compensation. They also expect a quality of work life that provides satisfying jobs.
- *Customers.* Customers want fair and honest representation of products and services. They expect the products to be safe and reliable. Customers want to be treated fairly and with respect.
- *Suppliers.* Suppliers expect to receive needed information in time to render quality service and supplies. They have the legal right to be treated according to the terms of their agreements. Also, they have an expectation of building relationships based on mutual trust.
- *Communities.* The overall community—including the environments and the governments that are affected by a company's operations—expect the quality of life to be respected and contributed to.

Today's business firms operate in an environment of interdependence. Society, government, and private enterprise must interact to ensure their mutual survival and success. Business managers cannot divorce their decisions, objectives, and resources from these influences. They must pursue their overriding goal of profit within a social and political framework.

In this respect, American business is in a pioneering era. It is dealing with

By participating in community activities, companies fulfull their role as good citizens.

relationships and challenges that were either nonexistent or of no concern to managers just a few decades ago. Therefore, the basic dilemma faced by managers is to balance conflicting demands as they attempt to allocate and manage their organization's resources.

As its first step, today's business must determine what specific responsibilities it has to society—what is the definition of good corporate citizenship? Then the organization needs to determine its specific philosophy toward social responsibility and what actions it will take to implement its philosophy. Equally important is deciding on the organization's code of ethical conduct—its basis, expectations, and sanctions. In this chapter we will explore the nature of both social responsibility and business ethics.

The Concept of Social Responsibility

As noted, businesses do not operate in a vacuum as they produce goods and services and pursue a profit. They operate in an environment of interdependence, exerting considerable influence on the general well-being of society. Regardless of whether a business is confined to a city, spans the nation, or has world-wide operations, its actions, products, and services directly affect the environment, the welfare of suppliers, and its customers' standard of living.

social responsibility A belief that business decisions should be made within the confines of both social and economic considerations.

Because of these influences, the need has developed for organizations to practice **social responsibility**—*a belief that business decisions should be made within the confines of both social and economic considerations.*

The concept of social responsibility is based on a sincere belief that as a business achieves its ultimate goal of profit, it should turn its attention to matters of public need that it can also pursue as profitable business opportunities.

An integral element of this concept is the belief that:

- What is good for society is good for the business firm.
- Social objectives actually enhance a firm's profitability over the long term.
- Companies should contribute to healthful social conditions to ensure that the society in which they earn their profits will remain so in the future.
- Companies with a high social consciousness further their own goals when they help to strengthen the social structure.

Though the rationale for an organization to incorporate social responsibility into its operating framework is comprehensive, perhaps no one provides a more thorough and eloquent argument than Robert D. Haas, president and CEO of Levi Strauss:

Corporations can be short-sighted and worry only about our mission, products, and competitive standing. But we do it at our peril. The day will come when corporations will discover the price we pay for our indifference. We must realize that by ignoring the needs of others, we are actually ignoring our own needs in the long run. We may need the goodwill of a neighbor to enlarge a corner store. We may need well-funded institutions of higher learning to turn out the skilled technicians we require. We may need adequate community health care to curb absenteeism in our plants. Or we may need fair tax treatment for an industry to be able to compete in the world economy. However small or large our enterprise, we cannot isolate our business from the society around us. Nor can we function without its goodwill.[2]

Acceptance of Social Responsibility

Businesses adopt varying approaches to the demands made on them for social responsibility. Some businesses eagerly seek ways to accommodate social needs, while others vehemently resist any externally imposed obligations. A business can take any one of three approaches to social responsibility: resist, react, or anticipate. Each approach represents different degrees of acceptance of social responsibility and levels of involvement.

The Resistance Approach

In the resistance approach, a company's professional managers are responsible to the owners and the owners' interests are primary. The only social responsibilities a manager has are to make profits and to obey the law.[3] As recently stated by Nobel Prize–winning professor of economics Milton Friedman:

- Managers are employed by owners to make as much money as possible while conforming to the law and to ethical custom.
- Managers are exclusive agents for their employers and owe primary responsibility to them.
- Managers are agents for stockholders and should not make decisions about social responsibilities and social investments, because they represent tax decisions. (These matters are government functions.)[4]

In short, social responsibility is not the business of business. As a result, companies actively fight to eliminate, delay, or fend off the demands being made on them—they persist in doing as little as possible. For example, when Toyota encountered problems with its 1987 to 1991 Camry models—some 890,000 vehicles had automatic door locks that could jam and lock owners out of the car or trap occupants inside the car—it cooperated with the investigation but, in spite of the evidence, maintained that a recall was not warranted. This despite the fact that consumer groups, the Center for Auto Safety, and *Consumer Reports* magazine recommend a recall.[5]

The Reactive Approach

Businesses taking the reactive approach wait for demands to be made and then respond to them by evaluating alternatives. This approach is often referred to as the hand-of-government approach because it is characterized by following the letter of the law but not its true intent or spirit. A business does only what it is mandated to do and does that with little enthusiasm. Little League teams are sponsored, managers attend business affairs, and quotas for minorities are set and, once reached, minorities are ignored.

In a recent example in Chicago's Lincoln Plaza area, neighbors complained about too many restaurants and bars in their neighborhood being open too late and having patrons who repeatedly caused disturbances. When their complaints went unheeded, the neighborhood groups began a petition drive to place a referendum on the ballot to ban the sale of alcohol in the area. Businesses mounted their own campaign to get people to remove their signatures. Eventually a compromise was worked out—the businesses would hire off-duty police to patrol during the late-evening hours. But it wasn't until a real threat to the businesses arose that the owners took actions to meet community demands.

The Proactive Approach

Companies taking the proactive approach continually look to the needs of constituents, constantly stay in touch, and try to find ways to assist them.

In this approach management has recognized that the long-range future of business is dependent on the health and well-being of the society of which it is a part. This view requires that business anticipate possible problems and changes and adopt an active approach to dealing with them. Business must understand it is a part of society and that anything that threatens society threatens the future of business.

This phase calls for business to partner with society—with labor, government, and religious and civic groups—in addressing society's needs. It also calls for business to assume the leadership role because it has the majority of the country's technical, financial, managerial, and professional resources. In short, business needs to be proactive, not reactive.

Companies that are proactive provide assistance where it is needed—donate cash, services, goods. Just Desserts' Elliot Hoffman teamed up with the San Francisco County Jail to turn a vacant lot adjoining his bakery into an elaborate organic garden tended by the parolees, the homeless, and other folk.[6] And Prudential Insurance Company received an award from the Business Enterprise Trust, a nonprofit organization that promotes socially responsible behavior, for creating the Living Needs Benefit, which allows certain seriously ill policyholders to redeem most of their life insurance benefits while still alive. About a third of the company's 3 million North American policyholders have signed up for the free option to date. Prudential has paid some $21 million on about 275 claims.[7]

Freedom of Choice

Figure 2.1 presents an overview of the social responsibility continuum—the choices available to organizations. Firms that choose to be proactive focus

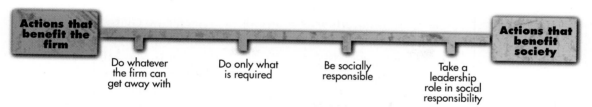

Figure 2.1

The social responsibility continuum.

their energies on specific social concerns, including small business, education and training, employment opportunities, the disabled in business, urban renewal, community involvement, environmental concerns, energy concerns, employee health, and consumer protection. Firms that pursue these areas do so with the purpose of investing their energies and resources toward the long-range goal of profitability for society—not as a philanthropic activity.

As the country moves through the 1990s, the challenge to business for social responsibility and social commitment will be in the forefront. Society, government, and business have all arrived at the same point at the same time. Society is moving away from "greed is healthy" to a more balanced approach. Business has observed this climate and the necessity to become a part of the solution, not a cause of the problem. It has the reason: business is a citizen of society and has a vested interest in its future health. And business has the resources, human and financial, plus the leadership skills to focus on society's needs.

In the next section we will examine areas for social responsibility.

Areas for Social Responsibility

In accepting its social responsibility, a business cannot be "all things to all people." Rather, it must seek the best match for its resources and interests—both the company and individual employees. Organizations have a wide choice for their social commitment, ranging from investing in the community to energy programs to consumer protection. All provide a return to society and to the organization.

Investing in the Community

Business has taken a proactive approach in the foundation of society—the community. Companies large and small have approached social responsibility from multiple directions: community involvement, small-business investment, and urban renewal.

COMMUNITY INVOLVEMENT It is a myth that only a big corporation or someone with lots of cash can make a powerful contribution to the community. A number of companies both large and small are creatively leveraging their products and skills to attack a variety of social problems. As an example, Figure 2.2 shows Rockwell International's commitment to the community. Companies make such commitments with the realization that the health and well-being of the community are major factors in recruiting and retaining talented employees. Here are some specific examples:

Figure 2.2
Rockwell
International's
community
involvement.

- Longfellow Clubs, a $4.5 million health and recreation company in Wayland, Massachusetts, donates the use of its swimming, tennis, and basketball facilities to kids with special needs. Through this action 80 percent of the children with disabilities in the Wayland area are served.
- Tom's of Maine, a producer of personal-care products in Kennebunkport, Maine, lets its employees donate up to 5 percent of their paid time as volunteers in efforts outside the company. The employees can spend two hours a week or one day a month working for a cause of their choice. Currently 33 percent of employees use the opportunity to work in schools, shelters, churches, or nonprofit organizations.
- Gilbert Tweed Associates, an executive search company, decided to use the company's skills to enhance nonprofit organizations. The company ran a lottery for nonprofits devoted to health care and education. The winners received free executive searches for a high-level position, human resources consulting services, or admission to one of the firm's seminars on selecting and retaining personnel.[8]

In addition to these company-based examples, the organizing campaigns for initiating mass transportation programs in southern cities of the United States have been strategically guided and publicly led by major community business leaders. And, more than 600 companies in the United States have some sort of formal volunteer program that encourages employee participation in the community. The programs range from granting employee release time at full pay, to work at schools and social agencies, to group projects such as Adopt-a-School or Partners in Education. Finally, millions of dollars have been contributed by businesses to establish or revive the arts programs of cities. Figure 2.3 summarizes the recipients of business donations of various types.

SMALL-BUSINESS INVESTMENT Businesses have taken a socially active role in providing substantial resources to assist the development of small-business

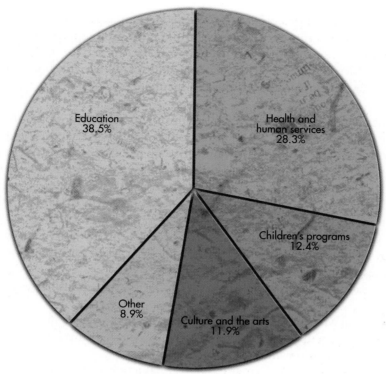

Figure 2.3
Splitting the business contribution dollar.

Source: Conference Board American Associates.

opportunities. Recognizing that a healthy business economy is built on the spirit of free enterprise found in small businesses, major corporations have committed financial, human, and technical resources to aid the formation and profitable growth potential of the small-business sector. Examples of this commitment are far ranging:

- Control Data Corporation has developed a wide range of services to assist small businesses, including financial assistance, data-processing services, education and training, management and professional consulting, and technology transfer. In addition, Control Data has established business and technology centers to provide combinations of consulting services. It has shared laboratory, manufacturing, and office facilities as well as other services to facilitate the start-up and growth of small businesses.[9]
- A number of companies, including Control Data, have either partnered with major corporations or formed their own small-business investment corporations (SBICs). These SBICs provide funds to finance the start-up of small business enterprises. Through their investments in SBICs the large corporations in essence take an equity position in the small business of tomorrow.
- Businesses have also become actively involved in small-business start-up activities through "small-business incubators." This innovative approach focuses on providing the opportunity for small businesses to set up in an

office building and receive specialized services to assist their growth: consulting in marketing, finance, accounting, and production; clerical assistance; computer support; and telephone answering service. Organizations such as IBM, Xerox, Procter & Gamble, and AT&T provide both financial and human resource support for such incubators.

Businesses have also made major commitments to promote the development of minority businesses. Shell Oil Company, General Motors, and other large firms have formed **minority enterprise small-business investment companies** (**MESBICs**), which are *venture capital firms designed specifically to provide funds to minority-owned small businesses.* MESBIC Ventures, Inc. of Dallas has eighty corporate shareholders, including NationsBank, Sun Company, Inc., Xerox, Frito-Lay, Mobil Oil Corporation, Arco Oil and Gas, Oryx Energy Company, and Coca-Cola Company. In the past twenty-three years it has been responsible for providing $28 million in capital for minority-owned companies; it invested $4 million in 1993.

Other examples of efforts to encourage minority-owned businesses include:

- Ark Capital Management, a Chicago firm, is attempting to raise $300 million to invest in up to fifteen small and medium-sized enterprises owned by minority men and women.
- The Mi Casa Resource Center in Denver has a new loan program designed to help low-income minority women obtain business loans of $500 to $5,000.[10]
- Anheuser-Busch, Shell Oil Company, Du Pont, and General Motors, among others, demonstrate their commitment to minority businesses by consciously doing business with and maintaining deposits in minority-owned banks.
- Numerous organizations, including AT&T, Du Pont, General Motors, and Pepsi-Cola, are committed to a minority vendors program. As an example, Tom Smith Industries, a major plastic injection molding and mold design company in Dayton, Ohio, recently announced it was awarding a $330,000 contract to black-owned Alex Industries of Jamestown, Ohio.[11]

URBAN RENEWAL   Another area for business commitment has been in direct investment in the inner city. Rather than deserting troubled cities at the first signs of urban decay, many firms now channel their resources toward **urban renewal programs,** *intensive efforts by businesses to refurbish old plants or offices or build new ones in cities, thus providing jobs and improving the city's economic health.*

Corporate involvement in urban renewal is more than two decades old. Hallmark built the $400 million Crown Center in Kansas City, Missouri in 1968, and four years before that Alcoa constructed a shopping complex and housing development in Pittsburgh. Responding to the inner-city riots that

minority enterprise small business investment companies (MESBICS)
Venture capital firms designed specifically to provide funds to minority-owned small businesses.

urban renewal programs
Intensive efforts by businesses to refurbish old plants or offices or build new ones in cities, thus providing jobs and improving the city's economic health.

broke out in several large cities in 1967 and 1968, Control Data built five manufacturing plants in the heart of such cities as Minneapolis, St. Paul, and Washington, D.C., providing employment for many persons who were once considered hard-core unemployed.

In recent years other corporations, such as Tandem Computers, have made major commitments that have resulted in the entire economic redevelopment of a geographic area. Tandem's plant in Maynard, Massachusetts has provided the one-time textile manufacturing town with a new lease on life. The plant was refurbished and employment opportunities became available once again.

In Chicago, the South Shore Bank is credited with revitalizing the South Shore neighborhood. For twenty years the bank made loans other banks wouldn't touch in a neighborhood where 97 percent of the residents are black and 20 percent are on welfare. South Shore not only made loans but founded City Lands, which invests in real estate projects, and the Neighborhood Institute, which locates government grants for major projects.[12]

Table 2.1

Survey results—corporations and education.

Education and Training

Another area for social responsiveness of business leaders is in education and job training. Recognizing that the future of their corporations, their communities, and America is directly linked to the opportunities for and quality of education and job training, corporations have committed funds, personnel, and equipment. Regardless of the industry—manufacturing, retailing, service—businesses are providing support to educational programs. The companies provide support, facilities, time, and management expertise in assisting high school and college students to gain both practical experience and an education. Table 2.1 shows the results of a survey of 250 of America's largest corporations. The 156 respondents proved that Corporate America is serious about education. Here are some specific examples of involvement:

- Exxon Corporation provided $127,500 to fund 75 internships in the Exxon Community Summer Jobs Program. With this pro-

	YES	NO
1. Is your company volunteering time and money to improve public education?	154	2
2. How would you characterize your involvement?		
Donate money or equipment	150	6
Adopt-a-school program	110	46
Employee-student mentor programs	110	46
Job training for high school students	84	72
Dropout prevention programs	83	73
School partnerships	87	69
Teacher development/training programs	74	82
Participate in school reform	98	58
Provide management training for education leaders	57	99
3. How much money did you commit to these efforts last year? (140 respondents)		
Under $100,000	53	
$100,000–$499,999	42	
$500,000–$999,999	16	
$1 million–$4,999,999	22	
$5 million or more	7	

Source: U.S. Department of Education.

gram college students are able to work with nonprofit agencies and practice their college majors.[13]

- General Electric, IBM, and other companies came to the rescue of the University of Vermont College of Engineering and Mathematics when a plan was announced to close the college to help reduce the university's projected $16 million deficit. The firms wrote letters, donated equipment, developed hands-on projects, and provided funds to keep the doors open.[14]
- Inter Voice, a Dallas voice automation company, recently donated new computer systems to the Jeffries Street Learning Center. They replaced computers stolen from the nationally acclaimed tutoring center in the gritty, inner-city neighborhood known as Jefferson-Meyers.[15]
- Tandy Corporation provided $2,500 stipends, $1,000 scholarships, ands Certificates of Achievement to "Champions of the Classroom." These awards are given to outstanding mathematics, science, and computer science students as well as outstanding teachers.
- Businesses have also supplied human resources to assist in education. Xerox has developed programs to provide for industry and college faculty exchange. The benefit from such a program: Current industry practices are brought into the classroom and the college instructors move into the "real-life" laboratory for skills updating. IBM grants fully paid leaves of up to a year to employees to teach or lend expertise to schools.

Employment Policies and Programs

In the area of employment, businesses are addressing wide-ranging areas of concern, from employment opportunities for minorities and women to family programs. Each area is continually shaped by the various stakeholders.

EMPLOYMENT OPPORTUNITIES FOR MINORITIES AND WOMEN Although business has long had the incentive of affirmative action programs (discussed in Chapter 8) to stimulate the development of employment opportunities for minority groups and women, total equality in employment opportunities has not been achieved. Progress has been made, but women and minority workers generally have not been given the needed experience to move into top-level positions. In an effort to correct this situation, businesses have committed to programs to provide these opportunities. For example:

- Many corporations have instituted Women's Advisory Councils. Their purpose is to develop recommendations and convey them to company decision makers on women employment concerns. As a result of various training and empowerment programs urged by the Women's Advisory Council at Tenneco, there are now nine senior women managers—up from two, five years ago.[16]
- Gannet Co. has developed specific career-advancement programs for minorities and women ranging from task force assignments, training, and

seminars to management bonuses tied to the advancement of women and minorities.[17]

- U.S. West has created the "Women of Color Project" to identify black, Hispanic, and Asian women—women of color—to fill leadership positions and to receive the training and development necessary to advance within the organization. Out of 1,800 applicants for the program, 50 were chosen. Selections were made based on managers' recommendations, leadership skills, and work experience. Once the participants were selected, they received extensive skills assessment, career planning, training and development classes, and the opportunity to take risks.

- In another sector of the economy, finance, the banking industry's efforts to recruit minorities and women are paying dividends. A recent study revealed that women and minorities are obtaining high-level management jobs at the nation's top banks at an ever-growing rate. The number of women filling top management positions has risen 166 percent in the last decade, while the number of blacks, Hispanics, Asians, and Native Americans has increased more than 100 percent. Now, 47 percent of top management positions at the nation's fifty largest banks are held by women. More than 57 percent of midlevel professional positions are held by women. In comparison, women accounted for 33 percent of top management positions and 41 percent of all professional jobs ten years ago in these same banks.[18]

THE DISABLED IN BUSINESS Another area of social concern for business is the employment of disabled workers. With the enactment of the Americans With Disabilities Act (the topic of Chapter 8's Manager's Notebook), employment policies and practices of all businesses will be modified and shaped to support the employment of disabled workers. But even without legislative

Many companies are actively seeking employees with disabilities, as such people tend to be dependable and highly motivated.

encouragement, many large companies are committed to both hiring disabled workers and modifying the physical work environment to accommodate them. For example, the Joseph Bulova School, which teaches watch repair to disabled workers, reports "an incredible change" in employer attitudes toward hiring the disabled. Employers not only have actively recruited workers; Control Data, IBM, Walgreen Company, and several Chicago banks have taught disabled employees to write computer programs at home.

As another example, the Atlanta-based Days Inns has tapped into the disabled population with great success. The workers have been found to be much more dependable, highly motivated, and eager to learn than many of their able-bodied colleagues. McDonald's, Kentucky Fried Chicken, and the Marriott Corporation have had successful experiences recruiting and employing mentally handicapped adults.

Although now required by law, many employers have voluntarily accommodated to the special needs of disabled employees by installing wheelchair ramps and electric doors; lowering elevator button panels, pay telephones, and water fountains; widening doorways; and providing wider than usual handicapped parking spaces close to buildings. When Days Inn hired its disabled workers it spent $10,000 redesigning its Atlanta reservations center to provide wheelchair ramps, wider doors, and lower lavatory fixtures. In addition, it purchased workstations, desks, and other furnishings that could easily accommodate wheelchair-bound people.

EMPLOYEE HEALTH At least 10,000 U.S. employers offer programs to improve or maintain employees' health. These programs, which first appeared in the mid-1970s, most often target health conditions that can be improved by changes in behavior. Such changes include stopping smoking, reducing cholesterol, exercising regularly, and controlling high blood pressure.

About 1,000 U.S. firms offer on-site, fully equipped fitness centers to promote good health habits. A pioneer in this field is Johnson & Johnson, whose "Live for Life" programs began in 1978. Workers at the company's New Brunswick, New Jersey headquarters have access to an 11,000-square-foot fitness center, with a half-mile indoor track for running or walking, as well as rowing machines and exercise bicycles. Aerobics and other exercise classes are available on a regular basis, as are talks on eating habits, AIDS, and alcohol abuse.

Another company committed to employee health and fitness is Tyler Corporation. Joe McKinney believes not only in the cardiovascular health and appearance bonus from a fit work force, but it's the "psychological fallout benefits" that really appeal to him: "People are more attractive not because they are lean, but because they have a more positive, everything-is-possible attitude. That alone makes them better dealmakers." McKinney has invested in exercise equipment, a jogging track, and policies to reward physical fitness.[19]

FAMILY FRIENDLY PROGRAMS As discussed in this chapter's Manager's Notebook, more companies are taking a proactive approach to balancing work and family with a realization that there is a link between family flexibility and high performance. Companies are building sound policies and programs. For example:

- NationsBank recently opened child-care facilities for 190 children in Charlotte, North Carolina. It is the latest in a string of workplace programs that has brought the company national recognition for creating a family-oriented work environment. Already in place are paid maternity, paternity, and adoption leave; a phase-in reduced-hour return-to-work policy; flexible work schedules; job sharing; adoption and child-care resource and referral services; and subsidized day care costs for low-income employees.[20]
- Companies like Affiliated Computer Systems, Mobil Corp., and Brown and Rout, Inc. provide toll-free hotlines that list child- and elder-care providers, provide subsidies for child care, arrange short-term help in case of illness or emergency, or subsidize summer or after-school programs.[21]
- Apple, Tandem, and McDonald's provide paid sabbaticals, sometimes called personal growth leaves. The concept allows people in high-stress professions to take time away from work to refresh and recharge.[22]

Environmental Responsibility

Environmental preservation, maintenance, and restoration must rank high on any corporation's list of social concerns. The advent of synthetic chemical compounds and materials and of exotic manufacturing processes means that the environment has become polluted. Actions have to be taken to eliminate the causes, and firms that are responsible must be held accountable. With this realization, there has been much environmental progress. Since Earth Day 1970, when Americans first began to "think green":

- Miles of polluted rivers and streams have been brought back to life.
- The number of cities with adequate sewage treatment plants has more than doubled.
- The pumping of sewage sludge into the ocean has ceased.
- Major air pollutants have been considerably reduced, as shown in Figure 2.4.

The business sector must continue its commitment. There are still problems in the areas of hazardous and solid waste and environmental maintenance.

HAZARDOUS WASTES The problem with **hazardous wastes**—*waste materials containing toxic substances*—is one common to land, water, and air pollution. According to recent estimates, industrial operations produce more than

hazardous wastes
Waste materials containing toxic substances.

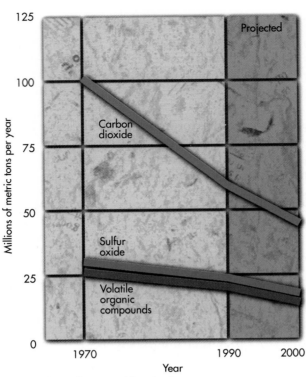

Figure 2.4
Reducing air pollution.

Source: Environmental Protection Agency.

50 million tons of hazardous waste each year, an average of 14.2 tons for each square mile of land mass in the forty-eight contiguous states. While generating products that benefit consumers in various ways, many manufacturing processes produce toxic chemical waste faster than it can be disposed of. Farsighted business leaders see this situation and give more than lip service to environmental concerns.

Recent data from the Environmental Protection Agency show that the toxic releases of U.S. manufacturers are falling. What's more, chemical makers that pump out the largest share of these poisons cut their emissions by 35 percent between 1987 and 1992, as shown in Table 2.2.[23]

One factor that has led to this decrease is the chemical industry's voluntary program to reduce toxic air pollutants below the standards set by the 1990 Clean Air Act. Nine of the nation's biggest polluters, including Du Pont and Monsanto, signed on with the understanding that they could

Table 2.2

A report card on the big polluters.

COMPANY	MILLIONS OF POUNDS OF POLLUTANT RELEASED	
	1987	1992
American Cyanamid, Westwego, LA	213.4	142.0
Shell Oil Company, Norco, LA	194.2	2.6
Monsanto, Alvin, TX	175.6	54.8
Kennecott-Utah-Copper, Bingham Canyon, UT	158.7	16.3

Source: Environmental Protection Agency.

Figure 2.5
A commitment by business to the world.

use the technology of their choice. At the same time, the Chemical Manufacturer's Association committed to pollution control, as shown in Figure 2.5. The results speak for themselves.

SOLID WASTES Besides hazardous waste, there is the basic problem of solid waste generated through packaging, bottling, and product construction. Experience and mistakes with waste disposal over the last three decades have shown that waste cannot be simply thrown away. About 64 percent of the country's growing mountain of waste is paper and paperboard, metals, glass, and plastics.[24]

In response to difficulties with solid waste disposal, organizations have attempted to provide alternative packaging that can help in the decomposition of products. Another area of emphasis has been to limit the manufacturing of new products by **recycling**, *the practice of reclaiming or producing materials from previously manufactured products and using them to make other items.* At the present time only 11 percent of solid waste is recycled.

Recycling opportunities exist in all areas of a business. Instead of discarding its cocoa-bean hulls, Hershey Foods Corporation reportedly grinds them up and sells them as garden mulch. Fiberboard and pressboard made from sawdust and wood chips enable economy-minded forest products firms to convert virtually every splinter of a tree into a salable product. In some manufacturing plants, heat from production processes is cycled through the heating system to heat the building. The Adolph Coors brewery once generated most of its needed electricity from recycled waste materials. The cumulative effects of recycling are impressive:

recycling
The practice of reclaiming or producing materials from previously manufactured products and using them to make other items.

- Mississippi River water is used at least eight times on its journey to the Gulf of Mexico.
- Forty percent of all new copper is made from recycled copper.
- Twenty percent of the glass we use comes from recycled scraps and shards that are melted down and mixed with new material.

Organizations that have committed to recycling are varied:

- Gardner's Supply, a mail order company in Burlington, Vermont, committed to a program that composts grass clippings and leaves for free in the local area. The program has been so successful that it collects 3,000 to 4,000 tons per year.[25]
- Yakima Products, Inc., a car-rack maker in Arcata, California, was unable to avoid using plastic and foam in packing its high-end roof-rack systems. The company created a way for customers to easily mail the packaging materials back—free. It then reuses the foam and polyethylene-shell portions of the container and recycles the outer chipboard.[26]
- The Boston Park Plaza Hotel has become immersed in recycling. Wooden pallets on which food is delivered to the hotel—up to 100 each week—are now returned to the vender and reused. The housekeeping staff makes chefs' aprons from damaged tablecloths. And, guests' returnable bottles are recycled—resulting in the purchase of several new vacuums.[27]

ENVIRONMENTAL MAINTENANCE In addition to solid waste problems, industry has another major social concern: overall environmental maintenance of water, air, and land. Business has begun to address this area. For example:

- E&J Gallo Winery gave $250,000 to the American Forestry Association's Global Relief Program, whose goal is to plant 100 million trees in the United States to counteract the greenhouse effect.
- Apple Computer donated $40,000 worth of computer equipment to Earth Day 1990.
- Timberland Shoes gave $250,000 to the Wilderness Society to assist in accomplishing its goals.
- Du Pont voluntarily spends $50 million each year on environmental projects beyond what the law requires, such as the $15 million it spent at a Texas plant to reduce the risk of dangerous gases being released.

Energy Programs

Companies have approached the energy situation from two directions: internal consumption efficiency and public programs. In the first area, organizations have attempted to use alternative means of energy, if possible, but many more have focused on developing or purchasing more efficient equipment.

For example, Fox River Mills, a manufacturer of gloves and athletic socks, spent $40,000 on measures to improve energy efficiency and reduced the company's monthly utility bill by about $3,000. The company installed energy-efficient ballasts in 600 fluorescent lights, moved the lights closer to the work being performed, added six inches of insulation to outside walls, installed white steel inner walls to reflect light, and directed wasted heat from air compressors and boilers inside its facility to heat part of the building in cold months.[28]

In the second area, firms have encouraged the use of van pooling. This public program has a twofold benefit: it reduces the amount of fuel consumed by using one vehicle instead of six, and it reduces traffic congestion on already snarled streets and freeways.

Consumer Protection

In recent years another major area of concentration for businesses has been **consumerism**—*activities undertaken to protect the rights of the consumer.* To genuinely partner with society, businesses cannot simply produce a product and place it on the market. Consumer protection involves consumer rights: the right to product safety, to be informed, to choose, and to be heard.

consumerism
Activities undertaken to protect the rights of the consumer.

PRODUCT SAFETY Businesses have spent time and money to improve the safety of products. Spurred on by the fear of lawsuits and consumer action, they have initiated a number of innovative ideas to ensure product safety.

Companies spend millions of dollars researching product safety. The auto industry has developed padded dashboards, shock-absorbing steering columns, and stronger gasoline tanks. Many companies have delayed the release of products until conclusive results of testing have been obtained, have initiated product recalls when their testing has discovered problems, and have attempted to identify product purchasers to make recalls less difficult.

CONSUMER INFORMATION Consumers have the right to have access to complete information about a product before they buy it, including information on potential dangers associated with the product. In response, companies have provided specific information on labels of food containers, and tags on clothing contain information on fabric composition and care. In addition, companies have co-sponsored, with retailers, workshops or clinics where consumers can see demonstrations of products and receive answers to their questions. Companies have produced extensive operating instructions, safety procedures, and practical uses of products to be provided to consumers at the time of purchase.

PRODUCT CHOICE Consumers have the right in the marketplace to choose between products offered by competing producers and marketers. This right is assured through the competition in the private enterprise system and by government antitrust laws.

YOU DECIDE

Identify a company in your community that is considered socially proactive. What areas of social responsibility is the company involved in? How do these efforts affect the community? How is this company viewed by the community for its actions?

VOICING CONCERNS Consumers have the right to be listened to and to have action taken when it is justified. A number of manufacturers have developed systematic programs to deal with consumer issues. A number of companies have established toll-free numbers for consumers to use to solve operating problems or receive product advice. Maytag introduced Red Carpet Service to improve its response to repair problems. General Electric operates the GE Answer Center, which handles consumer inquiries twenty-four hours a day, seven days a week, via a toll-free number. It receives 3 million calls each year. The center responds to questions from potential consumers and do-it-yourselfers and tries to resolve complaints from disgruntled customers.

Managing for Social Responsibility

An organization that accepts the view that it has obligations to persons other than its insiders and that makes managerial decisions on every level from this point of view is an organization that is socially responsible. Its leadership demonstrates this attitude by taking the lead in meeting social challenges.

Top Management Commitment

Executives in top management must commit the time and money necessary to make their organization socially responsible. They need to act as well as talk. They set the tone for the entire operation and establish its priorities. For an organization to be proactive, the following elements need to be in place:

- Top-level commitment and support
- Corporate policies that integrate socially responsible issues
- Effective communication between top management and the entire organization
- High degree of employee awareness and training
- Strong social auditing programs
- Establishment of responsibility for identifying and dealing with real and potential social responsibility problems

Social responsibility starts with the commitment in words and deeds of top management. Policies are written or revised to address social responsibility. Figure 2.6 provides a model that top management could follow in developing a policy statement, while Figure 2.7 shows how American Express has institutionalized its commitment to social responsibility.

Once top managers develops policies, they create programs for promoting an active role for their organization in meeting societal needs. Training is given to employees, emphasizing how they can contribute. Staff are encouraged to participate in their communities with time off and other incentives. When an organization is truly committed to meeting its social responsibilities,

Figure 2.6
A model policy for business social actions.

The following policy statement is suggested for companies reevaluating their responsibilities:

It is the policy of the company to take action in the name of social responsibilities but not at the expense of the rising profit level required to maintain the economic strength and dynamism desired by top management. Actions taken in the name of social responsibility should enhance the economic strength of the company and/or the business community. The overall mission of the company is two pronged: to set forth and achieve corporate objectives both internally and externally, that meet specified social challenges in areas ranging from product quality to quality of life; and to increase the company's earnings per share at a rate that meets shareowner/profit expectations *and* these new social requirements.

Source: George A. Steiner, "Institutionalizing Corporate Social Decisions," *Business Horizons*, December 1975, Copyright, 1975, by the Foundation for the School of Business at Indiana University. Reprinted by permission.

Figure 2.7
American Express's commitment to social responsibility.

At American Express, we measure performance by profitability and return on investment. There is, however, another significant measure: how we fulfill our responsibility to the communities from which our profits are derived. Public responsibility is a fundamental corporate value at American Express. It is visible in everything we do—from marketing to philanthropy, from our hiring practices to our consumer education programs. Some might call our traditions of caring and involvement enlightened self-interest. We call it common sense. Contributing to the quality of life in our communities is just good business.

Source: American Express Company, "American Express Public Responsibility: A Report of Recent Activities," 1987, p. 3. Reprinted by permission.

it reflects that commitment in its routine approach to management decision making and its ongoing planning operation.

The Social Audit

For social responsibility to be truly effective in an organization—as shown by McDonald's in Figure 2.8—it needs the backing of all managers. It needs to be part of daily operations, not subordinate to them. Managers and owners need to know what is being done in terms of social responsibility, what can be expected in the future, and what the results of past actions and plans have been. The means of achieving this is the **social audit**, *a report on the social performance of a business.*

Although no standard format exists, most proactive firms have developed some method for auditing their efforts and reporting the results to both insiders and outsiders. The social audit usually includes a summary of corporate activities under these headings: charitable contributions, support of local community groups and activities, employment of women, minorities, and the disabled, pollution control, support for minority enterprises, and efforts to improve the health and quality of work life for employees.

social audit
A report on the social performance of a business.

McDonald's people.
Serving customers and the community.

To McDonald's, people are everything.

Not only the people who work for us, but the people we serve as well.

The truth is, commitment, drive and talent are what make McDonald's people special. As many store managers will testify, you will start out in our Management Training Program and can end up managing a million dollar plus business.

The pace is fast, the atmosphere's fun and the spirit is catching, when you're a member of the McDonald's management team.

It's really all a matter of **pride.**

So it's not surprising that the people who take pride in their work at McDonald's are also proud to serve the community. Here are just a few of the projects our people are involved in:

There are the Ronald McDonald Houses.

These serve as homes away from home for more than 100,000 family members of seriously ill, hospitalized children every year.

There's our involvement in the Special Olympics.

This is the largest international program of physical fitness, sports training and athletic competition for the mentally and physically handicapped.

Then, of course, there's our involvement in high schools, with the McDonald's All American Band, Jazz Band and Basketball Team.

And these are but a few of the endeavors that our people take pride in supporting.

Which points to the fact that, throughout our team, McDonald's people are

special people.

So, if you're considering a career in management, consider McDonald's.

You'll not only find yourself in a satisfying job, you'll also find yourself getting involved in things which provide a deeper satisfaction.

Call 1-800-527-1737.
Always, An Equal Opportunity/
Affirmative Action Employer.

McDonald's
®

Powered by people with pride.SM

Figure 2.8
McDonald's is a part of the community.

ethics
The standards that govern moral conduct.

Progress may be stated in terms of goals set and met as well as in monetary terms. Those who benefit are clearly labeled, and the extent to which they benefit is quantified when possible. The results of the social audit should be shared with all stakeholders so that awareness of the commitment to and success of programs can be reinforced. Programs that have been successful should be continued and expanded if the need still persists. Programs that yield few positive results should be eliminated so that more productive ones may be initiated. People who have contributed to successful programs should be recognized and rewarded.

The Ethical Environment of Business

Whenever two parties interact in business, the quality of their relationship—the honest exchange of information, the openness, the "on the table" discussions—are the result of two forces: the laws that govern the transaction and the ethics of the two parties. **Ethics** are *the standards that govern moral conduct.* They have been narrowly referred to by people as "individual codes of conduct—the difference between right and wrong," "being honest," "fair play," and a "person's value system."

Regardless of how ethics are defined, they play a significant role in the business environment. Laws cannot and should not be developed to govern all business interactions. Rather, people must rely on the ethical practices of others to ensure the open conduct of business.

The Ethical Dilemma: What Is Unethical?

Ethics in the business world creates a dilemma for people. What makes a practice unethical? An action that is simply shrewd to one manager may be unethical to another. Practices in an organization that managers might condemn in profitable times might not seem so offensive when a firm is battling for its financial survival, with thousands of jobs and the welfare of supplier firms hanging in the balance. Following are some situations governed by ethics. Which of them would you consider to be ethical business practices?[29]

MANAGER'S NOTEBOOK

A New Responsibility to Family

Josephine Pigg, a former clerk with U.S. West, Inc. in Grand Junction, Colorado, was fourteen months from retirement when her thirty-two-year-old daughter, Tammie, was diagnosed with cancer. The prognosis was not good, and Pigg decided to stay with Tammie in Denver rather than travel 250 miles back and forth. At many other companies, Josephine would have been forced to leave. But her former boss, Penny Hubbard, figured out a way to keep Josephine working while she was sitting at her daughter's bedside. With the help of a human resources manager, Hubbard found Josephine a job with U.S. West in Denver. While it was a good deed, Hubbard wasn't just trying to be nice. "Josephine is valuable to our company—if employees have done a good job, we work to accommodate the situation."

Not all companies have this degree of commitment and social responsibility—but many companies are fast becoming the model of what ought to be. With record numbers of working women, single parents, two-career couples, and an aging population, more companies are coming face-to-face with the problems and demands of a diverse work force. The choices used to be: sacrifice the family for career or the career for the family. Now companies are creating a middle ground—success at home and at work—and everyone has to work together.

Increasingly companies are getting in step with the country's evolving social patterns. From Aetna Life and Casualty Co. to Alden Merrell Dessert Co., a cheesecake maker in Newburyport, Massachusetts, they are helping employees resolve work and family conflicts through such arrangements as job sharing, compressed work weeks, day care, family leave, working at home, and flexible scheduling. In the process they are increasing productivity, reducing turnover and absenteeism, and reinventing how work gets done.

At companies like NCR and Continental Corp., CEOs are driving changes. They're convinced that workplace flexibility is not an accommodation to employees but a competitive weapon. It frees workers to use their full potential on the job instead of fretting about taking a child to the doctor. Says NCR's Jerry Stead, "Everything we do must start with recognition of the balance between work and family. The only sustainable competitive advantage a company has is its employees. We have to recognize that people have lives."

(For more on business's new responsibility to family, see Michele Galen, "Work and Family," *Business Week,* June 28, 1993, pp. 80–86.)

- Paying suppliers net 60 days but expecting net 30 on your accounts receivable.
- Pretending your company has divisions to make it look bigger to clients and suppliers.
- Pirating software.
- Getting around privacy rights in job interviews.
- Writing a check for which you know you have insufficient funds, hoping it will be good by the time it's cashed.
- Using a copier machine on a thirty-day trial basis without intending to purchase it.
- Persuading dealers to buy more product than you think they need.
- Promising clients services you don't currently provide, or products you don't currently produce, and are not positive you can deliver.

Causes of Unethical Practices

What causes unethical conduct in business? Although the cause of every unethical action cannot be identified, there appear to be three major contributors: the competitive business environment, the organizational climate, and an individual's personal ethical values.

COMPETITIVE BUSINESS ENVIRONMENT Individuals and firms slip into questionable business practices as a way to keep pace with competitors, cut costs, increase efficiency, or meet ever-increasing sales quotas. For example:

- At Prudential Securities, senior executives debated for over seven years whether to dismiss a stockbroker for running roughshod over securities laws, making him the firm's second biggest producer. With annual commissions of as much as $5 million, the broker—Frederic Stovaska—made more than many Prudential branches—one reason he was protected for so long.[30]
- At the North Carolina–based Food Lion supermarket chain, the drive for efficiency induced employees to cut corners by selling spoiled meat and removing freshness dates on other products.[31]

ORGANIZATIONAL CLIMATE The organizational climate influences ethical behavior. Not only do individuals see a fellow worker or supervisor acting unethically and copy the actions, but organizational practices often encourage unethical behavior. For example:

- Offering unusually high rewards. Huge bonuses and commissions can distort a person's values, in much the same way that too much power can corrupt. People can be motivated without corrupting them by simply keeping rewards within the bounds of reason.
- Threatening unusually severe punishments. If people are desperate to avoid

GLOBAL PERSPECTIVE

Ethics in Japan

Breaches of ethics in the United States are pretty much isolated occurrences—Ivan Boesky, Michael Milkin, the illegal Treasury bids by Salomon Brothers. But "in Japan it's part of the system," privately confessed a director of Hitachi Ltd. shortly after his company was implicated in cases where securities firms were compensating their biggest customers for stock losses.

Unethical behavior is a longstanding problem, with origins deep in Japan's social and cultural tradition. "Loosely speaking, the Japanese think that whether one does business in a fair way or not is up to oneself," observes Tak Wakasugi, professor of finance at the prestigious Tokyo University.

At the foundation of this statement are two cultural guidelines: Japan's emphasis on personal relationships, and the commitment to not rocking the boat. In the first instance, Japan is a society based overwhelmingly on in-

sider relationships, as opposed to American society, which suppresses such tendencies and tries to create a system where all kinds of business transactions occur without collusion and where everyone has an equal chance.

The second guideline results in a belief that "You've got to look after the people around you and keep them happy." This principle appears to make Japanese accountants more willing to "cook the books." That is, they are more inclined to obey a boss who asks them to falsify accounts, because their first loyalty is to the company, not to a code of ethics.

(For more on ethics in Japan, see Edwin Whenmouth, "A Matter of Ethics," *Industry Week*, March 17, 1993, pp. 57–59.)

what they regard as a calamity, they will go to whatever lengths they must to avoid it. In this case, terror overcomes a person's conscience so that dirty work can be done.

- Emphasizing results and ignoring the means used by employees to achieve those results.[32]

INDIVIDUAL PERSONAL VALUES A person's own value system influences his or her ethical behavior. All of us have a set of standards or principles that dictate behavior. These principles are tested through experience—and some people's ethics may "stretch" more easily than others. Some individuals are able to rationalize more easily than others, which may lead to misconduct. Here are four common rationalizations:

- A belief that the activity is within reasonable ethical and legal limits—that is, it is not "really" illegal or immoral.
- A belief that the activity is in the individual's or the organization's best

interests—that the individual would somehow be expected to undertake the activity.

- A belief that the activity is "safe" because it will never be found out or publicized; the classic crime-and-punishment issue of discovery.
- A belief that because the activity helps the company, the company will condone it and even protect the person who does it.[33]

Encouraging Ethical Behavior

From a business standpoint it is undesirable to legislate ethics. Ethics and ethical practices can be influenced from two major sources: personal and company codes of conduct.

PERSONAL CODES OF CONDUCT An individual's personal value system is the greatest influence on the businessperson as he or she conducts business transactions. These personal codes of conduct, developed through personal experience, are the best barometers of "business right and wrong." Companies hire employees as well as their value systems, and with these comes a personal code of ethical behavior.

As a quick check of your personal code of conduct, which of the following statements most closely matches your views of ethics in business?

- I play by the rules, but I'll bend them to my company's advantage whenever I can.
- I tell the whole truth, all the time.
- All's fair in love and business, as long as you don't get caught.

Often within personal codes of conduct is the courage not to condone unethical practices of others. *Individuals who take action to inform their bosses, the media, or government agencies about unethical practices within their organizations* are referred to as **whistle-blowers**. At Teledyne Inc., whistle-blowers revealed that the defense contractor kept two sets of books, made illegal payments to a retired Egyptian Air Force general to secure lucrative contracts, falsified test results, and cut corners and sacrificed quality on military work.[34]

Whistle-blowers often risk their careers by reporting unethical behavior. They may be harassed, passed up for promotions, or fired.

whistle-blowers Individuals who take action to inform their bosses, the media, or government agencies about unethical practices within their organizations.

COMPANY CODES OF CONDUCT The actions of subordinate managers and employees reflect the standards, attitudes, and values of top management. Its willingness to condone or to ignore ethically questionable activities becomes an unwritten code in itself. For a company to maintain the highest possible level of ethical conduct by its employees, the senior executives must make a major commitment to ethics, clearly communicate standards of conduct to every employee, reward ethical behavior, and discourage unethical behavior. The key "is for an organization to never let up on its vigilance to achieve

Is the company:	Yes	No
1. Concerned about quality in its services, products, and operations?	___	___
2. Concerned about its employees' quality of life?	___	___
3. Proud of its reputation in the industry?	___	___
4. Proud of its reputation in the community?	___	___
5. Focused on the needs of its customers?	___	___
6. Honest in its dealings with you?	___	___
7. Honest in its dealings with customers?	___	___
8. Honest in its dealings with others?	___	___
9. Fair and equitable in the ways in which it decides on promotions?	___	___
10. Fair and equitable in the ways in which it compensates employees?	___	___
11. Open in its communications?	___	___
12. Trusting in its relationships with employees?	___	___
13. Concerned with developing and keeping its employees?	___	___
14. Actively promoting ethical conduct in all its operations and employees?	___	___
15. Actively searching for ways to better serve its stakeholders?	___	___
16. Carefully monitoring how decisions are made and checking them for their concern for ethical behavior?	___	___

Source: W. Plunkett and R. Attner, *Introduction to Management*, 5th ed. (Belmont, Calif.: Wadsworth, 1994), p. 767.

Figure 2.9

A checklist for determining whether ethical behavior is being supported.

ethical practices." Only then can an organization have a conscience.[35] Figure 2.9 provides a checklist to help management determine whether ethical behavior is being supported.

Many companies have addressed the problem by developing a written **code of ethics**, *formal guidelines for the ethical behavior of individuals in an organization, job, or profession.* The Conference Board, a business-funded research group, reported that "company codes of conduct are becoming increasingly sophisticated, and nearly one-third of the 264 chief executives surveyed had issued a personal statement or engaged in a formal discussion of ethics." These codes are effective only if companies live by them. The fact that a company has developed a code but ignores its presence in the conduct of business creates a question of credibility. Figure 2.10 presents General Electric's policy on business ethics.

code of ethics
Formal guidelines for the ethical behavior of individuals in an organization, job, or profession.

YOU DECIDE

Think of a newspaper story or news event reported on television that involved the ethical practices of a business. Was the action of the company illegal or unethical? What factors were reported to have led to this activity? What would you do if you were in the same situation?

Figure 2.10

A portion of General Electric's code of ethics.

*Ethical Business
Practices*
POLICY 20.4

Page 2 of 11
Issued April 1993
Supersedes all previous editions

- Be careful! Exercise due diligence when selecting a third party to represent GE, keeping in mind that GE and its employees may, in some circumstances, be held responsible for the actions of sales agents and other third parties. For example, it a sales agent make an improper payment to a government official, the GE employee who works with that agent, as well as the company, might be charged with a criminal violation of the Foreign Corrupt Practices act if the employee a) knew about the payment (or consciously disregarded information that the payment likely took place; *and* b) authorized it, either explicitly or implicitly. When selecting a third party to represent GE, consider the following:

  —Employ only reputable, qualified individuals and firms.

  —Understand and obey any requirements governing the use of third parties (for example, funding agency restrictions, or customer, country or ministry prohibitions).

  —Make sure that the compensation is reasonable for the services provided.

  —Follow the implementing procedures or component guidelines for selecting and paying third parties.

  —If you spot a "red flag" (an indication of a potential policy violation) involving a third party, make sure that it is promptly investigated and resolved.

  —Seek the assistance of company legal counsel and management in exercising due diligence and resolving any red flags.

Political contributions

- Obey the laws of the U.S. and host countries in promoting the company position to government authorities and in making political contributions.

- Political contributions by the company to U.S. federal, state or local candidates may be prohibited or regulated under the election laws. Any contribution of company funds or other assets for political purposes in the U.S. can only be made by GE's Vice President of Corporate Government Relations or Vice President of State Government Relations.

- Never make or offer, directly or indirectly, a payment or anything of value (such as a bribe or kickback) to any political party, party official, or any candidate for political office of a country outside the U.S. to influence or reward any governmental act or decision.

Source: Courtesy of General Electric Company. Reprinted by permission.

Ethical Business Practices
POLICY 20.4

Page 3 of 11
Issued April 1993
Supersedes all previous editions

Permissible payments

- You may provide customers with ordinary and reasonable entertainment and gifts only if they are permitted by

  —the law,

  —the customer's own policies and procedures, *and*

  —your business component's procedures.

  This policy does not prohibit lawful reimbursement for reasonable and *bona fide* expenditures—for example, travel and living expenses incurred by customers and directly related to the promotion of products or services, or the execution of a contract.

- Gifts and entertainment to officials and employees of the governments of the United States and other countries are highly regulated and often prohibited. Do not provide such gifts and entertainments unless you have determined that you are permitted by applicable law and regulations, and your business component's policies and procedures to do so.

- The Foreign Corrupt Practices Act does allow facilitating payments. Facilitating payments are gratuities paid to officials or employees of non-U.S. governments to expedite a service or routine administrative action that these individuals ordinarily perform and to which GE is entitled under the laws of that country. This policy allows facilitating payments in some countries (but not all countries) and only to low-level officials or government employees when they are customary in those countries. Seek the advice of the National Executive or your business legal counsel before visiting a country. Make sure that these payments are clearly and accurately reflected in financial reports.

Employee responsibilities:

- **Understand and keep up-to-date on the laws of the U.S. and other countries, funding agency regulations and customer requirements related to your job and each requirement of this policy. These requirements can be complex, and it is not unusual to have questions related to a transaction. If you have any questions related to matters covered by this policy, consult with business leaders, their designees, company legal counsel, component guidelines, implementing procedures or the GE National Executive in the country in which you are operating.**

SUMMARY

Today's business firms operate in an environment of interdependence with society and government. Out of this interdependence has come the realization that they must pursue their overriding goal of profit within a social and political framework. Business decisions must be made while evaluating their total effects on business's stakeholders: investors, employees, consumers, suppliers, and the community.

This in turn has led to an emphasis on social responsibility—the belief that business decisions should be made within the confines of both social and economic considerations.

Businesses can adopt one of three approaches to the demands made on them by social responsibility: to resist, to react, or to be proactive.

Many businesses have taken a proactive approach in the community. Companies have approached social responsibility from multiple directions, including community involvement, small-business investment, and urban renewal. Many business leaders have also made commitments to education. Recognizing that the future of their corporations, their communities, and their country is directly linked to the opportunities for and quality of education and job training, corporations have provided funds, personnel, and equipment.

In the area of employment policies and programs, businesses are addressing wide-ranging areas of concern, including employment opportunities for minorities and women, employing the disabled, employee health, and family-friendly programs.

Although a long way from perfection, businesses have been addressing environmental concerns. They have focused attention on disposal of hazardous and solid wastes and maintenance of air, land, and water resources. Business has also initiated programs to support energy conservation. Not only has business attempted alternative sources of energy, but it has initiated programs to reduce energy consumption through improved operations and van pooling.

Consumerism—consumer protection—has been a major concern for business. Companies have concentrated on improving product safety, providing consumer information, offering consumers a choice of products in the marketplace, and providing means for consumers to be heard.

Ethics are the standards that govern moral conduct. They are important because they affect all business transactions. The problem in the business environment is that ethics have been modified by changing situations. The factors that influence ethics include the competitive business environment, the organizational climate, and individual personal values. Business ethics depend on each employee's code of ethics and on the development and reinforcement of a company code of ethics.

KEY TERMS

code of ethics p. 59
consumerism p. 51
ethics p. 54
hazardous wastes p. 47
minority enterprise small-business investment
    companies (MESBICs) p. 42

recycling p. 49
social audit p. 53
social responsibility p. 36
stakeholders p. 34
urban renewal programs p. 42
whistle-blowers p. 58

FOR REVIEW AND DISCUSSION

1. Explain in your own words what is meant by social responsibility.
2. Why do you think companies have become socially responsive? Do you believe their actions have been voluntary or involuntary? Why?
3. Distinguish between the three approaches a company can take toward social responsibility. For each approach write one sentence that describes management's operating philosophy on social responsibility.

4. Why has business taken a leadership role in overall community involvement?

5. "Community involvement is the thing to do. It is expected." Evaluate this statement from the standpoint of social commitment.

6. Why do major business corporations invest in small-business opportunities?

7. Why would a company choose to participate as a shareholder in an SBIC or a MESBIC?

8. Evaluate this statement: "Companies that initiate programs for hiring and promotion of minorities and women are simply doing what the government demands."

9. Explain why businesses have been reluctant to hire disabled workers. Why has this reluctance been changing?

10. What specific benefit do employers and employees receive when a company health program is created?

11. Identify three specific family-friendly programs companies have initiated.

12. What actions have companies taken to reduce hazardous wastes?

13. "Energy conservation is just another phase. If it wasn't for the cost factor, we would not worry about it." Evaluate this statement from the standpoint of social responsibility.

14. Why are product safety programs and consumer information programs considered a function of social responsibility?

15. "Social responsibility is the job of every manager." Explain this statement as it relates to the social audit.

16. What effect does ethics have on business transactions? How can a company bring pressure on an individual that could create unethical practices? Can this be avoided?

17. What is the purpose of a company code of ethics?

APPLICATIONS

Case 2.1: Lotus in South Africa

Lotus Development Corporation, a leader in the field of spreadsheet software, has a long and highly respected reputation for taking clear positions on social issues. One of those issues is apartheid, the policy of racial segregation promulgated in the Republic of South Africa. Lotus suspended doing business in South Africa in 1985 because of apartheid and supported trade sanctions against the white, pro-apartheid political leadership in South Africa. But once the apartheid laws were overturned and the U.S. government lifted its sanctions in 1991, Lotus reentered the South African market. This action was widely criticized as opportunistic and irresponsible by those who maintained the need for sanctions. Indeed, Lotus had much to gain by reentering South Africa. The company made $7.5 million there the first year it was back. Lotus management held, however, that its focus was not on profit, but to promote democracy by investing in South Africa.

Such a reversal in corporate policy raises many questions concerning ethical investing and social corporate behavior. Contemporary views hold that companies must be socially responsible, acting in the best interests not only of the company's stockholders and investors but for the benefit of employees, consumers, and the society or community in which they do business. Increasingly, this community is becoming global. To assure that it was representing all interests properly, Lotus hired Macaw McLeod, a computer expert and antiapartheid social activist, to develop a socially responsible program in South Africa. The independent firm that McLeod headed was to be different than previous efforts at social involvement. Most companies in the past had invested in the country through "corporate social responsibility projects," which primarily meant gifts of money or equipment, that helped support various community projects. McLeod felt that these "gifts" were ineffective, doing more for the tax returns of the corporations that donated them than for the people who receive them.

McLeod trains trainers, who in turn teach others to use information technology and, of course, Lotus's software products. In addition, South Africans are selected for internships at the company's Cambridge, Massachusetts offices. By marketing his services to local community leaders, McLeod has found ways to make Lotus's investment more than an impressive expenditure. Planning projects such as a computerized national food bank, McLeod is finding ways to improve the quality of life for people of color in South Africa while giving Lotus the opportunity to take pride in profits that have nothing to do with little green pieces of paper.

Questions

1. How important is it for a company to have a policy concerning social responsibility?

2. Who should be responsible for determining social issues in a company?

3. What are the advantages to a company in taking a socially responsible stance on issues?

4. Do Lotus's profit motives conflict with the company's social responsibility agenda?

5. What role should individual employees play in these types of policies and issues?

For more information, see Myra Alperson, "Helping Lotus Do the Right Thing in South Africa," *The New York Times,* May 2, 1993, p. F12.

Case 2.2: Is "Pure and Natural" Just Marketing Hype?

In recent years, a dramatic shift has occurred in consumer behavior. Where once customers purchased products on the basis of convenience, performance, or prestige, today they favor healthiness, purity, and an absence of chemical additives in their products. Sometimes referred to as the "detox" or "green" movement, the trend toward pure and natural products is a response to the growing concern over environmental pollution.

Not every business takes the same approach to "pure and natural." Tom's of Maine has always produced pure and natural products; its toothpaste is made without sugar or chemicals. By abstaining from sweetened toothpaste and eliminating their intake of fluoride, some people hope to have cleaner teeth and longer lives. Other companies, such as Johnson & Johnson, are transforming existing products, such as cotton balls, into ones that are promoted as "all natural." The Johnson & Johnson swab is advertised as "Real Cotton," with no synthetic fibers and whitened without bleach. The new line, however, is identical to the company's normal products except that the cotton is not sterilized.

Johnson & Johnson and other companies are realizing huge profits from "pure and natural" products, one of the fastest growing segments of the health care market. Still others, such as Del Laboratories, are developing as-natural-as-possible products, using preservatives only when necessary and avoiding testing on animals.

Many consumers believe pure and natural products help them avoid toxic dangers or live a more healthful lifestyle and also feel more politically and socially responsible for using them. However, many are beginning to question the commitment of businesses to the ideals that have created this new industry. The profits are great, and it's often easy to position products as being "green." Is it just marketing hype? Are companies' commitments to "green" merely skin deep?

Questions

1. What are the business advantages to producing socially responsible products?

2. How does misleading advertising hurt a business?

3. Is it possible to produce "detox" or "green" products in response to consumer demand while not acting as a socially responsible business?

For more information, see Kathleen Deveny, "Marketscan," *The Wall Street Journal,* May 11, 1993, pp. B1–B8.

REFERENCES

1. Pat Widder, "More Corporations Learning That Ethics Are Bottomline Issue," *Chicago Tribune,* June 7, 1992, Sec. 7, pp. 1, 6.

2. Charles E. Watson, *Managing With Integrity: Insights from America's CEOs* (New York: Praeger), 1992, p. 321.

3. Kenneth E. Goodpaster and John B. Matthews,

Jr., "Can a Corporation Have a Conscience?" *Harvard Business Review,* January–February 1982, pp. 113, 138.

4. Milton Friedman, "The Social Responsibility of Business Is to Increase Its Profits," *New York Times Magazine,* September 13, 1970, p. 142.

5. Jacqueline Mitchell, "Toyota Finds Itself in Jam

on Door Lock," *The Wall Street Journal,* August 19, 1992, p. B1.

6. Brenton R. Schlender, "The Values We Will Need," *Fortune,* January 27, 1992, p. 77.

7. Gilbert Fuchsberg, "Business People Aiding Society Win Accolades," *The Wall Street Journal,* March 6, 1992, p. A3.

8. Ellyn E. Spragins, "Making Good," *Inc.,* May 1993, pp. 114–117.

9. "Social Needs and Business Opportunities," *Control Data Corporation Annual Report,* December 1992, p. 7.

10. Bradford McKee and Sharon Nelton, "Building Bridges to Minority Firms," *Nation's Business,* December 1992, pp. 29–33.

11. Ibid.

12. Paul Wiseman, "Chicago Bank Redefines Role in the Community," *USA Today,* January 8, 1993, pp. 1B–2B.

13. Jim Simnacher, "Exxon Puts Students to Work," *Dallas Morning News,* June 11, 1993, p. 2D.

14. Rick Tetzelli, "How Saving a School Paid Off," *Fortune,* December 28, 1992, p. 17.

15. Craig Flournoy, "Company Replaces S. Dallas Tutoring Center's Stolen Computers," *Dallas Morning News,* March 30, 1993, p. 17A.

16. Barbara Ettorre, "Breaking the Glass . . . Or Just Window Dressing," *Management Review,* March 1992, pp. 16–18.

17. Ibid.

18. Diane Kunde, "Power Struggle in Management Ranks," *Dallas Morning News,* January 24, 1993, pp. B1–B2.

19. Cheryl Hall, "Tyler Corp. CEO Finds Pipeline to Physical Fitness," *Dallas Morning News,* March 4, 1993, p. H1.

20. Cheryl Hall, "Taking Care of Employees No Child's Play to McColl," *Dallas Morning News,* May 17, 1993, pp. H1, H18.

21. Kathleen Kerwin, "Family Care: Tips for Companies That Are Trying to Help," *Business Week,* September 28, 1992, p. 36.

22. Diana Kunde, "A Little Corporate R&R," *Dallas Morning News,* March 27, 1993, p. D1.

23. Mary Beth Regan, "An Embarrassment of Clean Air," *Business Week,* May 31, 1993, p. 34.

24. Ibid.

25. Ellyn Spragins, "Making Good."

26. Ellyn Spragins, "Making Good."

27. Kevin Maney, "Conservation Effort Pays Off in Boston," *USA Today,* June 11, 1993, pp. B1–B2.

28. David Warner, "Ways to Save on Energy Costs," *Nation's Business,* August 1992, p. 29.

29. Christopher Caggiano, "Can You Afford to Be Ethical? *Inc.,* December 1992, p. 16.

30. Kurt Eichenwald, "Portrait of a Rogue Dallas Stockbroker," *Dallas Morning News,* May 25, 1993, pp. 1D, 16D.

31. Joseph Menn, "Food Lion's Smith Weathers Tough Blows," *Dallas Morning News,* November 25, 1992, p. 2D.

32. Saul W. Gellerman, *Motivation in the Real World* (New York: Dutton), 1992, pp. 265–267, 269–271, 273–274.

33. Saul W. Gellerman, "Why Good Managers Make Bad Ethical Choices," *Harvard Business Review,* July–August, 1986, pp. 88–89.

34. Eric Schine, "At Teledyne, A Chorus of Whistle-Blowers," *Business Week,* December 14, 1992, p. 40.

35. Christopher Caggiano, "Can You Afford to be Ethical?" *Inc.,* December 1992, p. 16.

3

THE UNINCORPORATED BUSINESS:
SOLE PROPRIETORSHIPS AND PARTNERSHIPS

*Y*ou don't get rich
by looking back-
ward . . . you've
got to be creative and find
a way to add value . . . We
are trying to figure out how
to build a better mouse-
trap.

Daryl Carter
Partner, Carter Primo

CHAPTER OBJECTIVES
After studying this chapter, you should be able to:
1. Explain the nature of a sole proprietorship as a form of business ownership.
2. Describe the process of creating a sole proprietorship.
3. List and describe the major advantages and disadvantages of a sole proprietorship as a form of business ownership.
4. Explain the nature of and process involved in creating a partnership.
5. List and describe the major advantages and disadvantages of a partnership as a form of business ownership.
6. Identify and distinguish between general and limited partnerships.
7. Describe the purposes and characteristics of a joint venture.

UP FRONT

What began as a childhood friendship has turned into an extremely successful business and an American household word: Ben & Jerry's. Ben Cohen and Jerry Greenfield met in their seventh grade gym class in Merrick, Long Island, New York and soon became fast friends. Their bond was a love of ice cream and feeling like outsiders: "We were the two slowest, chubbiest guys in the seventh grade," says Greenfield. "We were nerds." He went to Oberlin College with the intention of going on to medical school, while Cohen attended Skidmore College, majoring in pottery. After several postcollege odd jobs, they concluded that they wanted to do something that would be more fun, and they also wanted to live in a rural college town.

So in early 1977 the two men moved to Burlington, Vermont, home to the University of Vermont. They continued their education by completing a $5 correspondence course in making homemade ice cream. With $12,000—a third of it borrowed—and a rock salt ice cream maker, they opened Ben & Jerry's Homemade Ice Cream in a renovated gas station. That summer, they held their first free film festival, projecting movies on the outside wall of the building while viewers slurped down their ice cream. A year later, they were delivering their product to grocery stores and restaurants, and by 1980 they had moved into an old mill, where they packed their ice cream in pint-sized cartons for sale in stores to retail customers.

Even though it took some time to perfect their recipes, good taste and high quality were key to Ben & Jerry's ice cream success. The entrepreneurs concocted various flavors by adding chunks of chocolate, various fruits, and wild flavorings to their pure, all-Vermont dairy cream. Some of the flavors Ben & Jerry's has become famous for include Rainforest Crunch, Blueberry Cheesecake, Chocolate Chip Cookie Dough, and Cherry Garcia. This last flavor, a play on the name of the Grateful Dead's founder and lead guitarist, Jerry Garcia, was suggested by a customer in an anonymous postcard. Cohen and Greenfield spent two years tracking her down to thank her for her suggestion.

Developing Ben & Jerry's into a full-fledged business was a difficult transition for Cohen and Greenfield. They figured their lack of business ability would keep their operation small, but that was far from the truth. "When Jerry and I realized we were no longer ice cream men but businessmen, our first reaction was to sell," says Ben Cohen. "We were afraid that business exploits its workers and the community. We listed the company with a broker and actually had a buyer. We ended up keeping it, but we decided to adapt it so we could feel proud to say we were the businessmen of Ben & Jerry's."

One way they did so was by making the first public stock offering to Vermonters only. Another way they did so was to pay

Ben Cohen and Jerry Greenfield

BEN & JERRY'S HOMEMADE, INC.

Vermont dairy farmers more than the asking price for their cream, because they felt the farmers needed the money more than the company did. The co-founders also set up the Ben & Jerry's Foundation, to fund community projects with company profits. Each year since 1985, the company has donated 7.5 percent of its pretax earnings to this nonprofit institution to aid charitable organizations that apply for grants-in-aid. The goal is to support "projects which are models for social change; projects infused with a spirit of generosity and hopefulness; projects which enhance people's quality of life; and projects which exhibit creative problem solving."

The owners' social consciousness extends within the company as well. Employees have some latitude in the tasks they perform each day, so that the work does not become boring and monotonous; they're also entitled to free ice cream and back rubs. There are spontaneous visits throughout the factory by the Joy Gang, and celebrations such as Elvis Day. A Ben & Jerry's bumper sticker reads, "Practice Random Acts of Kindness and Senseless Beauty."

Ben & Jerry's Homemade, Inc. has grown from its partnership beginnings into a national corporation with 1992 sales of $132 million. In 1988 chairman and chief executive officer Cohen and vice chairman Greenfield were named U.S. Small Business Persons of the Year by the president. Over the years its operations have expanded, including a move to its corporate headquarters and ice cream factory in Waterbury, Vermont in 1985. Additional factories and operations are located in Springfield, Rockingham, and St. Albans, Vermont. Franchised Ben & Jerry's Scoop Shops are located across the United States and in Canada, Israel, and Russia. Ben and Jerry still host free concerts and festivals; in recent years these events have been held at the Killington ski area in Vermont, in Chicago, and in San Francisco's Golden Gate Park. Has business success gone to Ben and Jerry's heads? "I would say it's quite a shock to us, and quite frankly, it's a shock to anyone who knows us," Jerry quips.

The first two chapters introduced the broad framework for our study of business: the nature of business, the foundations of private enterprise, the economic systems, and the issues of ethics and social responsibility. Now we focus on the ways a business can legally organize.

Which Legal Form of Business Is Best?

One of the major decisions an entrepreneur must make is which legal form of business ownership to use in creating a business venture. He or she has three basic forms of business ownership to choose from: sole proprietorships, partnerships, and corporations.

Which of these legal forms of business ownership is best? There is no simple answer to this question. To decide, the entrepreneur must answer such questions as:

- How much money is needed to finance the business, and how easily will financing be found?
- How much decision-making control does ownership want?
- How much is the entrepreneur willing to risk—money invested in the business or personal property?

- How will the business be taxed, and who will be responsible for the taxes?
- Can the business easily attract employees?

The answers to these questions, plus the entrepreneur's personal goals, values, and work ethic, will determine which type of business organization is best.

A point to remember is that most businesses begin as sole proprietorships. As they grow, many become partnerships or corporations. As shown in Figure 3.1, sole proprietorships far outnumber corporations.[1]

In this chapter we will examine the two unincorporated business forms: sole proprietorships and partnerships—how they are created, their advantages and disadvantages. In Chapter 4 we will go on to provide an in-depth discussion on corporations.

Sole Proprietorships

A **sole proprietorship**, as the name implies, is *a business owned by one individual.* It is the oldest and most common type of business. As shown in

sole proprietorship
A business owned by one individual.

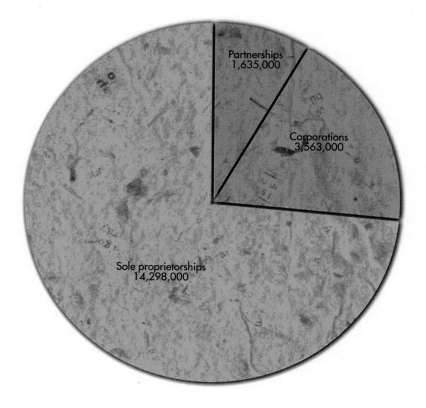

Figure 3.1
Distribution of the three basic legal forms of business ownership in the United States.

Partnerships
1,635,000

Corporations
3,563,000

Sole proprietorships
14,298,000

Source: Data from U.S. Bureau of the Census, *Statistical Abstract of the United States, 1992,* 112th ed. (Washington, D.C.: U.S. Government Printing Office, 1992), p. 519.

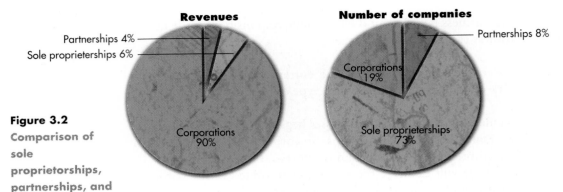

Figure 3.2

Comparison of sole proprietorships, partnerships, and corporations.

Source: Data from U.S. Bureau of the Census, *Statistical Abstract of the United States, 1992,* 112th ed. (Washington, D.C.: U.S. Government Printing Office, 1992), p. 519.

Figure 3.2, in recent years sole proprietorships have accounted for 73 percent of all businesses operating in the United States. That means sole proprietorships account for almost three out of four businesses. However, although they represent the vast majority of businesses, they produce only 6 percent of total revenues when compared with partnerships and corporations. That's because sole proprietorships are typically small-business operations such as drug stores, variety shops, and delicatessens or service-related businesses such as barbershops, repair shops, and lawn and garden services. Most sole proprietorships operate in the five categories shown in Figure 3.3.

In the eyes of the law, the owner and the company in a sole proprietorship are inseparable—the sole proprietor not only owns the business but also is responsible for its operation. In addition, in the eyes of the public and business suppliers, the sole proprietor is considered to be the business. But being a sole proprietor does not mean working alone: a sole proprietorship has as many managers and employees as the scope of operations requires.

Advantages of Sole Proprietorships

The popularity of the sole proprietorship is found in its many advantages— not the least of which are freedom of operation and simplicity. The main advantages are:

- *Ease of formation.* The sole proprietorship is the easiest and least expensive form of business to create. Normally, once a sole proprietor has decided on a product or service to sell, he or she is in business. Legal requirements are minimal. No permission is needed to enter business, with the exception of licenses for health and food services; permits for construction firms, beauty salons, and barbershops; and conformity to zoning requirements.
- *Retention of all profits.* As the sole owner, a proprietor is entitled to retain all profits. The profits of the business flow directly to the owner. The better the business operates, the greater the profit to the sole proprietor.

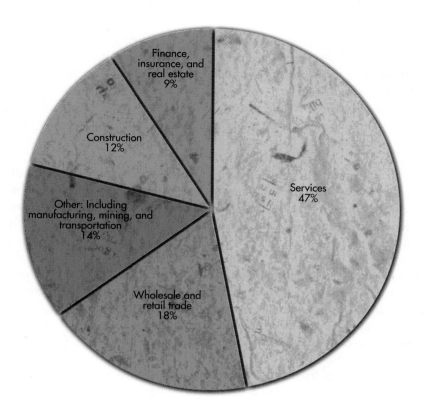

Figure 3.3
The most popular sole proprietorships.

Finance, insurance, and real estate
9%

Construction
12%

Other: Including manufacturing, mining, and transportation
14%

Services
47%

Wholesale and retail trade
18%

Source: U.S. Bureau of the Census, *Statistical Abstract of the United States, 1992*, 112th ed. (Washington, D.C.: U.S. Government Printing Office, 1992), p. 519.

- *Freedom in decision making.* As the owner and the boss, the sole proprietor enjoys freedom and flexibility in decision making. Decisions can be made promptly, without consulting others. This freedom and control also allows the sole proprietor to react quickly to changes in business conditions—without having to discuss the reasons why.

- *Personal satisfaction.* Sole proprietors enjoy the satisfaction that comes from personal achievement. Entrepreneurs who form sole proprietorships are highly motivated to achieve, desire independence, and place success or failure solely within their abilities. As a result of their actions, they personally can enjoy the rewards.

Most local retail stores and services are sole proprietorships.

- *Tax advantages.* Sole proprietorships are not taxed as a business. The profit from the business is reported on the owner's individual income tax return. The income of the business is combined with all other personal income of the owner and taxed as personal income.
- *Ease of dissolution.* A sole proprietorship can be ended as easily as it was begun. No one needs to be consulted. All the owner must do is pay the bills, close the doors, and cease operation.

With all of these advantages, it's no wonder that Cindy Somerville decided to enter business as the sole proprietor of Great Grooms, a mobile pet grooming salon, in Troy, Michigan. Cindy simply saw a need—people are burdened to the limit with activities and time demands—and acted to meet it. Cindy has met the need so well that Great Grooms has a growing list of customers for her services. She operates her business out of a van that she decided—with no other consultation—to turn into a mobile grooming studio. The van, equipped with hot and cold running water, plus electricity from the customer's house, allows Cindy to bathe, fluff-dry, clip, style, and groom her charges. The tab for a complete treatment runs from $30 to $45 depending on the size of the dog—and the profits are all Cindy's.[2]

Disadvantages of Sole Proprietorships

With all its advantages, a proprietorship also has its drawbacks:

- *Unlimited liability.* Remember that in the eyes of the law, the owner and the company in a sole proprietorship are inseparable. Therefore, the owner has **unlimited liability**—*the sole proprietor is personally responsible for any debts or damages incurred by the operation of the business.* If the business does not have enough money to pay its bills, the proprietor has to pay them with his or her own money and may be legally required to sell personal property to cover the bills.

  As an example, a sole proprietor of an Italian restaurant financed the necessary kitchen equipment, furniture, and fixtures by paying $8,000 from his personal savings and borrowing the rest from his bank. When several nationally known fast-food restaurants opened nearby, competition for customers became fierce. Business soon declined to a point where he could no longer make payments to the bank. The bank repossessed his equipment and sold it to satisfy the unpaid balance on the loan. Unfortunately, the proceeds did not cover the amount he owed, so the bank also attached (obtained the legal right to seize) and sold his new Nissan 300ZX and a piece of land that he had inherited from his parents.
- *Limited funds for expansion.* A sole proprietorship's financing consists of what the owner can contribute and borrow. The owner's personal contribution most often comes from withdrawing savings and investments, borrowing on personal life insurance, taking a second mortgage on a home,

unlimited liability The fact that a sole proprietor is personally responsible for any debts or damages incurred by the operation of the business.

or borrowing money from relatives. Getting financing from a bank or another lender depends on the value of the proprietor's business and personal assets. In addition, lenders may be somewhat reluctant to risk their funds on an unproved operation whose success depends on one person.

- *Lack of business and management skills.* By its nature a sole proprietorship places the demands for business and management skills on one person—the owner. One person can hardly be an expert in such broad and diverse fields as finance, accounting, marketing, production, and law. As a result, managing a sole proprietorship is often difficult, and success may be blocked by the owner's limitations. For example, Joe might be one of the best body-and-fender repairers in town, but that does not mean he has the business expertise to run his own repair shop profitably. A sole proprietor must be a jack-of-all-trades, which is no easy task—as many have discovered.

- *Difficulty in attracting employees.* An additional shortcoming of sole proprietorships is the difficulty of hiring and keeping highly talented, ambitious employees. The opportunities for development and advancement are quite limited in a small business. In addition, few sole proprietorships provide fringe benefits, because of their high cost.[3]

- *Personal time demands.* Many sole proprietors work ten to twelve hours a day, six or more days each week. It takes this type of personal commitment and sacrifice to make the business successful. In addition, the sole proprietor often has no one else to rely on; if an employee gets sick or quits, the owner is the one who usually fills in.

- *Limited life.* A sole proprietorship has a limited life as a business; it lacks continuity. If the owner dies or is permanently unable to continue operations because of a disability, the firm is legally dissolved. It cannot be handed down to the owner's heirs—only its assets can.

In spite of all these disadvantages, sole proprietorships are a significant factor in the world of business. For people who want to get into business and be independent, the sole proprietorship is an attractive choice. Table 3.1 sums up the advantages and disadvantages of sole proprietorships.

ADVANTAGES	DISADVANTAGES
Ease of formation	Unlimited liability
Retention of all profits	Limited funds for expansion
Freedom in decision making	Lack of business and management skills
Personal satisfaction	Difficulty in attracting employees
Tax advantages	Personal time demands
Ease of dissolution	Limited life

Table 3.1
Advantages and disadvantages of sole proprietorships.

Partnerships

The second major legal form of business organization is the partnership. The Uniform Partnership Act, the law that governs partnerships in most states, defines a **partnership** as *an association of two or more people who are co-owners of a business for profit.* Partnerships are created to pool talents, provide more financial resources than are possible with a sole proprietorship, and perhaps provide support for individuals who wish to enter a business but do not want to "go it alone."

> **partnership**
> An association of two or more people who are co-owners of a business for profit.

Forming a Partnership

A partnership may be entered into by simply discussing a business proposition with a prospective partner or partners and reaching an agreement. This approach has limitations: People may forget what they agreed to; difficult times may force the business to dissolve, which can result in decisions being made emotionally; and differences of opinion may create misunderstandings.

A better solution is to have an experienced lawyer draw up written **articles of partnership**, *a contractual agreement that establishes the legal relationship between partners.* Normally, a written partnership agreement identifies the names of the partners and the partnership and covers the following points: the management duties of each partner; the contributions of each partner in terms of skill, money, or equipment; how compensation will be determined (profits, salary); procedures for selling interests in the partnership; and how conflicts will be resolved, the business dissolved, and assets distributed. Figure 3.4 presents a typical articles of partnership agreement.

> **articles of partnership**
> A contractual agreement that establishes the legal relationship between partners.

Advantages of Partnerships

Like sole proprietorships, partnerships have many advantages:

- *Ease of formation.* Partnerships are easy to form. No state approval is required to form a partnership, nor does the partnership have to be in writing to be legal (though it is advisable, as previously stated). Once basic agreements on profits, responsibilities, finances, and termination procedures are resolved, a partnership can begin.
- *Pooling of knowledge and skills.* In a partnership, two or more persons can pool their knowledge and skills and operate more effectively than one person might. For example, one partner can provide management expertise while another provides marketing skills. Or, as in the case of Carter Primo, a real estate investment trust firm in Laguna Beach, California, the partners can combine complementary financial backgrounds. Initially high school friends, Daryl Carter and Quintin Primo went separate ways after graduation. Each got an MBA—Carter at MIT and Primo at Harvard. Carter joined Continental Bank after business school, specializing in construction lending and real estate investing. Primo joined Citicorp and ran its real estate investment banking operations. In 1991 they met and decided to join forces. They were tired of making deals for others and wanted to "chase

Figure 3.4

A typical articles of partnership agreement.

Partnership Agreement

This partnership contract and agreement entered into this   day of   19   , by and between

WITNESSETH: The parties hereto agree that they will become and be partners in a business for the purpose and on the terms and conditions hereinafter stated.

1. The name of the partnership shall be:

2. All of the partnership business shall be carried on in the partnership name.

3. The business or businesses of this partnership are as follows:

4. The principal place of business for the partnership is:

5. The period of duration of the partnership shall be from the date of the execution of this instrument until the   day of   , 19   .

6. The assets of the partnership are and were contributed as follows:

7. Each of the partners shall share in the profits and losses of the business equally.

8. Each of the partners hereby agrees to give his undivided time and attention to the business of the partnership, and to use his best efforts to promote the interests of the partnership.

9. It is understood and agreed that books of account of the transactions of the partnership shall be kept at the principal place of business of the firm, and shall be at all reasonable times open to the inspection of any partner.

10. Any or all of the partners shall be permitted to draw from the funds of the partnership as follows:
Such sums shall be charged to him and at the annual accounting shall be charged against his share of the partnership profits. In the event that his share of the profits shall not be equal to the sum so drawn, the deficiency shall be deducted from the sum to be drawn at the next pay period.

11. Checks on the bank account of the partnership may be signed by any partner, but only for partnership obligations, and no party shall sign checks to withdraw money for any purpose except to pay partnership debts or obligations.

12. Any or all partners shall, on every reasonable request, give to the other partner or partners a true account of all transactions relating to the business of the partnership, and full information of all letters, writing, and other things which shall come into his hands concerning the business of the partnership.

13. No partner shall, without the written consent of the other or others, become bail or surety for any other person, nor lend, spend, give, or make away with any part of the partnership property or draw or accept any bill, note, or other security in the name of said partnership.

14. Any partner may retire from the partnership at the expiration of any fiscal year on giving to the other partner or partners one month's written notice of his intention to do so.

15. When, in case of dissolution of the partnership by death, the survivors desire to continue the business, the value of the good will of said business shall be determined by appraisal. Said surviving partner or partners shall appoint one appraiser, the representative of the deceased shall appoint a second appraiser, and the two appraisers shall appoint a third. The decision of the three appraisers as to the value of the good will and other assets of the partnership shall be binding on the surviving partner or partners and the representatives of the deceased partner. The continuing partner or partners shall assume all of the existing firm obligations and hold the estate of the deceased partner harmless from all liability thereon.

16. In the event that the partnership shall terminate other than by death of one of the partners, the partnership business shall be wound up, the debts paid, and the surplus divided between the partners in accordance with their interest therein.

IN WITNESS WHEREOF we have hereunto set our hands this   day of   , 19   .

ACKNOWLEDGMENT

STATE OF TEXAS
COUNTY OF
BEFORE ME, the undersigned, a Notary Public in and for said County and State, on this day personally appeared

known to me to be the person whose name subscribed to the foregoing instrument, and acknowledged to me that he executed the same for the purposes and consideration therein expressed.
GIVEN UNDER MY HAND AND SEAL OF OFFICE, this the   day of   A.D. 19

_____
Notary Public in and for   County, Texas

their dream in earnest." Each brings a superior financial background to the partnership.[4]

- *More funds available.* By pooling their financial resources, partners have more money available to meet the financial needs of their business. These combined assets often give a general partnership a better credit rating than that of a sole proprietorship. In addition, because of the ability to offer a partnership to another person, the business has a method of attracting more funds for operations and expansion.

- *Ability to attract and retain employees.* One of the drawbacks of sole proprietorships is that they have trouble attracting and retaining superior employees because there are few opportunities for advancement. A partnership can overcome this problem, because valuable employees can be made partners in the firm. This is common practice in law and accounting firms, for example.

- *Tax advantages.* As with a sole proprietorship, the profit from a partnership venture is not taxed as a business. Any profits become personal income of the partners and are taxed as personal income.

Disadvantages of Partnerships

Those who think that the divorce rate is high should look at the statistics for partnerships. Business marriages, like personal ones, can fall apart quickly and with little warning. Anyone who enters into a partnership should recognize the potential pitfalls of the relationship in advance:

- *Unlimited liability.* As with sole proprietorships, each partner is personally liable for the financial obligations of the firm. If one partner incurs liabilities in the name of the partnership that exceed the wealth of the business and his or her personal wealth, the other partners' assets might be used to pay off the debts.

- *Limited life.* Partnerships lack permanence or continuity. When a change in partners occurs, the business must be formally ended under the old partnership and re-created under a new one. If one partner dies or becomes physically or mentally disabled, the partnership is legally dissolved. The same would be true if one partner decided to withdraw from the firm or a new partner were admitted. Problems of this nature sometimes can be minimized if the articles of partnership clearly define the action to take when a partner enters, leaves, or becomes incapacitated.

YOU DECIDE

What is the single most important advantage a partnership has over a sole proprietorship? What is the most important advantage a sole proprietor loses when a partnership is created?

- *Potential conflict between partners.* Partners sometimes have scant knowledge of each other's characteristics before they begin business. Is it any surprise that conflicts of personalities, ideas, and interests among partners can often be the downfall of a business? Disharmony can be a significant disadvantage to the partnership as a form of business organization. People as well as assets must be combined successfully. When combining forces, the individual partners' information on technology, people, and markets becomes invaluable. But a partnership can become a nightmare. Without trust, clear division of responsibility, and accountability to the other partners, the partnership won't work. According to Marsha Firestone, vice-president for training and counseling at the American Woman's Economic Development Corporation (AWED), "You see a lot of failures with these types of arrangements. It takes extraordinarily mature individuals to handle the situations."[5] (This chapter's Manager's Notebook focuses on how to make partnerships work.)

- *Difficulty in dissolving the business.* Once the partnership is formed, a partner cannot withdraw from the business by selling his or her partnership investment without the other partners' consent. If a partner decides that forming the partnership was a mistake, that partnership interest may be sold only to someone who is acceptable to all partners. Table 3.2 sums up the advantages and disadvantages of partnerships.

general partnership
An association of two or more people, each with unlimited liability, who are actively involved in a business.

general partner
A partner who has specific authority to act and bind the business, has operational responsibilities, and has unlimited liability.

Table 3.2
Advantages and disadvantages of partnerships.

Types of Partnerships

The two major types of partnerships are general and limited. A third type, the joint venture, is designed for short-term projects.

GENERAL PARTNERSHIP A **general partnership** is *an association of two or more people, each with unlimited liability, who are actively involved in a business.* In a general partnership each partner is a **general partner,** *who has specific authority to act and bind the*

ADVANTAGES	DISADVANTAGES
Ease of formation	Unlimited liability
Pooling of knowledge and skills	Limited life
More funds available	Potential conflict between partners
Ability to attract and retain employees	Difficulty in dissolving the business
Tax advantages	

business, has operational responsibilities, and has unlimited liability. There are approximately 1 million general partnerships in the United States, representing approximately 6 percent of all businesses. Most of these are service companies, such as real estate and securities brokerage firms, insurance companies, law and accounting firms, engineering firms, and medical and dental clinics.[6]

General partnerships, like sole proprietorships, are relatively simple to establish, but their operation is somewhat more complicated. Partners must work closely with each other, and the acts of one can legally commit or bind the rest. In a general partnership all partners can be held personally responsible for any business-related debts incurred by one partner.

In an attempt to clarify the rights and responsibilities of general partners, the Uniform Partnership Act was created. Adopted by all states except Louisiana and Georgia, it brings uniformity to several aspects of general partnership operations. It also sets forth the steps to be followed in dissolving a partnership. Any general partnership agreement must be constructed within the limits of this law in states that have adopted it.

Under this act each partner has the right to:

- Share in the management of the business
- Share in the profits
- Receive repayment for investments
- Receive repayment for payments made on behalf of the partnership
- Receive interest on any advances made to the business
- Have access to the financial records of the business
- Have a formal accounting of the financial affairs of the business

In addition, each partner has the obligation to:

- Contribute toward any losses incurred by the partnership
- Work for the partnership for a share in the profits rather than pay
- Agree to a majority vote or third party arbitration when differences of opinion occur
- Provide other partners with information known personally about the partnership
- Provide an accounting to the partnership of all profits made from the partnership arrangement

limited partnership
A partnership arrangement in which the liability of one or more partners is limited to the amount of assets they have invested in the firm.

limited partners
Partners who are legally barred from participating in the partnership's management but have limited liability for debts incurred by the firm.

LIMITED PARTNERSHIP The second type of partnership is **limited partnership**—*a partnership arrangement in which the liability of one or more partners is limited to the amount of assets they have invested in the firm.* A limited partnership must have at least one general partner to assume unlimited liability for the debts of the firm. It may then take in any number of **limited partners**, *partners who are legally barred from participating in the partnership's manage-*

ment but have limited liability for debts incurred by the firm. Limited partners stand to lose only the assets they have contributed to the company if creditors sue to recover unpaid debts.

Because they enjoy limited liability, limited partners' rights are restricted in several ways:

- Their names may not appear in the name of the business.
- They are not allowed to participate in management.
- They must not provide any services to the firm.

If a limited partner plays an active role in management, he or she may be stripped of limited liability and declared a general partner. For example, an attorney representing the creditors of a limited partnership obtained a document signed by a limited partner with the title *manager* after that partner's name. The court held that this was evidence of active management, and the limited partner was declared personally liable for $5,000 of the company's unpaid debts.

Why form a limited partnership? A limited partnership has some attractive features, including:

- The business can obtain additional funds without general partners having to share management decisions.
- The combination of limited partners can change (through death, withdrawal, or other circumstances) without causing the business to be legally dissolved.
- A limited partner can share in the profits without risking more than the amount of the investment.

With these advantages there are some limitations:

- The general partner or partners must assume the burden of full financial liability.
- If a general partner withdraws from the business, the partnership arrangement is terminated.

Limited partnerships are often created to raise venture capital for movie productions, gas and oil exploration, horse racing, and cable television. They have become increasingly attractive because of the return on investment to the limited partners. Jones Cable TV, the largest syndicator of cable television limited partnerships, has managed a 13.2 percent return on five completed partnerships.[7]

A limited partnership cannot be formed unless the

> **YOU DECIDE**
>
> What factors would you consider important in selecting one form of partnership over the other? Which form would you select? Why? If you selected a limited partnership, would you become a limited or a general partner? Why?

MANAGER'S NOTEBOOK

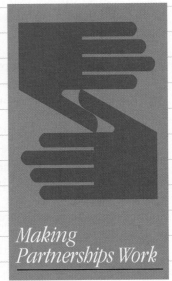

Making Partnerships Work

There is a big difference between making a partnership and making the partnership work. Even if partners have carefully planned, discussed, and structured the articles of partnership to cover every business possibility—compensation, individual contributions, procedures for bringing in new partners—living together in a partnership arrangement can and does bring personal conflict.

Often, business partners in conflict over each other's personal traits and management style conclude that a breakup is the only answer. But dissolution should not be looked at as the only outcome: The partners can make their business work and restore a good working relationship by cooperating.

The keys to cooperation are identifying areas of agreement on how the company should be run and recognizing that negatives one partner perceives in the other might actually be positives for the business. Partners Kenneth Ryan and Edward LeBeau of Airmax, a cargo management firm based at Chicago's O'Hare International Airport, offer a good example of cooperation.

Even though Airmax grew rapidly in its first four years of operation, Ryan and LeBeau underestimated the closeness of a business partnership and let it deteriorate. They had many common attitudes about how a business should be run, but they had a significant difference in style—Ryan was impulsive and intuitive and would become "impatient" with LeBeau's more methodical, "plodding" way of working.

In time the partners found themselves really disturbed with each other. The business was suffering and both partners wanted the conflict stopped. Seeing that they were on the road to splitting up, they chose another avenue—they sought out a psychologist who counsels business partners.

The psychologist first showed the partners that in fact they had similar goals for the firm but that their attitudes were keeping each from trusting the other to try it his way. The partners were taught two techniques for making the partnership work: take time out when talk gets heated, and reframe negative attitudes. The second approach helped Ryan and LeBeau turn negatives into positives. Rather than seeing LeBeau as "plodding," Ryan was encouraged to view him as "careful," while LeBeau now perceives Ryan as "energetic" rather than "impulsive."

As this example shows, the keys to success in partnerships are good old-fashioned hard work, positive thinking, and communication.

(For more on making partnerships work, see Janet M. Green, "Imperfect Partnerships: Vive La Difference," *Management Review,* May 1993, pp. 25–27; and Donna Fenn, "Selling Out Or Staying On," *Working Woman,* February 1993, p. 26.)

FACTORS	SOLE PROPRIETORSHIP	GENERAL PARTNERSHIP	LIMITED PARTNERSHIP
Liability	Unlimited	Unlimited	Limited for limited partners only
Formation	Minimum effort; low start-up costs	Minimum effort; hard to find suitable partners; low start-up costs	Documentation of type of partners; low start-up costs
Dissolution	Minimum effect	Agreement needed between partners	Agreement needed between partners
Duration	Life of the owner	Legally terminated at death or withdrawal of a partner	Legally terminated at death or withdrawal of general partner
Decision making	All decisions by owner	Cooperation required in decision making	Cooperation required in decision making if more than one general partner
Ability to acquire funds	May be difficult to raise additional capital	Easier to raise additional capital than in sole proprietorship	Unlimited ability to raise additional capital
Ability to acquire and retain employees	Little to offer potential or present employees	Can offer partnership	Can offer partnership
Business and management skills	Limited ability to possess all necessary business and management skills	Greater opportunity to have necessary business and management skills	Greater opportunity to have necessary business and management skills
Tax	Taxed as personal income	Taxed as personal income	Taxed as personal income

state allows it, and it must be registered with a state agency. Also, some states require a special notice to be filed in the county or district where the limited partnership is offered. Finally, to provide for consistent interpretation from state to state, all states except Louisiana have adopted the Uniform Limited Partnership Act to govern limited partnership operations.

Table 3.3 provides a comparison of sole proprietorships, general partnerships, and limited partnerships. Each has its advantages and disadvantages.

Table 3.3
Comparison of sole proprietorships, general partnerships, and limited partnerships.

The Joint Venture

As noted previously, although general and limited partnerships are the two major types of partnership arrangements, a third type exists that is designed for short-term projects. A **joint venture** is *a partnership established to carry out a specific project or undertaking*. It is usually dissolved after the objective has been achieved. For the duration of the agreement, each partner has unlimited liability. Joint ventures are fairly common in real estate: several persons pool their financial resources, purchase a large parcel of land, perhaps develop it, divide it, and resell it.

joint venture
A partnership established to carry out a specific project or undertaking.

GLOBAL PERSPECTIVE

Can Budweiser, the "king of beers," become as popular world-wide as Coca-Cola, Marlboro, and Levi's? Anheuser-Busch isn't sure, but the St. Louis–based brewery is giving it a shot.

Because overall U.S. revenue has been essentially the same since the late 80s, Anheuser is tapping into fast-growing international markets by creating joint ventures. In Japan Anheuser initiated an $80 million venture with that country's largest brewer, Kirin, to distribute Budweiser there. This deal was quickly followed by another venture uniting Anheuser with Mexico's biggest brewer, Grupo Modelo. In addition, Anheuser is looking at a half-dozen other joint venture development deals in Latin America, the Pacific Rim, and western Europe.

Creating a global beer brand will be difficult. Unlike other U.S. products— soft drinks, cigarettes, blue jeans— U.S. beers hold little prestige in many traditional beer strongholds. That is because American beers tend to be lighter, sweeter, and less robust than other brews. In addition, unlike fickle Americans who favor faddish beverages, such as light and dry beers, drinkers in countries such as Germany favor brands that are centuries old.

"We'd like to build a global brand, but I'm not sure we can ever be a Coca-Cola or a Levi's overseas," says Jack Purnell, chief executive of Anheuser's international division. "But right now, we don't know how high up is. We want to take it as far as we can."

Anheuser-Busch Pours Itself into Joint Venture

(For more on Anheuser-Busch's joint ventures, see Gary Struss, "Anheuser Pours into Global Pitch," *USA Today*, March 29, 1993, pp. 1B–2B.)

In an era when businesses are seeking opportunities in the international marketplace, a joint venture provides an exciting strategy for quickly entering the marketplace. It is becoming an extremely flexible and popular tool for a diverse number of organizations and geographies:

- Kimberly-Clark, in a bid to bolster consumer product sales in Europe, formed a joint venture with VP-Schickedanz AG of Germany, one of Europe's major makers of tissue products. The deal "leap frogged" K-C onto the continent. It provided a beachhead against rival Procter & Gamble in the lucrative and growing disposable diaper products market in Europe.[8]
- Hewlett-Packard Co. and Swedish telecommunications company Ericsson Telecom AB forged a joint venture to develop and market integrated computer network management systems. The alliance is designed to create a new market.[9]
- Chemical company W. R. Grace & Co. finalized a food-packaging joint venture in Moscow. The decision was made by Grace & Co. because of "the unlimited potential—regardless of the political situation."[10]

On the domestic scene the most striking example of a joint venture is a series of alliances between Apple Computer and former archrival IBM. One venture involves the development of the power PC, a new kind of Macintosh computer that uses superfast processors originally developed by IBM. Another project, Taligent, involves a new operating system that will enable programmers to write software more easily.[11]

SUMMARY

This chapter examined two categories of unincorporated businesses: sole proprietorships and partnerships. A sole proprietorship is a business owned by one individual. Legally, the owner and the company are inseparable. Sole proprietorships have a number of advantages, including:

- Ease of formation
- Retention of all profits
- Freedom in decision making
- Personal satisfaction
- Ease of dissolution
- Tax advantages

A sole proprietorship also has certain disadvantages:

- Unlimited liability
- Limited funds for expansion
- Lack of business and management skills
- Difficulty in attracting employees
- Personal time demands
- Limited life

A partnership is an association of two or more people who are co-owners of a business for profit. A partnership can be created orally or in writing. It is recommended that it be developed on paper through an articles of partnership agreement. A partnership has a number of advantages, including:

- Ease of formation
- Pooling of knowledge and skills
- More funds available
- Ability to attract and retain employees
- Tax advantages

As with sole proprietorships, it does have disadvantages:

- Unlimited liability
- Limited life
- Potential conflict between partners
- Difficulty in dissolving the business

There are two major types of partnerships: general partnerships and limited partnerships. A general partnership is an association of two or more people, each with unlimited liability, who are actively involved in the business. A limited partnership, on the other hand, is one in which the liability of one or more partners is limited to the amount of assets they have invested in the firm. A limited partnership must have at least one general partner who assumes unlimited liability. In a limited partnership the limited partner is legally barred from participating in managing the firm.

A joint venture is a partnership form developed for short-term projects. It is established to carry out a specific adventure or undertaking. It is usually dissolved after the objective has been achieved. For the duration of the agreement, each partner has unlimited liability.

KEY TERMS

articles of partnership p. 76
general partner p. 79
general partnership p. 79
joint venture p. 83
limited partners p. 80

limited partnership p. 80
partnership p. 76
sole proprietorship p. 71
unlimited liability p. 74

FOR REVIEW AND DISCUSSION

1. It has been said that in the eyes of the law, suppliers, and the public, a sole proprietor is the company. Explain.
2. "Forming a sole proprietorship is as easy as simply hanging out your shingle and beginning business." Explain.
3. Describe the major disadvantages of a sole proprietorship.
4. "A partnership does not have to be in writing to be legal, but it is a good idea to create an articles of partnership agreement." Discuss this statement.
5. Describe the advantages and disadvantages of a partnership as a form of business ownership.
6. Explain the rights and obligations of a partner under the Uniform Partnership Act.
7. Describe the burden placed on a general partner in a limited partnership arrangement.
8. What specific activity is a limited partner denied if limited liability is to be maintained?
9. What is the purpose of creating a joint venture?

APPLICATIONS

Case 3.1: IBM Looks for a Blockbuster

Computers are rapidly taking over our world. Not too many years from now, Americans are likely to own as many computers as they do TVs. Unfortunately, the explosion of the personal computer market has led to a decline in the demand for mainframe computers provided by companies such as International Business Machines. When revenues began declining, IBM initiated a new strategy designed to bring it back to prosperity: partnerships with other companies.

Many of IBM's "business partners" are companies in the computer business, but one of special note is the video rental company Blockbuster. The two companies have conceived a plan to produce and market machines that print compact discs at retail locations using a technology that a subsidiary of Blockbuster developed. A customer who wants a particular CD simply punches in an order, and the machine records music or computer data on the disc while it simultaneously prints the disc's booklet. Theoretically, after the six-minute process is done, the customer should have a product that is indistinguishable from a mass-produced disc.

To produce and sell their CD printers, Blockbuster and IBM formed two joint ventures. Fairway Technology Associates will build and operate the new systems, while Newleaf packages and markets them for individual retailers. The companies will be operated independently from the two parent companies.

When IBM was the dominant force in the computer industry, it seemed like things would never change. Unfortunately, due to management problems, slow development of new technology, and a steady, ongoing decline in its major market, IBM has had to face up to the fact that its glory days may be over. IBM needs some new friends and business partners to help it redefine itself.

Questions

1. What purposes do joint ventures between companies serve?
2. Why does IBM need partnerships with companies like Blockbuster?
3. How does a move into the consumer electronics field help IBM?
4. What risks does IBM face in its partnership with Blockbuster?

For more information see Laurence Hooper, "Co-ventures Planned by IBM, Blockbuster," *The Wall Street Journal*, May 11, 1993, pp. B1, B6.

Case 3.2: Women as Entrepreneurs

Joline Godfrey has done a little bit of everything. She had a go at Polaroid's corporate fast track but left the company to form a profitable venture of her own. Now, having written a book on entrepreneurial women, she is laboring to spread her knowledge of business from the woman's perspective. Her current project, a series of seminars titled "An Income of Her Own," sponsored by the Department of Labor, IBM, and the Kellogg Foundation, is aimed at giving young women across the country the tools and support to succeed in business.

Godfrey learned the difficulties of success the hard way. Starting in the human relations division of Polaroid, she spent ten years trying to work her way up, only to hit what is popularly known as a glass ceiling. The company's male-dominated structure simply would not allow her to be promoted higher. She left the company and started her own business creating learning games. Later she became an aggressive advocate of women in business, pointing out that despite the fact that women own 28 percent of American businesses, they are almost universally ignored. Outraged that even the U.S. Census does not keep data about women-owned businesses, she states, "We have better records on exotic cars in this country than we do on businesses owned by women."

Her interest consists of more than outrage, however. In her seminar series, she teaches young women, often coming from underprivileged backgrounds, to find their own paths to success. To Godfrey, this means starting their own businesses. She remarks, "Maybe the only place to be on a par with your male counterparts is to start your own business. It's a place where you at least get a shot." She makes a very convincing case—after all, she's done it. So have the female owners of multimillion-dollar businesses whom she invites as guest speakers for her workshops. Through her efforts, and the efforts she inspires in the upcoming generation of entrepreneurial women, the glass ceiling may soon be more than transparent—it may disappear altogether.

Questions

1. How can starting their own companies help women avoid the frustrations associated with glass ceilings?

2. What elements of a sole proprietorship would be appealing to an entrepreneurial woman?

3. What disadvantages of a sole proprietorship may create the biggest obstacle to an entrepreneurial woman?

4. What skills do young women need to start their own businesses?

For more information, see Penelope Rowlands, "Rebel with a Cause," *Working Woman*, March 1993, p. 52.

REFERENCES

1. U.S. Bureau of the Census, *Statistical Abstract of the United States, 1992*, 112th ed. (Washington, D.C.: U.S. Government Printing Office, 1992), p. 519.

2. Julie Candler, "It Pays to Deliver," *Nation's Business*, December 1992, p. 46.

3. Roger Thompson, "Benefits Costs Surge Again," *Nation's Business*, February 1993, p. 38.

4. Charles Burck, "The Real World of the Entrepreneur," *Fortune*, April 5, 1993, p. 65.

5. Donna Fenn, "Selling Out or Staying On," *Working Woman*, February 1993, p. 26.

6. U.S. Bureau of the ensus, *Statistical Abstract of the United States, 1992*, 112th ed. (Washington, D.C.: U.S. Government Printing Office, 1992), p. 519.

7. Jack Griffin, "Limited Partnerships Reap Rewards," *Business Week*, June 7, 1993, p. 47.

8. Jim Mitchell, "Kimberly-Clark Signs Huge Deal," *Dallas Morning News*, July 1, 1992, pp. 1D, 2D.

9. John Phelps, "Ericsson, Hewlett-Packard Announce European Venture," *Los Angeles Times*, January 11, 1993, p. H19.

10. Paul Wiseman, "U.S. Firms Waiting Out Upheaval in Russia," *USA Today*, March 29, 1993, p. B1.

11. John Markoff, "Beyond the PC: Apple's Promised Land," *New York Times*, November 15, 1992, Sec. 3, pp. 1, 10.

4

THE MODERN CORPORATION

I get paid to make the owners of the Coca-Cola Company increasingly wealthy with each passing day. Everything else is just fluff.

ROBERTO C. GOIZUETA
CEO, Coca-Cola Company

CHAPTER OBJECTIVES

After studying this chapter, you should be able to:

1. Summarize the nature and significance of the corporation as a form of business organization.
2. Describe the steps involved in forming a corporation.
3. Identify and explain the various categories of corporations based on place of chartering, restrictions on stock ownership, and reasons for existence.
4. Describe the internal organization of a corporation.
5. State in your own words the principal advantages and disadvantages of the corporate form of business organization.
6. Discuss the general conditions and benefits of organizing an S corporation.
7. Present the differences among an acquisition, a merger, and an amalgamation or consolidation.
8. Describe the various types of mergers that can occur among corporations.
9. List and describe the features of corporations formed for profit and those formed for nonprofit purposes.

UP FRONT

Apple Computer may be the best-known and most well-loved computer company in history. Started by two young men in a garage in 1976, its first commercial personal computer, the Apple I, quickly attained widespread acceptance. Then, in 1984, the world was rocked by the Macintosh, the first widely available personal computer made easy to use with a graphical user interface and "mouse" pointing device. Suddenly, Apple Computer became big business: revenues in 1985 reached nearly $2 billion. In 1993, ten years after joining Apple as chief executive officer, John Sculley turned the CEO responsibilities over to Michael Spindler and later that year resigned from Apple.

Spindler was born and educated in Germany, where he obtained a college degree in electrical engineering. He worked in his chosen occupational field for several years at Siemens, a German electronics and computer company, but found himself longing for more challenges. He found the opportunities for challenge and growth in the sales and marketing positions he took at Schlumberger, Intel, and Digital Equipment Corporation, ultimately leading him to the job of marketing manager of European operations at Apple in 1980.

A hard-working, goal-oriented man, Spindler saw great opportunities for Apple in Europe. Using his ability to speak many languages and his pan-European experience, he propelled Apple to success after success in the European markets, capturing over 8 percent of the market for personal computers. He was subsequently made president of Apple's European operations.

John Sculley, known as a brilliant mar-

keter and technological visionary at Apple, promoted the no-nonsense Spindler to chief operating officer in 1990. At the time, Apple's Macintosh was a mature product—and the competition was fierce. Sculley, Spindler, and the entire executive team gambled that a new pricing and production strategy would stimulate Apple's market share. As chief operating officer, Spindler led the implementation of this strategy, including the introduction of the low-priced Mac Classic as a replacement for the Mac Plus and SE. In addition, the team pushed product development cycles to nine months, from eighteen to twenty-four months, to get new products and innovations out the door and into the hands of customers faster.

At the same time, the executive team evaluated Apple's business model and concluded that to be more competitive with its computer pricing, Apple had to take steps to reduce its overall cost structure. As part of this restructuring, the company had to lay off 10 percent of its work force. Never a pleasant task, the downsizing nevertheless proved revitalizing and brought Apple shares to an all-time high in 1991.

These three activities—high innovation, competitively priced products, and shorter lead times bringing new products to market—have become the platform for Apple's long-term strategy. This strategy, first implemented in Apple's highly successful personal computer business, is being expanded into new and complementary businesses. Today Apple has five divisions: the

MICHAEL SPINDLER

CHIEF EXECUTIVE OFFICER, APPLE COMPUTER, INC.

Personal Computer Division; AppleSoft, its operating software division; Apple Business Systems, for large institution computing needs; the Personal Interactive Electronics division, which recently launched its first consumer product, the Newton MessagePad; and Claris, its application software subsidiary.

Apple is also involved in a number of industry alliances, including one with IBM and Motorola, in order to maximize technologic innovation and cut research costs. In addition, Apple is developing multimedia information services and hopes its new computers equipped with AV Technologies will take customers a step forward with voice recognition and other sophisticated digital features.

Michael Spindler has demonstrated his leadership ability, his strong, clear grasp of management, and his ability to drive technology at Apple. He has been in the industry, and at Apple, long enough to have a thorough grasp of the business trends. His global perspective will continue to be of value as world-wide trade continues to flourish. "The reality of the world today is that all economies are interlinked. Understanding this, and taking advantage of the opportunities it represents, will be a key to success in the coming decades."

corporation
A legal form of business organization created by a government and considered an entity separate and apart from its owners.

corporate charter
A document issued by a government that contains all information stated in the original application for a charter plus the powers, rights, and privileges of the corporation as prescribed by law.

shareholders or stockholders
A corporation's owners, but frequently not the individuals who control and manage the firm day to day.

stock certificates
Documents that provide legal evidence of ownership of shares in a corporation.

In Chapter 3 we examined two important legal forms of business ownership, the sole proprietorship and the partnership. In this chapter we explore a third legal form of business ownership: the corporation. Although there are approximately four times as many sole proprietorships in the United States as corporations, corporations are responsible for 85 to 90 percent of all sales. Corporation ownership is widespread, and corporations employ millions of workers. Their influence on society at all levels—local, national, and international—is substantial.

What Is a Corporation?

You learned earlier that forming a sole proprietorship or a partnership is relatively simple. You also learned that the owners of such unincorporated businesses ordinarily cannot be separated from their firms: they *are* the firms. A **corporation**, however, is *a legal form of business organization created by a government and considered an entity separate and apart from its owners.* In effect, it is an artificial person that has been created by law. Its birth certificate is the **corporate charter**, *a document issued by a government that contains all information stated in the original application for a charter plus the powers, rights, and privileges of the corporation as prescribed by law.*

A corporation can sue or be sued, make contracts, own property, and even be a partner in a partnership. In contrast to other legal forms of organization, the corporation does not cease to exist when its owners die. It is distinct and apart from its **shareholders** or **stockholders**, who are *a corporation's owners, but frequently not the individuals who control and manage the firm day to day.* **Stock certificates**, *documents that provide legal evidence of ownership of shares in a corporation,* are issued to the shareholders. Figure 4.1 shows an example of a stock certificate. Most shareholders have little or nothing to do with management, as you will see later in the chapter.

How to Incorporate

In the previous chapters we discussed what might happen when two people go into a business venture together. Let's assume that the two of you have considered both the sole proprietorship and partnership forms of organization but have decided to incorporate the business. How would you go about forming a corporation?

First, you would apply to the appropriate state official, frequently the secretary of state, for permission to incorporate. A lawyer can help you with this. A **certificate (articles) of incorporation** is *the application to incorporate that must be filed with the secretary of state, which becomes the corporation's charter after it is approved.*

Some states permit one person to form a corporation; others require a minimum of three. The people who form a corporation are called *incorporators* and usually serve as the corporation's directors until the first stockholders' meeting, when a board can be elected. If you wish to be the sole director of a corporation but the state requires three incorporators, you may ask relatives or your lawyer and accountant to serve. These two individuals may then bow out at the first meeting.

The charter describes the corporation's purpose and its intended business. Because the corporation cannot engage in any business not included in the charter, the articles of incorporation may list a wide variety of business

Figure 4.1

Sample stock certificate.

certificate (articles) of incorporation
The application to incorporate that must be filed with the secretary of state, which becomes the corporation's charter after it is approved.

activities. Doing so makes it unnecessary to apply for a charter amendment should the corporation enter a business different from its original one. A charter generally includes the following information:

1. Company name; names and addresses of incorporators; location of main office
2. Purpose for which the corporation is being formed
3. Length of life (may be perpetual)
4. Amount and kind of stock the corporation wants authorization to issue
5. Names, addresses, and powers of the original board of directors
6. Dates and times of shareholders' and directors' meetings
7. Names of initial subscribers to stock shares
8. Procedure to amend, alter, or repeal any provision contained in the original articles of incorporation (if the law permits)

Types of Corporations

Corporations fit into one of three categories, depending on where they are chartered. To illustrate, assume that a corporation is chartered in New Jersey. In that state, it would be a **domestic corporation**, *the term applied to a corporation in the state where it is incorporated.* In the other forty-nine states, it is considered a **foreign corporation**, *the term applied to a United States corporation in states other than the one in which it is incorporated.* If the same company does business in other countries, they would consider it an **alien corporation**, which is *a firm incorporated in a country other than the one in which it operates.* For example, Porsche, the German automobile manufacturer, is considered an alien corporation by the United States. Figure 4.2 presents these relationships visually.

Corporations may also be classified as open or closed. Those like General Electric and The Home Depot are considered **open corporations**; each is *a corporation whose stock can be purchased by anyone who can afford the price.* A **closed corporation** is *a corporation whose stock cannot be purchased by the general public; it is usually owned by a few individuals.* Often these are family members who agree not to sell stock to outsiders because they fear losing control of the firm. Corporations such as Ford Motor Company and Adolph Coors Company began as closed corporations and later "went public" (sold stock to the general public). Usually a corporation does this to raise additional capital for expansion. (The subject of financing with stock and the kinds of stock that may be sold will be explored in detail in Chapter 16.) Many large corporations, however, remain closely held to this day, including United Parcel Service, DHL Worldwide Express, Hallmark Cards, and Mars, Inc. Some additional examples appear in Table 4.1.

Going Public versus Staying Closed

The decision of whether to "go public" or to remain closely held may be one of the most difficult in a company's development.

domestic corporation
The term applied to a corporation in the state where it is incorporated.

foreign corporation
The term applied to a United States corporation in states other than the one in which it is incorporated.

alien corporation
A firm incorporated in a country other than the one in which it operates.

open corporation
A corporation whose stock can be purchased by anyone who can afford the price.

closed corporation
A corporation whose stock cannot be purchased by the general public; it is usually owned by a few individuals.

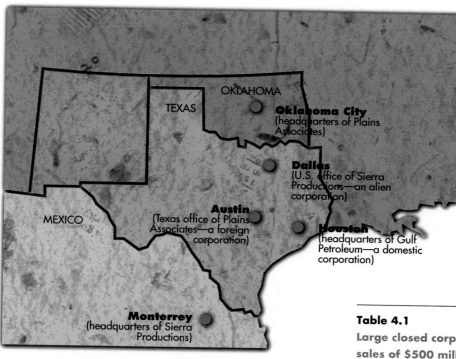

Figure 4.2
Three classifications of corporations: domestic, foreign, and alien.

Table 4.1
Large closed corporations with annual sales of $500 million or more.

INDUSTRY	COMPANIES	INDUSTRY	COMPANIES
Grocery stores	Publix Super Markets	Auto rental	Avis
	Grand Union		Enterprise Rent-A-Car
	Giant Eagle		Budget Rent a Car
	Kash n' Karry Food Stores		National Car Rental
Pizza	Domino's Pizza	Furniture	Levitz
	Little Caesar Enterprises		Ethan Allen
Accounting	Arthur Andersen & Co.	Management consulting	McKinsey & Co.
	Ernst & Young		Towers, Perrin
	Deloitte & Touche		Booz, Allen & Hamilton
	KPG Peat Marwick	Advertising	Leo Burnett
Apparel	Levi Strauss & Co.		D'Arcy Masius Benton & Bowles
	Polo Ralph Lauren		
	Guess?	Alcoholic beverages	Stroh Brewery
	Jordache Enterprises		E & J Gallo Winery
	Bugle Boy	Paper products	Fort Howard
			Sweetheart Holdings

Source: "Private Agenda," *Forbes*, December 7, 1992, p. 176. © Forbes Inc., 1992. Used by permission.

GLOBAL PERSPECTIVE

The abbreviation *Inc.* is commonly used to identify corporations in the United States. Here are the abbreviations that identify corporations in several other countries.

ABBREVIATION	COUNTRY	MEANING
AB	Sweden	Incorporated (Aktiebolag)
AG	Germany	Incorporated (Aktiengesellschaft)
A/S	Norway	Incorporated (Aksjeselskap)
Bhd	Malaysia	Incorporated (Berhad)
Cia	Spain	Company (Compania)
GmbH	Germany	Limited Liability Company (Gesellschaft mit beschrankter Haftung)
KK	Japan	Joint Stock Corporation (Kabushiki Kaisha)
Ltda.	Latin America	Limited Liability Company (Limitada)
NV	Netherlands	Incorporated (Naamlose Vennootschap)
Oy	Finland	Incorporated (Osakeyhtiot)
PLC or Ltd.	Britain	Public Limited Company
P.T.	Indonesia	Limited Company (Perusahaan Terbatas)
Pte	Singapore	Private Limited Company
Pty	Australia	Proprietary
SA	France, Spain, and others	Incorporated (Societe Anonyme/Sociedad Anonima)
S.A.R.L.	Brazil and others	Incorporated (Sociedad Anonima de Responsabilidade Limitada)
SPA	Italy	Incorporated (Societa per Azioni)

Many closed corporations prefer to stay closed because they can conceal more information about their finances, new product development, and various other activities. Also, less paperwork is required of closed corporations—only a fraction of that required by law once a company goes public. In addition, management enjoys more operating flexibility. Executives can devote their time to running the company instead of fielding inquiries from the news media, financial analysts, current and potential stockholders, and other interested parties. As long as creditors and customers are pacified, management is free to concentrate on long-term planning and success.

Top managers in open corporations, by contrast, must be concerned with short-term profitability, which is what the general public is mostly interested in and what key executives are perpetually held accountable for.

So why go public at all? The most compelling reason is money. Selling stock to the general public enables a company to obtain quick cash for rapid expansion. Successful closed corporations with a large backlog of unfilled orders may be handicapped by inadequate facilities and equipment to meet the growing demand for their products or services. Going public can bring a large infusion of cash to expand operations, improve existing products, develop new ones, and (they hope) increase sales and profits many times over. Aside from the benefit of raising large amounts of capital quickly, becoming an open corporation also enables the original stockholders to place a tangible value on the worth of their investment once the company's stock is actively traded on the stock market (see Chapter 16).

Going public is no picnic, though, as many executives will confirm. For one thing, there are many expenses and details involved:

- An investment banking firm must be employed to steer the company through its transition from closed to open corporation.
- Certified public accountants and attorneys must also be involved in the process, because the company must provide detailed financial, legal, and operating information to the Securities and Exchange Commission (SEC), the federal agency that regulates corporations' sales of stock to the general public.
- An open corporation must file annual, quarterly, and monthly reports with the SEC.

The stock market's condition at the time the stock is sold is another major concern. If investors are generally optimistic, the initial stock offering could bring a good price. But if market conditions are depressed, the stock may sell for much less than the corporation and its investment banker anticipated.

Beyond these concerns, the company must also reveal information on top executives' salaries and fringe benefits, background material on all top managers and directors, pending lawsuits that may be decided against the company, and business relationships that, although legal, may be embarrassing or ethically questionable. Securities and Exchange Commission regulations may also force a company to disclose trade secrets, new product development plans, and other material that competitors could take advantage of.

The alternative to going public, of course, is to remain closely held and pursue whatever sources of capital one can. For example, closed corporations might:

- Sell stock to their employees, if the workers can provide enough capital to satisfy the company's needs. Workers who wanted to sell their stock would be required to sell it back to the company or to other employees, but not to outsiders.
- Enter into a joint venture (see Chapter 3) with a larger company that would

provide the necessary funds for expansion in exchange for an attractive return on its investment.

- Sell off unprofitable or marginal parts of the company and invest the money in more profitable operations.
- Sell stock to a handful of wealthy new investors, but continue to remain privately held.
- Borrow the necessary funds. Interest must be paid on the loan, of course, and anxious lenders typically require the closed corporation's executives or stockholders to personally guarantee repayment if the company cannot pay.

YOU DECIDE

Describe at least two situations that might prompt the larger stockholders of an open corporation to purchase the shares of smaller stockholders and convert the company to a closed corporation.

professional corporation
A corporation formed by licensed professionals such as attorneys, physicians, or accountants.

This issue, like most others in business, has no clear-cut answer, no simple formula to apply. The "best" form of corporate ownership is a judgment call. One thing is certain, though: the course a company takes will have a major impact on its operations for many years to come.

In addition to open and closed corporations, there is a relatively new type of corporation called the **professional corporation,** or professional association (PA), which is *a corporation formed by licensed professionals such as attorneys, physicians, or accountants.* Professional corporations enjoy the usual benefits of being incorporated, and the laws in many states grant their stockholder/members limited liability for each other's actions. For example, a member of a PA may be liable only for malpractice charges that arise from services or advice that he or she personally provided to patients or clients.

How Corporations Are Organized

bylaws
Internal rules that govern the general operation of a corporation.

For the moment, assume that you and your friend have received a corporate charter and issued stock to twenty other persons. You would then call a meeting of the stockholders for the purpose of approving your **bylaws,** which *are internal rules that govern the general operation of a corporation.* The bylaws may repeat some of the charter's provisions and include the following points as well:

- Quorum required for holding stockholders' meetings
- Voting privileges of stockholders
- Number of directors; method of electing them; method of creating or filling vacancies on the board of directors
- Time and place of directors' meetings; requirements for a quorum
- Method of selecting officers; titles; duties; terms of office; salaries
- Transfer restrictions on stock certificates; procedure for recording new owners on company books
- Procedure for declaring dividends on stock
- Authority to sign checks
- Procedure for amending bylaws

	SOLE PROPRIETORSHIP	PARTNERSHIP	CORPORATION
Ownership	Proprietor	Partners	Stockholders
Management	Proprietor or person chosen by proprietor	Partners or person chosen by partners	Corporate officers who are chosen by board of directors, who are elected by stockholders

Table 4.2
Comparing ownership and management in the three forms of business.

Table 4.2 compares the ownership and management of a corporation to that in a sole proprietorship and a partnership. The owners of a corporation are the stockholders, but they do not run the business. They give the authority to develop the company's policies to the board of directors, who have been elected to represent them. The board members select the company's officers: president, treasurer, and secretary. A corporation's officers, rather than its board of directors, are responsible for carrying out its day-to-day activities. If the firm is large enough, it will employ and supervise specialized managers in fields such as marketing, production, finance, and personnel management.

Although sole proprietorships and partnerships can be managed by people who are not the owners, as Table 4.2 shows, such a practice is unusual. It is much more typical for the owners to manage these two forms of business.

Few stockholders in corporations, however, expect to exert control over corporate activities. If you own ten shares of General Motors (GM) common stock, you are a part-owner of a giant corporation. But you exercise little if any control over the firm because there are more than half a million other shareholders.

Stockholders tend to know or care little about the operation of the firm. They are more interested in the earnings or growth potential of their investment. Also, in many large corporations, no individual holds more than 1 percent of the outstanding stock, hardly enough to exercise control over corporate activities. In widely held corporations where stockholders are scattered and unable to contact each other conveniently, however, one stockholder could exert considerable influence with less than 51 percent of the stock. In fact, a person with 20 percent of the stock could gain effective control of the corporation.

Generally, however, the corporate management—the officers—control the internal affairs of most large corporations. And that management is largely self-perpetuating. Stockholders' influence can be felt only if they organize themselves into a group with a collective interest and vote their shares together to change the management or reject management policy. But as long as the stockholders feel that management is running the corporation well and that their own investment is secure and profitable, they will leave the management alone.

At a corporation's annual meeting, stockholders may express their concerns and recommendations to management face to face.

Management has to report to the stockholders in two ways: in the annual report, which describes the corporation's operations and financial status, and in the stockholders' meeting. The bylaws of each corporation specify when the meeting must be held. At the meeting, the stockholders have the opportunity to challenge management's decisions. Few stockholders attend these meetings, again because of the relatively small size of their holdings and their lack of interest in operational details.

Corporate management must obtain the stockholders' approval on certain issues. The bylaws always specify which matters this is true for, often including such things as the acquisition of another company or the issuing of new stock. Even so, not all stockholders will attend the meeting. A stockholder may mail the company a **proxy**, which is *a document that authorizes another party to cast a stockholder's votes at an annual meeting when he or she cannot attend in person*. Proxies are like absentee ballots in political elections, although the forms used to solicit them often state that if the proxy is not returned by a certain date, the stockholder's votes will be cast in a manner specified by management.

proxy
A document that authorizes another party to cast a stockholder's votes at an annual meeting when he or she cannot attend in person.

Advantages of Corporate Organization

Corporations have their advantages and disadvantages. One of the key drawbacks of sole proprietorships and partnerships—unlimited liability—is avoided under the corporate form of organization. Owners of a corporation enjoy **limited liability**, which is *a feature inherent in corporations; it means that stockholders' responsibility for debts is restricted to the amount of their investment in the corporation*. One practical point should be mentioned here. A corporation that decides to borrow money may have trouble doing so if its assets are inadequate security for the loan. A lender may then require one or more stockholders with substantial personal assets to cosign the loan agreement

limited liability
A feature inherent in corporations; stockholders' responsibility for debts is restricted to the amount of their investment in the corporation.

with the corporation. The stockholders who agree to such an arrangement voluntarily relinquish their limited liability for their company to borrow funds.

A second advantage is ease of expansion. Corporations can raise funds by selling stock, a financing device that does not exist for sole proprietorships or partnerships. Corporations can also borrow against the value of their assets by selling bonds. Both of these corporate securities will be explored in detail in Chapter 16.

A third advantage of corporations is the ease of transferring ownership. Stockholders can transfer their shares to someone else merely by endorsing the stock certificate in the space provided on the back.

Relatively long life is a fourth advantage. Corporations, unlike sole proprietorships and partnerships, can be chartered for perpetual existence. They do not terminate with the death or incapacitation of the stockholders/ owners. In fact, approximately twenty American corporations can trace their roots to before the Revolutionary War.

A fifth advantage of incorporation, especially if the company prospers, is the greater ability to attract and hire specialized management. As we said earlier, most sole proprietorships and partnerships are managed by the owners. One reason is that these people are often entrepreneurs who want to run their own business. Another reason is that these businesses are usually smaller and cannot afford to bring in sought-after managers. Larger corporations, on the other hand, have the facilities, money, and career opportunities necessary to attract top talent to management jobs in critical business areas such as labor-management relations, finance, marketing, manufacturing, and personnel. Unlike sole proprietorships and partnerships, large corporations can replace top managers if their performance is unsatisfactory.

Disadvantages of Corporate Organization

Corporations also have their disadvantages. One drawback is that they are normally more expensive and complicated to organize than the other forms of business. It is usually necessary to hire a lawyer to draft the articles of incorporation, and states require the payment of a charter tax, filing fees, and various other costs.

Taxation can be a further disadvantage. The Internal Revenue Service taxes the earnings of sole proprietorships and partnerships at the graduated personal income tax rate, which is often less than the 34 percent maximum tax rate applied to the earnings of corporations. Taxes are not a consistent problem, however. We mentioned earlier that expert managers could be hired, and often these experts can help a large corporation legally avoid the full 34 percent tax rate.

Exercising every citizen's right to take full advantage of federal tax laws, corporations, like individuals, can minimize their tax burden through such actions as:

1. Allocating certain kinds of revenue over several years' operations, which may reduce the total amount of tax paid on that revenue
2. Spreading certain kinds of operating losses over several years, which will reduce the firm's taxable income for each of those years
3. Selling unprofitable investments or subsidiary companies and using the loss to decrease taxable earnings over several years
4. Depreciating assets using the highest annual rate allowed under current tax laws, thus reducing the amount of revenue subject to income tax
5. Purchasing certain costly equipment or making major improvements whose value may be deducted from income taxes owed under current tax laws

In addition to federal income tax, corporations must pay taxes in each state where they do business, if the state levies a corporate income tax. Then the stockholders must pay personal income taxes on the corporate profits paid to them as dividends on their stock. The fairness of this double taxation has been questioned for many years by corporations, stockholders, and legislators alike.

Government restrictions and reporting requirements are generally more extensive for corporations than for other businesses. As a result, corporate activities lack the freedom and privacy enjoyed by the other forms of business ownership. In addition to federal reporting requirements and restrictions, corporations must comply with the demands of each state in which they operate. Depending on a company's operations and products, legally mandated paperwork can be mind-boggling. Most large corporations must report sources of revenue, debts, expenses, and a host of other financial information. This information, which often becomes a matter of public record, can be examined by competitors and other interested parties. Such loss of secrecy about operations can hurt a corporation's competitive position in the marketplace.

Finally, employees in large corporations may lack the personal identification with and commitment to corporate goals that those of smaller organizations often enjoy. This may be more the fault of management's attitude than of the company's form of organization.

Table 4.3 summarizes the advantages and disadvantages of the corporate form of organization, along with those of the sole proprietorship and general partnership you learned about in Chapter 3.

The S Corporation

S corporation
One that may elect, under Subchapter S of the Internal Revenue Code, to be taxed as a sole proprietorship if owned by one stockholder, or as a partnership if owned by several stockholders.

One way of avoiding the tax disadvantages of corporations while enjoying the advantages of incorporating is available to a business that qualifies as an **S corporation**. This is *one that may elect, under Subchapter S of the Internal Revenue Code, to be taxed as a sole proprietorship if owned by one stockholder, or as a partnership if owned by several stockholders.* If the owners choose this tax treatment, the corporation pays no corporate federal income tax. Instead, the shareholders declare their share of the firm's taxable income as personal

FORM OF OWNERSHIP	ADVANTAGES	DISADVANTAGES
Sole proprietorship	Easy to establish. Owner retains all profits. Owner enjoys relative freedom and flexibility in decision making. Owner gets satisfaction and independence. Easy to dissolve.	Owner has unlimited liability. Funds for expansion may be difficult to obtain. Owner's lack of business skills may impede success. Employees lack opportunities. Business lacks continuity; it dies when owner dies.
General partnership	Individuals with diverse talents can pool knowledge and skills. More funds may be more easily available than for sole proprietorship. There is the potential for a better credit rating than sole proprietorship can obtain. Valuable employees can be retained by allowing them to become partners.	Partners may have conflicting personalities, ideas, and interests. Business lacks permanence. General partners have unlimited liability. Investments are frozen. Value of partners' claims may be disputed.
Corporation	Owners have limited liability. Easy to expand. Easy to transfer ownership. Business can have relatively long life. First-rate, specialized managers can be hired and kept more easily.	More expensive and complicated to organize. Taxes are frequently higher. Government restrictions and reporting requirements can be costly and time consuming. Employees may lack identification with and commitment to corporate goals.

income (regardless of whether the amount was actually paid to them), and it is taxed at their personal income tax rate. This may be a clear advantage, because the maximum personal income tax rate is now 28 percent, while the maximum corporate rate is 34 percent.

The Subchapter S Revision Act of 1982 made several significant changes in the conditions and qualifications that apply to S (formerly called Subchapter S) corporations. Major conditions are:

1. The firm must be chartered in the United States.
2. Only one class of stock may exist.
3. A maximum of thirty-five stockholders is allowed.
4. Shareholders must be individuals or estates.

Table 4.3
Advantages and disadvantages of the three forms of business ownership.

5. Nonresident aliens and other corporations are not permitted to be shareholders.
6. All shareholders must agree to have their corporation taxed as an S corporation.
7. S corporation status may be terminated by a majority vote of the shareholders. (Under previous regulations, one minority shareholder could prevent the termination of S corporation status.)
8. The Internal Revenue Service may terminate S corporation status for a company whose passive income (from royalties, rents, dividends, and interest) exceeds 25 percent of annual gross sales for three consecutive years. Federal income tax must be paid on the excess amount in any given year.

If S corporation tax treatment sounds good to you, and you are able to meet the above conditions, you should still ask an experienced lawyer and accountant for their advice. It is possible, for example, that tax laws in your state do not recognize S corporations. That would mean that while avoiding federal corporate income taxes, your S corporation would still have to pay state corporate income taxes. Federal and state tax laws are quite complex, and they change from year to year.

Business Combinations

Businesses combine to achieve greater profitability, efficiency, and competitiveness. After forming a corporation—let's call it Yankee Pedaler Bicycle Corporation—your original company can be combined with others in one of several ways.

Acquisition

acquisition
Results when one firm buys a majority interest in another, but both retain their identities.

Acquisition *results when one firm buys a majority interest in another, but both retain their identities.* Corporations that want a reliable supply of parts and materials or guaranteed markets for their products often use this tactic. They simply purchase enough of the outstanding shares of a supplier or a customer to exercise a controlling interest in that firm.

To prevent periodic shortages of tires, tubes, and bicycle chains and to increase retail sales, you could buy controlling interest in Big Wheel Tire Company, Continuous Chain Corporation, and House of Spokes Bike Shops. Figure 4.3 shows the organization that would result. That should solve your supply and marketing problems.

Merger

merger
Occurs when two or more companies become a single enterprise; the controlling corporation retains its identity and absorbs the others.

A **merger** *occurs when two or more companies become a single enterprise; the controlling corporation retains its identity and absorbs the others.* Powerful entrepreneurs once eliminated competitors this way. United States Steel Corporation, Du Pont, and Standard Oil Company were born during the first

Yankee Pedaler Bicycle Corporation

Big Wheel Bicycle
Tire Company

Continuous Chain
Corporation

House of Spokes
Bike Shops

Owned by Yankee Pedaler

Figure 4.3
Yankee Pedaler grows by acquisition.

wave of mergers between 1881 and 1911. In 1899 alone, 1,028 companies completely disappeared as a result of merging with other firms.

In 1992 there were 2,578 announced mergers and acquisitions, an increase of 39 percent over the previous year and the highest number in six years. The biggest deal involved ITT Corporation's sale of 30 percent of its Alcatel operation to Alcatel Alsthom of France for $3.6 billion.[1]

There are three kinds of mergers. A **horizontal merger** *occurs when one firm purchases other firms that produce similar or competing products.* This results in greater production economies and reduced competition, but as you will see later, the Federal Trade Commission and the Department of Justice tend to regulate such mergers.

Despite potential government restrictions, horizontal mergers are quite popular today. In the candy industry, for example, Hershey Foods Corp. bought Peter Paul/Cadbury for $300 million in 1988 and recently paid $40 million for Gubor, a German chocolate manufacturer, and $180 million for 19 percent of the largest candy maker in Scandinavia.[2] Johnson & Johnson owns some seventeen companies that make pharmaceutical products, medical equipment, blood glucose monitoring systems, toiletries, and disposable contact lenses. Such mergers can be highly efficient, because the participating companies can integrate their research and development laboratories, marketing departments, and production facilities in ways that reduce expenses and increase sales more impressively than either could have done alone. If you staged a horizontal merger, you would buy bicycle companies, perhaps in other parts of the country, in exchange for stock in Yankee Pedaler, as shown in Figure 4.4.

Vertical mergers were common from 1921 to 1929. A **vertical merger** *occurs when one firm unites with others that contribute to its product's manufacture or distribution.* It is usually intended to guarantee sources of parts or sales outlets, so it can be used as an alternative to acquisition in attaining these goals.

horizontal merger
Occurs when one firm purchases other firms that produce similar or competing products.

vertical merger
Occurs when one firm unites with others that contribute to its product's manufacture or distribution.

Figure 4.4
Yankee Pedaler grows by horizontal merger.

Yankee Pedaler Bicycle Corporation

Easy Rider Bicycle Company

BMX Bicycle Corporation

Two-Wheel Transportation Company

Rapid Cycle Corporation

A company that merges vertically with others controls the raw materials, production, distribution, and marketing of a product. In their infancy automakers bought glass, adhesives, shock absorbers, batteries, and ignition parts from independent companies. Over the years suppliers of these items were acquired in vertical mergers, and most are now the exclusive suppliers of a parent firm. Vertical mergers have resulted in such entities as fully integrated oil companies like ARCO (Atlantic Richfield Company), which owns everything from offshore drilling rigs in the Gulf of Mexico to gasoline pumps at the corner service station. Vertical mergers are less likely than horizontal mergers to encounter antitrust difficulties.

If Yankee Pedaler Bicycle Corporation underwent a vertical merger, it would absorb companies that produced the chains, tires, wheels and fenders, handlebars and grips, seats, lights, and horns for its bicycles. Adding a chain of bicycle stores would complete the production and marketing system, as illustrated in Figure 4.5. After this kind of merging, the company would be virtually self-sufficient.

conglomerate merger
Occurs when one firm buys other firms that make unrelated products.

A **conglomerate merger**, which *occurs when one firm buys other firms that make unrelated products,* has become a natural response to government regulation of monopolies. The wave of mergers that occurred during the 1960s and early 1970s saw many of these.

To expand profitably is the main goal of a conglomerate merger. Another purpose of combining unlike firms is to diversify operations and thus vary sources of income for the parent company. Conglomerates avoid putting all their corporate eggs in one industrial basket. Hard times tend not to fall on all industries at once or with equal severity.

Alco Standard, a company with $4.9 billion in sales, owes its existence to conglomerate mergers. Since 1965 Alco has bought or sold more than 300 companies in 50 different lines of business, including liquor distribution, coal mining, and firms manufacturing a grab bag of products ranging from fish food and ice cream snacks to motor homes, electronic sports scoreboards, health services, food service equipment, and imported giftware. The company is now the largest paper distributor in the world and the leading seller and

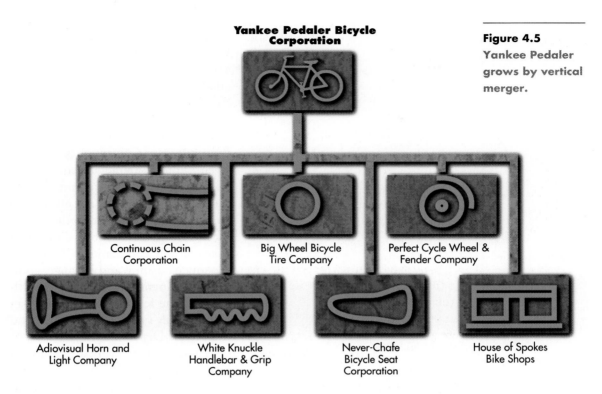

Yankee Pedaler Bicycle Corporation

Continuous Chain Corporation

Big Wheel Bicycle Tire Company

Perfect Cycle Wheel & Fender Company

Adiovisual Horn and Light Company

White Knuckle Handlebar & Grip Company

Never-Chafe Bicycle Seat Corporation

House of Spokes Bike Shops

Figure 4.5
Yankee Pedaler grows by vertical merger.

servicer of photocopiers and fax machines.[3] Johnson Controls, a company founded in 1885 to manufacture thermostats, has grown by conglomerate merger to acquire firms that manufacture car batteries (including the Sears DieHard), heating and cooling systems for office buildings, plastic beverage bottles, and automotive seats for Jeep Grand Cherokees and Chrysler LH cars.[4]

Table 4.4 presents selected subsidiaries or products owned by several large conglomerates. Note the variety of businesses these corporations are involved in. If the Yankee Pedaler Bicycle Corporation decided to undertake a conglomerate merger, it would purchase several well-managed firms that make a variety of products with promising consumer demand.

Amalgamation or Consolidation

An **amalgamation** *or* **consolidation** *occurs when one firm combines with others to form an entirely new company; former identities are relinquished.* This can be expressed as a formula:

$$\text{Company A} + \text{Company B} + \text{Company C} = \text{Company D}$$

Amalgamation is an alternative to the types of merger discussed previously. The companies sacrifice their former identities for the sake of a new combination and a fresh public image. Amalgamation is what happened in 1917 when the individual corporations that manufactured Oldsmobiles, Buicks, Pontiacs, and Cadillacs combined to form General Motors Corporation. (Two years later, this new firm absorbed Chevrolet in a merger.)

amalgamation *or* **consolidation**
Occurs when one firm combines with others to form an entirely new company; former identities are relinquished.

PARENT COMPANY	SUBSIDIARIES OR PRODUCTS
K mart	PACE Membership Warehouse
	Builders Square
	Pay Less Drug Stores
	Waldenbooks
	The Sports Authority
PepsiCo	Pepsi-Cola North America
	Pepsi-Cola International
	PepsiCo Worldwide Foods
	Frito-Lay, Inc.
	Pizza Hut Worldwide
	Taco Bell Worldwide
	Kentucky Fried Chicken Corp.
General Mills	Big G cereals
	Betty Crocker products
	Yoplait yogurt
	Gorton's frozen seafood
	Red Lobster USA restaurants
	The Olive Garden USA restaurants
RJR Nabisco	Nabisco Foods Group
	Nabisco International
	R. J. Reynolds Tobacco Company
	R. J. Reynolds Tobacco International, Inc.
Adolph Coors Company	Coors Brewing Company
	Golden Aluminum Company
	Graphic Packaging Corporation
	Coors Energy Company
	Coors BioTech, Inc.
	Coors Ceramics Company
	Golden Technologies Company, Inc.
Gillette	Waterman pens
	Paper Mate pens
	Liquid Paper correction fluid
	Jafra cosmetics
	Braun shavers and appliances
	Oral-B oral care products

Table 4.4
Parent companies and selected subsidiaries or products.

Applying this concept to your fictitious corporation, you could consolidate with other companies and adopt the new name and image of Amalgamated Manufacturing Corporation.

Regulation of Combinations

Even though mergers, acquisitions, and amalgamations are common in business, corporations are not free to engage in any combination they want. The U.S. government is concerned that colossal companies will control too much business and endanger competition. To monitor business combinations, the federal government uses the Federal Trade Commission and the Justice Department.

A government agency established by the Federal Trade Commission Act of 1914, the **Federal Trade Commission (FTC)** is *a quasi-judicial body empowered to issue cease-and-desist orders against companies whose combinations would significantly lessen competition.* A firm that disregards one of these cease-and-desist orders may be fined up to $10,000. The FTC also investigates false or misleading advertising claims, regulates product labeling and packaging, and ensures that borrowers are told the true cost of consumer loans and charge accounts.

The **Department of Justice**, *an arm of the federal government, works closely with the FTC to preserve competitive markets through investigations by its Antitrust Division.* This division investigates company activities that lead to one or a few firms so dominating an industry that they control the supply or cost of a product, enabling them to squeeze out competitors and charge extremely high prices.

Both of these regulators may dispute a proposed business combination. They also may bring legal action to break up large firms that have excessive control over products and prices within their industries. A Department of Justice case filed in 1970 sought to dissolve massive International Business Machines (IBM) but neglected to clarify precisely what illegal acts the firm was accused of. This case, nicknamed the Methuselah case, involved more than 300 lawyers and generated 66 *million* pages of depositions and other legal paperwork. As proceedings dragged on, IBM's share of the market decreased from 70 percent to an estimated 62 percent in 1981, owing to more aggressive foreign and domestic competitors and technological advances. The Department of Justice finally dropped the suit thirteen years later.

In recent years the Department of Justice has displayed more tolerance for business combinations. Discarding a 1968 guideline that marked a combination for investigation if fewer than five companies controlled 60 percent of the market, the department now applies a more precise and logical mathematical formula to proposed combinations. This yardstick considers both the number of firms in the market and the relative power of each.

Other Types of Corporations

So far we have discussed only private, profit-seeking businesses. Now we will look at some alternatives to private ownership: government corporations and nonprofit corporations, including cooperatives.

Government Ownership

A **government corporation** is *a corporation organized by a city, county, state, or federal government to serve a specific segment of the population.* First created during World War I to provide the financial and operating flexibility required by emergency programs, government corporations soon became common in most countries and at all levels of government.

The Tennessee Valley Authority (TVA) and the Federal Deposit Insurance Corporation (FDIC) are well-known examples of government corporations. In 1933, when President Franklin D. Roosevelt recommended that the TVA be established, he stated that "the government's purpose is to provide an agency clothed with the power of government but possessed of the flexibility and initiative of private enterprise." A more recent but now defunct example of a government corporation was the government's Synthetic Fuels Corporation. Set up in the late 1970s, it was created to finance companies that were willing to use new technology to produce energy from oil-bearing shale, garbage, solar power, geothermal sources, and windmills. Congress allocated $20 billion for disbursement. Eventually $2.7 billion was disbursed to pay for such ventures as a $1.2 billion coal gasification facility in North Dakota, a $900 million oil-shale plant in Colorado, and a $620 million facility to convert coal to gas in Louisiana. Falling oil prices made the development of alternate energy sources less attractive, however, and in 1985 President Ronald

Federal Trade Commission (FTC) A quasi-judicial body empowered to issue cease-and-desist orders against companies whose combinations would significantly lessen competition.

Department of Justice An arm of the federal government; works closely with the FTC to preserve competitive markets through investigations by its Antitrust Division.

YOU DECIDE
List at least three potential benefits that a small corporation might realize from merging with a company several times its size. List at least three potential benefits that a large corporation might realize from acquiring smaller companies in unrelated industries.

government corporation A corporation organized by a city, county, state, or federal government to serve a specific segment of the population.

Reagan signed a bill that terminated the Synthetic Fuels Corporation and placed its projects under control of the Treasury.

Government corporations at all levels have been created for many purposes. Some cities and townships, for example, carry out their governmental responsibilities under a corporate charter issued by the state. (They issue no stock.) Atlanta and San Francisco are examples of municipal government corporations. Pennsylvania, West Virginia, and several other states have created government corporations to control the sale of liquor. In these states, liquor can be bought only from one source—the state store.

Some government corporations are responsible for providing a public service regardless of profit or loss. Others must be self-supporting. Federal Prison Industries is an example of a self-supporting government corporation. This corporation is chartered by the federal government to sell goods and services to federal agencies through seventy-four industrial operations in thirty-five federal penal institutions.

When we discussed socialist economies in Chapter 1, we mentioned that in such an economic system the government owns the major industries. *The change from private ownership of an industry to government ownership* is a process known as **nationalization**. The banks of France were nationalized by President François Mitterrand. Many of the countries of Europe are socialist and have nationalized industries.

Nationalization also occurs in the countries of the Third World—Asia, Africa, and South America. The economically disadvantaged countries in these regions sometimes take control of important industries previously run by foreign companies.

Some government corporations compete directly with privately owned corporations for world markets. For example, Scandinavian Airlines System (SAS), a government-controlled airline, competes with Delta Airlines, a publicly held American corporation. Renault, a French government–owned automaker, competes with General Motors and Ford.

nationalization
The change from private ownership of an industry to government ownership.

nonprofit corporations
Organizations formed to further the interests and objectives of educational, religious, social, charitable, and cultural groups. No stock is issued, but members enjoy limited liability.

Many groups, including the Salvation Army, are organized as nonprofit corporations.

Nonprofit Corporations

Some corporations are considered **nonprofit corporations**. These are *organizations formed to further the interests and objectives of educational, religious, social, charitable, and cultural groups. No stock is issued, but the members of the organization enjoy the advantage of limited liability.* The American Automobile Association, most

MANAGER'S NOTEBOOK

McIlhenny Company

McIlhenny Company's famous product is a staple in kitchen cupboards around the world and a regular fixture on tables in both gourmet restaurants and backwoods barbecue joints. What is it? Tabasco brand pepper sauce.

Called "the wine of Louisiana," this simple concoction of red peppers, vinegar, and salt has a unique flavor and an almost cultlike following that has lasted for more than a century.

A closed corporation owned by descendants of founder Edmund McIlhenny, the McIlhenny Company, headquartered on family-owned Avery Island, Louisiana, began almost by accident after the Civil War.

The McIlhennys fled their island plantation in 1863 with Union troops on their heels. Two years later they returned to find their property virtually destroyed. Among the few things that survived were some red pepper plants that a family friend had brought from Mexico in the late 1840s.

Edmund began experimenting with sauces made from the fiery-flavored peppers, and by 1868 he had perfected a recipe that he believed he could sell. Descendants believe he chose the name Tabasco, an Indian name for "land where the soil is humid," just because he liked the sound. He bottled the product in women's cologne bottles that he found in the plantation's rubbish heap. Their shape endures in the design of today's Tabasco sauce bottle.

First-year sales hit a modest 350 bottles, but by 1872 sales had increased enough to justify opening a London office. Today the company sells more than 50 million bottles of Tabasco sauce a year in the United States alone. The product is marketed in almost 100 other countries; Japan accounts for more than 6 million bottles a year.

Today's Tabasco recipe is almost unchanged from the original. Peppers are handpicked at a precise shade of redness, ground up with distilled vinegar and 8 percent salt, and aged and fermented in white oak barrels. The aging process has been shortened from three years to "three warm seasons" because of product demand. When a batch is declared ready, the mash is strained, bottled, and shipped far and wide.

Although Tabasco sauce was once produced solely from Avery Island plants, the company now has several thousand acres of pepper plants in Mexico, Columbia, and Honduras. This geographic diversification enables the company to keep pace with demand and to guard against the possibility that pepper weevils, plant viruses, or a hurricane might devastate the original plots on Avery Island.

Just how profitable is this closed corporation? Family members decline to report profits, but they admit that making Tabasco sauce and two relatively new additions to the line (Bloody Mary mix and picante sauce) is a "very profitable operation." Stock certificates require stockholders to sell their shares back to the company.

Although they receive several attractive acquisition offers per year, the McIlhenny Company's close-knit owners remain as loyal to their heritage as their customers are to the product that made the business famous. Deep in the heart of Cajun country, these people still respect tradition.

(For more on the McIlhenny Company, see *The 100 Year History of Tabasco* [a centennial publication of McIlhenny Company], 1968, and *A Visit to the Tabasco Pepper Sauce Factory* [undated pamphlet published by McIlhenny Company].)

private colleges and universities, and the American Cancer Society are examples of nonprofit corporations.

As indicated by their name, nonprofit corporations do not exist to make a profit. They can, however, have a surplus of collections (dues, for instance) over expenses. This surplus can then be used by the nonprofit corporation to expand facilities or services or to give raises to employees. But that surplus is not a profit because it is not distributed as earnings to shareholders.

Cooperatives

Another type of enterprise can be included in our nonprofit classification—the **cooperative** or co-op. This is *an enterprise created and owned jointly by its members and operated for their mutual benefit.* It may be a group of consumers with a common interest or small producers whose objective is to gain greater economic power. By banding together the members enjoy the benefits of large-scale operations, as goods and services can often be bought more cheaply and sold more profitably in large quantities.

Some cooperatives are groups of consumers who combine their buying activities to receive quantity discounts and thus reduce their costs. Members also benefit from owning or controlling the facilities that make or sell the goods and services they desire. Many farming communities have cooperative stores that sell feed, seed, fertilizer, and equipment to members. There are also some 1,000 rural electric cooperatives that were formed in the 1930s to bring electricity and indoor plumbing to rural areas throughout the nation. Florida alone has eighteen such co-ops that supply power to 10 percent of its residents through 46,000 miles of transmission lines. Like most others, Florida's co-ops have no production facilities. They merely buy and distribute electric power from other companies. There are also cooperatively owned houses and apartment buildings, group health plans, insurance companies, and funeral homes. Some groups have created cooperatives that buy food in large quantities and sell it to members at low prices.

cooperative
An enterprise created and owned jointly by its members and operated for their mutual benefit.

One of the most common forms of cooperatives is the farmers' co-op, where growers join together to market their produce.

Cooperatives also exist for producers. Business owners have formed producer cooperatives to buy supplies more cheaply and sell products more profitably. Such cooperatives are most common in agriculture and also appear, though less frequently, in the fishing and petroleum industries.

SUMMARY

In this chapter we examined the third basic form of business organization, the corporation. This form accounts for more than 80 percent of all sales in the United States. A corporation is a legal entity separate from its owners. It can sue and be sued, enter into contracts, and buy, hold, and sell property in its own name. A corporation is created by the state, and its birth certificate is called a charter. Its owners are termed shareholders and hold stock certificates as evidence of their ownership.

Corporations are classified as domestic (within their home states), foreign (from another state), or alien (from another country), depending on where they were chartered and where they conduct their business affairs. Corporations are also classified as either open or closed, depending on whether their stock can be bought by the general public. Professional corporations are formed by professionals such as doctors or lawyers to enjoy the benefits of being incorporated. State laws may grant the stockholders/members limited liability for each other's malpractice. Corporations raise long-term funds or equity capital by issuing stock. They may also borrow by selling bonds. These subjects will be explored in depth in Chapter 16.

Stockholders with voting rights elect a board of directors, which is responsible for developing company policy and selecting top officers. A gap exists between ownership and true control in many larger American corporations. The average stockholder in a giant corporation has little involvement or interest in its affairs, caring only that the stock increases in value or the company pays regular dividends.

As is the case with sole proprietorships and partnerships, corporations have several advantages (in this case, ease of expansion, limited liability, and long life) and several disadvantages (expense of organizing, generally higher taxes, and government restrictions).

Business organizations are anything but static. New ones arrive on the economic scene daily, and older ones drop out. Some firms merge with others and lose their original identity. Some combine with others but retain their identity. Others voluntarily discard divisions or companies previously acquired. A few are required by the courts or regulatory agencies to divest themselves of previous acquisitions.

In addition to private corporations formed for profit, several types of corporations can be established for reasons other than profit making. These include government corporations, nonprofit corporations, and cooperatives.

KEY TERMS

acquisition p. 104
alien corporation p. 94
amalgamation *or* consolidation p. 107
bylaws p. 98
certificate (articles) of incorporation p. 93
closed corporation p. 94
conglomerate merger p. 106
cooperative p. 112
corporate charter p. 92
corporation p. 92
Department of Justice p. 108
domestic corporation p. 94
Federal Trade Commission (FTC) p. 108
foreign corporation p. 94

government corporation p. 109
horizontal merger p. 105
limited liability p. 100
merger p. 104
nationalization p. 110
nonprofit corporation p. 110
open corporation p. 94
professional corporation p. 98
proxy p. 100
S corporation p. 102
shareholders *or* stockholders p. 92
stock certificates p. 92
vertical merger p. 105

FOR REVIEW AND DISCUSSION

1. What is the purpose of a corporate charter? Why should its provisions regarding future activities be expressed in general terms?
2. Assume that the Kilobyte Personal Computer Company was incorporated in the state of Arizona. The company also has operations in Nevada, Texas, and Canada. How would the state of Arizona classify the firm? Nevada? Canada?
3. What is the difference between an open and a closed corporation? Why might a closed corporation decide to go public?
4. What is the difference between a professional corporation and a regular corporation?
5. What is the purpose of a board of directors?
6. Why is limited liability considered an advantage to the owners of a corporation?
7. What federal income tax option is open to the stockholders of an S corporation? What general conditions must be met before the company can elect this kind of tax treatment?
8. What are the main reasons some firms merge with or acquire other firms? State at least one potential disadvantage of business combinations to the controlling firm, the controlled or absorbed firms, and the general public.
9. Under what circumstances might it be better to combine several companies through amalgamation than to merge?
10. What is your attitude toward government ownership of such enterprises as the Tennessee Valley Authority (TVA) and the Federal Deposit Insurance Corporation (FDIC)? Discuss some of the alternatives.

APPLICATIONS

Case 4.1: Are CEOs Overpaid?

In 1980 the average CEO in the United States received $624,996 in compensation. By 1992 that figure had jumped an astonishing 614 percent to $3,842,247. The averages are not the only numbers to increase. In 1992 Thomas F. First, Jr., CEO of Hospital Corp. of America, earned over $127 million, while in the first half of fiscal 1993, Michael D. Eisner of Disney earned $197 million.

Whereas CEO income has reached historic highs, average CEO salaries have actually decreased since 1991. Instead of compensating CEOs with reported, and taxable, salaries, corporations have instead provided compensation through lucrative stock options. This sort of misrepresentation of income, as well as increasing stockholder concern, has prompted the Securities and Exchange Commission to expand the reporting responsibilities of corporations.

While Thomas F. First, Jr.'s gains were incredible, they may be well deserved. He made his $127 million by selling stock he purchased several years ago when the company went private and he invested his family fortune to forestall a takeover attempt. However, this sort of reward for risk taking may be the exception rather than the rule. Many executives reap huge profits through the inevitable rise of market values rather than through their own successes. For example, in 1992 Kenneth Olsen, CEO of Digital Equipment Corporation, pulled down $2.9 million while shareholders lost money.

In response to stockholder concern about overpaid executives, many companies, in addition to complying with new SEC regulations, are experimenting with more effective methods of tying compensation to performance. One method being tried is to sell stock options at a premium, often three times the current market value of the stock. This ensures that the company must increase its performance before an executive can make a gain on stock options. However, critics feel that such efforts are insufficient and that the value of options should be tied to trends in the market as well. While criticisms such as this are not new, boards of directors are now listening to them, and being a CEO may soon be much less lucrative.

Questions

1. Do you think corporate executives are being paid too much money? Why or why not?
2. What do you think might make a CEO worth more money than a worker or an engineer?
3. Should the government be involved in regulating CEO income? Why or why not?
4. What alternative methods might be used for compensating CEOs for performance?

For more information, see John A. Byrne, "Executive Pay" *Business Week*, April 26, 1993, pp. 56–79.

Case 4.2: Strategic Alliances
Make Strange Bedfellows

The computer industry, like many other high tech trades, was once a ground for astonishingly high-profit startups and equally quick failures. Multibillion-dollar companies such as Apple Computer and Microsoft, started on shoestrings, gained incredible prominence through excellent engineering or simple luck.

Today the industry is more mature and startups are less frequently successful. In fact, even major corporations have found it necessary to form strategic alliances in order to stay competitive. Computer companies in particular have found themselves constantly making and breaking alliances in order to gain market share.

An example of the constantly shifting alliances between computer giants is the relationship between IBM and Microsoft. Strong business partners in the early 1980s, the two companies had a falling out over a jointly developed product. Microsoft developed an operating system for IBM called OS/2, then later came out with a competing product named Windows NT. IBM retaliated by forming counter-alliances with other computer companies such as Apple. The ties between the companies were not severed, however, and when IBM was searching for a new CEO, the founder of Microsoft, Bill Gates, was informally consulted. The man who was chosen, Louis Gerstner, has met with Bill Gates and there has been a warming of relationships. This trend of improving relationships has not eliminated the competition between the companies, however. IBM has continued to position OS/2 as a competing product to Windows NT. With various divisions of IBM producing software that will compete with Microsoft and yet other divisions making products that will be sold with bundled Microsoft's Windows NT, it is clear that a great amount of alliance shifting will be going on in the future.

Strategic alliances are becoming prevalent in other high tech fields. New technologies, new standards, and new markets all cause major corporations to seek alliances with each other in order to share technology, resources, and clout as well as to become more competitive with Japanese firms. Other industries where alliances have become common are video and telecommunications. American A/V manufacturers have worked together to create technologies for the new high-definition television (HDTV) standard, while both telephone and cable companies are trying to dominate the emerging market for interactive television services.

Questions

1. How do alliances between corporations fit into the model of corporations presented in the chapter?

2. What disadvantages are brought about by the alliance/counteralliance business climate?

3. Does the business climate caused by alliances result in more competitive business or merely more complicated business?

4. What other major U.S. industries could use cooperative efforts to improve their performance against foreign competitors?

5. Should the government oversee or facilitate cooperative ventures? Why or why not?

For more information, see G. Pascal Zachary, "Chiefs of IBM, Microsoft Corp. Plan to Meet," *The Wall Street Journal*, May 10, 1993, p. A3.

REFERENCES

1. "Merrill Lynch Business Brokerage and Valuation Says Number of Mergers and Acquisitions Announced in 1992 Were the Highest in Six Years." (Press release issued by Doremus & Company, January 25, 1993)

2. Rita Koselka, "Candy Wars," *Forbes,* August 17, 1992, p. 76.

3. Seth Lubove, "How to Grow Big Yet Stay Small," *Forbes,* December 7, 1992, p. 64.

4. Rick Tetzeli, "Johnson Controls: Mining Money in Mature Markets," *Fortune,* March 22, 1993, p. 77.

5

THE SMALL BUSINESS AND FRANCHISING

G *oing into business for yourself, becoming an entrepreneur, is the modern-day equivalent of pioneering on the old frontier.*

PAULA NELSON

CHAPTER OBJECTIVES
After studying this chapter, you should be able to:

1. List three key people whose advice a new business owner should seek, and explain the need for each.
2. Describe the licenses and permits that must be obtained, and other general details that must be observed, in starting a new company.
3. List the things a small-business owner must know about to be successful.
4. List the roles of a business plan and the key areas it should cover.
5. Suggest several potential sources of capital for a small business.
6. Name several sources that provide continuing management advice after a small business begins to operate.
7. Describe how a franchise differs from an independent business and distinguish between the two main types of franchises.
8. State several important franchise terms that should be thoroughly investigated.
9. State the characteristics of a successful franchisee.
10. Recommend sources that can provide additional information about franchise firms.
11. Summarize how the FTC attempts to protect prospective franchisees.
12. State the potential advantages and disadvantages of entering into a franchise agreement.

UP FRONT

Ask Leslie Novak to describe herself and she'll tell you, "I'm a designer, product manager, and entrepreneur." Ask Leslie to describe her company and she'll tell you, "To provide products that solve people's problems and enhance the active lifestyle."

Her best-known product, the HowdaSeat, emerged from taking an old product and turning it into a new product for the 1990s. While moving from Iowa to Newburyport, Massachusetts, Novak came across a seat made of wood and canvas, circa the 1930s, designed to be used while sitting on bleacher benches at the circus. She was sitting with 350,000 people on the grassy lawn of the Esplanade in Boston, enjoying the Boston Pops Fourth of July concert, when the idea for the circus seat as something really useful and important came to her. "I realized I was sitting on something important," she recalls, "when I saw 350,000 people sitting uncomfortably on the ground. I saw 350,000 potential customers for a portable seat."

So in 1989 Novak set to work redesigning the circus seat. It took her a year. "I worked on the seat or some aspect of the business every day," she recalls. "One thing I realized early on was that I'd have to educate people to the need for this seat. That's called marketing, and among the HowdaSeat features we market are back support, durability, portability, all-natural and renewable materials, and made in Newburyport, Massachusetts, U.S.A."

The HowdaSeat, made of basswood slats and durable canvas, made its debut in the prestigious J. Peterman Company catalog in 1991. Home shoppers ordered it in droves; sales shot from 100 a week to 300, then 500, then 1,000. A number of other catalogs picked it up, and specialty retail stores carry it as well. The HowdaSeat's success has enabled Howda Designz to expand its offerings to a dozen different products, including accessories for the HowdaSeat itself. In 1992 the company began marketing its products internationally.

Today, Howda Designz employs ten people, some full-time and others part-time. "We try to manage and direct our human resources in a caring and renewable way, like we do our products, and so some people's skills or expertise we only need occasionally," says Novak. Another challenge for the company is trying to keep its products all-American: "We're hard pressed to keep production in the U.S. today, but it's been a very important aspect. We can maintain control over the quality and deliver in a more timely fashion. We see a growing trend overseas for American goods, which are viewed as 'high-design' products. We create good-looking, high-quality products, we respect human resources, we promote ecologically conscious manufacturing, and we're recognized throughout the world for it. For me, it's exciting to be able to manufacture in America while being conscious of the environment."

Novak says that running a small business means constantly redefining the company. "For example, we've found a third

LESLIE AISNER NOVAK

PRESIDENT, HOWDA DESIGNZ, INC.

major market for the HowdaSeat: the premium or incentive gift market for employees or customers. The HowdaSeat is selling well here. There are so many business opportunities out there that we often overlook because of self-imposed limits. The incentive market is certainly a good example. But it's not the outside world that places these restrictions on us. It's ourselves."

Leslie Aisner Novak offers this advice to would-be entrepreneurs: "Have faith in yourself, your design, your product, your vision. Let go of those self-imposed limits and restrictions. Believe in what you want to do, and focus on it. Keep your focus on that one thing, that starting point. Then you'll always know where you've come from, how far you've come, and where you stand.

"Do something every day for your business. Make a commitment to do one important thing that helps you move toward your vision. Never slack off, for starting your own business is a huge job. But if you do just one thing to help it along every day, have no fear. You'll get there."

Small Business Administration (SBA)
A federal government agency started in 1953 to give financial and managerial assistance to owners of small businesses.

Table 5.1
Guidelines defining a small business.

The more than 10 million small businesses in the United States account for more than 40 percent of the country's gross national product (these totals do not include farms or farm production). These companies provide livelihoods for their owners and employees while creating goods and services for millions of people. The definition of small business varies, but Table 5.1 lists some guidelines established by the **Small Business Administration (SBA)**, *a federal government agency started in 1953 to give financial and managerial assistance to owners of small businesses.*

Small-business owners require a unique combination of characteristics. Seeking economic independence outside the boundaries of traditional jobs and large, formalized employers, these individuals combine courage, determination, resourcefulness, ambition, self-confidence, and optimism into a business enterprise as unique as they are. The pioneer spirit is alive and well in dens, garages, small stores, and utility sheds nationwide.

INDUSTRY	DEFINITION
Manufacturing	A company with 500 to 1,500 employees, depending on the type of product manufactured
Wholesaling	A company with up to 100 employees
Services	A company with annual sales from $3.5 million to $14.5 million, depending on the industry
Retailing	A company with annual sales from $3.5 million to $13.5 million, depending on the industry
Agriculture	A company with annual sales from $0.5 million to $3.5 million, depending on the industry

Source: The Small Business Administration

According to the SBA, small businesses with fewer than 500 employees account for approximately 90 percent of all businesses in the United States and provide more than half of all jobs in existence.[1] The impact that small companies have on employment has become especially significant in recent years. *Fortune* magazine reports that small businesses accounted for 11.3 million of the 16.5 million net new jobs created between 1977 and 1987 and provided nearly all of the 2.7 million net new jobs created between 1988 and 1990. On the other hand, large companies *eliminated*

500,000 jobs during that time.[2] Small businesses, then, form a fundamental and significant pattern in today's economic tapestry.

In this chapter we will discuss starting and maintaining a small business and investigate the pros and cons of franchising. The discussion will be of special value to those who are planning to start their own companies or who have already done so.

A Board of Advisers

Input from an experienced lawyer, a certified public accountant, and an insurance counselor is vital to an infant business, helping pave the way to later prosperity. Few small-business owners are qualified to provide their own legal, accounting, or insurance advice.

Finding a competent professional in each of these fields is a challenge. One way is to ask friends and business acquaintances for recommendations. Local newspapers often interview outstanding local professionals who have earned special awards or recognition. Such service clubs as Rotary or Lions International usually have members who are active in these areas. The business owner must make an organized and thoughtful search; the people selected will be the firm's navigators, advising its owner, the pilot, on the direction he or she should take.

Lawyer

A lawyer provides in-depth legal advice on choosing forms of business organization (discussed in Chapter 3 and Chapter 4). If an owner decides to incorporate, a lawyer can prepare the required forms using the legal language needed to give the company maximum operating flexibility under its charter. The lawyer can also help by drawing up a partnership agreement for a business choosing that form.

In addition, a competent lawyer can help the small-business owner avoid legal confusion in such areas as:

- Contracts with outside parties (suppliers, landlords, creditors, customers, and service and repair firms)
- Liability for customer and employee injuries and for injuries caused by a product, service, or operating method
- Compliance with government regulatory agencies (Federal Trade Commission, Department of Justice, Occupational Safety and Health Administration, and others)

Accountant

An accountant helps ensure the financial success of a business venture. Certified public accountants, whom you will learn about in Chapter 19, provide advice on the tax aspects of operating as a sole proprietorship, a partnership, or a corporation and custom-build accounting systems to suit the legal and

Good things sometimes come in small packages. The collective sales and employment provided by small businesses make them a driving force in the nation's economy.

operating characteristics of a company. More specifically, an accountant helps a business owner:

• Determine how much beginning capital the firm requires
• Make decisions to lease or purchase major fixed assets
• Project cash collections and payouts to ensure that the firm has an adequate supply of cash on hand at all times
• Choose methods for raising short-term and long-term capital
• Manage finances so the owner receives the most favorable federal and state income tax treatment possible

Insurance Counselor

insurance counselor
An adviser who recommends a comprehensive program to protect a firm against insurable risks and to meet legal or quasi-legal insurance requirements.

A business's **insurance counselor** is *an adviser who recommends a comprehensive program to protect a firm against insurable risks and to meet legal or quasi-legal insurance requirements,* including workers' compensation insurance, mortgage insurance, or insurance required by a building lease. This risk expert should have the same professional concern for a firm's success as its lawyer and accountant. A conscientious insurance counselor should maintain close ties with the owner, recommending changes in coverage when changes occur in the company's size, the kinds of risks it faces, or the owner's personal circumstances.

Starting a Small Business

Entrepreneurs must comply with various legal requirements associated with starting a business and must understand the key factors that affect a company's success and profitability. Each of these elements should be reflected in a comprehensive business plan.

Legal Requirements

Small-business owners must follow several legal steps before offering a product or service to the public. That includes obtaining any necessary documents and approvals.

First, the business must meet applicable **zoning ordinances**, which are *city and county regulations defining the type of business activity that can be conducted at certain locations.* The firm must also obtain city and county business permits, and perhaps a state occupational license, if setting up shop as a cosmetologist, realtor, barber, electrician, or some other state-regulated profession. Local government officials will also inspect a company's building to verify that it conforms to local fire and safety codes. Retailers, who act as sales-tax collection agents for the state, must contact the state revenue department for registration forms and instructions on how to collect and pay sales tax.

The Internal Revenue Service (IRS) has various reporting requirements that affect every type of business. This agency provides a Business Tax Kit that describes the many taxes, deductions, and payment schedules companies must be aware of.

Most firms have to conform to a state's fictitious-name act. This means that if the name of the business is not simply the name or names of its owners, the owners' names must be registered at the county courthouse and published along with the company's name in the Legal Notices section of the newspaper.

Your advisers can provide detailed information on additional steps required in your city, county, and state.

zoning ordinances
City and county regulations defining the type of business activity that can be conducted at certain locations.

YOU DECIDE

Assume you own a successful business that employs 15 people and has openings for two more. You have two well-qualified relatives who have both asked you to hire them. What factors should you consider in deciding whether to hire them, instead of two equally qualified outsiders?

Factors to Consider

Infant companies have a fairly high mortality rate. The Dun & Bradstreet Corporation reports that approximately 36 percent of all business failures occur within the first 5 years.[3] The early years, then, are usually the most critical in a firm's life. There are many tasks to accomplish, and the owner's success in doing them will determine the success he or she will enjoy in the business. Figure 5.1 shows some of the factors that people who start their own businesses must consider. Let's look more closely at each one.

EXPERIENCE Any aspiring business owner should get experience in the line of business. Knowledge of finance, customer relations, marketing, inventory purchasing, personnel requirements, management, and technological developments is essential. Ira H. Latimer, executive vice-president of the American Federation of Small Business, suggests that would-be owners first become an employee in the kind of business they plan to start. They should avoid dead-end jobs that will isolate them from the rest of the organization and strive to become involved in every area of the company's business, however unfamiliar at first.

Figure 5.1
Factors for a new small-business owner to consider.

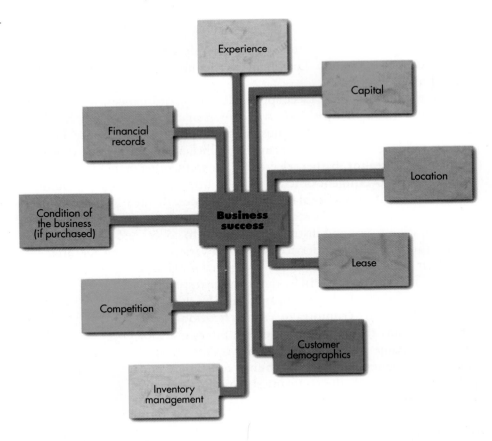

Experience doesn't have to come through one's main job, of course. A Department of Labor survey of people who worked two jobs revealed that, while 44 percent did so to pay their regular bills, almost 15 percent took a second job to gain career experience or to build a business that they might someday operate as their major source of income.

Dun & Bradstreet reports that 12 percent of all business failures are caused by the owner's inexperience. Figure 5.2 presents several kinds of inexperience that contribute to this cause. The areas cited in the figure build a strong argument for gaining sound experience before starting out on one's own. More than 56 percent of all companies that fail due to the owner's inexperience fail because the owner (1) doesn't know enough about the kind of business he or she has entered or (2) hasn't obtained adequate management experience—intimate, firsthand knowledge of the planning, organizing, staffing, directing, and controlling functions that we will discuss in Chapter 6.

Dun & Bradstreet, the nation's major source of statistics on business failures, reported that 96,857 businesses failed in one recent year alone. The effects of these failures extend far beyond the owners themselves, however, because companies never operate in a vacuum. Shock waves from a failed

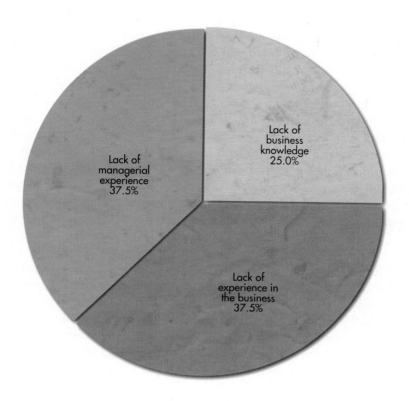

Figure 5.2
Causes of
business failure
related to
owner's
experience.

Source: *Business Failure Record* (New York: Dun & Bradstreet), 1993, p. 19. Courtesy Dun & Bradstreet Corporation.

company have an impact on many groups—employees, creditors, suppliers, customers, and governmental bodies (through lost tax revenue), to name just a few. Those 96,857 failed companies left behind debts of more than $91 billion.[4]

It is not necessary to start small to get the needed experience, though. Many small-business owners learn the basics of sound management in a large firm, then apply them to a small company of their own. Basic management practices remain the same regardless of a company's size. Some business owners have worked for low pay or even as volunteers to learn the basics of an industry, with an eye to the day when they would become their own boss. Keeping a diary of this work experience reinforces learning and helps make the most of the time spent. Courses and self-education supplement the lessons of experience. Business owners can also exchange ideas with one another by participating in service clubs and trade associations.

CAPITAL It is essential to start with sufficient capital. A company with inadequate financing is like a rowboat with a hole in the bottom: given enough time, it is bound to sink. Some small-business owners dream and save for so long that they reach the end of their patience and open the business come hell or high water. Rather than start a company on a shoestring, it is best either to wait until there is enough capital to ensure success or to begin on a smaller scale than originally planned. Both accountants and trade associations can help potential business owners decide whether they have enough capital to make a sound beginning.

How much capital does a business need? There is no easy answer. It depends on such variables as location, credit terms given by suppliers, distance from markets, and the nature of the product or service. It may take a construction company several months to complete its first projects, for example, but the owner must meet weekly payrolls, buy materials, make payments on leased or purchased equipment, maintain office facilities, and pay insurance premiums, taxes, utilities, and other business expenses in the meantime. These payments demand a large fund of operating capital.

LOCATION The business owner needs to pick a sound site for operations, a spot that favors the desired type of customer and the product or service that the firm will provide. A wag once declared that the three keys to business success are "location, location, and location." Neighboring businesses should be complementary. Undesirable neighbors can repel traffic, while several businesses with supporting lines or comparable target markets attract more customers than any one of them could alone. Many businesspeople also realize today that there is strength in numbers. This factor accounts for automobile alleys—rows of competing car dealers lined up next to each other—and shopping centers with two or more major department stores.

Site selection decisions often require a traffic study, an analysis of the traffic pattern around a location to confirm what type of person drives by, when, and

Many owners try to pick a location near complementary businesses, knowing that potential customers will already be attracted to the area.

why. Ideally, many people in the target area will need what the business sells and will find easy access to the premises. Traffic lights, pedestrian safety islands, and other traffic modifications should make it possible for customers to stop with a minimum of inconvenience. It also helps to consider plans for future street and highway improvements or business and housing developments. Such changes can make the area the hub or rim of traffic.

LEASE If a business owner decides to rent a facility, a lawyer should review the lease and explain what the tenant and the landlord are responsible for. Some business owners like to negotiate a short-term lease with an option to renew for a longer period, so they can see how the location actually works out before making a long-term commitment.

CUSTOMER DEMOGRAPHICS Before business owners can create effective advertising, sales promotion, or personal selling appeals, they must know customers' **demographics**. These are *statistics on such subjects as age, income, marital status, recreational habits, and ethnic customs for people who live within a given geographic area.* United States Bureau of the Census tracts help here, providing data on income, social characteristics, and occupations for as broad or as narrow an area as necessary. By combining census data with demographic reports from the chamber of commerce and the city and county government, business owners can define the population features of their trading areas clearly and accurately.

demographics
Statistics on such subjects as age, income, marital status, recreational habits, and ethnic customs for people who live within a given geographic area.

INVENTORY MANAGEMENT Demographic knowledge enables business owners to identify the most popular items to carry in inventory. Businesspeople who stock excessive inventory use too much storage space and pay too much for recordkeeping and insurance. Furthermore, the dollars invested in unneeded merchandise could be better spent on improved marketing efforts or more modern facilities and equipment. An understocked inventory is just as serious. The business can lose sales, goodwill, and customer loyalty if it cannot satisfy the needs of its clientele.

Major suppliers and trade associations provide information on seasonal trends and buying practices to help retailers stock the correct inventory at the desired levels throughout the year.

COMPETITION Still another aspect of running a successful small business is analyzing the practices of competitors. What do they do exceptionally well? Where could they improve? An alert newcomer, after observing the ways established competitors do business, can use their most effective practices and procedures from the beginning and avoid measures that they have found too costly, inefficient, or unproductive. One should examine competitors' approaches to such subjects as price, inventory selection, service, customer conveniences, and employee relations before committing oneself to any policy.

CONDITION OF THE BUSINESS An entrepreneur who buys an existing business rather than starting from scratch must investigate the business thoroughly. The prospective buyer's lawyer and accountant should obtain records that fairly present the business's legal and financial condition. A sole proprietor who claims that a business has earned $35,000 a year should be able to document that claim by showing copies of his or her personal income tax returns, for example. Equipment and merchandise should be physically inspected to verify its age and condition. Responsibility for any repairs should be clearly stated in the sales agreement between the current owner and the prospective owner. One novice restaurant owner who closed a deal without verifying the equipment inventory thought he was buying twenty more chairs than the building actually contained. On top of that, the seller had stopped servicing the equipment, which required expensive overhauling just after the sale was closed.

The buyer also should obtain a clear statement of which items will stay with the business and which will be taken by the seller, covering such things as drapes, special fixtures, paintings, wall hangings, and display equipment.

FINANCIAL RECORDS Doing it right the first time means keeping accurate and timely financial records. Knowing the current balances of accounts receivable and payable, levels of inventory, sales, expenses, and payment due dates gives an owner a view of the company's financial picture and of marketing trends and overall profitability. A certified public accountant (CPA) can develop an orderly accounting system that a bookkeeper can maintain with minimal effort. Sound and accurate accounting records let you monitor your financial condition from one period to the next and chart a course for success.

The Business Plan

business plan
A comprehensive summary of the key factors that will affect the operation of the proposed business.

Although it's important to appreciate how the elements just outlined affect a company's success, every small-business owner should prepare a formal **business plan**, which is *a comprehensive summary of the key factors that will affect the operation of the proposed business.* A business plan, which incorporates most of the elements in Figure 5.1, plays several important roles. First, it requires the owner to set clear, specific goals and work out steps by which to reach them. Second, it forecasts future business conditions that will affect the company's long-term success. Third, it provides data with which prospective investors can evaluate the potential risks and rewards of becoming investors in or creditors of the company. Finally, the business plan helps the owner monitor and evaluate the business's progress. The business plan should cover five main areas: mission statement, marketing, merchandise purchasing, organization, and financing.

MISSION STATEMENT The mission statement briefly defines the owner's reason for being in business and describes what the firm intends to do better or differently from competitors.

MARKETING The marketing section of the plan summarizes several elements that will affect company sales. For example, it profiles the company's target market demographics, including how many potential customers reside in the immediate area and how much they can be expected to spend for the business's product or service. This section also describes the proposed location, including a description of the building, the lease or mortgage terms, and the flow of nearby traffic. The plan must also state the image the owner wants the business to project, how that will be accomplished, and how this image will differ from that of competitors with respect to customer service, pricing, merchandise selection, product quality, delivery, financing, and other characteristics that can distinguish this company from the rest of the crowd.

The marketing portion of the plan should also discuss plans for advertising, including the types of ad media one plans to use (radio, television, newspapers, billboards, and so on), the size of each medium's target audience, how often ads will run, and what they will communicate about the business.

The plan should also outline practices for hiring and training salespeople and support personnel and should provide a diagram of the store's interior layout, including a description and location of furniture and fixtures.

Finally, the plan should thoroughly analyze nearby competitors—who they are, how long they've been in operation, the distinguishing characteristics of their business, and the most accurate estimates possible of their sales and expenses compared to the new business's projected figures.

MERCHANDISE PURCHASING This section of the plan lists the major suppliers the company expects to buy its inventory from. It should include information about their credit terms, delivery frequency, distance from the business, and the alternative sources to be used if a primary supplier cannot deliver what's needed.

ORGANIZATION The business plan should contain an organization chart that shows how key personnel (general manager, department managers, and supervisors) report and relate to each other (organization charts are discussed more thoroughly in Chapter 7). The plan should describe each person's main duties and responsibilities.

FINANCING This section should itemize start-up costs, including beginning inventory, licenses and permits, and promotional expenses for the grand opening. The plan should also show the amount of cash required to operate the business from month to month and the source of those funds (which, it is hoped, will be sales). The Small Business Administration offers the form shown in Figure 5.3 to help business owners estimate their starting cash needs.

The prospective business owner will probably need a loan to launch the business, so the plan should spell out what portion of start-up costs will be paid for by personal funds and how much will have to be borrowed. The plan should include a month-by-month forecast of sales and expenses and how

ESTIMATED MONTHLY EXPENSES			
Item	Your estimate of monthly expenses based on sales of $_____ per year	Your estimate of how much cash you need to start your business (See column 3.)	What to put in column 2 (These figures are typical for one kind of business. You will have to decide how many months to allow for in your business.)
	$ Column 1	$ Column 2	Column 3
Salary of owner-manager			2 times column 1
All other salaries and wages			3 times column 1
Rent			3 times column 1
Advertising			3 times column 1
Delivery expense			3 times column 1
Supplies			3 times column 1
Telephone			3 times column 1
Other utilities			3 times column 1
Insurance			Payment required by insurance company
Taxes, including Social Security			4 times column 1
Interest			3 times column 1
Maintenance			3 times column 1
Legal and other professional fees			3 times column 1
Miscellaneous			3 times column 1
STARTING COSTS YOU ONLY HAVE TO PAY ONCE			Leave column 2 blank
Fixtures and equipment			Estimate cost of fixtures you'll need and put total here.
Decorating and remodeling			Talk it over with a contractor.
Installation of fixtures and equipment			Talk to suppliers you buy these from.
Starting inventory			Suppliers will probably help you estimate this.
Deposits with public utilities			Find out from utilities companies.
Legal and other professional fees			Consult lawyer, accountant, and so on.
Licenses and permits			Find out from city offices what you have to have.
Advertising and promotion for opening			Estimate what you use.
Accounts receivable			Calculate what you need to buy more products until your credit customers pay.
Cash			How much do you need for unexpected expenses or losses, special purchases, etc.?
Other			Make a separate list and enter total.
TOTAL ESTIMATED CASH YOU NEED TO START WITH		$	Add up all the numbers in column 2.

Figure 5.3

Form for estimating small-business start-up costs.

Source: Small Business Administration.

much will be left over—the expected profit. Potential creditors will examine these estimates and the process by which they were arrived at very closely before deciding whether to grant a loan.

Finally, the plan should contain a personal financial statement that presents the value of everything the entrepreneur owns, everything he or she owes, and his or her net worth (the difference between the two). A history of managing personal finances wisely will count in the owner's favor if he or she must borrow money to start the business.

Sources of Financing

In Chapters 3 and 4 we introduced some fundamental points on the financing of sole proprietorships, partnerships, and corporations, and in Chapter 16 we will discuss the topic of finance at length. For now, however, it is necessary to explore specific sources of financing for small businesses.

Personal Savings

Personal savings is the source of financing used most often. Many observers advise small-business owners to avoid excessive borrowing. Firms that start off under the heavy weight of creditors' claims may take years to struggle out of debt, while their owners have to put up with the nervous questions and suggestions of the creditors. Still, under the right circumstances, a firm can profit impressively using the leverage of borrowed money. Thus the question of how much debt a firm should carry in relation to the owner's investment has no simple answer.

Credit from Suppliers

Businesspeople, especially retailers, buy inventory on trade credit or open-book accounts with suppliers. Under this arrangement, which will be discussed in Chapter 16, payment is not due for a credit period such as thirty, sixty, or ninety days, giving the buyer time to sell the goods before the bill is due.

A credit pyramid of sorts may arise within at least one of the distribution chains (discussed in Chapter 14). Assume that a manufacturer gives a wholesaler ninety days' credit and the wholesaler in turn decides to give its retail customers a sixty-day credit period. Under that relationship, the retailer could conceivably sell the goods to final consumers and pay the wholesaler, and that party could in turn pay the manufacturer so that each bill is paid within its respective credit period.

Manufacturer Financing of Equipment

Manufacturers (and sometimes distributors) of equipment and fixtures may be willing to finance purchases made by financially sound customers or help them to arrange financing through a commercial bank. Even if suppliers do not get involved directly, a supportive phone call from a well-established manufacturer to a bank lending officer might make it considerably easier for a customer firm to get a loan. An equipment manufacturer could also cosign for a loan along with the buyer or be a reference for that buyer at a bank where the manufacturer obtains financing.

Commercial Banks

A commercial bank may make a term loan that the small business can pay off within several years. In addition, commercial banks give qualified small businesses short-term loans. Naturally the business owner will have to provide financial statements listing personal and company assets and debts. Unfortunately, banks are often reluctant to lend money to new companies because of their failure rates unless the loan also is secured by the Small Business Administration.

The Small Business Administration

The federal government defines a small business as a profit-making concern with less than $9 million in assets, a net worth under $4.5 million, and profits below $450,000 for the last two years of operation. The SBA, however, uses different yardsticks to determine smallness among firms in different industries (see Table 5.1, page 120). A nearby SBA field office can provide you with specific standards for a business in a particular industry.

Under its guaranteed loan program, the SBA may secure up to 90 percent or $750,000 of a bank loan, whichever is less. If the bank declines to be involved in that arrangement, the SBA may lend up to $150,000 directly to the business.

Entrepreneurs who start a new firm instead of buying a functioning business are expected to contribute approximately half of the required funds before qualifying for SBA assistance. They must also present **pro forma financial statements**, which are *financial statements that forecast expected sales, expenses, profits, and other financial data for a future accounting period*. These statements are evidence that the owner can make payments on SBA loans and any other long-term debts incurred to finance the business. The SBA is prohibited from lending to a company that can borrow money from another source, so applicants must first attempt to borrow from such private lenders as commercial banks.

The steps in the SBA lending process are:

1. Describe the kind of business to be started.
2. List the owner's experience and management capabilities.
3. Estimate the amount the owner is prepared to invest and the amount he or she will need to borrow.
4. Prepare a personal financial statement listing the owner's assets and debts.
5. Develop pro forma statements of the business's sales, expenses, and profits for the first two years.

pro forma financial statements
Financial statements that forecast expected sales, expenses, profits, and other financial data for a future accounting period.

6. List the owner's collateral (security) for the loan, at current market value.
7. Ask a commercial bank for a letter stating the amount of the loan the owner requested, the interest rate, the payment terms, and the reason for rejecting the application.
8. If the bank agrees to be involved in the SBA's guarantee or participation plans (in which the bank joins with the SBA to make the loan), the banker will contact the SBA to negotiate the terms.
9. If the bank declines to be involved, contact the SBA for a direct loan.

Selling Stock

Some small businesses raise money by issuing and selling stock. Only corporations can sell stock, and open corporations, those whose stock is traded publicly, must comply with extensive state and federal regulations on stock sales. The founder of a company must also be concerned about surrendering control if a majority of the shares are sold to other persons. The firm could remain a closed corporation if the owner raises capital from a select and restricted group of investors. In Chapter 16 we'll discuss the kinds of stock a corporation can sell and the characteristics of each kind.

Venture Capital Firms

A **venture capital firm** is *a company that buys stock in new firms that make products or offer services with strong profit potential.* Venture capitalists take greater risks than such lenders as the SBA or commercial banks. Venture capital firms often are owned by successful entrepreneurs who have come up the hard way themselves. These companies shop for soundly managed firms with unique products or services in growing markets. Many specialize in specific industries (such as high technology, consumer products, or manufacturing companies). Recently companies with ideas for new minicomputers, electronic medical instruments, or communications equipment have been looked on favorably by venture capital firms.

Although venture capitalists are willing to take large risks, they also want large rewards. Typically they may want 50 percent or more of the fledgling corporation's stock in exchange for an infusion of cash and will require that their own people be seated on the small company's board of directors.

A really sound venture capitalist should provide far more than just capital, however. The small-business owner should deal with a firm that can help arrange short-term financing through a network of sympathetic commercial banking contacts. A venture capital firm should also be able to place the company in touch with potential customers for its products and help negotiate favorable contracts with suppliers. Companies such as Atari, Apple Computer, Compaq Computer, and Lotus Development Corporation (a producer of popular microcomputer software) all got assistance from venture capital firms during their infancy.

venture capital firm
A company that buys stock in new firms that make products or offer services with strong profit potential.

GLOBAL PERSPECTIVE

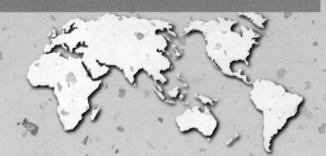

Trade Intermediaries Span the Globe

As business becomes more multinational, large and small companies alike have found it profitable to cultivate global markets. Given their limited resources, however, small businesses usually lack the knowledge and experience to market their products effectively in other countries.

That's where trade intermediaries come in. According to *The Wall Street Journal*, these entrepreneurs buy products for as much as 15 percent below a domestic producer's rock-bottom discount and resell them abroad.

The arrangement can work very well, because experienced trade intermediaries have developed sound networks of global sales contacts. Some intermediaries handle every phase of a transaction, including locating and extending credit to foreign buyers, paying the manufacturer for the goods, arranging for shipment, and collecting payments. High tech communications via computer, modem, and fax machine make contacting international prospects infinitely faster and easier than ever before.

One such intermediary, International Projects Inc., represents sixteen companies that manufacture everything from pleasure boats to air conditioner repair equipment to stationery.

The company sells about $8 million worth of products each year using just six people and seven computers. Another firm, Dreyfus & Associates, sends employees to drum up business at many foreign trade shows and has a global computer database of 1,500 distributors.

Using trade intermediaries has potential drawbacks, of course. For one thing, they may inflate the product's price. In addition, a client firm may find that intermediaries focus less energy on marketing its models over competing brands. Moreover, some overseas buyers prefer to work directly with a manufacturer instead of buying from a third-party company.

Nevertheless, small companies that appreciate the realities of today's global marketplace would be well advised to look hard at trade intermediaries when they look for sales abroad.

(For more on how small firms are turning to trade intermediaries," see *The Wall Street Journal*, February 2, 1993, p. B2.)

Sources of Continuing Help

Most small-business owners find they need advice after their business opens its doors. Among sources that can provide this ongoing assistance after the firm is on its feet are the SBA, SCORE, the National Family Business Council, business students, educators and consultants, trade associations, and wholesalers.

The SBA

The Small Business Administration has more than 300 free or inexpensive booklets with information on everything from procedures for incorporation to personnel selection. Approximately eighty field offices provide management advice and offer management training for owners with the assistance of nearby colleges and business schools. In addition, SBA assistance loans help companies that have been damaged by natural disaster or by the economic changes brought on by urban renewal or other government-funded construction programs. There are even loans to help small companies meet federal air and water pollution standards.

SCORE

The **Service Corps of Retired Executives (SCORE)** is *a volunteer organization of over 13,000 active and retired higher managers who advise small-business owners in conjunction with the Small Business Administration.* Business owners can request the assistance of a SCORE adviser whether or not they have received an SBA loan. They need only apply at an SBA field office. An adviser whose expertise fits the nature of the problem (finance, personnel, marketing) will meet with the owner to analyze the problem and develop a solution. A team of volunteers may be called on to attack problems with a broad scope. The advice is free, but the company will be expected to pay the SCORE volunteer's out-of-pocket expenses.

In addition to its free business counseling, SCORE members also conduct workshops on various specialized subjects at more than 750 locations nationwide. Attendees must pay a modest fee, which might be considered a bargain, considering that the average SCORE counselor has thirty-five years of business experience.

The National Family Business Council

The National Family Business Council (NFBC) consists of employees of family-owned companies who work in managerial or trainee positions and are related to the owners by birth or marriage. Any company that hires relatives of

Service Corps of Retired Executives (SCORE) A volunteer organization of over 13,000 active and retired higher managers who advise small-business owners in conjunction with the Small Business Administration.

Members of SCORE provide a valuable service by offering their expert advice to small businesses.

the owners—a common situation in closely held corporations—may benefit from joining this organization, which focuses attention on the unique interpersonal management problems found in family-operated businesses. In addition to its various chapters and management education programs, the NFBC publishes a newsletter and stages cooperative educational programs with leading universities and private management development firms.

Business Students

Many business professors include a small-business assistance project among the requirements for their graduate courses. Students may be called on to answer a business owner's request for help, analyze problems (possibly as part of a team or task force), and design and implement plans that will help a small firm back onto its feet. This type of program, which may be available through the business school at a nearby university, offers an inexpensive and reliable introduction to many of the latest concepts in the study of business operations.

Local Educators and Consultants

In his famous lecture "Acres of Diamonds," noted nineteenth-century clergyman and educator Russell Conwell dramatized how easy it is to overlook riches in one's own backyard. Business owners who live in a moderately or heavily populated area with colleges and universities nearby will find abundant management advice available from local business professors, authors of books on management, and consultants. Some recommendations of specific people to contact may be obtained from the local chamber of commerce.

Trade Associations

There is at least one trade association for practically every line of business, from funeral parlors to massage parlors. Some confine themselves to highly specialized fields, such as the Power Crane and Shovel Manufacturers Association and the Fir and Hemlock Door Association. Others, such as the National Association of Manufacturers and the National Retail Merchants Association, cover more ground. Trade associations can give advice on financing, inventory management, personnel management, accounting procedures, physical layout, marketing research, supplier relations, site selection, and advertising for their specific lines of business. They exist to help member firms prosper by communicating proven management practices and information.

Wholesalers

Well-equipped wholesalers can boost a small retailer's success in merchandise promotion by:

- Pooling orders from many customers, buying in large quantities, and receiving lower prices, thus allowing independent firms to offer prices that compete with those of chains and larger independents

MANAGER'S NOTEBOOK

High above the city of Santa Barbara, nestled in the heart of the San Marcos Pass, sits a 120-year-old small business that has endured since the days of the stagecoach—the Cold Spring Tavern.

Time, progress, and a succession of owners and operators have respected the dignity and character of this inviting, nostalgic time capsule. Standing on the dusty road leading up to the rustic wood-and-stone building, one can almost hear the crack of the whip and the rumble of hooves as an incoming stage barrels through the pass.

Local historians believe the tavern was built around 1868, when stagecoach travel was commonplace. No one knows the identity of the original builder. The property is now owned by freelance writer Audrey Ovington, who inherited it from her mother, who bought the tavern and surrounding land in 1941. It's run by Mark Larsen, a young southern California entrepreneur.

"Everyone who has ever owned the Cold Spring Tavern has been fanatical about keeping it authentic," says Larsen. "Our goal is to have people come back ten or twenty years later and have it look exactly the same."

That goal has been achieved, but not without considerable effort. When the roof needed repairs, for example, Larsen insisted on using all-original materials that could be safely removed from concealed parts of the building. Like its long succession of operators, nature has been a friend to the Cold Spring Tavern, too. The building, which has survived nearby forest fires, torrential rains, and unexpected snowstorms, includes the original tavern (which is primarily a restaurant) as well as a small stagecoach driver's quarters, now serving as a curio shop. There's also a nearby bunkhouse, which was built to house road workers, and a log cabin that once housed a springwater bottling operation. The cabin is an annex to the tavern.

In a world where many small businesses fail before their fifth birthday and original buildings are often remodeled, renovated, or razed to make room for new ones, the Cold Spring Tavern's longevity has ensured its special niche in time—and in the hearts of the many hungry, thirsty visitors who have welcomed its shelter for more than a century.

The Cold Spring Tavern Thrives in Its Second Century

(For more on the Cold Spring Tavern, see "Once a Wild West Stage Stop, Now a California Classic," a feature in *Anheuser-Busch Companies, Inc. Annual Report 1992*, pp. 26–27.)

- Selling certain items at cost, thus encouraging retailers to buy others later at regular prices
- Providing an inventory rotation plan to ensure fresh merchandise and ideal stock levels
- Distributing manufacturers' point-of-purchase displays to help retailers sell merchandise more effectively

They can make market information available by:

- Assessing market trends by monitoring trends in sales
- Distributing market information in newsletters and bulletins
- Forewarning customers of trends and changes in demand
- Providing information on competitors' prices and marketing practices
- Staying abreast of changing conditions that influence the supply of staple items
- Notifying customers of new products, improved store fixtures, and innovative equipment
- Advising on efficient store layouts, effective marketing practices, and productive floor displays

Wholesalers can give small retailers financial help, too, by selling merchandise on open-book accounts and by delaying billings for seasonal merchandise until the selling season arrives and sales improve. They can also provide accounting forms and booklets that help customer firms establish and maintain good recordkeeping habits, and offer accounting services through an umbrella contract with a local accounting firm.

Franchising

What Is a Franchise?

franchise
A license sold by one firm (the *franchisor*) to another (the *franchisee*), allowing it to produce and sell a product or service under specific terms and conditions.

A **franchise** is *a license sold by one firm (the* franchisor*) to another (the* franchisee*), allowing it to produce and sell a product or service under specific terms and conditions.* Franchised businesses are generally more successful than independent businesses because reputable franchisors have invested a great deal of time, effort, and money to develop and perfect effective marketing and management procedures for the products or services that franchisees sell. Although franchisees sacrifice considerable independence, the right to use the franchisor's proven techniques significantly increases the odds that their business will prosper.

Franchises are in many ways like a series of chain stores: the outlets look alike, each one makes and sells the product or service the same way, and each dealer adopts the same set of management techniques. Franchises differ from chain stores, however, in that the person in charge of a franchise is not an employee but rather the owner of the business. Franchisees are trained in effective management, marketing, and employee selection and training practices by the franchisor.

Franchises take two general forms. A **business format franchise**, which is often seen in retailing and service businesses, is *a franchise in which the franchisor gives franchisees a comprehensive, detailed plan for operating the business.* This plan may include, for example, an employee training program, promotional assistance and advice, and precise guidelines for operating every aspect of the business. Business format franchises are commonplace in fast-food, package wrapping and shipping, auto lubrication and oil change, and maid service businesses.

A **product** *or* **trade name franchise**, which is less common than a business format franchise, is *a franchise in which the franchisor allows the franchisee to sell products bearing the franchisor's trademark or logo.* Goodyear Tire and Rubber Company sells its products through this type of franchise.

business format franchise
A franchise in which the franchisor gives franchisees a comprehensive, detailed plan for operating the business.

product *or* **trade name franchise**
A franchise in which the franchisor allows the franchisee to sell products bearing the franchisor's trademark or logo.

Pizza Hut is one of the most popular franchises, not only in the United States but around the world.

Franchise opportunities exist for more than sixty types of businesses, ranging from daycare centers to funeral homes.

Since the 1960s, franchising has grown to have a significant impact on the nation's sales and employment levels. New franchise outlets now open at a rate of one every six and one-half minutes each business day. According to the International Franchise Association, $758 billion worth of goods and services—35 percent of all United States retail sales—were sold in one recent year through franchise outlets, providing jobs for more than 7 million people. Franchising is expected to grow especially fast in such areas as maid services, business assistance (accounting, personnel, and tax preparation), automotive repairs and services, weight control, temporary help, printing and copying, and hair salons.[5] Table 5.2 summarizes the benefits and drawbacks of owning a franchise.

Table 5.2

The benefits and drawbacks of franchises.

BENEFITS TO FRANCHISEE	DRAWBACKS FOR FRANCHISEE
• National reputation of franchisor • National advertising and sales promotion programs • Proven work layout refined for maximum efficiency in minimum space • Advice about site selection • Assistance in negotiating leases and purchase agreements for equipment and other items • Blueprints and bill of materials for constructing the building • Training in how to manage the business for maximum profitability • An accounting system developed to meet the needs of this business and the reporting requirements of the parent company • An employee training program • Grand-opening materials and the assistance of parent company employees • Group business insurance program through the parent company (at a lower cost than if the franchisee bought insurance alone) • Ability to purchase furniture and equipment from the parent at a lower cost • Advertising and sales promotion allowances • Advertising materials geared to various national promotions • Purchase of inventory items and supplies through the parent company at lower cost • Well-defined and protected territory • Financing assistance	• Investment of a minimum amount of capital • Payment of a percentage of gross profits (and possibly a fixed fee) to the parent company at specified times • Payment of several additional items as required • Approval from parent company for choice of location, installation of any furniture and fixtures, deviation from prescribed menu or inventory, purchase of disposables or inventory from anyone other than the parent company, pricing changes, involvement in any other business of a similar nature, and even changes in prescribed hours of operation • Full involvement in management and daily operations • Personnel required to present a specified appearance • No members of owner's family working in the franchise • Detailed accounting reports furnished to the parent company • Management techniques and methods of operation kept confidential • Minimum amount of insurance purchased as dictated by parent company • Shelf-life standards dictated by parent company for perishable inventory • Minimum amount of money spent each year for advertising and sales promotion • Periodic training as required by parent company at a specified location

Because franchisors sell proven techniques for success in a specific business, it's no surprise that their franchisees have a higher survival rate than independent businesses. According to a recent Gallup poll, 94 percent of franchise business owners are successful. They earned an average annual pretax income of $124,290.[6]

What Aspects Should You Investigate?

If you decide that you'd like to become a franchisee, you'll be given a franchise contract. It's important to be completely familiar with the franchise terms and to understand all aspects of the contract before you sign. Careful investigation, coupled with sound expert advice from an attorney and an accountant, can save hard feelings and possibly lawsuits later on.

EVALUATE THE FRANCHISOR'S TOP MANAGEMENT You can't know too much about the franchisor's higher executives. Read their résumés. Evaluate their business experience. Ask about the goals they have set for the parent company, how they plan to expand the number of franchised outlets, and their timetable for doing so. Ask about the techniques they use to monitor and respond to market trends for the franchise's product or service. Also note how long they have worked in franchising generally and how long they've been with *this* franchisor.

Finally, evaluate the compatibility of your personalities. Would you be comfortable entering into a long-term relationship with the executives you've dealt with so far?

EVALUATE MARKETING SUPPORT Clarify what ongoing marketing assistance you'll receive to promote your franchised business once you've opened your doors. For example:

What kind of assistance will the franchisor provide for your grand opening?

What percent of your franchise fees will be applied to promotional activities? How does this amount compare with that spent by competing franchises?

How often will the franchisor run advertising campaigns? What media will be used? Will the advertising appear locally, regionally, or nationally?

The answers to these questions will help you understand the quality and extent of the marketing support you can expect from the franchisor.

ASK ABOUT TRAINING Confirm the franchisor's commitment to provide both start-up and ongoing training for you and your employees. Clarify what specific types of training you're supposed to receive, where it will be held, and how frequently it will occur. Some training sessions may be held at the franchisor's home office; others may be provided on site at franchisees' locations. Ask to see examples of actual training materials such as videos, manuals, handouts, and recent training schedules and agendas. Inquire about the franchisor's policy on follow-up training to keep franchisees abreast of new marketing techniques, products, or equipment that may help them cut costs, increase sales, enhance productivity, and earn higher profits.

EXAMINE THE FRANCHISE CONTRACT After you've signed the contract, it may control your business life for as long as ten or twenty years. It is thus extremely important to ask your attorney to clarify all of its conditions and explain your rights and obligations as well as those of the franchise company. If you're not comfortable with the basic contract, ask your lawyer to recommend changes and additions that you can propose to the franchisor through a counteroffer. Make certain to ask the following questions:

1. What materials, supplies, and equipment must you purchase? Can you buy from any source, or must you buy directly from the franchisor?
2. What periodic reports will you have to submit to the franchisor? How often are they due? What format must they follow? Does the franchisor have a streamlined system to help you assemble the information with minimal expense and effort?
3. What periodic fees, royalties, or other payments must you make? How frequently? How will they be calculated—as a flat fee, percent of gross or net sales, percent of profits, or some other method? Are there penalties for late payments?
4. Does the franchisor have the right to assess franchisees one-time payments for special purposes? If so, under what conditions?
5. Will you need the franchisor's approval to change your menu, store layout, interior decor, external appearance, furniture, fixtures, or equipment?
6. Will the franchisor guarantee you a protected trading area? If so, how large will it be and for how many years?
7. Will you be given the first opportunity to purchase additional outlets the franchisor may open in your area before they're offered to other parties?
8. Under what circumstances may the franchise contract be terminated?

TALK TO EXISTING FRANCHISEES This is perhaps the best way to discover the true nature of the relationship between the franchisor and franchisees. Ask other franchisees how well the franchisor has met the terms of the contract and how they feel about the company's top management. Discuss areas in which the franchisor has treated them exceptionally well. Ask about conflicts and how they were resolved. Finally—and most important of all—ask whether they'd make the same decision if they had it to do over again.

EXAMINE THE FRANCHISOR'S FINANCIAL CONDITION Some novice franchise owners have discovered too late that the parent company didn't have enough money to deliver everything it promised. Some have ended up with little more than a colorful sign to hang on the front of the building. You can avoid that fate by having your accountant interpret and evaluate the franchisor's financial statements covering the last several years. You must feel confident that the franchisor is willing and able to afford all the training, marketing support, and other assistance referred to in the contract.

What Makes a Successful Franchisee?

Although franchised businesses are more likely to prosper than independent companies, the franchisee's commitment is absolutely vital to success. No one can expect to run a franchise as an absentee owner. No business system, no matter how well it functions, can be profitable without the owner's hands-on involvement and 100 percent support.

Successful franchisees tend to have the following traits:

- They can relate to and enjoy working with the type of product or service their franchise sells.
- They have adequate background, experience, and education to be able to operate their business successfully with the advice and support provided by the franchisor.
- They welcome constructive criticism, follow directions, accept supervision by the home office, and work within the operating rules and guidelines established by the franchisor.
- They're team players, willing to coordinate and cooperate with top franchise management and other franchisees for the benefit of everyone concerned.
- They accept the financial risk of starting a business and acknowledge that a franchise cannot guarantee success. It can only minimize the chance of failure.
- They're comfortable playing the many roles of a franchisee, including investor, general manager, supervisor, subordinate, and salesperson.
- They're willing to learn about and become involved in all aspects of operating the business, from keeping the books to sweeping the floor.
- They're willing to dedicate their energy, brainpower, and time—as well as their money—to help ensure that their business succeeds.

Being a franchisee is like driving a car with dual controls. The franchisor, like an experienced driving instructor, can intervene if the driver seems headed for trouble. The franchisee, the driver, finds a reassuring presence nearby. Information about popular franchises in several business areas appears in Table 5.3.

If you would like to know more about franchising, you might write to the Council of Better Business Bureaus in Washington, D.C., which has summaries of data on many franchise firms. The International Franchise Association (IFA) is another reputable source of data. This highly selective organization, whose membership consists of more than 750 sound franchisors, has a code of ethics that all members are expected to observe. Franchisors who wish to join

Franchises	Number of Franchised Units	Average Cash Investment ($)	Average Total Investment($)	Number of Years in Initial Contract	Franchise Fee ($)*
Printing and Packaging					
Mail Boxes Etc.	14,351	55 K	75 K	10	19.5 K
Insty-Prints	312	50–100 K	170–258 K	15	24.5 K
PIP Printing	1130	77 K+	201–211 K	20	40 K
Handle With Care Packaging Store	400	25–40 K	25–40 K	Infinite	15.5 K
Retail Foods					
Baskin-Robbins	3,355	27–34 K+	135–170 K	5	0
Heavenly Ham	46	30–60 K	84–134 K	10	25 K
Steak-Out	25	10–100 K	100–135 K	10	15 K
Domino's Pizza	4,153	10–30 K	83–194 K	10	1–3 K
Godfather's Pizza	350	55–120 K	72–291 K	15	7.5–15.0 K
Kentucky Fried Chicken	5,971	150 K	600–800 K	20	20 K
McDonald's	8,284	40–250 K	610 K	20	22.5 K
Tastee-Freez	400	50–150 K	125–450 K	10	10–25 K
Maid Services					
Merry Maids	524	30–35 K	30–35 K	5	18.5 K
Molly Maid	256	25–35 K	30 K	10	16.9 K
Motels/Hotels/Campgrounds					
Hampton Inns	233	0.6–1.5 MM	2–6 MM	20	35 K min.
KOA	620	85 K+	250 K+	5	20 K
Travelodge	361	20–150 K	4–40 MM	10	20–25 K
General Retail					
Computerland	694	250–900 K	0.2–1.0 MM	10	7.5–35.0 K
Wallpapers To Go	103	40–80 K	111–156 K	10	40 K
West Coast Video	700	240–350 K	240–350 K	10	40 K

* This fee is usually paid in addition to cash and total investment.
K = Thousand; MM = Million
Source: Robert E. Bond and Christopher E. Bond, *The Source Book of Franchise Opportunities*, 1991–92 ed.
(Homewood, Ill.: Business One Irwin), 1992.

Table 5.3
Franchising: Some specifics.

the IFA must have been operating for at least two years, be in sound financial condition, meet minimum requirements for number and age of outlets, comply with applicable state and federal laws, and supply satisfactory business and personal references.

How Can You Check Out a Franchisor?

The Federal Trade Commission (FTC) has come to the aid of prospective buyers of franchises with a Trade Regulation Rule adopted in 1979. The rule requires franchisors to provide information on twenty aspects of their business, including management experience, backgrounds of key managers, present or past bankruptcy or lawsuits, financial condition for the past year, and proof of the profits that franchisees may reasonably expect to make. Franchisees must be told of recurring fees required by the contract and the conditions under which the contract may be terminated, sold, or renewed by the franchisor. The rule also requires the parent firm to supply a list of the ten franchisees closest to a buyer's proposed location, the names of all franchisees in the United States, or the names of all those in a buyer's state. In addition, more than a dozen states now have disclosure laws that may require franchisors to report considerably more information than is demanded by this FTC rule.

Although the FTC's disclosure statement cannot guarantee a franchisee's success (or even that the parent company is as sound as it states), this document at least minimizes the likelihood that prospective franchisees will be defrauded or misled. FTC regulations help to ensure that franchisees will have enough information to make an informed decision about purchasing a particular franchise.

> **YOU DECIDE**
>
> Review the typical demands and obligations of a franchisee in light of your own personality, likes, and dislikes. Also consider the skills you now have and those you intend to develop through your college experience and other means.
>
> What personal characteristics suggest that you're the type of person who would be satisfied operating a franchised business? What characteristics suggest you might be happier working independently or for an employer? Do you think it would be worth the effort to try to acquire the characteristics that would make you a better candidate for success in a franchised business? Why or why not?

SUMMARY

Prospective small-business owners need a board of advisers (lawyer, accountant, and insurance counselor) to assist on technical matters of law, finance, and risk management. These individuals help ensure the company's success from the outset. It is also necessary to obtain certain licenses and permits, some of which vary with the firm's location and the nature of the business.

A small-business owner should have sound experience, adequate capital, a good location, and favorable lease terms if the building is rented. Entrepreneurs should know the demographics of their market, identify the most popular inventory to stock, and find out about competitors' operating techniques. Someone who buys an existing company must obtain accurate information on its condition from the seller before closing the purchase. Finally, the small-business owner must keep accurate, up-to-date accounting records to monitor the company's financial condition and profitability.

Prospective small-business owners have several avenues of financing available. Personal savings is the most obvious and popular one, but they can also buy merchandise on credit from suppliers, finance equipment through distributors or manufacturers, get a commercial bank loan, or borrow through the Small Business Administration. Corporations can sell stock to the general public or to a venture capital firm.

After a company starts operating, the SBA can provide continuing management advice, as can the National Family Business Council and SCORE, which works through the SBA to make the management expertise of retired and active executives available to small-business owners. Business students from nearby universities, local management authorities, trade associations, and wholesalers can also provide assistance.

Some entrepreneurs elect to buy a franchise, which is a license to sell a widely recognized product or service. There are many advantages to becoming a franchisee, but the franchisor's contract also sets forth various conditions and restrictions on operating freedom. The decision to buy a franchise should be made with the advice of a lawyer and accountant as well as some awareness of the experience of existing franchisees.

KEY TERMS

business format franchise p. 139
business plan p. 128
demographics p. 127
franchise p. 138
insurance counselor p. 122
pro forma financial statements p. 132

product or trade name franchise p. 139
Service Corps of Retired Executives (SCORE) p. 135
Small Business Administration (SBA) p. 120
venture capital firm p. 133
zoning ordinances p. 123

FOR REVIEW AND DISCUSSION

1. Name the three advisers you need before starting a business. Why do you need them? How would you choose them?

2. Describe the procedure a business owner must follow before a company opens its doors. Why would this procedure vary somewhat from area to area and from type of business to type of business?

3. Give at least one reason why a small-business manager must consider each of the following: experience in the type of business started, capitalization, location, lease terms, customer demographics, inventory management, competitors' practices, condition of a purchased business, and financial recordkeeping.

4. Why is it so important for a small-business owner to prepare a formal business plan? What specific areas should it contain, and what information should be covered in each?

5. Why might it be a good idea to finance a business as much as possible with your personal savings? How does this method of financing affect your chances of success?

6. What kind of financing do merchandise suppliers offer? How does this approach complement a retailer's sales activities?

7. Should distributors or manufacturers of equipment be concerned about helping you finance purchases from them? Why or why not?

8. Describe the types of loans available through the Small Business Administration. What prerequisite must you meet before becoming eligible for SBA loans?

9. How does the attitude of venture capital firms differ from that of such conventional capital sources as the SBA or commercial banks? What do you sacrifice when dealing with a venture capital firm?

10. Describe the type of management assistance offered by the SBA. How does it differ from that offered by the National Family Business Council?

11. Summarize the contributions of SCORE advisers to small-business managers.

12. Discuss the value and the limitations of graduate business students' advice to small-business managers as compared with that of SCORE volunteers.

13. How might local management authorities' advice be preferable to that of experts located several hundred miles away? In what ways could the distant advisers' views be preferable to those of local people?

14. Should you consider a trade association a source of highly specialized management assistance? Why or why not?

15. Discuss at least two areas in which wholesalers can help their retailer-customers. Why is it to their advantage to do so?

16. What causes franchised businesses to have a better success rate than independent businesses? What distinguishes them from chain stores?

17. What differentiates a business format franchise from a product or trade name franchise? Which type is most popular? What circumstances probably account for that popularity?

18. What franchise terms should a franchisee examine carefully before signing a contract? What problems can you foresee for the franchisee if these terms aren't thoroughly clarified and understood?

19. List at least five traits that are important to someone hoping to become a successful franchisee. How would you rank these traits in order of importance? Defend your ranking.

20. What organizations can you contact to obtain information on franchise firms?

21. How does the FTC's disclosure statement benefit prospective franchisees? Can they feel certain this statement gives them all the important information they'll need to decide whether to purchase a franchise? Why or why not?

22. List at least four benefits of entering into a franchise agreement. What must you be prepared to sacrifice? What suggestions would you offer to potential franchisees?

APPLICATIONS

Case 5.1: A New Life for Corporate Refugees

Corporate cost cutting is taking an increasing toll on the work force. More and more employees with high levels of experience and training are being laid off by America's large corporations. Additionally, the corporate environment, with its hierarchical management structure and high pressures, is driving some employees to seek their fortunes elsewhere. These two types make up an exciting group of new entrepreneurs, called "corporate refugees."

Having left corporate environments with substantial pay and benefits packages, corporate refugees frequently try their hands at buying or creating small businesses. While not all succeed, those who do tend to use their experience and prior business contacts to find profitable opportunities and exploit them.

One refugee, Peter A. Brewster, spent twenty-five years at Honeywell Information Systems before being squeezed out by the sale of his division. Using his unique knowledge of Honeywell's printer sales, he found a niche in upgrading older, but extremely expensive, high-speed printers to work with newer computers. Honeywell does not offer similar upgrades; instead, its sales staff refers interested buyers to Brewster, who sells them the $20,000 upgrade kits. As corporations eliminate more in-house services, many other corporate refugees have found business opportunities selling their services to their ex-employers.

Another high tech corporate refugee used his experience to revolutionize his parents' gravel business. Bruce W. Woolpert used his experience at Hewlett-Packard's personal computer software division to find a new way to accurately measure the amount of gravel and crushed rock that each customer receives and pays for. Using a computerized truck weighing system, Woolpert weighs a truck before and after filling, allowing him to sell a customer a more precise amount of gravel. His firm, Granite Rock Company, won the prestigious Malcolm Baldrige National Quality Award in 1992.

Questions

1. What strategies used by corporate refugees could be used by any entrepreneur in starting a business?

2. What advantages do corporate refugees have over beginning entrepreneurs?

3. How does the success of corporate refugees affect the prospects for other small businesses?

4. With small businesses outperforming in-house services, could corporations benefit by training entrepreneurs to operate in fields that provide essential services? Why or why not?

5. With the emergence of small businesses that are more efficient than corporate divisions, what is likely to be the future shape of large corporations?

For more information, see Bruce Nussbaum, "Corporate Refugees," *Business Week*, April 12, 1993, pp. 58–65.

Case 5.2: Government Small-Business Assistance

Small business has repeatedly been hailed as the savior of the American economy. With businesses of less than 500 employees accounting for 3.2 million new jobs between 1988 and 1990, it is easy to see why.

Because of this large job creation potential, small-business assistance has become a favorite cause among politicians. Several reforms proposed by the Clinton administration provide incentives for small businesses.

President Clinton proposed offering small businesses that have annual sales below $5 million a permanent investment tax credit for equipment purchased between 1992 and 1994, with credits for equipment purchased later, and a 50 percent capital gains tax break on profits from the sale of small company stock. The companies must not have raised more than $50 million in capital. Clinton also proposed the creation of fifty federal enterprise zones that give incentives to businesses that locate there.

Despite their good intentions, these programs were attacked for not affecting enough businesses. For one thing, the investment tax credit does not assist service-oriented businesses. Yet manufacturers are usually not included because of the low exclusion points. These concerns have left small businesses wondering how these programs are supposed to help.

Businesspeople are also worried about the harm another Clinton administration program may do. Many small businesses have voiced the concern that a national, mandatory health care program would result in their undoing. The additional employee costs that companies must pay may make it very difficult for small businesses to be the new job creators they are expected to be. On the other hand, many argue that low-level jobs that don't provide essential benefits aren't worth creating.

Questions

1. What are the advantages in having a government-sponsored small-business incentive program?

2. How would you structure an economic incentive program?

3. Should service-oriented or manufacturing-based small businesses be given preference by government incentive programs? Why?

4. Should government force businesses to provide health care services to workers, even at the expense of jobs and profitability? Why or why not?

5. Do businesses have an ethical responsibility to provide health care for their employees? Why or why not?

For more information, see James E. Ellis, "Tall Order for Small Businesses," *Business Week*, April 19, 1993, pp. 114–120.

REFERENCES

1. Small Business Association Answer Desk recorded message, April 1993 (phone 800-827-5722).
2. Terence P. Paré, "Why Banks Are Still Stingy," *Fortune*, January 25, 1993, p. 73.
3. *Business Failure Record* (New York: Dun & Bradstreet, 1993), p. 17.
4. *Business Failure Record*, p. 2.
5. *Franchise Fact Sheet* (Washington, D.C.: International Franchise Association, 1992), p. 1.
6. *Franchise Fact Sheet*, p. 1.

CAREER CAPSULE 1

Career Opportunities at General Mills

Echoing the slogan of its popular Wheaties breakfast cereal, General Mills calls itself "The Company of Champions." This global corporation recruits innovative, aggressive college graduates who thrive on challenge, relish competition, and pursue unlimited opportunity.

With annual sales of more than $7.1 billion, General Mills enjoys an enviable reputation not only in the packaged food industry but also as a restaurateur through its popular Red Lobster and Olive Garden restaurant chains. It's no surprise, then, that General Mills offers exceptional career opportunities for men and women in many fields. The company promotes from within; management assures employees that outstanding performance will be rewarded with advancement and incentives.

What's it like to work for General Mills? Here are profiles of several areas.

- Employees who work in *marketing management* have the opportunity to become involved with a broad range of products. They're challenged to be creative, decisive, and analytical and to work successfully with a broad range of people. The projects and products to which they're assigned provide a wealth of team-oriented general management experience that includes setting strategic sales and market-share goals; helping to develop and evaluate advertising campaigns; making plans for product promotional activities; and dealing with the production and distribution decisions required to bring General Mills's products to market. Such activities prepare them to reach their full potential during their career with the company.

- Employees who work in *finance* are responsible for improving the company's financial position and keeping production costs to a minimum. This requires a blend of analytical, managerial, and interpersonal skills, backed by a degree in business administration, accounting, finance, economics, or liberal arts. Graduates with bachelor's degrees begin work as financial associates, cost accountants, or financial auditors. They're responsible for financial analysis and for reporting information about ongoing company operations. Graduates with M.B.A. (master of business administration) degrees are immediately involved in evaluating and analyzing various projects and operations from a financial perspective.

- Employees in *human resources management* have often done graduate-level work in human resources, industrial relations, or business administration. After joining the company, they may be responsible for such activities as recruitment, hiring and placement, orientation, wage and salary administration, training, and labor relations. Human resources management employees may work in various plants or subsidiary companies or in divisions at General Mills's corporate headquarters in Minneapolis.

- Employees who work in *information systems* are exposed to every aspect of the business. After identifying key information that employees in other divisions need in order to make timely decisions, they design data processing systems to gather, summarize, and deliver that information quickly and accurately to colleagues throughout the company, who will use it to keep the business competitive and productive.

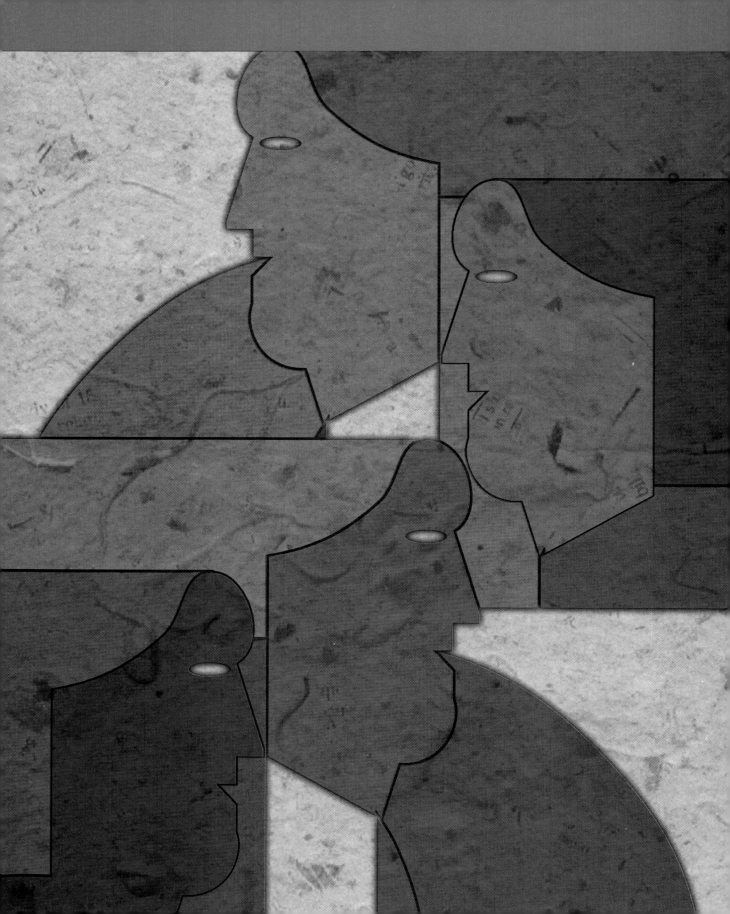

Part Two

The Human Side of Business

6

MANAGING BUSINESS ORGANIZATIONS

■ *believe there is a shortage of people who realize that a CEO's job is to lead.*

Mike H. Walsh
Chief Executive Officer, Tenneco

CHAPTER OBJECTIVES

After studying this chapter, you should be able to:

1. Explain why managers are necessary in organizations.
2. Describe the manager's environment.
3. Distinguish between the myths and realities of a manager's job.
4. Identify and explain the three levels of management in a firm.
5. Identify and explain the five management functions.
6. Explain how the management functions apply to all levels of management.
7. Describe the roles managers perform.
8. Describe the three skills—technical, human, and conceptual—required of a manager.
9. Explain the nature of and steps involved in managerial decision making.

UP FRONT

Sandor Schoichet has developed a keen sense of how businesses can apply information technology—computers and communications—to become more effective and successful. He's developed this knowledge by managing several successful small companies as well as by creating systems and technologies to solve problems for large client companies.

Schoichet attended the University of California at Santa Cruz, where he earned bachelor of science degrees in both philosophy and information sciences. He then spent three years designing logic systems and electronic circuits before attending the Massachusetts Institute of Technology, where he finished his master's degree in electrical engineering.

It was at MIT that Schoichet saw technology and business coalesce. He worked at the Artificial Intelligence Lab and with Michael Hammer in the Laboratory for Computer Science's office automation group. He also studied the management of innovation at MIT's Sloan School of Management. "Dr. Hammer was a very exciting, energetic guy to work with," he recalls. "We were trying to model business processes to understand professional office work. Instead of trying to de-skill people and turn them into data entry clerks, we sought ways to change work patterns. This led to the reengineering concept. It was never dull. Dr. Hammer was always interrupting our thesis-writing to send us off on consulting projects to places like New York and London."

Returning to the San Francisco Bay area after MIT, Schoichet worked in custom programming and systems development, writing proposals and helping design information systems for large, complex applications, such as collecting long-distance phone call data for billing purposes. This work led to managing development projects in Denmark, the United Kingdom, Canada, Japan, and Australia. "I learned what it means to run projects with people from diverse cultures, across time zones, and with a geographically distributed team of people. It was very interesting work."

It was work that would build Schoichet's skills in managing and operating an autonomous business unit—a company unto itself—as well. He rose from project manager to vice-president of marketing before he was lured away to help build a start-up company for Teknekron Corporation.

An enterprise launched by two University of California at Berkeley professors over a quarter of a century ago, Teknekron's mission is to accelerate the transfer of technology from the university to commercial use. Teknekron has launched over fourteen businesses, including Teknekron Communications Systems, which recruited Schoichet to manage its Network Applications division. TCS was very successful; it developed a single-chip modem and built large network applications for companies such as British Telecom and United Parcel Service.

But Schoichet soon became restless and

SANDOR SCHOICHET

DIRECTOR OF SYSTEMS INTEGRATION, TEKNEKRON PHARMACEUTICAL SYSTEMS

sought new opportunities and challenges in the form of a new Teknekron start-up, Teknekron Pharmaceutical Systems. "We saw a business opportunity to apply reengineering to the process of bringing new drugs to market," says Schoichet. He was able to apply nearly all of the management skills and techniques he had learned over the years in the new business. "We support people, we don't replace them. We use computers to speed up business processes. We help people learn to work more effectively in teams, and enable our clients to respond effectively to global competition by reducing the time and cost of getting to market."

Speaking of his management skills, Schoichet says, "I'm constantly wearing several hats. I have all the responsibilities of management in running a company: watching the financial picture, managing our internal resources, and working with people—hiring, evaluating, sometimes firing. I have to work continually with our clients, which means understanding and appreciating the complexity of their work and respecting the confidentiality that ex-

ists between us. And we're always running project teams, which must be kept on schedule and within budget. Project teams are typically made up of some of our people and some of the client's staff, so maintaining cohesion and keeping the communication channels open is a full-time job. With multiple projects for multiple clients, we use all known communications devices, from voice mail to cellular phones to electronic mail to fax to airplanes, to stay in communication. It's a real juggling act that requires discipline to draw the line between the details that matter and those which don't. It's like the proverbial piece of paper crossing your desk; you want to deal with it once and toss it, so you can move on to the next thing. Priority setting is a critical skill."

In its first year of operation, TPS grew to twelve people and brought in $1.5 million. Schoichet expects to see it grow to 200 people and $50 million before the end of the decade. "We will have lots of competition, but we sell ourselves as great people to have on your team, with an unusual range of critical skills," he says.

Why Managers Are Needed

Is management necessary? What does a manager actually do? What skills does it take to be a good manager? The answers to these questions, presented in this chapter, provide the foundation for managing a business. Nothing is more fundamental to understanding the operation of a business than realizing why managers are necessary.

Organizational Purpose of Managers

managers
People who direct the activity of others.

organization
A group of two or more persons that exists and operates to achieve clearly stated, commonly held objectives.

Managers, *people who direct the activity of others,* are necessary because organizations exist. The world is full of organizations: your school, Southwest Airlines, the Girl Scouts of America, the corner drugstore, the Internal Revenue Service, the Teamsters Union. Organizations vary in size, structure, resources, personnel, and purposes, but they have some characteristics in common.

Basically, an **organization** is *a group of two or more persons that exists and operates to achieve clearly stated, commonly held objectives.* Objectives are goals—targets to shoot for or outcomes to be reached through plans and actions.

These objectives have to do with providing goods and services to the organization's members or to others outside the organization.

Without any control, the members of the organization might do jobs that they thought would contribute to meeting the objectives when in fact they were working in opposite directions. To prevent this chaos from occurring and to ensure coordination of work to accomplish the objectives, managers are needed. A manager may be the owner or operator or founder (or all three) of an organization, or he or she could be someone hired to give it direction. Either way, a manager makes decisions and commits the organization's resources (personnel, capital, information, and equipment) to achieve its objectives. The manager is often a connecting link, catalyst, sparkplug, and driving force for change, coordination, and control in an organization.

The Universal Need for Managers

Managers are found in all organizations. Sometimes managers are narrowly defined as working strictly in the domain of private, for-profit businesses, but they are needed wherever organizations exist. When you visit a college dean, you talk to a manager. When you listen to the local director of the American Heart Association give a speech, you hear a manager. When you meet with the local PTA, you interact with managers.

Just what do managers do? Are all management jobs the same? If there are differences, what are they? In the following pages, we will examine the answers to these questions so you can get a better view of the manager's job.

What Management Is

Management is *the process of setting and achieving goals through the execution of five basic functions that use human, financial, material, and informational resources.*

There are a number of points to notice about this definition:

- Managers make conscious decisions to set and achieve goals. Decision making is a critical part of all management activities.
- Managers get tasks done through people. Once managers acquire financial, material, and informational resources for the organization, they work through the organization's members to reach the stated objectives.
- To achieve these goals, managers must execute the five basic functions. These **management functions** are *the five broad activities that managers perform to achieve organizational objectives: planning, organizing, staffing, directing, and controlling.*
- Managers work with both individuals and groups, not one or the other. They work with each subordinate and at the same time develop those subordinates into a coordinated work group. Both tasks demand skill—and patience.

Each of these points will be taken up in detail later in this chapter.

management
The process of setting and achieving goals through the execution of five basic functions that use human, financial, material, and informational resources.

management functions
The five broad activities that managers perform to achieve organizational objectives: planning, organizing, staffing, directing, and controlling.

The Manager's Environment

The real world of management is complex, demanding, exciting, exacting, and pressure-filled. As noted by Apple Computer Chairman John Sculley, "There's never a dull moment during my days."[1] Are these descriptors true for all managers?

For the majority of managers, yes. The manager's environment is becoming more complex. Look at the changes that have struck major businesses in recent years: shifts in business (UPS), changing structures (GE), downsizing (IBM and Sears), plant closings (GM and Ford), mergers (Time and Warner), and leadership vacuums (IBM, Sears, GM). Clearly, adjusting to such changes makes the day-to-day business of management complex and exacting. Managers of today have multiple demands on their time, on their capacity to absorb new technology, and on their flexibility to adapt to the new cultural diversity that is now representative of the work force.

Added to this setting are three issues facing today's managers: internationalization, ethical concerns, and the emphasis on total quality management. The way managers do business today has changed. Companies are venturing into the international arena, which requires them to adapt existing managerial practices to unfamiliar settings and to adopt workable elements from those settings. Even small businesses, as the suppliers of larger firms that compete in world markets or as businesses that face competition from foreign firms, are touched by the internationalizing of business. Additionally, society now demands that business be conducted more ethically. Finally, managers now see quality and total quality improvement as the gateway to survival, competitiveness, and long-range profitability. (Total quality management is discussed in this chapter's Manager's Notebook.) The new philosophies, cultural diversity, demands on leadership, and management techniques associated with a commitment to quality in all parts of the organization are revolutionizing the manager's job.

Managers must find a way to balance these multiple demands. As each new area of emphasis is adopted, the manager must attempt to understand its importance, consciously make a place for it within other critical priorities, and find another area to modify to provide the needed balance. With all these demands, a new type of manager is emerging. As shown in Table 6.1, this manager approaches the management job with a new philosophy.

The Myths and Realities of the Manager's Job

When Henry Mintzberg studied the effects of these multiple demands on managers, he found that the way managers actually work stands in sharp contrast to the myths that surround managers.[2]

Myth 1: The manager is a reflective, systematic planner. People believe that managers have time to plan and work their way through a day systematically.

OLD MANAGER	NEW MANAGER
Thinks of self as a manager or boss	Thinks of self as a sponsor, team leader, or internal consultant
Follows the chain of command	Deals with anyone necessary to get the job done
Works within a set organizational structure	Changes organizational structures in response to market change
Makes most decisions alone	Invites others to join in decision making
Hoards information	Shares information
Tries to master one discipline	Tries to master a broad array of managerial disciplines
Demands long hours	Demands results

Source: "The New Non-Managers," *Fortune*, February 22, 1993. © 1993 Time Inc. All rights reserved.

Table 6.1
The new manager.

Reality: The typical manager takes on so many tasks that he or she has little time to reflect. Daily events range from the trivial to various crises, with enough of the latter to keep the manager on the move. The average time spent on any one activity is only nine minutes. Managers face constant interruptions. Whether it is Roberto Goizueta, CEO of Coca-Cola (featured in this chapter's Global Perspective), or Gayle Patrick, a first-line supervisor at Texas Instrument's Dallas facilities, the manager has days that are long and full of interaction with others.

Myth 2: The effective manager has no regular duties to perform. According to this myth, the manager establishes everything in advance and then relaxes to watch others do the work.

Reality: Although their days may be interrupted by crises, managers have regular duties to perform. These duties include attending meetings, seeing community and organizational visitors, and processing information on a regular basis. To perform all their duties, managers often extend the day into the night.

Myth 3: The manager's job is quickly becoming a science. Managers work systematically and analytically determine programs and procedures.

Reality: The manager's job is less a science than art. Rather than relying on systematic procedures and programs, managers use intuition and judgment, even though they are depending on prepared information more heavily now than in the past. No management handbook could tell Roberto Goizueta how to change Coca-Cola Co. to make it more effective.

Who Managers Are

Depending on whom you talk to and whose business card you read, managers have all sorts of names and titles. The best way to answer the question "Who are managers?" is to examine levels and areas of management.

GLOBAL PERSPECTIVE

Coca-Cola Co.: Managing the World's Best Brand

"We used to be an American company with a large international business. Now we are a large international company with a sizable American business," states Coca-Cola Co. Chairman and CEO Roberto Goizueta. Coca-Cola's remarkably smooth evolution has been primarily envisioned and managed by Goizueta and his hand-picked management team.

Robert Goizueta spent the better part of the 1980s reengineering Coca-Cola—culturally, organizationally, and financially—to meet his vision of the future. From his beginning as CEO, he applied his management skills to a large, diverse, and traditional corporation. He methodically took the organization apart, examined each piece in the process, then decided what it should look like when he put it back together.

As a key element of the process, Goizueta recruited bright, young proteges. He took them into his confidence, heaped responsibility on them, and allowed them to take bold risks, and today they run much of the company they helped design.

The much more sophisticated Coca-Cola Co. that has emerged from Goizueta's managerial reworking is one of the simplest of all large corporations to define. Gone are the wine, coffee, tea, and industrial water treatment businesses that Goizueta inherited. Today, Coca-Cola is simply a beverage company—but what a beverage company!

Coca-Cola is a global soft drink company that holds 45 percent of the world market in carbonated drinks; it has 47 percent of the market outside the United States and plans to make that 50 percent in the next two years. It now earns 80 percent of its profits on the international front and has committed its resources and talents to this sector. "We have really just begun reaching out to the 95 percent of the world's population that live outside the U.S. Today, our top sixteen markets account for 80 percent of our volume, and those markets only cover 20 percent of the world's population," declares Goizueta.

To reach that population, Coca-Cola is directing billions of dollars toward building bottling plants and establishing joint ventures. Major developments are under way or in the negotiation process in Poland, Czechoslovakia, Romania, Russia, Albania, and Austria.

Under Roberto Goizueta's leadership, Coca-Cola is more focused, more single-minded, and more open about its intentions than it has been at any other time in its more than 100-year history.

(For more on managing at Coca-Cola, see John Huey, "The World's Best Brand," *Fortune*, May 31, 1993, pp. 44–54.)

Levels of Management

Are managers the same throughout an organization? The answer is both yes and no. Managers all perform the same management functions, but different positions in the company require different emphases. In most organizations the management group makes up a **management hierarchy**, or *the various levels of management, usually represented by a pyramid arrangement.* We can divide this hierarchy into three main levels, as shown in Figure 6.1.

Top management consists of *the organization's most important manager—the chief executive officer or president—and his or her immediate subordinates, usually called vice-presidents.* Top management is responsible for the overall management of the organization. It establishes organizational or company-wide objectives, goals, and operating policies, and it directs the company in its broader relations with the external environment. Sandor Schoichet of Teknekron Pharmaceutical Systems is in top management.

Middle management includes *all managers below the rank of vice-president but above the supervisory level.* Whether titled regional managers or group managers, they have subordinates who are other managers. They are responsible for implementing top management's objectives and policies. Some organizations have two or three levels of middle managers. Plant managers and sales managers are two examples of middle management.

First-line management, or supervisors, are *managers at the operating level, the lowest level of management.* They are responsible for managing their specific work groups and for accomplishing the actual work of the organization. Their subordinates are nonmanagement workers or operating employees—the group that all managers depend on for the execution of their plans. A night manager at a Holiday Inn is a first-line supervisor.

management hierarchy
The various levels of management, usually represented by a pyramid arrangement.

top management
The organization's most important manager—the chief executive officer or president—and his or her immediate subordinates, usually called vice-presidents.

middle management
All managers below the rank of vice-president but above the supervisory level.

first-line management *or* supervisors
Managers at the operating level, the lowest level of management.

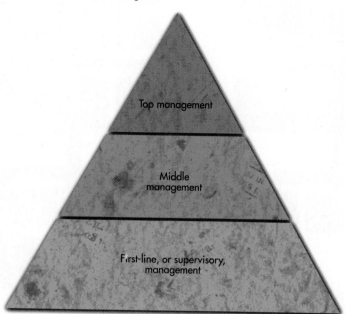

Figure 6.1
Management's pyramid structure.

Top management

Middle management

First-line, or supervisory, management

Specific titles of managers depend on the organizations they work in and the actual jobs they perform. In government organizations, titles such as administrator, section chief, and director are quite common. In business commonly used titles are supervisor, manager, and vice-president. Titles have little meaning outside the environment in which they are used, however. A district manager of one company could be the equivalent of a regional manager in a rival firm. This situation is illustrated in Figure 6.2, which presents the three levels of management in one organization along with the titles used for managers at each level.

Figure 6.2
Typical titles in the three levels of management.

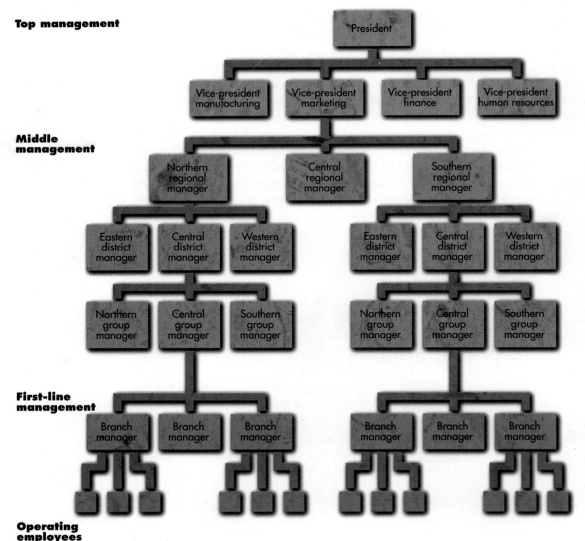

Top management

Middle management

First-line management

Operating employees

Areas of Management

Managers may also be identified by the kind of work, activity, or functions they handle. The most common kinds of management are marketing, operations, finance, and human resources.

MARKETING MANAGERS Marketing managers are responsible for research and for product development as well as for the pricing, promotion, and distribution strategy for an organization. In Figure 6.2 the vice-president of marketing is part of top management; regional, district, and group managers are all middle managers; and the branch manager is a first-line supervisor.

OPERATIONS MANAGERS Operations managers are responsible for the activities involved in creating the goods and services for the organization. They handle inventory control, plant layout, production control, and quality control. In Figure 6.2 the head of operations is the vice-president of manufacturing, a top-level manager; other managers are below this top manager in succeeding levels of the hierarchy, as is the case with the marketing managers.

FINANCE MANAGERS Finance managers are responsible for managing the financial assets of an organization. Individual managers in this area are responsible for accounting, investments, budgeting, and financial controls.

HUMAN RESOURCES MANAGERS Human resources managers are responsible for all the elements surrounding the human resources of an organization. Their tasks include forecasting the need for human resources; recruiting, selecting, orienting, training, and developing those resources; creating performance appraisal and compensation systems; overseeing labor relations; and handling all legal issues related to human resources.

Management Functions

We have defined management as the process of setting and achieving goals through the execution of five basic management functions that use human, financial, material, and informational resources. These five functions are planning, organizing, staffing, directing, and controlling.

Although we'll discuss these functions separately, in reality they are inseparable and interdependent. Managers are not able to say, "I'm going to plan in the morning, direct before lunch, organize between 1 and 2 P.M., and control from 2:30 P.M. until the end of the day." A manager must coordinate these functions. Implementing plans requires acquiring human resources (staffing) and structuring work groups (organizing). Subordinates must be guided to complete the plan (directing), and the plan's progress must be monitored (controlling). The management functions and managers' performance of those functions are dynamic, complementary, and mutually supportive. Following is an explanation of each function.

Planning

Planning is the first management function both because it lays the groundwork for all other functions and because it is the first step taken when performing the other functions. **Planning** is *the management function that involves identifying goals and alternative ways of achieving them.* It maps out courses of action that will commit individuals, departments, and the entire organization for days, months, and years to come. The very act of planning sets in motion the following processes:

1. Determining how personnel and other resources will be structured (organizing).
2. Obtaining the needed personnel and training them to accomplish the desired tasks (staffing).
3. Developing the foundation for the organizational environment in which work is to be accomplished (directing).
4. Determining a standard against which the progress toward objectives can be measured so that correction can be made if necessary (controlling).

LENGTH AND SCOPE OF PLANNING The amount of time managers spend planning and the scope of their plans vary according to the level of the manager. Top-level management's plans may cover three or five years; they are considered long-range plans. These plans may address the overall mission of the business or its expansion. At lower levels of management, the concern may be to plan for today's activities or next week's schedule.

INFLUENCES ON PLANNING Each manager's plans are influenced by the plans of other managers. Lower-level managers' plans must follow the direction of top-level managers' plans. Besides this vertical influence, horizontal influence comes from other managers on the same level within the same department. Add to these the influence of government rules and regulations, and you can see that planning is more complex than it appears. It does not occur in a vacuum.

CONTINUITY AND FLEXIBILITY Planning is a continuous function that must be performed as long as the organization exists. Plans are not always achieved as originally intended; managers must stay flexible because unexpected events and circumstances change original plans. Digital Equipment Corporation recently demonstrated how an organization must occasionally modify its plans. The company devised staffing plans based on meeting the needs of its business market. As the competitive environment changed, the company chose to shift its focus to meet new market opportunities. Thus the initial staffing plans had to be modified. The result: Digital revamped its operations and in the process eliminated 25 percent of its work force.[3]

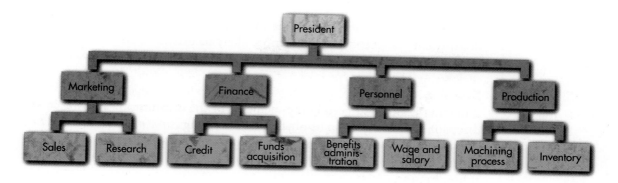

Organizing

Organizing is *the management function concerned with (1) assembling and allocating the resources necessary to achieve the organization's objectives, (2) establishing the authority relationships of the organization, and (3) creating the organizational structure.* Planning has established the goals of the company and how they are to be achieved; organizing develops the structure to achieve these goals.

The activities necessary to reach objectives are grouped into working divisions, departments, or other identifiable units primarily by clustering related tasks. The result is a network of interdependent units or departments known as an organizational structure, which can be charted as shown in Figures 6.2 and 6.3. Each unit (and each person in the unit) should have clearly defined authority or a clearly defined list of duties and one person to whom to report.

Organizing is not done once and then forgotten. As the objectives of the company change, the structure of managerial and organizational relationships may also change. One thing about organizing is certain—changes that occur both within and outside the organization will require new approaches, new plans, and new organizational units. Chapter 7 concentrates on the organizing function.

Staffing

Staffing is *the management function that attempts to attract good people to an organization and keep them.* Staffing attempts to locate prospective employees to fill the jobs identified as necessary in the organizing process. Staffing involves determining an organization's human resource needs (how many people are needed), attracting potential employees through newspaper ads and other sources, and reviewing the credentials of job candidates to match their abilities to job demands. After employees are hired, staffing involves orienting the employees to the company environment, training them for their jobs, and keeping them qualified. Staffing also involves developing and implementing a system for appraising performance and providing feedback for its improvement, as well as determining the proper pay and benefits for each job.

Figure 6.3
An organization structure.

organizing
The management function concerned with (1) assembling and allocating the resources necessary to achieve the organization's objectives, (2) establishing the authority relationships of the organization, and (3) creating the organizational structure.

staffing
The management function that attempts to attract good people to an organization and keep them.

Many aspects of this function are the responsibility of the human resources department—a staff department most likely to exist in a large organization. Chapter 8 examines the staffing function in detail.

Directing

Directing is aimed at getting the members of the organization moving in the direction that will achieve its objectives. **Directing** is *the management function that provides leadership, builds a good working climate, and arranges the opportunity for motivation.* Each manager must oversee the work of each of his or her subordinates.

When directing, the manager must provide leadership to the work group, build a climate in which individuals are motivated to perform their jobs effectively and efficiently, and communicate both operating expectations for performance and feedback on results. Directing places a premium on the manager's ability to work with people. There are no hard-and-fast rules: the manager needs to be sensitive to the individuals involved and to provide ongoing guidance, coaching, and information to them.

In practicing leadership, the manager does not simply give orders. Rather, he or she must decide how best to achieve goals through people. The dilemma for a manager becomes how to provide guidance, involve people in decisions, and build a work team when all people are different. Part of the solution is to create a work environment in which employees are motivated to work toward their goals and the goals of the organization. To do so, a manager must appreciate the uniqueness of each person in a work group and must attempt to provide an environment in which the personal needs of each individual are fulfilled. Dave Thomas, the founder of Wendy's restaurant chain, credits

directing
The management function that provides leadership, builds a good working climate, and arranges the opportunity for motivation.

Managers who are good leaders know that directing workers involves effective communication, including giving and receiving feedback.

much of his success to creating such an environment at his company. Through trial and error he learned to involve people, to stop trying to do everything himself, and to appreciate the uniqueness and talents of those around him.[4]

To exercise leadership and build such a supportive climate, a manager must keep communication channels open. A manager must communicate performance expectations, actively listen to employees, respond to employee concerns, and provide feedback on individual performance. There must also be a genuine exchange of ideas, concerns, and actions between manager and employee.

Controlling

Controlling is *the management function of establishing standards, measuring actual performance to see whether the standards have been met, analyzing the results, and taking corrective action if required.*

The controlling function is essential. Controlling attempts to promote success and to prevent failure by providing means for monitoring the performance of individuals, departments, divisions, and the entire organization. It attempts to prevent problems, to determine when problems do exist, and to solve those that occur as quickly and as effectively as possible.

The control process consists of four basic steps that are applicable to any persons, items, or processes being controlled:

1. Establish the standards to be used in measuring progress toward goals.
2. Measure performance against those standards.
3. Note and analyze any deviations from standards.
4. Take actions necessary to correct undesired deviations.

Sales-oriented companies such as Procter & Gamble and Frito-Lay establish sales quotas to monitor employee performance. At Chapparal Steel, production quotas are identified and serve as a measure of performance. For most managers budgets are control devices to monitor expenses.

controlling
The management function of establishing standards, measuring actual performance to see whether the standards have been met, analyzing the results, and taking corrective action if required.

YOU DECIDE
What function is the most difficult for a manager to perform effectively? Why?

Management Functions at All Levels

Regardless of title, position, or management level, all managers do the same job. They execute the five management functions and work through and with others to set and achieve the organization's goals. As you examine Figure 6.4, note that although all managers perform the same functions, managers at the various management levels require different amounts of time for each function. The points of emphasis in each function also differ.

TOP MANAGEMENT Top-level managers are concerned with the big picture, not the nitty-gritty. The planning function for the top managers at American Airlines, for example, consists of developing the major purpose of the organi-

Figure 6.4
Relative emphasis on each management function at various management levels.

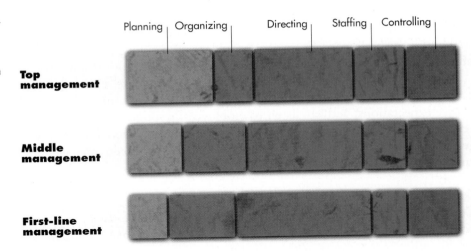

zation, the global objectives for organizational accomplishment, and the major policies to be implemented by middle and first-line managers. Organizing at the top level is a matter of developing the overall structure of the organization to support plans and to acquire resources. Staffing at the top level of management is concerned with developing policies in such areas as equal opportunity and employee development. Top management is also concerned with acquiring talent to fill upper-management positions. Directing consists of creating a company-wide management philosophy and cultivating an organizational climate for optimal employee performance. Controlling at this level emphasizes overall company performance relative to company objectives.

MIDDLE MANAGEMENT The middle manager's primary job is to develop strategies to implement the broad concepts determined by top management. For example, if the top managers at Dell Computers decide on a 10 percent profit objective, the middle managers of that company must define concrete goals of their own to attain that profit—whether to pursue new products, new customers, or new territories, for instance. Organizing at the middle level means making specific adjustments in the organizational structure and allocating the resources acquired by top management. Staffing focuses on implementing equal opportunity policies and employee development programs. Directing is a matter of providing leadership and support for lower-level management. Controlling is concerned with monitoring the results of plans for specific products, regions, and subunits and making any adjustment required to ensure that the organization's objectives are attained.

FIRST-LINE (SUPERVISORY) MANAGEMENT Whereas top managers are concerned with the big picture and middle managers with the implementation of overall plans, first-line managers are concerned only with their immediate responsibilities. For the first-line manager, say, a McDonald's shift supervisor, planning involves scheduling employees, deciding what work will be done first, and developing procedures to achieve immediate goals. Organizing may consist of delegating authority or assigning tasks to specific workers or groups. Staffing at this level consists of requesting a new employee, hiring that employee, and then training the person to perform the job. Directing includes communicating and providing leadership both to the group and to all employees individually. Controlling at this level focuses on ensuring that the group meets its production, sales, or quality objectives.

Management Roles

Our working definition describes managers, regardless of their level, as those who plan, organize, staff, direct, and control. To carry out these functions the manager must fill various roles. A **role** is *a set of expectations for a manager's behavior.* As a manager performs the management job and interacts with various members of the organization, he or she must wear different hats. These role requirements are influenced by the manager's formal job description, which grants certain authority and status, and by the values and expectations of the manager's superiors, subordinates, and peers.

Henry Mintzberg has analyzed management behavior as fitting into ten possible roles.[5] In turn, these ten roles can be grouped into three categories: those primarily concerned with interpersonal relationships, those primarily concerned with the transfer of information, and those primarily concerned with decision making. These ten roles are listed in Table 6.2 along with brief examples of how the work of CEOs demonstrates those roles. Following is an explanation of each category and the roles it encompasses.

Interpersonal Roles

Interpersonal roles deal with the manager's relationships with others. They arise directly from a manager's formal position and authority.

- *Figurehead* A manager is the head of his or her work unit, be it a division, department, or section. Because of this position, the manager must routinely perform certain ceremonial duties. For example, the manager may be required to entertain visitors to the organization, attend a subordinate's wedding, or participate in a group luncheon.
- *Leader* The manager creates the environment. She or he plays the leader role by working to improve employees' performances, reducing conflict, providing feedback on performance, and encouraging growth.
- *Liaison* Managers interact with others besides superiors and subordinates; they work with peer-level managers in other departments, staff specialists, other departments' employees, and outside contacts (suppliers, clients). In this role, the manager builds contacts.

Informational Roles

Partly as a result of the manager's contacts inside and outside the organization, he or she normally has more information than other members of the staff.[6] Three key roles are involved with the use and dissemination of information.

role
A set of expectations for a manager's behavior.

Table 6.2
Mintzberg's ten management roles.

ROLE	DESCRIPTION	IDENTIFIABLE ACTIVITIES FROM STUDY OF CHIEF EXECUTIVES
INTERPERSONAL		
Figurehead	Performs symbolic routine duties of legal or social nature	Attending ceremonies or other public, legal, or social functions; officiating
Leader	Motivates subordinates, ensures hiring and training of staff	Interacting with subordinates
Liaison	Maintains self-developed network of contacts and informers who provide favors and information	Acknowledging mail and interacting with outsiders
INFORMATIONAL		
Monitor	Seeks and receives wide variety of special information to develop thorough understanding of the organization and environment	Handling all mail and contacts concerned primarily with receiving information
Disseminator	Transmits information received from outsiders or subordinates to members of the organization (some information is factual, some involves interpretation and integration)	Forwarding mail into the organization for informational purposes, maintaining verbal contacts involving flow to subordinates
Spokesperson	Transmits to outsiders information about organization's plans, policies, actions, results, and so forth; serves as expert on organization's industry	Attending board meetings, handling mail and contacts involving transmission of information to outsiders
DECISIONAL		
Entrepreneur	Searches organization and its environment for opportunities and initiates projects to bring about change	Implementing strategy and review sessions involving improvement
Disturbance handler	Initiates corrective action when organization faces important, unexpected disturbances	Implementing strategy to resolve disturbances and crises
Resource allocator	Fulfills responsibility for allocation of organizational resources of all kinds—in effect, makes or approves all significant decisions	Scheduling, requesting authorizing, budgeting, programming of subordinates' work
Negotiator	Represents the organization in major negotiations	Negotiating

Source: From *The Nature of Managerial Work* by Henry Mintzberg. Copyright 1973 by Henry Mintzberg. Reprinted by permission of HarperCollins Publishers.

- *Monitor* The manager is constantly monitoring the environment to determine what is going on. The manager collects information both directly, by asking questions, and indirectly, by receiving unsolicited information.
- *Disseminator* As a disseminator, the manager passes on to subordinates some of the information that would not ordinarily be accessible to them.
- *Spokesperson* The manager is the person who speaks for his or her work unit to people outside the work unit. One part of this role is to keep superiors well informed; a second aspect is to communicate with those outside the organization.

Decisional Roles

The four decisional roles focus on the making of choices. Managers either make those choices (alone or with others) or influence the choices of others.

- *Entrepreneur* As the manager is exposed to new ideas or methods that may improve the work unit's operations, he or she assumes the entrepreneur role. In this role, the manager initiates activities that will allow and encourage the work unit to use the ideas or methods most advantageously.
- *Disturbance handler* When parts of the work environment get out of control (for example, schedule problems, equipment failure, strikes, or reneged contracts), the manager must handle these crises.
- *Resource allocator* The manager determines who in the work unit gets resources and how much each person gets. These resources include money, facilities, equipment, and access to the manager's time.
- *Negotiator* Managers are required to spend a good part of their time negotiating. Negotiating is required for contracts with suppliers and for

Managers must learn how to handle crises, which require quick decision making.

trading off resources inside the organization. The manager plays this role because he or she is the only one in the work unit with both the information and the authority that negotiators must have.

Roles and Managerial Functions

These multiple roles are what managers actually do to carry out the managerial functions. In planning and organizing, the manager performs the resource allocator role. Staffing requires the manager to play the leadership role by providing subordinates with feedback on performance. Directing includes the successful performance of disseminator, entrepreneur, and disturbance-handler roles. Controlling is aided through the performance of the monitor role.

Figure 6.5 illustrates the role behaviors expected by employees, peers, the formal job description, and the manager's supervisor. The ability to meet these multiple role demands makes the difference between a successful manager and an unsuccessful one. Any manager who has a problem wearing any of these many hats will have a work unit that suffers to some extent.

YOU DECIDE

What roles do you expect your manager to perform? What roles has the manager played successfully? Unsuccessfully? How did the results make you and your fellow workers feel?

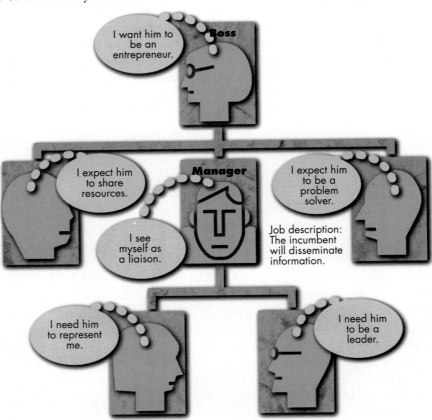

Figure 6.5

Conflicting role demands on a manager.

Management Skills

As a manager plans, organizes, staffs, directs, and controls, he or she must master skills that can be grouped in three clusters: technical, human, and conceptual.[7]

Technical Skills

Technical skills include *knowledge of and ability to use the processes, practices, techniques, and tools of the specialty area a manager supervises.* For example, a manager supervising accountants must know accounting. The manager does not need to be a technical expert. Rather, the manager needs enough technical knowledge and skill to do such things as intelligently direct employees, organize tasks, communicate the work group's needs to others, and solve problems. CEO Jack Stack at Springfield Remanufacturing is not a manufacturing expert, yet he has enough technical ability to communicate with the operations manager, first-line supervisors, and manufacturing employees about their concerns.

technical skills
Knowledge of and ability to use the processes, practices, techniques, and tools of the specialty area a manager supervises.

Human Skills

Human skills refer to *the ability to interact and communicate with other people successfully.* A manager must be able to understand, work with, and relate to both individuals and groups in order to build a team environment. The proper execution of one's human skills is often called human relations.

Human skills can be subdivided into two parts: leadership of the manager's subordinates and skill in intergroup relationships. A manager's human skills determine his or her ability to work effectively as a group member and to build cooperative effort within the group.[8] Herb Kelleher, CEO of Southwest Airlines, has used his human skills to build an outstanding rapport with his employees.

human skills
The ability to interact and communicate with other people successfully.

Conceptual Skills

Conceptual skills refer to *the ability to view the organization as a whole and to see how its parts relate to and depend on one another.* Conceptual skills, which deal with ideas and abstract relationships, also include the ability to imagine the integration and coordination of the parts of an organization—all its processes and systems. A manager needs conceptual skills to see how factors are interrelated, to understand the impact of any action on the other aspects of the organization, and to be able to execute the five basic management functions. Finally, conceptual skills include the ability to identify a problem, develop alternatives to solve it, select the best alternative, and implement that solution.

Michael Armstrong is a manager who illustrates the importance of good conceptual skills. After spending an entire career at IBM, he became the CEO of Hughes Aircraft. Because of his conceptual skills, he successfully moved into a new industry, company, and competitive environment.

conceptual skills
The ability to view the organization as a whole and to see how its parts relate to and depend on one another.

Importance of Skills According to Management Level

The importance of having each of the three management skills depends on a manager's level of management in the organization. Technical skills are critical for first-line managers and become less important as the manager moves up in the organization structure. For example, the supervisor of a word-processing department at Northwest Airlines needs to know more technical information about the systems, equipment, and methods of training than the president, who does not deal in the how to's of specific departments.

Human skills are important at every level in the organization. Nevertheless, the first-line manager's position places a premium on human skills because of the many employee interactions required.

Conceptual skills become increasingly important as a manager moves up the levels of management. The first-level manager focuses basically on her or his work group; therefore, the need for conceptual skills is at a minimum. Top-level management is concerned with broad-based, long-range decisions that affect the entire organization; therefore, conceptual skills are most important at that level. Figure 6.6 illustrates the relative amounts of each kind of skill needed by the three levels of management.

The Management Decision-Making Process

Now that we have examined the manager's job (functions), the behaviors necessary to perform the job (roles), and the skills necessary to manage, it is appropriate to look at decision making. Decision making is a part of all managers' jobs. A manager makes decisions constantly as he or she performs the functions of planning, organizing, staffing, directing, and controlling.

Figure 6.6

Relative amounts of management skills needed at various levels of management.

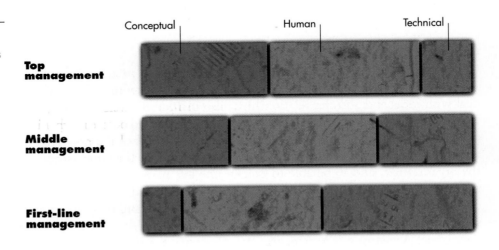

Source: Adapted from James A. F. Stoner/R. Edward Freeman, *Management*, 4th ed., 1989, p. 15. Used by permission of Prentice-Hall, Englewood Cliffs, N.J.

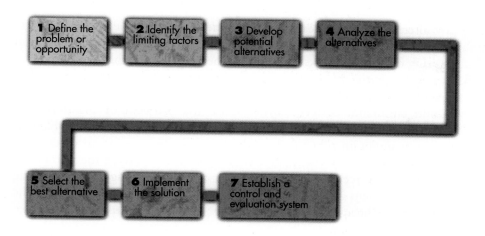

Figure 6.7

The decision-making process.

Decision making is *the process of identifying problems and opportunities, developing alternative solutions, choosing an alternative, and implementing it.*[9] Decision making is not a separate function of management but rather a common thread within the five management functions. Managers make big and small decisions daily. Whether planning a budget, organizing a work schedule, interviewing a prospective employee, watching a worker on the assembly line, or making adjustments to a project, the manager is performing a decision-making process.

The decision-making process consists of seven steps. They are logical and simple in themselves, but they are all essential to the process. The steps, diagrammed in Figure 6.7, are discussed briefly here.

1. *Define the problem or opportunity.* What is the particular problem or opportunity you have? Accurate definition of a problem affects all the steps that follow. If a problem is defined inaccurately, every other step in the decision-making process will be based on that incorrect point. A motorist tells a mechanic that her car is running rough, which is a symptom of a problem or problems. The mechanic begins by diagnosing the possible causes of a rough-running engine, checking each possible cause based on the mechanic's experience. The mechanic may find one problem—a faulty spark plug. If this is the problem, changing the plug will result in a smooth-running engine. If not, a problem still exists. Only a road test will tell for sure. The consequences of not properly defining the problem are wasted time and energy. And employees may become frustrated—"What, that again? We just solved that problem last month, or at least we thought we did."

2. *Identify the limiting factors.* Once the problem is defined, you need to determine the limiting factors of the problem. *Limiting factors* are those constraints that rule out certain alternative solutions. One common limitation is time. If a new product has to be on the dealers' shelves in one month,

decision making
The process of identifying problems and opportunities, developing alternative solutions, choosing an alternative, and implementing it.

any alternative that takes more than one month will be eliminated. Resources, personnel, money, facilities, and equipment are other common limiting or critical factors that narrow the range of possible alternatives.

3. *Develop potential alternatives.* At this point it is necessary to look for, develop, and list as many possible alternatives as you can. These alternatives should eliminate, correct, or neutralize the problem or maximize the opportunity. Alternative solutions for a manager faced with the problem of trying to maintain scheduled production may be to start an extra work shift, to schedule overtime on a regular basis, to increase the size of the current work force by hiring employees, or to do nothing. Doing nothing about a problem sometimes is the proper alternative, at least until the situation has been analyzed thoroughly. Occasionally just the passage of time provides a cure.

4. *Analyze the alternatives.* The next step is to decide the relative merits of each alternative. What are the positives and negatives of each? Do any alternatives conflict with the critical (limiting) factors that you identified earlier? If so, they must be automatically discarded.

5. *Select the best alternative.* By this point, you have listed the alternatives along with their corresponding advantages and disadvantages. Which should you select? Sometimes the best solution is a combination of several of the alternatives. In trying to select an alternative or combination of alternatives, you must find a solution that appears to offer the fewest serious disadvantages and the most advantages. You should be careful not to solve one problem only to create others.

6. *Implement the solution.* Managers are paid to make decisions, but they are also paid to get results from those decisions. A decision that just sits there hoping someone will put it into effect may as well never have been made. Everyone involved with it must know what he or she must do, how to do it, why, and when. In addition, a good alternative applied by uncommitted persons in a half-hearted way often will create problems, not solve them. Like plans, solutions need effective implementation to yield the desired results. People must be sold on their roles and know exactly what they must do and why. Programs, procedures, rules, or policies must be put into effect thoughtfully.

7. *Establish a control and evaluation system.* The final step in the decision-making process is to create a control and evaluation system. Ongoing actions need to be monitored. This system should provide feedback on how well the decision has been implemented, what the results are—positive or negative—and what adjustments are necessary to get the expected results.

For a manager who uses this decision-making process, the probability of successful decisions should be improved. Why? The manager is systematically approaching the problem rather than leaping from a problem to a solution with little or no analysis.

MANAGER'S NOTEBOOK

A not-so-quiet revolution is under way in organizations throughout the United States. This revolution focuses on the need to improve quality—quality as a gateway to survival, competitiveness, long-range productivity, and profitability.

For years managers gave quality a nod and then went about the business of the business—developing or delivering a product, process, or service. But, that product, process, or service did not necessarily contain the overall features and characteristics that truly satisfied the stated (or implied) requirements of either the producers or the users.

Today managers at all levels in an organization are becoming engulfed in the business of quality. This quality focus, called *total quality management (TQM),* involves much more than an individual manager's efforts. Rather, it is a company-wide effort to ensure that quality is an integral part of an organization's culture and operation. Companies such as Motorola, Hewlett-Packard, Ford, Texas Instruments, and Xerox have made the commitment to TQM.

In general, TQM embraces four essential elements:

1. Intense efforts to satisfy customers.
2. Accurate standards of measurement of every critical operation. These standards help identify problems and eliminate their causes.
3. Work relationships based on trust and teamwork. Central to TQM is *empowerment*—managers giving employees autonomy and support and motivating them to give their best. TQM must be a part of suppliers' culture and activities as well.
4. Continual improvement of processes, products, and services.

To be successful, TQM requires 100 percent commitment from everyone. Past efforts by companies to improve quality did not work because they were too dependent on a few people and not company-wide, committed efforts. Specifically:

- Top management must show a personal commitment to TQM. This commitment is expressed in actively discussing the need for quality improvement; developing written mission statements, value statements, and policies focusing on quality; removing fear from the workplace; and living the values of TQM.
- Middle managers must be active participants in planning for quality and quality control. They must have the authority and responsibility to execute plans and deal with problems. Middle management needs to develop systems that encourage and ensure cooperation and communication. Specific actions that can be taken include creating cross-functional teams, rearranging work flow and reassigning tasks, developing incentives and rewards to encourage cooperation, and creating accountability for internal customers.
- First-line management, team leaders, and employees must have a say in planning and in executing plans. First-line managers need to involve employees in decision making, to remove the fear of failure and blame for making mistakes, and to give workers the authority, training, and incentives to promote quality.

Total quality management is everyone's concern. To be successful, it requires total commitment at all levels.

Total Quality Means Total Commitment

(For more about total quality management, see Michael Barrier, "Putting Quality First," *Nation's Business*, May 1993, pp. 55–59.)

SUMMARY

The world is full of organizations. All organizations operate to achieve clearly stated, commonly held objectives. To achieve these objectives members of the organization must work together. To ensure the success of an organization, managers are necessary. Managers supply management—the process of setting and achieving goals through the execution of five basic management functions that utilize human, financial, informational, and material resources.

The management group in an organization consists of three basic categories: top management, middle management, and first-line management. Regardless of the management title, position, or level, all managers execute the five management functions.

Managers may be described by the kind of work or activity for which they are responsible. Typical categories are marketing, operations, finance, and human resources.

The five management functions—the broad activities that managers perform to achieve organizational goals—are planning, organizing, staffing, directing, and controlling. Planning is the management function that establishes organizational goals or objectives and creates the means for accomplishing them. Organizing is the management function concerned with (1) assembling the resources necessary to achieve the organization's objectives, (2) establishing the authority relationships of the organization, and (3) creating the organizational structure. Staffing attempts to attract good people to an organization and to hold onto them. Directing builds a climate, provides leadership,

and arranges the opportunity for motivation. Controlling is concerned with establishing standards, measuring actual performance to see whether standards have been met, and taking corrective action if required.

To accomplish management functions, managers must assume various roles. A role is a set of expectations for a manager's behavior. These roles are influenced by a manager's job description and the expectations held by superiors, subordinates, and peers. The ability to perform multiple roles is the difference between successful and unsuccessful managers.

Competent managers must draw on certain managerial skills to assemble and manage human and other resources for the achievement of organizational goals. The three required skills are technical, human, and conceptual. Human skills are equally important at all three management levels. Technical skills are most important at the first-line level and become less important as the manager moves up in the organization. Conversely, conceptual skills become increasingly important as a manager moves up the levels of management.

A part of all managers' jobs is decision making. A manager makes decisions constantly as he or she performs the functions of planning, organizing, staffing, directing, and controlling. The manager uses a seven-step decision-making process that includes defining the problem or opportunity, identifying the limiting factors, developing potential alternatives, analyzing the alternatives, selecting the best alternative, implementing the solution, and establishing a control and evaluation system.

KEY TERMS

conceptual skills p. 173
controlling p. 167
decision making p. 175
directing p. 166
first-line management *or* supervisors p. 161
human skills p. 173
management p. 157
managers p. 156
management functions p. 157

management hierarchy p. 161
middle management p. 161
organization p. 156
organizing p. 165
planning p. 164
role p. 169
staffing p. 165
technical skills p. 173
top management p. 161

FOR REVIEW AND DISCUSSION

1. Explain why managers are necessary in organizations. What specific contributions do they make?
2. Why is a manager's environment often described as complex?
3. What three myths are associated with a manager's job?
4. What are the three levels of management in an organization? Whom does each level manage? What responsibility areas does each level have?
5. Which management function is the most basic? Can the management functions be undertaken separately? Why or why not?
6. What occurs when managers perform the planning function? What is the importance of planning?
7. The organizing function includes what three parts? What is the result of the organizing process?
8. What is the purpose of the staffing function? What activities does the staffing function include?
9. What is the purpose of the directing function?
10. What is the purpose of the controlling function? What are the four steps in the control process?
11. What is meant by the term *role*? List and describe four roles managers are required to perform.
12. What three skills are needed by managers? Discuss how the need for two of these skills changes as a manager rises in the organizational hierarchy.
13. List the seven steps in the decision-making process. Why does decision making overlap all of the management functions?

APPLICATIONS

Case 6.1: Trouble at General Motors

General Motors Corporation's top management is struggling to make the company successful again. Over the years, GM's management has been a target of criticism from many corners. A documentary film, *Roger and Me,* portrayed former CEO Roger Smith as a distant monarch. Former presidential contender and successful businessman Ross Perot was so openly critical of GM's management that he was paid three quarters of a billion dollars to resign from its board of directors. And in recent years, a succession of company presidents have been hired and then fired for failing to turn the world's largest corporation around. The top management priority remains to return GM to productivity and profitability. As John Smith, GM's current president, states: "The issue is productivity. When we get productive we have a better shot at being more competitive in the marketplace."

But, unfortunately, management holds the largest share of blame for GM's current troubles. For example, GM has attempted to improve productivity by encouraging the development of new production techniques. In response, at one of the company's plants workers restructured a production line to increase productivity. This resulted in equipment that was less expensive than that used on the previous production line and employees who are three times more productive—fourteen workers could produce a thousand steering columns a day rather than four hundred. At the same time, quality control is better so the columns are seven times less likely to be defective.

The problem with this ambitious effort was management's response. Rather than capitalizing on the productivity gain, management determined that only one in three employees was still needed. Layoffs quickly followed, causing morale problems and union bitterness.

In another attempt to improve productivity, management supported creativity by allowing GM divisional managers to be autonomous in operating their separate divisions. Engineers and manufacturing personnel were given a free hand. The result? Inefficiency rather than efficiency. For example, GM uses 139 different types of hinges for their car hoods, whereas Ford uses one.

Despite these setbacks, Smith hopes to turn the corner at GM. He has directed management to find common tools and processes to create common products. He continues to focus on reducing overall employee numbers by closing plants throughout North America. But all of this will take time, and it is hard to know how much time General Motors has.

Questions

1. What does this case illustrate about the importance of coordination among the three levels of management in a company? Cite examples from the case to support your answer.

2. Which of the five functions of management are not being performed effectively at GM? Provide examples to explain your answer.

3. If you were a manager at GM, what actions would you recommend to John Smith to help turn the company around? Explain your recommendations.

For more information, see Joseph B. White, "GM Drive to Step Up Efficiency Is Colliding with UAW Job Fears," *The Wall Street Journal,* June 23, 1993, p. A1.

Case 6.2: Turning Enemies into Friends at Cam Systems

Geoffrey Knapp was just out of college and working for Triad Systems in 1980 when he decided to start his own company, Cam Data Systems. Triad sold business automation systems, and even though Knapp had targeted a different market segment, his product was the same. This did not please his former employer, and Triad immediately filed a multimillion-dollar damage suit against Knapp, charging unfair competition and breach of employment contract. These circumstances soured Knapp's relationship with his previous boss, Carl Smith.

In the next decade, Cam Systems grew very quickly. Unfortunately, Knapp was a good entrepreneur but a poor manager. Costs grew faster than revenues, and by the late 1980s, the company was consistently posting losses. Knapp was facing one of the most challenging problems that startups must deal with: changing from an entrepreneurial company to a professionally managed one. Knapp realized that he needed outside help. Looking for a new chief operating officer, he hired a successful young executive from a Fortune 500 company. Despite the man's perfect résumé, he was gone in 90 days, unable to deal with the shift to a small, money-losing company.

Then Knapp got a call from Carl Smith. Despite mutual reservations about working together again, they met and hit it off. Knapp offered Smith the president's post. Smith accepted on the condition that he would have total control over day-to-day operations. Knapp agreed and made Carl Smith both chief operating officer and chief executive officer in 1990. Smith set to work by cutting the work force by 20 percent, closing unprofitable branch offices, and setting goals that were directed toward making money for the company. His no-nonsense management style was a stabilizing influence for the company. After losing money for years, Cam Systems, under Carl Smith, made a profit for six consecutive quarters.

Freed to work on sales and procurement, Knapp has spent the last several years doing what he does best. Meanwhile, Smith has brought to the company a higher level of management skill. While not all entrepreneurs have the courage or temperament to hand control of their company over to someone else, Geoffrey Knapp has shown that it can be the best course of action.

Questions

1. How does this case illustrate the difference between managing a start-up organization and an established organization? Explain your answer.

2. What skills might be needed by a manager that an entrepreneur might not possess? Explain your answer.

3. What managerial skills did Carl Smith possess? Cite examples from the case to support your answer.

4. Which of the functions of management was Smith performing in the three actions he took after becoming chief executive officer? Explain your answer.

For more information, see John R. Emshwiller, "When Running a Company Is Harder Than Starting One," *The Wall Street Journal,* July 7, 1993, p. B2.

CHAPTER 6: MANAGING BUSINESS ORGANIZATIONS   181

REFERENCES

1. As quoted in John W. Verity, "Room at the Top," *Business Week*, March 9, 1992, p. 32.
2. Henry Mintzberg, "The Manager's Job: Folklore and Fact," *Harvard Business Review*, July–August 1975, pp. 49–61.
3. John Huey, "Managing in the Midst of Chaos," *Fortune*, April 5, 1993, p. 48.
4. John Bartholemew, "Front Line Management," *The Economics Press, Inc.*, Vol. 92, No 1, May 1992, p. 1.
5. Henry Mintzberg, "The Manager's Job."
6. Ibid.
7. Robert L. Katz, "Skills of an Effective Administrator," *Harvard Business Review*, September–October 1974, pp. 90–102.
8. David Holt, *Management Principles and Practices*, 2nd ed. (Englewood Cliffs, NJ: Prentice-Hall, 1990), p. 100.

7

DESIGNING AN ORGANIZATION STRUCTURE

We will never give up the principle of decentralization, which is to give our operating executives ownership of a business. They are ultimately accountable.

RALPH LARSEN
CEO, Johnson & Johnson

CHAPTER OBJECTIVES
After studying this chapter, you should be able to:

1. Explain the importance of the organizing process.
2. List and describe the five steps in the organizing process.
3. Identify the four forms of departmentalization and the situations in which each would be appropriate.
4. Define authority, and explain the differences among line, staff, and functional authority.
5. Explain the concept of power and its sources.
6. Relate the concepts of delegation of authority, responsibility, and accountability.
7. Explain the organizational concepts of span of control and centralization and decentralization.
8. Differentiate among line, line-and-staff, matrix, team, and network organization structures.
9. Explain the nature of the informal organization.

UP FRONT

"If you can dream it, you can do it," seems to sum up the birth and growth of the business known as Radius. The toothbrush company was born in March 1982 at the beach on the island of Tortola in the British Virgin Islands. Kevin Foley and his friend and associate James O'Halloran, both architects, had always talked about creating an extraordinary type of toothbrush. "Toothbrushes looked too dental," Foley recalls, "like a dentist's cleaning tool or mirror, not like something the average person either wants to use or would enjoy using." Now they had decided to take action.

Foley and O'Halloran moved to New York City, bought a five-story office building, and began developing the toothbrush. They decided that it should be comfortable, ergonomically designed for both right-handed and left-handed people. It should also be pleasurable to use, since most people brush their teeth first thing in the morning so that their mouth will taste and feel good. It ought to be effective yet gentle, so it should have a large head and many soft bristles. To find a name for this new product, they threw a party and asked people to vote on twenty possible names; the unanimous winner was Radius.

Radius occupied the second floor of the office building, while Foley and O'Halloran lived with their families on two of the upper floors. The molds for the Radius toothbrush were made and shipped to a contract manufacturing firm in Leominster, Massachusetts. The first Radius was introduced at the Accent on Design show in New York in 1984 and won first place,

resulting in two mail order catalog companies—Norm Thompson and Brookstone—picking it up. That first year, Radius had $188,636 in sales.

Foley became more active in running the company, and in 1985 it was just he, O'Halloran, and a secretary. "Using a personal computer allowed us to survive in a very competitive business environment," he says. "Because of the good information the computer provides, we know our sales, understand our customers, how much it costs to manufacture our toothbrush, and how many of them to ship. Many companies today still do not have information of this high a quality." Over time, the computer would be used to run every facet of the business, from inventory to manufacturing to order fulfillment to shipping.

The staff soon grew to four, and when people began standing in line to get at the computer, four PCs connected in a network were installed. In 1985, Foley recalls, "all paperwork and filing cabinets were thrown out. All company information was stored in the computer. Sales had thirty or forty file folders, but that was it."

Over the next three years, as business grew, Foley rethought the business. He and O'Halloran concluded that it would make sense to take over manufacturing so that they would have total control over every aspect of the business. "We wanted to know the *real* cost of making an item," says Foley, "the cost of materials, the cost

KEVIN FOLEY

PRESIDENT, RADIUS

of machines, the cost of labor. Then we'd know exactly how profitable we were, and how to enhance profitability."

Thus, in 1988 Radius moved its operations to an 1860 grain mill at the corner of Railroad and Peach Streets in Kutztown, Pennsylvania. There are only five knowledge workers at Radius, a direct indication of how the use of computers has streamlined operations and improved productivity. O'Halloran, the chairman, is in charge of all aspects of production, including the toothbrushes, displays, and manufacturing machinery. Foley, the president, is responsible for sales, marketing, administration, finance, public relations, and advertising. Lauren Pompilio is office manager and managerial accountant; Bernetta Fies handles customer order processing; Diane Rarick works with inventory and manufacturing; and Suze Foley handles order fulfillment and shipping.

"The Radius organization thrives on information, but it is driven by sales and marketing," says Foley. "No matter how good your product is, if you cannot sell it then you are no longer in business. We have sales brokers, nationwide sales representatives who sell our products into retail stores—gift shops, pharmacies, nutrition stores, and others. They receive a commission on their sales. This is primarily how

we offer the Radius toothbrush to the world, and everyone here in Kutztown is geared to support sales."

Even though they believe it is important to keep their staff to a minimum, Foley and O'Halloran also recognize that the company needs to grow—primarily by manufacturing and marketing new products. Plans are underway to introduce a different model of the Radius toothbrush and a new hairbrush. Doing so will require changing the organizational structure. "Although the current management technique has been to divide running the company between us, and even though it has provided us with a simple and flexible form for ten years, it will not provide the basis for a major increase in the size of Radius," says Foley. "In the future, we will need to provide serious management to deal with the expanded components of our business. We're going to need more organizational structure in sales, marketing, advertising, manufacturing maintenance and supervision, and industrial design and computer-aided design.

"The future of Radius lies in its ability to invest in new and creative products," he continues. "Our products aim to be very effective, well designed, and pleasing to own. Our aim is to make our customer into a fan of Radius."

"**Y**ou can't tell me what to do, only Larry can. He's my boss!"

"When did the advertising department start reporting to Frank? I thought it was part of John's department."

"Can I please have a decision on this requisition? Who do I need to go see? Who's in charge here anyway?"

If these words sound familiar, you have had practical experience with problems involving the second management function—organizing. In Chapter 6 you learned about the importance of planning in an organization. But planning alone cannot ensure an organization's success. A company that has taken the time, energy, and money to develop quality plans needs to organize its employees to implement these plans—and needs managers who understand the importance of organizing.

Organizing, like planning and the other managerial functions, is a process that must be carefully thought out and applied. It involves determining what work is needed, assigning those tasks, and arranging them into a decision-making framework. This framework provides an organizational structure for all jobs, making clear who has responsibility for what tasks and who reports to whom. Lack of structure can result in confusion, frustration, loss of efficiency, and limited effectiveness.

The Formal Organization

Remember, a business is an organization. It is created by owners and managers to achieve a specific goal: to provide a product or service to a customer at a profit. When managers create an organization, they are actually developing a framework in which to (1) operate effectively, (2) reach the organization's objectives, and (3) provide a profit. This framework establishes the operating relationships of people: who supervises whom, who reports to whom, what departments are formed, and what kind of work is performed in each department. This framework is known as a **formal organization**—*the official organization that top management conceives and builds.* A formal organization does not just happen; it is developed by managers through the organizing function of management.

formal organization
The official organization that top management conceives and builds.

Building an Organization: The Organizing Process

Managers use the organizing process to establish (and modify) the relationships between activities (what work people do) and authority (manager-subordinate relationships). The organizing process has five distinct stages, as shown in Figure 7.1. As you read the following description of the five-step process, refer to this figure to see how the organization structure is created for a hypothetical company, Excelsior Table Saw Corporation.

STEP 1: REVIEW OBJECTIVES AND PLANS A company's objectives and its plans to achieve them dictate its activities. Excelsior Table Saw plans to make and sell a top-quality table saw; its activities will be dictated by this objective. Some purposes, and thus some activities, are likely to remain fairly constant once a business is established. For example, the business will continue to seek a profit, and it will continue to employ people and other resources. But in time and with new plans, the ways in which basic activities are carried out will change. New departments may be created; old ones may be given additional responsibilities; some may cease to exist. New relationships between groups of decision makers may come into being as well. Organizing will create the new structure and relationships and modify the existing ones.

Examples of the relationship between planning and organizing—more specifically, how changes in plans affect the organization—can be seen in some of the changes taking place in business and industry:

Figure 7.1
The organizing process in action.

Step 1
Review objectives and plans

Excelsior Table Saw Corporation
Our aim: To manufacture and market the Mark IV table saw at a 10% return on investment.

Step 2
Determine activities

Hiring	Training	Assembling	Selling
Grinding	Shipping	Paying	Collecting
Bookkeeping	Inspecting	Recruiting	Compensating
Machining	Pricing	Advertising	Packaging

Step 3
Classify and group activities

Marketing	**Accounting**	**Personnel**	**Production**
Selling	Pricing	Recruiting	Machining
Advertising	Paying	Hiring	Grinding
Packaging	Bookkeeping	Training	Assembling
Shipping	Collecting	Compensating	Inspecting

Step 4
Assign the work and delegate authority

Benny Salazar Sales	Marcia Padilla Bookkeeping	Pat McCormick Payroll
Jacob Finsterbush Hiring	Sanjay Patel Collections	Lee Mai Advertising
Melody Kwan Assembly	Renée Montaigne Recruiting	Bill Vlasic Machining
Joyce Sabha Training	Frank Peña Shipping	Celeste Golushko Grinding

Step 5
Design a hierarchy

- Hughes Aircraft has realigned its divisions into units aimed at market segments—transportation, communication—instead of technology units. Hughes's new plans call for long-range development and application of military technology into peacetime use. The new structure will facilitate this goal.[1]
- CEO Paul Stern of Northern Telecom dismantled an organizational structure that divided the firm into units based on geographical boundaries. The new structure has created global product groups for research, manufacturing, and engineering so the firm can achieve its new objectives: (1) to make Northern Telecom a world, not just a Canadian, leader and (2) to help the firm create global, not regional, products.[2]
- United Technologies, following its plans to improve both its profitability and its competitive ability, reorganized its divisions to incorporate separate operating groups in the design and manufacture of commercial and military aircraft engines. Now Pratt & Whitney, Sikorsky Helicopter, and Hamilton Standard should be able to capitalize on the synergies that can exist among them.[3]

In addition to these specific company-related examples, a major organizational adjustment is taking place in business—downsizing. Companies are reviewing their operations and organizations and then **downsizing** by *eliminating positions, layers of middle management, and, in some instances, entire divisions, in light of competition, the economy, and global changes.* Companies are now "flatter," with fewer levels of management, and "leaner," with fewer employees on the payroll.

downsizing
Elimination of positions, layers of middle management, and entire divisions, in response to competition, the economy, and global changes.

STEP 2: DETERMINE ACTIVITIES The second step is for managers to ask what work activities are necessary to accomplish the company's objectives. Creating a list of tasks to be accomplished begins with identifying ongoing business tasks and ends with considering the tasks unique to this particular business. Hiring, training, and recordkeeping are part of the regular routine for running any business. But what, in addition, are the unique needs of this organization? Does it include assembling, machining, shipping, storing, inspecting, selling, advertising? It is important to identify all activities necessary, as is done for Excelsior Table Saws in Figure 7.1.

STEP 3: CLASSIFY AND GROUP ACTIVITIES Once managers know what tasks must be done, they can classify and group these activities into manageable work units. In Figure 7.1, this third step takes the jumble of Excelsior's tasks and creates four coherent groups of like activities. The principle of grouping together tasks that are similar in processes or needed skills is called functional similarity, or similarity of activity. This guideline is simple and logical to apply.

Managers perform three processes in carrying out this step:

1. Examine each activity identified to determine its general nature (marketing, production, finance, personnel, and so on).
2. Group the activities into these related areas.
3. Establish the basic department design for the organizational structure.

In practice, the first two processes occur simultaneously. Selling, advertising, shipping, and storing can be considered marketing-related activities. Thus they are grouped under the Marketing heading. Assembling, cutting, machining, welding, painting, and inspecting are manufacturing processes; they can be grouped as Production. Personnel-related activities include recruiting, hiring, training, and compensating.

As the tasks are classified and grouped into related work units (production, marketing, accounting, personnel), the third process, departmentalization, is being finalized; that is, a decision is being made on the basic organizational format or departmental structure for the company. **Departmentalization** is *the creation of groups, departments, or subdivisions that will execute and oversee the various tasks that management considers essential.* Management can choose one of four departmental types.

Functional departmentalization involves *the creation of departments on the basis of the specialized activities of the business*—finance, production, marketing, personnel (see Figure 7.2). The functional approach is the logical way to organize departments for most businesses. Excelsior Table Saw uses this approach. It is simple, groups the same or similar activities, simplifies training, and allows specialization.[4]

Geographical departmentalization *groups activities and responsibilities for each department according to territory* (Figure 7.2). Expanding companies often locate production plants, sale offices, and repair facilities in various areas of their markets to be near customers in order to serve them quickly and efficiently. Disney—with theme parks in Anaheim, Orlando, France, and Japan—uses geographical departmentalization for that aspect of its business.

Product departmentalization *assembles the activities of creating, producing, and marketing each product into separate departments* (Exhibit 7.2). This option is adopted when each product of a company requires a unique marketing strategy, production process, distribution system, or financial resources. Marketing oriented companies, such as Mattell, with many product categories, often capitalize on this approach.

Customer departmentalization *groups activities and responsibilities in departments in response to the needs of specific customer groups.* As shown in Exhibit 7.2, a company that markets products to three different customer groups—governments, businesses, and consumers—faces an extremely difficult task. Because each has different demands, needs, and preferences, each requires a unique strategy. Department stores have departments based on their customers: men, teens, women, children.

Although we have presented these department types individually, in reality

departmentalization
The creation of groups, departments, or subdivisions that will execute and oversee the various tasks that management considers essential.

functional departmentalization
The creation of departments on the basis of the specialized activities of the business.

geographical departmentalization
Groups activities and responsibilities for each department according to territory.

product departmentalization
Assembles the activities of creating, producing, and marketing each product into separate departments.

customer departmentalization
Groups activities and responsibilities in departments in response to the needs of specific customer groups.

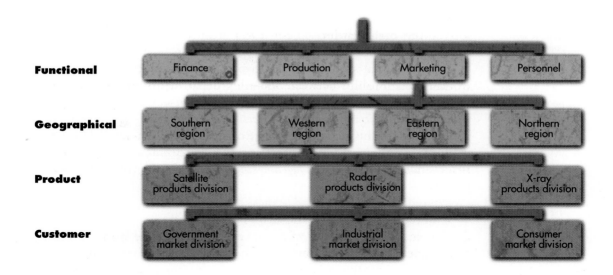

| Functional | Finance | Production | Marketing | Personnel |

| Geographical | Southern region | Western region | Eastern region | Northern region |

| Product | Satellite products division | Radar products division | X-ray products division |

| Customer | Government market division | Industrial market division | Consumer market division |

Figure 7.2
Methods of department-alization.

most companies use a combination of types to meet their needs. Large companies such as General Motors, AT&T, and Digital Equipment incorporate all these department types to meet their objectives.

STEP 4: ASSIGN THE WORK AND DELEGATE AUTHORITY Having identified the activities necessary to achieve objectives, classified and grouped these activities into major operational areas, and selected a departmental structure, management must now assign these activities to individuals and give them the appropriate authority to accomplish the task. This step is critical to the success of organizing.

When a company is reorganized, new departments or work groups need to be given tasks and authority. When Procter & Gamble inserted a new level into its management structure, the category manager, new activities were created, departmentalized, and assigned to that manager.[5] In the case of Apple Computer, a reorganization transferred responsibility for world-wide marketing of its software, hardware, enterprise solutions, and new personal electronics products from Apple USA to each of its product groups. As a result, the senior vice-president at Apple USA is no longer in charge of product marketing.[6]

STEP 5: DESIGN A HIERARCHY The final step is to determine the vertical and horizontal operating relationships of the organization as a whole. In effect, this step is putting together all the parts of the puzzle.

The vertical structuring of the organization results in a decision-making hierarchy that shows who is in charge of each task, each specialty area, and the organization as a whole. Levels of management are established from bottom to

YOU DECIDE

Consider an organization where you work now or have worked. What type of departmentalization is used? Why is this type used? What other departmentalization options would you recommend?

chain of command
The hierarchy of decision-making levels in the company.

span of control
The number of subordinates under the direction of a manager.

organization chart
A visual representation of an organization's structure and how its parts fit together.

Figure 7.3

The organization chart of Excelsior Table Saw Corporation.

top in the organization. These levels create the **chain of command**, or *hierarchy of decision-making levels, in the company.*

The horizontal structuring has two important effects: (1) it defines the working relationships between operating departments, and (2) it makes the final decision on the span of control of each manager. **Span of control** is *the number of subordinates under the direction of a manager.*

The result of this step is a complete organizational structure. This structure is shown by an **organization chart**, *a visual representation of an organization's structure and how its parts fit together* (see Figure 7.3). The organizational chart indicates:

1. Who reports to whom—the chain of command
2. How many subordinates work for each manager—the span of control
3. Channels of formal communication (the solid lines that connect each job)
4. How the company is departmentalized—by function, customer, or product, for example
5. The work being done in each job (the labels in the boxes)
6. The hierarchy of decision making (where the ultimate decision maker for a problem is located)
7. How current the organization structure is (if a date is on the chart)
8. Types of authority relationships (line authority, staff authority, and functional authority; these types of authority will be explained in the next section)

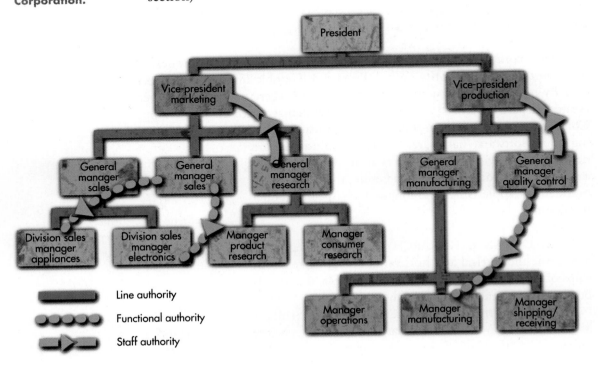

In addition, the chart is a troubleshooting tool. It can help managers locate duplications and conflicts that result from awkward arrangements. What the chart does not show are the degrees of authority, informal communication channels, and informal relationships, which we will discuss later in the chapter.

Benefits of the Organizing Process

The organizing process is not just important as a way to help the organization attain its purpose. It can also provide the following benefits:

1. *Clarifying the work environment.* Everyone knows what to do. The tasks and responsibilities of all individuals, departments, and major organizational divisions are clear. The type and limits of authority are determined.
2. *Creating a coordinated environment.* Confusion is minimized and obstacles to performance removed by defining the interrelationships of the various work units and establishing guidelines for interaction among personnel.

The organizing process, like all managerial functions, is ongoing. The initial application of the process results in the organization's first organizational structure and chart. As the organization begins its systematic pursuit of goals, management monitors and controls the company's actions, successes, and failures. Changes and reassignments will take place. New plans will dictate structural modifications after a new application of the organizing process. Thus, organizing should not be viewed as a one-time event.

Major Organizational Concepts

Now that we have discussed the organizing process, it is appropriate to examine some major organizational concepts and principles that managers apply in developing a workable system. These concepts include authority, unity of command, power, delegation, span of control, and the issue of centralization versus decentralization. A working knowledge of these concepts is essential to performing the organizing function.

Authority: The Concept and Application

When we discussed the fourth step of the organizing process—assignment of activities and delegation of appropriate authority—we introduced the concept of authority. In this section, we develop that concept in detail.

NATURE, SOURCES, AND IMPORTANCE OF AUTHORITY All managers in an organization have authority in varying degrees, depending on the level of management they occupy in the organization structure. **Authority** is *the formal, legitimate right of a manager to make decisions, give orders, and allocate resources.* It is the "glue" that holds the organization together, providing the means of command. How does a manager acquire authority?

authority
The formal, legitimate right of a manager to make decisions, give orders, and allocate resources.

Figure 7.4
The flow of line
authority.

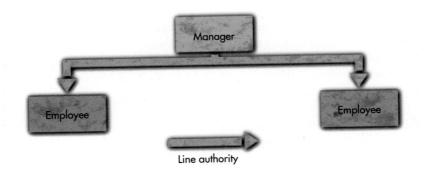

Line authority

It has been said that "authority comes with the territory," meaning that authority is vested in a manager because of the position he or she occupies in the organization. Thus, authority is defined in each manager's job description or job charter. The person who occupies a position has its formal authority as long as he or she remains in that position. As the job changes in scope and complexity, so should the amount and kind of formal authority possessed. As Albert Bersticker, CEO of Ferro Corp., a diversified organization composed of 100 individual business divisions, notes, "The Ivory Tower isn't dictating all corporate moves. What I stress from my management team is that they make the decisions. I won't tell a divisional manager what to do—I want him to decide how to fix it, tweak it, or get rid of it. The authority for decisions is theirs—that's what their job is."[7]

TYPES OF AUTHORITY In an organization, three different types of authority are created by the relationships between individuals and between departments.

line authority
Direct supervisory authority between a superior and a subordinate.

Line authority is *direct supervisory authority between a superior and a subordinate.* Any manager who supervises operating employees—or other managers—has line authority, allowing him or her to give direct orders to those subordinates, evaluate their actions, and reward or punish them. At Mrs. Fields Cookie Stores, the store manager has line authority over the employees. In an organization line authority flows downward directly from superior to subordinate, as Figure 7.4 illustrates.

staff authority
Authority to serve in an advisory capacity.

Staff authority is *the authority to serve in an advisory capacity.* Managers whose role it is to provide advice or technical assistance are granted advisory authority. This type of authority does not provide any basis for direct control over the subordinates or over activities of other departments with which the person holding staff authority consults; however, within the staff manager's own department, he or she can exercise line authority over subordinates. Staff authority, as advisory rather than direct control, will flow to the decision maker—usually upward. In Figure 7.5 both the legal department and the research department provide advice to the president.

functional authority
Authority to make decisions about specific activities undertaken by personnel in other departments.

Functional authority is *the authority to make decisions about specific activities undertaken by personnel in other departments.* Staff departments often have functional authority to control their systems' procedures in other depart-

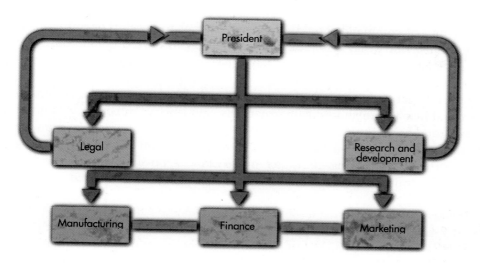

Figure 7.5
The flow of staff authority.

ments. This concept is shown in Figure 7.6, where the personnel manager must monitor and review compliance in operating departments for recruiting, selecting, and evaluation systems. But the personnel manager does not have the authority to tell the advertising personnel which products to promote or the manufacturing manager which products to manufacture.

Unity of Command

A concern of all managers in applying staff and functional authority is violation of the principle of **unity of command**: *the requirement that each person within the organization take orders from and report to only one person.*

unity of command
The requirement that each person in an organization take orders from and report to only one person.

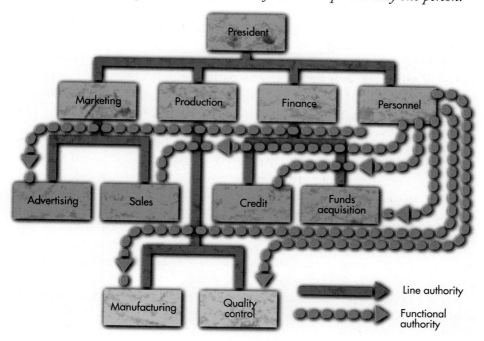

Figure 7.6
The flow of functional authority.

Unity of command should guide any attempt to develop operating relationships. But while it is ideal for each person to have only one boss, the operating relationships developed through staff departments mean that workers may have more than one supervisor in a given situation—or at least perceive that they do from the style with which advice is given. A departmental manager or subordinate may receive guidance or directives on a given day from the personnel department regarding employment practices, from the finance department on budget time frames, and from the data processing department concerning computer procedures. If possible, these situations should be minimized, or at least clarified, for the sake of all affected.

Power

Two managers could occupy positions of equal formal authority, with the same degree of acceptance of this authority by their employees, and still not be equally effective in the organization. Why? One manager may not possess the power to be as effective as another manager.

power
The ability to exert influence in an organization.

Power is *the ability to exert influence in an organization.* Having power can increase a manager's effectiveness by enabling him or her to influence people beyond what can be ascribed to the scope of formal authority. Authority is positional—it will be there when the incumbent leaves. Power is personal—it exists because of the person. Managers can acquire power from various sources:

- *Legitimate or position power.* Holding a managerial position, with its accompanying authority, provides a manager with a power base. The manager has the right to use power because of the position. The higher a manager sits in the organizational hierarchy, the greater is the "perceived

Managers wield legitimate power through the responsibilities assigned to them by their organization.

power"—power thought by subordinates to exist (whether or not it really does). Vice-presidents wield, or can wield, a lot of power.

Positional power also includes the power to reward or punish, because the manager has authority over raises, promotions, and preferential treatment. Likewise, the manager has the legitimate ability to withhold reward or initiate disciplinary action.

- *Referent power.* Power is also based on an individual's personality or charisma and how that personality is perceived by others. Adoration of and the desire to identify with and imitate a person are indications of this kind of power. It can be used effectively to motivate and lead others.

- *Expert power.* Expert power is held by persons who have demonstrated their superior skills and knowledge. They know what to do and how to do it. Others hope to stay on this person's good side to be able to benefit from his or her expertise.

> **YOU DECIDE**
>
> Which is more important to a manager, authority or power? Why? Can a manager be effective with only one, or are both necessary? Why?

Delegation

Delegation takes place because greater demands are placed on a manager as a company grows or because a manager wishes to develop subordinates. **Delegation** is *the downward transfer of formal authority from one person to another.*[8] Superiors delegate, or pass, authority to subordinates to facilitate work being accomplished.

> **delegation**
> The downward transfer of formal authority from one person to another.

One reason for a manager to delegate is to free himself or herself from some areas to be able to focus on more critical concerns. Delegation is also a valuable tool for training subordinates. Having capable subordinates can multiply the ability of a manager.

FEAR OF DELEGATION "When you fail to delegate, the monkey on your back gets fatter and fatter until it squashes you," says Paul Maguire, a senior partner of a management consulting firm.[9] But even knowing this, some managers do not delegate. Some managers fear giving up authority; others lack confidence in subordinates, worry that the employee may perform the job better than they do, are impatient, or are too detail oriented to let go. Some managers simply don't know how to delegate. Learning how to delegate is like learning to ride a bicycle—you have to learn to let go.[10] Delegation is not only a tool for survival, it is recognized as one of the key factors in a manager's success or failure.[11] The process itself involves two of the most important concepts in management: responsibility and accountability.

THE DELEGATION PROCESS Choosing to delegate authority sets a sequence of events in motion.

1. *Assignment of tasks.* The manager identifies specific tasks or duties to assign to the subordinate, then approaches him or her with those tasks. As an

example, Sharon's manager assigns her the task of designing an advertising campaign for the company's new client—The Hair Connection—a beauty salon.

2. *Delegation of authority.* For the subordinate to complete the duties or tasks, the authority necessary to do them should be delegated by the manager to the subordinate. A guideline for authority is that it be adequate to complete the task—no more and no less. In our example, Sharon is authorized to hire an artist and spend $10,000 on the campaign.

3. *Acceptance of responsibility. The obligation to carry out one's assigned duties to the best of one's ability* is called **responsibility**. Responsibility is not delegated by a manager to an employee; rather, the employee's acceptance of an assignment creates an obligation to do his or her best. When Sharon takes on The Hair Connection project and agrees to complete it by the deadline and within the budget, she becomes responsible to her boss for the project.

4. *Creation of accountability. Being answerable to others for the results of one's actions* is called **accountability**. It means accepting the consequences—either credit or blame—of these actions. When a subordinate accepts an assignment and the authority to complete it, he or she is accountable, or answerable, for his or her actions. At the same time, a manager is accountable for the use of his or her authority and performance and for the performance of subordinates. If Sharon misses the deadline, goes over the budget, or does not develop an acceptable advertising campaign, she is answerable to her boss—and her boss is accountable to his boss for assigning the project to her. On the other hand, if the project is completed as designed, Sharon will receive the credit—and the praise.

responsibility
The obligation to carry out one's assigned duties to the best of one's ability.

accountability
Being answerable to others for the results of one's actions.

Following this four-step process should ensure that the process of delegation produces clear understanding on the part of the manager and the subordinate. The manager should take the time to think through what is being assigned and to confer the authority necessary to achieve results. The subordinate, in accepting the assignment, becomes obligated (responsible) to perform, knowing that he or she is answerable (accountable) for the results.

Span of Control

As managers design the organizational structure, one of their concerns is the *span of control,* which, as we have seen, is the number of subordinates a manager directly supervises.

WIDE AND NARROW SPANS OF CONTROL As a general rule, the more complex a subordinate's job, the fewer such subordinates should report to a manager. The more routine the work of subordinates, the greater the number of subordinates that can be effectively directed and controlled by one manager. Because of these general rules, organizations always seem to have narrow

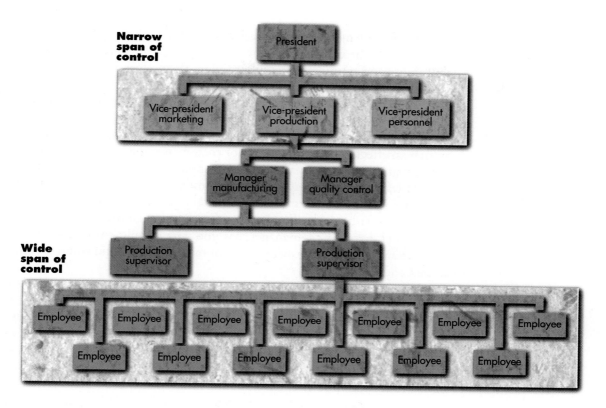

spans at their tops and wider spans at lower levels. The higher one goes in the organization's hierarchy, the fewer subordinates he or she will have (see Figure 7.7).

It is not uncommon to find a factory production supervisor with fifteen or more subordinates. Persons who can be well trained to follow procedures will, once they master their tasks, require less of their supervisor's time and energies. They will know what they must do and exactly how to do it to meet their performance standards.

Conversely, it is uncommon to find a corporate vice-president with more than three or four subordinates (Figure 7.7). Middle and upper managers perform little that is routine. Their tasks usually require ingenuity and creativity, and, because problems are more complex at this level, they are more difficult to resolve. These managers require more time to plan and organize their efforts. When they turn to their bosses for help, those bosses need to have the time available to render the assistance required. The only way to ensure having that time is to limit the number of people who will approach that boss for help—thus, a narrow span of control.

THE PROPER SPAN OF CONTROL Given these general rules, how many subordinates should any one manager have? The answer must be determined in terms of the specific manager and depends on many factors:

Figure 7.7

Narrow and wide spans of control.

- The complexity and variety of the subordinate's work
- The ability of the manager
- The ability and training of the subordinates themselves
- The supervisor's willingness to delegate authority
- The company's philosophy for centralization or decentralization of decision making

Setting an effective span of control for each manager is crucial to effectiveness. If a manager has too many people to supervise, his or her subordinates will be frustrated by their inability to get immediate assistance from or access to their boss. Time and other resources could be wasted, and plans, decisions, and actions might be delayed or made without proper controls or safeguards. On the other hand, if a manager has too few people to supervise, the subordinates might be either overworked or oversupervised and could become frustrated and dissatisfied.

Two managers who hold jobs at the same level in an organization should not automatically be assigned identical spans of control, because their abilities and those of their subordinates will differ. Managers' and subordinates' qualifications and experience must be considered when creating spans of control. The more capable and experienced the subordinates, the more that can be effectively supervised by one competent manager. The less time needed to train and acclimate people, the more time is available to devote to productivity. In general, spans can be widened as personnel develop experience and competence—thus the continuing need for training and development. Of course, this is true only up to the middle management level of the organization; there, the need for limited spans of control due to complexity becomes paramount.

Another factor that can influence a manager's span of control is the company's philosophy toward centralization or decentralization for decision making, as we will see in the next section.

Centralization Versus Decentralization

centralization
A philosophy of organization and management that concentrates authority within an organizational structure.

decentralization
A philosophy of organizing and management that disperses authority within an organizational structure.

Centralization is *a philosophy of organization and management that concentrates authority within an organizational structure*, while **decentralization** is *a philosophy of organizing and management that disperses authority within an organizational structure.*[12] Where authority resides is determined by an operating philosophy of management—either to concentrate authority for decision making in the hands of one or a few or to force it down the organization structure into the hands of many.

Centralization and decentralization are relative concepts. Top management may decide to centralize all decision making: purchasing, staffing, operations. Or it may decide to decentralize in part—setting limits on what can be purchased at each level by dollar amounts, giving first-level managers authority to hire clerical workers, and letting operational decisions be made where appropriate.

GLOBAL PERSPECTIVE

ABB, a global electrical equipment giant bigger than Westinghouse, has been described by a senior executive at Mitsubishi Heavy Industry as being "as aggressive as we are. I mean this as a compliment. They are sort of super-Japanese." This aggressiveness has been designed into the company by CEO Percy Barnevik.

In four years, Barnevik has welded ASEA, a Swedish engineering group, to Brown Boveri, a Swiss competitor, has bolted on 70 more companies in Europe and the United States, and has created a corporation that can go head to head with General Electric.

Barnevik has a formula and a working organizational design. When a business is acquired by ABB, the first step taken is to cut headquarters staff and decentralize. Barnevik's philosophy: "Ideally you should have a minimum of staff to disturb the operating people and prevent them from doing their jobs. When a company is acquired, the headquarters staff is reduced according to the following formula: 30 percent go into new companies, 30 percent are absorbed by operating units, and 30 percent are let go. By doing away with the centralized staffs, the decision making is in the hands of the line managers. The remaining staff at headquarters are truly coaches—rather than bureaucrats."

Barnevik has installed a matrix management structure that gives all employees two managers: a country manager and a business sector manager. The country managers run traditional national companies, while the business sector managers—such as for the power transformer business segment—provide leadership to that business. This matrix has resulted in allowing the use of technology and products from a variety of countries as well as providing for global coordination of each business segment. For example, every month the business segment headquarters tells all the factories in all the countries how each one is doing according to dozens of measurements. If one factory is lagging, solutions to common problems can be discussed and worked out across borders.

(For more on ABB, see Carla Rapaport, "A Tough Swede Invades the U.S.," *Fortune*, June 29, 1992, pp. 26–29.)

Swedish Giant ASEA-Brown Boveri: Designed to Compete

Honda's actions illustrate how the direction—centralization or decentralization—can change over the years. In March 1991 Honda President Nobuhiko Kawamoto abruptly reversed Honda's tradition of consensus management and shifted more decision making to the company's top executives. In June 1992, Kawamoto launched a reorganization that will decentralize authority back to lower levels of management. Referring to the initial decision as an interim move required to analyze the company's overall direction and operations, Kawamoto said the later decision is designed to give more decision-making authority to middle management. As Kawamoto noted, "I'm moving out of the day-to-day management. I have to take a broader view."[13]

To be effective, authority should be decentralized to the management level best suited to make the decision in question. A company president should not decide when to overhaul the engine in a forklift. Authority for that decision should be decentralized to the lowest possible level, in this case the plant maintenance manager.

More and more organizations see decentralization as a means to achieving greater productivity and rebuilding the organization. Decentralization is a way for managers to be closer to the action. As more organizations move toward "flatter" organizational structures with fewer levels of management, decentralization and accountability are becoming watchwords for management success.[14] Major corporations such as Mattel, General Foods, and Intercraft Industries are moving to a more decentralized philosophy of management.

Contemporary Organizational Structures

Formal organizational structures are developed by companies to help achieve their specific objectives. Since company objectives differ because of resources, stage of organizational development, and philosophies of management, the type of structure used to meet these objectives necessarily will differ. In addition, as companies and their objectives change, it is often necessary to adopt a new format. Management has five options from which to select. Three of those options—line, line-and-staff, and matrix structures—have been a foundation of organizational design for decades. But two other options—the team and network structure—are beginning to emerge in contemporary organizations.

The Line Organization Structure

line organization
A structure in which a straight line of authority originates from the top manager and connects each successive management level until it reaches the operating level.

The line organization structure is the simplest and the oldest form, having originated in military organizations. In **a line organization** *a straight line of authority originates from the top manager and connects each successive management level until it reaches the operating level,* as shown in Figure 7.8. The line

Figure 7.8
Line organization.

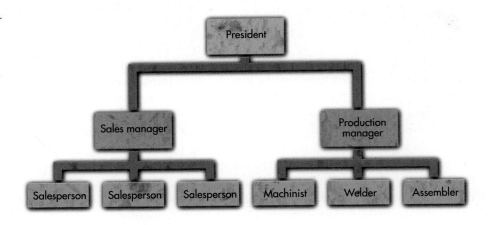

organization is based on direct authority. Each manager is responsible for making his or her own decisions. In making these decisions the manager is responsible for collecting and processing his or her own information without the assistance of specialists or staff advisers. This process provides for speed in decision making.

The line organization is most applicable to small businesses whose scope and volume of operations are limited. At Tony's Cafe in Plano, Texas, Tony Masillas is president and manager of this family-owned business. Tony is quite capable of handling all the responsibilities and performing the decision-making role.

The Line-and-Staff Organization Structure

As an organization grows in number of employees, complexity, and scope of operations, managers find it difficult to complete all their tasks with the same degree of effectiveness, because of time constraints or lack of special skills. Thus, large firms find it virtually impossible to operate effectively with a line organization. Widespread facilities, complex products, and sophisticated operations demand expert advice on such subjects as law, engineering, and human resources management. Consequently, growth forces a company to employ specialists in these areas and to convert to the second type of internal organization: line-and-staff.

The **line-and-staff organization** structure *blends into the line organization staff personnel that advise and serve the line managers.* The line managers make decisions and take actions that directly affect the firm's performance. The staff departments and their employees advise the line personnel and thus improve their decision-making effectiveness. Staff departments possess specialized or technical knowledge that enables them to provide assistance and expertise to line managers. Figure 7.9 presents an organization developed using the line-

line-and-staff organization
A structure that blends into the line organization staff personnel that advise and serve the line managers.

Figure 7.9
Line-and-staff organization.

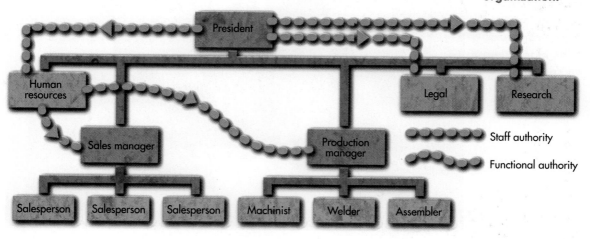

and-staff concept. In this organization the line manager is aided in decision making by human resources, legal, and research staff departments.

In a line-and-staff structure the three types of authority are present. Line managers possess line authority—direct supervisory authority over their departments and operations; they have the authority to make decisions and to compel action. Staff managers—human resources, legal, and research—possess staff authority. They are intended to advise line managers; they do not have the authority to give orders or force line managers to make certain decisions. Finally, some staff managers—human resources—are given functional authority: They have the authority to make decisions on specific activities undertaken by personnel in other departments.

The Matrix Organization Structure

The matrix approach to internal organization has received increasing attention in recent years. Sometimes referred to as a project organization structure, the **matrix organization** *temporarily groups together specialists from various departments or divisions to work on special projects.* When the project is completed, the specialists either return to their central area or are reassigned to another project.

The matrix approach is commonplace in aerospace companies where several simultaneous projects require the interaction of engineers, research and development scientists, and other specialized people. Figure 7.10 presents a matrix organization structure for an aerospace project. The departments—production, materials, human resources, engineering, and accounting—are permanent parts of the organization. The various project teams—Delta, Triton, and Corsair—are created as the need arises and are disbanded when the project is completed.

matrix organization
A structure that temporarily groups together specialists from various departments or divisions to work on special projects.

With a matrix organization, teams of experts from various departments are brought together for specific projects or tasks.

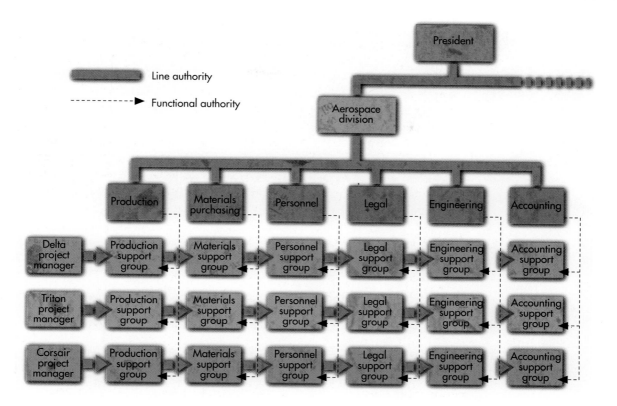

Figure 7.10
Matrix organization structure.

Members of the Delta project team are selected from the departments and are supervised for the duration of the project by the Delta project manager. During the course of the project, the technical team specialists have access to and can use the resources of their functional departments. The matrix approach utilizes the technical resources of an organization by efficiently allocating the expertise where and when it is needed.[15]

The Team Organization Structure

The newest and most potentially powerful approach to organizational structure is the team structure. The **team structure**—*organizing separate functions into a group based on one overall objective*—takes direct aim at the traditional organization hierarchy, whether line, line-and-staff, or matrix, and flattens it. Although the vertical chain of command is a powerful control device, it requires passing decisions up the hierarchy, which slows down the process. Such an approach also keeps responsibility at the top. The team approach calls for delegating authority, pushing responsibility down to lower levels, and creating teams of workers.

Rather than departments being structured by functional specialty, team departments are created. Team members representing various functions are grouped together, and a number of such teams report to the same supervisor. Although there are variations on this concept—some teams are responsible for a product, others for a process—the result is the same. The traditional

team structure
A structure that organizes separate functions into a group based on one overall objective.

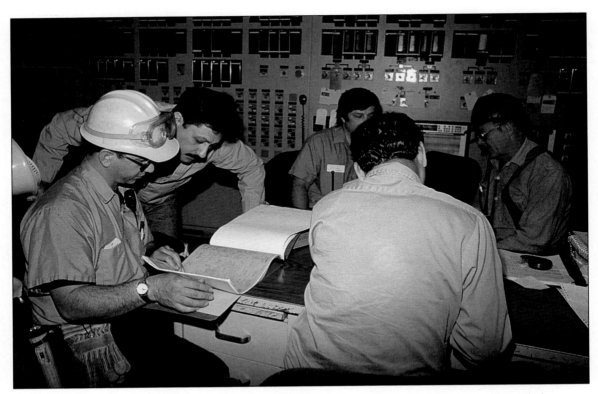

Under a team structure, team members jointly make important decisions, rather than leaving decision making to supervisors.

functions are reorganized, layers of management are removed, and the company becomes decentralized. An illustration of the reorganization of a line-and-staff functional structure to a horizontal team product structure is shown in Figure 7.11.

Although team structures can be found at Procter & Gamble, Quaker Oats, and General Foods, one representative illustration is GE's factory at Bayamon, Puerto Rico. The facility, which makes capacitors and power protection systems, employs 172 hourly workers and just 15 salaried supervisors-advisers, plus a factory manager. (A conventional plant would have twice as many salaried workers.) That translates to three layers of organization. Each hourly worker is on a ten-person team. The team owns part of the factory's overall work—assembly, shipping and receiving, and so on. But team members come from all areas of the plant, so that each group has representation from operations in the process. A supervisor-adviser sits in the back of the room and speaks up only if the team needs help.[16]

The team concept breaks down barriers across departments because knowing another person makes compromise easier. The team structure also speeds up decision making and response time: it is no longer necessary to go to the top of a hierarchy for approval. Another major

YOU DECIDE

Consider an organization where you work now or have worked. What type of organization structure is used? Do you consider it effective in meeting the company's objectives? Why? If a change were to be made in the type of organization structure, which one would you recommend? Why?

Figure 7.11
The development
of a team
structure.

From a line-and-staff functional structure . . .

. . . to the horizontal team structure

advantage is that employees are motivated. Taking responsibility for a project rather than a narrowly defined task results in enthusiasm and commitment. In addition, decentralization of authority eliminates unnecessary levels of managers, resulting in lower administrative costs.

The Network Organization Structure

The final approach to structure is known as the "dynamic network" organization. In the **network structure** *a small central organization relies on other organizations to perform manufacturing, marketing, engineering, or other critical functions on a contract basis.* In other words, rather than these functions being

network structure
A structure in which a small central organization relies on other organizations to perform manufacturing, marketing, engineering, or other critical functions on a contract basis.

Figure 7.12
A network
structure.

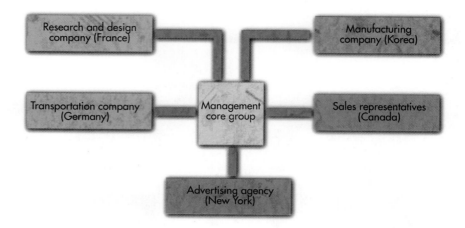

performed under one roof, they are purchased from outside services, as illustrated in Figure 7.12. This *practice of contracting with outside organizations to provide services normally performed inside a company* is known as **outsourcing**. The network structure is used by companies such as Nike and Esprit Apparel, which have booming businesses even though they own no manufacturing facilities and employ only a few hundred people. Rather than create the functions internally, they connect independent designers, manufacturers, and sales representatives to perform needed functions on a contract basis.[17] The network organization is the topic of this chapter's Manager's Notebook.

outsourcing
The practice of contracting with outside organizations to provide services normally performed inside a company.

Which Organizational Structure Is Best?

Because organization structures are created to achieve the objectives of the organization, there is no one best organization structure. A small business can best achieve its objectives through a line structure; a medium or large business would need the expert advice provided by the line-and-staff organization. A company specializing in custom production—car or van customizing—might select the team structure, while a company with an environment characterized by numerous projects may choose the matrix form. Each has its pros and cons. Table 7.1 examines the advantages and disadvantages of the five forms of organization.

The Informal Organization

Management has taken the time to develop the formal organization—departmental structures, decision-making guidelines, authority relationships, and designated managers—but existing within the formal organization is something management did not design: the informal organization.

**informal
organization**
A network of personal and social relationships that arises spontaneously as people associate in the work environment.

The **informal organization** is *a network of personal and social relationships that arises spontaneously as people associate in the work environment.*[18] It takes the form of the lunch bunch, the coffee-break group, the company bowling team, or just two

Table 7.1

Advantages and disadvantages of the five
major types of formal organizations.

TYPE OF ORGANIZATION	ADVANTAGES	DISADVANTAGES
Line	Decisions can be made faster. Authority, responsibility, and accountability are clearly placed. It is simple and sometimes less expensive to create and manage because no staff people are needed.	It omits the use of skilled specialists. All decisions tend to be made at upper levels, thus burdening top managers with minor details.
Line-and-staff	Staff employees provide specialized and technical information to line managers. Line managers need not be experts on highly technical subjects. Line managers' decisions may be better because of staff input.	Decisions may be delayed while staff people research problems and develop recommendations. Conflicts arise when some line managers resent staff's influence and expert status. Confusion results if staff-and-line authority and responsibility are not clear. Friction develops if staff members attempt to direct the activities of line personnel.
Matrix	Specialists in several functions can be assigned to various projects that require their expertise. Each project has a manager who devotes full time and effort to coordinating its success. Specialists benefit from working on a broad variety of challenging assignments.	Authority relationships between functional managers and project managers may be unclear. Employees may have difficulty serving two supervisors, the functional manager and the project manager. Project and functional managers may compete for recognition, status, and money. Specialists with long-term project assignments may identify more with the project than their functional area, thus distorting their perspective.
Team	Barriers between departments are removed. Employees are motivated because they have responsibility. Decisions and response times are faster.	Coordination time is increased because of numerous team meetings. Performance can suffer if the company does not provide training and time for learning.
Network	It provides flexibility because only the specific services needed are contracted for use. It keeps administrative overhead low.	Management has to rely on contracts, which results in less control. The reliability of supply is less predictable.

MANAGER'S NOTEBOOK

*Look Ma,
No Factory!*

What do Dell Computer, Chrysler, Nike, Reebok, and Brooks Brothers have in common? Besides profitability, each of these businesses has shunned the traditional organization structure and has evolved to a network organization. Each has chosen to focus on and nurture a few core activities—designing and marketing computers, autos, running shoes, or suits, for example—and has let outside specialists make the parts, handle deliveries, or do the accounting.

The network, or modular, organization is not a fad. Its streamlined structure fits today's fast-moving marketplace. Companies that have adopted the concept avoid becoming massive structures burdened with plants and bureaucracy. Instead they become exciting hubs surrounded by networks of the world's best suppliers. These manufacturing or service units are modular: they can be added or taken away with the flexibility of switching parts in a Lego set.

The adoption of the network organization and with it the outsourcing of noncore activities has two advantages: (1) it holds down the unit costs and investment needed to turn out new products rapidly, and (2) it frees companies to direct scarce capital where they hold a competitive advantage—doing market research, designing new products, hiring the best engineers, or training sales and service personnel.

The network organization works best when companies are able to achieve two objectives: collaborating smoothly with suppliers and focusing on the right specialty.

First, network companies need to find suppliers that are loyal, reliable, and able to rapidly retool their manufacturing facilities to rush out new products. Second, it is absolutely critical that the modular company has the vision to identify what the customers want, not just what the company is good at.

Two companies that have pioneered the network organization are Reebok and Dell Computer. Reebok has prospered by concentrating on its strength: designing and marketing high tech, fashionable footwear for sports and fitness. Reebok owns no plants. All footwear production is contracted to suppliers in Taiwan, South Korea, and other Asian countries.

Dell Computer prospers by concentrating on marketing and service, two areas where its competitors are vulnerable. Dell leases two small factories to assemble computers from outsourced parts. Freed from spending money on manufacturing plants, Dell pours it into training salespeople and service technicians and furnishing them with the best computers, databases, and software.

The network organization is a structure for the future. As more companies realize its potential, more will adopt the concept. Modular organizations are already flourishing in two industries that sell trendy products at a rapid tempo: apparel and electronics. But other important industries are becoming more network based, including steel, chemicals, and photographic equipment.

(For more on the network organization, see Julie Pitta, "Look, No Factory," *Forbes*, January 17, 1993, p. 113 and Shawn Tully, "The Modular Corporation," *Fortune*, February 8, 1993, pp. 106–114.)

people who meet to talk after work. It is a self-grouping of people because of shared interests, social and educational backgrounds, personalities, or needs.

The informal organization cuts across the formal organizational structure. It is not shown on the organization chart. People from different departments and different levels interact, find commonalities, support and assist each other, satisfy needs, and provide information. Membership in an informal group and in the informal organization is voluntary and is determined by the members of the group.

Managers need to understand and work with and through the informal organization. Why? Because it is present in all formal organizations, and ignoring it could lead to serious problems. Managers cannot prevent the informal organization from forming—people naturally interact and develop relationships. It is management's job to recognize and cultivate the informal organization. If approached correctly, the informal organization can aid in accomplishing the organization's objectives, provide stability, support the manager, and assist in providing information to members of the organization.

Figure 7.13 provides an illustration of the informal organization's communication system: the grapevine. Notice that most of the information is transmitted outside the formal channels. This system relies on word-of-mouth communication rather than memos. Information moves across as well as up and down the organization. By identifying and using the grapevine, managers can supply accurate information to combat rumors and to provide additional information to employees.

Figure 7.13

The informal organization's communication system: the grapevine.

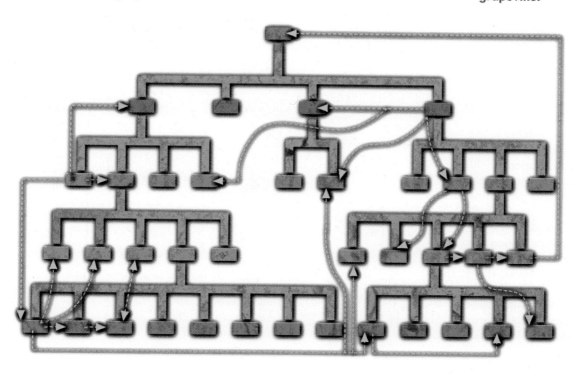

SUMMARY

A business is an organization created to provide a product or service to a customer at a profit. To reach these objectives, it must establish a framework of operating relationships of people and activities. This operating framework is known as the formal organization.

The formal organization is developed through a series of organizing steps: (1) review objectives and plans, (2) determine activities, (3) classify and group activities (functional, geographic or territorial, product, customer), (4) assign work and delegate authority, and (5) design a hierarchy of relationships. The result of this process is a formal organizational structure. This structure is shown visually by an organization chart.

Once the organization is developed, managers can apply several organizational concepts to assist the organization in achieving its objectives. These concepts include:

- *Authority.* The formal and legitimate right of a manager to make decisions, give orders, and allocate resources. There are three types of authority: line, staff, and functional.
- *Unity of command.* The requirement that each person within the organization take orders from and report to only one person.
- *Power.* The ability to exert influence in the organization. There are three sources of power: legitimate or position power, referent power, and expert power.

- *Delegation.* The downward transfer of formal authority to another person. It involves assigning tasks, conferring authority, exacting responsibility, and holding a person accountable.
- *Span of control.* The number of subordinates a manager directly supervises. There is no correct number to be assigned for each manager.
- *Centralization or decentralization.* A philosophy of management and organization that focuses on the selective concentration (centralization) or dispersal (decentralization) of authority within an organization structure. The application of this philosophy determines whether decision making is in the hands of a few or is forced down the organization structure.

There are five types of formal organizational structures: line, line-and-staff, team, matrix, and network. Each has its advantages and disadvantages. The structure selected will depend on the organization's objectives, stage of development, and philosophies of management.

Within the formal organization is the informal organization, a network of personal and social relationships that arises spontaneously as people associate with each other in the work environment. Managers need to recognize and work with the informal organization, as it assists them in meeting organization objectives.

KEY TERMS

accountability p. 198
authority p. 193
centralization p. 200
chain of command p. 192
customer departmentalization p. 190
decentralization p. 200
delegation p. 197
departmentalization p. 190
downsizing p. 189
formal organization p. 187
functional authority p. 194
functional departmentalization p. 190
geographical departmentalization p. 190
informal organization p. 208

line authority p. 194
line organization p. 202
line-and-staff organization p. 203
matrix organization p. 204
network structure p. 207
organization chart p. 192
outsourcing p. 208
power p. 196
product departmentalization p. 190
responsibility p. 198
span of control p. 192
staff authority p. 194
team structure p. 205
unity of command p. 195

FOR REVIEW AND DISCUSSION

1. What is a formal organization? How is it created?
2. List and explain each step of the organizing process.
3. What are the four forms of departmentalization? Under what situations would each be appropriate?
4. What information can be obtained from looking at an organization chart?
5. What is meant by the term *authority?* Where does a manager get his or her authority?
6. What is meant by the term *power?* How does it differ from authority?
7. What does the term *delegation* mean? How are delegation, authority, responsibility, and accountability related?
8. Is there a correct span of control? If your answer is no, what factors affect the span of control?
9. Distinguish between centralization and decentralization. What is the effect of each on decision making in an organization?
10. What are the advantages of a line organization? What size business should use a line organization?
11. What is the major difference between a line organization and a line-and-staff organization?
12. When would a matrix organization be applicable?
13. What are the advantages of team organization? What are the disadvantages?
14. What concept is basic to creating a network organization? What are the advantages of a network organization?
15. How does the informal organization come into existence? Who can be a member? What is the grapevine?

APPLICATIONS

Case 7.1: Downsizing: Recreating an Organization

Downsizing is currently a popular corporate tactic. Companies are laying off large numbers of employees in order to regain expected levels of profitability. Unfortunately, cutting out a company's human resources is a dangerous task. Although lowered labor costs do allow a company the appearance of "recovery" from tiny profits, they by no means ensure sustained, long-term growth.

A large downsizing effort dramatically changes the structure of an organization. Many companies fail to handle their downsizing efforts properly and lose key technical and management personnel. More important, layoffs often leave remaining employees with increased work responsibilities without increases in pay. The resulting morale and stress-related problems can cause major problems within an organization.

When considering a downsizing program, a company's leaders need to reevaluate their objectives and plans, establish which work activities are necessary, and redesign their chain of command and accountability. These steps must be performed, because the organization that emerges from a downsizing will be a different one from the one that entered it. In effect, the company will be re-creating itself.

Pointing out all of these requirements and problems, some analysts attempt to dissuade companies from downsizing, saying that the short-term results aren't worth it. One analyst points out that many valuable and experienced older employees have been lost by the early retirement efforts of downsizers. Other critics point out that there are better ways of restructuring, such as using retraining and new management techniques. Unfortunately, these criticisms are likely to be ignored, as companies continue with layoffs without considering the organization they will need to re-create.

Questions

1. In what ways is structuring a downsized organization like creating a new organization?

2. What changes in a company's plans or goals lead to downsizing efforts?

3. What are the advantages of downsizing?

4. What risks are involved in a downsizing?

For more information, see Joyce L. Kehl, "The New Trend in Downsizing," *Risk Management,* June 1993, p. 68; Robert Heller, "Turn-around Tricks Are a Short-Term Solution for Firms," *Management Today,* June 1993, p. 10; Madeleine A. Estabrook, "False Economics: Dowsizing as Cure Costs Valuable Older Workers," *Pension World,* May 1993, p. 10.

Case 7.2: Crises at GM

The future of General Motors is in the hands of President John Jack Smith—and he has his work cut out for him. The company continues to flounder. It lags behind its major competitors in almost every measure of efficiency. By some key standards—how many worker hours it takes to assemble a car, for example—GM is 40 percent less productive than Ford. In 1991 GM lost, on average, $1,500 on every one of the more than 3.5 million cars and trucks it made in North America. It ended 1991 with about 35 percent of the U.S. market; the company had sold fewer than 13 million new cars and light trucks that year. In comparison, in 1979 GM had commanded 46 percent of the market.

Salvaging GM, in the opinion of both insiders and outside observers, will require a radical restructuring. The company has a long tradition of being highly centralized and insulated from the rest of the industry. The current structure still reflects a time when the company had abundant time to work on any problem. The organizational problems that Smith faces include:

- The existence of separate marketing operations for each of it six car divisions: Chevrolet, Pontiac, Oldsmobile, Buick, Cadillac, and Saturn.
- The fact that GM, unlike any other auto company in the world, has a chief of design and a head of research who do not report to the auto-making side of the business. Instead, both report to the head of R&D, who in turn reports to another executive—a top-level manager who runs the aerospace division. This arrangement penalizes GM in two ways. Because designers do not work closely with vehicle engineers, development is long and costly. Second, scientists do not work with engineers, so GM is slow to apply new technologies even when GM developed them.
- A past history of poor managerial performance without accontability. Fewer than 100 salaried workers out of well over 100,000 were dismissed annually for poor performance between 1977 and 1983.
- A nonfunctioning decision-making structure. Middle managers—sometimes referred to as the "frozen middle"—have often been unable or unwilling to make decisions.

Questions

1. For each of the four situations noted, what organizational concepts apply? Explain.

2. As an adviser to President John Jack Smith, how would you resolve each situation?

For more information, see Alex Taylor, "Can GM Remodel?" *Fortune,* January 13, 1992, pp. 26–29, 32–34.

REFERENCES

1. James R. Healey, "Hughes Aircraft to Lay Off 9,000," *USA Today,* July 1, 1992, p. 1B.
2. Michael A. Verespej, "Stern Hand," *Industry Week,* February 17, 1993, p. 25.
3. Anthony L. Velocci, "United Technologies Restructures in Bid to Boost Profitability, Competitiveness," *Aviation Week and Space Technology,* January 27, 1993, p. 35.
4. R. L. Daft, *Organization Theory and Design* (St. Paul, Minn.: West Publishing, 1983), p. 227.
5. Briane Dumaine, "P&G Shouts for the Top," *Industry Week,* January 6, 1992, pp. 24–25.
6. Tom Quinlan, "Apple Shakes Up Marketing Division," *Info World,* March 16, 1993, pp. 1, 8.
7. Brian S. Moskal, "The Buck Doesn't Stop Here," *Industry Week,* July 15, 1992, pp. 29–30.
8. W. Richard Plunkett, *Supervision,* 6th ed. (Needham Heights, Mass.: Allyn and Bacon, 1992), p. 70.
9. Roz Ayers-Williams, "Mastering the Fine Art of

Delegation," *Black Enterprise,* April 1992, pp. 91–93.

10. Paul Hellman, "Delegating Is Easy, Deputizing a Posse Is Tough," *Management Review,* June 1992, p. 58.

11. Alex Taylor, "Chrysler's Next Boss Speaks," *Fortune,* July 27, 1992, pp. 82–85.

12. Harold Kountz and Cyril O'Donnel, *Management* (New York: McGraw-Hill, 1976), p. 375.

13. Clay Chandler, "Honda's Middle Managers Will Regain Authority in New Overhaul of Company," *Fortune,* July 27, 1992, p. 173.

14. Philip Spertus, "It's Easy to Fool the Boss," *Management Review,* May 1992, p. 28.

15. Lawton R. Burns, "Matrix Management in Hospitals: Testing Theories of Matrix Structure and Development," *Administrative Science Quarterly* 34 (1989), pp. 349–368.

16. Thomas A. Stewart, "The Search for the Organization of Tomorrow," *Fortune,* May 18, 1992, pp. 93–94.

17. Herbert G. Ramrath, "Globalization Isn't for Whiners," *The Wall Street Journal,* April 6, 1992, p. C27.

18. Keith Davis and John Newstrom, *Human Behavior at Work: Organizational Behavior,* 8th ed. (New York: McGraw-Hill, 1989), p. 262.

8

HUMAN RESOURCES MANAGEMENT

W

hen an industry
is in turmoil,
productivity and
people become the name of
the game. That's where we get
our edge.

W. J. CONATY
Vice-President of Human Resources
Aircraft Engines, Inc.

CHAPTER OBJECTIVES
After studying this chapter, you
should be able to:

1. Summarize the nature and importance of human resources management.
2. Explain the impact of equal employment opportunity and affirmative action programs on
human resources management.
3. Describe the process involved in
human resources planning.
4. Describe internal and external
sources for human resources recruitment.
5. Outline the selection process and
describe each step.
6. Describe the purposes of an employee orientation program.
7. Describe the purposes and methods of employee training and development.
8. Identify and explain the purposes
and types of performance appraisal.
9. Distinguish among employee promotions, transfers, demotions,
and separations.
10. List and explain the methods of
employee compensation.

UP FRONT

Jean Temkin graduated from the University of Maryland with a degree in personnel and labor relations. Over the next four years, she worked at a management consulting firm, at a pension administration firm, and at property management and construction companies, learning about her chosen field. She learned about recruiting, hiring, job applications, timesheets, job descriptions, performance appraisals, temporary agencies, health and education benefits, hiring and severance, pension plans, preparing quarterly and annual reports, and writing reports, personnel manuals, and company newsletters. This in-depth experience in a variety of positions led to her position as human resources manager at United Communications Group, an electronic information provider and publisher of over thirty newsletters. UCG, with headquarters in Rockville, Maryland and offices in New Jersey and Boston, employs over 200 people, many of whom are writers, editors, and people who collect and disseminate information in computerized databases.

Temkin's days are filled with a variety of activities, from planning and scheduling various company-related activities to meetings with managers and employees to using the company's computerized human relations information system. "I do a lot of computer work with the human resources information system," she says, "but I spend a lot more time with people. My job requires compassion and empathy, because I have to help UCG employees try to solve all kinds of differ-

ent problems. But sometimes I also need to be firm, because I'm responsible for representing the company's interests, too."

People come to Temkin for help with all kinds of issues. "People are often dissatisfied with a work situation or have a conflict with their supervisor or another employee. That's just part of life and work. They might have a question or a problem regarding their health insurance or their pension plan. I also get involved in new employee orientations and outplacement interviews. But whatever I'm doing, when someone comes to me with a problem, I have to set aside whatever I am doing and help them. People always come first."

Temkin performs a variety of administrative duties during the course of a normal work day. "You have to be very good at prioritizing in this work," she says, "because you wear many different hats and are constantly juggling tasks. I might be conducting a survey for health insurance programs, writing a new benefits brochure, planning a company event or function, administering the college tuition reimbursement program, updating the company's personnel manual, or evaluating the pension plan. And given that we're a rapidly growing company, I'm often in meetings with the director of human resources and the chief executive officer to find ways to improve human resources services."

JEAN TEMKIN

HUMAN RESOURCES MANAGER, UNITED COMMUNICATIONS GROUP

An ongoing task is researching and evaluating health benefits plans. "The services and costs are very competitive these days, and you have to constantly stay on top of things. I'm always shopping for a better plan. It's common today for companies to offer two plans to employees. One is the traditional indemnity plan, such as Blue Cross/Blue Shield, where you pay a deductible. The other is managed care, the health maintenance organization, or HMO, where services are provided for a flat fee. The trend seems to be toward managed care, and it will be interesting to see what role the federal government takes regarding public versus private health care over the next few years."

Jean Temkin likes working in human resources because it offers so much variety. "There are many ways to approach a career in HR; it's a very diverse field. It's also an essential part of business. Even though it isn't a revenue-producing job, a bad HR person can cost a company a lot of money. You can't run a modern company without it; that's why many HR directors report directly to the CEO. A happy worker is a good worker, and HR keeps workers happy."

"**Y**ou are only as good as your people" is an often-heard saying in management. An organization can have outstanding plans, but if it does not have the quality employees to carry those plans out, it is back to square one. For an organization to survive and prosper, it must be able to identify, select, develop, and retain qualified personnel. People are the most important resource of an organization. They supply the talent, skills, knowledge, and experience to achieve the organization's objectives.

The Importance of Human Resources Management

The importance of the human factor in an organization has been emphasized by Ben Tregoe, corporate strategy expert and chairman of Kepner-Tregoe:

> One of the most serious reasons for America's lack of competitiveness is that top management does not understand that human resources and human issues are critical to the organization. More and more companies, as they move into global competitiveness, see that the one thing that can make a difference in the world market is people. Raw material, technology, and systems are available to everybody. The right people can be a unique commodity.[1]

Through the planning function, management determines the objectives for the organization. In turn these objectives are analyzed through the organizing function to identify activities necessary to achieve the objectives. Ultimately, the activities form the basis for either creating or modifying job positions in the organization. The challenge at this point is for management to match personnel with the jobs identified and to provide for employees' long-range growth and welfare as members of the organization.

human resources management
The staffing function of an organization.

    Human resources management is *the staffing function of an organization.* Sometimes called personnel management, it includes such activities as human

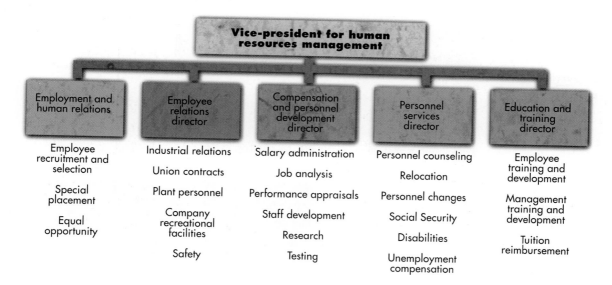

Vice-president for human resources management				
Employment and human relations	Employee relations director	Compensation and personnel development director	Personnel services director	Education and training director
Employee recruitment and selection	Industrial relations	Salary administration	Personnel counseling	Employee training and development
Special placement	Union contracts	Job analysis	Relocation	Management training and development
Equal opportunity	Plant personnel	Performance appraisals	Personnel changes	Tuition reimbursement
	Company recreational facilities	Staff development	Social Security	
	Safety	Research	Disabilities	
		Testing	Unemployment compensation	

resources planning, recruitment, selection, orientation, training, development, performance appraisal, and compensation. In small- to medium-sized organizations the individual manager tends to be responsible for the staffing function. As companies expand operations and need more people, a decision normally is made to employ a **human resources manager** (or a personnel manager), *a specialist who handles the more technical human resources matters.* The activities involved in human resources management are then grouped in a human resources or personnel department, as illustrated in Figure 8.1. Managers in this department, such as the director of education and training, assist line managers by planning, organizing, staffing, coordinating, controlling, and sometimes executing specific personnel and human resources management (P/HR) functions.

Figure 8.1

Example of the responsibilities and organization of a human resources department.

human resources manager
A specialist who handles the more technical human resources matters.

The Human Resources Process

The activities involved in human resources management can be grouped in a series of steps that managers and specialists perform to provide the organization with the right people in the right positions. Figure 8.2 illustrates the human resources process. The eight steps in the process are:

1. *Human resources planning.* The purpose of human resources planning is to ensure that the personnel needs of the organization will be met. An analysis of the plans of the organization will determine what skills will be needed. Then management can review the current inventory of skills of the organization and develop a plan to provide the quantity and quality of personnel needed in the future.
2. *Recruitment.* After the human resource needs are determined, managers undertake recruitment to locate prospective employees. They may do so through newspaper and professional journal advertisements, employment

Figure 8.2
The human resources process.

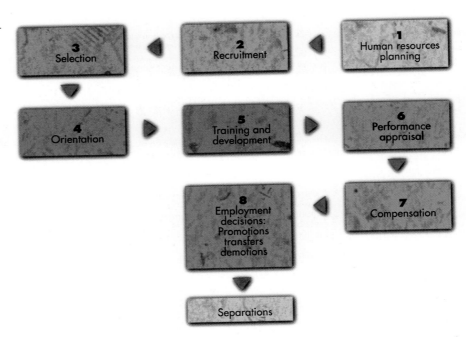

agencies, contacts at trade schools or colleges, or internal sources of the organization.

3. *Selection.* The selection process involves evaluating the candidates and choosing the one whose credentials match job requirements. The steps in the selection process may include application forms, interviews, reference checks, and physical examination.

4. *Orientation.* This step integrates the selected employee into the organization. Processes include being socialized into the work group and becoming acquainted with the organization's policies and rules.

5. *Training and development.* Both training and development are concerned with improving the employee's ability to contribute to organizational effectiveness. Training involves the improvement of employee skills. Development concerns the preparation of the employee for additional responsibility or advancement.

6. *Performance appraisal.* This step is one of appraising the employee's performance in relation to job standards and then providing feedback to the employee.

7. *Compensation.* Compensation involves determining an employee's initial wages, making changes to wages, and offering accompanying benefits.

8. *Employment decisions: promotions, transfers, demotions, and separations.* Performance appraisal results in management's making employment decisions that include transfers, promotions, demotions, layoffs, or firings.

Before we undertake an in-depth explanation of each step, it is important to examine some important factors that influence these steps—the legal and social-cultural environments.

The Legal and Social-Cultural Environments of Human Resources Management

The activities, actions, and decisions of all aspects of human resources management are subject to influence from external environments. The specific influences are from the legal and social-cultural environments.

The Legal Environment

Legislation has been enacted that directly affects managers with staffing responsibilities. Executive orders and laws generated by federal, state, county, and city agencies regulate how companies, usually those with fifteen or more employees, must conduct staffing. So complex are these regulations, and so great is the potential for harm due to noncompliance, that many large companies and institutions hire attorneys and specialists to deal with reporting and disclosure requirements.

Table 8.1 highlights federal laws regarding three topics: equal employment opportunity, affirmative action, and sexual harassment. Here we briefly review each topic.

Table 8.1

Legislation related to human resources management.

FEDERAL LEGISLATION	DESCRIPTION OF PROVISIONS
Equal Pay Act of 1963	Prohibits lower pay to employees of one sex than to employees of the opposite sex for doing roughly equivalent work. Applies to private employers.
Title VI 1964 Civil Rights Act	Prohibits discrimination in staffing decisions based on race, color, religion, sex, or national origin. Applies to employers receiving federal financial assistance.
Title VII 1964 Civil Rights Act—Amended 1972	Prohibits discrimination in staffing decisions based on race, color, religion, sex, or national origin. Applies to private employers of 15 or more employees; federal, state, and local governments; unions; and employment agencies.
Executive Orders 11246 and 11375 (1965)	Prohibit discrimination in staffing decisions based on race, color, religion, sex, or national origin. Establishes requirements for affirmative action plans. Applies to federal contractors and subcontractors.
Age Discrimination in Employment Act of 1967—Amended 1978	Prohibits age discrimination in staffing decisions against people over 40 years of age. Applies to all employers of 20 or more employees.
Title I 1968 Civil Rights Act	Prohibits interference with a person's exercise of rights with respect to race, color, religion, sex, or national origin.
Rehabilitation Act of 1973	Prohibits discrimination in staffing decisions on the basis of certain physical and mental handicaps by employers doing business with or for the federal government.

(continued)

Table 8.1

(continued)

FEDERAL LEGISLATION	DESCRIPTION OF PROVISIONS
Vietnam Era Veterans Readjustment Act of 1974	Prohibits discrimination in staffing decisions against disabled veterans and Vietnam era veterans.
Privacy Act of 1974	Establishes the right of employees to examine letters of reference concerning them unless the right is waived.
Revised Guidelines on Employee Selection, 1976, 1978, and 1979	Establish a single set of guidelines for discrimination on the basis of race, color, religion, sex, and national origin. The guidelines provide a framework for making legal employment decisions about hiring, promoting, demoting; for the proper use of tests; and for other selection procedures.
Pregnancy Discrimination Act of 1978	Prohibits discrimination in employment based on pregnancy, childbirth, or related medical conditions.
Equal Employment Opportunity Guidelines of 1981—Sexual Harassment	Prohibits sexual harassment if such conduct is an explicit or implicit condition of employment, if the employee's response becomes a basis for employment or promotion decisions, or if it interferes with an employee's performance. The guidelines protect men and women.
Equal Employment Opportunity Guidelines of 1981—National Origin	Identifies potential national origin discrimination to include fluency-in-English job requirements and denying employment because of foreign training or education. Identifies national origin harassment in the work environment to include ethnic slurs and physical conduct with the purpose of creating an intimidating or hostile environment or unreasonably interfering with work.
Equal Employment Opportunity Guidelines of 1981—Religion	Determines that employers have an obligation to accommodate religious practices of employees unless they can demonstrate this would result in undue hardship. Accommodation may be achieved through voluntary substitutes, flexible scheduling, lateral transfer, and change of job assignment.
Mandatory Retirement Act— Amended 1987	Determines that an employee cannot be forced to retire before age 70.
Americans with Disabilities Act of 1990	Prohibits discrimination in staffing decisions on the basis of physical or mental handicap.
Civil Rights Act of 1990	Permits recovery of punitive and compensatory damages for intentional discrimination and provides for jury trials, if requested.

EQUAL EMPLOYMENT OPPORTUNITY Some federal laws are designed to guarantee **equal employment opportunity**, *prohibiting discrimination in employment decisions.* **Discrimination** means *using illegal criteria in hiring.* Antidiscrimination laws are enforced by the Equal Employment Opportunity Commission (EEOC).

Under current federal law, it is unlawful for an employer:

1. To fail or refuse to hire or to discharge an individual solely on the basis of race, color, religion, sex, age, national origin, or handicap
2. To limit, segregate, or classify employees or applicants for employment in any way that would tend to deprive the individual of employment opportunities solely on the basis of race, color, religion, sex, age, national origin, or handicap

Federal law has created protected groups that include women, the handicapped, and the following minorities:

- Hispanics: Spanish-surnamed Americans
- Orientals: Asians or people from the Pacific Islands
- Blacks not of Hispanic origin: African Americans
- American Indians: native peoples of North America
- Alaskan Natives: Eskimos

By law, managers must refrain from employment decisions that produce a disparate impact on members of any protected group. A **disparate impact** refers to *any part of the employment process resulting in a significantly higher percentage of a protected group being rejected than the percentage of a nonprotected group.* Examples would be not hiring an applicant because she is a woman or using an employment test that eliminates a significantly greater percentage of Hispanics than whites. Both such actions would be considered discriminatory under law. The organization and the managers involved could be subject to criminal penalties.

To avoid breaking equal opportunity laws, managers should avoid using any criteria not related to the job when making decisions to recruit, hire, promote, train, develop, reward, or fire an employee. (This chapter's Manager's Notebook focuses on the Americans with Disabilities Act, which prohibits discrimination on the basis of physical or mental handicap.)

Seven states and about twenty municipal governments have added homosexuals to the list of protected groups. Doing so forbids, in applicable jurisdictions, employment discrimination on the basis of sexual orientation or sexual preference. Many firms have developed their own policies. MCA (a unit of Matsushita Electric Industrial Company and the parent of Universal Studios) has adopted nondiscrimination policies regarding homosexuals as have Fox, Inc. and Disneyland.[2]

equal employment opportunity
Prohibition of discrimination in employment decisions.

discrimination
Using illegal criteria in hiring.

disparate impact
Any part of the employment process resulting in a significantly higher percentage of a protected group being rejected than the percentage of a nonprotected group.

affirmative action
Requiring employers to make an extra effort to hire and promote members of protected groups.

AFFIRMATIVE ACTION Some laws go beyond prohibiting discrimination. Laws that mandate **affirmative action** *require employers to make an extra effort to hire and promote members of protected groups.* Affirmative action laws apply to employers that have, in the past, practiced discrimination or failed to develop a work force that is representative of the whole population of their community. (Under current laws, affirmative action is not required with regard to disabled Americans.) The fact that an organization has an affirmative action plan does not necessarily mean that the organization practiced unfair employment practices in the past, however. Managers of many organizations choose to develop affirmative action plans even when the law does not require them to do so. Affirmative action plans must identify how the organization plans to take aggressive or affirmative steps in recruiting, hiring, developing, and promoting, and ultimately how it will achieve greater representation of and equity for protected groups.

YOU DECIDE

Why do you think discrimination in employment occurs? If you were discriminated against, what would you do? Why?

sexual harassment
Unwelcome sexual advances, requests for sexual favors, or verbal or physical conduct of a sexual nature on the job.

SEXUAL HARASSMENT Title VII of the Civil Rights Act and guidelines established by the EEOC prohibit sexual harassment.[3] **Sexual harassment** includes *unwelcome sexual advances, requests for sexual favors, and other verbal or physical conduct of a sexual nature on the job* when

- Submission to such conduct is an explicit or implicit term or condition of employment.
- Submission to or rejection of such conduct is used as a basis for any employment decision.
- Such conduct has the purpose of unreasonably interfering with the individual's work performance or creating an intimidating, hostile, or offensive working environment.

This issue exploded into the national spotlight in 1991 when hearings of the Senate Judiciary Committee were broadcast on television. The hearings concerned allegations of sexual harassment made by Anita Hill, a University of Oklahoma law professor, about her ex-boss, Clarence Thomas, who was then a nominee for the Supreme Court. The hearings produced a renewed focus on the importance and consequences of sexual harassment. Managers in every industry should work to prevent harassment and establish procedures for dealing with it properly when it does occur. Sexual harassment can severely damage morale and undermine productivity and quality.

Violations of sexual harassment laws can be expensive. Settlements have been as large as $500,000. Louis W. Brydges, Jr., a management-labor attorney in Chicago, urges companies to create a policy statement telling everyone in the workplace that sexual harassment will not be tolerated and that those engaging in it will be disciplined.[4]

The Social-Cultural Environment

Issues and trends in the social-cultural environment also affect human resources management. These issues include cultural diversity, glass ceilings and glass walls, AIDS, and drug testing.

CULTURAL DIVERSITY The ethnic composition of the U.S. labor force is changing. This increased **cultural diversity** is evidenced by *the fact that minorities—African Americans, Hispanics, and Asians—are collectively becoming the majority in the workplace.* This cultural diversity requires new human resources management approaches.

In the past, most managers tried to create a homogeneous work force—to treat everyone in the same way and make people fit the dominant corporate culture. These efforts did not always build a stable, committed group of employees. What was needed—and what is rapidly appearing in enlightened corporations—was respect for what workers from different backgrounds bring to the workplace. Across America, managers are participating in workshops designed to facilitate understanding among diverse groups, not just tolerance of one another's existence.

One innovator in the effort to build respect for diversity is Levi Strauss & Co. of San Francisco. For several years the company has conducted workshops to help employees air grievances and dispel tension in the workplace. Through these sessions, workers and managers gain new insights and appreciation for differing perspectives and cultural values. With the growing emphasis on teams and the increasing presence of managers from other countries and cultures, employees and managers must learn to tap the power that comes from differing points of view.

GLASS CEILINGS AND GLASS WALLS The terms *glass ceiling* and *glass wall* refer to invisible barriers of discrimination that block the careers of women and other protected groups.[5] A **glass ceiling** is *discrimination that keeps women out of upper-level management jobs.* A **glass wall** is *discrimination that prevents women from pursuing fast-track career paths.* Do these invisible barriers exist? The data indicate that *something* is keeping women and other protected groups out of the top jobs. A federal study that surveyed ninety-four major corporations revealed that only 16.9 percent of managers at all levels were women and only 6 percent were minority group members. Among top managers, only 6.6 percent were women and 2.6 percent were minorities. These numbers suggest one reason why women earn about 72 cents for every $1 earned by men.[6]

Catalyst, a nonprofit research organization that focuses on women's issues in the workplace, conducted another survey about job discrimination. It revealed that human resources managers often steer women away from jobs in marketing and production. Stereotyped as support providers, women end up in staff positions. One reason for the continuation of the stereotype is that

cultural diversity
The fact that minorities—African Americans, Hispanics, and Asians—are collectively becoming the majority in the workplace.

glass ceiling
Discrimination that keeps women out of upper-level management jobs.

glass wall
Discrimination that prevents women from pursuing fast-track career paths.

Some companies are dealing with the "glass ceiling" by offering specialized training and mentorships for female managers.

many men, especially in the upper ranks of management, feel uncomfortable dealing with women. The Catalyst study suggested that women should "find out what type of experience companies require of their executives and then seek to get it." The report also suggested that "companies should create programs to encourage mentoring and career development and to discourage gender stereotyping."[7]

The cost of discrimination against women can be high in terms of lost morale, commitment, and productivity. Penalties can be high as well. State Farm paid $157 million to settle a case filed by 814 women. The women claimed that, because of their sex, State Farm had refused to give them lucrative sales jobs. In addition to the settlement, the women's claims led to changes in the way State Farm agents are recruited and hired in California. An affirmative action plan, in place since 1988, requires the company to hire women for 50 percent of the sales agent jobs to be filled through 1998.

Many companies recognize that glass ceilings and glass walls exist and have worked hard to eliminate them. American Airlines requires corporate officers to submit detailed, cross-functional plans regarding the development of all high-potential women in middle management and above.[8] Anheuser-Busch has a management development program that moves women and minorities from jobs in inventory to jobs as coordinators and then to supervisory positions. Johnson & Johnson, the pharmaceutical giant, operates workshops to sensitize managers and supervisors to the problems of those striving for the top. The company has a significant number of women and minorities in high positions.[9]

AIDS Acquired immune deficiency syndrome (AIDS) is a frightening condition that—until medical progress can prevent it—leads to death. HIV, the virus that causes AIDS, cannot be casually transmitted. But fear of AIDS is a reality in the workplace. Companies need policies telling employees and managers how to deal with the issue. Federal law prohibits discrimination against employees suffering from AIDS and any other contagious diseases. Will a company accommodate the employee who does not want to work with an employee who has HIV? What will management do when an employee's routine physical reveals that he or she is HIV-positive?

DRUG TESTING Most of America's largest companies have had experience with employees who are suffering from some sort of drug addiction. Yet fewer than half of these companies have drug policies. Employees addicted to drugs can and do cause losses to their companies, themselves, and others. Workers with drug problems compromise safety, quality, and productivity. One study estimated the loss from drug-related absenteeism and turnover in the United States to be nearly $50 billion a year.

According to the 1990 Americans with Disabilities Act, drug-addicted employees are protected from discrimination if they are currently enrolled in legitimate drug-interdiction programs or have completed such programs and are drug-free. Testing for drugs raises issues about employee privacy, because most drug tests involve blood and urine analysis. These tests can reveal conditions that an employer has no business knowing about. In addition, drug tests can produce false positive results. Many companies require drug testing for all applicants, and some require random testing of current employees involved in work that can be hazardous to themselves or others.

Human Resources Planning

Well-managed firms must forecast future personnel needs carefully. They are far too important to be left to guesswork. **Human resources planning** is *the process of forecasting the demand for and supply of personnel for an organization.* It has three parts: (1) forecasting personnel requirements, (2) comparing these requirements with the talents of current employees, and (3) developing specific plans for whom to train and develop (from inside) and how many people to recruit (from outside the company). Figure 8.3 illustrates the human resources planning process.

human resources planning
The process of forecasting the demand for and supply of personnel for an organization.

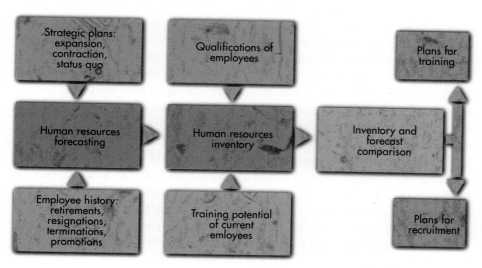

Figure 8.3

The human resources planning process.

Job Analysis

Before meaningful efforts can be made to determine personnel needs, all existing jobs need to undergo a **job analysis**, *a study that determines the duties associated with a job and the skills required to perform it.* Various methods exist for making an in-depth study of a job. Some companies use personnel/HR specialists (called job analysts) working with the job holder (where one exists) and the supervisor for each job under study. They use a combination of methods, including (1) observation of the job holder executing his or her duties, (2) questionnaires filled in by both the job holder and his or her supervisor, (3) interviews with these two parties by a skilled job analyst, and (4) formation of a committee to analyze, review, and summarize the results.

The result of job analysis is the preparation of two documents: the job description and the job specification. The **job description** *outlines the job's title, purpose, major work activities, levels of authority, equipment, machines and materials used, and physical demands or hazardous conditions (if any).* See Figure 8.4 for an example. The **job specification** *lists the human dimensions of the job, including the education, experience, skills, training, and knowledge required for a worker to perform the job successfully.* Care must be taken to list only those factors that are directly linked to successful work to avoid accusations of discrimination. See Figure 8.5 for a sample of a job specification.

Jobs need to be studied regularly (usually each year) to be certain that the descriptions and specifications remain an accurate reflection of what they really demand. Jobs evolve with time as changes in duties, knowledge bases, and equipment take place; these documents need to reflect that evolution. When new jobs are added to the organization, job descriptions and specifications must be created.

Human Resources Forecasting

Human resources forecasting attempts to predict the organization's future demands for people and for jobs. When forecasting the personnel requirements of the organization, managers need to consider the strategic plans of the company and the normal level of attrition that the company experiences. Strategic plans determine the direction for the company and influence the need for people. A long-term plan to stabilize the company at the current employment level will mean planning to replace those who leave.

We can see how a company translates strategic plans into actual personnel requirements with an example. Suppose a furniture manufacturer has decided to increase production by 30 percent to meet the needs of its forecast of rising long-term demand. Managers analyze the company's current capabilities, reject the use of overtime, and decide to add a third shift within three months. Using up-to-date job descriptions and specifications for the jobs to be added, they determine how many and what kinds of persons need to be hired—nine production workers. Then the managers look at the turnover they can expect from the existing shifts and related support personnel: Over the next three

Figure 8.4
Sample job description.

I. **Job Identification**

Position title: Customer-Service Representative

Department: Policyholders' Service

Effective date: March 1, 1995

II. **Function**

To resolve policyholders' questions and make corresponding adjustments to policies if necessary after the policy is issued.

III. **Scope**

a. Internal (within department)

Interacts with other members of the department in researching answers to problems

b. External (within company)

Interacts with Policy Issue in regard to policy cancellations, Premium Accounting in regard to accounting procedures and Accounting in regard to processing checks

c. External (outside company)

Interacts with policyholders, to answer policy-related questions; client-company payroll departments, to resolve billing questions; and carriers, to modify policies

IV. **Responsibilities**

The job holder will be responsible for:

a. Resolving policyholder inquiries about policies and coverage

b. Initiating changes in policies with carriers (at the request of the insured)

c. Adjusting in-house records as a result of approved changes

d. Corresponding with policyholders regarding changes requested

e. Reporting to the department manager any problems he or she is unable to resolve

V. **Authority Relationships**

a. Reporting relationships: Reports to the manager of Policyholders' Service

b. Supervisory relationship: None

VI. **Equipment, Materials, and Machines**

Personal computer, calculator, and VDT

VII. **Physical Conditions or Hazards**

95% of the duties are performed sitting at either a desk or a VDT

VIII. **Other**

Other duties as assigned

Figure 8.5
Sample job specification.

I. **Job Identification**

Position: File/Mail Clerk

Department: Policyholders' Service

Effective date: March 1, 1995

II. **Education**

Minimum: High school or equivalent

III. **Experience**

Minimum: Six months of experience developing, monitoring, and maintaining a file system

IV. **Skills**

Keyboarding skills: Must be able to set up own work and operate a computer and typewriter; no minimum WPM

V. **Special Requirements**

a. Must be flexible to the demands of the organization for overtime and change in workload

b. Must be able to comply with previously established procedures

c. Must be tolerant of work requiring detailed accuracy (the work of monitoring file signouts and filing files, for example)

d. Must be able to apply systems knowledge (to anticipate the new procedures that a system change will require, for example)

VI. **Behavioral Characteristics**

a. Must have high level of initiative as demonstrated by the ability to recognize a problem, resolve it, and report it to the supervisor

b. Must have interpersonal skills as demonstrated by the ability to work as a team member and cooperate with other departments

months, two new hires will be needed to replace retiring factory employees. Thus, the managers must acquire eleven new hires over the next three months.

Human Resources Inventory

The human resources inventory provides information about the organization's current personnel. In carrying out the inventory, an organization catalogs the skills, abilities, interests, training, experience, and qualifications of each member of its current work force. Managers will know who occupies each position and his or her qualifications, length of service, responsibilities, experiences, and promotion potential. This information is updated periodically and supplemented by the most recent appraisals given to job holders. What emerges is something similar to Figure 8.6, a plan for staffing changes in management ranks. Developing this chart makes management aware of strengths and weaknesses in the current personnel base and allows it to create what amounts to a potential managerial succession plan.

Forecast and Inventory Comparison

By comparing the inventory with the forecast, managers determine who in the organization is qualified to fill the projected openings and which personnel needs must be met externally. At the furniture company, the managers decide that most of the needed personnel must come from outside, because many of the positions are entry-level jobs and members of the existing work force will be needed to replace retiring workers.

If the managers decide to try to fill some of the vacancies from within, the first consideration is whether current employees qualify. If so, the managers should advertise the jobs within the company and encourage employees to apply for them. If current employees do not qualify, the next question is whether, through training and development, they can achieve the qualifications. If so, and if the company can afford the money and time, the managers should prepare a plan to provide the needed training and development.

Recruitment, Selection, and Orientation

With the forecast and inventory complete and job descriptions and specifications in hand, managers begin **recruitment**—*the process of locating and attracting a sufficient number of qualified candidates to apply for the jobs that need filling.* Sources of applicants should include employed and unemployed prospects and temporary help services.

Strategies for Recruiting

In our example at the furniture-making company, the managers decide to look outside for the needed applicants. This decision presents several options: They can call private or state-operated employment services. They can run ads in newspapers and other publications, including trade journals and papers that appeal to racial and ethnic minorities. They can ask current employees to recommend qualified friends and relatives. (Many companies offer bonuses to

recruitment
The process of locating and attracting a sufficient number of qualified candidates to apply for the jobs that need filling.

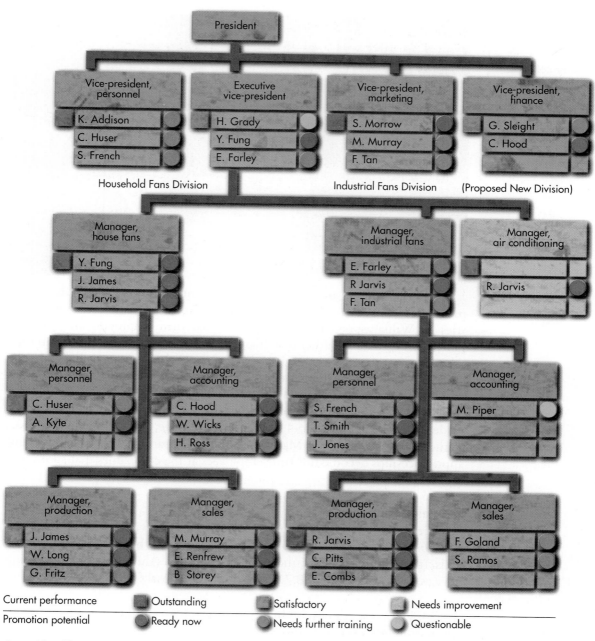

Source: Adapted from Walter S. Wikstrom, *Developing Managerial Competence* (New York: The Conference Board, 1964), p. 99. Used by permission.

employees who refer people who are eventually hired.) They can contact schools and offer a training program, and they can participate in job fairs. The managers can ask neighborhood and community groups to help them reach minorities and other protected groups and encourage them to apply for the jobs. If the company employs union labor, managers can contact trade unions in their search for skilled workers.

Figure 8.6
Management replacement chart.

Job recruiters are a common site on many college campuses.

Two other sources are internship and apprenticeship programs, which are a proven way to gain access to needed talent. Precision Metal Forming Industries of Williamsport, Pennsylvania, a small firm employing fifty people, joined forces with five other metalworking companies in its area to establish a school-to-work transition project. With six employers, seven high schools, and twelve students participating, the program (backed by private and government funding) gives students postsecondary credits and a certification of competence in entry-level metalworking skills. During the two-year program, students complete high school, earn minimum wage, and earn prejourneyman status in metalworking.[10] Many students who partake in internships and apprenticeships become full-time employees at the companies that sponsored them.

The Selection Process

selection
The process of deciding which candidates out of the pool of applicants have the qualifications for the jobs to be filled.

Selection is *the process of deciding which candidates out of the pool of applicants have the qualifications for the jobs to be filled.* Selection begins where recruiting ends. It attempts to identify the qualified candidates through several screening devices, as listed in Figure 8.7. Let's look more closely at these devices.

THE APPLICATION FORM   Usually, a prospective employee must fill out an application form as part of the selection process. An application form summarizes the candidate's education, skills, and experiences related to the job he or she is applying for. To avoid discrimination in the selection process, employers must not ask for information that is unrelated to the candidate's ability to perform the job successfully. Questions about home ownership, marital status, age, ethnic or racial background, and place of birth are usually irrelevant. When used properly, the completed application not only yields needed information, it indicates a person's ability to follow simple instructions and use basic language skills.

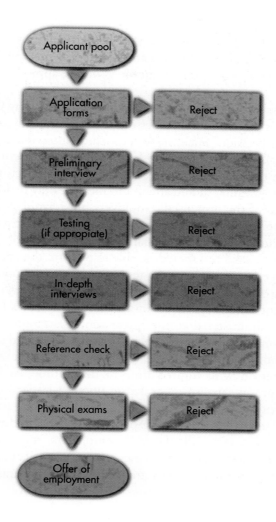

Figure 8.7
The selection process.

THE PRELIMINARY INTERVIEW In small firms, a job candidate's first interview at a firm may be conducted by the very manager for whom the person hired will work. In large companies, someone from the human resources staff may be the designated screening interviewer.

A preliminary interview may be structured—scripted with specific questions—or unstructured. An unstructured format allows an applicant relative freedom to express thoughts and feelings. An interviewer uses the preliminary meeting to verify details from the application form and to obtain information needed to continue the selection process. Interviewers must avoid topics that are not related to the applicant's abilities to perform successfully on the job. An ability necessary to perform a job is called a bona fide occupational qualification. For example, if a job involves work in a men's locker room, a question about the sex of the applicant is probably not discriminatory because it asks about a bona fide occupational qualification.

Employers and job candidates must be particularly sensitive to the potential for discrimination in interviews. Figure 8.8 presents some interviewing guidelines, which also apply to questions on the application form.

TESTING According to Equal Employment Opportunity Commission guidelines, a *test* is any criterion or performance measure used as a basis for any employment decision. Such measures include interviews, applications forms, psychological and performance tests, physical requirements for a job, and any other device that is scored and used as a basis for selecting an applicant. All tests used for screening should attempt to measure only performance of the job.

Regardless of the tests used, employers must avoid producing a disparate impact. Employers must also ensure that each test has *validity*—that is, is a good predictor of future performance on a specific job. A person receiving a high score on a valid test should be able to perform the related job successfully. Those who perform poorly on the test should perform poorly on the job. If test performance does not correlate to job performance, the test is probably invalid.

Assessment centers specialize in screening candidates for managerial positions. Tests administered at assessment centers attempt to analyze a person's ability to communicate, decide, plan, organize, lead, and solve problems. The testing techniques used include interviews, in-basket exercises (tests that present a person with limited time to decide how to handle a variety of problems), group exercises intended to uncover leadership potential and the ability to work with others, and a variety of hands-on tasks. The assessments usually last several days and take place away from the usual job site. Many large companies, especially Japanese employers, use assessment centers to determine who will make it into a company or up its corporate ladder. The results from assessment centers are usually more accurately predictive than paper-and-pencil exercises that assess managerial ability.

THE IN-DEPTH INTERVIEW An in-depth interview is almost always conducted by the person or persons for or with whom the applicant will work if hired. The goal of an in-depth interview is to determine how well the applicant will fit into the organization's culture and the department in which he or she would work. In-depth interviews may or may not be structured. They can be used to relay information specifically related to the job and its environment as well as to talk about benefits, hours, and working conditions. Applicants who have passed through the initial screening and progress to in-depth interviews need the endorsement of the person for whom they will work. Without this person's commitment to the success of the new hire, the applicant's future at that firm is in doubt. As is the case with application forms and preliminary interviews, interviewers must take care to avoid topics that could lead to accusations of employment discrimination.

YOU DECIDE

Think of a job you have applied for. Who interviewed you? What questions were you asked? Were any of the questions illegal? If so, why do you think you were asked these questions?

Discriminatory Topics

The best general guidelines to follow on employment application forms and in interviews is to ensure that information elicited relates to qualifications for effective performance on the job. The topics listed in bold in this exhibit are especially sensitive.

Age? Date of birth? In general, asking whether a candidate is under 18 or over 70 is permissible.

Arrests? Since an arrest is no indication of guilt and because, proportionally, minorities are arrested more than those in other segments of the population, questions about arrests are probably discriminatory.

Convictions (other than traffic violations)? Military record? Questions about convictions are generally inadvisable, though they may be appropriate for screening candidates who have been convicted of certain offenses and are under consideration for certain kinds of jobs. Questions about less-than-honorable military discharges are likewise inappropriate unless the job involves security issues. In general, a candidate can be asked what branch of service he or she served in and what kind of work the candidate did. If information about convictions or military discharge is necessary, exercise care in how it is used; avoid possible discrimination.

Available for Saturday or Sunday work? Although knowing when employees are available to work is important, a question about availability on certain days may discourage applicants from certain religious groups. If business requirements necessitate such a question, indicate that the employer will make an effort to accommodate the religious needs of employees.

Age and number of children? Arrangements for child care? Although the intent of these questions may be to explore a source of absenteeism or tardiness, the effect can be to discriminate against women. Do not ask questions about children or their care.

Credit record? Own a car? Own a home? Unless the person hired must use personal credit, must use a personal car, or do business from a home he or she owns, avoid these questions. They could discriminate against minorities and women.

Eye color? Hair color? Eye and hair color are not related to job performance and may serve to indicate an applicant's race or national origin.

Fidelity bond? Since a bond may have been denied for an arbitrary or discriminatory reason, use other screening considerations.

Friends or relatives? This question implies a preference for friends or relatives of employees and is potentially discriminatory because such people are likely to reflect the demography of the company's present work force.

Garnishment record? Federal courts have held that wage garnishments do not normally affects worker's ability to perform effectively on the job.

Height? weight? Unless height or weight relates directly to job performance, do not ask about it on an application form or in an interview.

Maiden name? Prior married name? Widowed, divorced, separated? These questions are not related to job performance and may be an indication of religion or national origin. These inquiries may be appropriate, however, if the information gained is needed for a preemployment investigation or security check.

Marital status? A federal court has held that refusal to employ a married woman when married men occupy similar jobs is unlawful sex discrimination. Do not ask about an applicant's marital status.

Sex? State and federal laws prohibit discrimination on the basis of sex except where sex is a bona fide occupational qualification necessary to the normal operation of business.

Note: If certain information is needed for employment purposes, such as in the administration of affirmative action plans, the employer can obtain it after the applicant has been hired. Keep these data separate from data used in career advancement decisions.

Source: Illinois Department of Employment Security.

Figure 8.8
Employment application forms and interviews: potentially discriminatory inquiries.

REFERENCE CHECKS A recent report found that most employers conduct fairly extensive background checks:

- 84 percent verify education and past employment claims.
- 60 percent contact persons listed as references.
- 63 percent review school transcripts.[11]

Checking an applicant's past can present problems. First, certain types of background checks are to be avoided, as they can be discriminatory. Checks of credit bureau and arrest records, for example, are discriminatory. Second, checking references can be difficult because most past employers either refuse to cooperate or avoid saying anything negative for fear of a defamation-of-character lawsuit by the ex-employee. According to one recent study, 41 percent of companies surveyed prohibited employees from giving references about ex-employees.[12]

THE PHYSICAL EXAM A recent article reported that of employers surveyed, 52 percent asked applicants to take a preemployment physical exam as part of the selection process, while 19 percent asked for a medical history without a physical exam.[13] Employers use physical exams and medical histories (1) to prevent insurance claims for illnesses and injuries that occurred prior to employment, (2) to detect communicable diseases, and (3) to certify that an applicant is physically capable of performing his or her job. If the job description cites physical demands, they must be valid. According to the Americans with Disabilities Act, employers must make reasonable accommodations for the physically impaired and not use physical barriers as an excuse for not hiring.

THE OFFER OF EMPLOYMENT After the screening process, the manager offers the job to the top-rated applicant. This step may involve a series of negotiations about salary or wages, work schedule, vacation time, types of benefits desired, and other special assistance the new person may need. With the diversity of the work force of today, an employer may have to accommodate an employee's disability, make time for him or her to get children off to school or be at home for them after school, or arrange for day care. Federal law requires that, within 24 hours from the time of hiring, the new employee must furnish proof of U.S. citizenship or the proper authorization needed to work in the United States as a legal alien.

orientation program
A series of activities that give new employees information to help them adapt to the company and their jobs.

Orientation

Once an employee is hired, he or she should be brought into the mainstream of the organization as quickly as possible. Organizations accomplish this by developing an **orientation program**—*a series of activities that give new employees information to help them adapt to the company and their jobs.* Although the previous steps in the selection process have done much to familiarize the newcomer with the company and the job, what the new hire needs now is a warm welcome so he or she can begin contributing as soon as possible.

The newcomer needs to be introduced to his or her workstation and co-workers. Managers and co-workers should answer the new employee's questions promptly and openly. Someone should explain work rules, company policies, benefits, and procedures and fill out the paperwork necessary to get the new person on the payroll. All employee assistance programs should be explained, and the new hire should be told how to take advantage of them.

All of this can be done in stages and by several different people. Human resource specialists may handle the paperwork while a supervisor takes charge of introductions to the work area and co-workers. All equipment, tools, and supplies that the newcomer needs should be in place when he or she reports for work.

It is important that first impressions and early experiences be realistic and as positive as possible. Orientation is the beginning of a continuing socialization process that builds and cements employees' relationships, attitudes, and commitment to the company. Orientation should be thoroughly planned and skillfully executed.

Training and Development

Training teaches skills for use in the present and near future, while *development* focuses on the future. Both involve teaching the particular attitudes, knowledge, and skills a worker needs. Both are designed to give people something new, and both have three prerequisites for success: (1) those who design training or development programs must create needs assessments to determine what the content and objectives of the programs should be; (2) the people who execute the programs must know how to teach, how people learn, and what individuals need to be taught; and (3) all participants—trainers, developers, and those receiving the training or development—must be willing participants.

American employers spend in excess of $210 billion each year to provide training and development. In most U.S. businesses, training and development are continual processes. The American Society for Training and Development named the Xerox Corporation as one of several businesses with the best training systems. Xerox spends about 4 percent of its payroll ($250 million to $300 million per year) for training its 110,000 employees. Xerox has its own training center in Leesburg, Virginia, and the corporation employs 120 trainers who train 12,000 employees annually. An additional 21,000 employees receive at least 40 hours of training each year at a district headquarters.

The Purposes of Training

Training *supplies the skills, knowledge, and attitudes needed by employees to improve their abilities to perform their jobs.* Training has five major goals: to

training Supplying the skills, knowledge, and attitudes needed by employees to improve their abilities to perform their jobs.

MANAGER'S NOTEBOOK

Americans with Disabilities Act: Revolution in the Workplace

In July 1990 Congress enacted the Americans with Disabilities Act—and with it the most sweeping changes to employment law in nearly 30 years. The regulations detail how employers must accommodate disabled employees and prospective employees—how they must interview applicants, make hiring judgments, and define jobs.

The rules on employing people with disabilities were preceded by a separate set of rules concerning how businesses must accommodate the public by assuring that all facilities conform to strict codes of access for people with disabilities. This second set of provisions prohibits discrimination against people with mental and physical handicaps—as well as the chronically ill.

The law defines a disability as (a) physical or mental impairment that substantially limits one or more major life activities (such as walking, speaking, or working), (b) a record of such impairment—such as a person with a history of cancer that is in remission, or (c) being regarded as having such an impairment (a person with high blood pressure that is controlled by medication, or someone who in the past was misdiagnosed with depression). In addition, the act also protects anyone who formerly abused alcohol or used drugs illegally and has since undergone treatment. Finally, employers may not discriminate against a person who has a relationship or association with someone who has a disability, such as a friend or family member for whom that person must provide care.

The law establishes specific guidelines in regard to elements of the employment process. These include:

- *Setting job qualification standards.* There are new guidelines for employers' job qualification standards—criteria for education and physical or mental requirements. The law allows such standards but requires that they be legitimately connected to the specific job.
- *Distinguishing essential job duties.* To decide whether a disabled person is qualified, employers must first distinguish between job functions that are essential and those that are peripheral.
- *Testing for fitness.* Employers who give applicants tests for physical agility before making a job offer—such as checking for the ability to climb trees for a pruning position—still may do so. However, such a test cannot be a medical examination or even seem like one.
- *Requiring medical exams.* No medical examination may be given to a job applicant before the employer makes a job offer. Employers may still give tests for current illegal use of drugs, which is not protected as a disability.
- *Interviewing.* Employers must make sure that people with disabilities can get to the interview site and participate fully in the process. Job notices and application forms should state that those needing disability-related accommodations for interviews should request them in advance. Employers may ask:
  - Whether a job task can be performed with or without accommodation.
  - How the individual would per-

form the tasks and with what accommodations.
- For a demonstration of how certain job functions would be performed, but only if every applicant for the job is required to do so, regardless of disability.
- Whether the individual can meet the job's work hour requirements, provided the hours truly apply to the job.

- *Adjusting so work is possible.* If a job candidate cannot perform the essential functions of the job outright, the employer must ask whether a reasonable accommodation would help the candidate carry out the task. A reasonable accommodation means removing unnecessary barriers to employment. The reasonable accommodation cannot cause undue hardship—significant difficulty or expense—to an employer. Examples of job accommodations may include restructuring jobs or reassigning tasks, changing work schedules, providing qualified readers or interpreters, or letting the employee bring equipment into the workplace that the employer is not required to provide.

The act incorporates the remedies found in Title VII of the Civil Rights Act. It allows employees to seek reinstatement and back pay. The act covered employers with twenty-five or more employees beginning July 1992. Employers with fifteen to twenty-four employees have two additional years to comply.

(For more on the Americans with Disabilities Act, see Bradford McKee, *Nation's Business,* June 1992, pp. 29–33; and Michael A. Verespej, "Sex, Age and Disability," *Industry Week,* February 17, 1992. p. 62.)

increase knowledge and skills, to increase motivation to succeed, to improve chances for advancement, to improve morale and the sense of competence and pride in performance, and to increase quality and productivity. In the culturally diverse work force of today, employees often need to improve their ability to handle English; to gain an appreciation of the organization's diverse cultures; and to learn how to cope with the many changes that occur on the job, such as new technologies, methods, and duties.

The Techniques of Training

A company can train employees in various places. Trainees can be sent to a job site, a corporate training center, a college classroom, or various workshops, seminars, and professional gatherings. When training is done by the employer in-house, the following methods are used:

- *On-the-job training (OJT).* In this approach, an employee learns while the job is being performed. Training proceeds through coaching or by the trainee observing proficient performers and then doing the work. Apprenticeships and internships are on-the-job training programs.
- *Classroom training.* In this system, training is conducted away from the pressures of the work environment. The employee learns the basic skills of the job and then is sent to the work force. An example of this technique is learning to use a computer. The trainees interact with a computer in an

On-the-job training programs are widely used in the fast-food industry.

environment that is usually controlled, and the interaction is one-on-one. The trainees proceed at their own pace or at a pace set by their training equipment.

- *Vestibule training.* This approach simulates the work environment by providing actual equipment and tools in a laboratory setting. The noise and distractions of a real work area and the pressure of meeting production goals are absent so that trainees can concentrate on learning.

Regardless of the techniques used, training must be realistic. It must teach necessary skills and knowledge in ways that can be directly applied to the work setting once training ends. Progress must be monitored to determine how well trainees are mastering the material.

The Purposes of Development

development
Preparing someone for the new and greater challenges he or she will encounter in another, more demanding job.

Development is *preparing someone for the new and greater challenges he or she will encounter in another, more demanding job.* Workers seek development opportunities to prepare for management positions; supervisors need development to prepare to move into middle management. All development is really self-development. Without a personal commitment, development cannot occur. People can be pressured into training just to keep their jobs, but development, when offered, can be rejected. Employees cannot depend on their employers for development. Small companies cannot afford it, and many large employers will not pay for development when it is not directly related to an employee's current job or career track.

GLOBAL PERSPECTIVE

Staffing the Japanese Way

Staffing practices of American and Japanese companies differ in important ways. Each approach is a product of its country's culture. The shrinking business world, however, means that human resources managers in each country must learn the strengths of practices used in the other. Here are some of the major aspects of the Japanese approach:

- Large Japanese companies competing in international markets offer lifetime employment to their employees. Once a person joins the company, company managers will do what is necessary to keep that person usefully employed.
- The Japanese prefer to train employees to do a variety of tasks. Job descriptions, where they exist, are usually broad and do not list specific duties. They focus instead on skills. People are expected to do what they know how to do when and where necessary.
- Before taking action, Japanese managers seek consensus—unanimous agreement by a group on what needs to be done and how to proceed. Even at the lowest level of a company, teams of workers conduct business in the same way.
- Japan lacks meaningful antidiscrimination laws; non-Japanese people as well as women are openly discriminated against. In foreign operations, however, Japanese companies must abide by the host country's laws.
- In Japan, recruiting for entry-level management jobs takes place at

schools and universities. From then on, management jobs are usually filled from within. Japanese employers promote by tapping the pool of employees who intend to spend their careers with just one employer.
- Japanese companies tend to use the techniques of the assessment center to screen applicants. They rely heavily on in-depth interviews and hands-on exercises to determine applicants' attitudes, commitment, and talents.
- Job rotation as a means for development and training is more common in Japan than in the United States. Japanese employees move through jobs in one area and also cross functional lines. Japanese managers tend to stay in a job for a longer period of time than the typical American manager does.
- In Japan, employee appraisals are part of the mentoring process. Those who conduct the appraisals try hard not to embarrass an employee. Japanese appraisals tend to be less formal than American appraisals.
- Salaries and promotions for Japanese employees are typically linked to seniority and experience. Wages and salaries are usually lower than they are in the United States.
- Forced retirements are still common in Japanese companies. They usually occur before an employee is over sixty years old.

The Techniques of Development

Development techniques include sending people to professional workshops or seminars, providing job rotation, sponsoring memberships in professional associations, paying for an employee's formal education courses, and granting a person a sabbatical (leave of absence) to pursue further education or engage in community service. An employee should regard a company-sponsored program as a reward and as a clear statement about his or her worth to the company. Such programs are conduits through which workers can gain prestige, confidence, and competence.

Development efforts should never end; indeed, they can be part of a daily routine. By reading professional journals and business publications regularly and by interacting with experts at professional meetings, employees can help keep themselves up-to-date. Another approach to development is volunteering for tough assignments. Meeting tough challenges encourages a person to expand his or her abilities.

Another form of development can be extremely significant: mentoring. *Mentors* are professionals who come from a person's current environment or from another organization. Whatever their affiliation, they are willing to share experiences and give competent advice about handling advancement opportunities, company politics, and self-development.

Performance Appraisal

performance appraisal
A formal, structured system designed (in line with legal limits) to measure the actual job performance of an employee by comparing it to designated standards.

In most organizations some assessment of job performance takes place every day, at least informally. When results for a given period are summarized and shared with those being appraised, **performance appraisal** becomes *a formal, structured system designed (in line with legal limits) to measure the actual job performance of an employee by comparing it to designated standards.* These standards are introduced and taught in the selection and training processes.

The Purposes of Performance Appraisal

Most organizations use appraisals to:

- Provide feedback about the success of previous training and disclose the need for additional training
- Develop individuals' plans for improving their performance and assist them in making such plans
- Determine whether rewards such as pay increases, promotions, transfers, or commendations are due or whether warning or termination is required
- Identify areas for additional growth and the methods that can be used to achieve it
- Develop and enhance the relationship between the person being evaluated and the supervisor doing the evaluation
- Give the employee a clear understanding of where he or she stands in relation to the supervisor's expectations and in relation to the achievement of specific goals

The Components of Appraisal Systems

Performance appraisal systems have two components: the criteria against which the employee is measured (for example, quality of work, knowledge, attitude) and the rating scale showing what the employee can achieve or perform on each criterion (good, 5 out of 10, 100 percent, etc.). As an example, consider that some of the criteria for measuring a student's performance are tests and classroom participation. The rating scale on a test might be 100 possible points; the rating scale on participating could be eight categories, ranging from "never volunteers" to "consistently creative participation."

Types of Appraisal Systems

Two basic types of appraisal systems can be used: subjective and objective. Most systems are variations of one or the other.

SUBJECTIVE PERFORMANCE APPRAISAL SYSTEM A **subjective performance appraisal** system is *one in which the performance criteria and rating scale are not defined.* Figure 8.9 provides an example of a subjective performance appraisal system. Notice the criteria—time management, attitude, knowledge of job, and communication. What does each category mean? What is attitude? What does "communication" refer to? Also notice the rating scale—excellent, good, fair, and poor. What does "excellent" mean to the rater? or to you? How about "good"? "fair"? "poor"? What is the difference between good and fair?

Rather than leading to dialogue about performance, the subjective approach can result in the manager and the employee trying to defend interpretations of performance. Because of the lack of specific criteria (described factors of performance) and of a specific rating scale (increasing or decreasing descriptors of performance), the subjective appraisal system can result in the citing of critical incidents, comparisons to other employees, and judgments based on personality traits (positive and negative).

subjective performance appraisal
Appraisal system in which the performance criteria and rating scale are not defined.

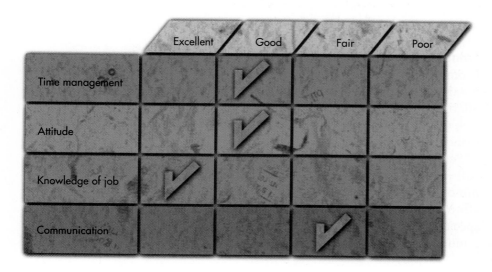

Figure 8.9
Subjective performance appraisal system.

Figure 8.10
Objective
performance
appraisal system.

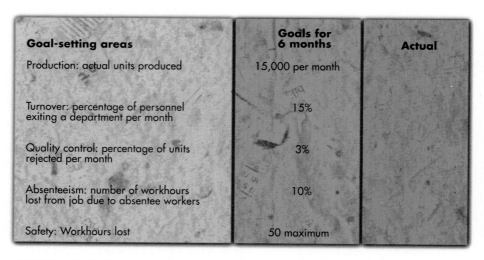

Goal-setting areas	Goals for 6 months	Actual
Production: actual units produced	15,000 per month	
Turnover: percentage of personnel exiting a department per month	15%	
Quality control: percentage of units rejected per month	3%	
Absenteeism: number of workhours lost from job due to absentee workers	10%	
Safety: Workhours lost	50 maximum	

objective performance appraisal
Appraisal system in which both the performance criteria and the method of measurement are specifically defined.

OBJECTIVE PERFORMANCE APPRAISAL SYSTEM With **objective performance appraisal** *both the performance criteria and the method of measurement are specifically defined.* Notice Figure 8.10. The criteria (production, turnover, quality control, absenteeism, and safety) are specific. The rating scale has been replaced by specific goals or objectives to be reached in performance. The production goal, for example, is 15,000 units per month.

In this system, the employee and the manager establish goals together. They know what performance is based on and how it will be measured. Feedback is provided through reports. The employer knows where he or she stands at all times.

Implementation of Employment Decisions

As noted earlier, employment decisions include decisions about promotions, transfers, demotions, and separations (voluntary or involuntary). These job changes are influenced by appraisals and by how an organization recruits, hires, orients, and trains. All employment decisions mean change—change that has a ripple effect throughout an organization.

Promotions

promotions
Job changes that lead to higher pay and greater responsibilities.

Promotions, *job changes that lead to higher pay and greater responsibilities,* reward devoted and outstanding effort. They serve as incentives as well, offering the promise of greater personal growth and challenges to those who seek them. Employees usually earn a promotion by exhibiting superior performance and going beyond that which is expected.

Sometimes past performance is not the sole criterion for a promotion. Affirmative action requires that underrepresented groups such as women and minorities be better represented at all levels within an organization. Therefore, affirmative action goals may dictate that members of these groups be given special status in hiring and promoting decisions. In many union agreements, seniority is the most significant factor influencing promotion decisions.

Transfers

Transfers are *lateral moves from one position to another having similar pay and a similar responsibility level.* The opportunity for transfer is becoming increasingly important. Opportunities for promotion are not as available now as they were only a few years ago. The leaner, flatter management structures of today and the trend toward teams mean there simply are not a large number of openings. According to Marilyn M. Kennedy, editor of the newsletter *Kennedy's Career Strategist,* transfers may be a company's only means of retaining talent:

> Companies that have restructured have taken steps to make sideways moves more palatable. RJR-Nabisco's Nabisco Foods Group (in New Jersey) recently added tiers to its pay scales so that workers who move sideways have a better chance of getting pay raises instead of cuts. Corning Inc., which has long wooed recruits by promising them they can "change careers without changing companies," recently began offering 5 percent raises to managers who make lateral moves. The policy comes on the heels of restructuring.[14]

For years companies have used lateral moves in attempts to train and develop employees. Doing so is one way of exposing people to different aspects of an operation and helping them see the big corporate picture. Transfers can help people advance by moving them from an area where few opportunities exist to an area that offers a less congested career track.

Demotions

A **demotion** is *a movement from one position to another that has less pay or responsibility attached to it.* In the business climate of today, demotions are rarely used as punishments. (Ineffective performers are fired, not retained.) Rather, they are used to retain employees who lose their positions through no fault of their own. Some people prefer taking a lower-status, lower-paying job to the alternative of being laid off. Others choose a demotion to free themselves of stress, allow themselves more freedom to pursue outside interests, or meet challenges such as having to care for children or an elderly parent.

Some companies have established what have become known as "mommy tracks"—temporary career interruptions for parents. Mommy tracks allow a parent to take care of children from pregnancy through the preschool years. By offering adjustments such as part-time work, a mix of telecommuting and office hours, and flexible work schedules, companies help valued employees cope with new interests and demands on their time.[15]

Separations

A **separation,** *the departure of an employee from an organization,* may be voluntary or involuntary. Voluntary separations include resignations and retirements. Involuntary separations include layoffs—temporary separations—

transfers
Lateral moves from one position to another having similar pay and a similar responsibility level.

demotion
A movement from one position to another that has less pay or responsibility attached to it.

separation
The departure of an employee from an organization.

and firings. Employers sometimes encourage voluntary separation by offering incentives to encourage employees to retire early. In May 1992 Digital Equipment Corporation offered 7,000 employees an early-retirement buyout; 3,000 accepted.[16] Involuntary separations seem to be on the rise in U.S. businesses. Factors from declining business to poor personal performance to company bankruptcies (as in the cases of Pan Am and Eastern Airlines) have cost millions of Americans their jobs.

As alternatives to separations, many companies are implementing other strategies. Some have enacted hiring freezes, which allow normal attrition to reduce the work force. Other strategies include restricting the use of overtime, retraining and redeploying workers, job sharing, reducing hours, and converting managers to paid consultants. Managers at Unarco, a manufacturer of shopping carts, pride themselves on the company's no-layoff policy. Unarco managers find useful employment for displaced workers by relying on retraining and normal attrition.

Unarco managers and managers everywhere have good reasons to avoid layoffs. Layoffs can be extremely expensive. Processing paperwork, closing facilities, paying severance costs, and covering higher unemployment insurance premiums can run in the thousands of dollars. The psychological costs are high as well. Those left behind after layoffs are fearful and insecure; those laid off are more likely than employed people to experience family problems, suffer divorce, or commit suicide.

Compensation

compensation
All forms of financial payments to employees: salaries and wages, benefits, bonuses, profit sharing, and awards of goods or services.

Compensation is a major part of the human resources environment. **Compensation** includes *all forms of financial payments to employees: salaries and wages, benefits, bonuses, profit sharing, and awards of goods or services.* The trend today is to offer increases in compensation in response to increases in performance that add value to the organization, its services, or its products. Increasing compensation is a way of retaining employees who have proved themselves valuable. This makes sense: As employees become more valuable, losing them becomes more costly.

The Purposes of Compensation

Compensation has three primary purposes: to attract, help develop, and retain talented performers. The level of compensation offered by a firm can increase or decrease a company's attractiveness to job seekers. Compensation should encourage people to continually improve themselves and to make themselves more valuable to themselves and their employers. It must also anchor valued employees to the company, discouraging them from leaving to find other employment. People who consider their compensation fair and adequate feel that they are being treated with recognition and respect. They feel that the organization is giving them a fair return on their investment of time, energy, and commitment. Finally, compensation should give employees a sense of security, freeing them to unleash their full energies without the distraction that comes with the inability to meet financial needs.

Factors That Influence Compensation

When designing a compensation package for employees, companies should be concerned about being equitable, meeting legal requirements, and linking compensation philosophy to various market factors. When certain types of workers are in short supply, managers may have to offer premium compensation to attract or hold them. Similarly, managers who decide to make their organization a leader in terms of the compensation it offers will probably be able to attract and keep the best employees.

The U.S. Fair Labor Standards Act, passed in 1938 and amended many times, relates to the payment of wages and overtime to workers under eighteen years of age. Other federal laws address the level of wages that must be paid to workers in companies doing business with the federal government. Some local and state laws affect compensation systems, and union contracts set wages and restrict compensation decisions in the organizations that are party to them.

How Compensation Is Set

Job evaluation is *a study that determines the worth of a job to an organization.* Each job is ranked in order of importance to establish its proper compensation. Factors such as responsibility, education, skill, training, and working conditions may be examined to help management decide where each job fits. The result is a job ladder, or hierarchy, that reaches from the company president to the lowest level of workers.

Once jobs have been evaluated and placed in their order of importance, management—taking into account such previously mentioned factors as legal requirements and supply and demand—creates pay grades. These are pay categories that relate dollar values to the job ladder developed through job evaluation. Each job may have a pay range of several thousand dollars, so jobholders do not have to be promoted to get a raise.

Types of Compensation

Compensation for a job is based on either time put into a job or what is produced on the job. **Wages** are *compensation based on hours worked,* while **salary** is *compensation based on weeks or months worked.* Both wages and salary are intended to provide pay for the time worked and not for what is produced. An hourly wage is the means of compensation generally provided for lower-level jobs in an organization. Managerial, professional, clerical, and secretarial employees are normally paid by salary.

After the base method of compensation is determined, management may also choose to provide bonuses, profit sharing, stock options, or fringe benefits. Let's examine each.

job evaluation
A study that determines the worth of a job to an organization.

wages
Compensation based on hours worked.

salary
Compensation based on weeks or months worked.

BONUS A bonus is incentive money paid to employees in addition to their regular compensation. It may be based on superior production, effective cost control, company earnings, or other performance factors. Some salespeople, for example, may receive a bonus for exceeding sales goals.

PROFIT SHARING Profit sharing refers to paying a portion of company profits to employees as a performance incentive in addition to their regular compensation. Firms such as Kaiser Aluminum & Chemical, Xerox, and IBM have long realized that sharing in a company's profits can give employees greater feelings of belonging and commitment, with a corresponding increase in motivation, morale, loyalty, and productivity.

STOCK OPTION A stock option is a plan that permits employees to buy shares of stock in the employee's firm at or below the current market price. Some firms have payroll deduction plans to encourage employee participation, and occasionally top managers receive stock options, bonuses, and salary in a total compensation package. Companies may set aside large blocks of shares to sell directly to employees.

benefits
Compensation that is not wages, salaries, or bonuses.

BENEFITS In addition to direct compensation for the job being performed, organizations build into the work environment **benefits**—*compensation that is not wages, salaries, or bonuses.* Most benefits fit into one of the following categories:

- Life, health, and dental insurance
- Paid vacations
- Sick pay
- Holidays, funeral leave, and emergency leave
- Discounts on merchandise or services
- Paid lunch and rest periods
- Tuition reimbursement

American employers are spending record amounts on employee benefits. On average, employers spend $13,126 a year per full-time employee to provide legally required benefits (Social Security, workers' compensation, and unemployment insurance) along with voluntary programs such as paid holidays and vacations, profit sharing, health and life insurance, retirement programs, and bonuses. Nationwide, employers spend an average of 39.2 percent of their payroll costs (over $1 trillion) to provide employee benefits.[17] The industry with the highest benefit costs—an average of $19,375 per employee—is the public utilities group. The group with the lowest cost is banks and finance companies—$9,797.

To accommodate a changing and diverse work force, many companies do manage to offer a number of innovative benefits. Many employees now have

An increasing number of companies are offering on-site day care for children of employees.

access to day care for their children through company-sponsored programs or child-care allowances. At some companies flexible scheduling allows employees to determine how they will fulfill their time commitments. They can choose to come early, leave late, or even work a four-day week—just as long as they work a specified amount of time and are present for specified hours.

Job sharing allows two people to split a job, each working part-time. (Job sharing and four-day weeks are discussed in Chapter 9.) Telecommuting allows workers to work at home while communicating through computers and fax machines. Parental leaves were growing in popularity even before they were mandated in 1993 by the first federal legislation signed by President Clinton. Parental leave offers new fathers and mothers time off (with or without pay) to care for newborns. For employers, these and other programs are alternatives to losing capable people who must cope with life changes.

An organization offers benefits, like other forms of compensation, so it can attract, develop, and retain talented and committed workers. As with wages and salaries, managers plan benefits according to their organization's financial resources and strategies and the market conditions the organization faces.

SUMMARY

Once an organization is developed, the challenge to management is to match personnel with the jobs identified and to provide for employees' long-range growth and welfare as members of the organization. Human resources management has this responsibility. In providing the staffing function for the organization, its activities include human resources planning, recruitment, selection, orientation, training, performance appraisal, and compensation.

The human resources area is influenced by both the legal and social-cultural environments. The legal environment includes equal employment opportunity, affirmative action, and sexual harassment issues. The social-cultural environment involves issues and trends relating to cultural diversity, glass ceilings and glass walls, AIDS, and drug testing.

The activities involved in human resources management should be viewed as a series of interrelated steps that managers and specialists perform to acquire and maintain the right people in the right jobs. These activities include:

- *Human resources planning,* which involves human resources forecasting, human resources inventory, and a comparison of these two to determine the need for recruiting. It also involves the development of job descriptions and job specifications as a result of a job analysis.
- *Recruitment,* which attempts to identify and attract candidates to meet the requirements of anticipated or actual job openings. Two sources for recruitment are inside and outside the company.
- *Selection,* which determines which candidates out of the pool of applicants developed in recruiting have the abilities, skills, and characteristics most closely matching job demands. The candidates go through a selection process that includes completing an application blank, a preliminary interview, testing, an in-depth interview, a reference check, and a physical examination.
- *Orientation,* which includes a series of activities that give new employees information to help them adjust to the organization and their new jobs.
- *Training,* which attempts to supply the skills, knowledge, and attitudes needed by individuals to improve their abilities to perform their jobs. Types of training are classroom, on the job, and vestibule.
- *Development,* which is preparing someone for the new and greater challenges he or she will encounter in another, more demanding, job.
- *Performance appraisal,* which measures an employee's job performance compared with established job standards. There are two types of appraisal—subjective and objective.

The results of the appraisal process and the actions of employees cause a number of employee-personnel actions. Employees may choose to resign or retire; management may choose to promote, transfer, demote, lay off, or terminate an employee.

Human resources managers are responsible for employee compensation. They must design a program to attract and retain qualified applicants. In doing so they rate the worth of each job and establish pay grades. Compensation is based on time or on output. Additional compensation in the form of bonuses, profit sharing, stock options, and pensions is also developed. Benefits—such as insurance and paid vacations—completes the compensation program.

KEY TERMS

affirmative action p. 226
benefits p. 250
compensation p. 248
cultural diversity p. 227
demotion p. 247
development p. 242
discrimination p. 225
disparate impact p. 225
equal employment opportunity p. 225
glass ceiling p. 227
glass wall p. 227
human resources management p. 220
human resources manager p. 221
human resources planning p. 229
job analysis p. 230

job description p. 230
job evaluation p. 249
job specification p. 230
objective performance appraisal p. 246
orientation program p. 238
performance appraisal p. 244
promotions p. 246
recruitment p. 232
salary p. 249
selection p. 234
separation p. 247
sexual harassment p. 226
subjective performance appraisal p. 245
training p. 239
transfers p. 247
wages p. 249

FOR REVIEW AND DISCUSSION

1. What is the importance of human resources management in the long-range development of a company?
2. What activities are included in human resources management?
3. What is the objective of equal employment opportunity legislation? How does this differ from affirmative action? What is sexual harassment?
4. What is meant by the term *glass ceiling? glass wall?*
5. What is the purpose of a job analysis? a job description? a job specification?
6. What steps are involved in human resources planning? What factors are considered in deciding to train or recruit?
7. What are the sources of internal recruiting? What are the sources of external recruiting?
8. What is the purpose of an employment application form?
9. What is the objective of a preliminary interview?
10. What limitations are placed on the use of testing for employment?
11. Who should conduct the in-depth interview? Why?
12. What fear is involved in reference checking?
13. What is the purpose of a preemployment physical examination?
14. What elements are included in an orientation program? What is the purpose of orientation?
15. Contrast on-the-job training with vestibule training. When might you use each?
16. What is the purpose of performance appraisal? Distinguish between subjective and objective appraisal.
17. Distinguish between transfers, promotions, demotions and separations.
18. What factors does a human resources manager analyze in developing a compensation program?
19. What are the two basic types of compensation? How do they differ?

APPLICATIONS

Case 8.1: Family Care as a Job Benefit

Compensation is no longer just a paycheck. For years businesses have been providing their employees with other forms of payment for their work. Most of these benefits have been a result of increased government regulation that requires employers to provide certain health care and retirement benefits. Companies have realized, however, that by providing superlative nonpay compensation, they can improve the quality of applicants they recruit as well as improve on-the-job performance.

Increasingly, employers have found that by providing various parent and family support services, they can relieve the conflict that often occurs when workers must juggle both family responsibilities and work scheduling. Parents who feel comfortable integrating their work life and their family life are happier, more efficient, and more loyal.

Companies such as Johnson & Johnson offer flexible scheduling, family care absences, relocation planning and spouse relocation, child care referrals, on-site child care, elder-care referrals, and adoption benefits. While these programs provide greater opportunities for abuse and allow more excuses for absenteeism, employers such as Johnson & Johnson have found nearly no abuses of the benefits, no increase in tardiness or absenteeism, and no decrease in productivity.

Quite the contrary, they have found that employees who take advantage of the program are the highest performers and are the least likely to leave the company or have disciplinary problems. Indeed, four years after Johnson & Johnson introduced its "Balancing Work and Family" program, three-quarters of employees said that the family policies were "very important" in deciding whether to stay with the company.

Questions

1. Is family care a human resources management responsibility? In what ways?
2. How does a company weigh the costs of providing family care against the perceived employee benefits?

3. Are all family care programs beneficial to management/employee relations, or would some, like on-site child care, distract employees from their work?

4. How does a family care program improve recruitment of employees?

For more information, see Barbara Presley Noble, "Making a Case for Family Programs," *New York Times,* May 2, 1993, p. F25.

Case 8.2: Sexual Harassment: Plague in the Workplace

The Anita Hill–Clarence Thomas hearings were eye-openers for many people in this country, not necessarily for those employers who have worked for years to rid the workplace of outmoded attitudes, but for all those other employers who have ignored the problem of sexual harassment for years.

For those who continue to ignore the problem or who choose to remain skeptical—chalking up sexual harassment as the latest liberal fad and convincing themselves that "this too shall pass"—the stakes are too high. Acts of sexual harassment carry with them significant consequences, not only for the victims but for the transgressors. The liabilities are measured not only in loss of careers or in the financial consequences of court-ordered punitive damages, but in the questioning of management's ability to manage by both the public and shareholders. In recent months:

- An automaker was ordered to pay $185,000 in back pay to a woman whose supervisor told her she was in a male-dominated field and had better get used to her co-workers discussing sex.
- A foodmaker was ordered by the court to pay victims $625,000 because of a manager who commented daily about an employee's figure and physical appearance, who suggested to women that they show him a "good time," and who imposed a dress code designed to show off women's legs.
- A publishing company that was told by the court to

pay $800,000 in punitive damages to an employee who proved that she was subjected to lewd remarks made by a supervisor about women and was twice passed over for promotion in favor of younger men, despite displaying exemplary qualifications for the particular promotion.

- A grocery store chain that settled out of court in a $14 million suit by an employee who charged that her supervisor made constant sexual advances and had sexual encounters with her. One piece of evidence presented to the jury before the out-of-court settlement was the trousers of her supervisor, which she had taken while he was harassing her.

These are the same companies where senior-level managers claim, "There's no sexual harassment going on in our company." In other instances, these same companies have had the subject of sexual harassment dismissed by executives with the casual disclaimer, "We're all adults; if there's a problem, we'll work it out." It's beyond time to ignore sexual harassment or pass it off with casual remarks.

Questions

1. What "attitudes" in the workplace have led to instances of sexual harassment?

2. What actions by management have contributed to sexual harassment practices? Cite examples from the case to support your answer.

3. If you were an executive in a company that had incidents of sexual harassment as noted in the case, what actions would you take? Why?

4. If you were asked to develop a policy addressing the issue of sexual harassment, what would you include?

For more information, see Diana Kunde, "A Painful Quest for Justice" *Dallas Morning News,* July 11, 1993, pp. 1H–2H; Jan Bohren, "Six Myths of Sexual Harassment," *Management Review,* May 1993, pp. 61–63; Joseph E. McKenna, "Dangerous Liaisons," *Industry Week,* February 17, 1993, pp. 56–61.

REFERENCES

1. Donna Brown, "HR: Survival Tool for the 1990s," *Management Review,* March 1992, p. 10.
2. David J. Jefferson, "MCA To Extend Health Insurance to Gay Couples," *The Wall Street Journal,* May 18, 1992, p. B5.
3. Jan Bohren, "Six Myths of Sexual Harassment," *Management Review,* May 1993, pp. 61-63.
4. Troy Segal, "Getting Serious About Sexual Harassment," *Business Week,* November 9, 1992, pp. 78-82.
5. Carol Kleiman, "Some Firms Breaking Glass Ceiling," *Chicago Tribune,* April 13, 1992, Sec. 4, p. 7.
6. Barbara Ettorre, "Breaking the Glass . . . Or Just Window Dressing?" *Management Review,* March 1992, pp. 16-22.
7. Gilbert Fuchsberg, "Study Says Women Face Glass Walls as Well as Ceilings," *The Wall Street Journal,* March 3, 1992, pp. B1, B8.
8. Ibid.
9. Carol Kleiman, "Some Firms Breaking Glass Ceiling."
10. Dana Milbank, "On the Ropes: Unions' Woes Suggest How the Labor Force in the U.S. Is Shifting," *The Wall Street Journal,* May 5, 1992, p. A1.
11. Carol Kleiman, "From Genetics to Honesty, Firms Expand Employee Tests, Screening," *Chicago Tribune,* February 8, 1992, Sec. 8, p. 1.
12. Elizabeth Evans, "Reference Checking," *Inc.,* November 1992, p. 38.
13. Carol Kleiman, "From Genetics to Honesty."
14. Quoted in Joan E. Rigdon, "Using Lateral Moves to Spur Employees," *The Wall Street Journal,* May 26, 1993, pp. B1, B5.
15. Joan Beck, "Matching the Workplace to the Work Force," *Chicago Tribune,* March 9, 1992, Sec. 1, p. 15.
16. John R. Wilke, "Digital's Offer to Employees Proves Popular," *The Wall Street Journal,* June 1, 1992, p. B6.
17. Roger Thompson, "As a Percentage of Pay, Benefit Costs Are Growing at a Faster Rate Than Wages," *Nation's Business,* February 1993, pp. 38–39.

9
MANAGING PEOPLE: MOTIVATION AND LEADERSHIP

■ f you're not thinking all the time about making every person more valuable, you don't have a chance. What's the alternative? Wasted minds? Uninvolved people? A labor force that's angry or bored? That doesn't make sense! If you've got a better way, show me. I'd love to know what it is.

Jack Welch
CEO, General Electric

CHAPTER OBJECTIVES
After studying this chapter, you should be able to:

1. Explain the importance of a manager's philosophy in developing a positive work environment.
2. Explain the influence of Theory X and Theory Y on leadership, motivation, and the work environment.
3. Explain the importance of managers' recognizing individual differences and needs and how they influence motivation.
4. Summarize the motivational theories of Maslow and Herzberg and explain the implications of each for employee motivation.
5. Describe the effect of leadership on employee performance.
6. Identify and explain the three factors that influence the choice of leadership style.
7. Describe the three major styles of leadership.
8. Describe techniques that managers and organizations can use to improve the work environment and increase motivation.

UP FRONT

William Wilson has a unique vantage point in the business world. As an employee who has risen from an entry-level job as an insurance broker to the position of vice-president at Johnson & Higgins, the world's oldest and largest insurance brokerage, he has seen changing management styles both within his company and at client companies. And in his current position as head of the office automation and computer systems infrastructure, Wilson is responsible for managing a group of professionals who work with other employees throughout the company.

Bill Wilson took his undergraduate degree in business administration at Miami University in Oxford, Ohio. On graduation, he went to work in Johnson & Higgins's Cincinnati office, continuing his education by earning an MBA from Xavier University. Johnson & Higgins is a privately held commercial insurance brokerage that employs 8,000 people in nearly every major city in the world. Started in 1845, its brokers have served the insurance needs of business by helping select the right types of casualty, property, employee benefits, and other types of insurance ever since.

When Wilson's manager was promoted to chief information officer, he promoted Wilson and transferred him to New York. "We were just getting into personal computers at the time," says Wilson, "and I was keenly interested in what they could do for the business. At first, there was a gap between the computer people and the business people, but we've made tremendous gains. You see, it's absolutely critical that the computer people understand the business and that we're trying to improve business operations with automation. Computers have to affect the bottom line. They have to have a positive impact on the business."

Wilson was concerned about productivity and felt the personal computer could either aid or hinder that goal. "There are always teams of up to twenty people working together on an account. Specialists come from different departments—risk management, casualty, and so on—and often work in different offices. That means lots of contact by phone and lots of meetings. We implemented a work group software application called Lotus Notes for our staff working with personal computers connected in a network. Then we developed an application suited to our own needs called J&H InfoEdge, that uses Notes. J&H InfoEdge makes it possible for our people to share information and communicate much more efficiently than they ever could using phones and meetings—which, of course, they still use, but far less frequently."

One benefit the computer system has provided is a more egalitarian environment for communication up and down the organization. "Even though we work in groups, and always have, we still have a hierarchical management structure," says Wilson. "I don't think you can have an organization without that. You still must have a manager, someone to report to, someone to ask for advice and counsel.

WILLIAM W. WILSON III

VICE-PRESIDENT, JOHNSON & HIGGINS

"Our management is very concerned about our people; they are truly our assets. We're a closely knit organization, and there's a low level of bureaucracy and politics here. Our president, even though he's busy with his own duties, wants to know what's on people's minds. Our computer system has a feature called electronic mail, which lets people write messages on the computer and send them throughout the company. The president now has an 'open electronic door,' and anyone can write him with comments. Our work group structure makes it possible to do that without somebody's boss feeling like the employee is going over his or her head. What we really have is a new network of relationships. More employees 'know' the president than ever before."

Wilson manages about forty-five people in his department, and they are often assigned throughout the Johnson & Higgins organization. "They join in work groups to install new software or PCs and help teams get trained and productive," he says. "This has really broken down the old barriers and has greatly streamlined our workflow and our operations. The technology is helping us change the way we work from 'What do you want to do?' to 'What do you want to *accomplish?*'

"I do a lot of management by walking around," Wilson continues. "My people are almost always involved in a project with a work group, and that's a fairly structured environment. They're expected to be self-starting and know what has to be done. But I like to get informal groups of people together over pizza and beer and just talk about things.

"There is a strong human factor in work that cannot be neglected. We need to interact with one another. I took a course in graduate school called Humanistic Leadership, but at the time I didn't have enough work experience to realize its true value. But now I feel it must have been one of the most important classes I've ever taken."

In Chapter 8 you were introduced to the concepts involved in staffing an organization. Once employees are hired, the manager needs to focus energy on working with these new organizational resources—developing a sound working environment, motivating workers, and providing leadership. People are the most important resource a manager has. With their support and skills, the organization—and the manager—will achieve objectives. Without a well-led and motivated work force, the organization is doomed to mediocrity or failure.

Developing a Positive Work Environment

morale
The attitude or feeling workers have about the organization and their total work life.

quality of work life (QWL)
Management efforts focused on enhancing workers' dignity, improving their physical and emotional well-being, and improving the satisfaction of individual needs in the workplace.

What do Southwest Airlines, Chili's restaurants, Chaparrel Steel, and Omni Hotels have in common? One answer could be success. Although these organizations offer different products in divergent marketplaces, they have all become successful. But if you have to peek through a window or, better yet, enter the workplace, you could tell the real difference. The **morale**—*the attitude or feeling workers have about the organization and their total work life*—is excellent in each organization. The CEOs of each company and their management teams have created a positive work environment. Each in his own way has implemented the philosophy and concepts associated with the quality of work life (QWL) movement.[1] With the **quality of work life** approach, *management efforts are focused on enhancing workers' dignity, improving their physical and emotional well-being, and improving the satisfaction of individual needs in the workplace.* The management teams at these companies, by providing leadership and focusing on developing a positive work environment, have captured the commitment of their employees. The result is employees who are truly motivated—they want to do their jobs well. Such commitment, combined with the skill to do the job, creates an energetic, highly competent set of partners to work with management. Figure 9.1 illustrates the factors that contribute to a quality work life.

The managers at Southwest Airlines, Chili's, Chaparrel Steel, and Omni Hotels have met one of the greatest challenges facing management—determining how to provide leadership and motivate employees. They have come to realize that motivation is not magic. Rather, it is supported by a positive work environment. The foundation for a positive work environment includes having a philosophy of management, treating people as individuals, providing support, and recognizing cultural diversity.

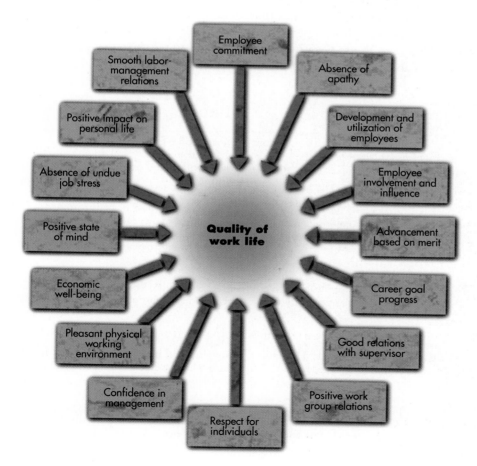

Figure 9.1

Factors that enhance the quality of work life.

Building a Philosophy of Management

One factor that sets the foundation for creating a positive work environment is a manager's **philosophy of management**, or *attitude about work and the people who perform the work.* A manager's philosophy incorporates and reflects his or her beliefs about human nature in the work setting—about the attitudes and characteristics of workers and about how management expectations influence behavior. A manager's philosophy influences the motivational approaches he or she will select. Managers who see subordinates as ambitious, eager, wishing to do work well, wanting to be independent, and enjoying work will take far different actions than managers who see subordinates in an opposite vein. These two opposing attitudes toward human nature have been dubbed Theory X and Theory Y.

THEORY X AND THEORY Y Douglas McGregor, a professor of industrial management, has said that management philosophy reflects one of two sets of assumptions about workers: Theory X or Theory Y.[2] **Theory X** is *a philosophy of management with a negative perception of subordinates' potential for work and attitudes toward work.* It assumes that workers dislike work, are poorly motivated, and require close supervision. A manager with these beliefs tends to control workers, to use negative motivation, and to refuse to delegate decision making. Table 9.1 provides a fuller description of Theory X.

Table 9.1

**Theory X and
Theory Y
assumptions
about workers.**

THEORY X	THEORY Y
People basically dislike work and avoid it whenever possible.	Most people find work as natural as play or rest and develop an attitude toward work based on their experience with it.
Because most people dislike work, they have to be closely supervised and threatened with punishment to reach objectives.	People do not need to be threatened with punishment; they will work voluntarily toward organizational objectives to which they are committed.
Most people prefer to be told what to do, have little ambition, want to avoid responsibility, and want security above all else.	The average person working in a good human relations environment will accept and seek responsibility.
Most people have little degree of imagination and creativity. They are not capable of solving problems. Rather, they must be directed.	Most people have a high degree of imagination, ingenuity, and creativity with which to solve organizational problems.
Most people have limited intellectual potential. Contributions above basic job performance should not be expected.	Although people have intellectual potential, managers only partially utilize it in modern industrial life.

Theory Y, on the other hand, is *a philosophy of management with a positive perception of subordinates' potential for and attitudes toward work.* It assumes, as shown in Table 9.1, that workers can be self-directing, will seek responsibility, and find work as natural as play or rest. The natural outcome of this belief is a manager who encourages workers to seek responsibility, involves them in decision making, and works with them to achieve their goals.

The important point about Theory X and Theory Y is that the manager's philosophy influences the type of work climate he or she tries to create and ultimately how people are treated. As Calvin Thomas, an assembly worker at Honda of America in Liberty, Ohio, says, "You give us the opportunity to have a say-so, and we can do a good job."[3]

DEVELOPING MANAGEMENT EXPECTATIONS: THE SELF-FULFILLING PROPHECY A second part of a manager's philosophy is that management expectations for performance and behavior need to be developed and directly communicated to employees; by doing so, managers get the results they desire. Research has shown that:

- Subordinates do what they believe they are expected to do.
- Less effective managers fail to develop high performance expectations.
- Managers perceived as excellent create high performance expectations that their employees can fulfill.[4]

This concept, often referred to as the *self-fulfilling prophecy,* is a key idea in management. Sam Walton believed in it so much that it became "Rule 3 of Sam's Rules for Building a Business: Motivate your partners. Money and ownership aren't enough . . . set high goals, encourage competition, and then keep score."[5]

Incorporating management expectations into a manager's philosophy involves two phases. First, the manager develops and communicates his or her expectations of performance, group citizenship, individual initiative, and job creativity. Second, the manager consistently applies these expectations. This consistency will promote stability, reduce anxiety, and eliminate guessing games by employees because they know what the boss expects.

Treating People as Individuals

A key ingredient in developing a positive work environment is to treat people as individuals. All of us are individuals. We have different personalities. We think differently. We have different needs, wants, values, expectations, and goals. We each change over time as well. Being linked to others may be important today; a year from now it may be more important to be recognized for what we have accomplished. Looking at the makeup of today's work force brings the concept of individuality into sharp focus. "Baby boomers," senior citizens, minority group members, new immigrants, and working mothers bring their own needs, goals, and values to the workplace.[6]

Theory Y
A philosophy of management with a positive perception of subordinates' potential for and attitudes toward work.

Managers need to recognize people as individuals and to work with their individual differences. This recognition goes one step further. Because each worker is an individual, each is motivated differently. The more managers know about motivation, the more successful they will be in working with people.

Providing Support

Essential to the development of motivated employees is a work climate in which their needs can be met. A starting point is to assist employees in attaining their individual goals—by removing barriers, developing mutual goal-setting opportunities, initiating training and education programs to enhance performance, encouraging risk taking, and providing stability.

Two other actions can provide support and enhance the environment. First, managers should openly appreciate the contributions of individual employees. As Jill Barad, president of Mattel USA, says, "Taking time to tell people how good they are is one of the best ways management can reward people for their efforts. We in management tend to focus on what's not being done, how people are not performing instead of recognizing that our people are performing. We must constantly remind people of their strengths so they can make the most of those behaviors."[7]

Second, managers should show sensitivity to employees' need for equity. Each employee must feel that she or he is receiving a fair exchange for his or her input into the company and in comparison to other employees. This point is supported by Norman Brinker, CEO of Chili's and the new Macaroni Grill restaurants: "Compensation has to be equitable. From the top to the bottom of the organization, the program must recognize the value of inputs into the company. Everyone is aware of everyone else."[8]

YOU DECIDE

How would you describe your work environment? What philosophy of management does your manager exhibit? Do you feel you are treated as an individual? Why? Do you receive support? Why? Does management value cultural diversity? Why?

Recognizing Cultural Diversity

Part of working with people as individuals is the ability to recognize and incorporate the value of cultural diversity within the workplace. As noted in Chapter 8, the ethnic composition of the work force is changing, and with it the needs, goals, and values of workers. Minorities—African Americans, Hispanics, and Asians—are collectively becoming the majority in the workplace.[9]

Managers need to respond to this diversity by understanding and appreciating cultural differences. As the mix in the work force continues to change, traditional programs for training, mentoring, and compensation may have to be modified.[10]

Umanoff and Parsons, a New York City Bakery, has recognized and incorporated the value of cultural diversity within the workplace. Its six-person—three women, three men—senior management team represents five

As cultural diversity continues to increase in the work force, management must respond with changes in training, mentoring, and other programs.

diverse cultures—Jamaican, American, Haitian, Hispanic, and Russian. Half of the bakery's workers are foreign born—from Haiti, Trinidad, Grenada, the Dominican Republic, and Russia. This diversity brings different viewpoints, experiences, and needs to the work environment. As a result, the company has designed training programs, developed mentor programs, and created cross-cultural teams.[11]

Motivating Workers

Enlightened managers understand that motivation is not something done *to* a person. Rather, it results from a combination of factors, the most important of which are the individual's needs, his or her ability to make choices, and an environment that provides the opportunity to satisfy those needs and create chances to make those choices. **Motivation** is *the result of the interaction of a person's internalized needs with external influences that determine behavior.*

People make conscious decisions that affect their own welfare. Why do you do what you do? Why do you choose to go to school and someone else does not? Why do you choose to study hard and someone else does not? Understanding motivation involves understanding what prompts people to act, what influences their choice of action, and why they persist in acting in a certain way. The starting point is to look at a person's needs by using a motivation model.

The Motivation Model

A person's needs provide the basis for a motivation model. **Needs** are *deficiencies that a person experiences at a particular time, creating a tension (stimulus)*

motivation
The result of the interaction of a person's internalized needs with external influences that determine behavior.

needs
Deficiencies that a person experiences at a particular time, creating a tension (stimulus) that results in wants.

Figure 9.2

Basic motivational model.

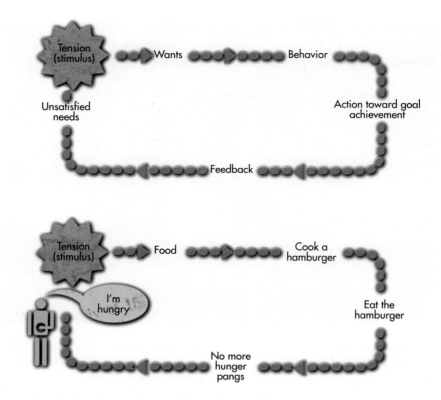

that results in wants. The needs may be physiological—bodily needs, such as food, water, and air—or psychological—such as affiliation with others or self-esteem. The person with a need develops a behavior or set of behaviors to satisfy the want that has been aroused. The behavior results in action toward goal achievement.[12]

Figure 9.2 shows this model in action: A person is hungry (need); recognizing this need triggers a want (food); the person chooses to cook a hamburger (behavior); he or she eats the hamburger (action to achieve the goal). Afterward, the person feels no hunger (feedback). This simple model becomes more complex with the recognition that a person's motivated behavior is subject to many influences. Why did the person choose a hamburger instead of cereal? Why did the person cook the hamburger instead of buying it? Has the behavior been used before? If so, did it satisfy the need? The integrated motivation model—by addressing what influences motivational choices—provides answers to such questions.

The Integrated Motivation Model

As a person is choosing a behavior to satisfy a need, he or she must evaluate several factors:

1. *Past experience.* All the person's past experiences with the situation enter into the motivation model. These experiences include the satisfaction derived from acting in a certain way, any frustration felt, the amount of effort required, and the relationship of performance to rewards.
2. *Environmental influences.* The choices of behaviors are affected by the environment, which in a business setting is composed of the values of the organization as well as the expectations and actions of management.
3. *Perceptions.* The individual is influenced by his or her perceptions of the expected effort required to achieve performance and by the value of the reward both absolutely and in relation to what peers have received for the same effort.

In addition to these three variables, two other factors are at work. *Skills* are the person's capabilities (usually the result of training) for performing, and *incentives* are factors created by management to encourage workers to perform a task.

Let's look at the process again, but this time from a business perspective, using a hypothetical first-level manager at General Electric:

1. Unsatisfied needs stimulate wants. The manager feels a need to be respected. She wants to be recognized by her boss as an outstanding employee.
2. Behavior is identified to satisfy the want. She identifies two behaviors that can satisfy the want: writing a report or volunteering to take on a special project. To decide between the two, she consciously evaluates the rewards or punishments associated with each (incentives), her abilities to take the actions (skills), and her past experiences, environmental influences, and perceptions.
3. Based on this analysis, she selects what she considers the best option (behavior) and then takes action to volunteer for the project.
4. The response that she gets from her boss constitutes the feedback. If that response is positive, the manager not only has her need met, but she is more likely to behave similarly in the future.

Figure 9.3 shows the integrated motivation model, illustrating how the various factors influence decision making.

With this model in mind we are now ready to explore some theories about motivation. The first two theories we'll look at emphasize the needs that motivate people. If managers understand workers' needs, they can include factors in the work environment to meet them, thereby helping direct employees' energies toward the organization's goals. The third theory explains how employees choose behaviors to meet their needs and how they determine whether the choices are successful.

Figure 9.3
Integrated
motivation
model.

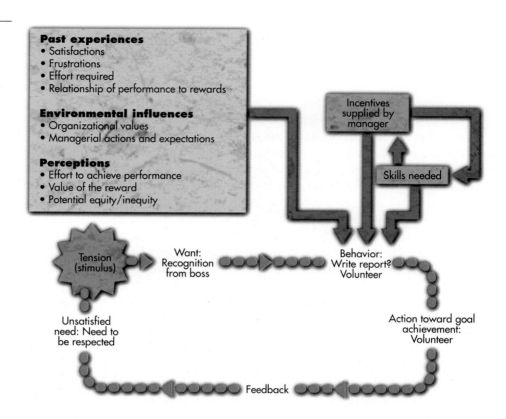

Maslow's Hierarchy of Needs

A tool that managers can apply to understanding human needs was developed by psychologist Abraham H. Maslow. His theory is based on four premises:

1. A person's needs are arranged in a priority order of importance. This priority, or hierarchy, goes from the most basic needs (water, food, shelter) to the most complex (esteem and self-actualization).
2. Only an unsatisfied need can influence behavior; a satisfied need is not a motivator. Thus, someone who has just been promoted is unlikely to feel the need for esteem.
3. A person will at least minimally satisfy each level of need before feeling the need at the next level. Someone must feel companionship before desiring recognition.
4. If satisfaction is not maintained for a need, it will become a priority need again. For example, for a person who is at the level of social needs, safety will become a priority once again if he or she is fired.[13]

MASLOW'S PYRAMID Figure 9.4 shows Maslow's hierarchy of needs in their order of priority. The first category consists of physiological (physical) needs.

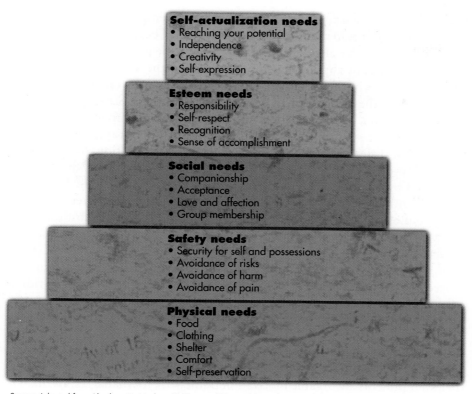

Figure 9.4

Abraham Maslow's hierarchy of human needs.

Self-actualization needs
• Reaching your potential
• Independence
• Creativity
• Self-expression

Esteem needs
• Responsibility
• Self-respect
• Recognition
• Sense of accomplishment

Social needs
• Companionship
• Acceptance
• Love and affection
• Group membership

Safety needs
• Security for self and possessions
• Avoidance of risks
• Avoidance of harm
• Avoidance of pain

Physical needs
• Food
• Clothing
• Shelter
• Comfort
• Self-preservation

Source: Adapted from Abraham H. Maslow, "A Theory of Human Motivation," *Psychological Review*, 50 (1943), pp. 370–396.

These are the primary or basic-level needs, including water, air, food, shelter, and comfort. In the working environment, management tries to satisfy these needs primarily through salary and wages that allow employees to buy the basic necessities. While the employee is at work, the company meets these needs with water fountains, clean air, no objectionable odors or noises, comfortable temperatures, and lunch breaks.

When physiological needs are met to the satisfaction of the individual, safety needs become a priority. Behaviors that reflect safety needs include joining unions, seeking jobs with tenure, and choosing jobs on the basis of insurance and retirement programs. All of us desire a work environment in which we can be free from threats to our physical and emotional sense of security.[14] Management attempts to satisfy safety needs primarily through salary, benefits, safe working conditions that are in place and enforced, and job security procedures.

Social needs become dominant when safety needs have been minimally gratified. People desire friendship, companionship, and a place in a group. Love needs include both giving and receiving.[15] These needs are met by frequent interaction with fellow workers and acceptance by others. The proverbial conversation at the water cooler reflects employees' needs to inter-act socially as well as in their official business roles. The groups that employees form at lunchtime are also a result of their need to be social. Management can meet social needs by supporting employee get-togethers.

The next level in the hierarchy, esteem needs, includes the desires for self-respect and for the recognition of one's abilities by others. Satisfaction of these needs gives pride, self-confidence, and a true sense of importance. Lack of satisfaction of these needs can lead to feelings of inferiority, weakness, and helplessness. Esteem needs can be met in an organization by successful completion of projects, by recognition of the merit or value of the person's work, and by organizational titles. The late Sam Walton of Wal-Mart recog-nized the importance of this need in creating his Rule 5: "Appreciate every-thing your associates do for the business . . . nothing else can substitute for a few well-chosen, well-timed, sincere words of praise."[16]

Maslow's highest need level, self-actualization or self-realization, is the need to maximize the use of one's skills, abilities, and potential. If an em-ployee wants a college degree, a manager can help meet this need by providing a flexible work schedule around classes, tuition reimbursement, and opportu-nities in jobs to learn the practical side of a class in theory.

IMPLICATIONS FOR MANAGERS Maslow's theory is a general needs theory. Its categories apply to all environments and not specifically to work. Never-theless, it presents a workable motivation framework for managers. By analyz-ing comments, attitudes, quality and quantity of work, and personal circum-stances, the manager can try to identify the particular need level an employee is attempting to satisfy. Then the manager can try to build into the work environment the opportunity for the individual to satisfy those needs. Table 9.2 presents examples of workers' circumstances, potential needs, and actions that can be taken.

A difficulty of working with needs theory is that people are unique in their perceptions and personalities. Thus, many workers can seek to satisfy the same need in many different ways. And just as one motive can lead to different behaviors, the same behavior can spring from different motives. For example, the act of working hard on a new project can come from many needs. Some people apply themselves to grow and develop. Others do so to be liked. Still others wish to earn more money to enhance their sense of security. And still others want the recognition that success will bring. For this reason, managers must be careful when attempting to read motives by simply observing a person's behavior.

A thwarted need can frustrate an employee and will remain an influence on behavior until it is satisfied. It might be satisfied off the job or on the job. It might be satisfied in a way that meshes with the organization's goals and processes or in competition with them. The esteem need, for example, can be satisfied by both unions and the informal group.

WORKERS' CIRCUMSTANCES	LEVELS OF NEED DEMANDING SATISFACTION	NEED-SATISFYING ACTIONS
Employee has two children entering college next year.	Physiological/safety	Increase pay or train and promote employee to higher-paying job if justified; confirm job security.
Worker feels concern about a competitor's purchase of the firm.	Safety	If possible, reassure worker that jobs will not be eliminated; otherwise, frankly admit that certain jobs will be abolished. Encourage and assist those affected to seek employment elsewhere.
Worker feels uncomfortable as a new addition to a closely knit work group.	Social	Invite workers to a social evening at your home, creating an opportunity for the newcomer to meet peers in an informal setting. Encourage the new worker to participate in company recreational activities. Sponsor the new worker for membership in professional organizations.
Employee feels unappreciated.	Self-esteem	Examine the employee's job performance and find reasons for praise. Accept the employee's suggestions where applicable. Build closer rapport.
Worker wants to get ahead in the organization and has a general idea of an ultimate employment goal in the company.	Self-realization/self-actualization	Provide specific guidance in pinpointing ultimate goal; help chart career path. Facilitate educational improvement. Provide opportunities for job experience and company recognition.

The level of satisfaction of needs always fluctuates. Once a need is satisfied, it will cease to influence behavior—only for a time. Needs never remain fully satisfied.

Table 9.2
Worker needs and appropriate managerial responses.

Herzberg's Two-Factor Theory

A second needs theory was developed by psychologist Frederick Herzberg and his associates. This theory, called the two-factor or maintenance-motivator theory, uncovered one set of factors that produce job satisfaction and motivation—called motivators—and another set of factors that lead to job dissatisfaction—called maintenance or hygiene factors.[17]

MAINTENANCE FACTORS **Maintenance factors**—often referred to as hygiene factors—are *aspects of a job's environment that must be provided in sufficient quality to avoid employee dissatisfaction.* These factors are extrinsic to the job—that is, they do not relate directly to a person's work, to its real nature. And when they are provided in sufficient quality, they will not

maintenance (hygiene) factors
Aspects of a job's environment that must be provided in sufficient quality to avoid employee dissatisfaction.

necessarily act as motivators—stimuli for growth or greater effort. They will only lead employees to experience no job dissatisfaction.[18] These factors include:

1. Salary—adequate wages and fringe benefits.
2. Job security—adequate company grievance procedures and seniority privileges.
3. Working conditions—adequate heat, light, ventilation, and hours of work.
4. Status—sufficient privileges, job titles, and other symbols of rank and position.
5. Company policies—standard organizational policies and fairness in administering those policies.
6. Quality of technical supervision—availability of supervisors to give answers to job-related questions.
7. Quality of interpersonal relations among peers, supervisors, and subordinates—adequate social opportunities as occasions for developing comfortable operating relationships.

Herzberg found that these factors are taken for granted. Workers feel that management is morally obligated to provide them, so when they exist the response is neutral. A package of standard fringe benefits such as sick leave, paid vacations, health and life insurance, and a pension plan will not make workers do more than they must. Take these benefits away though—cancel company-paid medical insurance—and employees will quickly become dissatisfied.

motivation factors
Aspects of a job that relate directly to the real nature of the work performed and that are necessary to job satisfaction.

MOTIVATION FACTORS **Motivation** (or growth) **factors** are *aspects of a job that relate directly to the real nature of the work performed and that are necessary to job satisfaction.* When an employer fails to provide these factors in sufficient quality, employees experience no job satisfaction. When provided in sufficient quality, they provide job satisfaction and high performance. People require different kinds and degrees of motivation factors—what stimulates one worker may not affect another. Motivation factors also act as stimuli for psychological and personal growth.[19] These factors include:

1. Achievement—opportunities to accomplish something and to contribute something of value when presented with a challenge.
2. Recognition—acknowledgment that contributions have been worth the effort and that the effort has been noted and appreciated.
3. Responsibility—acquisition of new duties and responsibilities, either through expansion of the job or by delegation.
4. Advancement—opportunities to improve one's position as a result of job performance.
5. The work itself—opportunities for self-expression, personal satisfaction, and challenge.

6. Possibility of growth—opportunities to increase knowledge and develop through job experiences.

Figure 9.5 illustrates Herzberg's factors. The maintenance factors range from causing no dissatisfaction, if they are present in the work environment, to causing high dissatisfaction, if they are not present in sufficient quality. Motivation factors, if present in the work environment, can provide low to high satisfaction. If they are not present, no job satisfaction can result.

IMPLICATIONS FOR MANAGERS Herzberg's theory has a number of implications for managers. They should use the theory to focus on ensuring presence of and quality in maintenance factors as a foundation on which to build motivation. In the absence of quality, employees may face an "unclean" environment, which can lead to dissatisfaction.

If you review the list of motivation factors, you will see that practically all supervisors have the power to make subordinates' jobs more rewarding by granting them more responsibility, praising their accomplishments, making them feel that they are succeeding, and so on. Company after company, whether du Pont, Tandem Computers, or Southwest Airlines, has come to the same conclusion: motivated employees are the ones who have responsibility, who are totally involved in their jobs. They feel that they have control over their jobs and can make a contribution. This conclusion serves as the basis for team management and the concepts of empowerment and intrapreneurship, which are discussed later in this chapter.[20]

Maintenance factors

High dissatisfaction · No dissatisfaction

Absence of factor · Presence of factor

Motivation factors

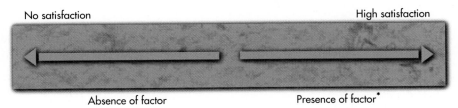

No satisfaction · High satisfaction

Absence of factor · Presence of factor*

*The quality of each factor present influences each employee's level of satisfaction or dissatisfaction.

Figure 9.5

Herzberg's job satisfaction factors.

Figure 9.6

Comparison of Maslow's needs hierarchy and Herzberg's maintenance and motivation factors.

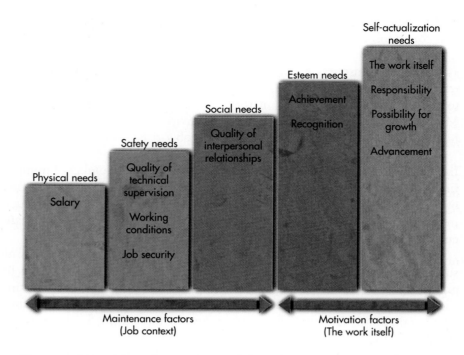

Maintenance factors
(Job context)

Motivation factors
(The work itself)

Figure 9.6 provides a comparison of the views of Maslow and Herzberg. Herzberg's maintenance factors are similar to Maslow's physical, safety, and social needs levels. Herzberg's motivation factors are similar to Maslow's esteem and self-actualization needs.

Vroom's Expectancy Theory

Up to this point, we have discussed two theories relating to the trigger for motivation—the needs of the individual. We are now ready to introduce a theory that explains why people choose a particular behavior to satisfy these needs. This theory discusses the influences on behavior illustrated in Figure 9.3: past experiences, environment, and perceptions.

expectancy theory
Vroom's theory that before choosing a behavior, an individual will evaluate various possibilities on the basis of how much work they involve and what the reward is.

Vroom's **expectancy theory** states that *before choosing a behavior, an individual will evaluate various possibilities on the basis of how much work they involve and what the reward is.* Motivation—the spur to act—is a function of how badly individuals want something and how likely they think they are to get it. It occurs in direct proportion to perceived or expected rewards. This theory includes three variables[21]:

1. *Effort-performance link.* Will the effort achieve performance? That is, how much effort will the performance take, and how likely is the effort to succeed?
2. *Performance-reward link.* What is the possibility of a certain performance leading to the desired reward or outcome? That is, how likely is the payoff to be worth the effort?

3. *Reward attractiveness.* How attractive is the reward? Will it fill an unsatisfied need of the individual?

AN EXAMPLE John Friedman's boss asks him at the last minute on Friday afternoon to develop a presentation on the six-month budget results by Monday morning. A quick analysis shows John that this project will take four hours. He sees two possibilities: stay and do the work, or take it home over the weekend.

Situation 1: Staying at work for the required four hours will result in a completed presentation by Monday (effort-performance link). John also knows from past experience that completing the project will be recognized by his boss and be lauded (performance-reward link). John has a high regard for this recognition because it will eventually lead to a promotion, but working late on Friday will interfere with plans and may cause domestic problems (attractiveness).

Situation 2: Both the effort-performance link and the performance-reward link remain the same as with situation 1. The difference is that by taking the work home, John will still receive his boss's recognition but not cause the negative consequences of interfering with social plans (attractiveness). John chooses this option.

In this process, John has gone through a series of questions: "Can I accomplish the task?" Yes, it will take four hours, but I have the ability to do it. "What's in it for me?" When I do the task it can bring both positive and negative results (situation 1) or just positive results (situation 2). "Is it worth it?" The positive is, but the negative isn't. Figure 9.7 provides a simplified illustration of this example of expectancy theory.

IMPLICATIONS FOR MANAGERS According to expectancy theory, behavior is heavily influenced by perceptions of possible outcomes. If an individual expects a certain outcome, possesses the competence to achieve it, and wants it

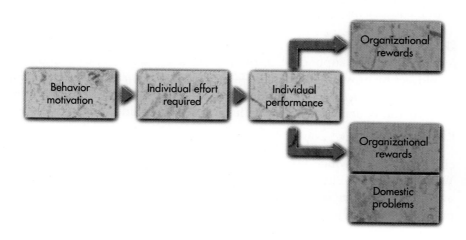

Figure 9.7
Expectancy
theory example.

badly enough, he or she will exhibit the required behavior. If a person expects that a specific behavior will produce an outcome that he or she perceives as undesirable, he or she will be less inclined to exhibit that behavior. In this light, a manager who knows each subordinate's expectations and desires can tailor outcomes associated with specific behaviors to produce motivation.

To motivate behavior, managers need to do the following things:

- Understand that managers get what they reward, not what they ask for. Employees measure the value associated with the assignment.
- Find out what outcomes are perceived as desirable by employees and provide them. Outcomes may be intrinsic—experienced directly by the individual—or extrinsic—provided by the company. A feeling of self-worth after doing a good job is intrinsic; the promotion that the job produces is extrinsic. For an outcome to be satisfying to an employee, it must be recognized by the employee as an outcome, must be related to his or her needs and values, and must be consistent with the individual's expectations of what he or she should receive.
- Make the job intrinsically rewarding. If this is a valued outcome, it is critical to provide it for the employee.
- Effectively and clearly communicate desired behaviors and their outcomes. Employees need to know what is and is not acceptable to the organization.
- Link rewards to performance. Once the acceptable performance level is attained, rewards should quickly follow.
- Be aware that people and their goals, needs, desires, and levels of performance differ. The manager must set a level of performance for each employee that is attainable by that person.
- Strengthen each individual's perceptions of his or her ability to execute desired behaviors and achieve outcomes by providing guidance and direction.

With the foundations of motivation established, we now move on to examine leadership.

Defining Leadership

Managers build a supportive work environment that encourages motivated employees by providing **leadership**—*the process of influencing individuals and groups to set and achieve goals.* **Influence** is *the ability to sway other people to one's will.* In the course of exerting influence, leaders guide, direct, show, and inspire.

Leadership involves three variables: the leader, those being led, and the circumstances in which leadership is exercised. All three change constantly. When head coach Phil Jackson of the Chicago Bulls prepares his team to take on an opponent, he is exercising leadership. Each opponent, game, and play presents the coach, his staff, and their players with new challenges and

leadership
The process of influencing individuals and groups to set and achieve goals.

influence
The ability to sway other people to one's will.

GLOBAL PERSPECTIVE

Creating a Motivated Work Environment

Japanese companies have a secret to their success. They have managed to break down the "us versus them" barrier that so often harms the American working environment by dividing management and labor. When an employee of Toyota thinks "us versus them," *them* is more likely to be Nissan or General Motors than Toyota's management. Japanese managers have achieved this attitude by creating a feeling that employees and managers share a common fate. A well-run Japanese corporation is of, by, and for its people.

The Japanese do not forget that a business organization is made up of people and can function no better than they do. Japanese managers believe that the company's employees, not its machines, are its most important assets and are therefore to be valued, nurtured, and, except in extreme situations, retained. As a result, Japanese companies train their employees, guarantee them job security, and offer career paths that are there if the company is successful.

Japanese companies—although they have management hierarchies—are run by their employees. Many top companies are run by consensus. Work is organized into teams, from the executive suite to the factory floor. Important ideas and decisions come up from below at least as frequently as they come down from the top. Ordinary workers are encouraged to make on-the-spot decisions rather than leave their brains at the door.

Japanese companies have been successful in incorporating the elements identified as supporting motivation. They have been rewarded by a committed, motivated work force.

(For more on creating a motivated work environment, see Alan S. Blinder, "How Japan Puts the Human in Human Capital," *Business Week*, June 11, 1992, p. 20.)

demands. When David Nagel, head of Apple Computer's advanced technology group, works with his teams to create new software and digital devices, he is leading. His teams' efforts are influenced by the quality of his leadership, by the abilities and motivations of team members, and by the internal and external limits and challenges they encounter in each situation.

What qualities must a leader have? Jeffrey Christian, president and chief executive officer of a Cleveland-based executive search firm, looks for managers who are

high-impact players, change agents, drivers, and winners—people who are extremely flexible, bright, tactical, and strategic, who can handle a lot of information, make decisions quickly, motivate others, chase a moving target, and shake things up. Previously, corporate recruiting emphasized credentials [schooling] and experience, which are still important, but . . . you can't teach good leadership or how to be excited about life.[22]

Robert K. Greenleaf, former director of management research at AT&T and founding director of the Center for Applied Ethics, says, "The leader exists to serve those whom he nominally leads, those who supposedly follow him. He (or she) takes *their* fulfillment as his principal aim." According to Greenleaf, the servant-leader takes people and their work seriously, listens to and takes the lead from the troops, heals, is self-effacing, and sees himself or herself as a steward.[23]

Leadership Traits

Early theories about leadership suggested that excellent leaders have certain traits, or personal characteristics, that lie at the root of their ability to lead. Following World War II, the U.S. Army surveyed soldiers in an attempt to compile a list of traits shared by commanders whom soldiers perceived as leaders. The resulting list, which included fourteen traits, was clearly inadequate to describe leadership. No two commanders displayed all the traits, and many famous commanders lacked several.

More recently, Gary A. Yuki constructed a list of traits and skills commonly associated with effective leaders.[24] Table 9.3 presents these traits. This list suggests that a leader is strongly motivated to excel and succeed.

No list of leadership traits and skills can be definitive, however, because no two leaders are exactly alike. Different leaders working with different people in different situations need different traits and skills. If people in charge

Table 9.3

Traits and skills commonly associated with effective leadership.

TRAITS	SKILLS
Adaptable	Cleverness (intelligence)
Alert to social environment	Conceptual ability
Ambitious and achievement-oriented	Creativity
Assertive	Diplomacy and tact
Cooperative	Fluency in speaking
Decisive	Knowledge about the group task
Dependable	Organizational (administrative) ability
Dominant (desires to influence others)	Persuasiveness
Energetic (high activity level)	Social ability
Persistent	
Self-confident	
Tolerant of stress	
Willing to assume responsibility	

Source: Gary A. Yuki, *Leadership in Organizations,* © 1981, p. 70.
Adapted by permission of Prentice-Hall, Inc., Englewood Cliffs, NJ.

MANAGER'S NOTEBOOK

"What kept me here is probably the most important question," says Shelley Lauten, director of Disney University at Walt Disney World. "Disney actually puts its philosophies of management to work—unlike many companies that say the right things in stated policies but don't practice them. Disney University is here to make sure that we focus on our people needs. That's a critical difference."

The critical difference is Walt Disney World's approach to people. The approach is actually quite simple—living up to it is the hard part. The philosophy includes:

- Training people to live the company's culture
- Communicating with all employees
- Recognizing people's talent and rewarding them for it in a variety of ways
- Ensuring a consistent approach to working with people

It is Shelley Lauten's job to help instill and nurture this philosophy in all the employees in The Magic Kingdom. As director of the Disney training facility, Lauten leads a full-time staff of 150 who last year taught 2,500 different classes—everything from basic training and refresher courses to executive development—to about 100,000 participants. She sees her personal charge as ensuring that cast members (employees) are happy so that they can focus on the guests (customers). "If employees are well taken care of, they will take care of the guests." With that said, Lauten sets about implementing the philosophy.

The goal of the training program is to create a sense of pride that assures employees they have picked the right place to work. Pride is seen at Disney as essential to productivity and quality service. With this in mind, everyone goes through Disney training—no exceptions, no condensed courses. In some instances new employees can experience severe cultural adjustment. But the training is designed to bring the new employees into the culture of the organization—and ease the transition.

As with its motion picture productions, Disney has found a winning formula: Define your philosophy, live it, train for it, and you'll be successful.

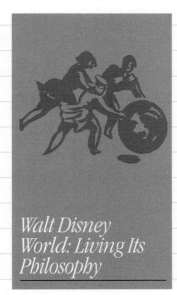

Walt Disney World: Living Its Philosophy

(For more on the Walt Disney World philosophy, see Cheryl Hall, "Disney School Fashions Workers in Its Image," *Dallas Morning News,* May 9, 1993, pp. 1H–3H.)

Figure 9.8

The relationship between management and leadership.

People who have both leadership ability and management ability

Leadership ability

Management ability

People who have leadership ability but are not managers

People who have management ability but are not leaders

possess what is needed when it is needed, they should be able to exercise effective leadership.

Management Versus Leadership

Management and *leadership* are not synonyms. Managers plan, organize, staff, direct, and control. They may or may not be effective in influencing their subordinates or team members to set and achieve goals. Ideally, leadership and management skills combine to allow a manager to function as a leader, as Figure 9.8 suggests. The manager who gives orders and explicit instructions to experienced people, for instance, is not leading but actually limiting productivity. Effective planning helps one to become a manager; enabling others to plan effectively is leading. Leaders empower—they give people the things they need to grow, to change, and to cope with change. Leaders create and share visions, generating strategies to bring the visions to reality. Table 9.4 provides even greater distinctions between management and leadership.

Choosing a Leadership Style

As noted earlier, leadership involves three variables: the leader, those being led, and the circumstances in which leadership is exercised. There is no one correct way to lead an individual or group. Leadership is situational. The **leadership style**—*the approach a manager uses to influence subordinates*—will depend on the situation. Managers' leadership styles consist of their choices of decision-making styles, their approaches to motivation, and their areas of emphasis in the work environment—whether they focus on tasks or on people.

leadership style
The approach a manager uses to influence subordinates.

MANAGEMENT TASKS	LEADERSHIP TASKS
Planning and budgeting. Establishing detailed steps and timetables for achieving needed results and then allocating the resources necessary to make them happen.	**Establishing direction.** Developing a vision of the future, often the distant future, and strategies for producing the changes needed to achieve that vision.
Organizing and staffing. Establishing a structure for accomplishing plan requirements, staffing that structure with individuals, delegating responsibility and authority for carrying out the plan, providing policies and procedures to help guide people, and creating methods or systems to monitor implementation.	**Aligning people.** Communicating the direction by words and deeds to all those whose cooperation may be needed to influence the creation of teams and coalitions that understand the vision and strategies and accept their validity.
Controlling and problem solving. Monitoring results in terms of the plan, identifying deviations, and then planning and organizing to solve these problems.	**Motivating and inspiring.** Energizing people to overcome major political, bureaucratic, and resource barriers by satisfying basic, but often unfulfilled, human needs.
Produces a degree of predictability and order and consistently achieves the key results expected by various stakeholders (for customers, being on time; for stockholders, being on budget).	*Produces change, often to a dramatic degree, that has the potential of being extremely useful (for example, developing new products that customers want or new approaches to labor relations that help make a firm more competitive).*

Source: John P. Kotter, *A Force for Change: How Leadership Differs from Management* (New York: Free Press), 1990, p. 6.
Copyright © 1990 by John P. Kotter. Reprinted with permission.

Decision-Making Styles

One element in a manager's leadership style is the degree to which he or she shares decision-making authority with subordinates. Managers' styles range from not sharing at all to completely delegating decision-making authority. Figure 9.9 shows the degrees of sharing as a continuum, with the range of styles categorized in three groups: autocratic style, participative style, and free-rein style. Which style a manager chooses should relate to the situation.

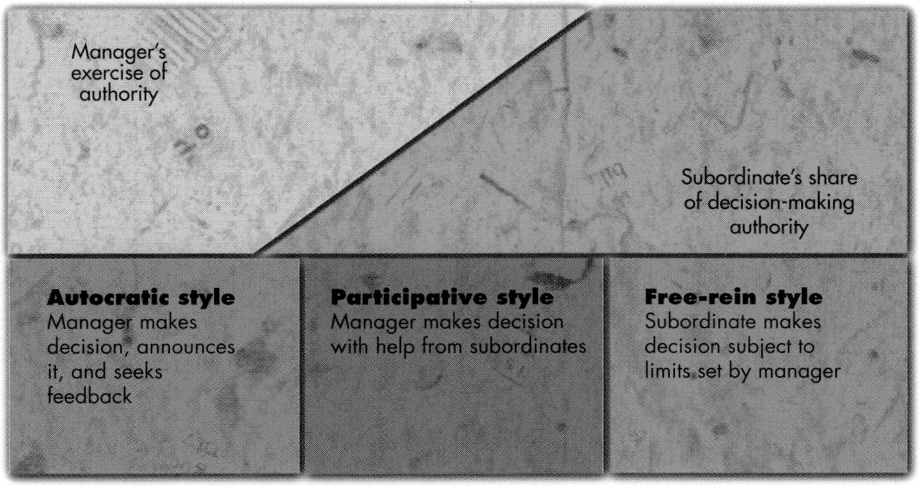

Table 9.4

The differences between management and leadership.

Manager's exercise of authority

Subordinate's share of decision-making authority

Autocratic style
Manager makes decision, announces it, and seeks feedback

Participative style
Manager makes decision with help from subordinates

Free-rein style
Subordinate makes decision subject to limits set by manager

Figure 9.9

Leadership styles and the distribution of decision-making authority.

autocratic style
A leadership approach in which a manager does not share decision-making authority with subordinates.

THE AUTOCRATIC STYLE With the **autocratic style,** *a manager does not share decision-making authority with subordinates.* The manager simply makes the decision and then announces it. Autocratic managers may ask for subordinates' ideas and feedback about the decision, but the input does not usually change the decision unless it indicates that something vital has been overlooked. The hallmark of this style is that the entire process is executed by the manager, who retains all the authority. Consequently, the autocratic style is sometimes called the "I" approach.

Under certain conditions, the autocratic style is appropriate. When a manager is training a subordinate, for instance, the content, objectives, pacing, and execution of decisions properly remain in the hands of the trainer. (The manager should seek feedback from the trainee, however.) During a crisis—a hazardous materials spill or a bomb threat, say—leaders are expected to take charge, issue orders, and make decisions.

To use the autocratic style effectively, managers must know what needs to be done and they must have technical skills. The autocratic style is effective when managers face issues that they are best equipped to solve, create solutions whose implementation does depend on others, and desire to communicate through orders and instructions. If these conditions do not exist, one of the other two leadership styles is probably more appropriate.

participative style
A leadership approach in which a manager shares decision-making authority with subordinates.

THE PARTICIPATIVE STYLE With the **participative style,** *a manager shares decision-making authority with subordinates.* The degree of sharing can range from the manager's presenting a tentative decision that is subject to change to letting the group or subordinate make the decision. Sometimes called the "we" approach, participate management involves others and lets them bring their unique viewpoints, talents, and experiences to bear on an issue. This style is strongly emphasized today because of the trends toward downsizing, employee empowerment, and worker teams.

This consultative and democratic approach works best for resolving issues that affect more than just the manager or decision maker. People affected by decisions support them more enthusiastically when they participate in the decision making than when decisions are imposed on them. Also, if others in a manager's unit know more than the manager does about an issue, common sense urges their inclusion in decisions concerning it.

Before subordinates can be brought into the process, mutual trust and respect must exist between them and their managers. The subordinates must be willing to participate and must be trained to do so. They must possess the related skills and knowledge needed to cope with the problems they are expected to solve. It takes time to give people the confidence and competence needed to make decisions. Managers must have the time, means, and patience to prepare subordinates to participate. But when employees participate, they devise solutions that they feel they own. This sense of ownership increases their commitment to making the solutions work.

THE FREE-REIN STYLE With the **free-rein style** (often called the "they" approach, or spectator style), *a manager empowers subordinates to function on their own, without direct involvement from managers to whom they report.* This style relies heavily on delegation of authority and works best when participants have and know how to use the tools and techniques needed for their tasks. Under this style, managers set limits and remain available for consultation. The managers also hold participants accountable for their actions by reviewing and evaluating performance.

Free-rein leadership works particularly well with professionals in engineering, design, research, and sales. Such people generally resist other kinds of supervision.

In most organizations, managers must be able to use the decision-making style that circumstances dictate. Lee is new, so he needs an autocratic approach until he develops the confidence and knowledge to perform independently or until he joins a team. Kim, experienced in her job and better at it than anyone else, will probably do well with a participative or free-rein approach. Because people and circumstances constantly change and because subordinates must be prepared for change, the effective manager switches from one leadership style to another as appropriate.

free-rein style
A leadership approach in which a manager empowers subordinates to function on their own, without direct involvement from managers to whom they report.

Positive Versus Negative Motivation

Another element of leadership style is the manager's approach to motivation, which can take the form of rewards or penalties.[25] Figure 9.10 presents a continuum containing positive and negative motivations. Managers with a positive leadership style motivate by using praise, recognition, or monetary

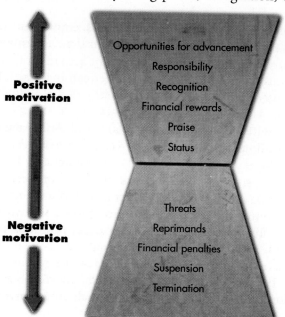

Positive motivation

Negative motivation

Opportunities for advancement
Responsibility
Recognition
Financial rewards
Praise
Status

Threats
Reprimands
Financial penalties
Suspension
Termination

Figure 9.10
Motivation continuum.

sanctions
Penalties such as fines, suspension, or termination.

rewards or by increasing security or granting additional responsibilities. Managers with a negative leadership style threaten or impose **sanctions**—*penalties such as fines, suspensions, or termination.* The manager who says, "Do it my way or else" employs negative motivation. Implied in this statement is the manager's willingness to exercise disciplinary powers; the subordinates' failure to comply would be an act of insubordination.

Positive leadership styles encourage development of employees and higher levels of job satisfaction. Negative leadership styles are based on the manager's ability to withhold items of value from employees. The result of negative leadership may be an environment of fear, where managers are viewed with distrust and seen as dictators rather than as leaders or team players.

Task Orientation Versus Employee Orientation

Yet another element of leadership style is the manager's philosophy about the most effective way to get work done. Leaders can focus on the work (a task orientation) or on employees (a relationship, or people-centered, approach). Depending on the manager's perspective and situation, these two approaches can be used separately or in combination.

A task-oriented manager emphasizes technology, methods, plans, programs, deadlines, goals, and getting the work out. Typically, such a manager uses the autocratic style of leadership and issues guidelines and instructions to subordinates. A task focus works well in the short run, especially with tight schedules or under crisis conditions. Used over the long term, however, a task focus can create personnel problems. It may cause the best performers, who desire flexibility and freedom to be creative, to leave the group, and it may increase absenteeism and decrease job satisfaction.[26]

The people-centered manager emphasizes employees' needs. He or she treats employees as valuable assets and respects their views. Teamwork, positive relationships, and mutual trust are important activities of the people-centered leader. By focusing on employees a manager can increase job satisfaction and decrease absenteeism.[27]

THE LEADERSHIP GRID Robert R. Blake and Ann Adams McCanse have created a two-dimensional model for visualizing the continuum from task focus to employee focus.[28] They call this model the Leadership Grid. As Figure 9.11 shows, the model presents two axes, one that rates concern for people and another that rates concern for production. The ratings are stated in terms of a 9-point scale, with 1 representing low concern and 9 representing high concern. The grid effectively summarizes positions that managers and leaders can take under a variety of circumstances.

If you are a manager, try to locate yourself on the grid in relation to a specific subordinate. If you are not a manager, try placing your boss's focus. Then ask yourself whether the focus is appropriate. Such an analysis typifies one use of the grid—it is an effective tool for management training and development.

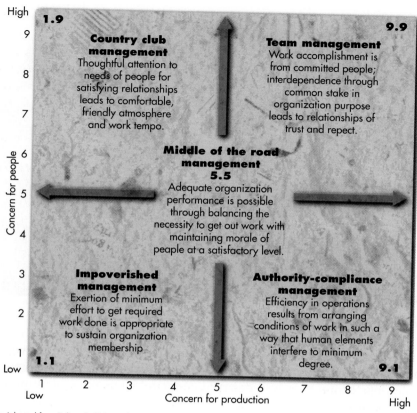

Figure 9.11

The Leadership Grid.

Source: Adapted from Robert R. Blake and Anne Adams McCanse, *Leadership Dilemmas—Grid Solutions* (Houston: Gulf Publishing), p. 29. Copyright 1991 by Scientific Methods, Inc. Used by permission.

In choosing a leadership style, a manager must adapt to the situation while evaluating decision-making style, motivational strategy, and the value of a task or employee focus. The style a manager chooses is influenced by his or her philosophy, background, and perceptions; the personalities, backgrounds, and needs of subordinates or team members; and external pressures, influences, and constraints.

Managing for Improved Motivation and Morale

With a well-rounded, people-centered philosophy, an understanding of individual needs and behaviors, and a leadership style based on the situation, a manager provides an environment for motivation to take place. In the next few pages we will examine additional actions a manager can take to increase motivation and morale: providing praise and recognition, implementing management by objectives, empowering employees, developing self-directed work teams, providing an effective reward system, redesigning jobs, promoting intrapreneurship, and creating flexibility in work.

YOU DECIDE

Think about a manager you have known. Which leadership style did the manager use? In what situations were different styles used? Were they effective? Why?

Awards
programs are
one way to give
employees
special recog-
nition for their
contributions.

Awards programs are one way to give employees special recognition for their contributions.

Providing Praise and Recognition

Giving deserved praise may seem like an obvious way to improve the work environment, but how many managers consistently do it? To most workers, honest praise and recognition are powerful motivators. Employees may redouble their efforts after well-deserved congratulations or recognition for a job well done. At Springfield Remanufacturing Corporation (SRC), praise and recognition are keystones of the company culture. Not only are individual employees singled out for dollar awards for improvement ideas, but entire departments and the total plant receive recognition for milestones. SRC has a traveling trophy for the outstanding department. When it is awarded, the entire department goes to retrieve it from the previous holder amid balloons, music, and dancing. When the company went 100,000 person-hours without an accident, the entire plant was closed for a beer bust featuring a barbecue and parades of decorated forklifts.

Implementing Management by Objectives

management by objectives (MBO)
A technique designed to improve motivation and commitment by having the manager and employee jointly set objectives, assess progress on the objectives, and evaluate the results.

One excellent motivational approach is **management by objectives** (**MBO**), *a technique designed to improve motivation and commitment by having the manager and employee jointly set objectives, assess progress on the objectives, and evaluate the results.* Management by objectives allows employees to understand goals fully. Because they are involved in a joint goal-setting process, they develop a greater commitment to meeting these goals. Finally, the employees know specifically how they will be evaluated.

The following steps are used in implementing MBO:

1. The employee and manager meet to review the employee's job description.

2. The employee and manager jointly develop the employee's goals for the agreed-upon time period.

3. The employee and manager meet periodically, at agreed-upon times, to review the employee's progress toward the goals.

4. At the end of the specified period, the employee and manager jointly evaluate the employee's performance on the goals.

If management by objectives is used in the entire company, it becomes both a planning system and a performance appraisal system. It will link all the levels of management together: Each manager will negotiate with the next lowest level of management on specific goals, which will help the people and the organization achieve their objectives.

Empowering Employees

"You want motivated workers?" asks Peter Fleming, vice-president of Prudential Insurance Company. "Just empower them and you will see what motivation and ownership means."[29] As defined by noted management consultant Tom Peters, **empowerment** is *giving individuals in an organization autonomy, authority, and trust and encouraging them to break the rules in order to get the job done.*[30]

Empowerment is designed to unshackle the worker and make the job—not just part of the job—the worker's. Employees at Prudential are now partners in the work setting. They make decisions that were formerly made by the manager. Empowerment results in greater responsibility and innovation and a willingness to take risks. Ownership and trust, along with autonomy and authority, become a motivational package.

Developing Self-Directed Work Teams

Hand-in-hand with empowering employees is creating a **self-directed work team**—a *work team that sets its own goals, creates its own schedules and budgets, and coordinates work with other departments.*

Self-directed work teams are used anywhere in the organization where work exists—in production, customer service, engineering, or design, for example. Companies using them report that team membership gives workers control over their jobs and a bigger stake in the company. "Self-directed work teams are," says Cecil Ursprung, CEO of Reflexite, "along with empowerment, the foundation for productivity, quality, and competitiveness in the marketplace. They wanted more than money—they wanted to be committed to something, and they wanted power over the decisions affecting their work lives. Give them that and they would repay the company a thousand times over." Empowerment, in the form of work teams responsible for production and quality, has given the employees at Reflexite (which makes reflective coatings, such as for signs) control over the decisions affecting their work lives. The teams plan the production operation, work with suppliers, respond to cus-

empowerment
Giving individuals in an organization autonomy, authority, and trust and encouraging them to break the rules in order to get the job done.

self-directed work team
A work team that sets its own goals, creates its own schedules and budgets, and coordinates work with other departments.

tomer questions, and are accountable for bottom-line decisions. The quality team, composed of members from all production operations, has established individual responsibility for quality assurance as an organizational value. At Reflexite the results can be seen in increased productivity, attainment of quality goals, and a committed work force.[31]

Providing an Effective Reward System

To motivate behavior the organization needs to provide an effective reward system that takes into account the fact that all people are individuals with different needs, values, expectations, and goals. An effective reward system has four elements:

1. Rewards must satisfy the basic needs of all employees. As an example, pay must be adequate, benefits reasonable, and vacations and holidays appropriate.
2. Rewards must be comparable to those offered by other, competitive organizations in the same area. For example, the pay offered should be equal to that for the same job in a competitive company, as should the benefits package and programs.
3. Rewards must be equally available to people in the same positions and should be distributed fairly and equitably. People performing the same job need to have the same options for rewards and should be involved in the decision on which rewards they receive. When employees are asked to complete a task or project, they should also be given the opportunity to determine their reward—a day off or extra pay.
4. The reward system must be multifaceted. Because people differ, a range of rewards needs to be provided, and rewards must focus on different aspects—pay, time, recognition, promotion. In addition a range of ways should be available to earn these rewards.[32]

This last point is worth emphasizing. With the move to empowerment, traditional pay systems are not viewed as working. In the traditional system, people are paid for the positions they hold, not the contributions they make. As organizations move toward an emphasis on teams, customer satisfaction, and empowerment, workers need to be paid differently. Companies such as Monsanto and Procter & Gamble have already responded. Monsanto has more than 40 pay plans—designed by employee teams—and P&G has a pay system that provides rewards based on skill levels.[33]

job redesign
The application of motivational theories to the structure of work for increasing output and satisfaction.

Redesigning Jobs

Jobs are important motivational tools because they can be a means to meeting an employee's needs. Managers need to determine what job elements provide motivation and then conduct a **job redesign**, *the application of motivational theories to the structure of work for increasing output and satisfaction.*

The two directions used to redesign jobs are job scope and job depth. *Job scope* refers to the variety of tasks incorporated into the job, whereas *job depth* refers to the degree of discretion the person has to alter the job. Approaches to job redesign include job enlargement, job rotation, and job enrichment. Let's examine each.

JOB ENLARGEMENT *Increasing the variety or the number of tasks a job includes, not the quality or the challenge*, is to practice **job enlargement**. Also called "job loading," job enlargement may attempt to demand more of the same work from an employee or to add other tasks containing an equal or lesser amount of meaning or challenge. Workers who can benefit from job enlargement are the underworked. These are people who need to be kept constantly busy and occupied with routine tasks that they understand and have mastered. Their sense of competence improves with their volume of output. Some people seek greater challenge, not more variety; job enlargement is not an appropriate strategy for them.

job enlargement
Increasing the variety or the number of tasks a job includes, not the quality or the challenge.

JOB ROTATION *Assigning people to different jobs or giving different tasks to people on a temporary basis* is called **job rotation**. The idea is to add variety and to expose people to the interdependence of a group of jobs in the organization. Managers involved in job rotation gain knowledge about the operations of various departments. Assembly-line workers may be assigned one set of tasks one month and another set the following month. Office workers may swap jobs for a time to learn additional dimensions of the office's responsibilities, to gain insights, and to be able to substitute for one another in times of need. At the Tony Lama Company, the El Paso bootmaker, each year six customer service department employees are assigned to work in the store, while salespeople work a week in the shipping department. Both sets of experiences have helped employees gain a broader perspective. Job rotation can be used to cross-train or to facilitate permanent job transfers or promotions. Workers who can benefit from job rotation are those who are interested in or ready for promotion, and those who need variety.

job rotation
Assigning people to different jobs or giving different tasks to people on a temporary basis.

JOB ENRICHMENT **Job enrichment** applies Herzberg's motivation factors by *designing a job to provide greater responsibility, control, feedback, and authority for decision making*. Herzberg refers to job enrichment as vertical job loading. It should include the following elements:

1. *Variety of tasks.* The employee should be given new and more difficult tasks not previously handled.
2. *Task importance.* The worker should be given a complete natural unit of work. Individuals should be assigned specific or specialized tasks that enable them to become experts.
3. *Task responsibility.* The manager should increase the accountability of

job enrichment
Designing a job to provide greater responsibility, control, feedback, and authority for decision making.

individuals for their own work. Also, employees should be given additional authority in their activities.

4. *Feedback.* Periodic and specialized reports should be made directly available to the worker himself or herself rather than to a supervisor.

Experiments with job enrichment have varied widely in their approach, scope, and content. Some companies merely establish regular meetings between supervisors and workers to discuss mutual problems, and they solicit employee suggestions on methods of improvement. Other companies encourage greater employee involvement. Volvo pioneered the concept of having a team of auto assembly workers produce a single car. The result was greater employee commitment, increased productivity, and decreased quality defects. Many manufacturers have allowed skilled machine operators to set up their machines, maintain them, plan their own work flow and pace, and inspect their own output.

Promoting Intrapreneurship

As an organization grows, it has a tendency to establish rules, policies, and procedures. The formal control systems that become established along with bureaucratic procedures cause it to lose innovative energy. Entrepreneurial employees caught in these environments often leave to form their own organizations because the corporate environment stifles their creative needs.

Recognizing this problem—and the losses they suffer as a result—many large corporations are trying to foster an environment for internal entrepreneurship, which has become known as intrapreneurship. Basically **intrapreneurship** is *entrepreneurship happening within the existing boundaries of a formal organization.*[34] It is in essence a process whereby an individual sees a need and can promote it within the organization. To create a climate for intrapreneurship, a manager might follow these guidelines[35]:

intrapreneurship
Entrepreneurship happening within the existing boundaries of a formal organization.

- Encourage action.
- Use informal meetings whenever possible.
- Tolerate—do not punish—failure and use it as a learning experience.
- Be persistent.
- Reward innovation for innovation's sake.
- Plan the physical layout to encourage informal communication.
- Reward or promote innovative personnel.
- Encourage people to go around red tape.
- Eliminate rigid procedures.
- Organize people into small teams for future-oriented projects.

Managers who really want to foster a climate of intrapreneurship cannot be timid. True intrapreneurs are different. They are not comfortable with structure—they will figure a way around orders that will block their dream. They will do any job that will make the project successful, always being true to their goals.

Creating Flexibility in Work

Another way managers can motive workers is to provide them with flexibility in work through flextime, a compressed work week, or job sharing/twinning.

FLEXTIME **Flextime** is *a program that allows employees to decide, within a certain range, when to begin and end each work day.* It thus lets them take care of personal business before or after work, vary their daily schedules, and enjoy more control over their lives. Companies that have adopted this approach have reported decreases in absenteeism, lower turnover, less tardiness, and higher morale.[36]

COMPRESSED WORKWEEK A **compressed workweek** is *a program that permits employees to fulfill their work obligation in less than the traditional five-day workweek.* The most often used model is four ten-hour days.

The approach—like flextime—provides time for personal business and recreation. Employees who adopt it report job satisfaction. Nevertheless, not all managers are supportive of the idea. Requirements that managers alter work schedules has caused concern. Some managers perceive that it will be harder to devise work schedules, that coverage of the department may not always be maintained because people are in and out; and others fear the loss of control.[37]

JOB SHARING OR TWINNING **Job sharing** or **twinning** is *a program that permits two part-time workers to divide one full-time job.* Such an occupational buddy system is ideal for parents who are raising school-aged children or those who prefer part-time employment. The benefit from an employer's standpoint is that two people share one salary—as well as one set of benefits—and ideas can be provided from two sources.

flextime
A program that allows employees to decide, within a certain range, when to begin and end each work day.

compressed workweek
A program that permits employees to fulfill their work obligation in less than the traditional five-day workweek.

job sharing *or* twinning
A program that permits two part-time workers to divide one full-time job.

With job sharing, two people fill one full-time position. For this program to work, the pair must meet regularly to compare notes and share information.

SUMMARY

Once an organization has acquired the best possible human resources to perform a job, managers are faced with the challenge of creating a positive work environment where employees can grow. The work environment is the key to developing and maintaining motivated workers who will achieve organizational objectives.

An influence on the work environment is the development of a management philosophy. Theory Y is a positive philosophy about people at work; Theory X is a negative philosophy. Other critical factors in developing a positive work environment include treating people as individuals, providing support, and valuing cultural diversity.

Enlightened managers understand that motivation is not done to a person. Rather, it results from a combination of factors, the most important of which are the individual's needs, his or her ability to make choices, and the existence of an environment that provides the opportunity to satisfy those needs and create chances to make those choices.

Maslow's theory identifies five main categories of needs motivating a person to behave in unique ways: physiological, safety or security, love or social, esteem, and self-actualization needs. Though approached differently, Herzberg's motivation and maintenance factors provide for the same needs identified in Maslow's hierarchy.

Vroom's expectancy theory identifies the factors that influence the choices a person makes to satisfy needs. A person's behavior is influenced by the value of the rewards, the relationship of the rewards to performance, and the efforts required for performance.

Managers aid in building a supportive work environment by providing leadership. Leadership involves three variables: the leader, those being led, and the circumstances. Management and leadership are not synonymous. Managers plan, organize, staff, direct, and control. They may or may not be effective in influencing their subordinates or team members to set and achieve goals.

Managers vary in their leadership styles—the approaches they use to influence subordinates. Leadership styles are composed of decision-making styles (autocratic, participative, or free-rein), approaches to motivation (positive or negative), and areas of emphasis in the work environment (task focus or people focus).

A manager can take a number of actions to increase motivation and morale in the work environment. These include providing praise and recognition, implementing management by objectives, empowering employees, developing self-directed work teams, providing an effective reward system, redesigning jobs, promoting intrapreneurship, and creating flexibility in work.

KEY TERMS

autocratic style p. 282
compressed work week p. 291
empowerment p. 287
expectancy theory p. 274
flextime p. 291
free-rein style p. 283
influence p. 276
intrapreneurship p. 290
job enlargement p. 289
job enrichment p. 289
job redesign p. 288
job rotation p. 289
job sharing or twinning p. 291
leadership p. 276

leadership style p. 280
maintenance (hygiene) factors p. 271
management by objectives (MBO) p. 286
morale p. 260
motivation p. 265
motivation factors p. 272
needs p. 265
participative style p. 282
philosophy of management p. 262
quality of work life (QWL) p. 260
sanctions p. 284
self-directed work team p. 287
Theory X p. 262
Theory Y p. 263

FOR REVIEW AND DISCUSSION

1. Why is it important for a manager to develop a positive work environment?
2. When a manager says, "We have a positive work environment here," what factors could he or she cite to defend this statement?
3. Why is it important for a manager to develop a positive philosophy of management?
4. Distinguish between Theory X and Theory Y as philosophies of management. How would the adoption of each by a manager influence the work environment?
5. In what ways are people different? Why is this important for a manager to recognize?
6. As a manager, how would you react to this statement: "It is up to the employee to satisfy his or her own needs; I don't have the time"?
7. Explain each of Maslow's five levels of needs. Why is Maslow's model known as a hierarchy of needs?
8. Differentiate between Herzberg's motivational and maintenance factors. What does the presence or absence of each mean to the work environment?
9. What is the importance of Vroom's expectancy theory? How does a person's analysis of potential outcomes affect motivation?
10. What is leadership? What three factors influence the choice of leadership style?

11. What three factors interact to create a manager's leadership style?
12. Under what conditions should a leader use autocratic style, participative style, and free-rein style?
13. For each of the following management techniques, explain how a manager's applying them will improve the work environment and motivation.
    a. Praise and recognition
    b. Empowerment
    c. An effective reward system
    d. Management by objectives
    e. Self-directed work teams
14. Distinguish between job enlargement, job rotation, and job enrichment. Which offers the most potential for employee motivation?
15. Why should an employer consider the use of flextime? What are the benefits to an employee?
16. Why would an employer not want to encourage job sharing? What are the benefits to both the employee and the organization?
17. Develop a proposal to present to management supporting the conversion of your job (or one you have held) to a four-day, forty-hour workweek. Include the advantages and disadvantages you can identify.

APPLICATIONS

Case 9.1: Building Commitment and Motivation

How does being obsessed with quality lead to motivated workers? According to John Wallace, CEO of Wallace Company, a winner of the Malcolm Baldridge National Quality Award, "It forces you to take a critical look at your entire operation—employees, systems, finances, suppliers, customer relations."

When Wallace Company committed to pursue quality in every facet of its operations, the company focused on the employees as the most critical ingredient. "If employees are not motivated and committed, they cannot and will not pursue quality, and they will be dissatisfied."

Responding to the challenge, Wallace provided new tools to employees who asked for them; put a fresh coat of paint on the offices, warehouse, and manufacturing facilities; and improved a company car plan that applied to outside salespeople.

The company began to address the administrative concerns of the employees by evaluating policies on vacation, sick leave, and personal leave. These policies were changed to be more competitive with those of other firms. The compensation system was redesigned to reflect the contributions made by the employees. Grievances over unfair policy administration were reduced to zero.

Wallace introduced a comprehensive training program for all levels of employees. "The training programs have been really important to a lot of us," noted a shipping supervisor. "Unlike some groups of employees in the company, many of the staff in our area didn't go to college or even finish high school."

Managers took two additional actions in the process of reshaping the organization. First, they recognized that the company needed a new mission statement. Several employees were asked to help develop an initial draft. The draft was distributed to all employees, who were asked to suggest changes or add their own values and views. Three drafts and six months later, the process produced the mission statement in use today.

The second action was to create teams. Teams were established to focus on quality, production, customer service, and order processing. Each team developed its own set of goals, evaluated its work, and made modifications when needed. The teams allowed employees to discover what they were capable of producing and the value of their products to themselves and the company.

The actions taken by Wallace Company resulted in a motivated work force. As people realized they had made a difference, a sense of unity emerged. On a daily basis, employees at all levels began to challenge old concepts and try new ideas.

Questions

1. Which motivation theories did Wallace Company apply in developing its overall motivation strategy? Explain your answer.

2. What specific elements of each theory did the company address with its actions? Provide examples to support your answers.

3. What specific techniques, cited in the chapter section "Managing for Improved Motivation and Morale," did the company use? Provide examples to support your answers.

For more information, see David Altany, "Cinderella with a Drawl," *Industry Week,* Jan:uary 6, 1992, pp. 49–51.

Case 9.2: Creating a Quality Work Environment

Happiness is something a company owes its employees. That's the gospel according to Hal Rosenbluth, the forty-one-year-old president and CEO of the Philadelphia-based corporate travel agency Rosenbluth International. Rosenbluth takes this philosophy so seriously that he has focused his energy and leadership style on creating a quality organizational climate. For example:

- The office motto is "the customer comes second," and Rosenbluth has asked customers who are rude to his employees to take their business elsewhere.
- The corporate culture includes an Associate of the Day (as employees are called to remove any thoughts

of inequity or subservience). The Associate of the Day gets to spend the day with a senior executive, following the executive around and observing him or her work.

- New employees receive several days of training in order to understand the company and its goals, philosophy, and values. From then on, they operate under their own authority with a minimum of supervision.

Rosenbluth's early work history helped mold his philosophy. As a college graduate in the mid-1970s, he worked as a reservation agent. What impressed him most was how the agents helped each other; "I fell in love with those people because I saw them working in natural teams without even knowing they were doing it."

As a result, Rosenbluth has become dedicated to hiring only those people who will work well in teams and then empowering the teams. When one candidate for a typing job failed the test, the company refused to pass on her because they liked her so much. She was told to practice typing for two weeks and come back. She did and was hired. Candidates for executive positions often join Rosenbluth on trips or in a game of basketball, which lets him evaluate how they function socially and in teams. One candidate looked promising until he blamed his teammates for losing the game.

The approach and the philosophy seem to be working. Under Rosenbluth's leadership, the travel agency has grown from 40 employees with just over $20 million in annual sales fifteen years ago to about 3,000 employees and $1.5 billion in sales today.

Questions

1. Using Figure 9.1 as a guide, what is your evaluation of the quality of work life at Rosenbluth International?

2. What leadership style does Hal Rosenbluth use? Provide examples to support your answer.

3. Which of Malsow's need levels are being met for the employees at Rosenbluth International? Provide examples to support your answer.

4. What management techniques has Hal Rosenbluth used? Provide examples.

For more information, see David Holzman, "When Workers Run the Show," *Working Woman,* August 1993, pp. 38–41.

REFERENCES

1. John Case, "Collective Effort," *Inc.,* January 1992, p. 32.
2. Douglas McGregor, *The Human Side of Enterprise* (New York: McGraw-Hill, 1960), pp. 23–27.
3. Myron Magnet, "The Truth About the American Worker," *Fortune,* May 4, 1992, p. 51.
4. John L. Single, "The Power of Expectations: Productivity and the Self-Fulfilling Prophecy," *Management World,* November 1980, pp. 19, 37–38.
5. Vance H. Trimble, *Sam Walton: The Inside Story of America's Richest Man* (New York: Signet, 1992), p. 109.
6. D. Quinn Mills and Mark D. Cannon, "Managing the New Work Force," *Management Review,* June 1992, p. 38.
7. Joyce Ann Oliver, "Mattel Chief Followed Her Vision," *Marketing News,* March 16, 1992, p. 15.
8. Cheryl Hall, "The Brinker Touch," *Dallas Morning News,* March 3, 1992, p. 15.
9. Howard Schlossberg, "Internal Marketing Helps Companies Understand Culturally Diverse Markets," *Marketing News,* January 21, 1993, pp. 7, 9.
10. Barbara Eltore, "Breaking the Glass . . . Or Just Window Dressing," *Management Review,* March, 1992, p. 17.
11. Sharon Nelton, "Winning with Diversity," *Nation's Business,* September 1992, pp. 18–21.
12. Keith Davis and John W. Newstrom, *Human Behavior at Work: Organizational Behavior,* 9th ed. (New York: McGraw-Hill, 1992), p. 105.
13. Abraham H. Maslow, "A Theory of Human Motivation," *Psychological Review,* 50 (1943), pp. 370–396.
14. Ibid.
15. Ibid.
16. Vance H. Trimble, *Sam Walton: The Inside Story of America's Richest Man* (New York: Signet, 1992), p. 109.
17. Frederick Herzberg, "One More Time: How Do You Motivate Employees?" *Business Classics: Fifteen Key Concepts for Management Success, Harvard Business Review,* 1975, pp. 16–17.
18. Ibid.
19. Ibid.
20. Larry Wilson, "Creating the Best Work Culture: How Managers Can Avoid the Trap of Ignoring the 'People' Skills in Dealing with Their Employees," *Nation's Business,* April 1992, p. 38.
21. Victor H. Vroom, *Work and Motivation* (New York: John Wiley & Sons, 1964).
22. Carol Kleiman, "1990s Will See Opportunity for New Breed of Manager," *Chicago Tribune,* March 22, 1992, Sec. 8, p. 1.
23. Walter Kiechel III, "The Leader as Servant," *Fortune,* May 4, 1992, pp. 121–122.
24. Gary A. Yuki, *Leadership in Organizations* (Englewood Cliffs, N.J.: Prentice-Hall), 1981, p. 70.
25. Keith Davis and John W. Newstrom, *Human Behavior at Work: Organizational Behavior,* 9th ed. (New York: McGraw-Hill, 1992), pp. 213–215.
26. Rensis Likert, "From Production-and-Employee-Centeredness to Systems 1-4," *Journal of Management,* 5, 1979, pp. 147–156.
27. Rensis Likert, *The Human Organization* (New York: McGraw-Hill, 1976).
28. Robert R. Blake and Anne McCanse Adams, *Leadership Dilemmas—Grid Solutions* (Houston: Gulf Publishing, 1991), p. 29.
29. Peter C. Fleming, "Empowerment Strengthens the Rock," *Management Review,* March 1993, pp. 34–37.
30. Tom Peters, "Time-Obsessed Competition," *Management Review,* September 1992, p. 18.
31. Myron Magnet, "The Truth About the American Worker," *Fortune,* May 4, 1992, pp. 49–52.
32. David D. Van Fleet, *Contemporary Management,* 2nd ed. (Boston: Houghton Mifflin, 1991), p. 371.
33. Michael A. Verespej, "Pay-for-Skills: Its Time Has Come," *Industry Week,* June 15, 1992, pp. 22–30.
34. Terry E. Winters and Donald L. Murfin, "Venture Capital Investing for Corporate Development Objectives," *Journal of Business Venturing,* Summer 1988, p. 207.
35. Donald F. Kuratko and Richard Hodgetts, *Entrepreneurship: A Contemporary Approach* (Chicago: The Dryden Press, 1989).
36. Jane Easter Bahls, "Getting Full-Time Work from Part-Time Employees," *Management Review,* February 1992, pp. 50–52.
37. Cheryl Hall, "Four-Day Week—The Jury Is Still Out," *Dallas Morning News,* February 16, 1992, p. D1.

LABOR-MANAGEMENT RELATIONS

n unity there is strength. Keep the faith, keep the unity. And we will win a contract.

WILLIAM RUDD
President, International Union of Electronics Workers, Furniture Division

CHAPTER OBJECTIVES
After studying this chapter, you should be able to:

1. Summarize the basic principles of unions and the primary objectives unions have for their members.
2. Trace the historical development of the labor movement.
3. Summarize the major legislation affecting labor-management relations and collective bargaining.
4. Identify the current trends and directions of the labor movement.
5. Discuss four reasons why people join unions.
6. Discuss each of the steps in the union organizing process.
7. Discuss the purpose of and issues involved in collective bargaining.
8. Contrast the tools management and labor have to achieve their objectives.
9. Describe the roles of mediation and arbitration in labor-management interaction.

UP FRONT

Brian Evans and Corey Green illustrate a redefinition of how employers and employees, management and labor, can work together in contemporary America. They are work unit module managers at Saturn, the GM auto company that was designed from scratch—from management to labor relations, from design to manufacturing—to address "the sins of the fathers" and become the American automaker of the future. If sales are any indication of success, we can note that Saturn is only the second automaker in U.S. history for which each of its dealers each sold over 1,000 cars in one year.

Although Evans and Green share the title of work unit module adviser, they represent two sides of the management-union coin. Evans is responsible for long-range planning and short-term problem solving, managing people, and addressing issues of product quality. Green represents the United Auto Workers and the plant workers, providing support and resources for people with concerns and needs. "We value people here," says Green, "and try to involve the union worker more in the processes of the auto business than has ever been done at any other company."

Each work unit module at Saturn is made up of several work teams. Each team, usually consisting of six to thirteen members, is represented by a work unit counselor (WUC). The WUC is elected by the team to represent them and is a counselor to the union. The WUCs report to the work unit module advisers (WUMA), in

this case Green and Evans, who are WUMAs in the final process area, the last stops for Saturn autos on the assembly line.

Green worked his way through General Motors at the Delco-Remy division, as a team leader, as an auditor, and in customer supplier relations. At Saturn he was a charter team member, the first person in one of Saturn's teams. He was a WUC before becoming a WUMA.

Evans came to Saturn from a college work-study program, first working in human relations to help hire the first Saturn employees and administer salary programs. He became an Equal Employment Opportunity counselor and helped administer the work-study program before asking for responsibility on the shop floor. "I didn't know a lot about building cars, so I got a job in the doors module," he says. Later, he was promoted to his current WUMA position in the final process work unit.

Brian Evans and Corey Green share an office, "where sometimes our distinct duties overlap, but all in all we try to keep a shared vision of our work," says Corey. "We beat up on ourselves daily, and sometimes we agree to disagree, but we get the issues out on the table and we deal with them," adds Brian. They work with their work teams to ensure that Saturn's goals are being met.

BRIAN EVANS AND COREY GREEN

WORK UNIT MODULE MANAGERS, SATURN CORPORATION

"We believe that people, when they are committed, work more effectively," says Green. "Saturn has a set of shared values that can be summed up in this way: Continuous improvement, commitment to excellence, teamwork, trust and respect for one another, and enthusiasm for satisfying the customer." Saturn employees share in the company's profits, so they are financially rewarded to strive for total quality in their work. For that reason, they are also responsible for many of the day-to-day decisions that are made concerning the work in their group. "There is a lot of peer support and peer critiques, too," says Evans. "We believe in letting them manage their own business, because it empowers them to ask, 'What is the best way to get the work done?' Auditing yourself and your work is encouraged. And since they have a vested interest, peers tend to keep each other on the right track."

Evans and Green meet daily with their WUCs, and whenever necessary with any other workers in the work teams. Their work is clearly people-intensive and designed to help people solve problems. "Another way people are empowered is by working from the head down, not just from the neck down," says Evans.

"But that's not the only thing, because we also believe work should be fun. I'm a great promoter of having fun," adds Green.

Evans sums up: "Individuals at Saturn are constantly recognized and rewarded for good work. Good people build good cars."

Mentioning the word *union* at a social gathering rarely draws neutral reactions. Some people see unions as unnecessary, too powerful, a cause of problems for business, and a major contributor to low productivity in America. Others view unions as essential to protecting workers, as an aid in providing a quality work life, and even as a partner with management for long-range profitability.

Regardless of the perception, unions and management will continue to interact in the work environment. Why do some organizations have unions while others do not? What role does a union play within an organization? How do unions and management function together through collective bargaining? The answers to these questions will be provided in this chapter. But first, a good starting point is a brief discussion of what unions are and why they exist.

What Is a Labor Union?

labor union
An organization of workers who have united to negotiate their collective wages, hours, and working conditions with management.

A **labor union** is *an organization of workers who have united to negotiate their collective wages, hours, and working conditions with management.* Labor unions are created by workers to provide a method for dealing with management more effectively. The "collective voice" of a union in essence offsets the power of management.

For many people, union membership is a way of life, with the whole family participating in union rallies and activities.

Why Labor Unions Exist

When workers feel they are not treated fairly, are not listened to, and are dominated in all aspects of their life by management, forming a labor union is a natural choice. In other words, management can develop a work environment that either discourages or encourages unionization. An enlightened management team that is sensitive to the needs of workers, treats them fairly, develops written policies and grievance procedures, and provides for quality of work life probably will not be unionized. Companies like Texas Instruments, Motorola, and Springfield Remanufacturing Corporation provide for the needs of employees and are not unionized. But when employees feel that they cannot fulfill their needs, that their voices are not being heard, and that they are not treated equitably, unionism is a viable alternative.

The Principles and Objectives of Unions

The labor movement has as its cornerstone certain basic principles that serve as the foundation for the primary objectives unions have for their members.

BASIC PRINCIPLES Unions are based on three principles:

1. *Strength through unity.* A union is founded on the collective voices of many, thinking, acting, and speaking as one.
2. *Equal pay for the same job.* Pay for the equivalent job should not be left open to discrimination or favoritism.

3. *Employment practice based on seniority.* All promotions, raises, and layoffs should be made on the basis of seniority in the organization.

PRIMARY OBJECTIVES When unions represent their members in negotiation with management, they have four specific objectives:

- Improved job security
- Higher pay
- Shorter hours of work on a daily, weekly, or annual basis
- Improved working conditions—both physical and psychological

From the very beginning of unions, these principles and objectives have been the basis for all union activities with management and all actions taken against management. Initially, and continuing for many decades, these cornerstones of the labor movement served the members well. But in recent years, their viability has been questioned.[1]

With this in mind, it is appropriate to briefly review the history of the labor movement. Figure 10.1 serves as a guideline for the important events in the history of labor-management relations.

A Brief History of the Labor Movement

Figure 10.1

Important events in the history of labor-management relations.

Unions have existed in the United States in one form or another for nearly 200 years. They began in 1792 with an alliance of cordwainers (shoemakers) in Philadelphia. By 1800 unions of carpenters and printers had sprung up in Baltimore, Boston, and New York.

These fledgling unions rarely survived for long, because the courts of the day had declared them unlawful conspiracies "pregnant with public mischief

Civil War 1861–1865

1792
Cordwainers union formed in Philadelphia; first craft union

1842
Commonwealth of Massachusetts v. Hunt; court rules that unions can legally be formed

1869
Knights of Labor formed

1886
American Federation of Labor begins

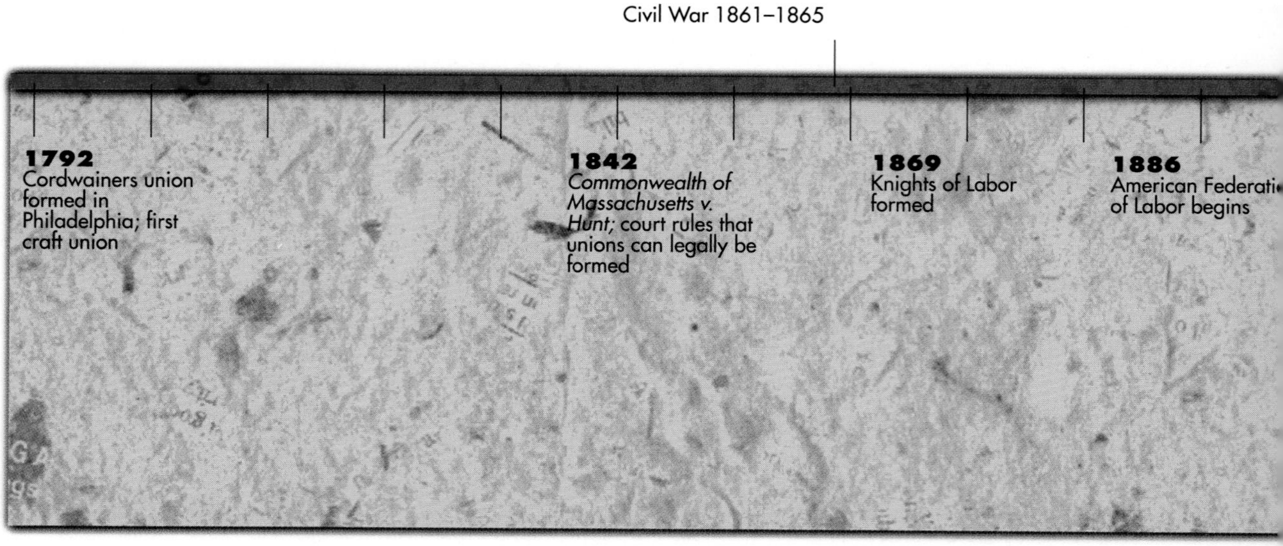

and private injury."[2] Finally, in the 1842 case of *Commonwealth of Massachusetts* v. *Hunt*, Chief Justice Lemuel Shaw of the Massachusetts Appellate Court reversed precedent by declaring, "We cannot perceive that it is criminal for men to agree together to exercise their own acknowledged rights in such a manner as best to subserve their own interest." For the first time in American history, a court ruled that workers (in this case shoemakers) could legally form a union to promote better working conditions as long as they pursued "virtuous ends by virtuous means."[3]

Although the Massachusetts ruling opened the door for union formation, it was not opened too wide. Until the 1930s, workers had to struggle for whatever power they could get to influence their working conditions, wages, hours, or benefits. Despite the fact that unions were no longer illegal, those that formed had little or no power.

The Early Craft Unions

Most of the early unions were considered **craft unions**, which are *associations of workers with a specific craft, trade, or skill,* such as iron molders, locomotive engineers, carpenters, or printers. The first truly national union, the Knights of Labor, formed in 1869 as a secret, somewhat ritualistic society of garment cutters, came out of hiding in 1878. It numbered as many as 700,000 members by 1886.

The Knights wanted to create one huge, centrally managed organization to represent farmers, laborers, and other groups of working people, regardless of skill. They attempted to achieve their goals through political action and social reform. As a result of poorly defined goals and a series of unsuccessful strike actions, their membership began to dwindle. By 1890 membership had declined to 100,000 workers; the Knights were dissolved in 1893.

craft unions
Associations of workers with a specific craft, trade, or skill.

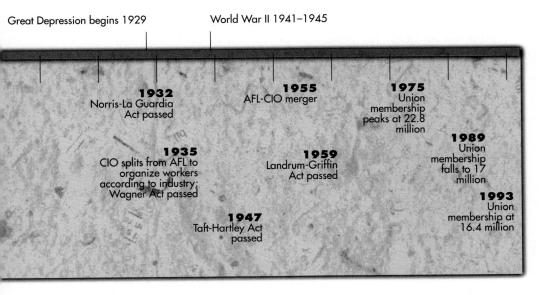

Great Depression begins 1929   World War II 1941–1945

1932
Norris-La Guardia
Act passed

1935
CIO splits from AFL to
organize workers
according to industry;
Wagner Act passed

1947
Taft-Hartley Act
passed

1955
AFL-CIO merger

1959
Landrum-Griffin
Act passed

1975
Union
membership
peaks at 22.8
million

1989
Union
membership
falls to 17
million

1993
Union
membership at
16.4 million

Creation of the American Federation of Labor

The dissension that caused the end of the Knights of Labor eventually resulted in the establishment of the American Federation of Labor (AFL). Several disenchanted Knights of Labor members initially formed the Federation of Organized Trades and Labor Unions, which in turn became the American Federation of Labor, a union of trade unions, in December 1886. Its members consisted primarily of skilled workers.

The person chosen by the members to provide leadership to the AFL was Samuel Gompers—one of its founders. Gompers set his sights on the "bread-and-butter" interests of his members. The union focused its energies on raising the wages of its members and improving working conditions. The result: by 1887 unions representing more than 600,000 people were affiliated with the AFL. By 1920 almost three-fourths of all organized workers belonged to unions that had joined the coalition. The decision to permit member unions considerable independence over their affairs (unlike the Knights of Labor, which had sought to centralize control) aided the AFL's growth.

Establishment of the Committee for Industrial Organization

Although the AFL recruited unions organized according to craft, militant coal miner John L. Lewis believed that greater emphasis should be placed on creating **industrial unions**—*associations of workers employed within a given industry,* such as coal mining or steel or automobile manufacturing, regardless of skill. In 1935 this philosophical difference caused Lewis to establish the Committee for Industrial Organization (CIO), which separated from the AFL and quickly rivaled it in size.

industrial unions
Associations of workers employed within a given industry.

The AFL-CIO: A Merger

After two decades of intense competition between the AFL and the CIO, the two groups set aside their collective differences and merged into one national organization in 1955: the American Federation of Labor and Congress of Industrial Organizations (AFL-CIO). The AFL-CIO gathered together unions representing 16 million workers—more than 85 percent of all union members in the United States at that time. The person chosen to lead the 16 million workers was George Meany, a former plumber from the Bronx. He served as the AFL-CIO president until his death in 1979.

Labor and the Law

Early efforts to organize unions were met with so much opposition by business and the legal system that the years leading up to the 1930s are sometimes called the repressive phase of the labor movement. Because many judges came from wealthy backgrounds, they tended to represent the interests of their peers. Without laws or court decisions to aid them, unions were generally ineffective when it came to recruiting members and representing workers in negotiations with management. In addition, many people considered union activity unpatriotic until the Great Depression of the 1930s.

The Depression, during which unemployment approached 25 percent, shifted public sentiment away from business and toward unions. With the 1932 election of Franklin D. Roosevelt (who sympathized with working people despite his wealthy background), the pendulum swung to the unions' side, and the Norris-LaGuardia Act and the Wagner Act were passed, promoting the formation of unions. As a result, total union membership grew from fewer than 4 million in 1935 to almost 15 million by 1945. As we look closer at these acts and related legislation, refer to Table 10.1 for a summary of our discussion.

Norris-LaGuardia Act (Federal Anti-Injunction Act)

The first major pro-union legislation was the Norris-LaGuardia Act of 1932—also known as the Federal Anti-Injunction Act. Prior to the act, a business that faced a labor strike or picketing could get an **injunction**, *a court order prohibiting a party from performing unjust, injurious, or inequitable acts.* The **Norris-LeGuardia Act** basically *prohibited the courts from issuing injunctions against labor's nonviolent protest activities* such as striking and picketing. The Norris-LaGuardia Act also outlawed another anti-union tactic: requiring employees to sign a **yellow dog contract,** *an agreement by workers, as a condition of employment, that they will not join a union.* If they violated the agreement, they would be fired.

Wagner Act (National Labor Relations Act)

The **Wagner Act** of 1935, also known as the National Labor Relations Act, *encouraged the formation of labor unions by prohibiting management from interfering with employees' rights to organize, join, or assist a union.* The Wagner Act also protected workers by specifying and prohibiting **unfair labor practices**—*actions designed to keep workers from joining a union.* As an example, it prohibited the use of **blacklists:** *the names of pro-union workers circulated among firms to keep workers from being hired.*

Finally, the Wagner Act established the **National Labor Relations Board** (**NLRB**), which is *a federal agency authorized to supervise union certification elections and to investigate complaints of unfair labor practices.*

Taft-Hartley Act (Labor-Management Relations Act)

The Wagner Act was considered to be pro-union, and with it the power of unions overshadowed management. Congress, in an attempt to swing the pendulum back, amended and supplemented the Wagner Act with the **Taft-Hartley Act** (also known as the Labor-Management Relations Act) in 1947. As noted in Table 10.1, the law *defined specific unfair labor practices by unions, established emergency strike procedures, and prohibited unions from charging excessive or discriminatory fees or dues.* It also empowered states to pass **right-to-work laws,** *which allow workers to obtain and keep jobs without having to join or pay money to a labor union.* Finally, the act established the Federal Mediation and Conciliation Service, which we will discuss in detail later in the chapter.

---

injunction
A court order prohibiting a party from performing unjust, injurious, or inequitable acts.

Norris-LaGuardia Act
Also known as the Federal Anti-Injunction Act of 1932. A federal law that prohibited courts from issuing injunctions against labor's nonviolent protest activities.

yellow dog contract
An agreement by workers, as a condition of employment, that they will not join a union.

Wagner Act
Also called the National Labor Relations Act of 1935. A federal law that encouraged the formation of unions by prohibiting management from interfering with employees' rights to organize, join, or assist a union.

unfair labor practices
Actions designed to keep workers from joining a union.

blacklist
The names of pro-union workers circulated among firms to keep the workers from being hired.

National Labor Relations Board (NLRB)
A federal agency authorized to supervise union certification elections and to investigate complaints of unfair labor practices.

LAW, YEAR	PROVISIONS
Norris-LaGuardia Act (Federal Anti-Injunction Act of 1932)	Prohibits courts from issuing injunctions against labor's nonviolent protest activities, such as strikes and picketing.
	Requires an open hearing before the issuance of an injunction.
	Outlaws yellow dog contracts, in which employees agree not to join a union.
Wagner Act (National Labor-Relations Act of 1935)	Prohibits management from interfering with threats or from questioning employees' right to organize, join, or assist a union.
	Prohibits management from giving financial or other support to a union, to avoid having a union dominated by or dependent on the employer.
	Prohibits management from using employment practices to discriminate against pro-union workers or reward anti-union workers: it prevents companies from firing or demoting current employees, from refusing to rehire employees who participated in a strike, and from refusing to hire qualified applicants because of union membership.
	Prohibits management from discharging or otherwise discriminating against an employee who files charges or testifies against the employer in labor relations cases.
	Requires management to bargain in good faith about wages, hours, and other employment conditions with the union that workers lawfully chose as their bargaining representative. (Management is not required to agree with or concede to union demands, but it must agree to meet at reasonable times and be open to discussion.)
	Establishes the five-member National Labor Relations Board to supervise employee elections for union representation, and to prevent and remedy unfair labor practices by either employers or unions.
Taft-Hartley Act (Labor-Management Relations Act of 1947)	Permits the president of the United States to seek an eighty-day injunction to delay a strike or lockout if evidence suggests that the strike would "imperil the national health and safety."
	Declares the following union activities to be unfair labor practices:
	1. Closed shops and secondary boycotts
	2. Featherbedding (forcing an employer to hire unnecessary workers)
	3. Refusal to bargain in good faith
	Empowers states to pass "right-to-work" laws, permitting employees to work without joining or paying dues to a union.
	Prohibits unions from charging excessive or discriminatory initiation fees or dues.
	Establishes the Federal Mediation and Conciliation Service.
Landrum-Griffin Act (Labor-Management Reporting and Disclosure Act of 1959)	Requires union officers to permit members to nominate candidates for union office, vote in elections, and dispute union election results.
	Stipulates that all union members must be allowed to examine the contracts negotiated between the union and management.
	Requires unions to file copies of their constitution, bylaws, and various reports (including financial statements) with the secretary of labor, where they become public record.
	Bars persons convicted of certain felonies from serving as union officers.
	Requires that union officers be bonded (insured) if the union has property and annual dues collections of more than $5,000.

Table 10.1 Major federal labor legislation since the 1930s.

Landrum-Griffin Act (Labor-Management Reporting and Disclosure Act)

In 1959 the **Landrum-Griffin Act**, officially called the Labor-Management Reporting and Disclosure Act, was passed after congressional investigations uncovered rigged union elections, bribery, poor financial management, and extortion among union leaders. This act, known as the bill of rights of union members, gave every union member the right to:

- Nominate candidates for union office
- Vote in union elections
- Attend union meetings
- Examine union accounts and records

In addition, unions were required to file copies of their constitutions, bylaws, and financial statements with the secretary of labor—where they became public record.

The Unions Today

The unions of today face an uncertain future. Concerns over membership trends, image, and long-range strategy present union leadership with multiple challenges.

Union Membership

From a peak in total membership of 22.8 million workers in 1981, union membership has declined to 16.4 million in 1993. In addition, the percentage of the total work force that belongs to unions declined from 33 percent in 1958 to 20.1 percent in 1983 and 15.8 percent in 1993. Figure 10.2 traces these union membership trends.

Taft-Hartley Act
Also known as the Labor-Management Relations Act of 1947. A federal law that defined specific unfair labor practices by unions, established emergency strike procedures, and prohibited unions from charging excessive or discriminatory fees or dues.

right-to-work laws
State laws that allow workers to obtain and keep jobs without having to join or pay money to a labor union.

Landrum-Griffin Act
Also called the Labor-Management Reporting and Disclosure Act of 1959. A federal law that defined the rights of union members in regard to internal union operations and access to union organizational and financial information.

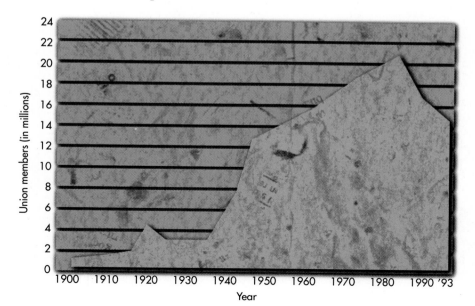

Figure 10.2
United States labor union membership, 1900–1993.

Overall, there are 9.7 million union members in private industry and 6.7 million in government. In the private sector, the industry group with the largest union membership is manufacturing (3.7 million), followed by services (1.4 million), wholesale and retail trade (1.3 million), and transportation (1 million).

Among the major occupational groups, operators, fabricators, and laborers (including machine and vehicle operators, assemblers, and helpers) have the highest union proportion, 27 percent. Close behind are precision production, craft, and repair workers (including mechanics and electricians), and similar skilled trade workers with 26 percent. Membership proportions are lowest in technical, sales, and administrative support groups, and in farming, forestry, and fishing occupations. Table 10.2 outlines the largest union memberships.

When looking at individuals in the work force, union membership is higher among men (20 percent) than women (13 percent). Workers age thirty-five to sixty-four are more likely to be union members than either younger or older workers. Finally, union membership is higher among blacks (22 percent) than among either whites (16 percent) or Hispanics (15 percent).[4]

In addition, the following membership statistics have been reported:

- Union membership of all eligible wage and salary earners ranges from a high of 29 percent in Hawaii to a low of 5 percent in North and South Carolina.
- For right-to-work states, the average union membership for all eligible

Table 10.2

Membership of the largest labor organizations.

ORGANIZATION	MEMBERSHIP (IN THOUSANDS)
National Education Association	2,095
International Brotherhood of Teamsters	1,510
United Food and Commercial Workers International Union	1,300
American Federation of State, County, and Municipal Employees	1,250
Service Employees International Union	1,000
International Union of Automobile, Aerospace, and Agricultural Implement Workers of America	900
American Federation of Teachers	790
International Brotherhood of Electrical Workers	788
International Association of Machinists and Aerospace Workers	729
United Steelworkers of America	570
United Brotherhood of Carpenters and Joiners	405

Source: AFL-CIO and NEA Membership Reports, 1993.

Union recruiters are having difficulty locating new groups of workers to sign up.

wage and salary earners is 8.5 percent, compared with 20.3 percent for free collective bargaining states.

• Membership has dropped in 33 states and the District of Columbia. In the remaining states membership remains at the same level.[5]

Problems Behind the Numbers

Unions are at a critical juncture in their existence. While most Americans support unions in principle, far fewer do it in practice. As perceived:

> Unions affirm the democratic vision in authoritarian companies by balancing the power of management and strengthening the relatively powerless employee. They guarantee due process in the workplace. They protect free speech. They try to achieve a more equitable distribution of rewards. They stand for the rights and dignity of individuals.[6]

Yet despite this ideology, unions have been losing their clout since the early 1960s. A number of reasons have been provided. These include:

1. Employees see less reason to join a union than they did in the past, as managers have learned to be more responsive to employee needs.
2. Unions do not connect with a new generation of knowledge workers. These employees—technicians, programmers, and sales and service workers—have more schooling than previous generations and are oriented to a personal career and a possible future in management. They seek continuous learning and personal development and do not necessarily expect to stay with one company. They tend to be critical of and frustrated with union-backed seniority rules that block merit rewards.
3. Management may not be the enemy. Unlike workers of the past, the new

generation may not see managers as the enemy or as members of a different social class but rather as team leaders with an important job to do.

4. Unions face problems in internal leadership. Union leadership has come from old-style table pounders who rely on power tactics. This image and its impact on employee-union-management relations weakens rather than helps the cause.

5. Unions have been slow to adjust their recruiting message. One of the basic objectives of unions has always been to achieve higher wages. Through a combination of international competition and deregulation, employers have been forced to cut costs—and upward union wage patterns were the first to go. So unions that address the single issue of higher wages cannot deliver.

6. Employers are becoming bolder in their resistance to unionization. They have been motivated to do so because of global competition, which makes it more urgent to cut costs and gain flexibility in work rules. The demand for quality and customer service requires employees who care about the company. A we-they, company-versus-union culture can be detrimental to competitiveness.[7]

Future Trends and Directions

As noted, the general direction of union membership has been downward. A number of business trends will continue to influence this downward spiral. As a result, unions will need to pursue alternative directions.

TRENDS Specific business trends that will continue to effect union membership include:

1. *The restructuring and downsizing of American businesses.* The natural result of restructuring and downsizing is the elimination of jobs and workers, which in turn translates into a reduction in the number of union members.

2. *The relocation of plants and manufacturing facilities because of labor costs.* The continued emphasis on lower labor costs, achieved through relocation of plants or manufacturing capabilities to the American South and Southwest or to other countries, continues. These actions remove or eliminate work opportunities and present threats to union employees.

3. *Technological change in manufacturing.* The continued emphasis on more efficient technology, robotics, and advanced computerization leads to fewer workers on the assembly line.

4. *An increased emphasis on efficiency as a result of global competition.* With less margin for error, quality demands, and more competitors in the marketplace, companies are learning to do more with less—fewer workers, fewer union members.

5. *Changes in the composition of the work force.* The number of workers in the traditionally heavily unionized industries—manufacturing, transportation, construction—has been decreasing, while the number of workers in both

the service area and the public sector have been increasing. Union organizing efforts and resources have not been redirected to focus on the changes.

DIRECTIONS In dealing with these trends, the union movement is changing its focus in the following directions:

- Maintaining the current percentage of organized workers (16 percent), which requires an average yearly addition of 650,000 organized workers to keep up with work force growth and to replace exits from the work force
- Unionizing federal, state, and local government employees; currently 37 percent of union-represented employees are government workers
- Targeting workers in the service industries for unionization
- Organizing white-collar employees in insurance, banking, and retail trades
- Directing efforts to unionize the emerging numbers of career women and minorities in the work force
- Developing negotiation programs based on job security
- Exploring ways to cooperate with management through quality of work life programs, common-interest forums, and joint labor-management retraining programs
- Devising and implementing new tactics, such as implementing corporate campaigns and making better use of public goodwill and lobbying

Table 10.3 lists the individual unions that have been "winners" and "losers" in

Table 10.3
Changes in union membership.

UNION WINNERS AND LOSERS	MEMBERSHIP (IN THOUSANDS)		PERCENT CHANGE
	1981	1993	
Winners			
Service Employees International Union	600	1,000	+67%
National Association of Letter Carriers	151	210	+39%
American Federation of Teachers	575	790	+37%
American Federation of State, County, and Municipal Employees	970	1,250	+29%
National Education Association	1,717	2,095	+22%
Losers			
United Steelworkers of America	1,037	570	−45%
International Ladies' Garment Workers	296	130	−44%
Amalgamated Clothing and Textile Workers	239	146	−39%
American Federation of Government Employees	223	149	−33%
Hotel Employees and Restaurant Employees International Union	362	258	−29%
International Association of Machinists and Aerospace Workers	950	729	−23%

Source: AFL-CIO and NEA Membership Reports, 1993.

GLOBAL PERSPECTIVE

In Sweden Unions Achieve Lagom

In Sweden, unlike the United States, unions and management have historically worked together to achieve *lagom*—fairness. *Lagom* is the belief that cooperation means wealth. Swedish unions demand that wages be *lagom* enough to create solidarity among workers.

It is said that the word *lagom* comes from the Viking drinking horn that was passed around among a circle of villagers. Each person was expected to drink not too much and not too little, but just enough that the horn would be emptied. The value of *lagom* permeates Swedish culture—Swedish children learn that putting either too much or too little on their plate is not *lagom*—and is a way of minimizing the envy and rivalry that could destroy management and union relations.

In the early history of Swedish unions, workers marched for their rights. But the eventual outcome was a social contract based on a vision of a prosperous economy in which everyone participates and no one suffers starvation. In the 1940s and 1950s, unions, employers, and government worked out agreements on sharing wealth that were essential for creating prosperity. In return for supporting mechanization and productivity improvement, Swedish workers gained high wages and the promise of continuous employment. All Swedish groups—unions and management together—share the belief that the first priority is to create work and prosperity.

(For more on *lagom*, see Michael Maccoby, "Cooperation Means Common Wealth," *Utne Reader*, March/April 1993, p. 86.)

the struggle to adjust and react to the trends and new directions. (In addition, this chapter's Manager's Notebook provides an analysis of the future of unions.)

In light of present-day trends, let's examine why people join labor unions and what the organizing process is.

Why Do Workers Join Unions?

There is no single reason why almost 17 percent of today's work force belong to unions. But the main reason is that unions provide some things that workers need and that management has failed to supply. The key point is that workers have historically created and maintained unions because they provide balance to managerial thinking and actions.

Reasons to Join Unions

In the best of all possible worlds there would be no need for trade unions:

- Managers would make rational decisions based not only on profits and financial considerations but also on the effects they might have on employees, their families, and the communities in which the company operates.

- Workers would give their best efforts to the company, knowing that doing so would increase profitability and productivity. They would be consulted in any decisions affecting their jobs and would be represented on the shop floor in workers' committees.
- The enlightened management would then reward its employees' efforts with increased wages and benefits, after paying an equitable percentage of the profits to shareholders as dividends.

Unfortunately, the perfect environment does not exist: employees do not always have control over the work situation; employees are not always paid fairly; working conditions can be unsafe; and employees are given a voice in the operations only if management wants to offer it. As a result, there are a number of reasons workers join unions, including to acquire power, provide job security, and improve their economic position and working conditions.

POWER The collective voice is more powerful than a single voice. Management is management and has the power of the company and the authority contained in the job description. A single worker voicing a safety demand, questioning a work policy, or protesting against perceived arbitrary management practices faces the immediate possibility of being fired. But the power in a united work force with a spokesperson that management *must* listen to can offset and equalize management power. Numbers acquire power.

JOB SECURITY Union membership provides job security. Union members view their union as a defense against arbitrary personnel decisions by management. Labor-management contracts specify the procedure that management must follow when assigning work to union members, taking disciplinary action (including firing), laying off workers, or recalling those who were previously laid off. Worker seniority figures prominently in the procedures followed for layoffs, recalls, and work assignments.

In the face of international competition and cost-cutting moves by employers, unions have focused on job security as a major bargaining issue. In recent years the United Mine Workers of America, among other unions, has bargained for job security either through a guarantee of all jobs to union members or a guaranteed percentage of jobs. Other unions have agreed to retraining and job flexibility programs to ensure job security.

ECONOMIC POSITION One of the basic objectives of unionism is to raise the wages and other benefits of employees. Many workers believe that union membership is the best route to a higher standard of living. Once again, the collective voice and the collective ability to withhold services is a strong bargaining tool. In addition to higher wages, many labor-management contracts provide automatic pay increases when prices rise; a number of paid holidays each year; paid vacations; health, life, and dental insurance; and, in some industries, a guaranteed retirement income.

Concern over long hours and dangerous working conditions in early factories gave impetus to the labor movement.

WORKING CONDITIONS In the initial days of the union movement, improving working conditions was one of the most important reasons for union development. Unions might not have reached their current strength if early managers had been more concerned about the welfare of their employees.

Long hours and unsafe working conditions were commonplace. In 1900 the average workday was ten hours, six days a week.

Thirteen-year-old boys labored in iron foundries and coal mines for as little as 50 cents a week. Many clothing factories rightfully earned the label *sweatshop*. If workers were injured on the job—even because of the employer's negligence—the courts of the day usually applied the assumption-of-risk doctrine, ruling that the employees worked at their own risk. Workers found that the only way to overcome these oppressive conditions was to organize. Today the concern—especially in the case of the United Mine Workers and unions in the construction trades—is to establish and maintain safe working conditions and monitor the quality of the work environment.

Now that we know why people join unions, let's examine the organizing process.

Union Organizing Process

A number of steps are involved in organizing a union. As shown in Figure 10.3, the steps include:

1. *Organizing campaign.* An *organizing campaign* is the first step in a non-union employer becoming unionized. Its purpose is to create widespread interest among the employees in forming a union. The campaign may be started from within by employees who contact a union, or a national union may target a company for an organizing drive.

   Regardless of how the campaign is initiated, both management and unions become involved in a contest—each trying to convince the employees to believe in them. Management attempts to persuade the employees not to unionize, while unions argue the opposite.

2. *Authorization cards.* Eventually during the campaign workers are asked to sign *authorization cards,* which signify the workers' interest in having the union represent them. During this time, as in all elements of the organizing process, the National Labor Relations Board governs the behavior of both the union and management. As an example, it is illegal for management to interfere with the authorization card campaign or to threaten any worker's job security for signing a card.

3. *Certification election.* If the union gets signed authorization cards from at least 30 percent of the eligible workers, it can send a request to the National Labor Relations Board for a *certification election.* In response, the NLRB posts an election notice and defines the *bargaining unit*—those workers who are eligible to vote. The election is then conducted by secret ballot.

4. *Certification of union.* If the union receives a majority of the votes, it is certified as the exclusive bargaining agent for the employees—and collective bargaining on the contract may begin immediately. If the union is rejected by the voters, the NLRB will not authorize another election for one year.

The fifth step is collective bargaining, which we explore in detail in the next section.

Figure 10.3

Steps involved in organizing a union.

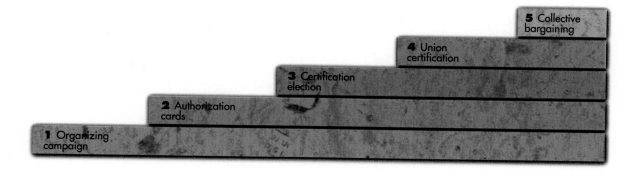

5 Collective bargaining

4 Union certification

3 Certification election

2 Authorization cards

1 Organizing campaign

Collective Bargaining

Once a union is certified, **collective bargaining** takes place. This is *the process whereby employer and employee representatives jointly negotiate a contract that specifies wages, hours, and other conditions of employment.* Collective bargaining is a process and a set of governing guidelines under which management and labor work through the negotiation of contractual terms. In addition, collective bargaining includes the ongoing relationship between management and labor in administering and enforcing the contract.

In collective bargaining, management and labor meet together to hammer out the terms of the contract. Over a period of days, weeks, or months, the two parties work on the eventual agreement. Under law, both parties are required to negotiate wages, hours, and the terms and conditions of employment in "good faith." This means that when one party makes an offer, the other side agrees or matches it with a counteroffer. It does not mean that either management or labor must agree to a proposal or that either party must make a concession.

Management and Labor Bargaining Issues

Negotiation sessions differ from industry to industry, but normally bargaining is done on wages, conditions of work, employment procedures, grievance procedures, safety, management's rights, and union security. It is during this process that the balance of power in an organization is determined. What management "gives up" labor receives, and vice versa. Table 10.4 provides a list of topics normally bargained for and included in a contract. Though all are important, three are the foundation for all future management and labor relations and need further discussion: union security, management rights, and grievance procedures.

Table 10.4

Topics normally included in a labor contract.

Employment Practices
Hiring procedure
Discharge
Layoff plan
Reinstatements
Terminations
Seniority
Transfers
Job-posting practices

Work Assignments
Workloads
Work hours
Work breaks
Subcontracting

Management and Labor Rights
Management rights clause
Union security

Grievances
Grievance procedure
Arbitration (voluntary, mandatory)
Disciplinary procedures

Wages
Bonus payments
Piece rate
Shift differentials
Severance pay
Overtime pay
Job evaluation
Base wages

Benefits
Discounts on company products
Profit sharing
Sick leave
Group insurance
Vacations
Pensions

UNION SECURITY The issue of *union security*—the definition of the strength of the union's position as the workers' bargaining agent—is critical. A union's strength is its ability to represent the workers in collective bargaining. This strength comes directly from the number of members it represents. The greater the percentage of union members, the stronger and more secure the union is.

In negotiating contracts, union and management ultimately define union security by agreeing on union membership conditions. These conditions are designated through various types of "shops"—closed, union, agency, maintenance, and open:

- *Closed shop.* Before the Taft-Hartley Act, strong unions negotiated **closed shop** *agreements stipulating that employees had to be union members at the time they were hired.* Although this practice is formally outlawed today, it is often practical for a person wanting a job to join a union. In states without right-to-work laws, union membership may be required for regular employment in such occupations as printing or construction. In addition, some labor-management agreements stipulate that management will first go to the union hiring hall to fill any openings. The likelihood of a nonunion applicant's being hired is remote in such a case.
- *Union shop.* States without right-to-work laws can have **union shop** *agreements stipulating that a company's new employees must join a union within a certain number of days after being hired in order to keep their jobs.* In essence this is joining a union as a condition of employment.
- *Agency shop.* Although union membership is not mandated in an **agency shop**, *nonunion members must pay union dues* because the union acts as their agent when bargaining with management. That alone is normally a reason to join the union officially.
- *Maintenance shop.* In a **maintenance shop** *employees do not have to join a union, but those who do must maintain membership for the length of the contract.*
- *Open shop.* In an **open shop** *workers do not have to join the union or pay dues.*

MANAGEMENT RIGHTS In collective bargaining management wants to retain as many of its decision-making rights as possible. Management does so by negotiating for and developing a management-rights clause in the contract. It defines those areas that management will control—hiring, work scheduling, discipline. Obviously, the union negotiates to limit these rights.

GRIEVANCE PROCEDURES Regardless of how well the contracts are worded, a **grievance**, *a dispute caused by contract violations or different interpretations of contract language,* can arise at any time. As a result, virtually all contracts include a **grievance procedure**, *a series of steps to be followed by an employee who has a complaint about a contract violation.* Grievance procedures enhance industrial relations by providing a safety valve for tensions and a remedy for disputes that arise between management and workers.

---

closed shop
Agreements stipulating that employees had to be union members at the time they are hired.

union shop
Agreements stipulating that a company's new employees must join a union within a certain number of days after being hired in order to keep their jobs.

agency shop
Agreements stipulating that nonunion members must pay union dues.

maintenance shop
Agreement stipulating that employees do not have to join a union, but those who do must maintain membership for the length of the contract.

open shop
Agreement stipulating that workers do not have to join the union or pay dues.

grievance
A dispute caused by contract violations or different interpretations of contract language.

grievance procedure
A series of steps to be followed by an employee who has a complaint about a contract violation.

The steps in a grievance procedure are not standardized in all labor-management contracts, but a typical sequence of events, as shown in Figure 10.4, is as follows:

union steward
An employee who has been elected by fellow union members to serve as their representative.

Step 1. An employee with a grievance takes his or her complaint to a **union steward**—*an employee who has been elected by fellow union members to serve as their representative.* Both the shop steward and the employee present the grievance to the employee's supervisor. Normally both the grievance and the supervisor's response are put in writing.

Step 2. If the union steward and the supervisor cannot reach agreement, the matter will be forwarded to the chief union steward and the supervisor's boss. The supervisor, union steward, and employee participate.

Figure 10.4
Steps in a grievance procedure.

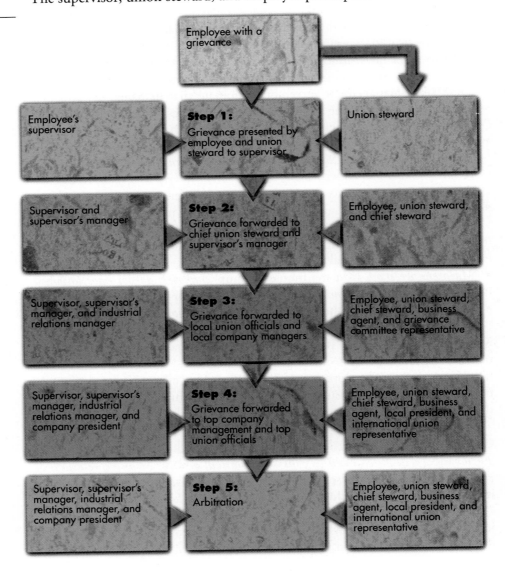

Employee's supervisor	**Step 1:** Grievance presented by employee and union steward to supervisor	Union steward
Supervisor and supervisor's manager	**Step 2:** Grievance forwarded to chief union steward and supervisor's manager	Employee, union steward, and chief steward
Supervisor, supervisor's manager, and industrial relations manager	**Step 3:** Grievance forwarded to local union officials and local company managers	Employee, union steward, chief steward, business agent, and grievance committee representative
Supervisor, supervisor's manager, industrial relations manager, and company president	**Step 4:** Grievance forwarded to top company management and top union officials	Employee, union steward, chief steward, business agent, local president, and international union representative
Supervisor, supervisor's manager, industrial relations manager, and company president	**Step 5:** Arbitration	Employee, union steward, chief steward, business agent, local president, and international union representative

Step 3. If the parties in Step 2 cannot reach a mutually acceptable settlement, the dispute is referred to local union officials and local company managers, who sometimes meet as a committee to resolve the grievance.

Step 4. If the dispute is not settled at Step 3, top company management and top union officials confer on the matter.

Step 5. If the parties in Step 4 cannot agree, the matter is typically referred to arbitration. **Arbitration** is *a process in which an impartial third party called an arbitrator makes the decision to settle a grievance.*

Ratification by Members

When the management and union representatives have tentatively agreed to a contract, it is submitted to the members of the union for ratification. The ratification process may be complex or simple. In the case of a local union, the contract needs only to be voted on by that membership. For a national union (such as the United Auto Workers or Teamsters), each local union affected by the national agreement must vote to accept or reject the contract.

Management and Labor Negotiating Tools

During contract negotiations both management and labor have powerful tools they can use to influence each other. Management can use lockouts, strikebreakers, management-run operations, injunctions, and plant closings for direct action. Unions can use strikes, picketing, boycotts, and corporate campaigns.

Management Tools

LOCKOUT One way to counteract employee demands is the **lockout**, *a tactic in which management locks the doors and prevents workers from entering the building.* Although effective in crushing workers' demands during the 1930s, the lockout is rarely used today because it produces too much negative publicity for management.

Also, normally management cannot sustain a lockout because a work stoppage loses sales, profits, and market share to competitors. As an example, the lockout of 1,120 steelworkers at Boston Gas Co. facilities was ended after four months primarily because of revenue concerns. Local municipalities, sympathizing with the union, had voted to stop payment of their gas bills while the lockout continued. It quickly ended.[8]

STRIKEBREAKERS Companies may attempt to operate during a strike by employing outside **strikebreakers** (called scabs by the strikers and their supporters): *workers who perform jobs until striking workers come to terms with management.* Strikebreakers are an effective tool. Coupled with the ability to permanently replace workers on strike, this tool can bring labor back to the bargaining table. In the five-month strike between Caterpillar, Inc. and the United Auto Workers, the key move was Caterpillar's threat to hire replacement workers.[9]

arbitration
A process in which an impartial third party called an arbitrator makes the decision to settle a grievance.

lockout
A tactic in which management locks the doors and prevents workers from entering the building.

strikebreakers
Workers who perform jobs until striking workers come to terms with management.

MANAGEMENT-RUN OPERATION As an alternative to hiring strikebreakers, some firms attempt to keep minimum production flowing by having supervisory, technical, or clerical personnel run the equipment when regular operators walk off the job. Several large oil companies have used this method to keep refineries operating in the wake of strikes by the Oil, Chemical, and Atomic Workers International Union, which represents most refinery workers. Firms in the telephone industry, such as the "Baby Bells" and GTE, have used this technique for years during contract renegotiation phases.

INJUNCTION In certain instances, management can obtain an injunction ordering employees back to work. As noted earlier, the Norris-LaGuardia Act requires management to supply specific evidence of potentially irreparable injuries before the courts will order workers to stop their protest activities.

In the past, injunctions have been issued to prevent strikes. One such instance was the use of an injunction to prevent a strike by the Brotherhood of Locomotive Engineers against Conrail, the federally subsidized Northeast Corridor rail freight line. The injunction was issued because the strike threatened to interrupt interstate commerce and deprive a section of the country of essential transportation service.

plant closing
A tactic in which management stops operations or sells a plant and moves away rather than surrender to labor's demands.

PLANT CLOSINGS In what is referred to as **plant closings**, *management stops operations or sells a plant and moves away rather than surrender to labor's demands.* This was the case when the textile industry migrated from New England to the South to find cheaper, nonunion labor. Some firms have put individual plants on the market in the wake of wage demands that they said would make it impossible for them to operate at an acceptable profit. A major policy decision by the National Labor Relations Board, which allows employers to move operations to a nonunionized facility to avoid the higher costs of a union contract, probably has resulted in more plant closings. The NLRB stated that such moves are legal as long as companies satisfy their obligation to bargain with the union and as long as the contract does not specifically restrain it.

Unions believe that the plant-closing tactic has been used when it has not been justified—that management really did not satisfy its obligation to bargain. As an example, during negotiations with Local 455 of the United Food and Commercial Workers Union, representing 1,700 workers, Kroger Co. stated that unless the contract concessions were approved by the membership, Kroger would pull out of San Antonio and shut down its fifteen stores there.[10]

To provide an early warning system when a company plans to close a plant, Congress passed the Plant Closings Act in 1988. This law requires that employers with one hundred or more employees give sixty days' notice for plant closings or mass layoffs—even those affecting as few as fifty workers. In addition to covering plant closings, the act covers the closings of operational units, the discontinuance of product lines, and the discontinuance of operations previously performed in-house.

MANAGER'S NOTEBOOK

Unions—collaborators or adversaries? The future of the labor movement may hinge on the answer to this question. Facing the fact that union membership has been consistently on a downward spiral for more than a decade, labor leaders are being forced to reassess the elements of their strategy.

This self-analysis requires a review of goals, leadership, recruiting practices, political activities, and resource allocations. Examining these elements, while not easy, does not cause the degree of uneasiness or pain for senior labor leaders as does a nonprejudicial examination of labor's traditional adversarial role.

Being management's adversary has been the expectation. But labor leaders are having to accept the fact that this traditional role is not effective in today's environment. Times have changed and so has business. Global competition is not a vision of the future—it is here. Business must cut costs, be more efficient, and have the flexibility to adjust and respond. If it can't, it won't exist—and neither will the jobs.

Within the ranks of labor leaders a reform movement has begun—not by all leaders, but by enough. Their goal is to be proactive, not reactive. They are focusing on preserving the industrial base, rather than helping it self-destruct. Their approach is to work jointly with management, using the intelligence and initiative of the group to make world-class facilities. They are acting as collaborators, not adversaries.

Collaboration takes many forms with many names: quality of work life teams, quality circles, employee involvement programs, and empowerment. But within these is a common core: recognition of the union, involvement of the worker in decision making, and mutual respect between management and labor. As Jack Sheinkman, president of the Clothing and Textile Workers notes, "The key is that it is a true partnership with workers. We are playing an active role in the success of the company. These programs require the company to deal with workers with respect and honesty."

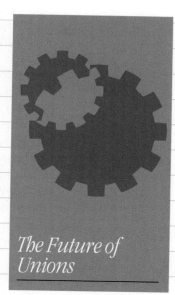

The Future of Unions

The reformers are hard at work in the steel, rubber, textiles, and communication industries. At companies like Goodyear, AT&T, Xerox, and Ford, as well as GM's Saturn plant, the partnership programs are in place. But being judged successful requires collaboration over the long haul and not just in hard times. Only time will tell if the collaboration strategy works.

(For more on the future of unions, see Peter Nulty, "Look What the Unions Want Now," *Fortune,* February 8, 1993, pp. 128–135; Michael Byrne, "Unions Show Partnerships Help Companies, Workers," *AFL-CIO News,* March 1, 1993, p. 8.)

OTHER TOOLS In addition to these direct-action tools, management has three other options to help in its efforts. These include the media, employers' associations, and lobbying.

For example, when a labor dispute arises, management can try to influence public opinion through the media. This involves not only seeking publicity opportunities but also purchasing advertising space and broadcast time. For instance, when giant grocer Food Lion, Inc. and the United Food and Commercial Workers Union were locked in a dispute over employment practices, Food Lion used direct mail to send flyers to households stating its position and denying union charges of illegal labor practices.[11]

employers' association
A group that represents several companies in bargaining with a union that has organized their workers.

Sometimes competing firms will form an **employers' association**, *a group that represents several companies in bargaining with a union that has organized their workers.* Because master contracts often cover many firms and thousands of employees within one industry, employers' associations provide management with greater bargaining strength. Bargaining through associations is common in the coal, steel, construction, railroad, and trucking industries, where firms share the cost of highly qualified negotiators—a significant advantage for firms that cannot afford to hire their own. For example:

- Rail carriers formed the National Railway Labor Conference to bargain with twenty unions representing several groups of railroad workers.
- More than 600 trucking companies formed Trucking Management, which acts as their agent in contract negotiations with the giant International Brotherhood of Teamsters.
- Coal producers have dealt with the United Mine Workers of America through the Bituminous Coal Operators' Association, which is authorized to act for 130 coal companies in fourteen states.

lobbying
Employing persons to influence state and federal legislators to sponsor laws that further one's own interests or inhibit those of one's opponents.

Management may also resort to formal **lobbying**, which is *employing persons to influence state and federal legislators to sponsor laws that further one's own interests or inhibit those of one's opponents.* Large companies, employers' associations, and trade associations of companies in various industries hire professional lobbyists to represent the interests of management to legislators.

Labor Tools

Labor has its own set of tools to counter management actions: strikes, picketing, boycotts, and corporate campaigns.

strike
A temporary work stoppage by employees to bring pressure on management to meet their demands.

STRIKES A **strike** is *a temporary work stoppage by employees to bring pressure on management to meet their demands.* The purpose of a strike is to stop work and cut off the labor supply. It is only effective if it does just that and if it can be sustained. Former AFL-CIO president George Meany once asserted that "It is the right to strike that gives meaning to collective bargaining. It is the right to strike that gives a union spokesperson some measure of equality at the

Strikes are the most visible tool used by unions in their efforts to counter management actions.

bargaining table." Most employers would at least agree with Meany that the strike is a powerful weapon, one that can have a lasting impact on an employer, an industry, or even an entire nation—it is a very real threat, and it is used. For instance, in 1993 the United Mine Workers of America (UMWA)—one union that has historically used strikes as a weapon—employed a series of selective strikes to force a new contract. Embroiled in heated contract negotiations with the two largest coal companies, Peabody Holding Co. and Consol Energy, Inc., the UMWA triggered strikes in six states involving 14,000 workers.[12]

PICKETING "It pays to advertise," an old Advertising Council slogan, applies to workers' grievances too. **Picketing** is *a tactic in which workers publicly air their complaints against an employer by staging a demonstration outside the building, with protest signs and explanatory leaflets.* Although most picketing occurs during strikes, some is informational, designed to acquaint the public with the workers' side of a dispute that has not yet escalated into a strike. Figure 10.5 illustrates material distributed during a picketing action.

BOYCOTT Another union tactic, the **boycott**, is *a refusal to do business with a given party until certain demands are met.* There are two types of boycotts: primary and secondary boycott. A **primary boycott** *occurs when union members agree not to purchase goods or services from the firm they are in dispute with.* For example, the AFL-CIO recently called for a boycott by all of its union members of the Iron Age Protective Shoe Company. The company, which makes items such as steel-toed shoes, was locked in contract negotiations with

picketing
A tactic in which workers publicly air their complaints against an employer by staging a demonstration outside the building, with protest signs and explanatory leaflets.

boycott
A refusal to do business with a given party until certain demands are met.

primary boycott
Occurs when union members agree not to purchase goods or services from the firm they are in dispute with.

Figure 10.5
Informational
picketing
literature.

Please Don't Shop at Colonial Plaza Mall Stores

The working men, women, and retirees of Carpenter's Local Union 1765 urge you not to shop at Colonial Plaza Mall Shops because of the builders, Thompson Construction Company, Contract Construction, Scandia Inc., Kelley's Concrete, and their contributions to substandard wages.

Colonial Plaza Mall stores under construction are being built by Thompson Construction Company, Contact Construction, Scandia Inc., and Kelley's Concrete who pay substandard wages and fringe benefits. The use of contractors who pay substandard wages and benefits is a drain on our local economy. The payment of substandard wages diminishes the purchasing power of working persons who are also customers and neighbors in this community. Our members cannot maintain their living standards due to the substandard wages paid by Thompson Construction Company, Contract Construction, Scandia Inc., and Kelley's Concrete at Colonial Plaza Mall construction sites. Moreover, the use of the contractors paying substandard wages undermines the business of fair labor contractors who build with skilled labor under union standards.

With so many shopping centers in the area, why not purchase your merchandise at one built by contractors using union labor, which ensures skilled labor under union standards?

We ask you to support our protests against substandard wages and working conditions by refusing to buy any merchandise at the Colonial Plaza Mall Stores until the building contractors, Thompson Construction Company, Contract Construction, Scandia Inc., and Kelley's Concrete, are willing to pay wages consistent with the area.

The picketing is informational and does not have organization, recognition, work jurisdiction, or bargaining as an objective. Employees of this and other employers are not requested to refrain from working or performing services.

Please Do Not Litter

Source: Courtesy United Brotherhood of Carpenters and Joiners of America. Figure is for educational purposes only.

Teamsters Local 636. The boycott was credited with being the major factor in gaining the contract.[13]

secondary boycott
Pressure aimed at businesses that buy or sell to a firm that is engaged in a labor-management dispute.

A **secondary boycott** consists of *pressure aimed at businesses that buy from or sell to a firm that is engaged in a labor-management dispute.* These third-party companies may be boycotted or have other pressures brought to bear on them if they continue to do business with the target firm. Although the Taft-Hartley Act initially outlawed secondary boycotts, a 1988 Supreme Court ruling gave unions the right to use them—as long as they do not involve any picketing.

An example of a secondary boycott is the decision by Archibald Candy Corp., the nation's largest candy chain, to no longer buy walnuts from the Diamond Walnut Growers' Association. The company was pressured into this decision by a corporate campaign, our next labor tool.[14]

CORPORATE CAMPAIGN The **corporate campaign** is *a tactic designed to influence the opinions of a large corporation's suppliers, customers, creditors, directors, stockholders, and the public to bring pressure on the corporation in bargaining with the union.* In using this tactic the union researches the corporation to determine its vulnerable areas and sources of power and income. The union digs into the backgrounds of the corporation's officers and directors. Then the campaign begins wherever the corporation has a weakness.

In addition to the example of Archibald Candy Corp., the Teamsters successfully used the corporate campaign in a contract dispute with Hasbro, Inc. After learning that Hasbro's Playskool unit had purchased licensing rights to make products featuring Barney the Dinosaur—the children's television character—the union arranged to send look-alikes of the purple dinosaur to the American International Toy Fair in New York. There, Barney would proclaim that Hasbro unfairly locked out eighty warehouse workers in Rhode Island. The Teamsters did not have to carry out the action—just the threat helped with the contract.[15]

OTHER TOOLS Just as management has indirect tools, so does labor. These include the use of the media and lobbying and political activities.

Unions realize, as do companies, that it is important to create and project a favorable public image to consumers and potential members. Examples include labor's ongoing campaign for Americans to buy union goods, promoted through print and television commercials. In addition, the AFL-CIO has developed the AFL-CIO Union Industries Show to promote union-made products and union skills.[16]

Unions, like management, have a strong professional lobbying effort. They attempt to influence the direction of legislation and enlist the support of legislators sensitive to labor's concerns. Figure 10.6 provides a list of labor's extensive agenda for the 103rd Congress.

As an alternative to striking, unions may engage in a boycott, encouraging members and others not to do business with the target employer.

corporate campaign
A tactic designed to influence the opinions of of a large corporation's suppliers, customers, creditors, directors, stockholders, and the public to bring pressure on the corporation in bargaining with the union.

YOU DECIDE

Think of a labor-management situation you have read about or seen on television. What tools of labor were being used? What tools was management using? How effective was each side in dealing with the situation?

AFL-CIO's legislative agenda, determined by the Executive Council's Legislative Priorities Committee, is nonexclusive and not in order of priority. It may be changed during the course of the 103rd Congress as events warrant.

Airline Employee Protections

Anti-Recession Program
- Infrastructure
- Aid to local and state governments

Asbestos Removal

Bankruptcy

Black Lung Reform

Budget
- Constitutional Balanced Budget Amendment
- Line Item Veto

Buy America

Campaign Finance Reform

Carbon Taxes

Cargo Preference

Civil Rights

Construction Safety

Davis-Bacon Reform

Economic Conversion
- Defense Budget

Education/Skills Training

Family and Medical Leave

Federal Employee Health Benefit Program Overhaul

Fish Inspection

Flight Attendants Duty Time

Fringe Benefits
- Taxation of Health Benefits
- Education
- Legal

Hatch Act Reform

Health Care
- Retiree Health

Highway/Mass Transit
- Funding

Housing

Indoor Air

Maritime Issues

Minimum Wage

National Service issues

NLRA Amendments
- Security Guards
- University Professors
- Performing Arts

Public Employees/Collective Bargaining
- Privatization

Nuclear Waste/Toxic Waste

OSHA Reform

Pension Reform
- ERISA preemption
- Investment
- Public Employees (PERISA)

Railway Labor Act

Railway Safety

Railroad Retirement

Revenue Foregone

Striker Replacement

Tax Reform
- Taxation of Foreign Corporations
- Personal Income Tax Changes

- Eliminate Tax Incentives for Runaway Plants
- Tax Modification Section 936
- Intangibles Timber Employment

Trade
- China MFN
- GATT
- GSP reform
- NAFTA
- Textile and Apparel
- Voluntary Restraints
- Worker Rights
- TAA
- Trade Deficit Reduction

Universal Voter Registration

Unemployment Compensation

Welfare Reform issues

Source: Courtesy of the AFL-CIO Institute of Public Affairs.

Figure 10.6
Labor's agenda for the 103rd Congress.

mediation
A process by which an impartial person acceptable to both sides in a labor dispute encourages them to communicate, bargain, and work toward a satisfactory compromise.

Additionally, unions back political figures who have strong labor views. By providing financial and election-worker support, the unions attempt to get people elected who will promote labor's programs.

Mediation and Arbitration

When representatives of labor and management reach a stalemate in negotiations, they may resort to **mediation**, *a process by which an impartial person acceptable to both sides in a labor dispute encourages them to communicate, bargain, and work toward a satisfactory compromise.* The mediator, who has no authority to decide the issue, proposes solutions to the dispute and acts as a friend to both parties. Mediation can fail, however, when labor and management are poles apart and a strong adversarial relationship exists.

In severe disputes that mediation fails to settle, or when mediation is simply bypassed, *arbitration* may take place. In this scenario labor and management empower an impartial third party (an arbitrator) to act as judge and hand down a

The AFL-CIO Industries Show is an opportunity to promote union-made products to the public.

legally binding decision that both sides have agreed in advance to accept. Arbitration is voluntary when both parties agree to submit disputed issues to a final judgment. The law may also call for compulsory arbitration when deadlocks arise, for example, between city governments and such groups as firefighters, law enforcement officers, or other employees whose jobs affect the public welfare and safety. Almost all labor-management contracts contain an arbitration clause.

When the need for third-party help arises, labor and management can turn to two important agencies—the Federal Mediation and Conciliation Service or the American Arbitration Association—to help them resolve disagreements peacefully. Each can provide the following services:

1. Examine labor-management disputes with greater objectivity
2. Devise creative solutions to a dispute that neither side may have considered
3. Recommend specific contract terms and language that has been acceptable to both parties in similar cases
4. Provide data that may help labor and management clarify their respective demands and smooth the way for successful negotiations
5. Inform the parties of current trends in labor-management relations in other parts of the country

The Federal Mediation and Conciliation Service

The Federal Mediation and Conciliation Service (FMCS), a federal agency, will help settle a broad range of labor-management disputes. Functioning under a director appointed by the president of the United States, the FMCS, as noted earlier, was created by the Taft-Hartley Act to resolve disputes before they reach a crisis or to help settle existing strikes or lockouts rapidly.

Mediation through the FMCS is free and voluntary, and it can be requested by either party to help settle a conflict. In fact, the Taft-Hartley Act requires parties to a labor-management contract to file a dispute notice if they cannot agree on a new pact thirty days before their current one expires. An FMCS mediator then meets with them to see whether they want assistance. (Approximately 95 percent of such cases are usually settled without mediation.)

The FMCS also maintains and makes available a roster of over 1,300 independent arbitrators who are qualified to handle disputes on subjects such as wages, hours, working conditions, fringe benefits, and job assignments. Labor and management jointly choose an arbitrator and share the arbitrator's fee equally. Arbitrators on the FMCS roster must adhere to the ethical standards and procedures contained in the code of professional responsibility for arbitrators of labor-management disputes, and their impartiality is rarely questioned. The purpose and spirit of the Federal Mediation and Conciliation Service was reflected on matchbooks commemorating the service's 30th anniversary. They read, "Call us before striking."

The American Arbitration Association

The American Arbitration Association (AAA), a private nonprofit group, can also be used to resolve disputes. This organization follows a procedure similar to that of the FMCS in providing a list of suggested arbitrators containing more than 1,800 names. It stands ready to handle anything from property boundary arguments and partnership friction to labor-management issues.

The AAA charges an administrative fee per case, and the arbitrator selected by the parties charges a separate fee for services rendered. The AAA helps to settle over 16,000 labor-management disputes every year.

Both mediators and arbitrators have grown in national recognition in recent years. As a result of strikes in professional sports—football, baseball, and basketball—the use of the third party to work through contracts has become well known. In a famous, bitterly fought UMWA and Pittston Company strike in 1991, a federal mediator was appointed and successfully assisted in helping the parties negotiate what both sides described as a win-win situation. In another strike, between the Allied Pilots Association and American Airlines, a federal mediator was brought in at the request of management to assist in resolving the dispute. With the mediator's assistance the dispute was resolved to the satisfaction of both parties.

SUMMARY

A labor union is an organization of workers who have united to negotiate their collective wages, hours, and working conditions with management. Labor unions are created by workers to provide a method to deal with management more effectively and to equalize the balance of power. Unionism is based on three principles: strength through unity, equal pay for the same job, and employment practices based on seniority.

Labor unions, considered illegal conspiracies in the United States until 1842, have come a long way since the turn of the century. Beginning with craft unions, which organized skilled workers, they had expanded by the 1930s to recruit workers in various industries. Major union organizational accomplishments included the development of the AFL, the CIO, and the eventual union of both to create the AFL-CIO.

Union growth during the 1930s was accompanied and encouraged by the passage of the Norris-LaGuardia Act and the Wagner Act, federal laws that protect workers' rights to strike and to form unions. These rights were modified somewhat by the Taft-Hartley Act of 1947. The Landrum-Griffin Act of 1959 addressed the financial responsibility of union officials and members' rights.

Today's labor movement faces a downward spiral in total membership. Factors that have led to the decline include the facts that employees have fewer reasons to join, unions have failed to connect with the new generation, management is not necessarily seen as the enemy, unions have internal leadership problems, unions have been slow to adjust their recruiting message, and employers are becoming bolder in their resistance to unions.

Besides these problems, unions are influenced by general business trends such as the restructuring and downsizing of American companies, the relocation of plants and manufacturing facilities due to labor costs, technological changes in manufacturing, global competition, and changes in the work force.

Workers form unions for many reasons: to acquire more power, to provide job security, to improve economic position, and to improve working conditions. Through unionization they are able to have a collective voice to deal with management.

Once workers decide a union is needed, the steps in the organizing process include (1) conducting the organizing campaign, (2) obtaining enough signatures on authorization cards to force an election, (3) holding a certification election, and (4) obtaining certification of the union as the bargaining agent by the NLRB.

Once a union is certified, the collective bargaining process between management and labor begins. Both parties are charged with bargaining in good faith. Normally, contracts include conditions on wages, hours, time off, benefits, and procedures for laying off or discharging employees.

Both parties have their respective tools to influence the other in collective bargaining. Management may use lockouts, strikebreakers, management-run operations, injunctions, plant closings, the media, employers' associations, and lobbying. Labor's tools include strikes, picketing, boycotts, corporate campaigns, media and public relations, lobbying, and political activities.

If contract negotiations stall, a third party, either a mediator or an arbitrator, may be utilized. To receive help in mediation or arbitration cases, labor and management may call on the Federal Mediation and Conciliation Service or a private organization, the American Arbitration Association.

KEY TERMS

agency shop p. 317
arbitration p. 319
blacklist p. 305
boycott p. 323
closed shop p. 317
collective bargaining p. 316
corporate campaign p. 325
craft unions p. 303
employers' association p. 322
grievance p. 317
grievance procedure p. 317
industrial unions p. 304
injunction p. 305
labor union p. 300
Landrum-Griffin Act p. 307
lobbying p. 322
lockout p. 319
maintenance shop p. 317

mediation p. 326
National Labor Relations Board (NLRB) p. 305
Norris-LaGuardia Act p. 305
open shop p. 317
picketing p. 323
plant closing p. 320
primary boycott p. 323
right-to-work laws p. 305
secondary boycott p. 324
strike p. 322
strikebreakers p. 319
Taft-Hartley Act p. 305
unfair labor practices p. 305
union shop p. 317
union steward p. 318
Wagner Act p. 305
yellow dog contract p. 305

FOR REVIEW AND DISCUSSION

1. Why do labor unions exist?
2. What are the three guiding principles of unionism? How have those been translated into labor's basic objectives?
3. Distinguish between the types of unions that would affiliate with the original AFL and the original CIO.
4. Summarize the key points of each of the following:
   a. Norris-LaGuardia Act (Federal Anti-Injunction Act)
   b. Wagner Act (National Labor Relations Act)
   c. Taft-Hartley Act (Labor-Management Relations Act)
   d. Landrum-Griffin Act (Labor-Management Reporting and Disclosure Act)
5. What is the status of union membership today in terms of percentage of the total work force?
6. Identify four reasons union membership is declining.
7. Comment on the statement "The bread-and-butter days of unionism are over. Unions have to develop new directions."
8. Identify four new directions unions will be focusing on.
9. Does a union give employees a greater voice? Is this true in all companies? Why or why not?
10. What are the steps in the union organizing process?
11. What is meant by collective bargaining? What does bargaining in "good faith" mean?
12. Comment on the statement "The collective bargaining process establishes the balance of power in an organization."
13. What is a union shop? An agency shop?
14. What is a grievance? How can it be resolved?
15. Why do you think management has increased the use of strikebreakers?
16. What is the key legal ingredient in management's being able to close a plant or move operations as a tool in contract negotiations, according to the National Labor Relations Board?
17. What is the purpose of an injunction? Under what conditions is it granted by the courts?
18. Distinguish between a primary boycott and a secondary boycott.
19. Distinguish between mediation and arbitration; between voluntary and compulsory arbitration.

APPLICATIONS

Case 10.1: Strike! You're Out!

As former AFL-CIO president George Meany once stated, "It is the right to strike that gives a union spokesperson some measure of equality at the bargaining table." Historically, this statement has been true. The threat of a strike or a union's ability to deliver a strike action has served unions well—that is up until the early 1980s.

In 1981 the nation's air controllers' union was making demands on their employer, the U.S. government—demands for improved wages, improved staffing, and improved safety. When the demands fell on deaf ears, the air controllers went on strike and in the process crippled the nation's air transportation. President Ronald Reagan, taking a hard-line approach, fired the striking controllers and hired a new group. The action not only broke the controllers strike but sent a strong message to future strikers—beware of the consequences.

In 1992 another series of events occurred that threatened the value of a strike as a tool of labor. For months Caterpillar and the United Auto Workers sparred on provisions for a new contract. Finally, when neither side would budge, the union workers attempted to break the deadlock situation with the only effective way left to them. They struck.

Caterpillar responded with its own threat—report back to work, or all 12,000 workers would be replaced permanently with new nonunion workers. To carry out the threat, Caterpillar placed ads in all Illinois newspapers. With unemployment at all-time high levels, Caterpillar received 10,000 calls a day from people interested in the $16+ an hour positions—among the highest-paying jobs in Illinois. The threat of permanent replacement took the heart out the the union's bargaining position, and it was forced to back down.

Many supporters of organized labor cried foul over management's tactics and have pushed for legislative action to rebalance things and give the unions back the ability to strike. If the legislation is passed, it would prohibit the hiring of replacement workers during a strike and put the teeth back into a strike action.

Questions

1. What is the economic purpose of a labor union going on strike?

2. Noting the number of weapons or tools a union has, when should a labor union strike? Explain your answer.

3. How does management's ability to hire permanent replacement workers limit the power of a strike? Explain your answer.

4. Would you vote for legislation banning the hiring of permanent replacements during strikes? Explain your answer.

For further information, see Bob Secter, "Caterpillar, UAW Agree to Talks but Cling to Demands," *Los Angeles Times,* April 11, 1992, p. A1; Amy Harmon, "UAW Chief Issues Warning to Auto Firms," *Los Angeles Times,* June 15, 1992, p. D2; Amy Harmon, "Is UAW Taking Right Path to Regain Clout?" *Los Angeles Times,* June 22, 1993, p. D1.

Case 10.2: Work Slow to Make a Point

In Decatur, Illinois, union employees are using a new tactic to gain management's attention—and agreement to their contract demands—while keeping their jobs. Because of fears about the risks of staging a full-scale strike and potentially losing their jobs, employees have chosen to implement slowdown strikes. For example:

- Lance Vaughn, an installer at one of the Caterpillar's Decatur plants, is now doing his job backward.

Vaughn's job is to install a set of hoses on the huge, off-highway trucks produced at Caterpillar. Up until recently, he installed a set of small hoses inside *before* attaching the larger hose on the outside. But now he puts on the large hose first, as described in the assembly manual, and then reaches around it to put the small hose in place.

- Patricia Zilz, an employee at Staley Corporation, a Decatur beer supply company, does her job by the rules. Working twelve-hour shifts three to four days a week, Zilz drives her water sampling truck at the company speed limit of 15 miles per hour rather than the 25 miles per hour, which has been company precendent—and is more productive.

In both examples, the strategies result in workers doing no more than the absolute minimum while gumming up production. Most important, management is brought back to the bargaining table—while workers keep their jobs.

Questions

1. What are the risks—for both management and labor—of a strike?

2. When a slowdown occurs, which side benefits the most? Why?

3. How can a slowdown hurt a company's performance?

4. What are the risk to employees who participate in slowdown efforts?

For further information, see Jesse Green, "Out and Organized," *New York Times,* June 13, 1993, p. F1.

REFERENCES

1. Kevin G. Salwen, "Labor Letter," *The Wall Street Journal,* April 13, 1993, p. A1.
2. *A Short History of American Labor* (Washington, DC: AFL-CIO, 1993), p. 1.
3. Ibid., p. 2.
4. Rudy Oswald, *Historical Trends in Union Membership: Department of Labor Statistics* (Washington, DC: AFL-CIO, 1993), p. 2.
5. Ibid.
6. Michael Maccoby, "The New Unionism," *Utne Reader,* March/April 1993, p. 85.
7. Ibid.
8. Candice Johnson, "Locked-Out UAW Workers Stand Strong," *AFL-CIO News,* May 3, 1993, p. 6.
9. Kevin Kelly, "Caterpillar's Don Fites: Why He Didn't Blink," *Business Week,* August 10, 1992, p. 56.
10. Steven Lee, "Kroger Expects to Be out of San Antonio by the End of August," *Dallas Morning News,* July 2, 1993, pp. 1D, 11D.
11. Martin Zimmerman, "Food Lion, Union Taking Their Cases to the Consumer," *Dallas Morning News,* June 2, 1992, p. 4D.

12. James B. Parks, UMWA Strike Swells to 14,000 in 6 States," *AFL-CIO News,* June 28, 1993, p. 7.
13. John Oravec, "AFL-CIO Lifts Boycott After IBT Local Gains Pact," *AFL-CIO News,* June 14, 1993, p. 9.
14. "Candy Maker Joins Boycott of Diamond," *AFL-CIO News,* January 11, 1993, p. 3.
15. Robert Rose, "Unions Hit Corporate-Campaign Trail," *The Wall Street Journal,* May 20, 1993, p. B7.
16. "Union-Made Products and Skills Exhibited," *AFL-CIO News,* June 14, 1993, p. 20.

CAREER CAPSULE 2

Career Opportunities at R. R. Donnelley

Textbooks, catalogs, magazines, the Bible, computer software documentation, maps, telephone books—the list goes on. R. R. Donnelley produces virtually every type of publication imaginable. As the largest commercial printer in the United States, this company sells more than $3.5 billion worth of printing services each year and provides a host of challenging and rewarding career opportunities to college graduates.

ADMINISTRATION

Most of Donnelley's administrative professionals have earned bachelor's degrees in accounting or finance; some have MBA (master of business administration) degrees. Graduates who work in the accounting or finance areas can expect to become involved in cost accounting, budgeting, inventory control, financial reporting, or forecasting as well as investments and risk management. Employees in Donnelley's price administration area often do considerable research and analysis to prepare a price quotation that sales professionals will relay to a potential customer who has asked the company to bid on a major printing job. The administrative area also offers career opportunities in credit administration, where employees evaluate a customer's financial condition and develop an acceptable payment schedule based on the nature and size of the printing job. Credit representatives may also be responsible for collecting payments and negotiating new payment terms with a customer if the need arises.

MANUFACTURING

Those who go to work in the manufacturing area usually have degrees in engineering, manufacturing management, or a related field. Trainees begin in Donnelley's Manufacturing Management Training (MMT) program, which rotates them through an entire range of plant operations, including customer service, the pressroom and bindery, distribution, human resources, waste reclamation, purchasing, and shipping. Once they're thoroughly familiar with the manufacturing process, it's common for trainees to become supervisors in one of the areas they rotated through. The key prerequisites to success in manufacturing are flexibility, sound human relations skills, the ability to communicate effectively, initiative, energy, and a commitment to providing top-quality service to Donnelley's customers.

SALES

Donnelley operates more than two dozen sales offices throughout the United States and Canada. Sales professionals usually have a four-year degree in business, in liberal arts, or in a technical field, plus a high level of self-motivation and self-confidence. Trainees usually start by learning the basics of the printing industry through plant tours and meetings with seasoned technical employees. They're also exposed to pricing and credit operations, effective sales techniques, and information about the various types of customers they'll eventually meet. This foundation makes them more knowledgeable about the company and its services when they begin working in the field.

R. R. Donnelley's commitment to employee success goes far beyond the training mentioned here, however. Management urges employees to further their education and offers tuition assistance to help them do so. The R. R. Donnelley employment experience is geared to provide employees with rewarding challenges, gratifying growth opportunities, and satisfying personal development throughout their entire careers.

Part Three

Production and Marketing Activities

11

PRODUCING THE PRODUCT

ne way to increase productivity is to do whatever we are doing now but faster. . . . There is a second way. We can change the nature of the work we do, not how fast we do it.

ANDREW S. GROVE

CHAPTER OBJECTIVES
After studying this chapter, you should be able to:

1. Discuss the influence of production on people's standard of living.
2. Differentiate between processing and manufacturing companies.
3. List the three kinds of factors to consider when choosing a plant site, and give examples of each.
4. Contrast motion study and time study and evaluate their use in production management.
5. Compare the four major production processes, giving examples of each.
6. Summarize the nature and relationship of computer-aided design, computer-aided manufacturing, and computer-integrated manufacturing.
7. Discuss how robots may be used for certain production jobs and how their use may benefit both labor and management.
8. List the steps involved in a typical purchasing procedure and summarize the purchasing policies that management may follow.
9. Summarize the characteristics and advantages of a just-in-time inventory system.
10. Describe the steps involved in production control.
11. Contrast total quality management with an organization's quality assurance program and explain how departments must relate to one another to apply TQM.

UP FRONT

Mention the name of one of America's foremost companies, General Electric, and most people might think of light bulbs. But the truth is, GE is a highly diversified company that produces not only light bulbs but kitchen appliances and jet aircraft engines. Take GE Transportation Systems, a manufacturing facility in Erie, Pennsylvania, for example. This division makes motorized wheels for earthmoving equipment, propulsion systems for transit cars, and railroad locomotives. Next time you board a train, it might be pulled by a Genesis Series 1 locomotive built by GE Transportation Systems.

Tony Aiello oversees the final stages of locomotive manufacturing at GE Transportation Systems. Raised in Jersey City, New Jersey, Aiello attended Stevens Institute of Technology in Hoboken, earning a B.S. in electrical engineering. He spent a summer working at a Du Pont plant where nylon was manufactured. "At the time, I thought factory automation was a good way to go with my career," he recalls. "But I was also interested in manufacturing. Many people don't realize the complexity of how things are made. I was interested; I wanted to stay flexible and keep my options open."

In his senior year, Aiello was recruited by GE to enter its Manufacturing Management Program (MMP). "The program requires you to work at four different jobs over a period of two years, to gain broad manufacuturing experience," he explains. "First I was assigned to the GE plant in Syracuse, New York. For six months I was a quality engineer, then I spent another six months supervising twenty people in sub-

assembly for sonar systems. By necessity, you learn a lot, quickly.

"I was then transferred to Burlington, Vermont, where armament systems are made. Many people are not aware that GE made weaponry for jet aircraft, helicopters, and ships. I was a plant engineer for six months, working on projects for improving the physical plant, then was made a product control specialist for electronic subassemblies. My chief responsibilities were to make sure that the product was built and that it shipped on time."

After completing the two-year Manufacturing Management Program, Aiello had a number of interviews with different GE companies. "The hiring process is conducted throughout GE, to find the job you're looking for," he says. "I had thought I wanted to work with technology, but the Syracuse experience had piqued my interest in management and working with people. I found what I was looking for in Erie."

Tony Aiello went to work as a maintenance supervisor at the Erie manufacturing facility. He was responsible for twenty-three maintenance people and about $2 million worth of machine tools and shop equipment. During this time, he began studying at the Behrend College campus of Penn State University, where he earned an MBA degree. Following his maintenance assignment, he moved to the locomotive operation as a quality engineer. "I worked

TONY AIELLO

BUSINESS LEADER, GE TRANS-PORTATION SYSTEMS

on the second shift, in the locomotive final inspection and testing, then on first shift in cab assembly. Not all locomotive cabs are alike. Every locomotive we build is a custom order for railroads such as Conrail, Santa Fe, Union Pacific, Amtrak, and others. They specify what they want in the cab and how it's to be designed. Our job was to assure that the plans and materials were all correct and that the proper gauges, controls, radios, refrigerators, and electronics were in place."

From there, Aiello was promoted to business leader of the paint, test, and prep-to-ship function. This is the last phase of locomotive manufacture. "My group is about a hundred people, who take the locomotive from final assembly to painting, assembling the windows and gaskets, and final testing, where we run the locomotive on a test track for about one hundred miles. Once it has passed, we present it to the customer inspector for acceptance; then it's ready to ship."

Building a locomotive is no simple feat, yet the Erie plant turns out eight to ten a week. Conventional diesel locomotives have a 4,000-horsepower engine and cost $800,000 to $2 million. Engineers at GE Transportation Services designed two locomotives. One is the Genesis Series 1, a concept originally designed for Amtrak. The GE 2000 incorporates alternating current, or AC, technology, to give the locomotive higher operating efficiencies. "AC is the way to go in the future," says Aiello. "Technologically, it's a cut above."

Tony Aiello is constantly finding diversity in his work. "I may want to move into other management areas myself at some point. I work with a lot of different people in the company—sales, marketing, field service, engineering, and other functions. It helps me get a broad picture and a sense of future directions.

"Just when this job starts to seem routine is about the time something happens to make you realize how exciting building a locomotive really is. Above all the hard work and frustration, the most unique thing is the satisfaction of seeing a completed locomotive go out the door."

In this part of the book, we will focus on the central functions of business: making, selling, promoting, and distributing products. Production is an integral part of this business activity: you cannot sell what you have not made. The age-old questions of production are at the heart of business: how can I make more products, make them cheaper, and make them better?

The Nature of Production

People in the United States enjoy a high standard of living because companies make goods in adequate numbers to fulfill consumer demand. In doing so, they create jobs for millions of Americans and encourage a flourishing service industry to maintain and repair the articles made. Here are a few of the support industries that provide the auto industry with required materials, parts, and supplies:

- Glass
- Metals
- Fiberglass
- Plastics
- Rubber
- Leather
- Abrasives
- Paint
- Carbon
- Cork
- Paper
- Textiles

Production, whether in the form of processing or manufacturing, is fundamental to business.

That is not all; various other businesses rely on cars for their livelihood by servicing existing autos or auto owners:

- Maintenance and repair businesses
- Replacement parts firms
- Aftermarket businesses selling such items as radios, paint, and tires
- Petroleum-based products dealers
- Insurance companies

The Motor Vehicle Manufacturers' Association reports that 14.3 percent of the United States work force has jobs somehow related to the automobile industry. Production is clearly a significant factor in the world of business.

What Is Production?

Production is *a business activity that uses people and machinery to convert materials and parts into salable products.* Two types of companies engage in this activity: processing companies and manufacturing companies. A **processing company** is *a firm that converts natural resources into raw material.* Forest products, petroleum, steel, bauxite, meat-packing, citrus, and leather-tanning companies are processors. A **manufacturing company** is *a firm that converts raw materials and component parts into consumer and industrial goods.* Farm equipment, stereo, computer, and appliance makers are manufacturing companies. They are what most people have in mind when they think of production: long assembly lines where workers add parts to a growing object until it finally appears as the product. Our discussion will concentrate on manufac-

production
A business activity that uses people and machinery to convert materials and parts into salable products.

processing company
A firm that converts natural resources into raw material.

manufacturing company
A firm that converts raw materials and component parts into consumer and industrial goods.

turing firms, but many of the principles discussed and introduced are important in both kinds of production.

Products are often used to make other products, so one firm's finished product may be another's component part. This kind of interdependence is common. Tens of thousands of firms rely on one another for essential parts, subassemblies, and supplies that support or become part of an end product.

Managing Production

Production management is *the job of coordinating and controlling all the activities required to make a product.* It begins well before actual production. Managers who represent production, marketing, finance, and other areas must decide jointly what product to make, based on their analysis of consumer wants and needs (more on this in Chapter 12). Once a product has been chosen, management determines where and how to produce it. Materials, parts, equipment, supplies, subassemblies, and employees must appear in the right quantities, places, and times. Effective production managers coordinate people, dollars, machines, and materials as economically and efficiently as possible to create a marketable product.

Choosing a Plant Site

Actual production cannot begin until a plant is built, but the original plants of many prominent manufacturing companies were situated in humble and sometimes illogical places. Liquid Paper correction fluid was first brewed up in a kitchen. Everest & Jennings International, a world-wide producer of wheelchairs and other medical equipment, began in 1933 in Harry Jennings's one-car garage. Several years later Jennings and his partner, Herbert Everest, tripled the size of their physical plant—by moving to a three-car garage. Hewlett-Packard Co., TeleVideo Systems, and hundreds of other well-known companies have begun in such modest surroundings.

No matter how accidental or casual the origin, the management of a thriving company must eventually select a permanent plant location. This is a matter for careful thought and investigation.

Location Decisions

A plant location always leaves something to be desired. A site with an exceptionally good supply of skilled workers may be remote from prime market centers, raw materials, or both. Available transportation may not be the most economical or efficient to ship parts and materials in and finished products out. State and local regulations can weave a web of red tape around an otherwise attractive location. The point is to select the best site available—the one with the greatest advantages and the fewest drawbacks.

Location decisions are often made by committees of top executives who examine and weigh every factor, from taxation and transportation to community services and climate. They may evaluate several potential sites, because the firm will have to live with the decision for years to come.

GLOBAL PERSPECTIVE

Manufacturing: A Transnational Activity

Multinational manufacturing has become a way of life. American manufacturers routinely make parts and assemble final products in other countries, while their foreign competitors set up shop in the United States. For example:

- General Motors employs approximately 68,000 people in Mexico to build vehicles and assemble components such as electrical wiring harnesses from parts manufactured in the United States.
- Rubbermaid planned to invest between $1.3 million and $1.5 million in 1993 to upgrade its plastics and rubber molding plants in Mexico. The plants make approximately 120 products from trash cans to tool boxes.
- Levi Strauss & Co. has eighty-two production, finishing, and customer service facilities in twenty-three countries and usually manufactures clothing in the countries or regions where they will be sold.
- There are more than 1,500 Japanese-affiliated factories in the United States. Most of them are entirely owned by a Japanese firm. Honda now has more than 25 percent of its manufacturing capacity in the United States. The company has invested $3 billion in the United

States and $230 million in Canada to build research and development, toolmaking, engine production, and vehicle assembly facilities.
- More than 200 German companies, including such giants as BMW and Siemens, have spent $4 billion to build plants in North and South Carolina.

These examples imply at least one thing: manufacturers who compete in the global business arena tend to ignore artificial and geographic boundaries when they establish or expand production facilities. Building component or final-assembly plants in other countries often enables firms to take advantage of lower labor and real estate costs and to minimize the shipping expense to get their finished products to a major market.

(For more on foreign companies in the United States and vice versa, see Mike Allen and Jim Dunn, "America Goes International," *Popular Mechanics*, October 1992, p. 37; Bill Bregar, "Rubbermaid Upgrading Mexican Plant," *Plastics News*, February 22, 1993, p. 1; "Japan's U.S. Plants Up 9% in 1991," *Fortune*, April 20, 1992, p. 16; and Robert M. Ady, "Why BMW Cruised Into Spartanburg," *The Wall Street Journal*, July 6, 1992, p. 10.)

Loctite Corporation, which makes a variety of adhesives and sealants including the popular Super Glue, recently built a plant in Ireland to manufacture adhesives for many of the eighty-odd countries in which the company's products are sold. (Different languages pose no problem; a computerized system prints labels in the language of the country where the product is being shipped.[1])

Figure 11.1
The "Three Ps" of
plant location.

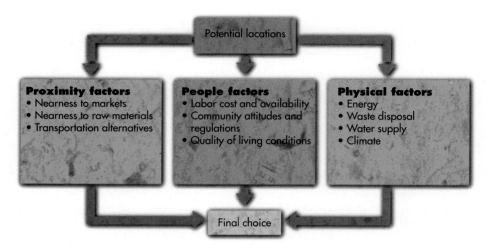

Although plant site requirements vary with the individual firm, product, and intended market, a location decision is based on three general concerns, referred to as the "Three Ps": proximity, people, and physical factors (see Figure 11.1).

Proximity Factors

Proximity to customers or to raw materials is often an either-or decision. That is, manufacturers must choose between locating a plant near customers or near raw materials. Someone in the dairy business, for example, may want to avoid the need to refrigerate and ship perishable eggs and milk over long distances, and so may locate near major markets. ARCO Pipe Line Company, a subsidiary of Atlantic Richfield Company, recently relocated from Independence, Kansas to Houston, Texas. Management decided to make the move because the petrochemical business is well established in Houston and the city is a major center for petroleum refining and foreign crude oil imports.[2]

On the other hand, for those who make television sets or stereo equipment, nearness to customers is less important because customers are not concentrated in specific areas, the goods are not perishable, and shipping costs are relatively low in relation to the selling prices of the items.

Occasionally, closeness to raw materials overrides the advantage of being close to markets, especially when these materials are expensive to ship. Timber, for example, is heavy, and shipping it great distances is costly, so the paper mills of Maine and Georgia and the furniture plants of North Carolina are located near forests. Steel mills in Pennsylvania and West Virginia are built near iron ore and coal deposits, which give them access to both fuel and raw materials. Glass container manufacturing plants are located near large bodies of sand in Pennsylvania and West Virginia.

The third proximity factor that affects a plant site decision is the availability of transportation. The options include rail, highway, air, water, and pipeline.

The best choice depends on the individual case. If management is worried about perishability or rush shipments, nearness to airports might be important. Dole pineapples, for example, are transported from Hawaii by plane instead of ship because of their perishability. Heavy, bulky products such as earthmoving equipment are shipped cheapest by rail or water, and fluids by pipeline. Highway transportation is popular for most products.

Along with its primary shipping method, a firm needs alternatives available in emergencies or when bad weather, strikes, or other unforeseen events temporarily shut down the main choice. Furniture plants, for example, may ship mainly by rail but use trucks for emergency shipments. Nissan officials chose Tennessee for a truck plant because 60 percent of the parts needed to build the trucks must be shipped in by rail or highway, and Tennessee is crisscrossed by key railroads and interstate highways.

People Factors

People—their numbers, skills, and attitudes—also influence the choice of a plant site. Although some firms actually have attracted a skilled work force to a plant site with otherwise appealing features, producers usually try to build where an adequate supply of skilled labor already exists. A company may, however, have to shoulder the burden of training a large supply of willing but unskilled applicants.

Aside from labor supply and skills, another people factor is the prevailing wage. If companies in a region pay higher-than-average wages, management of a firm intending to move may look for a location in an area where pay tends to be lower.

Community attitudes toward new businesses are a concern, too. Area business leaders may become hostile toward a new company that pays significantly higher wages than existing businesses, because this would pressure established firms to pay more or lose workers to the newcomer. Production processes that threaten the environment may place community pressure on city, county, or state regulatory bodies to deny the company operating permits.

State and local regulations and restrictions should be studied before a location decision is made. It may take several months to several years to obtain operating permits for certain kinds of processing or manufacturing plants, such as petroleum refineries.

Regulatory agencies frequently require firms to submit an **environmental impact study**, which is *a report describing how a proposed plant will alter the quality of life in an area,* covering such topics as air, water, and noise pollution; wildlife displacement; effect on natural plant life; and increased load on transportation facilities, sewage treatment plants, and water and energy supplies. This kind of preliminary work can be very expensive and time consuming, and there is no guarantee that once it is completed the necessary approvals will be granted.

environmental impact study
A report describing how a proposed plant will alter the quality of life in an area.

On the other hand, many states and cities try to sell a large company on the advantages they can offer, because new manufacturing plants mean jobs, prosperity, and increased revenues. A large plant employing several thousand people can make the difference between economic distress and prosperity in some regions—which states, counties, and local business associations acknowledge in their appeals to new corporate residents.

Many states and communities make enormous concessions to attract new manufacturing plants. For example, South Carolina gave BMW $130 million (which included $71 million in tax concessions) to build an auto plant there. In addition, the state bought the land for the plant site and agreed to extend the runway at the Greenville-Spartanburg airport to accommodate large cargo planes.[3] Other communities actively advertise the attractiveness of their locations. Figure 11.2 shows an advertisement placed by Volusia County, Florida emphasizing the county's benefits.

Management may also want to evaluate the community's living conditions—housing, educational, recreational, and cultural facilities—because they help to attract employees and keep them content once they are hired.

Figure 11.2

Cities, counties, and states attempt to influence firms in their location decisions.

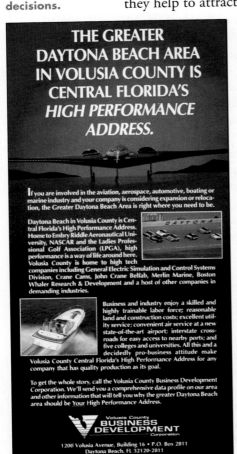

Physical Factors

Operating a manufacturing plant without heat, light, and power would be as difficult as running your car without gas, oil, and water. Managers who research suitable plant sites must investigate the supply and the cost of electricity and other forms of energy. If a plant's projected energy demands would overtax existing supplies, management must either negotiate with the suppliers to expand their facilities to accommodate the plant's needs or look for a location with better service.

In addition to energy supplies, other physical factors that might be considered, depending on the nature of the product, include waste disposal facilities, climate, and water supply.

Productivity Studies

Managers must estimate each worker's productivity during a work period to employ enough workers to produce a certain quantity of units on schedule. Productivity estimates are also used in drawing up a budget for labor costs and perhaps constructing a piece-rate wage system based on each employee's output.

Motion and time studies are needed whenever management must know how many units a worker can produce in a certain situation. These studies also allow the firm to add a portion of each worker's hourly wage to each unit's total cost. Companies that do not perform motion and time studies may hire too many or too few workers to do the jobs at hand or may compute a unit price too low to recapture the product's cost, let alone earn a profit. In addition, it is important for management to design production jobs with enough motions and variety to make them challenging to workers. Repetitious, unchallenging jobs often cause high turnover—workers are virtually bored to death with their tasks.

Motion Study

A **motion study**, conceived and refined by management pioneer Frederick W. Taylor, is *a study that identifies the number and kind of movements required to perform a given operation*. The purpose is not to make employees work *harder* but to help them work *smarter*—to condense the job into an economical series of steps that are more efficient and less tiring than those used before. Often employees find that they can produce more with less effort after their motions have been studied and refined.

Total simplification is not a desirable end, though. Extremely menial jobs can be terribly unmotivating and boring. So while you want to eliminate wasted motion, the work should offer enough challenge that employees are not dehumanized. Nevertheless, workers who now stand may have their work layout rearranged so they can sit down, and those who pick up and lay down several hand tools to perform a series of operations may be given a device that does the work of several of the old tools with a single squeeze.

Copying machines that collate and staple documents after they have been copied are a good example of motion-reducing machinery. They save the motions that would be required to hand-collate and staple the pages. A product's design naturally has an impact on motion studies, too. By redesigning its Elite model vacuum cleaner and the production process by which it is made, the Hoover company reduced the number of fasteners that hold the machine together from fifty-six to only twelve. Bill Machrone, publisher and columnist at *PC Magazine*, claims he saves 40 feet of finger travel by writing his columns on a notebook computer (which requires a 2 mm stroke to depress a key) instead of a standard desktop PC (which requires approximately 4 mm keystrokes).[4]

motion study
A study that identifies the number and kind of movements required to perform a given operation.

Time Study

A **time study** is *a study that determines the amount of time an average worker takes to perform a given operation*. After motion study has been used to refine movements and gain efficiency, a time study of a large cross section of workers doing the same task allows management to determine the average time it takes to complete a particular job. This permits supervisors to estimate production volume per work shift and lets management prepare budgets accordingly. Firms that pay production workers on a piece-rate wage plan, as discussed in Chapter 8, use motion and time studies to establish average production volume per worker and to create a base pay rate from there.

time study
A study that determines the amount of time an average worker takes to perform a given operation.

Perhaps the most familiar production process is the assembly line.

Applying Productivity Studies

Many jobs lend themselves to motion and time studies. Meter readers are expected to read a certain number of water or electrical meters in a typical residential area each day; telephone operators are responsible for processing a certain number of operator-assisted calls an hour. When you had your car fixed, the repair shop probably used a flat-rate manual to compute its labor charges. That book lists standard times required to perform specific maintenance and repair jobs on various makes and models of cars.

Workers tend to be wary of motion and time studies, believing that management is trying to get more work for less pay. As a result, they may try to mislead the observer by reducing their normal work pace while under study. Observers, who are usually industrial engineers, can adjust for this normal worker reaction mathematically.

Management should explain in advance what the motion and time studies are intended to do, emphasizing the budgeting and personnel planning purposes mentioned earlier in this section. Supervisors, working closely with industrial engineers, should notify workers when they will be observed and reassert the reasons for these studies.

Production Methods

Not all products can be made the same way: the nature of the product determines how it will be produced. Traditionally, production methods have been classified as analytic, synthetic, continuous, and intermittent. In the following sections, we examine each one briefly.

Analytic and Synthetic Processes

analytic process Production method in which raw materials are broken down to form new products.

In the **analytic process**, *raw materials are broken down to form new products*. An example is found in the citrus industry, where oranges are processed and converted into several end products, as shown in Figure 11.3.

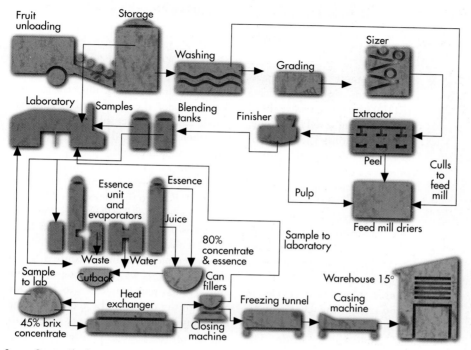

Figure 11.3
Analytic
production
process: orange
juice and related
products.

Source: Courtesy Florida Department of Citrus.

In a sense, the **synthetic process** is the opposite of the analytic process, because *materials are combined to form a certain product.* Glass manufacturing illustrates the synthetic process, because it combines lime, sand, potash, soda, and other elements to make a product with a unique appearance and characteristics different from any of these ingredients. Aluminum production is another example because processed bauxite is combined with lime and ash. The synthetic process has two variations, the fabrication and the assembly processes.

The **fabrication process** is *a variation of synthetic production in which new products are created from those already manufactured by changing their form.* Levi's 501 jeans, for example, are created from cloth, buttons, and thread joined together according to a pattern. Shoes and handbags, kitchen cabinets, baked goods, tires, and flashlight batteries are also produced by fabrication.

The **assembly process** is *a variation of synthetic production in which materials or parts are combined without substantial changes.* For example, Ford Motor Company is planning to invest $1.2 billion to develop and build a new family of V-6 engines, $700 million of which will be spent to modify the Cleveland plant where the engines will be assembled. Ford also made $700 million worth of changes at its Chihuahua, Mexico engine plant, which began assembling a multivalve four-cylinder engine in 1993.[5]

Meanwhile, General Motors has simplified the assembly process for its cars and trucks by reducing the number of basic frames from twenty to seven—a

synthetic process
Production method in which materials are combined to form a certain product.

fabrication process
A variation of synthetic production in which new products are created from those already manufactured by changing their form.

assembly process
A variation of synthetic production in which materials or parts are combined without substantial changes.

MANAGER'S NOTEBOOK

Right- or Left-Hand Drive?

AT HONDA'S MARYSVILLE, OHIO PLANT, IT'S NO BIG DEAL

The Japanese and European market for right-hand drive (RHD) cars is impressive. Ford is developing a RHD Probe, Chrysler is doing a Jeep Cherokee, and GM has firm plans to produce an RHD Saturn.

The engineering and production line changes required to manufacture both right-hand and left-hand drive cars frustrate some manufacturers, however. They claim the difference doubles engineering efforts and causes major bottlenecks in production line changeovers. Honda, in contrast, has taken the challenge in stride. The company's Marysville, Ohio plant builds either model on the same production line without duplicating tools or increasing the number of employees. RHD cars are built in lots of 60, with little more than a hood sheet to alert employees that the next batch will be made for export.

How so?

To start with, Honda made the left and right sides of the engine compartment as close to mirror images as possible. The engine was unchanged. Engineers also positioned underdash and engine compartment components so they won't have to be moved no matter which side the steering column is mounted on. The firewall is the only stamping that's unique to RHD models, and more than 80 percent of the parts are identical for either model. Designers made sure that the space allocated to parts that fit under the dashboard is approximately equal on either side to permit room for either a right-hand or left-hand steering column and pedals.

As far as production methods go, Marysville engineers designed workstations that will "flop" to the other side of the line to build a batch of RHD models. Parts are routed to the proper side about an hour before a changeover takes place.

The employee training required to orchestrate all this was, of course, considerable. Honda sent employees to Japan for two months to learn the techniques the company had perfected there to build both models on the same line. After returning, employees underwent another two to three months of training, starting with an on-site training line and progressing to building training bodies, which were disassembled and inspected for quality.

Perhaps the most impressive fact of all is that Honda considered engineering for left-hand or right-hand drive more of a cultural change than an engineering challenge. Says Raita Musumiya, associate chief engineer for Honda R&D North America, "Once you have made the commitment to design a car this way, anybody can do it. It's making the commitment from the start that's important."

(For more on Honda's approach, see Gerry Kobe, "Engineer for Right-Hand Steer: How Honda Does It," *Automotive Industries*, March 1992.)

decrease of 65 percent. This move will significantly reduce both product development costs and the time required to produce new models.[6]

Continuous and Intermittent Processes

Production processes are called analytic or synthetic because of what is done to raw materials. Another way of classifying production methods is by how they are performed over time. A **continuous process** is *a production method that uses the same machinery to perform the same operations repeatedly over relatively long periods of time.* Synthetic fibers, chemicals, Bic pens, and Gillette razor blades are made by this process. Machinery runs for months at a time with few if any changes in methods or equipment (Gillette's Sensor razor blades are produced by high-speed equipment that makes fifteen laser welds in a fifth of a second).[7] A continuous process is used for making cars. Understandably, plant closings to retool for new models that will be made with a continuous process require several months: Many tools and dies must be replaced and other extensive changes are necessary.

The moving assembly line, which was actually born at Ford Motor Company, celebrated its eightieth birthday in 1993. An engineer in the company's production area first used the continuous production process on April 1, 1913, to make ignition parts. It was tried in the Model T's final assembly area in October of that year. The chassis was pulled along the line by a rope as 150 workers installed the necessary parts. Although it was primitive, this technique increased worker productivity impressively. Moving assembly lines soon became standard procedure for manufacturing most high-volume, standardized products.

A firm that uses an **intermittent process** is engaged in *a production process that shuts down equipment periodically and readjusts it to make a slightly different product;* production does not run the same day in and day out. The intermittent process is used by **job shops**, *companies that make products to customers' individual specifications.* Custom gunsmiths and guitar makers use an intermittent process: no two units are identical. One extreme example of a job shop is the legendary James Purdey and Sons, a London gunsmithing firm that has been in business for more than 175 years. Purdey shotguns, which are custom-fitted to the individual, are so unique that the barrels and stocks cannot be interchanged. The company produces only seventy shotguns per year.

The security vehicle (armored car) firms that have flourished with the epidemic of international terrorism are vivid examples of intermittent process production. They do custom work by reworking a Cadillac or Lincoln Continental, in the spirit of James Bond, enabling it to conceal machine guns, spread oil slicks in the path of pursuing vehicles, release smoke bombs, start by remote control (to check for booby traps), and withstand grenade and machine gun attacks with armor plate and bulletproof glass.

Management's choice of a continuous or intermittent process is governed by the nature of the product and the market the product is meant for. Custom-

continuous process
A production method that uses the same machinery to perform the same operations repeatedly over relatively long periods of time.

intermittent process
A production process that shuts down equipment periodically and readjusts it to make a slightly different product.

job shops
Companies that make products to customers' individual specifications.

made products must be manufactured by intermittent process because manufacturing must stop with the completion of each unit. Mass production of identical units lends itself to a continuous process, but even some mass-produced items have elements of an intermittent process. Printers manufacture thousands of books in a continuous process, for instance, but must make changes when they print another book.

CAD, CAM, and CIM

The more sophisticated and competitive companies use computers to design and manufacture their products.

computer-aided design (CAD)
A process that uses highly specialized computer graphics programs to create three-dimensional models of products on a computer screen.

Computer-aided design (CAD) is *a process that uses highly specialized computer graphics programs to create three-dimensional models of products on a computer screen.* CAD programs have made drafting instruments, pencils, and templates obsolete. After a product's design and materials data are stored in a computer database, engineers and designers can retrieve, manipulate, and modify these data using keyboard and mouse commands to produce a three-dimensional model of the product. They can then modify the model and ask "what if" questions about its shape, size, and material without having to build a wire-and-clay version. CAD systems simplify product design work just like word processors simplify the writing and editing of documents.

After the necessary data are entered, the computer can calculate the part's dimensions, figure the center of lines and arcs, allow designers to view it from any angle, cut it into cross sections, and position it in relation to adjacent parts (to confirm that it will fit inside the allotted space). Engineering drawings that once took hours to produce with traditional drafting instruments can be produced by a CAD system in minutes. The savings can be enormous—one engineer with a CAD system can be as productive as several engineers producing designs by hand.

In addition to producing engineering drawings, a CAD system can test the computer model to reveal how the part's materials and design will react to changes in stress, pressure, temperature, and other variables it will encounter in actual use. Auto manufacturers have used CAD to simulate and analyze the conditions that occur inside the combustion chamber of a running automobile engine.

CAD's ability to compress design and testing time enables manufacturers to make design changes much faster and to introduce new models weeks or months earlier than they otherwise could.

computer-aided manufacturing (CAM)
A manufacturing system in which computers direct, control, and monitor production equipment to perform all the steps required to perform a task.

Computer-aided manufacturing (CAM) is *a manufacturing system in which computers direct, control, and monitor production equipment* (which usually includes robots) *to perform all the steps required to perform a task.* After a part has been designed by a CAD system, CAM calculates the movements a machine must make to produce the part and converts those movements to a set of computer instructions that the machine understands. Production changeover costs in highly automated, state-of-the-art CAM system can be virtually nil. The computer merely directs the machine to perform a different task (such as machining, grinding, honing, drilling, punching, or assembling) than it did on the last job. Such flexibility reduces traditional machine setup time enormously and makes small-lot production runs both practical and economical.

Computer-integrated manufacturing (CIM), which combines CAD and CAM, is *a system in which all production-related activities, from product design through manufacturing, are controlled by a computer.* A true CIM system merges manufacturing with other operations, including materials purchasing, physical distribution, inventory control, and cost accounting. The National Science Foundation has said that CIM has greater potential to increase productivity than any invention since electricity. CIM systems are found only in the most highly automated factories.

Robots on the Production Line

The last two decades have brought a pronounced trend toward the use of robot assembly techniques in a number of manufacturing companies. In the context of manufacturing, a **robot** is defined by the Robot Institute of America as *a reprogrammable, multifunctional manipulator designed to move material, parts, tools, or specialized devices through variable programmed motions to accomplish a variety of tasks.* First installed on General Motors and Ford Motor Company assembly lines in 1961, robots are used today for repetitive

> **YOU DECIDE**
>
> What advice would you have, given CAD, CAM, CIM, and other high-technology aspects of manufacturing, for someone whose ambition is to go to work in a production-oriented job?

computer-integrated manufacturing (CIM)
A system in which all production-related activities, from product design through manufacturing, are controlled by a computer.

robot
A reprogrammable, multifunctional manipulator designed to move material, parts, tools, or specialized devices through variable programmed motions to accomplish a variety of tasks.

The use of computers in manufacturing allows for highly sophisticated robots to perform all the steps in a particular production task.

jobs such as spray painting, spot welding, and grinding; handling plutonium or other hazardous materials; and working in environments that are otherwise hostile to humans.

Although robots may require changes in a plant's layout and work flow (total costs to buy and install one may exceed $100,000), ultimate savings can be impressive—$6 per hour to operate some robots compared with $19 per hour in wages and benefits paid to an auto assembly worker. Productivity naturally improves because these machines may be operated nonstop, twenty-four hours per day if necessary. Robots also may be reprogrammed to perform different sequences of rote movements, so they are not limited to just one specialized task. Some are only "down" (in need of service or repairs) an average of 2 percent of the time. Manufacturers have reported increases in output ranging from 30 to 300 percent after robots were installed. At Honda of America's $670 million Anna, Ohio engine plant, which is one of the most automated auto engine plants in North America, robots load and unload castings into shot-blasting machines and deliver them to machining areas for further processing. With 48 percent of its operations automated, this plant easily produces one engine every 27 seconds.[8]

The impact of robots is even more dramatic at Next Computer's state-of-the-art production line, where there are thirteen robots for every five employees. Next engineers have built robots so sophisticated that they can apply 1,700 tiny drops of solder 1/100th of an inch thick on circuit boards and install 150 parts per minute following the soldering operation. Only fifteen to seventeen out of every 1 million of these robot-soldered connections fail. Although robots replace some employees, they create jobs for programmers, engineers, and hydraulic and electronic technicians to maintain them.

Materials Management

Once a company has chosen a product, built a plant, planned for workers' productivity, and determined which production method to follow, it must buy and control the materials needed to make the product. Materials management is a crucial concern in the production of anything from skateboards to computers. Consider that minor miracle, the car. If thousands of such seemingly insignificant parts as rubber seals, mounting brackets, and door handles had not been brought together at the required assembly points, hundreds of workers would have been idle and thousands of dollars lost as the assembly line ground to a halt. Problems of this type do happen from time to time, of course, and few manufacturers are immune to them. Business historian and author Harold C. Livesay once saw a grim group of Chrysler Corporation employees attack a locked boxcar in a railroad yard to get the bolts they needed. With no time to unload the boxcar, the crew began cutting holes in it with an acetylene torch. Citing a cost of $40,000 per hour to stop the production line, the workers swore that the company would pay for the damaged railroad car and any fines associated with their assault.

The Purchasing Function

Production thrives on machinery, raw materials, parts, and supplies, all of which may be bought. As a firm expands, it will centralize and coordinate responsibility for buying the items it needs in a purchasing, or procurement, department.

A **purchasing agent** (sometimes called a PA or a procurement specialist) is *a company's in-house expert on where to buy various products.* Each will buy a broad or narrow line of products, depending on the size and complexity of the company and the characteristics of its end product. In a very small machine shop, for example, the owner may make all the buying decisions. In companies the size of McDonnell Douglas, you may find one purchasing agent in charge of buying electronic components, another who buys only steel, and one who buys janitorial supplies and office equipment.

Although purchasing agents make many buying decisions, their authority is limited. Purchases that exceed a certain dollar amount may require the purchasing manager's approval or even that of top company management. Regardless of who does the purchasing, most companies establish a **purchasing procedure**, *a series of steps that a company follows when buying products.* Figure 11.4 shows a typical purchasing procedure.

Proper specifications are vital when buying something from an outside supplier or vendor. A producer may use the vendor's regular specifications—these exist for such standard items as fasteners, steel, and various electrical components—but some producers prefer to dictate custom specifications that the vendor must meet.

purchasing agent
A company's in-house expert on where to buy various products.

purchasing procedure
A series of steps that a company follows when buying products.

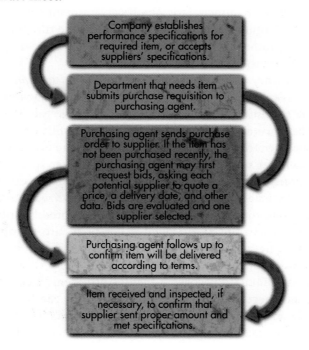

Company establishes performance specifications for required item, or accepts suppliers' specifications.

Department that needs item submits purchase requisition to purchasing agent.

Purchasing agent sends purchase order to supplier. If the item has not been purchased recently, the purchasing agent may first request bids, asking each potential supplier to quote a price, a delivery date, and other data. Bids are evaluated and one supplier selected.

Purchasing agent follows up to confirm item will be delivered according to terms.

Item received and inspected, if necessary, to confirm that supplier sent proper amount and met specifications.

Figure 11.4

A typical purchasing procedure.

on-site inspection
The buyer's inspectors examine purchased items throughout the supplier's manufacturing operations.

hand-to-mouth purchasing
Purchasing an item in small quantities, as needed.

forward purchasing
A policy of purchasing relatively large quantities to fill needs over longer periods of time.

anticipatory purchasing
A purchasing agent stockpiles an extremely large supply of an item, well in advance of need, anticipating future problems.

Companies that buy products whose failure could cause serious harm or financial loss may even conduct **on-site inspection**, in which *the buyer's inspectors examine purchased items throughout the supplier's manufacturing operations.*

Purchasing Policies

Companies may follow several purchasing policies, depending on the nature of the product, consumer demand, storage space, and the availability of funds. The first three of these policies involve deciding how much purchasing to do; the last three help the purchaser determine whom to buy from.

POLICIES ON QUANTITY As might be expected from its name, **hand-to-mouth purchasing** involves *purchasing an item in small quantities, as needed.* If your end product has an uncertain market demand, it may be wise to buy parts on a hand-to-mouth basis so you will not be stuck with a large inventory should demand disappear. Other factors that suggest the use of this approach are lack of funds to buy a larger supply, perishability or limited shelf life, and lack of storage space.

Forward purchasing is *a policy of purchasing relatively large quantities to fill needs over longer periods of time.* Normally the purchase price, shipping charges, and purchasing and receiving expenses will be lower as a result of forward purchasing. Producers may charge less per unit on a larger order because fixed production costs will be spread over more units. Shipping in bulk also saves money, and purchasing and receiving expenses will be lower because the paperwork is cheaper to process for one large shipment than for a series of small ones. Forward purchasing assumes that you have the funds to spend, a place to store the product, long shelf life, and a market that will remain strong long enough for you to use this large supply.

Under **anticipatory purchasing**, *a purchasing agent stockpiles an extremely large supply of an item, well in advance of need, anticipating future problems* such as a shortage or a drastic price increase. This is a kind of gambling: the buyer, betting that the uncertain condition will materialize, fills up a warehouse. If the expected problem does not arise, the purchasing agent could be criticized for spending so much money and using so much storage space for so long.

Final consumers followed this practice during a rumored toilet paper shortage several years ago. The shortage never materialized, but some householders were buying the stuff by the case. Gasoline stored in privately owned underground tanks and sugar stockpiled at low prices are examples of anticipatory purchasing by final consumers and companies alike.

POLICIES ON SUPPLIERS Purchasing agents must identify suitable suppliers, but this does not necessarily mean those firms with the highest quality or lowest price. In addition to quality and price, the suitable supplier must be able to offer adequate production capacity, meet delivery schedules, offer a sound guarantee, and provide reliable service. The purchasing agent for a given item should keep records of suppliers who meet these conditions. To ensure supply, quality, or reliable delivery, a company may try to create a **captive supplier**, which is *a vendor firm in which the customer firm owns controlling interest or from which it obtains an exclusive supply contract.* The latter arrangement gives the buyer a legal right to all the units that the vendor produces. When shortages occur within an industry, it can be comforting to have a captive supplier and thus be assured of adequate stock.

Many purchasing agents are wary of **single-source purchasing**, which is *buying a product from one company only.* Rather than putting all their eggs in one basket, some firms buy standard items from several vendors. Then, if one vendor cannot fill an order, more units can be requested from one or more of the others.

Although many producers buy from several sources to lower the risk of interrupted shipments or price gouging from a single source, a few companies actually prefer single-source buying. For example, one 3M plant reduced its list of suppliers from 2,800 to a mere 300 in just two years. Vendors responded by improving the quality of their products, streamlining price negotiations and delivery schedules, and investing in state-of-the-art tooling that produces parts cheaper, faster, and better than before.

In the same vein, some manufacturers have improved vendor relations and locked in a source of supply by agreeing to buy the entire output of a vendor's plant or department. For example, orders from a furniture manufacturer that agreed to buy the entire production from one portion of a textile mill kept four of the mill's looms running twenty-four hours a day. Such an arrangement gives the customer firm a distinct advantage over competitors whose orders are filled on a first-come, first-served basis. Moreover, it may also cut the lead time required for delivery 90 percent or more.[9]

Bid purchasing is *a policy of requesting bids from several vendors and selecting the most attractive one.* This choice is not always the cheapest, because the purchasing agent considers such factors as the vendor's production capacity, quality, guarantee, and others referred to earlier. One private college in Florida displayed this kind of reasoning when it bought Japanese-made photocopy machines instead of a less expensive domestic brand. Although the Japanese machines cost more, they were easier to service, were more reliable, and produced better-quality copies than the cheaper American model. Firms that buy strictly from low bidders may find that in the long run they have not saved money at all: a cheap part might fail to hold up, or the vendor might provide poor service and repairs.

After decades of paying nonnegotiated prices and buying from all the major steel companies, General Motors (GM) adopted a bid-purchasing policy for its steel requirements in the early 1980s. In addition to making demands for improved quality, the company also informed bidders that it would evaluate such criteria as financial condition and the range of products each firm's

captive supplier
A vendor firm in which the customer firm owns controlling interest or from which it obtains an exclusive supply contract.

single-source purchasing
Buying a product from one company only.

bid purchasing
A policy of requesting bids from several vendors and selecting the most attractive one.

facilities could produce. General Motors requested price quotations on more than 5,000 items used at fifty-three manufacturing plants throughout the country.

This revolutionary change by one of the nation's largest steel customers had positive results. At least one steel company offered a volume discount and extended credit for thirty days, while helping GM to reduce the various standards for thickness by half. Shipments were consolidated as GM reduced the number of mills it dealt with from 341 to 272. Demands for improved quality caused the steel companies themselves to address quality as never before, which caused rejected material to drop to just a few hundred tons per year.

Contract purchasing occurs when *the company and supplier negotiate a contract that defines prices, delivery dates, and other conditions of sale.* This type of purchasing is common practice with the United States government, especially the armed forces, which contract for everything from fighter planes to backpacks. Most contracts are quite complex, and lawyers may be needed to represent each party in establishing and clarifying all the terms. Contract purchasing is also a good way to assure an adequate supply if a shortage develops.

A **make versus buy** *or* **in-house versus out-of-house** policy decision answers *an either-or question: whether to create one's own supply of an essential item or rely on an outside producer to make it.* Some suppliers already have the specialized equipment, engineering, materials, and assembly personnel to turn out a superior part. It is usually more practical to buy from them than to try to do it oneself. For example, Intel Corporation is the world's largest supplier of computer chips to personal computer manufacturers.[10] Shopsmith Inc., which used to manufacture most of the parts that went into its multipurpose woodworking machine, recently subcontracted production for many of them to outside suppliers.[11] Ball Corporation manufactures metal cans for such companies as Anheuser-Busch, PepsiCo, and Coca-Cola.[12]

A manufacturer that decides to make a part must be able to allocate production space to it, buy material and equipment, and hire or train workers to produce it. Demand for the item must be strong enough to justify committing resources to it, and the final unit cost for in-house manufacture should be equal to or less than that of using outside suppliers.

General Motors's Inland Fisher Guide subsidiary makes many of the plastic-composite parts in-house for the popular Camaro and Firebird models, but the dent-resistant plastic doors are molded out-of-house by Budd Company.[13]

The make-or-buy question should be asked periodically about heavily used items. Changing conditions may suggest and prompt a move to the alternative.

Inventory Control

Inventory control is *balancing the need for adequate stock against the costs of purchasing, handling, storing, and keeping records on it.* Such control demands that management evaluate current consumption rates and anticipate future needs. Inventory control is an attempt to keep enough material on hand to satisfy production requirements and at the same time avoid tying up too much capital in inventories. Imagine the challenge Ford Motor Company faces controlling its reported 50,000 production items. Even smaller products such as the one-cylinder engines that Briggs & Stratton Corporation manufactures for power mowers and snow blowers may contain up to 500 parts.

Inventories represent a considerable investment, and the related costs of carrying them, listed in Table 11.1, make efficient control even more important. Inventory shortages can trigger as many difficulties as excesses can. A producer who runs out of an essential item loses sales and customer goodwill. Inventory shortages also increase costs. The unavailability of one indispensable part will stop a production line, and workers will be idle until the missing piece arrives. If delays caused by inventory shortages have to be made up through overtime work,

STORAGE COSTS

1. Cost of building the storage facility, including interest on borrowed funds
2. Value of the storage space assigned to the inventory
3. Additional cost of purchasing other items in smaller quantities because of space now occupied in the warehouse

HANDLING COSTS

1. Equipment and materials (forklifts, conveyors, pallets, bins, racks, dollies, record cabinets, requisition forms)
2. Personnel (warehouse workers, record clerks, managers to supervise their work)

OTHER COSTS

1. Loss caused by obsolescence, seasonal changes, shifts in customer demand, and physical wear while in storage
2. Inventory taxes that may be levied by government agencies
3. Interest paid on money borrowed to buy the inventory

Table 11.1
Costs associated with carrying inventory.

the producer may lose money on the order if the overtime wages cannot be passed on to the customer. Finally, machines that are run faster or longer than usual to reduce the backlog will suffer greater-than-normal wear and tear.

Inventory control managers often apply the standard of an **economic order quantity (EOQ)** to their work. This is *the point at which the cost of an item and the cost to store it are equal.* To derive this figure, a purchasing agent compares the cost of buying an item in various quantities with the cost of carrying these units in stock. The point at which they are equal is the best amount to buy. This computation is shown graphically in Figure 11.5.

An inventory control system will also determine consumption rates for each item and identify the point at which it is necessary to order additional stock. This should not be when all units are gone. Some units, called *safety stock*, should be on hand to meet production demands until the new order arrives. In determining reorder points, purchasing agents and inventory control em-

economic order quantity (EOQ) The point at which the cost of the item and the cost to store it are equal.

Figure 11.5
Determining economic order quantity.

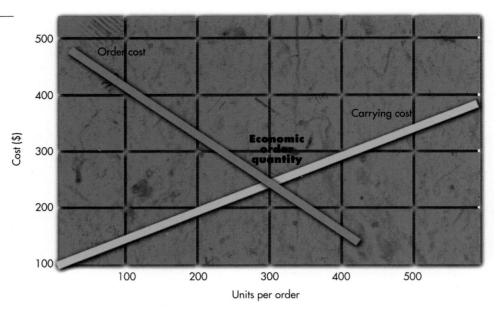

lead time
The time a supplier requires to process and ship an order.

ployees must be aware of **lead time**, *the time a supplier requires to process and ship an order.* When lead time changes, purchasing agents have to revise their schedules to keep production flowing smoothly.

Just-in-Time Inventory Systems

just-in-time (JIT) inventory system
An inventory system that delivers parts to the production line exactly when needed.

A **just-in-time (JIT) inventory system** is *an inventory system that delivers parts to the production line exactly when needed.* Companies that refine their purchasing, materials handling, and manufacturing operations to this degree either eliminate or drastically reduce the inventory carrying costs listed in Table 11.1. Moreover, factories can be smaller because of less need to store large supplies of parts in warehouses and near the assembly-line point where they're added to the final product. Manufacturers that use a JIT inventory system must develop extremely cooperative relationships with suppliers, because substandard quality or late deliveries would be catastrophic.

In addition to maintaining seamless relations with outside vendors, manufacturers that use a JIT inventory system must also ensure a synchronized flow of parts that are made in-house. CAD, CAM, and CIM contribute greatly to this effort, as do factory layout and materials-handling techniques. For example, Harley-Davidson used to hoard up to three months' worth of in-house components in bins until they were needed. Sometimes the parts sat so long they rusted or were damaged in handling. Moreover, design and manufacturing defects sometimes wouldn't be detected until parts reached the assembly line. By adopting JIT and other modern production and inventory control methods, however, Harley-Davidson has become an outstanding model of successful manufacturing practices:

- Parts are generally used within hours of being produced, which means mistakes can be caught and corrected quickly.
- A CAM system directs machines that make engine components. Changeover time is minimal. Parts are produced in small lots and are moved directly to the next production step. Computers notify employees when a machine's cutting tool should be replaced.
- All the machines required to produce some parts are grouped in one production area or "cell" so they can be monitored by the same operator. These production cells make an entire part from start to finish.
- Both suppliers and employees are more concerned about making defect-free parts, because there's little safety stock to fall back on if a batch of parts is made incorrectly. Everyone works harder to prevent mistakes.

YOU DECIDE

What geographic and post–World War II characteristics of Japan, unlike those of most if not all other industrialized nations, have contributed to its ability to use JIT in manufacturing plants?

Production Control

Production control, one of the most important concerns in making a product, is *coordinating the interaction of people, materials, and machinery so that products are made in the proper amounts at the required times to fill orders.* Six steps are involved: planning, routing, scheduling, dispatching, follow-up, and quality assurance. The sequence of these steps is illustrated in Figure 11.6.

production control Coordinating the interaction of people, materials, and machinery so that products are made in the proper amount and at the required times to fill orders.

Planning

Successful production, like other successful business activities, is based on planning. Production planners know what materials, equipment, processes, and working time must be allotted to make a given item. Often they are former production workers themselves, so they can visualize the end product at various stages of completion, knowing from experience what remains to be done.

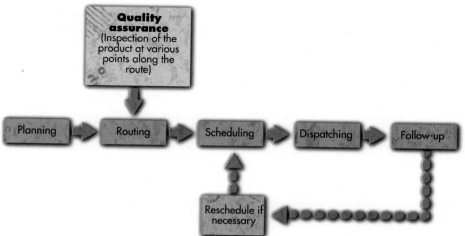

Figure 11.6

Steps in production control.

The **production plan** is *a document that contains a list of materials and equipment needed to manufacture a finished product and also specifies which operations will be performed in-house or out-of-house.* In addition, this plan reveals any operations that require special machinery or equipment to be brought out of storage or purchased and set up when the product reaches a particular stage of completion.

Production planners are like orchestra conductors. They coordinate the performances of purchasing, manufacturing, shipping, and marketing, all of which contribute to or need information about the status of an order at various stages of completion.

Routing

Routing is *the production control step in which a logical sequence is established for the operations that the product must undergo on its way to completion.* Each job's path is defined, thus determining what work will be done at what point. The person handling routing for a brewery must take into account all of the following steps: germinating the barley grain, cleaning it, milling it, weighing it, cooking it, blending it with water, removing the grain solids to produce a clear liquid, brewing the liquid, straining out hops, cooling the liquid, fermenting it, and aging, filtering, and packaging the beer.

Trident, a German cutlery manufacturer, claims that thirty-eight precision operations are involved in manufacturing its paring knives. Wooden pencils, which required five steps to manufacture, were slowly replaced with plastic ones beginning in 1973. Although today's plastic pencils sharpen and look like wooden ones, they can be produced in just one manufacturing step. The now-defunct High-Standard Sporting Firearms claimed that the manufacturing process to produce its precision target pistol involved more than 400 operations, more than half of which were performed on the frame. Rolex reports that more than 150 production operations are needed to make the case for its Rolex Oyster Perpetual Sea-Dweller. The case is produced from a solid block of metal; the movement contains more than 220 parts. Each of these examples shows how management must acknowledge both planning and routing concerns in production operations.

Scheduling

Scheduling is *the production control step that allots time for each operation along the route.* Knowledgeable production planners are an asset here. Schedules that allow too much or too little time can lead to slack periods in various departments, causing wasted time and perhaps employee layoffs, or create bottlenecks that back up work at certain points, causing late deliveries and canceled orders. Production planners also have to take nonwork time into account. Once they are painted, auto bodies have to sit in a drying booth for some time before further work can be done. A production planner who does not know how much time to allow will leave workers idle at the next step along the route.

A product rarely follows the original schedule from start to finish. Production planners must reschedule work in process because of canceled orders and customer requests for earlier delivery dates or because of machinery breakdowns, design changes, strikes, and inclement weather, all of which can cause lost work time and delays in the delivery of essential materials.

Dispatching

Dispatching occurs after jobs have been planned, routed, and scheduled. This is *the production control step in which a production planner releases a job to the first production department on its route.* Before dispatching, production control employees must gather up the materials and parts required by the production plan and issue them to the correct department.

dispatching
The production control step in which a production planner releases a job to the first production department on its route.

Follow-Up

Follow-up is *the production control step in which production planners monitor each job's progress along its route and report and attempt to deal with any delays or difficulties that occur.* A job is usually identified by number so it can be traced from one operation or department to the next. Large manufacturing plants may be working on thousands of jobs simultaneously, many of which become subassemblies of others. Follow-up is essential in these cases to ensure that work moves according to schedule. When delays occur, production planners should be notified so they can bring the job back on schedule or reschedule it.

follow-up
The production control step in which production planners monitor each job's progress along its route and deal with any delays or difficulties that occur.

Quality Assurance

A firm does not always want to make the best product possible but rather a product that suits its reputation and its customers' expectations and price requirements. Exceedingly high quality almost always is accompanied by a higher price, and not everyone wants or can afford the best. A company's quality standards are set with its market, reputation, and budget in mind.

Some progressive manufacturers have created the job of *quality engineer*. The people who do this work are responsible for improving product designs, tools, machines, and production operations so that well-designed products are made from the start. For example, they may:

- Install computerized measuring devices on existing equipment to provide instant process control and inspection.
- Develop fast, simple changeover procedures to switch machines from making one part to another.
- Color-code parts and the tools used to assemble them so production workers can select the proper tools without delay.
- Standardize designs, raw materials, and components (such as wiring harnesses, trim, nuts, bolts, screws, or gear wheels) among several models of the same product to keep the number of assembly tools and parts inventories to a minimum.

Some manufacturers have had excellent success with these practices. For example, Harley-Davidson discovered that the oil-access holes in two sizes of crankshafts were drilled at different angles merely because they had been designed by separate engineering teams. Changing the design to make the angle identical reduced drilling-machine changeover time from 114 minutes to 12. Bell & Howell designed a new projector with a molded plastic housing that cut the number of metal parts from more than 100 to only 6.[14]

The number of units inspected will vary. If product failure causes serious injury, financial loss, or both, companies might inspect each unit. This is the case with strategic missiles, communications satellites, astronauts' spacesuits, and complex electronic health care equipment. It is often impractical or unnecessary, however, to inspect every unit. If products pour off the machines by the thousands per hour (as with pencils, plastic trash bags, or nails), management makes random, or spot, inspections. This technique detects any major or repeated flaws caused by production routines or equipment, but it allows for and considers acceptable the occasional minor defect that escapes detection.

Problems may arise at various points along the production route, which creates a need for **quality assurance**. This is *the production control step in which the product is inspected at various stages along the route to ensure that it meets standards.* Quality assurance ought to be preventive as well as corrective. It should identify deviations from standards as quickly as possible and correct them before units must be rejected. Some rejected pieces may be sent through a rework area, where the flaw can be corrected. If the flaw is irreparable, however, the part must be recycled or scrapped. Quality rejects in automobile paint, upholstery, or trim are reworked, flawed steel castings are melted down and recast, and faulty pop-top can lids are discarded.

Manufacturers that do not inspect a critical part of the product, or that do not inspect it as thoroughly or as rigorously as need be, suffer the consequences. Products may fail as customers try to use them, leading to recalls. In early 1990, General Motors announced that it planned to recall every Pontiac Fiero ever made—all 244,000 of them—in a major attempt to correct a problem with engine fires that influenced management to discontinue producing the car at the end of the 1988 model year. Earlier the company recalled 125,000 of its 1984 Fieros after engine fires occurred in one out of every

Regular inspection at key production steps is a part of quality assurance programs.

quality assurance The production control step in which the product is inspected at various stages along the route to ensure that it meets standards.

400 cars. Recalls are hardly confined to domestic products, however, as some American manufacturers quickly point out. Several hundred thousand Hondas were once recalled to rectify severe rusting of front suspension and body parts. A lesser-known but unusual recall occurred when a university recalled more than 3,000 diplomas awarded to a graduating class because the ink faded. While that case was not really damaging to the manufacturer—or to the university—instances of defective products may expose manufacturers to extremely expensive product-liability suits from injured customers. (These will be discussed in Chapter 17.)

Total Quality Management

Total quality management (TQM) is a *comprehensive effort to improve the quality of every department's product or service and achieve increasingly higher levels of customer satisfaction.* TQM can be applied to every type of organization, no matter what it does. For example, TQM:

- Helped Florida Power and Light reduce customer complaints by 80 percent
- Increased production at Motorola by 30 percent
- Reduced paint flaws on metal folding chairs at MECO Corporation by 88 percent
- Saved Holston Valley Hospital $8,985 per year by simplifying patient discharge procedures
- Reduced annual customer complaints from 44 to 3 and increased sales by nearly 45 percent at Globe Metallurgical[15]

total quality management (TQM)
A comprehensive effort to improve the quality of every department's product or service and achieve increasingly higher levels of customer satisfaction.

TQM programs have a ripple effect. When a big company moves to TQM, suppliers tend to follow. Says Noel Pooler of Pooler Industries, which makes high-precision parts for auto manufacturers, TQM "doesn't just change how those folks do business. It changes how everybody who deals with them does business. They're attempting to reduce the number of suppliers that they have—they want long-term contracts, fewer and fewer suppliers, and better and better quality."[16]

TQM embraces every aspect of a company, from the way secretaries answer the telephones to how quickly the data processing department delivers a special report. TQM is a way of life; it makes a universal commitment to quality throughout the entire organization. "Customers" are not only those who buy the company's products or services but also the departments who use information, services, or parts produced by other departments inside the company. In fact, departments *are* each other's "customers" as a result of the web of mutually supportive, interdependent relationships that connects them all. Employees work as teams to eliminate waste, inefficiency, and defects. They are empowered to identify quality problems and develop and implement solutions that will eliminate the problems entirely.

(Note: total quality management is discussed further in the Manager's Notebook for Chapter 6.)

SUMMARY

Perhaps the most fundamental production concern is where to build a plant. Managers examine the combined effects of certain proximity factors, people factors, and physical factors at various potential sites. The final choice is almost always a compromise.

The nature of the product and the market dictate which production method a firm uses. The analytic process breaks down raw materials to form new products, while its opposite, the synthetic process, combines materials—by fabrication or assembly—to form new products. A production process can be termed *continuous*, if it makes identical units by following the same steps over a long period of time, or *intermittent*, if the product is made to customers' specifications and procedures and equipment are adjusted accordingly. State-of-the-art manufacturers use computer-aided design, computer-aided manufacturing, and computer-integrated manufacturing techniques to streamline design and manufacturing operations as thoroughly as possible.

Robots, which were first installed on auto assembly lines, are now used by an increasing number of manufacturing companies. Although changes in plant layout and production flows are usually necessary, these reprogrammable automatons can increase productivity impressively while reducing wage and benefit costs and working in environments that are unpleasant or hostile to humans.

Production requires materials, parts, supplies, and equipment, so management creates a purchasing, or procurement, department and employs purchasing agents to buy the items it needs. These purchasing agents will use a combination of several purchasing policies, depending on the nature of the item, consumer demand, storage space, and available funds. Inventory control balances the need for adequate stock against the costs of acquiring, handling, and keeping records on it. Inventory control employees and purchasing agents work together to determine consumption rates for various products and ensure that enough stock is available to satisfy production requirements. Manufacturers that can forge cooperative relationships with suppliers and synchronize the production and movement of in-house parts may able to minimize inventory carrying costs and factory size by creating a just-in-time inventory system.

Management controls production through planning, routing, scheduling, dispatching, and follow-up, so that enough units are made when they are needed to fill orders. Management also inspects products so that the products meet standards of acceptability.

Many companies have adopted the practice of total quality management, which attempts to improve the quality of products or services produced by every department and employee.

KEY TERMS

analytic process p. 348
anticipatory purchasing p. 356
assembly process p. 349
bid purchasing p. 357
captive supplier p. 357
computer-aided design (CAD) p. 352
computer-aided manufacturing (CAM) p. 352
computer-integrated manufacturing (CIM) p. 353
continuous process p. 351
contract purchasing p. 358
dispatching p. 363
economic order quantity (EOQ) p. 359
environmental impact study p. 345
fabrication process p. 349
follow-up p. 363
forward purchasing p. 356
hand-to-mouth purchasing p. 356

intermittent process p. 351
inventory control p. 358
job shops p. 351
just-in-time (JIT) inventory system p. 360
lead time p. 360
make versus buy *or* in-house versus out-of-house p. 358
manufacturing company p. 341
motion study p. 347
on-site inspection p. 356
processing company p. 341
production p. 341
production control p. 361
production management p. 342
production plan p. 362
purchasing agent p. 355
purchasing procedure p. 355

FOR REVIEW AND DISCUSSION

1. How does production contribute to the nation's economic health?
2. Comment on the following statement: "A plant site should be picked by a committee. One manager is not qualified to evaluate all the factors accurately and objectively."
3. List the proximity factors, people factors, and physical factors that companies examine when selecting a plant site. Why are most site decisions compromises?
4. What is the difference between motion study and time study? Offer examples from your own experience of how they affect your job or your personal life.
5. How do companies use motion and time studies? How might employees react to them? What would you recommend management do to encourage a positive reaction?
6. List some products made by the analytic and the synthetic production processes. What is the difference between the two processes?
7. How would you describe the fabrication process? Compare it with the assembly process. Is it usual for a company to make a product using one or the other exclusively? Why or why not?
8. Under what conditions would a continuous production process be preferred to an intermittent one? Find several local firms that use each.
9. What benefits would a company realize by using CAD?
10. What benefits would a company realize by installing CAM? Which practice, CAD or CAM, is a company most likely to adopt first? Why?
11. How are CAD, CAM, and CIM related? What types of factories are most likely to use all three? Why?
12. Justify the use of robot assembly techniques in enabling American producers to respond to foreign competitors. What impact should this trend have on employee training?
13. Comment on the following statement: "Purchas-

ing agents, by the nature of their jobs, are subject to a number of ethical pressures that most other employees do not encounter." What might these pressures be? How do you think most purchasing agents react to them? Explain your answer.
14. Describe a typical purchasing procedure, including circumstances under which the purchasing agent would solicit bids from several vendors.
15. Summarize the distinguishing features of the following purchasing policies, and the conditions under which each may be used: hand-to-mouth, forward, anticipatory, bid, and contract purchasing, and make-versus-buy decisions.
16. What factors combine to fix an economic order quantity (EOQ)? How does this statistic influence a purchasing agent's decisions? What conditions might prompt a purchasing agent to buy more or less than the EOQ?
17. Explain why purchasing agents and inventory control employees should be concerned with the matters of reorder point, safety stock, supplier lead time, and economic order quantity.
18. What benefits should a company expect to realize from installing a just-in-time inventory system? How would this system alter its relationship with suppliers and the responsibilities of departments that make in-house parts?
19. Would CAD, CAM, or CIM improve the operation of a just-in-time inventory system? Why or why not?
20. Why are production planners essential to a successful manufacturing operation? Is hands-on production experience helpful to them in their jobs? Why or why not?
21. "When I'm right no one remembers: when I'm wrong, no one forgets." Why might this lament be particularly true in the production planner's job?
22. Discuss at least two circumstances that would require jobs in process to be rescheduled after they have been dispatched.
23. Do you believe follow-up could be eliminated

from production control responsibilities if the various departments involved did their jobs efficiently? Why or why not?

24. Justify the need for quality assurance. Under what conditions would you recommend spot inspections, and when would inspection of every piece, or a "zero defects" philosophy, be preferable?

25. How does quality assurance relate to total quality management (TQM)? What types of organizations are likely to have success with a TQM program? How might such a program affect suppliers, customers, and other departments within a company?

APPLICATIONS

Case 11.1: Innovative Cost Cutting at Key Tronic

American companies, while strong on innovation, have trouble maintaining a competitive edge because of cheap overseas labor. Foreign manufacturers can be successful in the U.S. market because their low wages can absorb even the high shipping costs of flying products here. As a result, many American manufacturers have moved their operations out of the country in order to take advantage of lower labor costs. With strong management and vision, however, such a drastic move is not necessary.

Several years ago, Key Tronic Corporation was close to shutting its doors. Once the largest manufacturer of computer keyboards, Key Tronic found itself continually undercut by foreign manufacturers that could assemble keyboards much more cheaply. In 1992 the company's board hired turnaround expert Stanley Hiller, Jr. despite his complete inexperience in running a high tech company.

Hiller's first step was to bring in a board of high-powered advisers to provide him with the technical and marketing expertise to compete in the computer industry. All of the company's problems could be traced to the lack of cost-competitive keyboards. By focusing on this basic issue and assigning a full-time team of engineers to solve it, Hiller has reversed Key Tronic's fortunes.

Nicknamed Kermit, the new keyboard designed by Hiller's engineers has undercut keyboards manufactured overseas. Designed to be a low-cost, high-quality keyboard, Kermit uses only 17 parts rather than the typical 150. The result is greatly decreased assembly costs. Additionally, a highly automated assembly process allows Key Tronic to pump out 2,400 keyboards a day—with only fourteen workers, compared to the forty workers required by competitors. By designing the labor costs out of its product,

Key Tronic found an innovative way to compete against cheap foreign labor.

Questions

1. What other industries could use better automation and design to cut labor costs?

2. When should a company put its energy into developing new products rather than trying to reengineer existing products to be more competitive?

3. Is knowledge of a particular field necessary to manage the production of a product? Why or why not?

4. How can managers maintain the level of innovation necessary to keep ahead of foreign producers?

5. What issues, besides labor costs, help or hinder manufacturers located in the United States?

For more information, see Dori Jones Yang, "The Keyboard Repairman Leading Key Tronic," *Business Week*, May 10, 1993, p. 72.

Case 11.2: Luring Industries with Incentives

How much is a job worth?

To the Kentucky state government a job is worth $350,000. Like many states, Kentucky is involved in heavy marketing to attract industry. In a recent lure, the state offered $140 million in potential tax credits to Dofasco Inc. and Co-Steel Inc. to build a minimill that would create 400 jobs in a northern rural county. Job for job, it was the biggest deal sweetener on record.

While many industries have benefited from location incentives, the airline industry has been one of the biggest recipients. Job intensive, the airlines are popular with state governments because of the chance to acquire the valuable prize of a flight "hub." United Airlines was offered $300 million to move a maintenance facility to Indiana. Although this was a larger overall package than the Kentucky incentive, it averaged much less for each of the 6,300 jobs that would be created.

Incentive programs for big businesses are popular with politicians for their flashy local gains. While offering benefits for smaller companies or a consistent, low tax structure might provide a stronger long-term boost to the state's economy, few politicians can resist the lure of making the big catch and creating large blocks of new jobs.

Companies should be wary of these incentives, however. Other factors may be more important to business growth and should be considered before the gains from short-term tax incentives. Among these factors are access to suppliers and markets, the quality of the work force, and the overall cost of living. California, for example, has found it hard to attract business, even with tax incentives, because of the lower quality of its available work force and the high price of housing.

Questions

1. Why are states offering attractive tax incentives to businesses?

2. What better uses could state governments put this money to?

3. What are the disadvantages of accepting a tax incentive?

4. What factors should companies review before accepting an incentive?

5. When is it appropriate for government to provide monetary incentives for some businesses rather than others?

For more information, see Tim Ferguson, "Locales Still Shopping for a Corporate Catch," *The Wall Street Journal*, July 6, 1993, p. A13.

REFERENCES

1. Tim Smart, "Why Ignore 95% of the World's Market?" *Business Week, Reinventing America 1992* (special edition), p. 64.

2. Gwen Fisher, "Southern Exposure," *Spark* (an employee publication of Atlantic Richfield Company), April 1993, p. 8.

3. Michael J. McCarthy, "Why German Firms Choose the Carolinas to Build U.S. Plants," *The Wall Street Journal*, May 4, 1993, p. A1.

4. "How to Stroke a Key," *Fortune*, January 13, 1992, p. 88.

5. "Ford Is Ready to Invest $1.2 Billion to Develop a New Group of Engines," *The Wall Street Journal*, February 24, 1992, p. B3.

6. Gregory A. Patterson, "GM to Cut Number of Vehicle Frames to 7 from 20," *The Wall Street Journal*, May 15, 1992, p. A2.

7. Edmund Faltermayer, "Poised for a Comeback," *Fortune*, April 19, 1993, p. 174.

8. William R. East and Virginia D. Smith, "Quality and Quantity Achieved at Honda's Anna Engine Plant," *Foundry Management and Technology*, June 1991 (reprint; no page number).

9. Roy L. Harmon, *Reinventing the Factory II* (New York: Free Press, 1992).

10. Ken Yamada, "Intel Became World's Largest Supplier of Semiconductors in 1992, Study Says," *The Wall Street Journal*, January 5, 1993, p. B6.

11. Ralph E. Winter, "Shopsmith Says It Can't Assess Retailing Shift," *The Wall Street Journal*, January 29, 1993, p. B8A.

12. James P. Miller, "Ball Is Preparing to Clean Out Its Corporate Cupboard," *The Wall Street Journal*, February 24, 1993, p. B10.

13. Roger Rowand, "Plastics Muscle In on Steel in Muscle Cars," *Plastics News*, March 1, 1993, p. 11.

14. Roy L. Harmon, *Reinventing the Factory II* (New York: Free Press, 1992).

15. Promotional brochure for a seminar on total quality management published by SkillPath, Inc.

16. Michael Barrier, "Small Firms Put Quality First," *Nation's Business*, May 1992, p. 22.

12

MARKETING AND PRODUCT STRATEGY

All of our people
understand what
the Holy Grail is.
It's not the bottom line. It's
an almost blind, passionate
commitment to taking care
of customers.

ARTHUR BLANK
President, Home Depot

CHAPTER OBJECTIVES
After studying this chapter, you
should be able to:

1. Describe the importance of marketing in a company's success.
2. Describe the evolution of an organization from production orientation to consumer orientation.
3. List and explain the functions involved in marketing.
4. Explain the marketing concept and its effect on the role of marketing in an organization.
5. Describe the marketing process.
6. Define what a market is and distinguish between industrial and consumer markets.
7. Discuss the importance of and processes involved in market segmentation.
8. Describe each of the four elements of the marketing mix.
9. Explain what a product is and distinguish between the two major categories of products.
10. Explain the importance of brands and packaging as components of product strategy.
11. Explain the four stages of the product life cycle.
12. Identify the six steps in product development.

UP FRONT

Bill Dodge is a clear example of the philosophy "Do what you love and love what you do." Raised in upstate New York, Dodge developed an appreciation for the outdoors, especially bicycling and skiing. When he entered college, his major was biology, but he soon found that he was far more interested in business. Recreation and vocation came together when he began working in retail ski shops and bicycle shops. "I was an avid cyclist and skier, so what seemed ideal to me was to bike in the summer and ski in the winter, while working in a related business," he recounts.

Working in the ski shop, Dodge came to know some of the people who worked for Salomon, a French company that makes Alpine (downhill) ski boot bindings. Salomon was founded in Annecy in 1947 by Georges Salomon, to make steel edges for skis. Over the years, Salomon introduced its bindings, boots, and a revolutionary downhill ski design. Today it is the world's largest winter sports company, with nearly 3,000 employees in France and at subsidiaries in North America, Scandinavia, Japan, and elsewhere. Dodge was offered a job as a Salomon North America representative.

"One of the things the ski industry is noted for is dealer training," says Dodge, "and I began working in an education program to help retailers sell, maintain, mount, and adjust bindings on skis." After ten years, with various responsibilities in the field, Dodge was promoted to manager of product information. "I helped develop strategies for launching the new Salomon ski and the Alpine boot line called 'The

Integral,'" he says. "This was a very important introduction for Salomon. At first it was just the bindings; then in 1980 we introduced the boots, and in 1990 the monocoque ski." The company invests 7 percent of its revenues in research and development, with the goal of becoming a market leader through innovation. Its products are often introduced first for professionals, then released to the broad consumer market. This strategy has paid off well: Salomon is number one in the binding, boot, and ski markets in which it competes.

"Salomon is known for launching innovative products," says Dodge. "Our first boot was a rear-entry racing boot, for example. When we introduced Nordic (cross-country) ski equipment, we integrated the boot and ski. Salomon is a conservative company, and we do our homework before we enter a market. Then we innovate."

In talking about Salomon's entry into the hiking boot market in 1991, Dodge notes, "The way we enter a market is time-consuming and expensive, because we want to learn everything there is to know. First, we want to understand the market by talking to people to find out what's needed. Second, we try to provide solutions to problems our market research has identified. This may seem logical, but not many companies do it. At Salomon, it's second nature. Third, once the innovative ideas are developed, we test the product. Over half

BILL DODGE

PROJECT DIRECTOR FOR OUTDOOR PRODUCTS, SALOMON NORTH AMERICA, INC.

our time is spent in the field to assure the product will be accepted.

"This is a conservative market, so when we showed hikers our new Adventure 9 hiking boot, they told us we were crazy, that it would never sell. We figured the way to convince people was to let them see for themselves, so we let trendsetters and journalists try them out. At the annual trade show, we let 200 retailers put on a pair and go for a hike on fairly serious terrain. After that, everyone at the show was talking about us."

Bill can take pride in the way the Adventure 9 hiking boot has found market acceptance; *Outside* magazine said that it "delivered mountaineering features . . . at a fraction of the weight of traditional leather boots of equivalent performance." Since all Salomon products are launched worldwide, he has to assure that products are suitable for the North American market. "I love my work," he says from his office in Georgetown, Massachusetts. "It's time-consuming, but I'm not sure any good jobs aren't hard work." In his role as manager of outdoor products, he travels extensively across the United States and Canada, "and I go to Annecy at least five times a year." Salomon is continuing to explore new market opportunities, to which it will bring its design innovation and strong marketing.

Bill Dodge offers this advice for people interested in a career in the sports and recreation industry: "The broader your experiences, the more the company will be interested. We look for a good educational background, but also experience in retailing, manufacturing, distribution, and marketing—the more, the better. I got involved because I wanted to learn the industry and build a good business foundation, while having a good time. I wouldn't expect quick promotions to management. It's a small industry, and it's not easy to get into, but the business trends look good for us through the year 2000, so I believe there are some opportunities for highly motivated people."

Most people, when asked what marketing is, would define it as selling a product or service. They would be partially correct. Selling is a part of marketing—but only a part. Marketing is much, much more. It involves a wide range of activities, including market research, consumer behavior, product development, promotion, product distribution, and product pricing. Surprised? Curious? This chapter will introduce you to the dynamic nature of marketing.

Marketing Defined

marketing
A group of interrelated activities designed to identify consumer needs and to develop, distribute, promote, and price goods and services to satisfy these needs at a profit.

Marketing is *a group of interrelated activities designed to identify consumer needs and to develop, distribute, promote, and price goods and services to satisfy these needs at a profit.* Whether an organization is large or small, whether it produces goods or provides a service, its long-range future is linked to successful marketing practices.

The old saying "Build a better mousetrap and the world will beat a path to your door" is not true. "They" must *need* the product, know about it, be able to get it when and where they want it, and be able to afford it. Marketing provides the means to make the organization successful in the long run. What happens when marketing is not practiced well? The answer can be seen in the experiences of three well-known companies: Coca-Cola, J. C. Penney, and Sears.

- Coca-Cola, long renowned for its marketing expertise, experienced a marketing fiasco with its introduction of New Coke to replace the age-old Coca-Cola formula. When introducing the sweeter, reformulated Coke—designed to match archrival Pepsi—Robert Goizueta, Chairman of Coca-Cola, proclaimed: "Thousands of consumers across the width and breadth of this entire land have told us this is the taste they prefer." Shortly thereafter, millions overruled "thousands." The humiliated company brought back its original formula— as Coca-Cola Classic—three months later. Coke Classic now rules the sales charts, while New Coke— now named Coke II—struggles for its existence.[1]

- J. C. Penney has finally rediscovered its calling. A disastrous marketing decision almost undid years of solid business decision making. In a bid to become middle America's favorite department store, Penney's pushed into higher-priced goods. It started offering trendier looks and courting makers of well-known brands usually found in better department stores. The image makeover did not work with customers—they did not and could not associate Penney's with high-priced fashion goods. With the cash registers ringing at a slower pace, Penney's returned to its roots as a moderately priced merchant carrying respected brand names and brighter fashions.[2]

- Sears, the store America grew up with, has plummeted in the marketplace. Touted for years as the cornerstone of retail marketing, Sears forgot about marketing, raised unresponsiveness to consumers to an art, and forgot who its market was. It is desperately fighting to turn around these marketing mistakes. It is now committed to truly understanding who its market is— the female customer (40 percent of its tire sales are to women). Sears is also focusing on only three core products: apparel, home furnishings, and automotive supplies. These actions, along with upgrading the store image, are hoped to boost Sears' fortunes.[3]

Ineffective marketing can be disastrous for a business because it does not result in satisfied customers. Effective marketing does just the opposite: it

Marketing encompasses all aspects of creating, promoting, and distributing products, including such familiar activities as in-store displays.

utility
The ability of a good or service to satisfy a consumer need.

form utility
Value created when a firm's production function manufactures a product.

time utility
Value created when a product is made available when consumers want and need it.

place utility
Value created when marketing makes a good or service available where the consumer wants it.

possession utility
Value created when ownership (or title) is transferred from buyer to seller.

creates value or utility. Simply, **utility** is *the ability of a good or service to satisfy a consumer need.* There are four types of utility: form, time, place, and possession.

Form utility is *value created when a firm's production function manufactures a product* such as a car, jeans, or hamburger. Although production primarily creates form utility, marketing helps by gathering market research data on what consumers want in a product—sizes, shapes, features.

Marketing directly creates time, place, and possession utility for the consumer. **Time utility** is *value created when a product is made available when consumers want and need it.* Newspapers are distributed at the crack of dawn so people can read the sports page, supermarket ads, or business section at breakfast. In turn, *when marketing makes a good or service available where the consumer wants it,* **place utility** is created. When newspapers are delivered to homes or hotel rooms, and sold at vending machines, newsstands, drugstores, supermarkets, and convenience stores, they are available anywhere the consumer wants them.

Possession utility is *value created when ownership (or title) is transferred from buyer to seller.* In the case of newspapers, ownership is created by putting coins into a vending machine, paying for home delivery, or giving money to a store clerk.

The Marketing Concept

From our discussion it is obvious that marketing has value to both businesses and consumers. But this was not always the case—marketing as we know it today did not always exist. The marketing concept has evolved over the years.

The Evolution of Marketing

Marketing was unheard of in the early 1900s. This period can best be described as one when people needed far more consumer goods than companies were able to manufacture. This intense demand on manufacturing led to organizations dominated by production management. Companies had a **production orientation**, in which *the number-one priority is to produce a good to keep up with demand.* All energies and talents were placed in the production function. Selling a good was incidental; determining consumer needs was unheard of. The company's calling card: "I've got the product. It's here if you want it."

production orientation
The number-one priority is to produce a good to keep up with demand.

As manufacturers increased their production capabilities, the supply of goods available increased and inventories of goods accrued. The emphasis switched to selling. This led to a **sales orientation**, in which *the energy of the company is focused on selling the products produced.* The salesperson's job was (1) to make the desires of the consumers "fit" the products the company manufactured and (2) to convince the consumer to buy. The company's goal was to "send the wagon out full and bring it back empty."

sales orientation
The energy of a company is focused on selling the products produced.

As more producers began competing for consumer dollars by making such high-demand products as automobiles, vacuum cleaners, and refrigerators, the supply of goods began to exceed the demand. Companies had to find a way to identify consumer needs. Organizations began to shift to a **consumer orientation**, which is *an emphasis on identifying the needs and wants of specific consumer groups, then producing, promoting, pricing, and distributing products that satisfy these needs and earn a profit.*

Implementing the Marketing Concept

Companies that are consumer oriented have adopted a philosophy known as the marketing concept. The **marketing concept** is *a belief that the firm should adopt a company-wide consumer orientation directed at long-range profitability.*[4] It includes the belief that all efforts of the organization should be directed at identifying and satisfying the needs of the consumer at a profit.

A prime example of a person who did not initially adopt the marketing concept (and who was actually production oriented) is Henry Ford. Through the early 1920s, Ford Motor Company mass-produced more than 1 million Model-T Fords off the assembly lines. When questioned about altering the style, color, or features of these cars, Ford's response was, "They can have any color they want as long as it's black." A more appropriate answer was given by Alfred Sloan of General Motors (GM), who began redesigning the cars in GM's wide product lines each year to offer buyers styling, accessories, and luxuries that Ford's rugged, reliable Model-T lacked.

A modern company that got carried away with its own desires and lost sight of consumer needs is American Express. It lost not only its prestigious image, but 2 million cardholders as well, because management failed to understand that consumers preferred value to prestige and wanted a card that could be used anywhere—not just in fine restaurants.[5]

The marketing concept has been adapted by many of today's most successful businesses. The honor roll includes Hertz, Bank One, Singapore Airlines, Lexus, Dell Computer, The Four Seasons Hotel chain, and Home Depot. (Home Depot is the subject of this chapter's Manager's Notebook.) What each business has in common is:

- The customers and the customers' needs come first. Each company continually spends time, energy, and money to identify consumer needs.
- The customers' needs drive the development of products or services to meet the needs. In turn, the product is surrounded with matching promotion, pricing, and distribution strategy.
- The entire organization, not just the marketing department, is committed to satisfying the customer.[6]

consumer orientation
An emphasis on identifying the needs and wants of specific consumer groups, then producing, promoting, pricing, and distributing products that satisfy these needs and earn a profit.

marketing concept
A belief that the firm should adopt a company-wide consumer orientation directed at long-range profitability.

YOU DECIDE

Give two examples of companies you have dealt with that have adopted the marketing concept. Why do you feel that they have? Are there businesses you know that have not adopted the concept? Why? What effect has it had on your business relationship?

MANAGER'S NOTEBOOK

Home Depot

**MEETING
CONSUMERS' NEEDS**

Visit a Home Depot, a retail Disneyland for residential fixer-uppers, and you will see marketing at its best. The arena-sized emporiums are packed to the rafters with plywood, paint, power tools, and 35,000 other pieces of whatever you might need for your home. The people who operate this marketing showcase have carefully crafted a model of low-price, low-frills, low-hassle, high-customer-coddling service.

CEO Bernard Marcus and president Arthur Blank, who built their first store in Atlanta just 14 years ago, are so good at mixing low prices with high-grade service that they are being lauded for running the best marketing organization in America today. As a basis for that recognition, Marcus's customer-oriented philosophy is, "Every customer has to be treated like your mother, your father, your sister, or your brother."

Home Depot so excels at implementing this philosophy that last year the company's net income rose 45.6 percent, to $362.9 million, based on $7.1 billion in sales. The secret to this phenomenal performance is customer retention. Typical shoppers spend an average of $38 per visit, but since they drop in 30 times annually, year after year, they end up shelling out $25,000 each in a lifetime.

The key to retention is that Home Depot not only offers the lowest price, but delivers value, a concept that goes beyond price, and it delivers that value in a cost-effective way. For example, Home Depot:

- Spends money only on what directly benefits customers. Customers shop in cement-floored, warehouse-style outlets with the ambiance of airplane hangers, but the prices they pay are 20 to 30 percent below those of old-style hardware stores and are guaranteed to be the best in town.

- Encourages employees to build long-term relationships with customers. Workers are trained in home-repair techniques and can spend as much time as it takes to educate shoppers. Employees are on straight salary, and there are no high-pressure sales tactics.

- Trains salespeople not to let customers overspend. "I love it when shoppers tell me they were prepared to spend $150 and our people showed them how to do the job for four or five bucks," Marcus says.

- Pays its people as partners. Instead of receiving discounts on merchandise, workers get shares in the company. "To satisfy customers consistently, you must have a committed work force," notes Marcus. As evidence, scores of the 224 store managers have accumulated $1 million or more in Home Depot stock.

- Identifies and responds to the shoppers' ever-changing needs. Marcus spends at least a quarter of his time prowling the stores asking his favorite question to customers, "Did you find what you want?" Also, Home Depot employees do research every day by talking to the customers. And Thompson Associates, a retail research firm in Ann Arbor, Michigan, interviews more than 5,000 customers annually for Home Depot. Thompson president Bob Buckner notes: "They keep closer track of customer satisfaction than any other company we work for. Unlike a lot of clients, they always react to what we hear."

In short, Home Depot is committed to meeting its customers' needs.

(For more on meeting customers' needs, see Patricia Sellers, "Companies That Serve You Best," *Fortune,* May 31, 1993, pp. 74–88.)

Marketing Functions

At the beginning of the chapter we defined marketing as a group of interrelated activities designed to identify consumer needs and develop, distribute, promote, and price goods and services to satisfy these needs. What are these activities?

Figure 12.1 presents the three broad categories of these activities: exchange functions, physical distribution functions, and facilitating functions. Let's examine each.

Exchange Functions

The **exchange functions**, *buying and selling,* are *activities that relay products to their intended users.* Each consumer buys for his or her personal use, but other parties must perform buying functions that lead up to the final sale. *Wholesalers,* for example, are firms that distribute goods to other sellers. *Retailers* are businesses that sell to ultimate consumers. Retailers perform a buying function when they obtain merchandise from manufacturers or from wholesalers. (The roles of wholesalers and retailers are explored in Chapter 14.)

Selling—the other exchange function—is the critical counterpart of buying. It includes not only face-to-face meetings between salespeople and potential customers but also such sales support activities as advertising and sales promotion, some of which are examined in Chapter 13.

exchange functions
Buying and selling—activities that relay products to their intended users.

Figure 12.1
Principal activities involved in marketing.

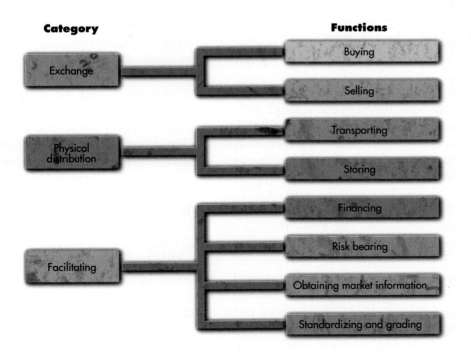

Physical Distribution Functions

Physical distribution functions are *activities involved in transporting and storing goods.* Because members of a market segment usually are scattered throughout the country, these functions place products where they are wanted.

Products are shipped regularly by air, water, truck, rail, and pipeline. The method of transportation that a given producer uses depends on such factors as the perishability, durability, bulk, and weight of the good, rates charged by the carrier, and how urgently the customer needs the item. Live Maine lobsters, a highly perishable product, are flown across the country packed in wet seaweed. Oil and natural gas, because of their bulk and fluidity, can be transported conveniently by pipeline, oceangoing tankers, and rail tank cars. Forest products are shipped in bulk by rail and truck, and iron ore by rail and water.

Storage, another physical distribution function, allows firms to distribute goods to strategic areas and place them on retail store shelves when buyers need them, eliminating coordination problems caused by seasonal and uncertain demand. Toys, which sell best during the Christmas season, may be shipped several months early and stored until the season nears. Storage enables manufacturers to produce enough units to meet demand for most of the year and release them to the market as demand dictates. Products such as Coppertone suntan lotion and Scotts lawn fertilizer rely heavily on storage as a physical distribution function.

Facilitating Functions

Four other activities facilitate or assist companies in performing the exchange and distribution functions. These are the **facilitating functions**—*financing, risk bearing, obtaining market information, and standardizing and grading.*

FINANCING   The financing function aids marketing by making the exchange functions (buying and selling) easier to accomplish. Businesses may offer credit to customers, which allows them to pay for purchases over several weeks or months. Firms may also borrow funds to buy materials and parts used in the end product, which makes financing important even before the product is ready to be marketed.

RISK BEARING   Some element of risk is inherent in any business activity, especially marketing. Firms that are sales oriented instead of market oriented face greater likelihood of financial loss, but all companies face the risk of loss caused by competitors' marketing tactics, changes in product life cycle, and disappointing sales or profit potential.

OBTAINING MARKET INFORMATION   Successful marketing is no accident. Managers make it happen by conducting extensive **marketing research,** which is *the facilitating function of gathering, recording, and analyzing data on cus-*

tomer demands and characteristics so that firms can develop new products and sell existing ones profitably. Marketing research is a powerful tool in the marketing process. Major consumer products companies such as Frito-Lay, Hallmark Cards, McDonald's, and the Marriott Courtyard chain use marketing research extensively to gather data about consumer needs as well as market potential, buying power, and profit potential. Table 12.1 lists data that marketing research can supply. Of equal importance is how the data are used. Accurate marketing research is used to:

- Conceive and develop new products to meet consumer wants, needs, and expectations. Burger King's dinner service is a result of consumer research by individual franchise owners and the corporation.[7]
- Improve and modify existing products to better satisfy customer needs. Gillette redesigned its Sensor razor for women with a wider handle and moisturizing strips on the blade cartridges.[8]
- Develop advertising campaigns and messages that have maximum impact on the buyers in the target market. General Motors's Camaro campaign—targeted at "twentysomethings," predominantly female—is a product of extensive marketing research.[9]
- Distribute a product in stores and in locations where members of the target market shop. Soon, wherever there are eaters, Pepsi will be hawking food. PepsiCo's fast-food restaurant chains—Pizza Hut and Taco Bell—are popping up at airport terminals and supermarkets, as they try to be "in easy reach everywhere an American stomach growls."[10]
- Develop prices based on the market. Procter & Gamble, with research data revealing a steady decline in disposable diaper market share, cut the prices of Pampers by 5 percent and Luvs by 16 percent.[11]

Marketing research provides the data for critical marketing decisions. Although we have discussed its importance here, the processes used and types of data collected are described in Chapter 18.

Table 12.1

Data that marketing research can supply.

1. Personal data
   a. Age
   b. Sex
   c. Income
   d. Occupation
   e. Marital status
   f. Educational level
   g. Hobbies, favorite recreation
2. Product use
   a. Frequency
   b. Reason (personal, professional, commercial)
   c. Most popular time of year (if applicable)
3. Type of store at which product is likely to be bought (supermarket, hardware store, discount store, department store)
4. Source from which consumer is most likely to learn about product (magazine, television, radio, or newspaper advertising; friends; direct mail promotion; store displays)
5. Brands or models previously owned
6. Factors that influence a buying decision (price, warranty, design, brand name, ease of operation)
7. Housing (own or rent house or apartment; live with parents; own vacation home)
8. Credit cards that may be used to buy the product

STANDARDIZING AND GRADING The facilitating functions of standardizing and grading permit buyers and sellers to make transactions without physically examining the product in question. If it were not for standards or grades, customers would often have difficulty comparing one product with another. Imagine, for example, the problems producers and retail stores would have with shoes or clothes if sizes were not standardized. The same holds true for light bulbs, bed sheets, flashlight batteries, tires, and the eggs you have for breakfast.

The Marketing Process: Developing a Marketing Strategy

Now that we have examined the activities involved in marketing, one major question needs to be answered: How does a company actually market a product or service? Figure 12.2 provides an illustration of the overall process involved in marketing a product or service. Briefly, an organization:

- Identifies a potential target market of consumers (age, income, location, benefits desired, lifestyle)
- Analyzes the needs of the identified target market
- Researches the potential of the target market for demand, sales, buying power, and profit
- Creates a good or service intended to satisfy the needs of the target market
- Distributes, prices, and promotes the good or service to the target market
- Ensures satisfaction through after-sales services

marketing strategy
An overall plan of marketing activities to meet the needs of a market.

These overall steps describe how a firm develops **marketing strategy**—*an overall plan of marketing activities to meet the needs of a market.* An organization develops a marketing strategy by (1) selecting a target market and (2) designing a marketing mix (a combination of product, price, promotion, and distribution) that will meet the needs of the target market.

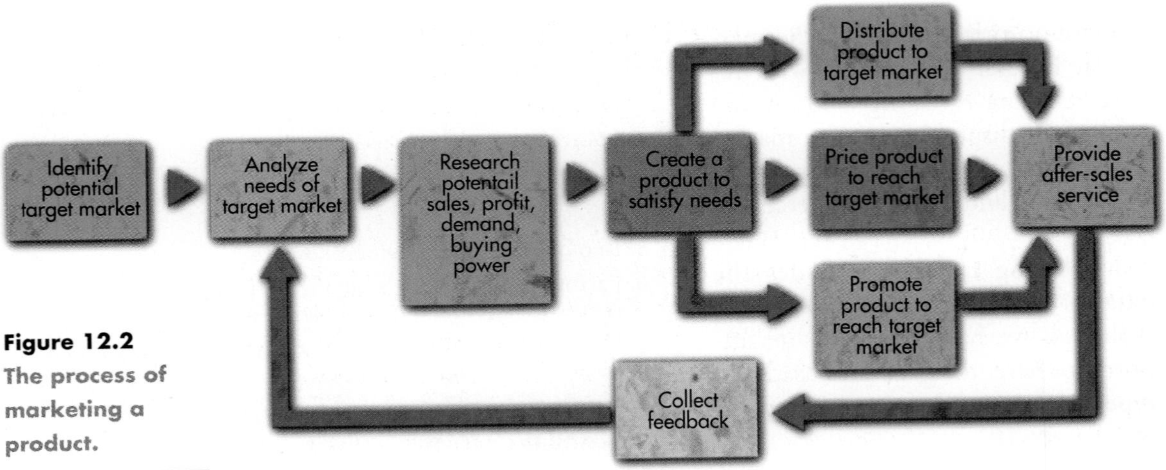

Figure 12.2
The process of marketing a product.

With this in mind, the starting point is identifying a market. A **market** is *a group of potential customers with the authority, ability, and willingness to purchase a particular good or service that satisfies their collective demand.* The important part of this definition is that people alone do not make a market. The people in the market, whether individual consumers or individuals buying for a business, must have the authority to make the purchase decision, have the money to be able to buy, and be willing to make the purchase. Marketers must be careful to qualify the market.

Markets are categorized by who buys the products and for what purpose the purchase is intended. Markets are subdivided into two major markets—consumer and industrial.

- The **consumer market** consists of *individuals who buy products for their personal use.* The products targeted for this market are known as consumer products. (Consumer products will be discussed later in the chapter.)
- The **industrial market** consists of *businesses, government agencies, and other institutions that buy products to use either in their operations or in making other products.* These purchases, which amount to billions of dollars' worth of goods each year, directly or indirectly support the production of consumer goods and other industrial items. Examples of industrial goods are iron ore, office supplies, drill presses, packaging machinery, and most computers.

While such products as iron ore are clearly industrial (no consumers purchase it), the buyer's intent determines whether other products fall into the category of industrial goods or consumer goods. Typing paper, for example, is an industrial good when purchased by a business for its correspondence and a consumer good when bought by a college student to write a term paper. Fertilizer, pickup trucks, and vegetables also fall into both categories, depending on how the buyer plans to use them.

Market Segmentation: Identifying Target Markets

Whether a market is consumer or industrial, one observation can be made: there are numerous customers with very different and specific needs in the market. For example, companies that market cars have recognized a simple fact: The same car cannot be sold to everyone who drives. Some people want economy, others luxury. Some people will buy a Porsche, others a Honda Prelude. It is more logical and practical to develop products for the preferences, habits, special uses, or general lifestyles of a particular group of users and market them to that group. In doing so the marketer is practicing **market segmentation**—*the process of dividing a total market into subgroups with similar characteristics and product needs.* When a market has been segmented the organization can decide which segment or segments will be its **target market**—*the particular customer group at which the company will aim its marketing*

market
A group of potential customers with the authority, ability, and willingness to purchase a particular good or service that satisfies their collective demand.

consumer market
Individuals who buy products for their personal use.

industrial market
Businesses, government agencies, and other institutions that buy products to use either in their operations or in making other products.

market segmentation
The process of dividing a total market into subgroups with similar characteristics and product needs.

target market
The particular customer group at which the company will aim its marketing activities.

Table 12.2
Automobile
market segments.

LIFESTYLE/AGE	INCOME		
	$0–$20,000	$21,000–$35,000	$35,000–$50,000
Single/22–30	Subcompact car	Compact car	Sports car
Single/31–40	Compact car	Midsized car	Foreign sports car

activities. The automobile maker that appeals to particular market segments—the high fuel economy market, the larger-family market, and the youth market—may capture most of such homogeneous markets by satisfying its members' specific needs. Table 12.2 illustrates how the automobile market can be segmented into smaller markets.

Now, knowing the logic for market segmentation and target marketing, let's look at the marketing process in detail, dividing it into two main steps.

Step 1: Identifying the Characteristics and Needs of the Market

As we saw in Figure 12.2, the first step involves identifying the characteristics and needs of the potential target market. By using marketing research (one of the marketing functions we discussed earlier in the chapter), marketers can acquire the necessary information on consumer characteristics and needs to segment the markets. The information might include:

- Data on family income, race, sex, and age
- Behavior patterns (e.g., amount of a specific product consumed, benefits wanted, brand loyalty)
- Psychological traits (e.g., personality characteristics, hobbies, lifestyle)
- Geographic location, climate, terrain

With this general information, the potential market can be analyzed and segmented in four ways:

- *Demographic segmentation* classifies the market into like groups based on characteristics such as age, sex, education, income, and household size.
- *Geographic segmentation* identifies where the consumer actually lives, such as Portland, Maine or Dime Box, Texas.
- *Psychographic segmentation* identifies like groups based on lifestyles such as peoples' activities, interests, and opinions.
- *Benefit segmentation* focuses on the benefits expected from a good or service. For example, diet soda may be expected to provide great taste for one group of individuals, while another group may seek the soda's low-calorie benefits (see Figure 12.3).

Demographic segmentation (because of the ease of reaching specific groups of consumers) and psychographics (because of the ability to consider consumers' perceived or desired lifestyle) are the two most commonly used bases for segmentation.

Companies spend countless hours and enormous sums of money on segmenting the market. Identifying the "right group" of people can mean tapping a goldmine. Marketers are currently setting their sights on three market segments: ethnic markets, the aging baby boomers, and the up-and-coming "busters." The baby boomers, all 76 million of them, have marketers scrambling to deliver products and services. The busters, the "X" generation, or twentysomethings, are 46 million Americans, ages eighteen to twenty-nine, who make up the next generation after the boomers. The ethnic market, composed of Asians, African Americans, and Hispanics, make up almost 25 percent of the U.S. population.[12]

An example of ethnic marketing is Kentucky Fried Chicken's "Neighborhood KFC" concept. Seeking to appeal to the preferences of people in predominantly ethnic neighborhoods, KFC restyled its restaurants to feature additional food items, new employee uniforms, in-store art, and a more hip blend of music. Targeted at African American and Hispanic areas, the results have been positive, with sales at Neighborhood KFCs increasing 5 to 30 percent.[13]

Stouffer's® makes a real mean Lean Cuisine®.

Figure 12.3
Benefit advertising.

Step 2: Analyzing the Potential of the Market

The next activity undertaken in segmenting the market is to analyze its (1) sales potential, (2) demand potential, (3) buying power, and (4) profit potential.

SALES POTENTIAL Important market segments have sales potential, which means a sufficient number of prospective buyers exist to justify risking capital and human resources to make and market the product. This is why, to use exaggerated examples, snowmobiles are not sold in Hawaii or air conditioners in Alaska.

Figure 12.4

Many marketers are targeting the sales potential in ethnic markets, such as African Americans, Hispanic Americans, and Asian Americans.

Forward-looking companies are especially concerned with anticipated changes in sales potential. Predictions that a segment's population will decrease, or will grow at a slow rate, may discourage entrepreneurs from appealing to that segment.

As previously noted, if you are focusing on the baby boomer or buster market, the sales potential is 76 million and 46 million, respectively. The ethnic population totals 62 million people. An ad targeted to African Americans is shown in Figure 12.4.

DEMAND POTENTIAL Another concern in evaluating a market segment is customer demand. Customers must either demonstrate an urgent, justified need for a particular product or indicate that they can be made to want it by a company's promotional activities. The difference between the two is primarily necessity. The Frisbee, for example, is not a necessary product, but millions of customers were convinced that they wanted it. Products such as smoke alarms and antibiotic drugs, however, are sold in response to needs.

The demand potential for companies that market health and financial services to baby boomers is unlimited. Boomers have a true need for goods and services that they hope can keep them fit and financially stable. They are living longer and think of themselves as active and vibrant, not bored and static. Nevertheless, few have saved for retirement. Rather, most have been and continue to be spenders—but now need to plan for retirement.[14]

BUYING POWER People are not potential customers for a product simply because they need or want it. They must also have buying power—cash or credit that enables them to buy the product. Many college students may want a Porsche, for example, but without sufficient cash or credit they will never get beyond the tire-kicking stage. Buying power separates casual lookers from serious prospects. An important market segment needs enough buying power to warrant producing the item. And they must be willing to spend the money.

Buying power is evident in the three markets we have noted:

- In the baby boomer market, the "seniors" control $250 billion of spending power.
- The ethnic market reveals equally impressive buying power: Hispanics, $141 billion; African Americans, $172 billion; and Asian Americans, $196 billion.
- Even though the busters have not entered their peak earning years, they already have $125 billion of buying power.[15]

PROFIT POTENTIAL The fourth important factor in attributing importance to a market segment, and the key to all the others, is profit potential. This is the likelihood that an entrepreneur will earn sufficient profit from the units sold to justify the risk involved. Successful firms minimize the frequency and severity of bad decisions by confirming that a market segment exhibits these four features to an acceptable degree before they commit themselves to production.

In the process of segmenting a market, we have identified a group of consumers that have similar needs and characteristics—a target market—and we have assured ourselves that they have the authority and ability to buy. Now we must develop plans for reaching the target market or markets by creating the marketing mix.

The Marketing Mix

The tools or variables a marketer works with to reach the target market are product strategy, promotion strategy, price strategy, and distribution strategy. *The effective meshing of product, price, promotion, and distribution strategies to achieve success* is known as the **marketing mix**. Figure 12.5 shows the relationship of the marketing mix ingredients as they blend together to focus on a target market segment.

marketing mix
The effective meshing of product, price, promotion, and distribution strategies to achieve success.

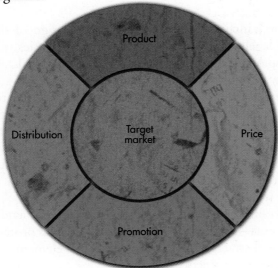

Figure 12.5
Elements in the marketing mix.

GLOBAL PERSPECTIVE

The ultimate test for marketing is to create or adapt a product for a specific target market. The challenge for American pizza giants Domino's and Pizza Hut was to accept the fact that good old pepperoni and cheese wouldn't cut it in Japan—and then develop products for that culture.

Each company spent millions developing outlets and convincing Japanese consumers to accept the idea of pizza as desirable. But what the Japanese did not want or accept totally was "American" pizza—pepperoni, cheese, anchovies. The cash registers weren't ringing until the two giants listened to the consumers. Then they got creative.

Domino's began to offer apple or rice pizza, German sausage and potato pizza with mayonnaise sauce, squid and tuna topping, curry topping, and barbecued beef with sauteed burdock root. Outdoing itself in creativity, Domino's introduced a 10-inch chicken teriyaki gourmet pizza for $15, including Japanese-style grilled chicken, spinach, onion, and corn.

Not to be left behind, Pizza Hut introduced barbecued chicken pizza, as well as burdock root and potato and macaroni salad. And, stretching to reach the most exotic taste buds, it quickly followed with shrimp in chili sauce on a sweetened pizza crust and a chicken, seaweed, and shredded bonito topping with sauce made from fish stock.

With this array of pizza pleasers, the cash registers are ringing and the streets of Tokyo are abuzz with the sound of pizza-delivery scooters.

(For more on product marketing, see Yumiko Ono, "Pizza in Japan Is Adapted to Local Tastes," *The Wall Street Journal*, May 6, 1993, p. B1.)

One Curry Pizza with Squid— To Go!

Product strategy includes decisions about the design of the product and about brands, labels, trademarks, packaging, warranties, guarantees, new product development, and the product life cycle. Table 12.3 indicates how product strategy designs products for market segments.

Pricing strategy is concerned with establishing prices for products that will return a profit. Pricing decisions are influenced by how responsive a target market is to a high or low price, the psychological images created by prices (cheap versus quality), and the actions of competitors. William Wrigley implemented price strategy successfully by marketing a product with a low-price, high-volume potential: chewing gum for a nickel a pack. (We will explore pricing strategies in Chapter 14.)

Promotional strategy involves developing the correct blend of the promotional mix elements—advertising, personal selling, sales promotion, and publicity. Promotional strategy is the communication element of the marketing mix. (Promotion is the subject of Chapter 13.)

Distribution strategy involves the distribution systems and channels used to place the product in the customer's hands. Decisions are made concerning what shipping methods to use, how and where to store the product until it is sold, what intermediaries to use, and what sales outlets will be used in specific locations throughout the country. (Distribution is the subject of Chapter 14.)

PRODUCT	MARKET SEGMENT
Hero dog food	Owners of large dogs
Cycle dog food	Owners of dogs at different stages of life
Gaines Burgers	Dog owners seeking convenience
CD dog food	Owners of dogs needing special diets
Good Houskeeping	Homemakers
Working Woman	Female entrepreneurs and executives
Vogue	Fashion-conscious women
Flintstones vitamins	Children
Fem-iron tablets	Adult women
Geritol	Elderly people

Table 12.3
Variations of products designed for market segments.

Products and Product Strategy

The product and product strategy play the key role in marketing mix planning. Developing a good or service to satisfy a consumer need is the critical first step. The other elements are based on product planning.

What Is a Product?

A product is more than meets the eye. It is the total package that brings satisfaction to a consumer. A **product** consists of *the basic physical offering and an accompanying set of image and service features that seek to satisfy needs.*[16] It includes the tangible features that can be seen and the intangible image and service features that we cannot see but that make the product what it is.

As an example, a VHS videocassette recorder by Panasonic:

- Is a rectangular box with wires connecting it to a television set (physical characteristics)
- Has a warranty and service facilities (service characteristics)
- Has prestige associated with ownership of a particular brand name, Panasonic (image)

These characteristics, whether tangible or intangible, are designed to produce consumer satisfaction.

product
The basic physical offering and an accompanying set of image and service features that seek to satisfy needs.

Categories of Products

Product strategy involves deciding on the category of good to offer. Different types of products are intended for particular target markets. A products category or type in large part determines what promotion, pricing, and distribution strategies will be used. There are two categories of products: consumer and industrial.

Products are anything available for sale designed to meet particular buyers' needs.

CONSUMER PRODUCTS   *Products intended for the personal use of the consumer* are **consumer products**. The products in this category can be identified according to the differences in buying behavior that occur from one group of goods to another. There are three categories of consumer goods: convenience goods, shopping goods, and specialty goods.

consumer products
Products intended for the personal use of the consumer.

convenience goods
Products purchased with a minimum of effort.

shopping goods
Items purchased after comparative shopping based on quality, design, cost, and performance.

specialty goods
Items that buyers prefer strongly because of their unique characteristics or image.

Convenience goods are *products purchased with a minimum of effort.* They are usually inexpensive and are purchased frequently. Milk, newspapers, pencils, and motor oil (see Figure 12.6) are examples of convenience goods.

Shopping goods are *items purchased after comparative shopping based on quality, design, cost, and performance.* Potential purchasers undergo an extensive shopping campaign, investigating and comparing products at competing stores. Televisions, clothes, shoes, and appliances generally fall into this category.

Specialty goods are those *items that buyers prefer strongly because of their unique characteristics or image.* Consumers are willing to expend considerable energy and time to acquire these goods. Some people, for example, have specific, nonnegotiable demands for Carver stereo amplifiers, Martin guitars, or Mobil 1 motor oil. Generally, if the specific product is not available, many customers will not accept a substitute.

It is important to realize that the boundaries between these three types of goods are personal. One person's specialty item may be another's convenience good, a difference in perception that sometimes depends on spendable income (as with jewelry) and sometimes on the effect that peer opinions and promotional efforts have on the buyer's attitude (as with motor oils, razor blades, and sporting goods). General classifications help producers construct broad promotion and distribution strategies that will succeed with most consumers who want or need the product.

INDUSTRIAL PRODUCTS *Goods or services purchased for the production of other goods and services or to be used in the operation of a business* are **industrial products**. The classifications of industrial goods include installations, accessory equipment, fabricated parts and materials, raw materials, and industrial supplies.

- **Installations** are *large, expensive capital items that are the major assets of the business.* Examples are storage facilities and factories.
- **Major equipment** includes *machinery and large tools used for production.* Examples are lathes, milling machines, and brewing vats.
- **Accessory equipment** refers to *items that are less expensive than major equipment and are standardized.* Examples are hand tools, calculators, and typewriters.
- **Component parts** are *prefinished items that are put into the final product.* Batteries and spark plugs for automobiles illustrate this type of product.
- **Raw materials** are *natural and farm products that become part of a final product.* Minerals, sand, oil, and barley are examples of raw materials.
- **Supplies** are *items necessary in the daily operation of a business.* They do not become part of the final product. Supplies include light bulbs, repair supplies, stationery, and pens.
- **Industrial services** are *items used to plan or support company operations.* Examples include legal, printing, janitorial, and accounting services.

The Fountain of Youth.

Eternal youth? In a container of motor oil? Ah, but it's no conventional motor oil. It's Mobil 1. And it can actually help your engine defy the aging process. What's Mobil 1's secret?

Amazing synthetic diet

Mobil 1 is an advanced-formula synthetic. And in the realm of motor oil, synthetic is superior to the real thing. In fact, Mobil 1 synthetic fights engine wear far better than leading conventional oils. And don't worry. It's ok to switch to Mobil 1 after using a conventional oil.

200,000 miles without aging

In tests we drove an engine 200,000 miles using Mobil 1. And?

Virtually no wear. The engine was still running like new. The vital engine parts even looked like new. In fact, key parts met the manufacturers' specs for new parts.

Any questions?

For instance, can I use Mobil 1 in my new car? Absolutely. In fact, Mobil 1 actually exceeds the standards set by major car manufacturers. For answers to other questions, call

1-800-366-3333.

Meanwhile, it's nice to know that Mobil 1 advanced-formula synthetic motor oil will help keep your engine from aging for the life of your car. Too bad it can't work for people.

Mobil 1

It keeps your engine running like new.*

*Regular oil filter changes and scheduled maintenance. © 1993 Mobil Oil Corporation   Protect the environment. Take your used motor oil to an approved collection center.

Advanced Formula

Mobil 1

Formula 5W-30

Race Proven

Fully Synthetic Motor Oil

1 QUART (.946 LITER)

Figure 12.6

An advertisement for a convenience good.

industrial products
Goods or services purchased for the production of other goods and services or to be used in the operation of a business.

Product Strategy: The Use of Brands

A major concern in developing product strategy is to distinguish one's product from all others. Part of a product as we defined it earlier is its image. To create an image, companies adopt a strategy of branding. A **brand** is *a name, symbol, design, or combination of them that identifies the goods or services of a company.*

There are three distinct brand identifications:

- A **brand name** is *a letter, word, or group of letters or words used to identify a product.* Campbell's Soup, Mrs. Smith's Pies, IBM, Coke, and Lite Beer are brand names.
- A **brand mark** is *a symbol or design used to identify a product and to distinguish it.* Shell Oil Company's shell, McDonald's golden arch, and the Nike "swoosh" are examples of a brand mark.
- A **trade character** is *a brand mark that has a human quality.* Ronald McDonald, Tony the Tiger, and the Pillsbury Dough Boy are examples.

A brand identification has such value to a company that it should be protected. To do so, firms obtain a **trademark**—*a brand name, brand mark, or trade character that has legal protection.* Companies obtain the exclusive legal right to trademarks by registering them with the U.S. Patent and Trademark Office. When registered, the trademark is followed by an ®. Examples of trademarked names include Coca-Cola and Xerox.

THE VALUE OF BRANDS Developing and protecting a brand has a number of advantages in the marketplace. Branding makes the product recognizable and distinguishable. Chef-Boy-R-Dee's smiling face and Fruit-of-the-Loom fruits aid customers in distinguishing these products from others.

PROJECTING A MESSAGE Brands project a message of quality and consistency. This message of quality is intended to increase consumer acceptance of the product and to help move it through the following three stages of brand acceptance:

1. *Brand recognition.* A newly introduced product becomes familiar to the public. If the product is part of a branded group of products, this stage is facilitated. "Oh, Kellogg's has a new cereal."
2. *Brand preference.* Consumers who rely on previous experience with a brand choose it over competitors. "I know it's good because all their products are good."
3. *Brand insistence.* Consumers will accept no alternatives. "If you don't carry Campbell's soup, I'll shop at a store that does."

Brands are so effective at projecting a message that a brand can get the ultimate promotion: becoming the company name. Recently United Brands Company changed its name to Chiquita Brands International, Inc., in honor of Chiquita brands. The reason: to reflect the company's position as a major marketer of fresh fruit and vegetables.

BRAND STRATEGIES The use of brands is such an effective strategy that a number of approaches have evolved. Some companies, such as General Electric, use a family brand: the company's products are identified by one name.

On the other hand, the strategy of individual branding uses separate brands for each item or product marketed by the firm. Manufacturers develop their own brands, called *national brands*, while retailers and wholesalers put their own "private" brands on the market.

trademark
A brand name, brand mark, or trade character that has legal protection.

BRAND EXTENSIONS The enormous impact of a successful brand in the marketplace has made brand extension or brand leveraging—the use of an established brand name to propel a new, sometimes totally unrelated product into the marketplace—the name of today's marketing game. Marketers today are making brands jump across whole categories of goods. Sun-Maid's familiar logo and red packaging appear on the bread shelf as well as in the dried fruit section. Häagen Dazs is a liqueur as well as an ice cream brand, and Turtle Wax products will clean your home, not just your car.

YOU DECIDE

Think of your favorite brand of products. Which stage of brand acceptance—recognition, preference, or insistence—applies to the product? Why?

The second brand extension tactic is to develop variations of existing products. Of the 15,866 food, household, and personal care products launched last year, nearly 70 percent were brand extensions. Well-known examples of this type of brand extension include:

- RJR Nabisco packaging its fifty-eight-year-old Ritz cracker into Ritz Bits.
- Kellogg enjoying success with Rice Krispies Treats, a cereal version of a fifty-year-old snack recipe.
- Quaker Oats rolling out flavored rice cakes. New flavors such as nacho cheese have boosted annual revenue 50 percent.[17]

GENERIC BRANDS: COMPETITION FOR ALL Some organizations have chosen an opposite approach to brands, brand names, and brand marks—**generic brands**. These are *products that carry no brand name.* Generics do not have expensive packages or promotional support.

generic brands
Products that carry no brand name.

The difference between generic and brand-name products is often minimal. Generics may be slightly inferior in color, size, or quality of ingredients, but with little effect on nourishment or flavor. The grade difference, coupled with the fact that the producer spends no money on promotion, enables generics to sell for as much as 30 to 40 percent less than brand-name items. Manufacturers typically use excess production capacity to process generics, so regular operations may be unaffected. While generics return a lower profit per unit, they can sell in large enough volume to supermarket outlet chains that the producer enjoys satisfactory profits.

Product Strategy: The Use of Packaging

Packaging is more than putting the product in a box, bottle, or wrapper. Package design has a significant impact on the company's image. The proper

use of shape, color, and material is an element of product strategy. Kleenex comes in decorator boxes, Pangburn's Chocolate Millionaires are in a gold box, and Lowenbrau beer has gold foil wrapped around the neck of the bottle. An accident? Hardly.

In addition to the use of color, multiple use and ease of handling are conscious decisions made by marketers. Would you rather buy five 1-quart oil cans or one 5-quart plastic oil container, which you can use to store the old oil? Would you prefer plastic or glass quart bottles of cold drinks for a long car trip? Skillful marketing product designers help you with those decisions—and help you buy their products.

Packaging is playing a more magnified role in today's marketing plan. Comments from marketers, such as "Packaging is the least expensive form of advertising" and "Every package is a five-second commercial," provide testimony to packaging's importance (see Figure 12.7).

Figure 12.7

Packaging—part of product strategy.

product life cycle
The succession of phases including introduction, growth, maturity, and decline of a product in its market.

The Product Life Cycle

Products, like people, pass through several stages between birth and death. These are called collectively the **product life cycle,** *the succession of phases including the introduction, growth, maturity, and decline of a product in its market.* The length of the stages and the profits received at each stage vary according to the specific product, as Figure 12.8 illustrates.

Successful marketers are concerned about a product's position in the life cycle. It not only influences the marketing strategy that will be applied at any given moment, it also indicates the need to introduce new products. The product life cycle is a useful tool to a marketer. It reminds him or her of the necessity to watch the product and adjust the elements of the marketing mix as needed in the various stages. It also shows the vulnerability of a product and the need for new product development. Let's examine each stage in the product life cycle.

Introduction

Sales and profits are typically low during a product's introductory stage. The company may spend a great deal of money to inform potential customers

Figure 12.8
**The product life
cycle.**

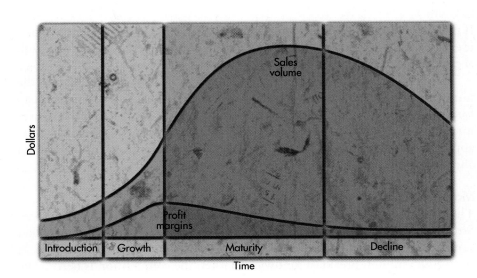

about the product and convince them that it will satisfy their needs and wants. Because people are not familiar with the product and may doubt its useful- ness, the introduction stage is a crucial get-acquainted period. A product currently evolving through the introductory stage is Tab Clear, a transparent cinnamon-tinged version of Coca-Cola's original diet soft drink. Billed as "the ultimate soft drink," Tab Clear allows Coke to take on Crystal Pepsi without endangering its flagships—Coke and Diet Coke.[18]

Seasoned marketing managers usually prefer to spend a relatively small amount of money marketing a new product to small geographic regions rather than offer it nationwide from the start. In a nationwide introduction, poor consumer response would cause enormous losses; so "risk a little, lose a little" usually seems a more prudent course to follow. This small-scale introduction, called **test marketing**, involves *introducing a product in strategic geographic locations, rather than everywhere, to assess consumer response.*

A company that is no stranger to test marketing is Taco Bell Corp. In the fierce, competitive fast-food business, Taco Bell is looking for an edge on its major rival, Taco Bueno. With this in mind, it is trying an assault on stay-at- home diners with a line of taco shells, salsa, and refried beans. To see whether this is a wise decision, Taco Bell is testing the line in 1,000 supermarkets in the South and Southwest.[19]

On the other hand, sometimes companies choose not to test market a product. Moving directly into mass production and distribution can be a risky business, but some companies choose to do it for good reasons. Owens Country Sausage introduced microwavable Border Breakfasts, a spicy com- bination of scrambled eggs, cheese, and sausage, directly into twenty-seven market areas with no test marketing. The reason: not to tip off competition. Within the first six months the product raked in $3 million in retail sales and the company's production tonnage was six times greater than projected.

test marketing
Introducing a product
in strategic geo-
graphic locations,
rather than every-
where, to assess con-
sumer response.

Growth

If the new product sells briskly in test areas, confirming management's hopes, it enters the growth stage, during which it may be marketed nationwide with accompanying increases in sales and profits.

Through hard work, Lever Brothers has seen its Lever 2000 grow into the number-one position in the soap category by touting it as a multipurpose soap for the whole family. No longer does a family have to have a moisturizing soap for mom, a deodorizing bar for dad, and a mild soap for the kids. The approach has been so successful that sales are ringing up at $113 million annually.[20]

Maturity

The third stage—maturity—is an important one for original manufacturers. Strong sales and profits up to this point will encourage other firms to market similar products, and cut-throat price reductions may occur. For example, in the $109.5 million breakfast sandwich market, the competition is fierce. The lure of sales revenue has attracted Jimmy Dean Sausage 'n Biscuits from Sara Lee, Great Starts Breakfasts from Campbell Soup, New Traditions Breakfasts from Hormel, Weight Watchers Breakfasts by Heinz, and both Breakfast Biscuits and Border Breakfasts from Owens Country Sausage.

When a product is in the maturity stage, sales reach a peak and profits decline rapidly, suggesting that it is time to introduce a new product or revitalize the current one's appeal and begin the life cycle anew. This is a sound time to practice brand extension.

Decline

Some products, such as fountain pens, retain consumer popularity for decades before they enter the fourth stage, decline. During this stage demand virtually disappears, because the product no longer suits consumer needs, lifestyles, habits, or tastes. Men's oily hair cream, washboards, straight razors, and slide rules are products that have passed through the decline stage.

Products that satisfy wants instead of urgent needs sometimes appeal to a very fickle market segment, being popular today and forgotten tomorrow. Their life cycle often resembles a pyramid. Many toys and grocery items, for example, have relatively short life cycles; approximately 60 percent of the toys you see for sale today were not available two years ago, and over half the items now sold in supermarkets did not exist ten years ago. Klackers, pet rocks, and mood rings are products that sped through their life cycles very quickly.

New Product Development: A Necessity

The product life cycle has a very loud message: all products eventually pass through the stages and have to be removed from the market. It is critical for the success of a company to have new products planned as replacements for existing ones or to find new uses for old products.

An excellent example of a company that constantly monitors the product life cycle and puts new products in the marketplace is the Gillette Company. The firm has made it a practice over decades to innovate in the face of competition and present other product alternatives to the consumer. The change from the Gillette "Blue Blade" and the Wilkinson Stainless Steel Blade to Gillette's Trac Two and from the swivel razor to Trac II Plus and the Sensor is a magnificent analysis and use of the product life cycle.

Developing new products is not a simple task. Thousands of new products are introduced annually with a failure rate ranging between 60 and 70 percent. Products fail for many reasons, including design problems, insufficient research, or poor timing of the product's introduction to the marketplace. To minimize these risks a firm can use a well-thought-out six-step process to develop new products, as outlined in Figure 12.9. Let's review each step.

1. *Generation of ideas.* Ideas for new products are generated to help the company achieve its objectives. Ideas can be generated from anywhere—researchers, engineers, customers, suppliers.
2. *Screening of ideas.* The initial set of ideas are screened against a number of criteria, including whether they match the firm's objectives, whether the company has the expertise to develop the ideas, and the availability of financial resources. If the idea passes the criteria, it is evaluated further.
3. *Business analysis.* In this phase the product's market potential is evaluated. An analysis is made of potential sales, costs, and profits. If the product is promising, the idea is sent to product development.
4. *Product development.* In this phase the company develops a prototype or

Figure 12.9
New product development process.

working model of the product idea. The company conducts a feasibility study in an effort to determine whether it is technically feasible to produce the product and what the costs will be to offer the product on a large scale.

5. *Test marketing.* As noted earlier, test marketing is introducing the product on a limited scale in an area that represents the entire market. This phase allows the company to experiment with the product and the other marketing mix variables.

6. *Commercialization.* If the product is successful in test marketing, the company makes plans for production and distribution of the product. During this phase, refinements are made to the product itself, as well as to other elements of the marketing mix.

SUMMARY

Marketing is a group of interrelated activities designed to identify consumer needs and develop, distribute, promote, and price goods and services to satisfy those needs at a profit. A company's long-range future is tied to the successful application of marketing.

Effective marketing creates value, or utility. There are four types of utility: form, time, place, and possession. Marketing influences form utility and directly affect time, place, and possession utilities.

The practice of marketing has evolved from a production orientation to a sales orientation and finally to a customer orientation. An organization that is customer oriented has adopted a philosophy known as the marketing concept—a belief that the firm should adopt a company-wide consumer orientation directed at long-range profitability.

Marketing includes both activities and a process. Marketing activities are grouped in three major areas: exchange (buying, selling), physical distribution (transporting, storing), and facilitating (financing, risk bearing, obtaining market information, and standardizing and grading). These activities are undertaken while completing the marketing process.

The marketing process involves developing a marketing strategy: a target market and a marketing mix. The overall process includes:

- Identifying a potential target market
- Analyzing the needs of the identified target market
- Researching the potential of the target market for demand, sales, and profit
- Creating a good or service intended to satisfy the needs of the target market

- Distributing, pricing, and promoting the good or service to the target market
- Ensuring satisfaction through after-sales service

The efforts of marketing are directed at a market. A market is a group of potential customers with the authority, ability, and willingness to purchase a particular good or service that satisfies their collective demand. There are two major markets: consumer and industrial. The consumer market is composed of individuals who buy products for their personal use. The industrial market consists of businesses, government agencies, and other institutions that buy products to use either in operations or in making other products.

The large industrial and consumer markets need to be subdivided into smaller markets. This process of dividing a total market into subgroups with similar characteristics is called market segmentation. By using demographic, geographic, psychographic, and benefit segmentation, large markets can be divided to identify the characteristics and needs of the target market. In turn, the market is analyzed for sales potential, demand potential, buying power, and profit potential.

Once a company selects a particular segment as its target market, a marketing mix needs to be developed. The marketing mix is the effective meshing of product, promotion, price, and distribution strategy to achieve success.

Product strategy is the key in marketing mix planning. A product consists of the basic physical offering and accompanying set of image and service features that seek to satisfy needs. There are two categories of products: consumer products and industrial products. Consumer products include convenience goods, shopping goods, and specialty goods. Industrial goods include installations, major equipment, accessory equipment, component parts, raw materials, supplies, and industrial services.

An element of product strategy includes the decision to use branding. A brand is a name, symbol, design, or a combination of them that identifies the goods or services of a company. Companies choose branding to aid in recognition and to project a message. Companies choose to use brand names, brand marks, and trade characters. Today generic brands compete with family, manufacturers', and private brands.

A second element of product strategy is the choice of packaging. The proper use of shape, color, and material is important to the image, multiple use, and ease of handling of products.

Marketers need to be concerned about a product's life cycle, which is the succession of phases that includes introduction, growth, maturity, and decline of a product in its market. The cycle affects promotion, pricing, and distribution strategies as well as the importance of new product development.

New product development involves a six-step process: generation of ideas, screening of ideas, business analysis, product development, test marketing, and commercialization.

KEY TERMS

accessory equipment p. 391
brand p. 391
brand mark p. 392
brand name p. 392
component parts p. 391
consumer market p. 383
consumer orientation p. 377
consumer products p. 390
convenience goods p. 390
exchange functions p. 379
facilitating functions p. 380
form utility p. 376
generic brands p. 393
industrial market p. 383
industrial products p. 391
industrial services p. 391
installations p. 391
major equipment p. 391
market p. 383
market segmentation p. 383
marketing p. 374

marketing concept p. 377
marketing mix p. 387
marketing research p. 380
marketing strategy p. 382
physical distribution functions p. 380
place utility p. 376
possession utility p. 376
product p. 389
product life cycle p. 394
production orientation p. 376
raw materials p. 391
sales orientation p. 376
shopping goods p. 390
specialty goods p. 390
supplies p. 391
target market p. 383
test marketing p. 395
time utility p. 376
trade character p. 392
trademark p. 392
utility p. 376

FOR REVIEW AND DISCUSSION

1. What is utility? What types of utility does marketing directly create? Give an example of each.
2. What is the marketing concept? What stages might a company go through before it is ready to adopt the marketing concept?
3. What are the three major marketing functions? What activities are included in each?
4. What is marketing strategy? What are the two elements of marketing strategy?
5. Marketers refer to marketing as "the application of the marketing process." What is included in the marketing process? What is it attempting to accomplish?

6. What is a market? What elements are necessary for a group of people to be called a market?

7. What are the two major markets? How do they differ?

8. How is a market segmented? What do demographic, geographic, psychographic, and benefit segmentation accomplish?

9. Once a target market segment has been identified, what four areas are analyzed for potential?

10. What is the purpose of the marketing mix? What are its four elements?

11. What is a product? Take one product that you are

familiar with and describe its physical, image, and service features.

12. What is the purpose of adopting branding as a product strategy?

13. Distinguish among brand names, brand marks, and trade characters; among family brands, manufacturers' brands, and private brands.

14. Explain the importance of the product life cycle to a marketer. What are its four stages?

15. Why is it important for a marketer always to be developing new products? What are the six steps in product development?

APPLICATIONS

Case 12.1: Procter & Gamble: To Russia with Love

When Sergei Dmitriev bought the perfect anniversary present for his wife—Oil of Olay Night Cream, called Oil of Olay in Russia—it was a tribute to the powers of Procter & Gamble's marketing. The $2.40 tab is no small extravagance considering Sergei's $25 monthly salary. That same sum would have fetched more than a dozen tickets to the Kiren Ballet, 50 loaves of bread, or 500 subway rides.

Brand-name giant Procter & Gamble has spent millions of dollars researching the Russian consumer's mind. P&G has been aggressive in conducting the same painstaking market research that it does for Ivory, Crest, and Tide at home in Cincinnati. It hired a local company to do the door-to-door consumer interviews about household cleaning habits and discovered that:

- Russians usually store detergent in cramped bathrooms, so the box must be strong enough to sustain water damage.
- Because the state-made detergents were so weak, Russians tended to soak their clothes for hours in a tub; P&G notes that its powerful detergent eliminates that need.
- Many Russians boil clothes after washing them, so P&G notes that its soap is safe at high temperatures.

Focusing on the results of the marketing research, P&G is blitzing the airwaves with commercials that

offer almost comic contrast to the dismal hardships of everday life. It is introducing the Russians, accustomed to brown paper packaging, to distinct brands that tout unheard of benefits such as dandruff control. And it is emphasizing marketing tactics that are radical in Russia, such as samples and gifts with purchases.

The efforts to understand the Russian consumer and adjust their marketing strategy is paying off for P&G. On gift-giving occasions such as New Year's Eve and Women's Day, Russians wrap bars of Camay soap and bottles of Pert Plus shampoo (marketed in Russia as Vidal Sassoon Wash & Go) to bestow on their loved ones. That in itself is no small tribute to P&G's marketing, considering that a consumer could buy eight bars of Russian soap for the 37 cents that Camay costs in Russia.

Questions

1. Using Figure 12.2 as a guide, which steps of the marketing process have been used by Procter & Gamble in its Russian marketing efforts? Cite examples from the case to support your answer.

2. What specific information related to demographics and benefits did marketing research reveal about the Russian consumer? Cite examples from the case to support your answer.

3. Which of the marketing mix ingredients were affected by the market research? Cite examples from the case to support your answer.

For more information, see Valerie Reitman, "P&G Uses Skills It Has Honed at Home to Introduce Its Brands to the Russians," *The Wall Street Journal*, April 14, 1993, pp. B1, B3.

Case 12.2: Behind the Time at Timex

In 1982 Timex, the internationally known manufacturer and marketer of watches, was approached by a tiny Swiss company with a business proposition. The Swiss company had developed a new concept in watches but needed someone to provide marketing and distribution. With no effective way to bring the product to market, the Swiss company offered Timex the opportunity to be the marketer and distributor of the watch—worldwide.

The Timex executives, conservative by reputation and practice, liked the deal but felt that the strange, colorful timepieces would fall flat in the marketplace. So, they rejected the offer and lost the opportunity for exclusive rights to market Swatches.

This was not the first time Timex had made a mistake. In fact, it was good at making mistakes on new trends and products. It had trouble changing from its earlier successes. The company had become the industry leader in sales by producing simple, inexpensive watches, watches that were functional and dependable. Clinging to the concept that "proven is best" Timex failed in the 1970s to recognize and jump on the digital revolution. It continued to make only analog watches and lost market share for years.

When C. Michael Jacobi became president of Timex, one of his first moves was to significantly expand the company's marketing research efforts in an attempt to make the company more responsive. He recognized that the wristwatch had become a fashion item more than a timepiece. With market statistics showing that the average American owns five watches, Timex needs to be responsive to consumer desires for more than a functional, inexpensive, reliable watch.

Questions

1. How does this case illustrate the importance of meeting consumer needs?

2. How does this case illustrate the importance of the product life cycle to a company's success?

3. In the 1970s, at which stage of the product life cycle were Timex's analog watches? Explain your answer.

For more information, see Chris Roush, "At Timex, They're Positively Glowing," *Business Week*, July 12, 1993, p. 141..

REFERENCES

1. John Huey, "The World's Best Brand," *Fortune*, May 31, 1993, pp. 44–54.
2. Wendy Zellner, "Penney's Rediscovers Its Calling," *Business Week*, April 5, 1993, pp. 51–52.
3. Ellen Neuborne, "Streamlined Sears Shopping for New Image," *USA Today*, February 12, 1993, p. 7B.
4. Joel R. Evans and Barry Berman, *Marketing*, 5th edition (New York: Macmillian), 1993, p. 12.
5. Patricia Sellers, "Companies That Service You Best," *Fortune*, May 31, 1993, p. 76.
6. Ibid.
7. Andrew Berg, "Sid Fellenstein Is Having It His Way," *Business Week*, November 22, 1993, p. 64.
8. Gary Strauss, "Marketers Touch Up Products to Appeal to Women," *USA Today*, November 11, 1992, p. B1.
9. Martha T. Moore, "Ford Tunes Up to the MTV Generation," *USA Today*, March 29, 1993, p. B5.
10. Amy Barrett, "Detergent, Aisle 2, Pizza Hut, Aisle 5," *Business Week*, June 7, 1993, p. 82.
11. Valerie Reitman, "P & G Cuts Prices in Baby Market," *The Wall Street Journal*, April 14, 1993, p. B8.
12. William Dunn, "The Move Toward Ethnic Marketing," *Nation's Business*, May 1993, p. 39.
13. Barry Bloomberg, "Getting a Leg Up," *USA Today*, April 14, 1993, p. D1.
14. Howard Schlessberg, "Aging Boomers Give Marketers a Lot of Changes to Consider," *Marketing News*, April 12, 1993, p. 10.
15. Laura Zinn, "Move Over, Boomers," *Business Week*, December 14, 1992, pp. 74–82.
16. Evans and Berman, *Marketing*, p. 12.
17. Gary Strauss, "Extending a Bit Too Far," *USA Today*, April 19, 1993, p. B7.
18. Martha T. Moore, "Coke Issues Clear Challenge to Pepsi," *Fortune*, December 28, 1992, p. 64.
19. Amy Barrett, "Detergent, Aisle 2, Pizza Hut, Aisle 5," p. 82.
20. Susan Caminiti, "Finding More Ways to Sell More," *Fortune*, July 27, 1992, p. 101.

13

MARKETING PROMOTIONAL STRATEGY

Savvy marketers find clever new ways to promote their products into the spotlight, and in doing so, build brand loyalty.

GAIL CONGER
Product Manager, Heinz U.S.A.

CHAPTER OBJECTIVES
After studying this chapter, you should be able to:

1. Identify the principal buying motives of final consumers and of industrial purchasers.
2. Describe the role and importance of promotional strategy.
3. Identify the four elements of promotion and explain how they are combined to form an effective mix.
4. Identify the eight elements of the communication process.
5. Define personal selling and present the seven steps in the selling process.
6. Define advertising and identify the two types of advertising.
7. List at least four advertising media and describe the advantages and disadvantages of each.
8. Define publicity and discuss its importance.
9. Define sales promotion and describe some of the sales promotion devices that can be used to appeal to middlemen and final consumers.

UP FRONT

Sarah Rolph is someone who has learned wisely and well from her experiences. Like any good craftsperson, she has assembled a set of skills and has accumulated knowledge that now serve as the core of her business: marketing communications.

Rolph was born and raised in Los Angeles but left the warm southern California beaches in favor of attending Evergreen State College in Olympia, Washington. "The academic program at Evergreen is interdisciplinary, so students don't declare a major as at most colleges. Instead, they study a variety of subjects in the context of a theme that helps tie them together—for example a comparison of ancient Athens to modern America. The heart of the Evergreen philosophy is that independent thinking requires the ability to look at things from a number of perspectives. I spent my last year focused on writing, but the Evergreen philosophy became part of my way of thinking about things."

After returning to Los Angeles, Rolph took a job as an editorial assistant at *Datamation*, a monthly magazine for computer and management information systems professionals. When *Datamation* moved its offices to New York, Rolph and most of the staff moved, too. There she had her first hard lesson in the business world: losing her job for reasons that had to do with office politics. "It's not really clear why it happened, although I will say that the editor who fired me got rid of everyone who worked with her at one point or another. It was painful, but in the end it was a good experience. I learned to separate my identity from my job, which I

think a lot of people never do. Once I got over the trauma, I became much less fearful and more creative. "

Rolph did what so many others in publishing have done when fired: she began freelancing. She found it to be fun, and relatively lucrative, but she wasn't able to stay busy full time. "I wasn't ready to be in business for myself," she says. "Psychologically, I needed more stimulation, the kind of support you get from colleagues. And from a business perspective, what was missing was sales. I hadn't yet learned to sell myself."

She answered an ad for a writer/editor in the publications group at MITRE Corporation, a government contractor in Bedford, Massachusetts. She worked there for five years, doing a wide variety of projects, from writing the annual report to producing a recruitment videotape. "I learned a tremendous amount at MITRE," she says. "One of the most valuable things was project management, which includes putting together a budget and schedule and sticking to it. This experience is one of the things that sets me apart from my competition. There are plenty of freelance writers out there, but not many people who can handle a project, with all its planning, coordination, and problem solving, from start to finish."

Sarah Rolph continued her education at her next job with a startup software company. "I began as a writer working for

SARAH ROLPH

SARAH ROLPH COMMUNICATIONS

the marketing director, and before long I was involved in every aspect of marketing. Two years later, I was in charge of it all. In addition to writing and producing product literature, I wrote technical documents, managed trade shows, did public relations, and provided sales support." But three years later, Rolph was looking for work again—the startup had failed to meet its revenue targets, investors had grown impatient, and the staff was pared back from thirty to ten people. "Of course it was upsetting, but I have no regrets because I learned so much. It was a challenging, interesting job, and it made me realize I now had the skills to manage my own business. I had learned to sell."

She took an office in a beautiful old converted Victorian home and took on some freelance writing projects while building her marketing communications clientele. "I got in touch with every contact I had from my previous two jobs and soon had a few good-sized clients," Rolph recalls. "One of the most enjoyable aspects of my work is helping a company find the right mix of marketing tools to successfully support its sales efforts. There are so many choices: sales literature, magazine articles, presentations, technical papers, videotapes. I begin by helping them with project management and planning. We analyze how the product is sold, what marketing tools are needed to support the business goals, and who the audience is and what they want to know. I extract all the essential information, for example from management, the sales people, and technical staff. I bounce ideas around with my graphic designer, prepare some written samples, then present the marketing communications plan to the customer's team for reactions and feedback. We make adjustments, then I begin to implement it. What really sets my work apart is all the forethought and planning, my high standards for thoughtful and conscientious work. I strive to understand business needs so that I can help my clients realize the benefits of marketing communications and present effective information about them in written and graphic form. Finally, I try to do all this within the budget I've been given, and on schedule," she notes.

"I'm working now to build up the consulting aspect of my business, so I can spend more time on the thinking and planning that allow clients to create an integrated set of marketing tools to help them be really successful. One thing is clear in this business: you can't stop selling," says Rolph. "My biggest client one year is a nonclient the next—sometimes companies go through hard times or their interests wax and wane, so you always have to have some irons in the fire."

"**Y**ou can't sell what people don't know about" is a truism that emphasizes the importance of marketing promotional strategy, the second element of the marketing mix. Regardless of how outstanding, useful, superior, or needs satisfying a product might be, marketers must inform potential customers of its existence and its merits before they are likely to purchase it. Through a well-developed marketing promotional strategy, consumers can learn about and gain access to the goods and services they need and want.

In this chapter we will explore the buying motives of potential consumers, the role and objectives of promotional strategy, and the roles of the four elements of promotional strategy: personal selling, advertising, publicity, and sales promotion.

Identifying Buying Motives

Those who are involved in marketing promotional strategy must understand why consumers buy the things they do. Have you, for example, ever thought about why you bought a particular good or service? What motivated you to pick one brand or model over the other? Did you make a rational buying decision, or did emotions influence your purchase? If you are like most consumers, your buying motives vary substantially depending on the particular product you buy and the mood you are in at the time you buy it.

Marketers want to know what makes their customers buy a given product, because buying motives form the basis of effective promotional strategies. Final consumers and industrial buyers have different buying motives.

Consumer Buying Motives

Consumer buying motives are *factors that cause someone to purchase a product for personal use.* They reflect the person's needs and wants, attitudes, and self-image. They also reflect a person's experiences and the influences of social groups, culture, and family. People buy things for emotional, rational, or patronage reasons—sometimes for a blend of all three.

EMOTIONAL MOTIVES Consumers are often unaware of the emotional motives that influence their buying decisions, but these are important motives for marketers to appeal to nonetheless. **Emotional motives** are *buying reasons that arise from impulse and psychological needs rather than careful thought and analysis.* Table 13.1 summarizes the most common emotional buying motives for various goods and services. They do overlap, and several of them may act simultaneously on a prospective buyer.

Many products become successful by appealing to one or more emotional buying motives. Many people purchase designer jeans out of a desire to express themselves and seek social approval by being fashionable. Teenagers are bombarded with buying messages for the "right" clothes and the "right" shoes—direct appeals for prestige and social approval from peer groups. Ads for vacations and romantic getaways play directly to people's needs for fun and excitement.

Consumers sometimes buy products because the products appeal to their self-image—the kind of person they believe or wish themselves to be. In turn, marketers work hard to ap-

consumer buying motives
Factors that cause someone to purchase a product for personal use.

emotional motives
Buying reasons that arise from impulse and psychological needs rather than careful thought and analysis.

Table 13.1
Emotional buying motives and products or services that appeal to these motives.

EMOTIONAL BUYING MOTIVE	GOODS OR SERVICES
Fear and safety	Smoke and burglar alarms Fire extinguishers Insurance
Love and social approval	Grooming aids Flowers Singing telegrams
Fun and excitement	Vacation tours Rock concerts Sporting goods Sports cars
Pride and prestige	Luxury cars Jewelry Maid service
Self-expression	Guitar lessons Personalized license plates Do-it-yourself books

RATIONAL BUYING MOTIVE	GOODS OR SERVICES
Economy and cost	Home freezers
	Day-old baked goods
	Extended warranties on cars and appliances
Quality and dependability	Top-quality watches
	Lifetime automobile batteries
Convenience	Fast-food restaurants
	Dry cleaning
	Dishwashers
	Remote-control television sets

Table 13.2
Rational buying motives and products or services that appeal to these motives.

rational motives
Buying reasons that arise from careful planning and analysis of information.

patronage motives
Buying reasons based on the characteristics of a specific retail outlet or brand of product.

peal to the buyer's self-image by sending convincing messages. Air Jordan basketball shoes, Levi's 501 Jeans, and Absolut Vodka are promoted through highly focused appeals to self-image. While emotional buying behavior is not necessarily logical, it is extremely important for marketers to take into account.

RATIONAL MOTIVES Although the distinction between emotional and rational buying motives may not always be clear in a consumer's mind, rational motives are easier for buyers to justify: they make good sense and do not lead to guilt. **Rational motives** are *buying reasons that arise from careful planning and analysis of information.* They are based on facts and logic. Consumers who carefully shop and compare prices on tires, clothes, and televisions are responding to rational motives in making their final decision. The person who decides to pay a little more for the top-of-the-line paint because it will last seven years rather than three years is buying because of quality and dependability. Homeowners who install automatic lawn sprinkler systems want the assurance that their lawns will be watered regularly whether they are at home or away. Ads that illustrate how much a simple investment of $2,000 will be worth in ten years are trying to provide a logical reason for choosing this alternative rather than spending the money on a car or a vacation.

Examples of rational buying motives are summarized in Table 13.2. Although it sounds easy, few consumers purchase goods for purely rational reasons.

PATRONAGE MOTIVES Another classification of motives, **patronage motives**, are *buying reasons based on the characteristics of a specific retail outlet or brand of product.* Once we have made a decision to buy a product, patronage motives may surface. Some of us are loyal to a particular brand or a specific store because of past satisfactions. Patronage motives make a given brand a specialty good to some buyers. Table 13.3 lists several reasons that have been given for regularly patronizing a firm. Do some of these factors cause you to buy repeatedly from the same retailer? Ads like "You're in good hands with All State," or those for Pennzoil and Quaker State motor oil, appeal directly to patronage motives.

Industrial Buying Motives

Industrial buying motives are *factors that cause an industrial buyer to recognize a need or want and to make a purchase that satisfies it.* They reflect the particular needs of the business and industry of the buyer. They are also a product of the development of a specific set of criteria for purchasing the products. Even though the industrial buyer makes the decision, the criteria have already been established by the purchasing system. Business purchasers primarily buy for rational reasons—the best price, the best quality, the best service, or a combination of these criteria as identified in Table 13.4.

In addition to the rational motives, some firms engage in **reciprocal buying**, *a practice in which two or more companies become mutual customers, buying each other's goods and services.* An auto repair shop, for example, may buy all of its parts from one auto parts store; the store, in turn, has its delivery fleet tuned up and repaired at the repair shop. Mutual sales mean mutual profits.

Finally, despite the fact that industrial buyers purchase for their companies (instead of themselves) and spend their firms' money (instead of their own), marketers of industrial goods should realize that emotion can be and is often an industrial buying motive. For example, an administrative assistant respon-

PATRONAGE MOTIVES
Convenient location
Pleasant salespeople
Positive public image or reputation
Cleanliness
Customer services (delivery, gift wrapping, advice on product installation and use)
Prices (high for status appeal, competitive or low to appeal to economy motives)
Variety of merchandise
An atmosphere of goodwill

Table 13.3
Patronage motives that cause customers to shop regularly at a particular store.

industrial buying motives
Factors that cause an industrial buyer to recognize a need or want and to make a purchase that satisfies it.

reciprocal buying
A practice in which two or more companies become mutual customers, buying each other's goods and services.

BUYING MOTIVE	RATIONALE
Profit	Long-range profitability is the goal of businesses. Most promotional efforts for industrial goods ultimately appeal to this motive.
Price	Price is related to performance and efficiency. Industrial buyers often look beyond actual dollars for a product's impact on long-range operations.
Quality	Quality is a critical factor in industrial buying decisions—but often it is reconciled with price. Firms do not want to pay for more quality than they need.
Salability	Components and ingredients that make an end product more appealing to customers influence industrial buyers. A product that will make another product—paint on a new Corvette—look more attractive, perform better, or take on a unique characteristic can influence a buyer's decision and can be appealed to.
Service	Industrial buyers need assurance that effective service will be provided for vital equipment. The concern for service may offset a higher price.

Table 13.4
Rational industrial buying motives.

sible for company printing purchases places all the orders with a printer who is her husband's best friend. In another instance a person continues to use the same vendor to design advertising brochures because the person dreads doing comparison shopping and feels comfortable with the current vendor—even though the price is higher and it takes longer for a job to get done.

Once the buying motives of the potential target markets, industrial or consumer, have been identified, the next step for the marketing manager is to design a promotional strategy to appeal to these buying motives.

Promotional Strategy: Role and Objectives

Promotional strategy is the second element of the marketing mix. It is the communication ingredient in the marketing mix for reaching specific target markets. Communication to the target market is achieved through the development of a **promotional mix**—*the correct blending of personal selling, advertising, publicity, and sales promotion.*

The role of promotional strategy is to inform, persuade, and remind people about the firm's goods, services, and image. By using the special strengths of each element of the promotion mix, a marketing manager can focus the communication messages from four different angles to influence a prospective buyer's decision. Table 13.5 illustrates the role of promotional strategy in the marketing mix.

Developing the proper promotional mix for effective communication requires the marketing manager to understand the **communication process**—*the method by which promotional messages travel to reach the consumer.* Figure 13.1 diagrams the communication process. Let's examine each element:

- The *sender* is the company (or person representing the company) that presents a message to the target market. The sender may be a company employee, a celebrity, a paid actor, or a customer.
- *Encoding* is the process of translating an idea into a message. During this time a decision is made on what the message will be: price, quality, pride, love, or whatever.
- The *message* is developing the actual combination of words and symbols to be directed at the target market.
- The *medium* is either the personal or nonpersonal means of sending the message. One personal medium is a salesperson. Nonpersonal media include television, radio, billboards, and coupons.
- *Decoding* is the process of interpreting the message by the target market. The sender's message is influenced by a person's experience, culture, and family.

promotional mix
The correct blending of personal selling, advertising, publicity, and sales promotion.

communication process
The method by which promotional messages travel to reach the consumer.

Table 13.5
The role of promotional strategy in the promotional mix.

FUNCTIONS OF PROMOTIONAL STRATEGY

Create awareness of new products and services

Provide information about the benefits and features of products and services

Influence customers to try products and services

Distinguish a company and its products and services from competitors

Call for action to close a sale

Increase the amount and frequency of use of a good or service

Notify consumers of sales, specials, and price increases

Build a company image

Communicate to retail and wholesale channel members in order to develop loyalty and enthusiasm

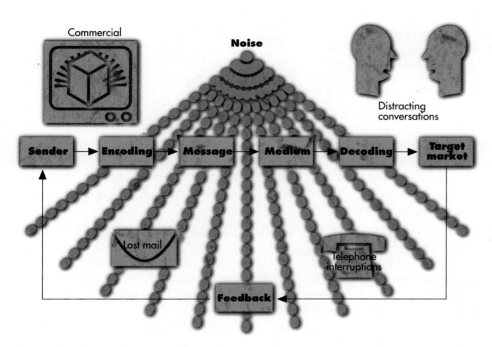

Figure 13.1
The communication process.

- The *target market* is the focus point for the sender's message. It is either the industrial or the individual consumer.
- *Feedback* is the target market's actions as a result of the message. It may be a decision to purchase or not purchase or simply a new way of looking at the product or service.
- *Noise* is any possible interference with the communication process. It can occur at any time in the process. Examples include conversations during broadcasts, lost mail, and interruptions during sales presentations.

In Figure 13.1 we can see all the elements of the communications process—including noise—in action.

Here is an example of how marketers use the communication process. NordicTrack, a rapidly growing developer and marketer of exercise equipment and accessories, has decided to aggressively promote its new line, NordicTrack Gold—a complete body conditioning system—to buyers of NordicTrack's other exercise equipment, the target market. As the sender, NordicTrack encodes its ideas and develops the specific message—traditional quality, complete workout, convenience. As an aggressive marketer, NordicTrack chooses to use television commercials, direct mail, and 800-number telemarketing. If, and only if, the target customer is listening to the television when the commercial is aired—and is not at the refrigerator or distracted by other conversations—or receives the direct-mail package, or is not interrupted during the telephone presentation, will the promotional message have a

Figure 13.2
Tuning out ads.

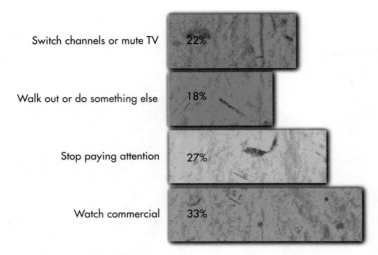

Switch channels or mute TV — 22%

Walk out or do something else — 18%

Stop paying attention — 27%

Watch commercial — 33%

Source: *USA Today*, June 15, 1993, p. 18. Copyright 1993, USA Today. Used with permission.

chance of being attended to. Overcoming noise is a very real problem to a marketer. Figure 13.2 presents the various tactics TV viewers use to tune out ads. Which is your favorite?

Having discussed the communication challenge facing marketers, now let's examine each element of the promotional mix, beginning with personal selling.

The Promotional Mix: Personal Selling

The first element of the promotional mix that can be used to communicate to a target market is personal selling. **Personal selling** is *a personal attempt to persuade prospective customers to buy a given good or service.* This technique is essential when marketing many kinds of shopping goods, and it plays an especially significant role in the marketing of industrial goods.

personal selling
A personal attempt to persuade prospective customers to buy a given good or service.

The Value of Personal Selling

Personal selling provides the company with the opportunity to:

- Focus closely on a specific target market
- Give customers individual attention
- Identify a customer's problem and design specific solutions for it
- Adapt a message to the unique needs of a customer
- Receive immediate feedback on the promotional message
- Provide the opportunity to close the sale
- Build a long-term relationship with a customer[1]

When used correctly—for the right product and the right target market—personal selling is a powerful promotional tool. Companies like Du Pont, Home Depot, Toyota, Wal-Mart, and Nordstrom, in industries ranging from pharmaceuticals to financial services, are fine-tuning their personal selling efforts. Those companies that are leading the way in personal selling strategy are featured in Table 13.6.

The Selling Process

As you can see in Table 13.6, although there are many types of salespeople who have varied responsibilities and sales settings, salespeople share one thing in common: the **selling process**. This is *a series of seven steps that salespeople*

selling process
A series of seven steps that salespeople follow when persuading prospective customers to make purchases.

Table 13.6
Leaders in personal selling.

COMPANY	WINNING SALES STRATEGIES
Du Pont	Pioneered team selling 10 years ago: Groups of sales reps, technicians, and factory managers work together to solve customer problems, create and sell new products.
Merck	Tops in turning salespeople into experts. Merck trains its reps over 12 months in pharmaceuticals and trust-building sales techniques. Continuing refresher courses are mandatory.
Reynolds Metals	A model of perseverance and innovation. Spent 25 years cultivating Campbell Soup before winning an aluminum-can contract. Has developed team selling to educate customers such as auto makers on new uses for aluminum.
Wal-Mart Stores	Built customer confidence by selling the basics: everyday low pricing, items always in stock, cashiers always available. Demanded simplified selling from vendors such as Procter & Gamble in the form of data linkups and coordinated inventory management.
Nordstrom	Proving that department stores need not die. Intense, personalized attention to the customer pays off in high shopper loyalty and steady growth.
Home Depot	The boss as salesman-in-chief. Founder Bernard Marcus preaches smart selling and follows up with endless training.
Dell Computer	How to sell a complicated product by phone and mail. The secret: Advanced technology to keep track of the customer and intense training.
Toyota Motor	Lexus luxury line uses customer satisfaction as a key measure for setting dealer compensation, turning Lexus showrooms into the new standard for U.S. auto dealerships.
General Electric	Revamping selling on many fronts: It's training salespeople to work long-term with customers, experimenting with team-based compensation, assigning staff full-time to customers' factories, and forging deep relationships with its own suppliers.
Vanguard Group	A mutual-funds marketer that has perfected the low-key sell. Uses reliable customer service, easy-to-understand products, and super-low fees to lure investors who don't like the hard sell of brokers looking to earn hefty commissions.

Source: *Business Week*, August 3, 1992, p. 48. Copyright © 1992 by McGraw-Hill, Inc. Used with permission.

Figure 13.3
Steps in the selling process.

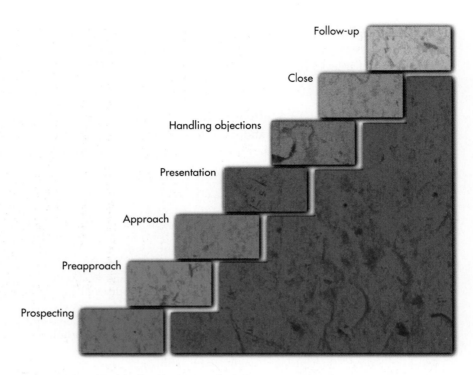

follow when persuading prospective customers to make purchases. Figure 13.3 diagrams this sequence of steps.

prospecting
The step in the selling process that identifies potential customers for a product.

Prospecting is *the step in the selling process that identifies potential customers for a product.* Although it is rarely done by retail salespeople (customers usually come to them), prospecting is essential when selling most industrial products or when selling to middlemen. Companies such as EDS and Travelers Insurance, for example, seldom wait for potential customers to make the first move. Instead, their sales "reps" spend their time seeking out potential buyers.

Salespeople may get prospects from several sources: referrals from existing customers, replies to direct-mail and other promotional messages, impromptu cold-canvassing calls, or the salesperson's own ingenuity. When prospecting, salespeople must also confirm that a potential buyer is qualified (i.e., can afford the product, has the authority to buy it, and genuinely wants or needs it). Qualifying the customer increases the likelihood that a sale will be made.

preapproach
The second step in the selling process, in which the salesperson researches the qualified prospect's background.

Preapproach is *the second step in the selling process, in which the salesperson researches the qualified prospect's background.* By reviewing census data, contacts in the industry, and company records, the salesperson attempts to put together a personal profile of the prospect. The more useful information that is gathered, the more focused will be the sales presentation.

approach
The third step in the selling process; the salesperson makes actual contact with the prospect and prepares to deliver a sales presentation.

The **approach** is *the third step in the selling process; the salesperson makes actual contact with the prospect and prepares to deliver a sales presentation.* A creative, planned approach, using information gathered in the preapproach,

Personal selling allows businesses a chance to solve customers' problems and build a long-term relationship.

helps the salesperson achieve rapport with and gain a more positive reception from the prospect. Each approach is tailored to the individual and the circumstances: no two are identical.

Next comes the **presentation**, *the fourth step in the selling process, in which the salesperson shows how the prospect can benefit by owning the product.* The salesperson must explain how the product will satisfy the prospect's wants or needs.

Some creative dramatization, including a demonstration and audiovisual appeals (charts, videos, or comparative tables), can turn a mediocre presentation into a lively, exciting experience for both parties.

Objections, a basic part of the selling process, are *a potential customer's verbal or silent forms of resistance to the salesperson's message.* They must be overcome before the prospect will buy. Effective salespeople anticipate most objections and address them, stating counteracting benefits early in the presentation. Typical customer objections concern price, product characteristics, company service, or the salesperson as an individual.

A sale does not actually occur until the **close**, which is *the point in the selling process when the prospect agrees to buy.* Closing, which is the true measure of a salesperson's ability, is often considered one of the most challenging parts of selling. Some salespeople have difficulty closing because they fear rejection, misunderstand the prospect's needs or wants, appeal to the wrong buying motives, or mishandle one of the other steps.

For most professional salespeople, repeat business is the key to long-term profits, and repeat business comes from satisfied customers who feel strong patronage motives. Consequently, we see the importance of **follow-up**, *the final step in the selling process; it builds and maintains customer loyalty and goodwill.* In the process, the salesperson confirms that the buyer has received

presentation
The fourth step in the selling process, in which the salesperson shows how the prospect can benefit by owning the product.

objections
A potential customer's verbal or silent forms of resistance to the salesperson's message.

close
The point in the selling process when the prospect agrees to buy.

follow-up
The final step in the selling process; it builds and maintains customer loyalty and goodwill.

everything that was originally promised and clearly understands the benefits of owning the product.

The Promotional Mix: Advertising

The second element of the promotional mix is advertising. **Advertising** is *any nonpersonal message paid for by an identifiable sponsor to promote goods, services, or ideas.* It is an important part of many companies' promotional mix.

Why Advertise?

Effective advertising, placed where it reaches members of the right target market, is intended to increase the likelihood that consumers will buy the good or service. Specifically, advertising is used to inform, persuade, and remind the target market about the goods or services. Advertisements can build customer awareness of products and provide information on use, quality, and performance. In addition, advertisements help create demand for products by answering prospects' questions and objections to buying. Advertising also can remind customers about a company and its products between salespersons' visits.

Companies obviously see the value of advertising based on their decisions to spend money on it. Even in hard economic times, companies like Philip Morris ($2.1 billion ad budget), Procter & Gamble ($1.8 billion), PepsiCo ($790 million), and McDonald's ($780 million) continue to believe in the promotional benefits of advertising.[2]

Types of Advertising

Companies use two types of advertising: product and institutional. Each has its own unique characteristics and objectives.

Product advertising is *advertising intended to promote demand for a good or service,* such as ads for Coca-Cola or Oscar Mayer hot dogs. Product advertising can be directed at informing, persuading, or reminding the target market. If marketing research determines, for example, that the market segment is not aware of the new services a bank is providing, advertisements will be created to provide the information. In other instances, consumers may need to be persuaded about the benefits of the good or service either by focusing strictly on these benefits or by comparing the product with a competitor's. Finally, reminder advertising may be called for, especially in the maturity stage of the product life cycle, to keep the product before the public. Figure 13.4 illustrates product advertising. What is the message?

Institutional advertising is *advertising done to enhance a company's public image rather than to sell a product.* It has the long-term objectives of goodwill and image creation. Stressing such themes as equal employment opportunity for women, environmental protection, energy conservation, and public issues such as competition, institutional advertising highlights a company's efforts

MANAGER'S NOTEBOOK

James Dean and Marilyn Monroe cashed in their chips years ago, but they are just beginning to cash in on their marketing potential. Along with the Marx Brothers and Malcolm X, they are among the hottest of the dead personalities making major endorsement deals.

These deceased celebrities, and many others, are being brought back to life by marketers looking for famous faces to hawk their goods and services. Here are some examples:

- Buddy Holly is the pitchman for Maxell tapes, and the singer will soon get his very own lottery ticket. Introduction of the new Iowa State Lottery game, "It's So Easy," will be supported by an ad campaign featuring Holly.
- General Mills is tapping into baseball legends Lou Gehrig and Babe Ruth with two Wheaties collector's boxes featuring the two personalities.
- Marilyn Monroe ads for the Alaska Visitor's Association feature a photo of the actress without her famous beauty mark. The caption reads, "The picture may have changed, but her beauty hasn't. The same is true of Alaska."
- Images of James Dean have been used to sell everything from Champion sparkplugs ("something the rebel was never without") to Converse sneakers. In Japan, Levi's gives Dean the starring role

in its marketing campaign. Levi's decided to go with Dean because of the high awareness among young consumers that associate Levi's with him.

The major reasons for this trend include instant recognition and the public's fascination with the rich and famous. "We are not dealing with dead celebrities. We're dealing with Hollywood legends," states Roger Richman, whose Beverly Hills agency represents the heirs of a slew of famous faces, including Albert Einstein, W. C. Fields, the Marx Brothers, and Marilyn Monroe.

In addition to the fame, the dead stars are popular because morality problems won't arise—everyone already knows everything there is to know about W. C. Fields, Marilyn Monroe, and Steve McQueen. The marketer is not going to suffer huge embarrassment or have to close down a commercial because of a spokesperson's current behavior, as Pepsi had to do with Michael Jackson, for example.

(For more on marketing of Hollywood's legends, see Cyndee Miller, "Some Celebs Just Now Reaching Their Potential— And They're Dead," *Marketing News,* March 29, 1993, pp. 2, 22.)

Advertising Is Alive with Hollywood's Legends

**Figure 13.4
Product
advertising.**

toward becoming a responsible, concerned citizen. Figure 13.5 is an example of an institutional ad.

Once the type of advertising is decided on, the best method or medium to convey the message needs to be selected.

Where to Place an Ad: Advertising Media

Advertising media are *the nonpersonal means of sending a promotional message to a target market.* Marketers have a number of media options to select from, including newspapers, magazines, television, radio, direct mail, and outdoor. In deciding which option is best, marketers must consider such factors as target audience behavior, cost, lead time, and the company's overall promotional budget. Let's examine each option.

NEWSPAPERS   The most popular advertising medium in the United States, especially for retailers, is newspapers. The amount spent on newspapers is about 26 percent of the total advertising dollar.

On the plus side, newspapers provide local or concentrated market coverage. Advertising dollars are not wasted on reaching people who are outside the company's market area. Cost is relatively low—based on overall readers. Finally, lead time is minimal—advertisements can be prepared or changed quickly.

The primary downside of newspapers is that marketers cannot target specific markets—the audience is general. In addition, there is heavy ad competition—not only within the newspaper but on television and radio. Finally, color reproduction is often poor and creativity is limited.

MAGAZINES   If carefully selected, magazines can reach specific target markets. There are magazines for jogging, home improvement, fashion, investment, and any other topic you can think of. Magazines provide high-quality reproduction and high-quality color options, have a longer life span than newspapers, and if they are targeted well can actually have a lower cost per reader.

For all their positives, magazines require a long lead time—thus are less flexible. In addition, they have limited frequency of publication.

TELEVISION Television ranks second to newspapers in share of advertising dollars spent—23 percent—and is used primarily by national manufacturers and large retailers. Television reaches a large audience at a low cost per viewer, and it provides a wide variety of options for creativity.

The major disadvantages of television include the long lead time required to prepare commercials and the high minimum total cost to reach a market that can simply switch a channel and never see or hear the message. Finally, television commercials have a very short life span—15, 30, or 60 seconds. If the commercial is missed, it may be gone forever.

RADIO Like magazines, radio offers selectivity; radio stations have specific programming to appeal to specific audiences—news, country western, rock, oldies, classical. Radio advertising offers a low cost per listener and is flexible—messages can be changed.

Figure 13.5
Institutional
advertising.

Radio does have some drawbacks. Primarily, it has no visual impact, and commercials are subject to station switching.

DIRECT MAIL How well direct mail—promotional material mailed to consumers directly from advertisers—is used determines whether it is effective in reaching its target market. Direct mail is the most selective medium, if the mailing list and the promotional material are of high quality. The potential, as well as the results, is so attractive that 18 percent of all advertising dollars are invested in direct mail.

Unfortunately for advertisers, the majority of direct-mail advertising has low credibility with consumers and suffers from a high throwaway rate.

OUTDOOR Outdoor advertising consists of billboards, posters, bus signs, taxi signs, and skywriting. By nature it is fairly inexpensive, is flexible, and can be developed quickly, but it is limited to a few words to allow time for the consumer to absorb the message.

Each of the media has its strengths and limitations. In turn, the choice made by the marketer is critical. Table 13.7 provides a comparison of the media options.

MEDIUM	MARKET COVERAGE	BEST USES	ADVANTAGES	DISADVANTAGES
Newspaper	Entire metropolitan area; local editions sometimes used	Large retailers	Short lead time, concentrated market, flexible, pass-alongs, surrounded by content	General audience, heavy ad competition, limited color, limited creativity
Magazines	National (most with regional editions) or local	National manufacturers, mail order firms, local service retailers	Color, creative options, affluent audience, permanence of message, pass-alongs, flexible, surrounded by content	Long lead time, ad clutter, geographically dispersed audience
Television	National or regional	Regional manufacturers and large retailers, national manufacturers and largest retailers	Reach, low cost per viewer, persuasive impact, creative options, flexible, surrounded by programs	High minimum total costs, general audience, long lead time, short message, limited availability
Radio	Entire metropolitan area	Local or regional retailers	Low costs, selective market, high frequency, immediacy of messages, surrounded by content	No visual impact, commercial clutter, station switching, consumer distractions
Outdoor	Entire metropolitan area or one location	Brand-name products, nearby retailers, reminder ads	Large size, color, creative options, frequency, no clutter of competing messages, permanence of message	Legal restrictions, consumer distractions, general audience, inflexible

Source: Adapted from *Essentials of Marketing*, 4th edition, by Joel R. Evans and Barry Berman. Copyright 1990 by Macmillan Publishing Company.

Table 13.7

A comparison of advertising media.

Truth in Advertising

Through the years, many marketers have abused advertising's power and consumers' gullibility to sell products that have not been all they claim to be. Consider, for example, the outrageous claims in the early advertisement shown in Figure 13.6. As newspaper and magazine circulation increased and radio coverage spanned the nation, deceptive advertising naturally increased, as did consumer distrust.

The level of trust has not improved. Recent survey data reveal that:

- more than 50 percent of consumers distrust most promotional claims
- only 2 percent of U.S. consumers believe the accuracy of nutritional claims on package labels
- 25 percent of consumers believe marketers are abusive about the health benefits of their product
- 70 percent of consumers do not trust marketers' environmental claims[3]

Not only has the level of distrust remained high, but the volume of claims filed with the Federal Trade Commission (FTC), the government agency charged with handling false or misleading advertising claims, has risen consistently in recent years. The FTC has the power to issue cease-and-desist orders as well as require a company to run corrective advertising if the original message gave consumers a lasting and grossly incorrect impression of the product's capabilities. To comply with FTC guidelines, advertisers must have proof of claims in hand when the ad is disseminated. Instances of companies that have not followed these guidelines—and that the FTC has received decrees on—include:

- Campbell Soup, on its chicken soup helping to prevent heart disease
- Perrier, on its water being natural
- Kraft, on its single cheese slices containing calcium of five ounces or more.[4]

Another area where marketers have crossed the lines of legality and deceptive advertising is the imitation of voices of well-known personalities in advertisements. Claims arising from these cases, dubbed sound-alike claims, arise when a celebrity's voice or singing style has been imitated or copied without his or her permission. One highly publicized sound-alike claim involved Bette Midler and the Ford Motor Co. After Midler declined to participate in the commercials by singing a song she had popularized, "Do You Want To Dance," Ford hired another singer and instructed her to sound as much like Midler as possible. The singer's rendition was so good that a number of people thought they were actually listening to Bette Midler. Midler sued and was awarded $400,000 in damages.[5]

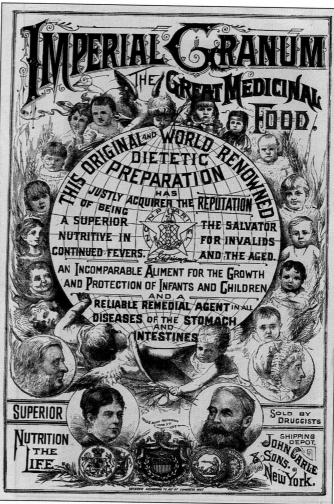

Figure 13.6

Deceptive advertising at its most obvious.

The Promotional Mix: Publicity

The third element of the promotional mix is publicity. **Publicity** is *nonpaid, nonpersonal communication to promote the goods, services, or image of a company.*

publicity
Nonpaid, nonpersonal communication to promote the goods, services, or image of a company.

GLOBAL PERSPECTIVE

Harleys: Rumbling Around the Globe

How do you say "Angel Mama" in Japanese or German? Harley-Davidson's aggressive promotional program has the Harley mystique spreading around the globe. In Japan's countryside, across the Australian outback, on roads winding through Germany's Black Forest, and on Mexico City's crowded streets, scores of riders are discovering the thrill of hopping on a Harley. Bike sales abroad are expected to hit $285 million this year, or 24 percent of the company's $1.2 billion total, up from $115 million and 14 percent of sales in 1989.

Harley's global marketing requires it to customize its U.S. promotional package for other cultures. For Harley that means creating HOGs (clubs) overseas so customers can exchange tips and biker talk. It means publishing Harley magazines in various languages and staging beer-and-band rallies. But it also means changing ads and tweaking its tried-and-true methods of building customer loyalty.

For example, until recently corporate headquarters had insisted that the Japanese divisions use the American print ad campaign. But the desolate scenes and the tag line "One steady constant in an increasingly screwed-up world" didn't win over Japanese riders.

The campaign had to be modified—and it was. Japanese images replaced American ones: American riders passing a geisha in a rickshaw, Japanese ponies nibbling at a Harley motorcycle. The campaign's effect on sales has been gratifying—waiting lists for Harleys in Japan are as long as six months.

Harley has also had to modify its promotional program in Europe. Biker rallies are less widespread in Europe than in the United States—and the customs are different. To overcome the first limitation, Harley encouraged dealers to host open houses and lectures. Different customs required Harley to extend the hours of its first rally in southeastern France, where people tend to keep later hours than in the United States. Harley supplied beer and rock 'n' roll until midnight, then turned off the lights. For the French, the evening had just begun. The Harley rep had to reopen the bar and persuade the band to keep playing until 4 A.M.

(For more on Harley-Davidson's global marketing, see Kevin Kelly, "The Rumble Heard Round the World: Harleys," *Business Week*, May 24, 1993, pp. 58–60.)

It is an important element of the promotion mix that can be overlooked because of its nature.

The Nature of Publicity

Publicity for the goods, services, or image of the company is an ongoing goal for marketing managers, but gauging its success is often difficult. For example, how can you measure the impact of a popular radio talk show host who

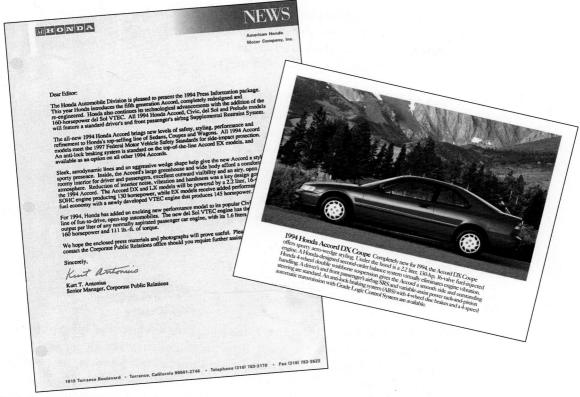

declares that "Henri's has the best, I mean the best, combination of food, service, and environment I have ever experienced," or of a well-known newspaper columnist who reveals that "Hair E Natural is *the* place to have your styling done"? Publicity has a few unique advantages:

- *Timeliness.* Publicity can be tied to real-time news coverage. Thanks to satellite technology, such events as grand openings and press conferences can be broadcast live.
- *Adaptability.* Publicity can work in concert with advertising, personal selling, or sales promotion.
- *Credibility.* A unique feature of publicity is "third-person endorsement," or the "halo effect." When a reporter talks about a product, there is an implied endorsement. Wouldn't you believe a movie reviewer rather than the claims of a movie advertisement?
- *Cost efficiency.* The cost of publicity is minimal when compared to advertising.
- *Mobility.* Publicity can be gained anywhere a marketer's imagination will go—locally or nationally.[6]

Publicity is given to a company by independent media. The media—television, radio, newspapers, or magazines—are independent because public-

> Press releases with accompanying photos are a standard means of publicizing new products and company activities.

ity is nonpaid. To take advantage of the opportunity for publicity, companies have to prepare newsworthy items and send them to the media, provide the opportunity for members of the media to observe the event, hold news conferences, and maintain personal or telephone contacts.

Types of Publicity

Various means of gaining publicity are available to a company, including:

- News publicity dealing with events of local, regional, or national importance
- Business feature articles—stories about the company or its products—that are given to the business media
- Financial releases directed toward business magazines and financial writers for newspapers

The Two Faces of Publicity

Publicity has two faces: positive and negative. A company must work hard to achieve positive publicity. Negative publicity just happens.

POSITIVE PUBLICITY Firms provide an ongoing stream of positive publicity: information about new products, major accomplishments, or other, similar stories. Frieda Caplan, of Frieda's Finest in Los Angeles, is an excellent example of someone who knows how to get publicity and use it. Frieda is always available for interviews, has been the subject of numerous magazine articles by a variety of publications (*Savvy, Ladies Home Journal, Inc., Los Angeles Times*), and has appeared on David Letterman's late night talkshow displaying one of her exotic fruits. Frieda Caplan really works to get publicity. Other successful examples are:

- *The California Raisins.* Although the dancing California Raisins' television commercials were extremely effective, the Raisin Board went even further with an extensive publicity effort. With the objective of sparking repeat sales and keeping old relationships alive, the publicity effort incorporated a fan club that required multiple purchases and brought the famous dancing raisins to the stores for cameo appearances with shoppers.
- *Fig Newtons.* Recently, the Fig Newton celebrated its 100th anniversary with a grand barbecue and a special performance by singer Juice Newton. The birthday party provided a national spotlight for Fig Newton and was covered by *Newsweek*, CNN, and David Letterman.[7]

NEGATIVE PUBLICITY Other firms have been the victims of negative publicity. The outcome, at the least, is loss of credibility and, at the worst, is loss of sales. Companies that have felt the backlash of negative publicity include:

- *Jack in the Box.* The tragedy began with a $2.69 "Kids Meal" bought for a two-year-old in Tacoma, Washington. Within ten days the boy died of kidney and heart failure. Over 300 other patrons of Jack in the Box got sick from the same *E. coli* bacteria that had contaminated the child's hamburger. Although the company immediately scrapped 20,000 pounds of hamburger patties prepared at plants where the bacteria were suspected to have originated, nervous customers defected to other hamburger spots. A once-crowded Jack in the Box on Wilshire Boulevard in the Los Angeles business district became practically deserted, and sales at most Jack in the Box restaurants went down more than 20 percent.[8]
- *General Motors.* An Atlanta, Georgia jury ruled that General Motors Corp. owed $4.24 million to the family of a teenager killed when his pickup truck erupted into flames after a drunk driver broadsided it. With that decision, GM began another trial—in the court of public opinion. In the years before the decision, GM had sold nearly 600,000 full-sized pickup trucks at a profit of $4,000 to $5,000 apiece. The image of the company is now at stake, and sales have been affected.[9]

The Promotional Mix: Sales Promotion

The fourth element of the promotional mix is sales promotion. The American Marketing Association defines **sales promotion** as *"those paid marketing activities, other than personal selling and advertising."*[10] This definition encompasses a host of devices—coupons, samples, trade shows—some geared toward middlemen, others toward final consumers.

sales promotion Those paid marketing activities other than personal selling and advertising.

Sales promotion supports the other three elements in the marketing mix. When focused on the final consumer, it assists in (1) increasing brand awareness, (2) developing impulse sales, (3) initiating a trend of a new product or service, and (4) encouraging repurchase of goods. When directed at middlemen, it aids in encouraging distribution, obtaining shelf space in stores, developing middleman cooperation, and increasing sales.

Promoting to Final Consumers

Both manufacturers and retailers use sales promotion devices to appeal to final consumers' buying motives.

COUPONS One common way to bring potential consumers and products together is by placing money-saving coupons outside or inside a product package. Cents-off coupons are also printed in magazines and newspapers, mailed directly to consumers' homes, and distributed at retail store counters. Processed foods, fast foods, consumer cleaning products, and patent medicines are examples of consumer products that have been promoted this way. Producers hope that coupon offers will generate enough new sales volume to offset the lower coupon price.

Technology has added another dimension to coupons. To help encourage

Figure 13.7

An example of a promotional coupon.

customers to switch from another cookie brand to, say, Nabisco's Chips Ahoy, a computer system spits out a discount coupon for Chips Ahoy each time a checkout scanner reads the barcode for a rival brand.[11] Figure 13.7 provides an example of a cents-off coupon.

SAMPLES Some firms place products in consumers' hands by giving away samples. This form of promotion was used for General Mills's Cluster cereal, for Delicare cold-water wash for fine washables, and for Lever Brothers's Snuggle fabric softener. It acquaints consumers with the product in the hope of making them more likely to buy the regular size when they use up the free amount. Manufacturers of products that are used in or with certain appliances or other durable goods may arrange to distribute their product free with each of the larger items sold—a box of Bounce fabric softener comes free in every Frigidaire clothes dryer, for example. At the grocery store shoppers can "eat" their way through a shopping trip. On many days the consumer can begin the "tour" with samples of cheese, pizza, or nacho appetizers, graduate to grilled chicken or ham slices accompanied by sample breads, rolls, or crackers, wash it all down with a new soft drink or fruit drink, and have dessert—ice cream, yogurt, or cookies. When accompanied by a coupon—which the consumer ideally should use immediately—the promotion is successful.

premium
Something of value given free or at a nominal charge as an incentive to buy a product.

PREMIUMS Another appeal to final customers, a **premium**, is *something of value given free or at a nominal charge as an incentive to buy a product.* Premiums have special appeal to children, who in turn influence adults to buy the product. Magazines like *Sports Illustrated* offer free sports videos and novelty items with any purchase of a subscription. Oscar de la Renta provides a premium gift package of women's toiletries with any purchase of $35 or more. But the classic example of a premium is the prize that comes in every Crackerjacks box.

SPECIAL SERVICES Some merchants appeal to patronage motives by offering consumers special services. A hardware and garden supply store, for example, may hold free classes in ornamental horticulture or lend fertilizer spreaders

One of the best-known contests used to promote a company's products is the annual Pillsbury Bake-Off.

without charge. Some paint and wallpaper stores hold free classes in paper-hanging. Banks offer such services as free travelers' checks and money orders to depositors, and department stores sometimes hold such events as makeup or hair-styling shows.

CONTESTS AND SWEEPSTAKES Contests, another popular method of promoting products, require entrants to compete for prizes by doing such things as naming a new product, writing a slogan containing the firm's or the product's name, completing a poem or limerick, or even baking a cake. Reader's Digest, Coca-Cola, and many chain supermarkets have run contests to increase product use and buyer loyalty. The home-shopping QVC Network gave viewers a chance to win a $10,000 shopping spree on Rodeo Drive in Beverly Hills. As an added bonus, the winner got to hobnob with comedienne Joan Rivers.[12]

Sweepstakes entrants submit their names on forms that are entered in a drawing to determine the winners. Prizes vary from exotic vacations to Walkman radios. A three-month sweepstakes sponsored by Cruise Line International Association attracted 130,000 entries for 112 free cruises.[13]

TRADING STAMPS Once a popular promotional device that built patronage for gas stations, supermarkets, and other retail outlets, trading stamps have been eliminated by most stores in an effort to control escalating prices.

YOU DECIDE

Think of the last time you were in a supermarket. Were there any food products—soft drinks, sausage, cheese and crackers—being sampled? Did you use any coupons? Was the store having a contest? How effective do you believe such promotional techniques are?

There are, however, a few holdouts—primarily supermarkets—that continue to use stamps as promotional attractions. Retailers give trading stamps to customers according to how much merchandise they have purchased. The stamps are collected in books and can be redeemed for merchandise exhibited through a catalog or in a showroom.

REBATE OR REFUND OFFERS Money refund offers have been used to encourage sales of Purina dog food, Kraft food products, and even (through factory rebates) new automobiles. With this device, the producer returns part of the purchase price to customers who submit a proof of purchase.

Promoting to Middlemen

Manufacturers use several sales promotion devices to influence the sales activities of wholesalers and retailers—firms that help to move products from producers to consumers.

point-of-purchase displays
Promotional devices that are placed where sales transactions occur.

POINT-OF-PURCHASE DISPLAYS Many manufacturers promote their products with **point-of-purchase displays**, *promotional devices that are placed where sales transactions occur.* They include posters, life-size cardboard mannequins, display racks, and dummy packages. Although these attractions ultimately appeal to final consumers, they can be considered promotional appeals to middlemen, as retail stores sometimes agree to carry a product only if the manufacturer provides an effective display. L'eggs hosiery, Hartz Mountain pet supplies, and Spice Islands spices are sold with the help of these visual enticements.

One of the newest concepts in point-of-purchase strategy is the video commercial. While the shopper is at the checkout stand, short commercials appear on the video screen.[14]

cooperative advertising programs
Programs in which the manufacturer agrees to pay part of the advertising costs for the product.

COOPERATIVE ADVERTISING PROGRAMS Some manufacturers engage in **cooperative advertising programs**, *programs in which the manufacturer agrees to pay part of the advertising costs for the product.* Teledyne, for example, extends such a program to retailers that regularly sell its Water Pik oral hygiene appliance. The fact that producers will share the dealer's advertising costs makes dealers more willing to promote the products. Cooperative advertising is especially useful for smaller, independent retailers, who otherwise might be unable to afford advertising and thus be unable to compete effectively with chains.

specialty advertising
Providing "frequent reminder" items that build goodwill and keep a firm's or product's name within the prospect's view.

SPECIALTY ADVERTISING Another appeal to middlemen, and also to final consumers, is **specialty advertising**, which is *providing "frequent reminder" items that build goodwill and keep a firm's or a product's name within the prospect's view.* Such items range from relatively cheap ballpoint pens, calendars, and matchbooks to staplers, coffee cups, and even skywriting. The choices have one thing in common: they all identify the product or the company.

The list of specialty advertising objects is confined only to the marketer's imagination. Domino's Pizza hands out magnets in the shape of a Domino's pizza box; logo hats bearing corporate emblems promote everything from Coors beer to Mack trucks to Red Man chewing tobacco; bumper stickers sporting the call letters of radio stations are passports to contests; drinking glasses carrying Mobil logos tout local sports teams across the country; and T-shirts sing the praises of Coca-Cola, Pizza Hut, and Chili's restaurant.

TRADE SHOWS Both producers and retailers find trade shows popular. At these shows, a great array of products from one or several competing firms are exhibited, attracting thousands of prospects within a region. Typical trade shows feature boats, automobiles, or mobile homes. Because these events attract such a high volume of traffic, participating companies make many sales on the spot. They also gather the names of prospects for future sales, often by having attendees register for a drawing that awards an attractive prize. The names and addresses of those who register become a valuable mailing list after the show.

PUSH MONEY As an added incentive for salespeople to devote extra personal selling effort to their brands, some producers offer **push money** (also called "PMs" or "spiffs"), which is *a manufacturer's commission paid to salespeople for selling one particular brand over all others.* This extra commission offers an incentive or "push" to motivate salespeople.

push money
A manufacturer's commission paid to salespeople for selling one particular brand over all others.

Developing Promotional Strategies

The four elements of the promotional mix need to be blended to communicate effectively to a target market. Each type of promotion serves a different function and therefore should support the other elements. (Table 13.8 summarizes the function and value of each promotional alternative.) The blending

Table 13.8
Function and value of promotional mix elements.

RATING CRITERIA	PERSONAL SELLING	ADVERTISING	PUBLICITY	SALES PROMOTION
Goal	To present an individual message, to problem solve, to close the sale	To reach a mass audience; to inform, persuade, and remind	To provide a mass audience with unbiased information	To complement other promotional elements; to increase impulse sales
Type of message	Individual, specific, focused	Same message to all individuals	Same message to all individuals	Will vary depending on the specific sales promotional device
Flexibility	High flexibility	Medium flexibility	Low flexibility	Medium flexibility
Cost	High per sales call	Low per person contacted	No or low cost	Medium per customer
Control of message material	High control	High control	No control	High control

of the elements results in a promotional strategy. There are two potential promotional strategies: push strategy and pull strategy.

A **push strategy** is *a strategy directed at the members of the marketing channel rather than the consumer.* This strategy depends heavily on personal selling, with support provided by sales promotion techniques of cooperative advertising programs and push money. For example, a manufacturer might decide that the most successful way to promote a product is to first sell the "idea" to a wholesaler, who in turn will sell the idea—with incentives—to the retailer. Now, the retailer—with point-of-purchase displays and a commitment for cooperative advertising—will "push" the product onto the customer.

A **pull strategy** is *a strategy aimed at getting consumers to demand that a product be available in the distribution channel.* To accomplish this strategy, marketers rely on the advertising, sales promotion, and publicity elements of the promotional mix. As an example, the manufacturer purposely bypasses the wholesaler and retailer and appeals directly to the consumer. An advertising campaign bombards the consumer with information, offers coupons via direct mail and magazines, and provides samples in the Sunday newspaper. The desired result: consumers clamor for the product to the retailers, who in turn "pull" the product from the manufacturer.

push strategy
A strategy directed at the members of the marketing channel rather than the consumer.

pull strategy
A strategy aimed at getting consumers to demand that a product be available in the distribution channel.

SUMMARY

Managers who are responsible for developing promotional strategy need to understand why consumers and industrial buyers purchase the things they do. Consumers buy products under the combined influence of emotional, rational, and patronage motives. Industrial buyers buy for rational reasons—price, profit, quality, salability, and service—as well as reciprocity and emotion.

Once the buying motives have been identified, the next step is to create a promotional strategy—the communication ingredient in the marketing mix. A promotional strategy is composed of the four elements of the promotional mix: personal selling, advertising, publicity, and sales promotion. The promotional strategy is developed with an understanding of the communication process, which includes sender, encoding, message, medium, decoding, target market, feedback, and noise.

The first element of the promotional mix is personal selling. It is a personal attempt to persuade the prospective customer to buy a product. Salespersons use a seven-step sales approach that includes prospecting, preapproach, approach, presentation, handling objections, closing, and follow-up.

The second element of the promotional mix is advertising, which is any nonpersonal message paid for by an identifiable sponsor to promote goods, services, or ideas. There are two types of advertising: product (intended to promote demand for a good or service) and institutional (done to enhance a company's public image). Once the type of advertising is determined, marketers have to select the medium for presenting the message. They may select from among newspapers, magazines, television, radio, direct mail, and outdoor advertising. Each medium has its strengths and limitations. Regardless of the media used, all advertising must be done within legal guidelines that prohibit false or misleading advertising claims.

The third element of the promotional mix is publicity. It is nonpaid, nonpersonal communication to promote the goods, services, or image of the company. The development of the publicity element of the promotional mix requires the firm to take advantage of all opportunities to present material to independent media. Types of publicity include news publicity, business feature articles, and financial releases.

Sales promotion is the fourth element of the promotional mix. It involves paid marketing activities other than personal selling and advertising. Some types of sales promotion devices are intended for the consumer: coupons, samples, premiums, special services, contests and sweepstakes, trading stamps, and refund offers. Other types are directed at the middleman: point-of-purchase displays, cooperative advertising programs, specialty advertising, trade shows, and push money.

The four ingredients of the promotional mix are blended to communicate effectively to a target market. In blending these elements the manager has a choice of two types of promotional strategy: push strategy or pull strategy. Push strategy is directed toward the marketing channel, whereas pull strategy is aimed at the consumer.

KEY TERMS

advertising p. 416
advertising media p. 418
approach p. 414
close p. 415
communication process p. 410
consumer buying motives p. 407
cooperative advertising programs p. 428
emotional motives p. 407
follow-up p. 415
industrial buying motives p. 409
institutional advertising p. 416
objections p. 415
patronage motives p. 408
personal selling p. 412
point-of-purchase displays p. 428

preapproach p. 414
premium p. 426
presentation p. 415
product advertising p. 416
promotional mix p. 410
prospecting p. 414
publicity p. 421
pull strategy p. 430
push money p. 429
push strategy p. 430
rational motives p. 408
reciprocal buying p. 409
sales promotion p. 425
selling process p. 413
specialty advertising p. 428

FOR REVIEW AND DISCUSSION

1. What is the relationship between buying motives and promotional strategy?
2. Evaluate this statement: "Consumer buying motives are more emotionally oriented than industrial buying motives are."
3. Explain the role of promotional strategy in the marketing mix.
4. Identify each of the elements of the communication process and explain what occurs during each part of the process.
5. Summarize the seven steps in the selling process. Should one of the steps be considered more important than the others? Why or why not?
6. Why do companies advertise?
7. Distinguish between the two types of advertising.

8. Identify four advertising media and discuss the advantages and disadvantages of each.
9. What role does publicity play in the promotional mix? How can a company guarantee that it will receive publicity?
10. What is meant by the "two faces of publicity"? Provide a recent example of negative publicity.
11. What function does sales promotion perform in the promotional mix? Whom can it be targeted to?
12. Explain the purposes of four promotional devices used to appeal to middlemen and four used to appeal to final consumers.
13. Explain how the four elements of promotion are blended to create the promotional mix.
14. Discuss the purposes of a promotional push strategy and a promotional pull strategy.

APPLICATIONS

Case 13.1: Buying a Market?

Companies are finding it takes cold hard cash—or at least a gimmick or giveaway—to warm consumers' hearts these days. Companies are slugging it out in the market trying to add value to products without altering the products themselves.

In recent promotional campaigns:

- Burger King and Disney offered 100 million prizes to fast-food customers, luring them with free food, 200 trips to Disney World, and a $100,000 grand prize.
- PepsiCo's Frito-Lay unit gave consumers 8 million prizes from free chip coupons to $50 vouchers in 2- to 3-ounce snack packs.
- Confectioner M&M/Mars offered refunds of five cents per candy bar wrapper.
- Coors Beer distributed talking cans in 30,000 twelve-pack cases. Instead of beer, the cans contained light-activated microchips telling consumers they had won prizes from compact discs to stereos.
- PepsiCo and Polaroid offered consumers a chance to rub shoulders with facsimiles of celebrities. As part of PepsiCo's "Uh-huh!" campaign, a consumer could have a photo taken next to life-sized cardboard cutouts of Ray Charles and the Uh-huh Girls at 4,000 U.S. locations.

In some product categories, these types of promotional programs have been the rule, not the exception. Faced with a glut of competing products and higher marketing costs, companies see a contest or other sales promotion device as a cheap way to push a product. Perhaps a better measure would be whether such methods are effective.

Questions

1. In addition to contests, what sales promotional devices are marketers incorporating in their promotional campaigns? Cite examples from the case to support your answer.

2. Are the sales promotions noted in the case designed to boost short-term or long-term revenue? Explain your answer.

3. Does the use of sales promotional devices noted in the case help or hurt efforts to build long-term brand loyalty? Explain your answer.

For more information, see Thomas A. King, "Film Ads Blast Away with Both Barrels," *The Wall Street Journal,* April 16, 1993, p. B1; Gary Strauss, "Sometimes the Best Ads in Life Are Freebies," *USA Today,* March 19, 1993, p. 1B.

Case 13.2: Big Brother and Little Brother Are Watching

Marketers beware: Big Brother (government) is watching you and Little Brother (consumer) wants him to do it even more, and better. With survey data showing that more than half of consumers distrust most marketing claims, marketers are at a crossroads with promotional strategy: clean up your own act, or the government will step in and do it for you.

The burden is on the marketers. From the consumer standpoint, the marketers are the experts on the benefits of their products. It is not the consumer's job to be the expert. The consumers have to trust the marketing community not only for the right information, but for information delivered the right way to the right target market.

Unfortunately, marketers fail on all three counts. Survey data show that consumers more often than not believe marketers intentionally exploit kids, women, and minorities; show no respects for the public's intelligence; reduce the amount of product in packages; give misleading competitive claims; exaggerate health and environmental claims; and don't give accurate information in general.

Although all marketers are not to blame, everyone gets lumped in the same category. And, remember, Big Brother is watching.

Questions

1. What responsibility does a marketer have to the consumer in developing and delivering promotional messages?

2. What actions should be taken by marketers to eliminate the problems noted in the case? Cite specific problems and their solutions.

3. What role should government play in this situation?

4. What are the advantages and disadvantages associated with government involvement in marketing practices?

For more information, see Rahul Jacob, "Beyond Quality and Value," *Fortune,* Autumn/Winter 1993, pp. 10–11; Patricia Sellers, "The Best Way to Reach Your Buyers," *Fortune,* Autumn/Winter 1993, pp. 14–17.

REFERENCES

1. Christopher Power, Lisa Driscoll, and Earl Bohn, "Smart Selling: How Companies Are Winning Over Today's Tougher Customer," *Business Week,* August 3, 1992, pp. 46–48.
2. *Advertising Age,* September 23, 1992, p. 3.
3. Howard Schlossberg, "Marketers Told to Heed Consumers Before Big Brother Steps In," *Marketing News,* April 27, 1993, p. 10.
4. Ibid.
5. Maxine S. Lans, "Sound-Alikes Sound Like a Legal Violation," *Marketing News,* January 18, 1993, p. 7.
6. David Drobis, "Building Broad Equity with Public Relations," *Management Review,* May 1993, p. 52.
7. Ibid, pp. 53–54.
8. Ronald Grover, "Boxed in at Jack in the Box," *Business Week,* February 15, 1993, p. 40.
9. Paul Magnuson, "Now the Court of Public Opinion Has GM Worried," *Business Week,* February 22, 1993, pp. 38–39.
10. Joel R. Evans and Barry Berman, *Marketing,* 4th edition (New York: Macmillan, 1989), p. 457.
11. Ronald Grover, "Big Brother Is Grocery Shopping with You," *Business Week,* March 29, 1993, p. 60.
12. Gary Strauss, "Sometimes the Best Ads Are Freebies," *USA Today,* April 1, 1993, p. 1B.
13. Ibid.
14. Ronald Grover, "Big Brother Is Grocery Shopping with You," p. 60.

14

DISTRIBUTION AND PRICING STRATEGY

We try to associate the price of our services not with our costs—but with the value customers assess for our services. That way, price has nothing to do with profit.

LESTER M. ABERTHAL
Chairman, Electronic Data Systems Corp.

CHAPTER OBJECTIVES
After studying this chapter, you should be able to:
1. Describe the importance of distribution strategy.
2. List and explain the primary distribution channels for industrial goods and consumer goods.
3. Discuss the various types of middlemen and their roles as channel members.
4. Explain the components of a physical distribution system.
5. Describe the importance of pricing strategy.
6. Explain how prices are determined by supply and demand, the cost-oriented approaches of markup and break-even analysis, and the market approach.
7. Describe pricing strategies marketers can adopt.

UP FRONT

David Bond's business life is a perfect example of the goals he set for himself in earning his bachelor's degree in communications from the University of Massachusetts at Amherst. "I structured my college experience so that I would become a more well-rounded person. I wanted to get a little knowledge in a variety of areas. I guess you could say I sought, and got, a classical education. This may not have meant coming out of college able to start a vocation or career, or to immediately attain wealth, but I'm still satisfied with my decision. I didn't want to narrow my horizons."

After graduation, Bond, who grew up in a small town near the Massachusetts seacoast, moved to Boston and got involved in one of his first loves: music. His degree helped him land a job with a recording studio, then he became a road manager for a rock and roll band. "I've always liked high technology, which led me to working in the computer industry for a while. But what happened to change my life is what I call the 'cathartic summer,'" he recalls. "My mother fell ill with lung cancer and I decided to quit smoking, became interested in health and fitness, and took up bicycling. I pretty much shut the door on my old lifestyle."

Fortuitously, Bond bumped into an old college roommate, Kyle Schmeer, and told him about his new interests. "Kyle owned a bike shop, and mentioned that he knew of an opening for a sales representative in the bike business, and I said I might be interested. A few days later I got a phone call to discuss the job of New England sales rep for Mid Atlantic Cycle Specialties. A

week after that I was on an airplane, heading for the industry's big trade show in Anaheim, California.

"I'll always remember that Kyle said how small the business is, but when I walked into the Anaheim Convention Center I found myself in a huge hall, filled with bikes as far as I could see. Then I walked into another huge hall filled with bikes, and then another. The experience certainly dispelled any ideas I had about this being a quaint little business. It's a multibillion-dollar industry," he says.

Over time, Bond's territory and responsibilities grew; he now works with retail bicycle shops in Massachusetts, Rhode Island, Connecticut, Maine, New Hampshire, Vermont, and upstate New York. "In essence, I telecommute for fifteen employers, acting as the sales and marketing representative for their products. As district manager, I am responsible for everything: new product introduction, pricing, terms, discounts, distribution, and order fulfillment. I make sure my customers get what they want, when they want it.

"A few companies in the industry, such as the bicycle manufacturers, have their own factory reps. I'm an independent, and there are about ten to fifteen others in New England. I represent a number of different product lines: bicycles, cycling clothing, helmets, accessories, saddles, wheels, child carriers, shoes, pedals, car racks, just about anything for bikes. We even used to dis-

DAVID BOND

NEW ENGLAND REGIONAL DIRECTOR, MID ATLANTIC CYCLE SPECIALTIES

tribute Gatorade. The product line changes from year to year.

"I visit about a hundred dealers on a regular basis, but I service a total of about 400," Bond continues. "My job is to keep them informed about new products and make sure they have the stock on hand they need. Basically, I drive around with a bunch of things for them to look at. For example, one of my accounts brought out a new computerized shifting system, so I mounted it on my own bike and took it with me for the dealers to test ride. Once they've decided what to order, they can either call me or call the company direct. A lot of this is computerized, so orders are filled quickly and drop-shipped directly from a factory or warehouse."

Even though bicycling is seasonal in the Northeast, David Bond works year round. "August to November is the time to book preseason orders, so manufacturers can figure out how much to build. Dealers get special terms and discounts for ordering. January to March is the 'at once' order period, when I take orders in person or over the phone for immediate shipment. Summer is new orders and replenishment orders, and maintaining good customer relations by visiting the shops, going out on their afternoon rides, just keeping in touch."

"I try to provide a high level of service for my dealers. I have an 800 line for them to place orders, I return calls promptly, I get the orders in right away, and I call them back if something is out of stock. Most of them appreciate this. I telemarket to the smaller shops that I can't see on a regular basis, using my personal computer and special telemarketing software that helps me organize calls and in general be more efficient."

What does David Bond foresee for the bicycling industry? "I like the business and I like the people in it," he says. "They're into health and their families. One problem I see is that in a less than vibrant economy, retail volume drops and all of us reps earn less money. But there will always be a need for independent reps to market the smaller lines. I'm on the road four days a week visiting bike shops, because one of the most powerful things you can do is let a dealer actually touch and see a new product. New England is a beautiful place to travel around. I like the freedom that comes with being an independent, distributing for a number of companies, setting my own hours and working from my home. But sometimes that freedom means working longer hours than you would at a regular outside job!"

Distribution strategy and pricing strategy are the third and fourth ingredients in a company's marketing mix. When these elements are "blended" with product and promotional strategy (discussed in Chapters 12 and 13, respectively), the organization has created its marketing strategy to reach the selected target market. In this chapter we will examine the importance, objectives, and components of distribution strategy. We will also investigate pricing: its objectives, methods of determination, and potential strategies.

The Importance of Distribution Strategy

Distribution strategy encompasses physical distribution systems and the channels used to place the product in the customer's hands. It is responsible for getting the product to the right place at the right time. A firm can have the best products in the world (product strategy) and people can know about them and want them (promotional strategy), but all this will be useless if people cannot get the products when and where they want them.

Distribution involves (1) the routes goods take and the people involved in that process and (2) the activities involved in getting the goods to the consumer—a physical distribution system. Element 1 deals with the channels, choices of channels, and channel members. Element 2 deals with the actual components of a physical distribution system—transportation, warehousing, order processing, materials handling, and inventory control.

Channels of Distribution

A **channel of distribution**, or **marketing channel**, is *a route that goods follow on their journey from manufacturers to consumers.* Distribution channels are composed of organizations or people known as channel members, middlemen, or intermediaries: **wholesalers**—*those who sell products to other sellers of goods*—and **retailers**—*those who sell products to the ultimate consumer.* The channels and the organizations that compose them serve as pipelines by which the manufacturer moves goods to the final customer—either an individual consumer or industrial buyer.

Based on these two types of customers, there are two major distribution channel categories by market: the industrial goods market and the consumer goods market.

Channels for Industrial Goods

Industrial goods channels tend to be more direct than consumer goods channels—many industrial goods are designed solely for the end user. For example, Otis Die and Casting Company designs and manufacturers tool dies for Cummings Tool. But in other instances—accessory equipment, supplies—longer channels are required. Figure 14.1 illustrates the four main

channel of distribution or marketing channel
A route that goods follow on their journey from manufacturers to consumers.

wholesalers
Those who sell products to other sellers of goods.

retailers
Those who sell products to the ultimate consumer.

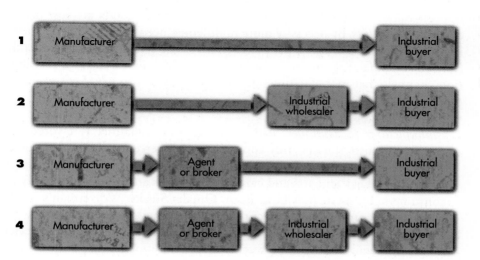

Figure 14.1
Distribution channels for industrial goods.

distribution channels that producers can use to reach the industrial goods market. Let's discuss each of them:

1. *Manufacturer to industrial buyer.* The shortest and sometimes most practical way for a manufacturer to distribute industrial goods is to sell them directly to industrial customers. Direct distribution is used if goods are awkward to handle, the market segment is small, the seller must train the buyer's employees to operate the product, or, as previously noted, the product is specifically designed for the end user. Computers, textile manufacturing equipment, and iron ore often are distributed in this way.

2. *Manufacturer to industrial wholesaler to industrial buyer.* Industrial goods with a broad market, such as welding rods, printing paper, and construction materials, need wider distribution. They utilize a distribution channel featuring wholesalers known as *industrial distributors*. These distributors resell to the industrial buyer.

3. *Manufacturer to agent or broker to industrial buyer.* In some instances the product being sold does not require the intermediate warehousing service provided by a wholesaler but still needs some intermediary to sell the products. An agent or broker can serve as the contact point for the manufacturer without taking possession of or title to the goods and can provide the necessary sales support.

4. *Manufacturer to agent or broker to industrial wholesaler to industrial buyer.* Small manufacturers often need to contract with an agent or broker to represent products to wholesalers. The agent serves the purpose of bringing the wholesaler and manufacturer together but does not take title to the goods.

Channels for Consumer Goods

Consumer goods channels tend to be longer and more complex than industrial channels. Because a large number of consumer goods are low-priced convenience goods, by necessity more middlemen need to be involved. Chewing gum, razor blades, and paper plates cannot be effectively marketed directly from the manufacturer to the consumer. Figure 14.2 shows the four distribution channels that manufacturers of consumer goods can use. Let's examine each:

1. *Manufacturer to consumer.* Although the direct channel is favored for reaching industrial users, only approximately 5 percent of consumer goods are moved in this way. Such products as plants at nurseries, vegetables at farmers' markets, and arts and crafts items at fairs are often sold directly to consumers. Firms such as L. L. Bean, Omaha Steaks, Wolverman's (muffins, bagels, crumpets) sell direct through their mail-order catalogs.

2. *Manufacturer to retailer to consumer.* Some manufacturers choose to select their own retail outlets to represent them. Automobiles and large house-

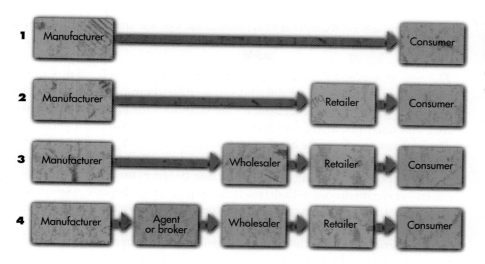

Figure 14.2
Distribution channels for consumer goods.

hold appliances are products that traditionally are distributed directly to retailers without the need for wholesalers.

3. *Manufacturer to wholesaler to retailer to consumer.* Some products—magazines, combs, lipstick, hair spray—need a broad channel of distribution. This is provided by incorporating a wholesale and retail link in the channel. The wholesaler aids in allocating the product to the retailers in order to have the product available when and where needed by the consumer. The success of consumer product manufacturers such as Gillette and Schick is related directly to the distribution networks the firms have developed. As convenience goods, the products are placed in supermarkets, convenience stores, drug stores, and discount stores across the country.

4. *Manufacturer to agent or broker to wholesaler to retailer to consumer.* When goods are produced by a large number of small companies—canning, frozen-food packing, meat packing—an agent or broker brings the buyers and sellers together. In some cases the agent or broker contacts the wholesalers, who in turn buy from the producers. In other instances the wholesaler may be seeking a source of supply.

Selection of a Distribution Channel

Which of these distribution channels should a manufacturer use? The decision is based on a number of variables, such as:

- *The market segment.* As we have seen, a major factor in the decision is whether the product is intended for the consumer or industrial market. Industrial purchases normally deal directly with the manufacturer, while consumers make most purchases at retail stores.
- *The size and geographic location of the market segment.* A market that is large and geographically dispersed, as in the case of many consumer goods,

requires the use of marketing intermediaries. On the other hand, a direct channel is more effective when the manufacturer's potential market is small and geographically concentrated.

- *The type of product.* Product type also dictates channel selection. Convenience goods require broad distribution to have them available where the consumer wants them—therefore a long channel with multiple intermediaries. Specialty goods are distributed directly to retail stores.

- *The ability to perform the marketing functions.* A critical factor is whether the manufacturer can perform the required marketing functions (selling, transporting, storing, financing, risk bearing) or has the need for others—intermediaries—to do so. If a company has adequate resources—managerial, financial, marketing—it feels less pressure to use intermediaries.

- *The competitor's distribution strategy.* Sometimes it is necessary to respond to a competitor's distribution strategy. Dell Computers, by bypassing retail outlets and going directly to the consumer, revolutionized computer sales and forced similar actions by IBM.

- *The degree of market coverage.* Adequate market coverage—the number of dealers or outlets where the good can be purchased—for some products could mean one store for 70,000 people, while for another it may mean one store for 200,000. As seen in Figure 14.3, there are three degrees of market coverage: intensive distribution, selective distribution, and exclusive distribution. A firm that markets convenience products will want **intensive distribution**, *widespread market coverage that utilizes a large number of wholesalers and retailers.* Another manufacturer

intensive distribution
Widespread market coverage that utilizes a large number of wholesalers and retailers.

Figure 14.3
Degrees of market coverage.

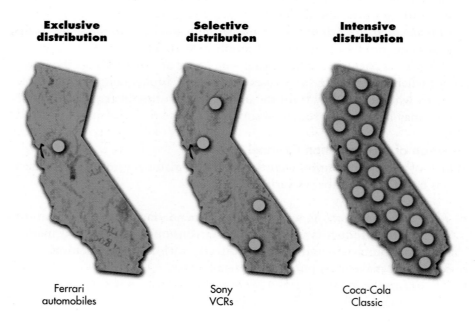

Exclusive distribution — Ferrari automobiles

Selective distribution — Sony VCRs

Intensive distribution — Coca-Cola Classic

that markets shopping goods may wish to emphasize image and a good sales volume through **selective distribution,** *utilizing a moderate number of retailers and wholesalers.* Finally, for a specialty good, a manufacturer may use **exclusive distribution:** *limiting distribution to one retailer or wholesaler in a geographic area.*

With these factors in mind, let's examine the roles of the two major channel members.

Channel Members

As mentioned earlier in the chapter, the various channels of distribution we have examined are composed of organizations or people known as *channel members, middlemen,* or *intermediaries.* These intermediaries perform the marketing functions of buying, selling, storing, transporting, risk taking, and collecting marketing information for the manufacturer. In addition, marketing intermediaries are vitally important in creating time, place, and possession utilities. The intermediaries ensure that products are available when and where they are needed.

Two types of middlemen operate between the manufacturer and consumer or industrial user: wholesalers and retailers. In the next sections we will discuss each.

Wholesaling Middlemen

Wholesalers are middlemen who sell goods to retailers, to other wholesalers, and to industrial users, but who do not sell in significant amounts to the final consumer.[1] As shown in Figure 14.4, if wholesalers did not exist, retailers would have to spend a great deal of time dealing with many different manufacturers, attempting to coordinate numerous product orders and shipments, and acquiring and maintaining huge stock inventories.

Not all wholesalers are the same. Some take title to the goods (merchant wholesalers); others do not (agents and brokers). Some provide a full range of services. As shown in Table 14.1, full-service merchant wholesalers provide credit, store and deliver, and provide sales and promotional assistance. On the other hand, limited-service merchant wholesalers simply resell goods and provide little or no service. Table 14.2 provides a sampling of the various types of wholesalers and their characteristics.

Retailing Middlemen

Retailers are the last stage in the channel of distribution: they perform the business activities involved in the sale of goods and services to the ultimate consumer for personal use. The activities may include buying and selling of products, transportation or delivery, storage of inventory, financing, and risk bearing. Retailers can be classified by type of ownership and where business is conducted.

selective distribution
Utilizing a moderate number of retailers and wholesalers.

exclusive distribution
Limiting distribution to one retailer or wholesaler in a geographic area.

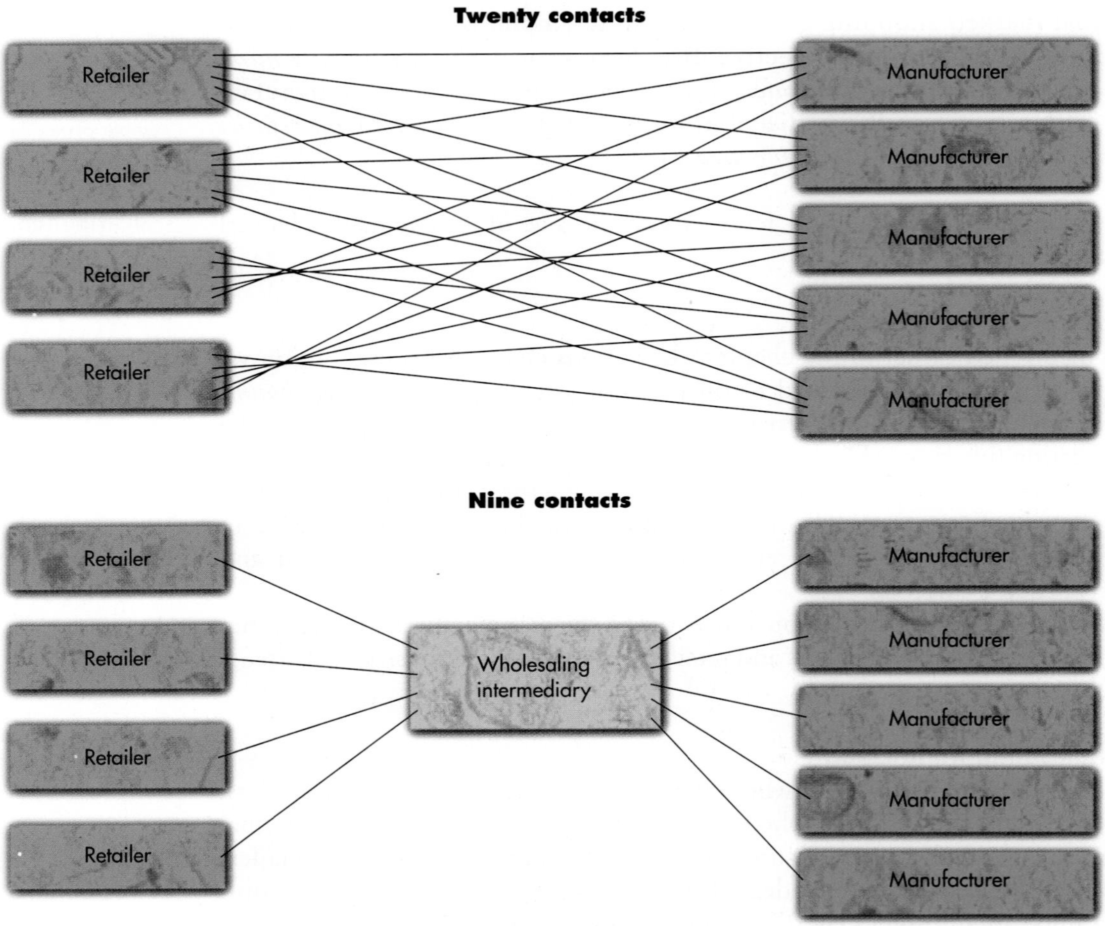

Twenty contacts

Nine contacts

Figure 14.4
The value of the wholesale middleman.

Table 14.1
Typical services provided by full-service wholesalers.

SERVICES TO MANUFACTURERS	SERVICES TO RETAILERS
Relay market information from retailers	Advise retailer on layout, promotional activities, bookkeeping practices, inventory planning, and sources of credit
Employ sales force to sell products	Tell of new products that manufacturers are bringing to market
Save manufacturers work by extending credit to retailers	Deliver merchandise faster and in smaller quantities than producers are willing to do
Store products before resale and deliver them when sold	Simplify retailers' recordkeeping and inventory-handling activities by gathering many manufacturers' products into a single delivery and billing
Bear risk of market changes that may reduce demand for the product	

WHOLESALER	CHARACTERISTICS	TAKES TITLE
Manufacturers' agent*	An agent who sells products made by several manufacturers	No
	Has little authority to approve customer requests for price concessions, expedited delivery, or credit	
Selling agent*	An agent who sells a producer's entire output	No
	Usually has broad authority to approve customer requests for price concessions, expedited delivery, or credit	
Auction house*	Brings buyers and sellers together in one location	No
	Allows buyers to inspect products before purchase	
Commission merchant*	An agent who represents producers	No
	Sells products for the best price possible; takes possession of goods	
	Sells agricultural products	
Broker	An agent who represents either buyer or seller for a commission on sales or purchases made	No
	Arranges for products shipped directly to the purchaser	
	Distributes such products as coal, grain, and produce	
Rack jobber	A type of consumer-goods wholesaler	Yes
	Sets up manufacturers' point-of-purchase displays in stores and restocks them as needed	
	Distributes such products as magazines, panty hose, and candy	
Drop shipper	An intermediary who does not take physical possession of goods	Yes
	Provides selling and credit	
	Does not provide advertising or merchandising support	
	Distributes primarily raw materials	
Truck wholesaler	An intermediary who sells and delivers goods at the same time on a regular sales route	Yes
	Provides merchandising and promotion support	
	Distributes potato chips, bakery, and dairy products	

Table 14.2
Types of wholesalers and their characteristics.

*Manufacturers' agent, selling agent, auction house, and commission merchant are all categorized as *agent* channels of distribution.

OWNERSHIP OF RETAIL STORES One way to distinguish retailers is by the number of outlets or stores owned and operated by the company: an independent retailer or a chain store. An **independent retailer** is *a company that operates only one retail store.* Independents are usually a family-owned business—Nelson's Donut Shop, Tony's Cafe, Hardy's Mower Sales and Service. More than three-quarters of all American retailers are independents. This large number is attributable to the ease of entry into retailing because of low investments and little technical knowledge. But because of poor management skills and inadequate resources, many independent retailers do not succeed—about one-third of new retailers do not last one full year, and two-thirds do not make it past the first three years.[2]

Most independents sell a relatively narrow line of products, such as auto parts or records and tapes. Few have the sophisticated management training programs that J. C. Penney or other large retailers run. Most obtain merchandise through the wholesalers, not having the capital, sales volume, or storage space to justify buying large quantities directly from manufacturers.

The second type of store ownership is the **chain store**—*one of two or more similar stores owned by the same company.* There are national chains like McDonald's and regional chains like Winn-Dixie Grocery Stores. Although chains operate less than one-quarter of all American retail outlets, they account for well over half of total retail store sales. Only a few hundred chains operate a hundred or more units, yet they are responsible for over 30 percent of all store sales in the United States.

Chains like Wal-Mart, the nation's largest retailer, K mart, and Target have one great advantage over independent stores—they can make volume purchases through a central buying office, allowing the chains to pay lower prices for goods than independents can. In addition, chains can use layout specialists, sales training, and computerized merchandise inventory and ordering.

Regardless of the type of ownership, a retailer conducts business either in-store or out-of-store. Both independent and chain ownership is found in either category.

IN-STORE RETAILERS In-store retailers use store facilities to provide products and services to the ultimate consumer. In-store retailers operate various types of stores, including department stores, discount stores, specialty stores, off-price stores, supermarkets, superstores, hypermarkets, convenience stores, catalog stores, warehouse clubs, and factory outlets.

Department stores, such as Dillard's, Nordstrom, and Macy's, are *stores organized by departments that provide an extremely wide variety of merchandise,* including home furnishings, clothing, appliances, cosmetics, furniture, and dry goods. Department stores also provide a full line of services, such as gift wrapping, home delivery, and credit. In addition, a number of department stores offer gourmet cooking classes, fashion shows, seminars, and investment and career counseling programs to attract women.

independent retailer
A company that operates only one retail store.

chain store
One of two or more similar stores owned by the same company.

department stores
Stores organized by departments that provide an extremely wide variety of merchandise.

MANAGER'S NOTEBOOK

Power Retailers Rule the Marketplace

The face of retailing is undergoing dramatic change. In category after category, giant "power retailers" are using sophisticated inventory management, purchasing clout, and above all internal cost management to crowd out weaker players. If this trend continues, it is predicted that retailers now accounting for half of all sales will disappear by the year 2000 through bankruptcy, mergers, or other reorganizations. Triumphant over them will be the superpowers, including Wal-Mart, K mart, Toys 'R' Us, Home Depot, Circuit City Stores, Dillard's Department Stores, Target Stores, and Costco.

Leading the pack is Wal-Mart. The nation's number-one retailer is expected to grow 25 percent this year to some $55 billion in sales. In comparison, retailers as a whole will be lucky to grow 4 percent.

Consumers are flocking not only to Wal-Mart but to new retailing channels. They are now loyal to warehouse clubs and "category killers"—large specialty stores that are taking over sales of everything from tires to toys.

It all adds up to a power shift to a privileged circle of merchants. More and more, this group is telling the mightiest of manufacturers—Whirlpool Corp., Procter & Gamble, Rubbermaid—what goods to produce, in what colors and sizes, how much to ship, and when. They are forcing suppliers to rethink whom they sell to, how to price and promote their products, and how they structure their own organizations. The approach of the giants is "We want this. Either you do it, or we'll get it from somebody else."

In addition to pressuring suppliers, the giants are continually squeezing costs out of their own distribution systems. Wal-Mart holds its operating and selling expenses to 15 percent of sales, versus 28 percent for Sears. Much of these savings are passed on to consumers in the form of better service or lower prices. The super-efficient warehouse clubs—Costco, Sam's—offer prices 26 percent below regular prices at traditional supermarkets.

The final ingredient in this formula is that the best retailers are using powerful information systems to stock what customers want, when they want it—and they expect suppliers to act quickly on that knowledge. At Wal-Mart, for instance, more than half of its 5,000 vendors get point-of-sale data. At K mart, 2,600 of 3,000 suppliers have some sort of electronic linkup.

The combined tactics have multiple effects. The companies are dominant in the marketplace and in turn control the futures and fortunes of many supplier-manufacturers. When suppliers have a significant percentage of their sales dollar committed from a "power retailer," they are placed in a less-than-enviable bargaining position. This conclusion is supported by the following sales data:

- Haggar gets 22.6 percent of sales from J. C. Penney, 10 percent from Wal-Mart.
- Mr. Coffee gets 21 percent of sales from Wal-Mart, 10 percent from K mart.
- Mattel gets 13 percent of sales from Toys 'R' Us.
- Hasbro gets 75 percent of sales from ten customers, 17 percent from Toys 'R' Us.
- Royal Appliances gets 52 percent of sales from five retailers, including 26 percent from Wal-Mart and 16 percent from K mart.
- Huffy gets 23 percent of sales from K mart and Toys 'R' Us.

The power retailers indeed rule the marketplace.

(For more information on power retailers, see Zachary Schiller and Wendy Zellner, "Clout: More and More, Retail Giants Rule the Marketplace," *Business Week,* April 21, 1993, pp. 66–73.)

Specialty stores, such as gift shops, bakeries, and florists, can often be found grouped in strip malls.

discount store
A store that has low prices, a broad line of merchandise, and limited or self-service.

A store that has low prices, a broad line of merchandise, and limited or self-service is a **discount store**.[3] Such stores rarely offer their own credit cards, although they accept such bank credit cards as Visa and MasterCard. They avoid home delivery, gift wrapping, and other services that would force them to raise their prices. Discount stores base their operations on (1) their ability to make volume purchases at lower prices and (2) their willingness to buy regular-priced merchandise and take a lower percentage of profit on the goods. As a result, these stores sell billions in goods and services annually. The major product lines sold are toys and games, housewares, gifts, small electric appliances, jewelry, and apparel. Together, K mart, Wal-Mart, and Target account for $104 billion in annual sales in the United States.[4]

off-price retailer
A retailer that buys manufacturer's overruns, odd lots, and closeouts and then sells them at deep discounts.

An **off-price retailer** *buys manufacturer overruns, odd lots, and closeouts and then sells them at deep discounts.* Ross, T. J. Max, and Marshalls all sell goods at prices 25 percent or more below those of traditional department stores.

specialty store
A store that offers many models or styles of a specific product.

Specialty stores like Toys 'R' Us, Pier I Imports, and Circuit City *offer many models or styles of a specific product* such as toys, home furnishings, or electronics. These stores make up the majority of retailers located in regional shopping centers anchored by one or more full-service department stores. Specialty stores are most successful in the apparel, gourmet food, appliance, toy, electronics, and sports product lines.

supermarket
A store that provides a wide variety of food items along with a limited amount of household goods in a large, self-service facility.

One type of retail store everyone is familiar with is the **supermarket**, which *provides a wide variety of food items along with a limited amount of household goods, in a large, self-service facility.* Large supermarket chains like Kroger, Safeway, Winn-Dixie, A & P, and Jewel try to provide convenient locations, ample parking, and low prices—everything attractive to the consumer for one-step shopping.

A warehouse club isn't pretty, but shoppers are more concerned about getting the discount prices.

superstore
A giant retail store that sells food and nonfood items but also additional product lines that are purchased routinely.

hypermarket
A gigantic discount retail complex that combines the features of supermarkets, department stores, and specialty stores under one roof.

convenience store
A conveniently located store that carries a wide selection of popular consumer items and stays open long hours.

The original supermarket has evolved into the **superstore**, *a giant retail store that sells food and nonfood items but also additional product lines that are purchased routinely.* Superstores carry not only the food and household items found in supermarkets but also hardware, garden supplies, clothing, personal care items, automotive supplies, pet products, and small appliances. Superstores normally have 25,000 to 50,000 square feet of selling space to operate with. The potential of the superstore is so attractive that Wal-Mart is beginning to muscle its way into the $383 billion grocery business. Already operating forty-two supercenters, it plans to add ninety-four more by mid-1994.[5]

Popular in France, Japan, and Germany is the **hypermarket**, *a gigantic discount retail complex that combines the features of supermarkets, department stores, and specialty stores under one roof.* Such stores typically have 200,000 or more square feet of selling space, compared to a superstore's 25,000 to 50,000. One of the most successful hypermarkets is Meijers Thrifty Acres in suburban Detroit. The 245,000-square-foot store has forty checkout registers and sells food, hardware, soft goods, building materials, auto supplies, appliances, and prescription drugs. It also has a restaurant, beauty salon, branch bank, and bakery. But for the most part, hypermarkets have not generally caught on in the United States.[6]

One type of retail outlet spelled the demise of the small mom-and-pop grocery store: the **convenience store**. It is *a conveniently located store that carries a wide selection of popular consumer items and stays open long hours.* As the name indicates, the main attraction is convenience: many operate twenty-four hours a day, seven days a week, in areas of high population or heavy highway traffic. Speedy Mart, 7-Eleven, Mini-Market, and Jiffy Stores are well-known convenience stores. Despite charging high prices for most items, their long hours, popular merchandise, and strategic locations combine to attract an ever-increasing number of customers.

Stores that send catalogs to customers and also make them available in stores are known as **catalog stores**. Service Merchandise, Best Products, and Lurias display sample items in the store, have clerks take orders, and then provide the customers with the take-home merchandise from an attached warehouse.

Open to members only, **warehouse clubs** *provide a broad range of name-brand merchandise at deeply discounted prices.* At Sam's Wholesale Club, PACE Membership Warehouse, and Costco Wholesale Club members normally pay $25 for the privilege of shopping for food, beverages, appliances, tires, and clothing at prices 20 to 40 percent lower than those of discount stores or supermarkets.

Factory outlets are *retail stores set up by manufacturers, where they can sell directly to the retail customer.* Companies such as Levi Strauss, Dansk, and Ship 'n Shore market closeouts, factory seconds, and canceled orders from their own stores.

OUT-OF-STORE RETAILERS Out-of-store retailing is conducted by retailers that do not use conventional retail facilities. This category includes in-home or door-to-door selling, mail-order retailing, home shopping, and vending machine retailing.

A retailer that calls on prospective customers in their homes is an **in-home or door-to-door retailer**. Salespeople may go door to door, telephone prospects for appointments, or arrange sales parties—as with Tupperware. Brushes, cosmetics, encyclopedias, kitchen utensils, and vacuum cleaners are sold in this way. Fuller Brush, Amway, Avon, Encyclopaedia Britannica, Mary Kay Cosmetics, and Electrolux have built thriving businesses using this approach.

Asking buyers to order products from catalogs or brochures sent to their homes or via order blanks in newspapers and magazines is called **mail-order retailing**. Some companies, such as Lands End (clothing), Omaha Steaks (meats and gourmet poultry), Clifty Farm (gourmet meats, poultry, and cheese), and Arlene's ("specializing in fine cutlery by mail since 1955") distribute most or all of their products through the mail. Others, such as Hammacher Schlemmer, I. Magnin & Company, Victoria's Secret, and Nordstrom, use catalogs to supplement in-store retailing efforts.

A fast-growing area in out-of-store retailing is **home shopping**, *the use of cable television to merchandise products via telephone orders.* Home shopping was introduced by the Home Shopping Network, Inc., and today half of all American households with television sets watch one or more home shopping networks. The dynamic potential of home shopping has brought Liz Claiborne, the country's largest women's apparel manufacturer, to join a growing list of

catalog stores
Stores that send catalogs to customers and also make them available in stores.

warehouse clubs
Member-only stores that provides a broad range of name-brand merchandise at deeply discounted prices.

factory outlets
Retail stores set up by manufacturers, where they can sell directly to the retail customer.

in-home *or* door-to-door retailer
A retailer that calls on prospective customers in their homes.

mail-order retailing
Asking buyers to order products from catalogs or brochures sent to their homes or via order blanks placed in newspapers and magazines.

home shopping
The use of cable television to merchandise products via telephone orders.

GLOBAL PERSPECTIVE

DISCOUNTERS IN MEXICO

The discounters that revolutionized retailing in the United States are now focusing on Mexico. The result: they are underselling not only the department stores and specialty shops but sometimes even the street vendors, kiosk operators, and other merchants in the large, informal economy.

The invasion began after the Mexican government lifted import restrictions on most American consumer goods in anticipation of the North American Free Trade Agreement (NAFTA). Soon Wal-Mart with its Sam's Club set up shop in a former candy factory on one side of Mexico City, and the Price Club opened one of its warehouse-like stores on the other side.

The two primary goals of both discounters are (1) to attract all Mexicans, including the thousands who migrated to the United States, lived there for a while and became shoppers at warehouse clubs before returning to Mexico, and (2) to sell to wholesalers, small businesses, mom-and-pop shops, and street merchants who cart off their purchases in a van or pickup truck.

The last goal may have the most revolutionary effect. The street vendors account for more than 15 percent of the nation's total economic activity, but the two discounters are beginning to challenge them. They offer the quality, spare parts, service, and warranties that the street vendors can't provide.

(For more on discounters in Mexico, see Stephanie Anderson, "U.S. Discounters Try Approach in Mexico," *Business Week*, May 31, 1993, p. 88.)

---

retailers and designers trying to tap into the lucrative $2.5 billion television shopping market.[7]

Two other major retailers have already taken the plunge—R. H. Macy & Co. and Nordstrom. Macy's is creating its own shopping channel—and plans to be a big star on the tube. For a relatively limited investment, the chain can reach new customers—10 to 20 million in a matter of a year or two—particularly in the middle of the country where it has no stores.[8] Nordstrom, with an announcement that "It is our intention to be a major player in this new arena," is exploring both interactive TV and home shopping broadcast channels.[9]

A final popular out-of-store method of marketing such convenience items as soft drinks, snack foods, newspapers, candy, and gum is **vending-machine retailing,** *distribution of products to consumers by coin-operated or card-operated machines.* Even though most individual sales are less than a dollar, there are so many vending machines, and they are so conveniently placed, that total sales are high.

vending-machine retailing
Distribution of products to consumers by coin-operated or card-operated machines.

Vending-machine sales are concentrated in a narrow product line, with beverages, cigarettes, and food items representing 97 percent of the total in the United States. Newer technology allows vending machines to make change for dollar bills, talk to consumers, use video screens to display merchandise, and "cook" the food.

Another product being molded to the vending options is water—the world's most popular beverage. Water Point Systems has signed a twenty-year exclusive contract with Cadbury Beverages that will allow Water Point to sell purified water by the gallon from special machines using Cadbury's Canada Dry trademark.[10]

The Physical Distribution System

For goods to reach their target market, whether they are intended for the industrial or the consumer market, organizations have to create a physical distribution system. The **physical distribution system** is *the activities that take place as goods move through channels.* These activities include warehousing, order processing, materials handling, transportation, and inventory control. Let's discuss each briefly.

Warehousing

Warehousing is *receiving, identifying, and sorting goods.* The warehouse function can be provided by company-owned (private) or public warehouses. Within the framework of warehousing the following activities normally take place:

physical distribution system
Activities that take place as goods move through channels.

warehousing
Receiving, identifying, and sorting goods.

At distributors' warehouses, goods are received, logged, sorted, and then selected as needed for distribution to customers.

- *Receiving goods.* The goods are delivered and the warehouse signs for them and accepts responsibility for them.
- *Identifying goods.* The received goods are marked, coded, or tagged for identification. Inventory records are updated.
- *Sorting goods.* Goods may be sorted by size, color, quantity, or other criteria before being stored.
- *Picking goods.* As orders are received, selected items are taken from the store for shipment to a customer.

Order Processing

Order processing includes *the grouping of products specified by the customer and the accompanying paperwork.* The activities include development of the shipping orders, requisitions from inventory, and collection of the physical goods. Order processing begins as soon as the customer places an order—by fax, telephone, mail, or computer. The order is then sent to the warehouse, where the items are "picked" from storage, assembled for shipment, packaged, and shipped.

order processing
The grouping of products specified by the customer and the accompanying paperwork.

Materials Handling

Materials handling includes *the activities involved in physically handling goods while they are in the warehouse.* The goal of a sound materials handling system is to move goods as quickly as possible while minimizing the number of times they are handled. The use of conveyer belts, palletizing boxes, and containerization—packing goods in a container and then shipping the entire container rather than individual boxes—all provide for efficiency.

materials handling
The activities involved in physically handling goods while they are in the warehouse.

Transportation

Transportation includes *the modes or means of shipping goods.* There are five major modes: railroads, trucks, waterways, airways, and pipelines. Each has its strengths and weaknesses as shown in Figure 14.5.

transportation
The modes or means of shipping goods.

RAILROADS Almost 40 percent of all products are shipped by rail. Railroads carry a wide range of products such as coal, lumber, chemicals, and automobiles. They are capable of reaching a large number of locations and are cost-efficient.

TRUCKS Trucks are the most flexible carriers. They can travel anywhere there are roads, and they provide door-to-door service in almost every community in the United States. Trucks carry livestock, clothing, produce, furniture, and other valuable, nonbulk items. Combining trucks with containerization—introduced in materials handling—makes for great efficiency. Containerized shipments can be loaded on a truck, then the truck can be loaded onto a train, ship, or airplane and taken to its destination and offloaded, and the goods can be delivered to the customer. The names attached to these forms of hitchhiking are *piggyback, fishyback,* and *birdyback.*

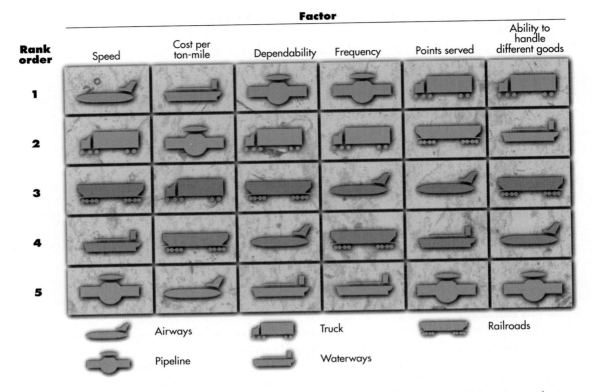

Figure 14.5
Advantages of basic transportation modes.

WATERWAYS Transportation by water includes use of barges and cargo ships. Though they are the least costly, they are the slowest and least dependable and are limited to cities that have ports. Goods commonly carried include chemicals, petroleum, and iron ore.

AIRWAYS Normally, the fastest way to ship goods is by air—and it is also the most expensive. Goods shipped by air usually are of high value (emergency parts and diagnostic or technical equipment) or are perishable (flowers, lobsters).

PIPELINE The products shipped by pipeline include oil, coal (in a watery mixture called slurry), and natural gas. Pipelines provide a continuous flow of products but have inflexible routes and limited capacity.

Inventory Control

inventory control
Monitoring of the physical inventory of goods, monitoring inventory levels, and minimizing reorder costs.

Inventory control includes *monitoring of the physical inventory of goods, monitoring inventory levels, and minimizing reorder costs.* Inventory control attempts to maximize usable inventory and minimize the costs to the organization of that inventory.

Wal-Mart, as well as other "power retailers" featured in this chapter's Manager's Notebook, has installed inventory technology to meet the needs of consumers. Using a combination of handheld terminals, personal computer networks, and satellite communications, stores can order directly from suppliers, rather than awaiting central processing.[11]

The Importance of Pricing Strategy

The fourth element of the marketing mix is pricing strategy, which involves establishing prices for a product that will return a profit. The organization's pricing decisions are critical for the long-term survival of the company. The prices and the volume of goods sold at those prices determine the revenue received by the firm and eventually its profits. If the wrong price is charged, products can be priced right out of the market.

Pricing decisions are important from the consumer's viewpoint. To a consumer, **price** is *the exchange value of a product expressed in monetary terms.* What is a fair or an unfair price to a consumer? That question can be answered only if and when the consumer buys the product. The price paid by the consumer is not just for the tangible product features but also for the intangibles, such as being the first to own a product or having the newest product.

A company develops a pricing strategy to accomplish organizational objectives. A firm can select from among three general pricing objectives: sales volume objectives, profitability objectives, and status quo objectives.

- *Sales volume objectives* emphasize growth in sales or growth in market share.
- *Profit objectives* emphasize the maximizing of profit or earning a specific return on investment.
- *Status quo objectives* are set by companies that want to maintain their present position. They may be driven by a need to meet competitors' prices, to maintain a good relationship with government agencies and channel members, and to create a good public image by focusing on developing a perception of fair and ethical pricing.

price
The exchange value of a product expressed in monetary terms.

Determining Prices

How does a marketer determine the price of a product or service? Three distinct approaches can be taken: the supply and demand approach, the cost-oriented approach, and the market approach. Even though each is a distinct alternative, in essence they complement each other. Through their use, the company is assured that it will cover its costs, make a profit, respond to competition, and adjust for what the consumer thinks the product is worth.

Supply and Demand Approach

Supply and demand describe the marketplace. Their interaction is an informal, invisible bargaining table where producers and consumers constantly negotiate the amount of a product they are willing to make or consume at a given price. Producers who are able and willing to satisfy consumer demand at

supply
The quantity of a product that producers are willing to make available at a given price.

demand
The quantity of a product that customers are willing to buy at a particular price.

equilibrium price
The point at which what the consumers are willing to pay is equal to what producers are willing to accept for a product.

Figure 14.6
Supply and demand curves and equilibrium price for hand-held electronic calculators.

a price that both find acceptable will prevail over competitors who are either unable or unwilling to adjust their prices to align with consumers' actions.

Supply refers to *the quantity of a product that producers are willing to make available at a given price.* When prices are high, producers are willing to supply more. Low prices encourage them to supply less. Part A of Figure 14.6 presents a hypothetical supply curve for hand-held electronic calculators. Notice that companies are not willing to supply as many calculators at a price of $5 as when the price is $25.

Demand is *the quantity of a product that customers are willing to buy at a particular price.* High prices discourage demand, as consumers seek substitutes or simply live without a product rather than pay what producers are asking. In the case of hand-held calculators, customers may elect instead to make mathematical calculations mentally or with pencil and paper. Low prices, on the other hand, may attract more new customers to the product and may encourage current users to buy more than one. Part B of Figure 14.6 presents a hypothetical demand curve for hand-held electronic calculators. Notice that if a company chose to lower its price from $25 to $5, consumers would demand 20,000 more units.

Equilibrium price is *the point at which what the consumers are willing to pay is equal to what the producers are willing to accept for a product.* At this point the quantity supplied equals the quantity demanded. Part C of Figure 14.6 shows how the supply curve and the demand curve meet to determine the equilibrium price.

Determining the equilibrium point and price requires adjustment. The initial high prices above equilibrium that encourage producers to make and

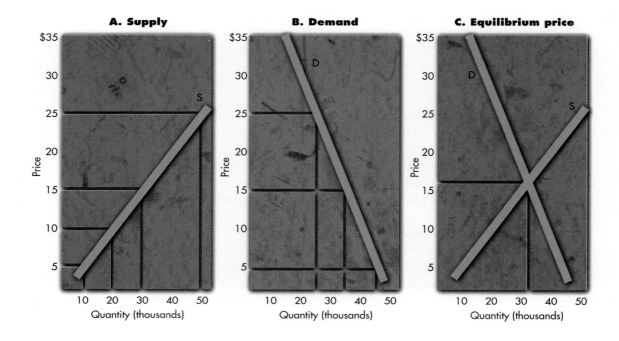

sell the product drive some consumers away. A surplus of goods results. Manufacturers may respond by lowering the price to get rid of the excess inventory. In doing so they will eventually reach an equilibrium price—an amount that both buyers and sellers find acceptable. The situation also works in reverse. An originally low price below equilibrium attracts many consumers. The resulting scarcity prompts manufacturers to supply more and charge higher prices. The price climbs until an equilibrium is reached.

The interaction of supply and demand in pricing can be seen when new companies enter the marketplace and compete with established firms. The new firms supply more goods, which in turn adds to the total supply on the market. The total supply is now more than the consumers need. This "glut" is responded to by some sellers lowering the price to attract buyers. The seesaw action of supply, price, and demand will continue until a market or equilibrium price is established.

Supply and demand analysis is correct with regard to the overall market for a product, but companies still face the problem of setting the price for an individual product. It is difficult to determine in advance the amount of a product that will be bought at a certain price. Thus, business has tended to adopt cost-oriented approaches.

Cost-Oriented Approach

Some companies adopt the **cost-oriented approach**—*determining price by focusing on costs of merchandise, accompanying services, and overhead costs, and then adding an amount for desired profit.* There are two basic approaches: markup pricing and break-even analysis.

MARKUP PRICING Companies can use **markup pricing** by *calculating all the costs associated with a product and then determining a markup percentage to cover the costs and expected profit.* The markup percentage is calculated in the following manner:

$$\text{Markup percentage} = \frac{\text{Selling price} - \text{Merchandise cost}}{\text{Selling price}}$$

For example, if all the costs of a product (shipping, overhead, merchandise) are $6 and the selling price is $8, the markup is $2 and the markup percentage is 25 percent:

$$\text{Markup percentage} = \frac{8 - 6}{8} = 25\%$$

Markup pricing is used by many retailers and wholesalers. It is part of distribution channel tradition and is easy to apply. But it has one major

cost-oriented approach
Determining price by focusing on costs of merchandise, accompanying services, and overhead costs, and then adding an amount for desired profit.

markup pricing
Calculating all the costs associated with a product and then determining a markup percentage to cover the costs and expected profit.

break-even analysis
A method of determining the number of units that must be sold at a given price to recover costs and make a profit.

total costs
The total of fixed costs and variable costs.

fixed costs
Costs that remain constant regardless of the number of units produced.

variable costs
Costs that arise when the first unit is produced and that increase with production.

total revenue
A figure determined by multiplying price times the number of units sold.

break-even point
The point at which sales revenue equals total costs.

shortcoming: the correct percentage as an absolute is difficult to determine. Setting a 40 or 50 percent markup because it is tradition does not take into consideration the effect of consumers' wishes or competitors' actions.

BREAK-EVEN ANALYSIS Companies also may choose to use **break-even analysis**, *a method of determining the number of units that must be sold at a given price to recover costs and make a profit.* In this approach a firm can compare the results on profits of using different prices.

In doing break-even analysis, the company is comparing total costs with total revenue. **Total costs** are *the total of fixed costs and variable costs.* **Fixed costs** are *costs that remain constant regardless of the number of units produced.* Rent, fire insurance premiums, payments on production equipment, and managers' salaries are examples of fixed costs. **Variable costs** are *costs that arise when the first unit is produced and that increase with production.* Salespeople's salaries, production workers' wages, raw materials, and energy used to operate production equipment are examples of variable costs. **Total revenue** is *a figure determined by multiplying price times the number of units sold.*

Figure 14.7 shows how fixed costs, variable costs, and total sales revenue combine to fix the **break-even point**—*the point at which sales revenue equals total costs.* Above that point, additional sales result in increasingly larger profits; below it, the firm operates at a loss. In our example, the firm must sell 22,000 calculators at the $16 equilibrium price to break even.

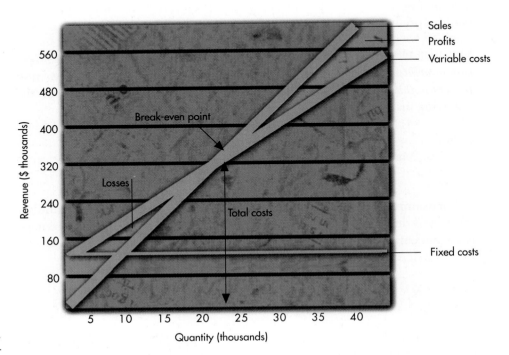

Figure 14.7
Determining the break-even point.

A break-even point (BEP) can also be determined by using the formula:

$$\text{BEP (units)} = \frac{\text{Total fixed costs}}{\text{Price per unit} - \text{Variable costs per unit}}$$

A product selling for $15 has total fixed costs of $30,000 and variable costs of $5 per unit. For the company to break even, it must sell 3,000 units:

$$\text{BEP} = \frac{30,000}{15 - 5}$$

$$= \frac{30,000}{10} = 3,000$$

Both cost-oriented approaches must be compared with the market demand for product, as previously noted. In markup pricing the markups desired may have to be adjusted based on consumers' reaction. Companies have to be willing to take less profit. In break-even analysis the company can evaluate various prices and their profit potential. It will then have to use market research to determine what the potential sales volume is at each price.

Market Approach

Another variable to be considered is the impact of the current market prices based on the **market approach**, *a method of price determination that recognizes that variables in the marketplace influence price.* These variables include competition, political factors, the social and cultural environment, individual perceptions, and timing. The market approach has been quite evident in the computer industry. In the ongoing industry price war, consumers have benefited from the major players—Apple, Dell, IBM—taking aggressive action to increase sales. In one action, Apple slashed prices twice within a two-month period. The first resulted in a 16 percent cut in some computer prices and a 29 percent reduction in some printer prices. In the second round, both computer and printer prices were reduced by 10 percent.[12]

All these approaches—supply and demand, markup pricing, break-even analysis, and the market approach—need to be combined to determine prices effectively. Each has strengths. If one is used without the other, gaps in information will result. Figure 14.8 illustrates the elements of overall price determination.

market approach
A method of price determination that recognizes that variables in the marketplace influence price.

Potential Pricing Strategies

Once the basic price is established by using a combination of supply and demand, cost, and market considerations, the next step is to apply various pricing strategies. Companies have a number of potential pricing strategies to

Figure 14.8
Elements of price determination.

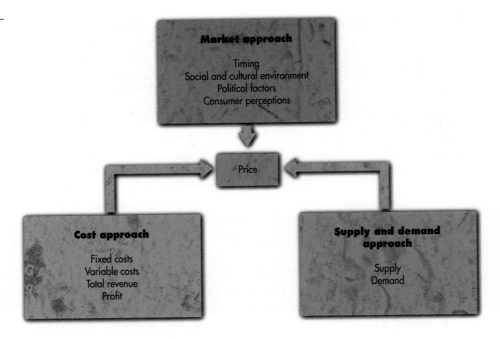

implement. The choice depends on company objectives, stage of the product life cycle, and competition.

NEW PRODUCT STRATEGIES When introducing new products to the market, companies can choose skimming pricing or penetration pricing.

Skimming (as in "skimming the cream off milk") is *charging a relatively high price when a product first appears on the market.* Makers of new high-technology products that cost a great deal to invent, perfect, and manufacture want to recover those product development costs as soon as possible, and skimming is a logical policy to follow. Apple computers, Hewlett-Packard printers, and Nintendo electronic games are all examples of products introduced with a skimming price policy.

Another introductory pricing strategy is **penetration pricing**, which is *introducing a product at a low price intended to capture the mass market for the good or service.* The objective is to penetrate as much of the market as quickly as possible and to build brand loyalty. This strategy was followed by Lewis Galoob Toys, a San Francisco–based manufacturer, in introducing Bouncin Babies dolls. The retail price of the dolls was set at under $10 each, with volume as the target.

PSYCHOLOGICAL PRICING STRATEGIES Psychological strategies encourage consumers to make buying decisions based on emotional rather than rational motives. The strategies include prestige pricing, odd pricing, multiple-unit pricing, price lining, and leader pricing.

skimming
Charging a relatively high price when a product first appears on the market.

penetration pricing
Introducing a product at a low price intended to capture the mass market for the good or service.

Prestige pricing is *setting the price high to convey the image of quality*. Although price and quality are not always related (we do not always get what we pay for), many consumers believe that they go together, and producers react accordingly. In fact, some marketers who experimented with prestige pricing for shopping and specialty goods have found that their unit sales actually increased after raising prices. Rolex uses prestige pricing strategy for its watches. The company not only produces a quality product, it also has developed the price-quality image in the consumer's eye. This approach has taken Rolex "out of competition."

With **odd pricing**, *the seller selects as prices amounts that fall just below an even number*, such as $29.99, $19.98, or $9.95. Although we realize that those amounts are only pennies short of $30, $20, or $10, they still cushion the blow of round figures. Everything from men's cologne to used cars is priced in this manner.

A practice in which a company offers consumers a lower than unit price if a specified number of units are purchased is **multiple-unit pricing**. For example, products that are six for $1.50 or two for $.99 are known to be more attractive than items that are $.30 or $.50 each.

When a company develops more than one model of product, a price lining strategy can be used. **Price lining** is *setting distinct prices for the different models in a product line*. Each model in the line is of different quality and sold at a different price. Sears sells its paints under a price lining strategy; it offers distinct qualities of paint with accompanying prices of $9.98, $14.98, and $19.96 per gallon.

Firms involved in retailing may use **leader pricing**, *selling attractive items at lower than normal prices*. The objective is to increase customer traffic in the store. Low prices on soft drinks, sugar, and coffee may be offered to the consumer as attractive invitations.

DISCOUNTING STRATEGY A strategy used by nearly all organizations in one form or another is price discounts to encourage purchases. **Price discounts** are *deductions allowed from the established price*. Discounts include cash discounts (prompt payment), trade discounts (given to a channel member by another channel member for performing marketing services), and quantity discounts (buy fifty cases and get a 10 percent discount).

COMPETITIVE PRICING STRATEGIES Companies often set prices in response to competition. There are two basic approaches: relative pricing and follow-the-leader.

A **relative pricing** strategy is *a decision to set prices above the competition, below the competition, or at the same level as the competition*. The company

---

prestige pricing
Setting the price high to convey the image of quality.

odd pricing
Selecting as prices amounts that fall just below an even number.

multiple-unit pricing
A practice in which a company offers consumers a lower than unit price if a specific number of units are purchased.

price lining
Setting distinct prices for the different models in a product line.

leader pricing
Selling attractive items at lower than normal prices.

price discounts
Deductions allowed from the established price.

relative pricing
A decision to set prices above the competition, below the competition, or at the same level as the competition.

YOU DECIDE

Think of a supermarket or superstore you have been in recently. What type of goods were priced using multiple-unit pricing strategy? What specific products were priced as leaders? What examples of psychological or odd pricing were evident? Were there examples of prestige pricing in the ice cream section? If so, which brands?

makes a conscious strategy decision to base its pricing on what its direct competitors are doing.

Under the philosophy of **follow-the-leader pricing,** *companies do not set prices but react to others' prices.* With this approach, smaller companies or conservative companies choose to let others determine prices. The plumbing and steel industries, for example, have mature companies with the economic strength and market control to set the pace in product pricing. This condition generally is referred to as *price leadership* or *administered prices.* Smaller firms, which are content to avoid rocking the boat, will raise their prices along with the industry leaders rather than keep their prices low and risk triggering a price war.

follow-the-leader pricing
Companies do not set prices but react to others' prices.

One approach to competitive pricing is to undercut the competition in everyday pricing.

SUMMARY

Distribution strategy is the third element of the marketing mix. Distribution involves (1) the routes goods take and (2) the activities involved in getting the goods to the consumer—a physical distribution system.

The two major channels of distribution are for industrial goods and consumer goods. Each type of good has four potential channels to use for distribution. Each type can potentially be distributed directly from manufacturer to actual user. In addition, each has potential channels using wholesalers and agents. Only the consumer goods channel utilizes retailers.

The actual routes, or channels, of distribution selected by a manufacturer are determined by a number of variables, including the market segment, the geographic location of the market segment, the type of product, the ability to perform the marketing functions, the competitors' distribution strategy, and the degree of market coverage.

The channels of distribution are composed of wholesalers and retailers. Wholesalers sell goods to retailers, to other wholesalers, and to industrial users but do not sell in significant amounts to the final consumer. Retailers perform the business activities involved in the sale of goods and services to the ultimate consumer or user.

Goods move through the channels by means of a physical distribution system. A physical distribution system includes the activities of warehousing, order processing, materials handling, transportation, and inventory control.

Pricing strategy is the fourth element of the marketing mix. It is involved with establishing prices (exchange value of a product expressed in monetary terms) that will return a profit. These prices are developed to accomplish organizational objectives: sales volume, profitability, or status quo objectives.

There are three approaches for determining price: supply and demand, cost-oriented (markup and break-even analysis), and the market approach. While each offers a distinct alternative, in essence they all need to be used to determine a price. They complement each other and provide information for the company to cover its costs, make a profit, respond to competition, and adjust for what the consumer thinks the product is worth.

Companies may select different pricing strategies depending on company objectives, the product life cycle, and competition. These potential strategies can be categorized into new product strategies (skimming and penetration pricing), psychological pricing strategies (prestige pricing, odd pricing, multiple-unit pricing, price lining, and leader pricing), discount strategy, and competitive strategies (relative pricing and follow-the-leader pricing).

KEY TERMS

break-even analysis p. 458
break-even point p. 458
catalog store p. 450
chain store p. 446
channel of distribution *or* marketing channel p. 439
convenience store p. 449
cost-oriented approach p. 457
demand p. 456
department stores p. 446
discount store p. 448
equilibrium price p. 456
exclusive distribution p. 443
factory outlets p. 450
fixed costs p. 458
follow-the-leader pricing p. 462
home shopping p. 450
hypermarket p. 449

independent retailer p. 446
in-home *or* door-to-door retailer p. 450
intensive distribution p. 442
inventory control p. 454
leader pricing p. 461
mail-order retailing p. 450
market approach p. 459
markup pricing p. 457
materials handling p. 453
multiple-unit pricing p. 461
odd pricing p. 461
off-price retailer p. 448
order processing p. 453
penetration pricing p. 460
physical distribution system p. 452
prestige pricing p. 461
price p. 455

price discounts p. 461
price lining p. 461
relative pricing p. 461
retailers p. 439
selective distribution p. 443
skimming p. 460
specialty store p. 448
supermarket p. 448
superstore p. 449

supply p. 456
total costs p. 458
total revenue p. 458
transportation p. 453
variable costs p. 458
vending-machine retailing p. 451
warehouse clubs p. 450
warehousing p. 452
wholesalers p. 439

FOR REVIEW AND DISCUSSION

1. Evaluate the statement "A firm can have the best products in the world, people can know about them and want them, but all this will be useless if they cannot get the products when and where they want them."
2. What four channels are available for industrial goods? When would each be selected?
3. Why would a manufacturer choose to use direct distribution to the ultimate consumer?
4. Why would manufacturers choose to use a channel that includes both an agent and a wholesaler?
5. What variables influence the choice of distribution channels?
6. What is meant by intensive, selective, and exclusive distribution?
7. Distinguish between a wholesaler and a retailer.
8. List six types of in-store retailers. For each type identify a store in your community that fits the category.
9. What type of goods are normally sold by mail-order retailing?
10. What is the difference between volume and profitability price objectives? Why would a company set volume objectives rather than profitability objectives?
11. Explain how supply and demand interact to arrive at an equilibrium point and price.
12. When markup and break-even analysis are used to determine price, what important factor is not included? How can a company correct this problem?
13. What type of information does the market approach to pricing provide management? How does this approach complement the cost-oriented and supply and demand approaches?
14. Is there any difference between skimming price strategy and prestige price strategy? If so, what is it?
15. What is the advantage of adopting a price lining strategy?

APPLICATIONS

Case 14.1: Value Pricing: Just Another Discount Tactic?

U.S. automakers are trying a price strategy that gives consumers more car for less money while simplifying manufacturing and cutting costs. The strategy is called value pricing, and it seems like a no-brainer—add popular options to a car, cut its price substantially, then stand back while buyers flood the showrooms. And, as an added bonus—to Detroit's delight—it is a strategy that Japanese automakers, hurt by unfavorable currency exchange rates, probably can't match.

Value pricing is a huge change from business as usual. It gives customers the features they want at a relatively low price, often in the least expensive models. It is also helping to push GM, Ford, and Chrysler's price advantage close to $3,000 over comparable Japanese models.

For years, Detroit went in the other direction, using the good-better-best system. The trick: Advertise a low-price stripped model to get shoppers in the showroom. The salesperson then tells the shopper that the cheaper model is good, of course, but suggests that he or she would be happier in a pricier, better model with extra features. From there it is a short step to the high-dollar best model with all the options the customer wants—plus lots he or she doesn't want but can't avoid paying for. So the customer winds up with too much car, too little cash, and a sour attitude.

Value pricing could solve the problem for both consumer and manufacturer. Consumers can balance the price-value equation in their minds without all the horse trading and dickering that makes most customers cringe at the thought of buying a car. On the other hand, manufacturers, by reducing the number of variations, can cut the number of parts needed, thus lowering inventory costs, saving assembly time, and making it tougher to install the wrong parts.

As good as value pricing looks, it will require two radical changes to occur. First, automakers have to eliminate the rebate cushion they pack into every sticker price—as much as $4,000 on some models—which hurts their ability to offer clearance-sale rebates. And dealers must accept shrunken profit margins that hurt their ability to negotiate with buyers. These changes may be difficult to accept—but they may offer more long-range profitability.

Questions

1. In order for value pricing to work, what do manufacturers need to consider about the consumer when they set prices? Explain your answer.

2. If you were an automaker, how would you respond to the statement "Value pricing is just another discount tactic"? Explain your answer.

3. Have automakers used supply and demand, costs, and market considerations to establish prices? Cite specific examples from the case to support your answer.

For more information, see James. R. Healey, "Automakers Shifting to Value Pricing," *USA Today*, July 9, 1993, pp. 1B–2B; Micheline Mayward, "GM Slams Door on Rising Prices," *USA Today*, June 4, 1993, p. 1B.

Case 14.2: Price Club Fails to Compete

One of the dilemmas involved in building a successful business is to balance the desire to grow and expand—the attraction of greater profits, more markets, and more stores can be almost irresistible to a new business—with the need to maintain a lean, debt-free organization. Sometimes organizations are able to accomplish both objectives through careful planning, but more often than not one objective

dominates the other. Such was the case with Price Club.

In 1976 Sol Price opened a 100,000-square-foot discount warehouse store in San Diego. His simple, yet revolutionary, marketing idea was like an earthquake in the retail business. Building on a strategy of carrying a select number of products (a tenth of the 30,000 products traditionally carried by the typical supermarket) offered in bulk at discount prices, Price Club was instantly successful with both businesses and individual consumers. By 1980 Price Club had sales of $148 million. It went on to achieve eleven straight years of increased sales and earnings.

Despite this success, throughout the 1980s the company carefully refused to expand much beyond its California base. Even when other competitors entered the scene early in the decade, Price Club did not respond to the threat by expanding into other markets. Rather, Sol Price insisted on moderate expansion in order to maintain tight control over costs and overall operations.

When Price Club finally made a large push toward expansion in the early 1990s, it found the markets around the country already dominated by other warehouse stores, including Sam's, PACE, and Costco. Unable to compete with the new larger warehouse stores, Price Club surrendered to a merger with Costco. After almost two decades of business, Price Club now finds itself under the management of Costco CEO James Sinegal and operates as a new company, Price/Costco.

Questions

1. What risks are associated with a strategy of rapid expansion?

2. Is it necessary for a company to treat the two objectives of growth and being debt-free as mutually exclusive—can both be accomplished simultaneously? Explain your answer.

3. If you were a marketing consultant, what advice would you have given Sol Price? What specifically would you have said to him?

4. If you had been in Sol Price's position, what would you have done? Explain your strategy and how you would have carried it out.

For more information, see Amy Barrett, "A Retailing Pacesetter Pulls Up Lame," *Business Week*, July 12, 1993, p. 122.

REFERENCES

1. Peter D. Bennet (ed.), *Dictionary of Marketing Terms* (Chicago: American Marketing Association, 1988), p. 183.

2. Russel Mitchell, "From Dirty Towels to the Top of the Heap," *Business Week,* March 10, 1993, p. 63.

3. Joel R. Evans and Barry Berman, *Marketing,* 5th ed. (New York: Macmillan, 1993), p. 423.

4. Zachary Schiller, "Clout: More and More, Retail Giants Rule the Marketplace," *Business Week,* December 1992, p. 67.

5. Wendy Zellner, "When Wal-Mart Starts a Food Fight, It's a Doozy," *Business Week,* June 14, 1993, pp. 92–93.

6. Steven H. Lee, "Hypermarkets Struggle with Bigness of Business," *Dallas Morning News,* April 12, 1993, p. 1H.

7. Jeane MacIntosh, "Liz Claiborne's TV Debut Slated for Sunday at 9," *Women's Wear Daily,* May 14, 1993, pp. 1, 11.

8. David Moin, "TV Could Be Macy's Hottest Sales Channel," *Women's Wear Daily,* May 3, 1993, pp. 1, 6.

9. Ellen Neuborne, "Nordstrom Turns to Home Shopping," *USA Today,* May 18, 1993, p. B1.

10. Marla Halkias, "Purified Water to Be Sold in Vending Units," *Dallas Morning News,* April 19, 1993, p. 1D.

11. Tom Steinert-Threlkeld, "Global Network Under Firm Control," *Dallas Morning News,* June 13, 1993, p. H1.

12. John Sarno, "Apple Plans Price Cuts, Rebates, Newspaper Says," *Dallas Morning News,* June 14, 1993, p. 6D.

CAREER CAPSULE

Management Opportunities at Agway, Inc.

If it has anything to do with agriculture, Agway, Inc. probably does it. This *Fortune* 500 company is involved in a smorgasbord of business areas, including agricultural supplies, consumer products, energy, food, and financial services. Its employees make, process, market, and deliver an enormous range of products and services to hundreds of thousands of customers each day.

Agway is justifiably proud of the career opportunities and work environment it offers the newly minted college graduates it recruits. The company enjoys a unique combination of size and diversified operations and a family atmosphere not always found in a business its size.

Agway's Management Development Program gives trainees twelve months of comprehensive training along with the hands-on experience they need to become management leaders. Trainees are first assigned to a certified trainer who oversees their development and progress throughout the program. During this important time, they also spend about ten weeks attending seminars and workshops at Agway's training center in Syracuse, New York. This combination of field and classroom experience enables trainees to apply what they've learned at their respective field locations while acquiring many additional skills through their workshops and seminars.

The company is quite selective about the people it recruits into this program, and for good reason: Agway invests more than $50,000 in each trainee. The program also brings recruits into the orbit of many seasoned Agway employees, who share their knowledge and expertise. The result? Trainees with the self-confidence, experience, and knowledge to succeed and to qualify for promotion from within as future opportunities arise.

After completing the program, trainees may work in management in one of several areas, including Agway stores or petroleum plants. The company is quick to point out that most of the college graduates who complete its Management Development Program are still employed by Agway five years later. This demonstrates how the company's people-oriented philosophy helps keep employees satisfied and moving forward.

Part Four

Finance and Management Information

15

MONEY AND FINANCIAL INSTITUTIONS

t's good to have money and the things money can buy. But it's good, too, to check up once in a while and make sure you haven't lost the things that money can't buy.

GEORGE LORIMER

CHAPTER OBJECTIVES
After studying this chapter, you should be able to:

1. Describe the functions of money in a society and list the items that make up the money supply of the United States.
2. Contrast the two causes of inflation and discuss how the Consumer Price Index monitors it.
3. Summarize the operations of a commercial bank.
4. Define the three kinds of thrift institutions and compare their operations.
5. Evaluate the role of the Federal Reserve System and discuss its organization and operation.
6. List and evaluate the devices that the Federal Reserve uses to regulate the money supply.
7. Comment on the need for the FDIC and describe its role in building public confidence in the banking system.
8. Summarize the status of interstate banking.

UP FRONT

Jim Howard is a New Hampshire native through and through. Born and raised in Lebanon, New Hampshire, he attended the University of New Hampshire in Durham, where he took his baccalaureate degree in piano performance. On graduating, he realized he might not land a job as a concert pianist, so he took a summer job as a bank teller. "I quickly learned that I enjoyed banking," he recalls, and he was soon working in the loan department of a savings bank in his hometown.

Howard learned a lot about commercial loans and consumer lending in those first few years. "But I soon realized I'd need more business education to do my job well, so I entered the executive MBA program at the University of New Hampshire. During the next two years I acquired broad management training and studied advanced accounting and finance and business law." It was a rigorous program; in addition to doing regular coursework, MBA candidates had to spend two weekends each month at the campus, and a full week each summer. "One of the greatest benefits was learning how to manage time effectively. Most of us had to balance between our full-time job, coursework, and family. Juggling these three made you learn and develop good time management skills."

In 1991 New London Trust decided to open a loan office in what is known as the Upper Valley region of New Hampshire, centered around Lebanon and Hanover. Jim Howard, with his banking experience

and knowledge of the region, accepted an offer to head the new loan office. "One of the keys to successful banking is knowing the market you serve," says Howard. "That means the area and its people. One of the most pleasurable parts of my job is watching businesses that I helped grow and become successful, and to see people buy their homes and raise their families."

Howard makes most of the lending decisions for his branch in Hanover, located just a few blocks from Dartmouth College. "I look at the credit history, income, the ability to repay, the collateral, and the person," he says. New London Trust is conservative in its lending and sticks to the fundamental credit decision criteria that make for a good loan decision. It's one bank that didn't get into a lot of speculative lending in the 1970s and 1980s.

"I feel I can do a better job for New London Trust because I live here. I'm on the street a lot. I can feel the pulse of the community, especially when I'm financing a new business or an expansion. I use this philosophy in my lending practices, and I've seen on a number of occasions when I've decided against making the loan that it was the right decision. Lending is a business where you've got to be right most of the time. There isn't a great margin for error!"

JAMES HOWARD

VICE PRESIDENT, LOANS, NEW LONDON TRUST

barter system
An economic system in which two parties trade certain goods and services that each needs to survive.

money
Any object that a group of people uses to pay its debts and buy the goods and services that it needs.

Most nations can point to a time in their history when they operated on the **barter system**, *an economic system in which two parties trade certain goods and services that each needs to survive.* The farmer would exchange a cow for seed, the cobbler would swap shoes for flour, and the country doctor, with a service in great demand, could trade medical care for practically everything.

This system, which flourished while we were living in agrarian societies, grew awkward and obsolete as households became less self-sufficient and specialization arrived with the Industrial Revolution. Given enough time and economic growth, every society eventually requires some form of money.

Money is *any object that a group of people uses to pay its debts and buy the goods and services that it needs.* In addition to money, however, an advanced economic system needs financial institutions that regulate demand for that money and make it possible for organizations and individuals to save, borrow, and transfer money as they carry out daily transactions. In this chapter we will examine money and the various institutions, such as commercial banks, the major thrift institutions, the Federal Reserve System, and the Federal Deposit Insurance Corporation, that affect its flow within our economy.

Putting Money in Perspective

Money performs several important functions for both companies and individuals. Its value also has a major impact on their ability to buy the goods and services they need to maintain or improve their standard of living.

What Money Does

A society's money functions as a medium of exchange, a measure of value, and a store of value, as is shown in Figure 15.1. To do so it must be relatively scarce and widely accepted. Objects that are used as money also must be durable, portable, and divisible if they are to serve people conveniently over a long period of time.

A MEDIUM OF EXCHANGE   Money makes it easier for us to accomplish the exchange functions of marketing that you learned about in Chapter 12—buying and selling. Although we sometimes think of money only as the bills and coins we carry in our wallets and pockets, certain societies and cultures have used some of the following unusual objects as money:

- Bison robes
- Bird-of-paradise feathers
- Bricks of tea
- Woodpecker scalps
- Manga bird feathers
- Elephant tail hair

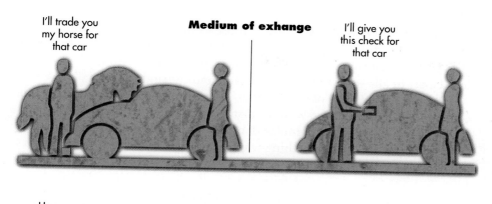

Figure 15.1
Functions of money.

A MEASURE OF VALUE   A society's money is a universal measure of worth. The value of everything from livestock to common stock can be expressed in a common denominator: money. This makes communication infinitely easier, because the parties to a transaction can express worth in the same units.

A STORE OF VALUE   We can convert our labor and any products we own into money of a certain value and store it in that form indefinitely. People regularly store their value in such other objects as real estate, precious metals, gems, and rare coins, but these are not as *liquid* (easily disposed of) as money. If you have stored your value in nonmonetary objects and want to purchase something like a stereo, you will have to convert those valued objects into money. This process can be costly and time consuming; you may need to have the items appraised to establish their value, and then find a buyer. Money is the most liquid asset of all—easily transferred from hand to hand.

It should be obvious, of course, that money must have a relatively stable value before people will be willing to store very much of their wealth in it. When the value of money declines, people rush to convert it to something whose value will hold steady or increase as time passes.

Counterfeiting naturally decreases the value of all the legitimate money in circulation. Although this practice has been a problem for centuries, there have been some recent interesting developments that frustrate attempts to counterfeit paper money. For example, the Reserve Bank of Australia has developed a device that places a hologram on Australia's plastic $10 bills.[1] Color photocopying machines have been used by would-be forgers in the United States for several years, but Canon recently invented a computer chip that enables its copy machines to identify paper money and produce a blank piece of paper instead of a color copy.[2]

> **YOU DECIDE**
>
> Live-aboard boaters who sail the South Pacific often must barter their skills in exchange for the services or products they need. What general and nautical-related skills would be most valuable to barter in remote ports of call? What conditions make money relatively worthless there?

The Federal Reserve System's high tech money sorting equipment has a battery of sensing devices that can detect all but the very best counterfeit money. For example, the paper in genuine bills contains red and blue fibers, and the black and green ink has a special magnetic composition that the sorting equipment's sensors recognize. In addition, genuine bills are printed by a complex intaglio technique that requires an enormous investment in equipment.[3]

Money in the United States

The money supply of the United States consists of three items: coins and paper (collectively called *currency*) and checking accounts. Federal law has declared coins and paper money to be *legal tender,* which means they must be accepted when tendered as payment for debts.

Paper money takes three days to print—one day for the front, one day for the back, and one for the overprinting of such data as the serial number and the seal of the Federal Reserve Bank that will issue it. The Bureau of Engraving and Printing produces approximately 1.6 billion $1 bills each year.

The mechanics of printing and replacing paper money pose problems. Constant passing from hand to hand wears out $1 bills in eighteen months. Larger denominations last slightly longer. Commercial banks return worn, damaged, and dirty bills to the Federal Reserve Bank in their district, where the Treasury Department exchanges the bills for new ones and destroys them. Damaged coins are melted down and recycled by the U.S. Assay Office.

Paper money is printed by the U.S. Bureau of Engraving and Printing and issued by Federal Reserve Banks.

A **check** *or* **demand deposit**, the third component of the United States money supply, is *a bank depositor's written order instructing the bank to pay a certain sum to a third party.* The bank, which owes the deposited money to the customer, provides this third-party payment, usually for a fee or service charge. Although they are not legal tender, 90 percent of all money spent is in the form of checks. Three of every four persons in America has a checking account.

A **savings account** *or* **time deposit** is *a sum of money, deposited with a bank, that cannot be withdrawn by writing a check.* Because the bank may require advance notice for withdrawal, time deposits are not considered part of the money supply.

Inflation

Inflation, which is *a decrease in the value of a society's money,* affects both individual and business purchasing power. If it becomes acute, public opinion of money's value erodes and economic chaos may result. Inflation has two general causes.

Demand-pull inflation *occurs when producers raise prices in response to strong consumer demand.* Items subject to demand-pull inflation have relatively inelastic demand. When market segment members appear willing to pay a higher price or view the product as a specialty item, entrepreneurs are tempted

check *or* demand deposit
A bank depositor's written order instructing the bank to pay a certain sum to a third party.

savings account *or* time deposit
A sum of money, deposited with a bank, that cannot be withdrawn by writing a check.

inflation
A decrease in the value of a society's money.

demand-pull inflation
Occurs when producers raise prices in response to strong consumer demand.

cost-push inflation
Occurs when producers pass rising labor, materials, and other costs on to consumers by increasing prices.

Consumer Price Index (CPI)
A figure that measures changes in purchasing power and the rate of inflation by expressing today's prices in 1982-1984 dollars.

to charge more and reap a higher return for their risk. In essence, consumer tolerance encourages producers to raise prices, almost as at an auction.

Cost-push inflation, the second type, *occurs when producers pass rising labor, materials, and other costs on to consumers by increasing prices.* Sometimes called *market power inflation,* this is a reaction to escalating costs. In the past two decades inflation has affected every country in the world. One of the major causes of this inflation has been escalating energy costs, a cost-push cause of inflation.

Inflation leads to witch hunting: management, labor, and consumers look for someone to blame. Management may accuse labor of a thirst for higher wages and more costly benefits, while labor criticizes management's lust for steadily increasing profits, and consumers complain even louder as they pay even more. In essence, everyone is responsible for inflation to some degree. This does not ease the intense pressure it places on corporate and household budgets, however.

The Consumer Price Index

The **Consumer Price Index (CPI),** computed by the U.S. Department of Labor's Bureau of Labor Statistics, is *a figure that measures changes in purchasing power and the rate of inflation by expressing today's prices in 1982–1984 dollars.* Prices for this standard base period represent 100 percent, and current prices are references to them. A CPI of 126, for example, means that consumers pay an average of $12.60 today for items that cost an average of $10.00 between 1982 and 1984.

Although the Bureau of Labor Statistics will continue to publish certain CPI data based on the former base year of 1967 as a convenience to some users, referencing data to the 1982–1984 base period began in January 1988. Comparing today's consumer prices to such a recent time makes them more relevant and meaningful.

There are actually two Consumer Price Indexes. The broadest one, CPI-U, tracks the impact of inflation on all urban consumers—approximately 80 percent of all citizens. The other index, CPI-W, assembles data on the purchasing power of wage earners and clerical employees and disregards self-employed and professional persons.

Early in 1983 the Department of Labor altered its method of calculating the CPI-U. One change involved adjusting the home ownership component so figures would more accurately reflect the true cost of shelter. The present CPI-U now disregards interest charges, real estate taxes, and other satellite costs of home ownership. The weights assigned to the 364 items involved in calculating this gauge of purchasing power were also adjusted. Gasoline, food, and clothing, for example, now receive greater emphasis.

The CPI is the most popular measure of how inflation dilutes buying power. The CPI-W is also a standard for computing increased benefits to military and civil service retirees and persons receiving Social Security payments. In addition, labor-management contracts covering more than 8.5 million workers tie wage increases to this measure of inflation. Each 1 percent increase in the CPI triggers approximately $1 billion in increased payments to these groups.

Commercial Banks

A **commercial bank** is *a profit-making corporation that accepts customers' deposits and lends them out to businesses and individual borrowers.* These banks accept both demand deposits (checking accounts) and time deposits (savings accounts), paying interest on the latter. Since December 31, 1980, both banks and savings and loan associations (which we will discuss later in this chapter) have been permitted to offer customers interest-bearing checking accounts called *NOW* accounts (for "negotiable order of withdrawal").

commercial bank
A profit-making corporation that accepts customers' deposits and lends them out to businesses and individual borrowers.

Banks' Lending Role

Commercial banks earn most of their income from interest on loans, but they also invest large amounts in interest-bearing United States government securities. The balances in depositors' accounts are actually debts that the bank must pay at some future date, and a bank could have difficulty paying depositors if many of them demanded their money at the same time.

Given their role as moneylenders, commercial banks occupy an influential position in our economic system. Their widespread lending operations can act as an accelerator or a brake on inflation and profoundly affect growth trends and public attitudes nationwide.

Commercial banks give their largest, most secure corporate borrowers a **prime rate of interest,** traditionally defined as *a lower rate of interest than that charged to most borrowers.* Although this definition has some validity, the concept of a prime rate has lost credibility within the last several years. A House Banking Committee survey of the nation's ten largest banks disclosed that each regularly lent money at less than its publicized prime rate. That figure often was merely a point at which potential big borrowers could begin interest-rate negotiations. A Federal Reserve Board study found that more than half of the large business loans made by several New York banks in one month were at less than the prime rate.

This discrepancy implies that the prime rate is a benchmark, or general guideline, and not the lowest rate available.

prime rate of interest
A lower rate of interest than that charged to most borrowers.

Certificates of Deposit

Commercial banks also issue **certificates of deposit (CDs),** *bank obligations that pay higher interest than regular savings accounts because the depositor agrees to leave the money on deposit for a certain length of time.* Depositors who need the funds before the certificates mature may cash them in, but the bank will

certificates of deposit (CDs)
Bank obligations that pay higher interest than regular savings accounts because the depositor agrees to leave the money on deposit for a certain length of time.

GLOBAL PERSPECTIVE

Banking has been a global industry since the days of the Phoenician traders. In fact, the largest banks are located in the Far East. Here's a list of the world's ten largest banks according to assets (amounts are in billions of U.S. dollars):

1. Agricultural Bank of China ($919.88)
2. Dai-Ichi Kangyo Bank ($425.51)
3. Sumitomo Bank ($406.11)
4. Sakura Bank ($405.96)
5. Sanwa Bank ($400.74)
6. Fuji Bank ($396.45)
7. Mitsubishi Bank ($380.44)
8. Credit Lyonnais ($306.33)
9. Deutsche Bank ($298.16)
10. Banque Nationale de Paris ($289.75)

Banking Across Borders

Source: Data from *Euromoney 500* (annual), June 1992, p. 108.

YOU DECIDE

What circumstances lead people to put their money in certificates of deposit instead of potentially higher-paying instruments such as common stock?

pay a lower rate of interest than if they had been held until maturity. Certificates of deposit are sold in denominations from $100 to $100,000 and up, generally for terms of six months to five years.

Major Thrift Institutions

The term *thrift institution* refers to three kinds of organizations: savings and loan associations, credit unions, and savings banks. These institutions encourage people to save for a rainy day, and they lend their deposits to other people who want to buy or build homes or purchase certain consumer goods.

Savings and Loan Associations

savings and loan associations (S&Ls)
Thrift institutions that accept time deposits and lend them to a variety of borrowers, especially to buyers of single-family homes.

Originated in Philadelphia in 1831, **savings and loan associations (S&Ls)** are *thrift institutions that accept time deposits and lend them to a variety of borrowers, especially to buyers of single-family homes.* These institutions may be organized in one of two ways.

MUTUAL S&LS Mutual S&Ls record deposits as shares of ownership, unlike deposits in commercial banks, which are considered debts or liabilities of those organizations. Payments on such shares are termed *dividends*—not interest—but the term *savings account* more recently has replaced the label *shares* in referring to deposits.

Hundreds of savings and loans went out of business during the S&L crisis. Here customers stand in line to withdraw their funds from a failed S&L in Paterson, New Jersey.

STOCK S&LS Stock-issuing S&Ls are owned by stockholders, like any other profit-making corporation. Mutual S&Ls may be chartered by the federal government or by an individual state (more than half are state chartered), but there is no federal provision for chartering stock S&Ls.

THE S&L CRISIS: AN INDUSTRY ON THE REBOUND The 1980s saw an epidemic of failures in the savings and loan industry. The problem began with abrupt interest rate increases in the early 1970s, when commercial banks and S&Ls were heavily regulated by the federal government.

As interest rates escalated, depositors withdrew money from S&L accounts (which were prohibited by law from paying higher interest) to invest in areas that offered a higher rate of return. This action, which left S&Ls short of cash, did not harm commercial banks as seriously because many of their deposits consisted of business checking accounts that paid no interest. S&Ls, by contrast, were prohibited from offering checking accounts and therefore found themselves at a competitive disadvantage.

Savings and loan associations coped with this outflow of funds by borrowing money to meet their cash needs. They received some minor relief in 1980, when Congress deregulated interest rates, but their financial woes persisted for at least one fundamental reason: the interest S&Ls were now able to pay to attract new depositors exceeded the fixed interest rates that they were earning on long-term loans that they had made to homeowners—the only major type of lending they were allowed to do until 1982, when S&L lending rules were relaxed.

S&Ls responded to the government's liberalized lending rules by selling off many of their old low-interest loans for a fraction of their value in order to get money to lend for business ventures that they hoped would help them to recover some of their losses and regain financial stability. That was not to be.

Many savings and loan executives were ill-prepared and not trained to wheel and deal in the more volatile world of speculative loans and investments. Mismanagement, economic downturns, risky lending practices, and alleged fraud by managers of many large S&Ls caused them to lose billions of dollars during the 1980s. In 1985, the Federal Savings and Loan Insurance Corporation (FSLIC), which insured depositors' funds in S&Ls, ran out of money. Congress issued $10 billion in government bonds and used the money to cover depositors' claims, but by that time many S&Ls were well on their way to failure.

Widespread emergency relief was the only way to avert an industrywide collapse, and Congress responded by passing the Financial Institutions Reform, Recovery and Enforcement Act in 1989. Under the terms of this law, the functions of the Federal Home Loan Bank Board, a government agency that regulated S&Ls in the same fashion that the Fed regulates commercial banks, were shifted to a newly created Treasury Department organization called the Office of Thrift Supervision. The now-bankrupt FSLIC was terminated. Its functions were taken over by the newly created Savings Association Insurance Fund (SAIF), which is controlled by the FDIC. This legislation also created the Resolution Trust Corporation (RTC), which is responsible for selling repossessed commercial and residential real estate and other collateral held by failed S&Ls. Commercial property included such diverse holdings as a karate studio and a bingo parlor in Louisiana, a mortuary in Texas, an airport in Colorado, and assorted hotels, restaurants, golf courses, churches, private hospitals, and marinas.

Observers claim in retrospect that the FSLIC failed to regulate S&Ls with a firm hand and to sound the alarm when loans turned sour. Prescribed lending and management guidelines were not enforced, and the problem was compounded by misleading accounting practices that obscured the real scope of the S&L crisis until the entire industry was in jeopardy.

Although previous estimates for the S&L bailout have been as high as $500 billion, it appears that the total cost may now amount to less than $300 billion.[4] The RTC hopes to complete liquidating failed S&Ls' collateral within a year or two, and its recent practice of auctioning off huge assets in bulk has greatly simplified the job. The agency hopes to finish all of its work in connection with the S&L crisis by 1996, which is the legally mandated deadline.[5]

Credit Unions

credit union
A mutual savings and lending society for people with a common bond.

A **credit union** is *a mutual savings and lending society for people with a common bond,* such as the same employer or union. It accepts their savings at rates comparable to those of savings and loan associations and lends them money at

MANAGER'S NOTEBOOK

What can you do if eccentric Uncle Sherman stashed some cash that has become damaged over the years? The situation may not be as bad as it looks. The Department of the Treasury's Bureau of Engraving and Printing handles some 30,000 claims and redeems mutilated currency valued at more than $30 million each year.

Paper bills have been abused and mutilated in every way imaginable. The bureau's Office of Currency Standards has a staff of experts who will examine currency that has been burned; involved in explosions; buried; damaged by rodents, liquids, or chemicals; or otherwise converted from crisp new bills to a nasty-looking pile of debris. If the currency falls within the bureau's guidelines for replacement, it will issue a Treasury check for the value of whatever is declared redeemable.

According to the bureau, currency is mutilated if less than one-half remains or it is in such poor condition that its value is questionable and it requires a special examination to determine what it's worth. (You can exchange notes that are merely soiled, defaced, torn, or disintegrated at your local bank, which will send them to the Federal Reserve Bank in its district).

Finders of mutilated currency should ship it to the bureau along with a letter stating the estimated value and explaining how the currency was damaged. Each case is carefully examined by a mutilated currency expert. The amount of time needed to process each case varies according to the examiner's workload and the nature of the damage. For example, people have found paper money that relatives had buried in coffee cans in the backyard, concealed between the walls of a decaying old building,

or squirreled away in outhouses for almost a century.

Although Treasury examiners can usually determine the amount and value of mutilated currency, these packaging guidelines make the process easier:

Damaged Money? Maybe the Treasury Can Help

- Do not disturb the fragments more than is absolutely necessary.
- Pack brittle currency in plastic and cotton and place the package in a secure container.
- If the currency was mutilated inside a container, leave it in the container to minimize further damage. If you must remove it, send the container along with the currency fragments and other contents from the container that may have pieces of currency attached.
- If the currency was flat when damaged, don't roll or fold it; if it was rolled when damaged, don't unroll it.

Senders should mail currency "Registered Mail, Return Receipt Requested" and insure it for its estimated value. If they prefer not to mail it, they can deliver it in person to the Office of Currency Standards during prescribed business hours. The Bureau of Engraving and Printing will provide confirmation of receipt for cases that are expected to take more than four weeks to process. The director of the Bureau of Engraving and Printing has the final authority over the settlement of mutilated currency claims.

(For more on mutilated currency, see "Preparation and Redemption of Mutilated U.S. Paper Currency," a publication of the Department of the Treasury, Bureau of Engraving and Printing.)

Credit unions provide financial services for the employees of thousands of companies and nonprofit organizations nationwide.

reasonable rates. The concept was originated in 1849 by Friedrich Wilhelm Raiffeisen, mayor of Flammersfeld, Germany, to enable drought-stricken farmers to avoid borrowing from unethical moneylenders who charged exorbitant interest rates. Technically speaking, members' savings represent shares in the organization. The group elects a board of directors, and members may volunteer their time to handle clerical and administrative duties. Larger, more sophisticated credit unions employ a salaried general manager and a full-time paid staff.

Most credit union loans are secured by such consumer products as major appliances and automobiles, but members can obtain unsecured "signature" loans up to a certain amount. Larger credit unions make both consumer goods loans and real estate loans.

Credit unions, like commercial banks and S&Ls, may be chartered by federal or state governments. Approximately 7,800 have federal charters and some 5,400 are chartered by states. The National Credit Union Administration (NCUA), a federal agency established in 1970, examines and supervises the federally chartered groups and insures their deposits (shares) in the same way that the FDIC insures deposits in commercial banks. All federally chartered credit unions must have this insurance.

Savings Banks

savings bank
A thrift institution that accepts time deposits and lends them for a variety of purposes, but especially for home purchase and construction.

A **savings bank,** which was formerly known as a mutual savings bank, is essentially the same as an S&L: *a thrift institution that accepts time deposits and lends them for a variety of purposes, but especially for home purchase and construction.* In several states savings banks accept demand as well as time deposits. If qualified, they may become members of the FDIC.

Although federal law now allows savings banks to be federally chartered, most are chartered in approximately fifteen states, primarily in New England, New York, and New Jersey. The Fed reports approximately 420 state-chartered savings banks in existence. Some of the largest are located in New York City.

The Federal Reserve System

Commercial banks keep only a small percentage of deposits on reserve, lending the rest to borrowers. Unusually heavy withdrawals, therefore, can exhaust a bank's cash, no matter how sound its loans might be. When this happens and word spreads among the bank's depositors, there can be a run on the bank, with most or all depositors demanding their money at once, causing the bank to fail.

One such panic, in 1907, led Congress to pass the **Federal Reserve Act of 1913,** *a law that created the Federal Reserve System, commonly called the Fed, and made it responsible for managing the nation's supply of money and credit.* The Fed, which has been called "the nation's banker," monitors the demand for money and credit nationwide and regulates their availability so that managed, responsible economic growth can occur.

Federal Reserve Act of 1913
A law that created the Federal Reserve System, commonly called the Fed, and made it responsible for managing the nation's supply of money and credit.

Organization and Membership

The Federal Reserve System consists of a seven-member board of governors, appointed by the president and confirmed by the Senate. Each member serves a fourteen-year term, but terms are staggered so that one seat is vacant every two years. As Figure 15.2 shows, the Fed has established a dozen Federal Reserve Banks in strategic parts of the country. These serve as "bankers' banks" for commercial banks that belong to the Federal Reserve System.

Commercial banks may be chartered by the federal government or by the states in which they are founded. Those with federal charters are called

Figure 15.2

Federal reserve banks and districts.

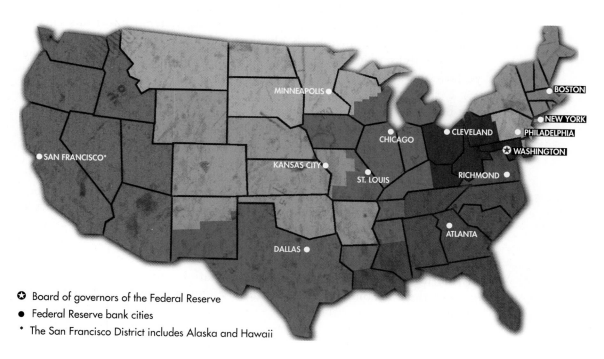

● Board of governors of the Federal Reserve
● Federal Reserve bank cities
* The San Francisco District includes Alaska and Hawaii

national banks and must belong to the Federal Reserve System. You can identify one by the word *national* in its name or the letters *N.A.* (meaning nationally associated) appearing after it. State-chartered commercial banks, called *state banks,* may join the Federal Reserve System if they wish, and most of the large ones have done so.

Approximately 38 percent of the nation's 12,000 commercial banks belong to the Fed, and they hold nearly 72 percent of all commercial bank deposits. Just under 1,000 of these Fed members are state chartered; more than 7,000 state-chartered banks are not members. Commercial banks operate under a dual banking system: they must comply with both federal and state banking laws and regulatory agencies. The Fed sets the maximum interest rates that member banks can pay on time deposits, approves mergers, and establishes specific bank management rules that its members must observe.

Reasons for Joining the Federal Reserve System

Commercial banks join the Federal Reserve System chiefly for the privilege of borrowing from the Fed to meet temporary cash shortages and to have access to the Fed's system of collecting checks written by depositors. Federal Reserve membership allows a bank to borrow from its district bank when depositors make heavy withdrawals—for Christmas spending, to pay income taxes, or to finance summer vacations, for example—thus depleting the bank's cash supply. In addition, the Federal Reserve "bankers' banks" have a nationwide check-collection network that speeds a check's trip through the banking system. The Federal Reserve Bank of Minneapolis estimates that more than half of all checks are mailed to other cities and must be returned to the bank on which they are drawn through the banking system. The Fed's check-clearing service saves member banks the time, cost, and effort of sorting and mailing checks to their home banks. Instead, the Federal Reserve Banks perform this service, processing some 35 billion checks per year.

The Bank Examiner

To confirm that state-chartered member banks are following regulations, bank examiners from the Federal Reserve System may arrive unannounced and audit (inspect) their records and management practices. National banks, which receive their charters from the federal government, are examined in the same manner by the comptroller of the currency. Examiners visit at least once a year and may stay from one week to several months, depending on the bank's size.

Regulating the Money Supply

As the legally mandated regulator of the nation's money supply, the Fed governs the availability of money—and therefore the rate of inflation—with three complementary devices:

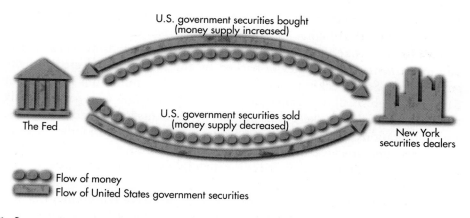

U.S. government securities bought
(money supply increased)

The Fed

U.S. government securities sold
(money supply decreased)

New York
securities dealers

Flow of money
Flow of United States government securities

Figure 15.3
The federal reserve's open market operations.

1. Its own open market operations (buying and selling United States government securities on the open market)
2. The reserve requirements it mandates for member banks
3. The discount rate it sets for loans to member banks

These tools are employed simultaneously to increase or decrease the amount of money available for borrowing and, therefore, spending.

OPEN MARKET OPERATIONS Using **open market operations,** the most flexible money supply adjuster, *the Fed buys or sells billions of dollars of United States government securities daily through securities dealers in New York City.* It works in the following manner.

When the Fed wants to decrease the money supply, it sells government securities. The money that the purchasing dealers pay is kept out of circulation by the Fed, and eventually borrowing declines and interest rates rise as lenders find that there is less money to meet potential borrowers' requests.

When the Fed wants to increase the money supply, it buys government securities. Money is created the moment the Fed pays the dealers, and it filters down into the general economy as the dealers pay it to the businesses and individuals whose government securities they sold.* Figure 15.3 summarizes the effect of open market operations.

There are three types of United States government securities: Treasury bills (which have a three-, six-, or twelve-month maturity), Treasury notes (which have a one- to seven-year maturity), and Treasury bonds (which mature in seven years or more). Although the physical certificates had a long and honorable history, the United States Treasury stopped printing them in 1986 in favor of giving buyers a simple document that looks like a bank statement. The Treasury predicted that it would save $46 million

open market operations
The Fed buys or sells billions of dollars of United States government securities daily through securities dealers in New York City.

---

* Critics point out that the Fed's ability to incur debts and pay them back with interest by printing money fuels inflation. As new money enters circulation in this way, the money issued earlier immediately decreases in value.

by not having to print such ornately engraved securities and send them to buyers by registered mail.

Treasury bills, like all U.S. government securities, are considered extremely safe investments because they're backed by the full faith and credit of the government. Sold weekly in lots of $5,000 (with a minimum purchase of $10,000), their small denominations and short maturities (three months, six months, or one year) make T-bills popular investments for individuals, banks, and corporations alike. They can be purchased directly from the treasury when first sold; after the original sale, T-bills may be bought or sold before maturity at prevailing market prices through banks and stockbrokers.

reserve requirement
A percentage of deposits that member banks must retain on deposit within their own walls or at the Federal Reserve Bank in their district.

RESERVE REQUIREMENTS The Fed stipulates a **reserve requirement,** *a percentage of deposits that member banks must retain on deposit within their own walls or at the Federal Reserve Bank in their district.* When the Fed raises the reserve requirement it tightens the money supply, making loans more costly because member banks must hold a greater percentage of deposits on reserve than before. Lowering the reserve requirement instantly frees some existing reserves for lending. The Fed rarely uses this device to regulate the money supply, however. It is an extreme measure—like driving a tack with a sledgehammer. Changing the reserve requirement just a fraction of a percent liberates or restricts millions of dollars within the commercial banking system, because as was noted earlier, members of the Fed hold approximately 72 percent of the nation's total money supply.

Member banks earn no interest on required reserves, and the Fed may charge a penalty to members whose reserves fall below the required level. Reserve requirements, which vary according to a member bank's deposits, range from 3 to 10 percent on demand deposits. The reserve requirement does not apply to time deposits.

This reserve requirement, when coupled with open market operations, has a considerable multiplier effect on the money supply. Let's assume, for example, that the Fed wishes to increase the money supply and buys just $1 million in government securities on the open market while the reserve requirement is 10 percent. The effect at each stage as this money is deposited and lent by a succession of banks is illustrated in Figure 15.4.

discount rate
The interest rate that the Fed charges member banks for loans.

THE DISCOUNT RATE As was mentioned earlier, Fed members may borrow from their district banks when depositors' heavy withdrawals endanger a bank's required reserves. The **discount rate** is *the interest rate that the Fed charges member banks for loans.* Usually this loan privilege is used only in emergencies, so the discount rate plays a relatively minor role in regulating the money supply. The discount rate at the time of this writing is 3 percent, which is the lowest it has been in more than twenty-five years.

Because the discount rate clearly signals the Fed's position with respect to regulating the money supply, however, changes tend to have a domino effect

Level 1

The Fed pays securities dealers $1 million for United States government securities that it buys.

$1,000,000

Level 2

Banks that accept the securities dealers' $1 million lend out 90%.

$900,000

Level 3

Receiving banks for Level 2's loans lend out 90%.

810,000

Level 4

Receiving banks for Level 3's loans lend out 90%

729,000

Level 5

Receiving banks for Level 4's loans lend out 90%

656,100

Level 6

Receiving banks for Level 5's loans lend out 90%

590,490

Level 7

Receiving banks for Level 6's loans lend out 90%

531,441

Level 8

Receiving banks for Level 7's loans lend out 90%

478,297

Total created by all transfers $4,695,328

Figure 15.4

How open market operations and the reserve requirement affect the money supply.

on interest rates in general. For example, a decrease in the discount rate usually triggers a drop in the prime rate of interest within several hours. This event leads to lower interest rates on home equity loans, small-business loans, and other loans whose interest rates are related to the prime rate. Eventually the interest rate on home mortgages will follow suit. It's interesting to note, however, that the interest on bank credit cards has remained high despite declines in other interest rates. Banks justify this by pointing out that their losses on bad credit card debts have not decreased, which prompts them to maintain higher interest rates on credit card balances.

The Federal Deposit Insurance Corporation

Between 1921 and 1933, more than half the commercial banks in the United States failed—9,000 of them after 1929 alone. This prompted Congress to pass the Banking Act of 1933 and create the **Federal Deposit Insurance Corporation (FDIC),** *a public corporation with a threefold purpose: to build confidence in the nation's banking system, insure depositors' account balances, and promote sound bank management.*

Federal Deposit Insurance Corporation (FDIC)
A public corporation with a threefold purpose: to build confidence in the nation's banking system, insure depositors' account balances, and promote sound bank management.

Figure 15.5

Percentage of banks insured by FDIC.

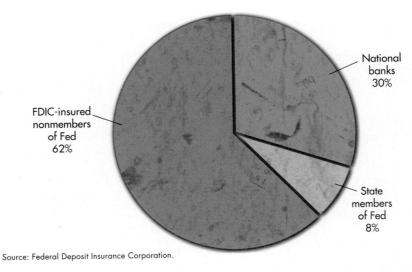

Source: Federal Deposit Insurance Corporation.

All banks that belong to the Federal Reserve System must also belong to the FDIC. Others may join if they meet its standards and conditions. As Figure 15.5 shows, virtually 100 percent of all commercial banks are members of the FDIC.

Insurance Provisions and Examinations

The FDIC insures individual and joint accounts up to $100,000. If a bank fails, the FDIC usually begins paying depositors' claims within ten days of its closing. The corporation is funded by premiums assessed on its member banks.

The FDIC, like the Federal Reserve System and the comptroller of the currency, has a staff of examiners. Member banks are subject to their scrutiny and management guidelines. When examiners find that a bank has not followed sound practices, the FDIC may issue a cease-and-desist order. It is even empowered to remove officers of state-chartered banks that do not belong to the Fed if their personal dishonesty damages the bank financially. The FDIC's problem list carries the names of banks that may have made risky loans, suffered employee embezzlement, or violated prescribed management practices. Problem banks are monitored closely until they regain their financial health. Approximately 1,000 banks are currently on the FDIC's problem list.[6]

The Federal Deposit Insurance Corporation Improvement Act (FDICIA), which became law in 1991, attempts to decrease the likelihood of bank failures by increasing the FDIC's power to regulate commercial bank operations. This law requires examiners to evaluate the quality of a bank's assets, the methods it uses to disclose interest rates on loans, and the techniques and paperwork used to document the loans it makes.[7] In addition, FDICIA requires the FDIC to take specific actions to help a bank regain its financial strength if losses decrease capital below specified levels. FDICIA also increased the FDIC's ability to borrow from the U.S. Treasury from

When a bank fails, the FDIC liquidates its assets and takes over as receiver for the bank's loan payments.

$5 billion to $30 billion to cover any losses in the FDIC's bank insurance fund. (Borrowed funds must be repaid to the Treasury within 15 years.) FDICIA grants the FDIC the power to increase the insurance rates it charges member banks more often than semiannually if necessary and to impose special assessments on member banks if required to repay loans from the U.S. Treasury.

Bankers have not been pleased about the impact of FDICIA. They complain about the forms and checklists they must fill out in the process of evaluating and deciding on a loan application, paperwork that keeps them from interacting with customers and generating more business. Most loans require approximately the same amount of paperwork, no matter how large or small.[8] (The paperwork associated with one $11 million construction loan—while admittedly an extreme example—reportedly filled a dozen boxes and two portable file carts.[9])

If a Bank Fails

If the value of a bank's loans and other assets ever falls below its depositors' claims against it, a disaster that frequent bank examinations are designed to prevent, the FDIC may lend the bank money and accept its assets as collateral. If the possibility of recovery seems remote, the FDIC may simply pay off the bank's depositors. In this case the FDIC becomes the receiver (caretaker) of the bank's loans and collects them as they come due. It *liquidates* (converts to cash) such assets as land and equipment. FDIC liquidators have sold off such unusual items as a Houston brothel, a burning Pennsylvania coal mine, an X-rated movie theater, a dog kennel, a sunken tugboat, a goat farm, and a thoroughbred stud with venereal disease. Most of these items had been

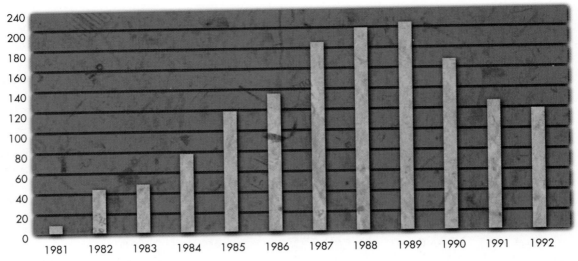

Source: Federal Deposit Insurance Corporation.

Figure 15.6

Commercial bank failures, 1981–1992.

pledged as collateral on loans that later became uncollectible. The largest FDIC payoff to insured depositors occurred in January 1992 when the Independence Bank of Encino, California failed. The FDIC paid off $575.4 million in depositors' claims.[10]

The number of commercial bank failures has declined in recent years, as shown in Figure 15.6.

Interstate Banking Gains Momentum

A pronounced trend toward interstate banking developed in the early 1980s as several huge "money center" banks in New York City found ways to expand operations beyond the borders of their home state. Federal deregulation of the banking industry has enabled megabanks such as Citicorp to offer a smorgasbord of services in several states by purchasing a controlling interest in banks or savings and loan associations already established there. Citicorp and other large New York banks also belong to computerized teller systems such as CIRRUS and PULSE that form nationwide networks of automated teller machines. Equipped with a computer-coded plastic card and a personal identification number (PIN), customers can withdraw money, make payments, transfer funds between accounts, and conduct various other transactions (except for making deposits) in their accounts with out-of-state banks.

State law permitting, banks may now acquire competitors in other states. A reciprocal agreement allowing regional mergers now exists between Massachusetts, Connecticut, and Rhode Island, and similar agreements exist in several southern and Atlantic seaboard states. For example, NationsBank has managed through a series of mergers to establish some 1,800 branches in nine states from Maryland to Texas.[11] Although such regional mergers may thwart the growth of true interstate banking, observers believe they may be done to prevent gigantic banks like Citicorp and Manufacturers Hanover Trust from swallowing up smaller banks when all legal barriers to interstate banking are eventually removed.

SUMMARY

Money enables citizens in a modern society to purchase goods and services conveniently, thus eliminating the need for barter. It serves as a medium of exchange, a measure of value, and a store of value. Money in the United States takes the form of coins and paper (collectively called *currency*) and checking accounts (also called *demand deposits*) in commercial banks.

Inflation, which decreases the value of a society's money, has a serious effect on purchasing power when it rises unchecked. This occurs when producers raise prices in response to strong consumer demand or when they pass rising labor, materials, and service costs on to consumers through increased prices. The Consumer Price Index (CPI), calculated by the U.S. Department of Labor, is the federal government's inflation barometer. It expresses today's prices in 1982–1984 dollars so concerned government agencies can monitor the rate of inflation from one period to the next and take action to bring it under control.

Commercial banks play a unique role in controlling inflation through their lending operations. Most of the larger ones, holding approximately 72 percent of all commercial bank deposits, belong to the Federal Reserve System.

In addition to commercial banks, savings and loan associations, credit unions, and savings banks (collectively called *thrift institutions*) also encourage deposi-tors to open savings accounts. Such institutions lend funds for home buying and building and for the purchase of various consumer goods.

The Federal Reserve System (the Fed) coordinates the nation's banking policy. The Fed's board of governors monitors inflation's growth and responds by regulating the availability of money and credit through open market operations and by adjusting reserve requirements and the discount rate for member banks.

While many commercial banks choose not to belong to the Fed, nearly all of them belong to the Federal Deposit Insurance Corporation (FDIC), a federal government corporation that will pay depositors up to $100,000 on their individual and joint accounts should a bank fail. The FDIC, the Fed, and state banking regulators examine commercial banks' management practices and financial positions periodically to reduce the likelihood of failure.

Although federal law still prevents banks from accepting deposits across state lines, recent deregulation has encouraged larger banks to offer most other services in several states by buying control of banks or savings and loan associations already established there. Banks may also operate across state lines by joining one of several nationwide automated teller machine networks. A few regions of the country have reciprocal agreements allowing banks to buy competitors in neighboring states.

KEY TERMS

barter system p. 474

certificates of deposit (CDs) p. 479

check *or* demand deposit p. 477

commercial bank p. 479

Consumer Price Index (CPI) p. 478

cost-push inflation p. 478

credit union p. 482

demand-pull inflation p. 477

discount rate p. 488

Federal Deposit Insurance
    Corporation (FDIC) p. 489

Federal Reserve Act of 1913 p. 485

inflation p. 477

money p. 474

open market operations p. 487

prime rate of interest p. 479

reserve requirement p. 488

savings account *or* time deposit p. 477

savings and loan associations (S&Ls) p. 480

savings bank p. 484

FOR REVIEW AND DISCUSSION

1. Under what circumstances would a barter system work? Present several situations in which barter could function in our society.

2. What three functions does money perform for a society?

3. What items make up the money supply of the United States? Why are savings accounts not included?

4. Differentiate between demand-pull inflation and cost-push inflation, and give examples of each type.

5. How does the Consumer Price Index (CPI) help the federal government monitor inflation? How does this barometer affect certain citizens' incomes?

6. Discuss the functions and the purpose of commercial banks. What consideration do they give to their most secure corporate borrowers? What instrument do they offer to depositors who agree to leave money on deposit for a certain length of time?

7. What is the difference between a thrift institution and a commercial bank? How would you characterize the role of each in our economy?

8. Describe the ownership philosophy behind both types of savings and loan associations.

9. How is a credit union different from a savings and loan association and a savings bank? Through what federal agency are credit union accounts insured?

10. How do the lending policies of savings banks compare with those of savings and loan associations? What is their relative importance in the field of thrift institutions?

11. Describe the organization of the Federal Reserve System. Why do banks join? How are they regulated after they become members?

12. Summarize how the Fed may use each of the following activities to regulate the money supply: open market operations, reserve requirements, and the discount rate.

13. Why was the Federal Deposit Insurance Corporation (FDIC) created? How does it affect the attitudes of commercial bank depositors?

14. How does the FDIC monitor a commercial bank's condition? What may the FDIC do if a bank gets into financial difficulty? If it fails?

15. How may out-of-state banks offer most of their services in other states despite the fact that federal law prohibits them from accepting deposits there? How have the states themselves promoted the growth of interstate banking?

APPLICATIONS

Case 15.1: Do Banks Discriminate?

In 1993 the Federal Reserve Bank of Boston released a study claiming that banks discriminate against African American and Hispanic applicants for home loans. This study was based on denial rates of whites and minorities with similar incomes, credit histories, and so on. The study showed that while Hispanics and African Americans were rejected more often, Asian Americans were given loans more often than whites.

Critics of the study have noted that many characteristics of applicants are not assessed. For example, previous records of chronic late payments and other factors are not used in considering whether a minority person is equivalent to a white. Because of the difficulty in obtaining these data, many studies that show discrimination are believed to be faulty. The Boston Fed study examined average default rates in the Boston area and did not find greater default rates

in minority tracts, but the lack of individual data is thought to be a significant flaw. Further, critics have noted that banks that specialize in loaning to African Americans are generally not profitable.

One critic, Gary Becker, uses what he calls a "simple method" of assessing marketplace discrimination. He holds that the only way to assess whether banks discriminate against minorities is to show that they would make more money if they did not. By proving that banks give up valuable customers because of race, a study could show definitively that unfair and unreasonable practices are in effect.

Questions

1. What harms are caused by discrimination in lending?

2. Do you believe the government should seek out and discourage discriminatory banking practices? Why or why not?

3. Discuss the strengths and weaknesses of Gary Becker's proposed method of studying discrimination.

For more information, see Gary S. Becker, "The Evidence Against Banks Doesn't Prove Bias," *Business Week,* April 19, 1993, p. 18.

Case 15.2: Bank Branches
Become Fewer and Far Between

Mendocino, California is a nice small town. It was always convenient to have a branch of San Francisco's giant Bank of America in town. Unfortunately, as in many other areas, the Mendocino branch was closed down. Along with the branch went the only ATM in town. Not only were locals inconvenienced, but both customers and merchants were faced with a problem: The cash that made for impulse purchases had dried up.

Across the country, banks are closing branches. From 1990 to 1992 nearly 4,000 bank and thrift branches were closed. Bank of America, having acquired Security Pacific, had trimmed 568 branches by 1993 and was planning to close more. Banks have become increasingly intolerant of the overhead of maintaining branches and paying tellers. Additionally, mergers are making many branches redundant. Analysts have predicted that there could be as many as 15,000 closed branches by the end of the decade.

Accompanying these closings, banks have been moving from small, local branches to larger offices. Optimal branch sizes are targeted at $40–$50 million in deposits, up from the desired $15–$20 million considered satisfactory a decade ago. Instead of using staffed branches, banks are installing larger networks of ATMs and are encouraging customers to use telephone banking services. Citibank has installed a depot at New York City's Grand Central Station that consists of twenty ATMs and no tellers. Electronic banking may prove to be more cost effective than maintaining branches, but for the moment, people in Mendocino still can't get any cash.

Questions

1. What are the advantages to consumers of using electronic banking instead of personalized service?

2. Do banks have a responsibility to provide local services to customers? Why or why not?

3. Should the national banking system, as a whole, be required to maintain services within a certain distance of customers? Why or why not?

For more information, see Kelly Holland, "Next Bank, 100 Miles," *Business Week,* May 10, 1993, p. 55.

REFERENCES

1. Kate McIlwaine, "Australian Forgery-Detection Device Wins Patent in U.S.," *Plastics News,* February 8, 1993, p. 3.
2. "Cunning Copiers: Manufacturers Puzzle over Ways to Foil Counterfeiters," *The Wall Street Journal,* December 31, 1992, p. A1.
3. Rick Wartzman, "Counterfeit Bills Confound Detectors at the Fed, Sleuths at the Secret Service," *The Wall Street Journal,* July 3, 1992, p. A8.
4. "Bailout Keeps on Growing," *The Orlando Sentinel,* March 17, 1993, p. A-1.
5. Martin Mayer, "Turnaround at the RTC," *The Wall Street Journal,* December 22, 1992, p. A10;

Mark D. Fefer, "Time to Speed Up the S&L Cleanup," *Fortune,* November 16, 1992, p. 116.
6. Kenneth H. Bacon, "Bankers Aim to Slash Red Tape Imposed by FDIC's 1991 Law on Supervision," *The Wall Street Journal,* February 1, 1993, p. B5.
7. Terence P. Paré, "Why Banks Are Still Stingy," *Fortune,* January 25, 1993, p. 73.
8. Brad Kuhn, "Stricter Regulations Rile Bankers," *The Orlando Sentinel,* February 21, 1993, p. F-1.
9. Ibid.
10. FDIC Press release dated January 30, 1992.
11. "Nothing Comes to Those Who Wait," *Fortune,* December 28, 1992, p. 54.

16

FINANCING FOR PROFITS

B ulls and
bears aren't
responsible
for as many stock
losses as bum steers.

OLIN MILLER

CHAPTER OBJECTIVES
**After studying this chapter, you
should be able to:**
1. Describe the short-term financing
   instruments that companies may
   use, and compare the financing
   institutions used to raise capital.
2. Discuss the contribution of retained earnings in raising long-
   term capital.
3. Summarize four major laws that
   regulate securities sales.
4. Distinguish among common and
   preferred stock and mutual funds
   and summarize their features.
5. Describe the nature of a sinking
   fund.
6. Compute a bond's current yield
   and yield to maturity.
7. List and define the types of bonds
   companies may issue.
8. Give reasons for investing in
   bonds versus common or preferred stock.
9. List the advantages and disadvantages of a company's selling common stock, preferred stock, and
   bonds.
10. Explain the concept of leverage.
11. Contrast the New York and
    American stock exchanges and
    the over-the-counter market.
12. Discuss the role of a stockbroker.
13. Describe three alternative invest-
    ment objectives, the role of the
    specialist, and ways to hold secu-
    rities.
14. Summarize the investment strate-
    gies of short selling and margin
    buying.

UP FRONT

Clarke Kawakami isn't your typical chief financial officer. But then, Black Diamond Equipment isn't your typical business, either. Kawakami graduated from Harvard University, then joined the U.S. Navy. After his military service he attended the Wharton School at the University of Pennsylvania, where he earned his MBA in finance and accounting. Then, somewhat uncharacteristically, he spent some time working with computer systems and "at the business end of a software company."

During this time, Kawakami developed an interest in rock climbing. One day, while reading a climbing magazine, his eyes fell on a climbing equipment company's ad for a chief financial officer. He applied for and got the job, at Black Diamond Equipment, Ltd., of Salt Lake City, Utah. "I think it helped that I understood what the business is all about, but the job is so demanding that I probably do less climbing today than I'd like to," he says.

Black Diamond Equipment is a U.S. manufacturer and distributor of high-quality rock climbing, mountaineering, backpacking, and cross-country skiing equipment. A privately held corporation with about 100 employees, it was formed in 1989 out of the bankruptcy of a larger entity. Employees bought the company and moved the operations from Los Angeles to Salt Lake City, partly to lower costs and mostly because they would be closer to skiing and climbing. "Most of the people here have active, outdoor lifestyles using our equipment," says Clarke. The company manufactures carabiners, pitons, belay-rappel devices, and other climbing devices, which it distributes along with cross-country skis, boots, and outdoor gear made by other companies. "When I came on board, it was to create the financial infrastructure. We had a thriving business; we were good at manufacturing, but it was my job to build a finance department.

"I was at it for twelve to fifteen months," Kawakami recalls, "mostly me and some clerical help. Over time, we discovered just how complex financial management work really is. For example, there is manufacturing cost accounting versus the kind of accounting you do in a service company. You could say manufacturing accounting is grown-up accounting."

Once the rudimentary reporting systems were in place, Kawakami began building a financial organization. "I got to select and hire the people as I needed them: a bookkeeper, a technical accountant, the controller, the credit manager. I've got excellent people. Today, I could take off for a year and the system would run itself."

However, that was only part of the job. Next, Clarke Kawakami had the opportunity to use his experience with computers in setting up the management in-

CLARKE K. KAWAKAMI

CHIEF FINANCIAL OFFICER, BLACK DIAMOND EQUIPMENT, LTD.

formation system (MIS) for Black Diamond. "I think my experience on the systems side made me responsible for the computer automation by default," he says. "But bringing in a computer and getting the order, inventory, and accounting systems set up on it was one of the big accomplishments of my first year. We were proud to say we brought it up on time and within budget."

Kawakami has four people in finance who report to him and is also responsible for the staff of the personnel and MIS departments. "Compared to other companies our size, we're very strong financially," he says.

Black Diamond is a rapidly growing company. "The climbing market is incredibly strong," says Kawakami. "We're the leader in the United States, Japan, and Australia, but we feel there will be competition coming from stronger, older companies in Europe over the next few years."

short-term *or* working capital
Money spent on business operations covering a period of a year or less.

long-term *or* fixed capital
Money used to buy fixed assets, which are long-lived, and (with the exception of land) manufactured items that will be used to produce goods and services for several years.

A company must raise two kinds of capital, categorized by the way in which the funds will be used. The first kind, called **short-term *or* working capital**, is *money spent on business operations covering a period of a year or less*. Working capital is used to purchase inventory and to pay daily operating expenses such as wages and salaries, insurance premiums, rent, and utilities. The demand for working capital can be enormous. Large companies may require more than $50 million each working day.

The second kind of capital is called **long-term *or* fixed capital.** This is *money used to buy fixed assets, which are long-lived, and (with the exception of land) manufactured items that will be used to produce goods and services for several years.* These fixed assets can be a microcomputer system to link all the departments in a textile plant of Burlington Industries; computer-controlled robot welding machines for a Ford Motor Company auto assembly line; or three new cargo jets for Federal Express. Unlike short-term capital, which is used to sustain a company from one day to the next, long-term or fixed capital is spent for lasting improvements that will enhance a company's ability to produce goods or services superior to those of competitors, improve or expand its existing line of products, invent new products, or even purchase the stock of other companies in one of the business combinations that you learned about in Chapter 4.

Sources for capital are as distinct as the uses to which capital may be put. In this chapter we will examine ways to obtain both kinds of capital, along with the practices and financial instruments associated with each.

Short-Term Capital

Businesses need short-term capital to amplify purchasing power and increase profit. Firms use short-term capital to buy more merchandise than they can afford to buy out of pocket. This money may be borrowed; the larger inventory that it buys should earn an increased profit when sold, even after interest payments. As a result, the business is further ahead than it would have been had it bought merchandise on a cash-and-carry basis.

Short-term capital is also used to pay current debts, when cash receipts from sales and from credit customers fall below expectations. Like us, businesses have expenses that remain steady throughout the year—insurance premiums, utilities, rent, and managers' salaries, for example. Cash flowing into the business, however, is sometimes insufficient to pay such obligations, especially during slack periods. Again, management may have to find money for a short period of time.

Short-term capital also helps businesses meet unexpected expenses when sales remain steady. Even when sales and cash receipts are constant, management may have to do unanticipated maintenance or repair equipment, or it may have to pay increased insurance premiums, higher-than-expected taxes, or professional fees of attorneys or accountants. When these unpleasant surprises demand more money than a firm has on hand, it must secure short-term funds.

Short-Term Financing Instruments

Table 16.1 summarizes several tools or instruments that play a part in raising short-term or working capital. We will discuss their characteristics at this point; later parts of this chapter will refer to some of them.

Table 16.1

Instruments of short-term financing.

INSTRUMENT	CHARACTERISTICS
Promissory note	A debtor's promise to pay a certain sum of money at a future date. Usually carries interest at a fixed rate. May be secured or unsecured.
Draft	Completed by a creditor ordering a debtor to pay a specific sum of money. Does not become a binding obligation until accepted by the debtor. *Sight drafts* are payable immediately; *time drafts* give the debtor a stated length of time after acceptance to produce the money.
Commercial paper	An unsecured promissory note of a large corporation (sometimes referred to as a *corporate IOU*). Used to borrow large amounts for short periods of time.
Check	A kind of draft used to make payments in financial transactions. Two kinds of checks may be used aside from a check drawn on a business's own account. A *cashier's check* is written by a commercial bank against its own money. Generally considered the safest kind of check, it may be purchased by giving the bank the amount to be paid plus a modest fee. The other kind, a *certified check,* is a depositor's own check that the bank certifies to be good. The popularity and convenience of obtaining cashier's checks has made certified checks relatively uncommon today.

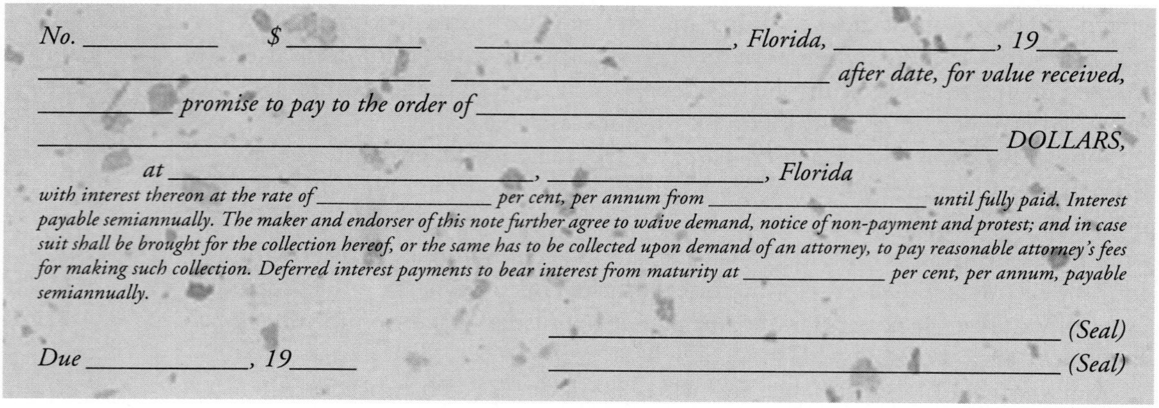

No. _____ $ _____ _____, *Florida*, _____, *19*_____
_____ _____ *after date, for value received,*
_____ *promise to pay to the order of* _____
_____ *DOLLARS,*
at _____, _____, *Florida*
with interest thereon at the rate of _____ *per cent, per annum from* _____ *until fully paid. Interest payable semiannually. The maker and endorser of this note further agree to waive demand, notice of non-payment and protest; and in case suit shall be brought for the collection hereof, or the same has to be collected upon demand of an attorney, to pay reasonable attorney's fees for making such collection. Deferred interest payments to bear interest from maturity at* _____ *per cent, per annum, payable semiannually.*

_____ *(Seal)*
Due _____, *19*_____ _____ *(Seal)*

Figure 16.1

Form for an unsecured promissory note.

promissory note
A short-term financing instrument, given by a debtor (called the *promisor*) to a creditor (called the *promisee*) as a legal and binding promise to pay a certain sum of money at a future date, usually with interest at a fixed rate.

draft
An instrument completed by a creditor ordering a debtor to pay a specific sum of money.

commercial paper
(Sometimes referred to as *corporate IOUs*), the unsecured promissory notes of large, financially sound corporations.

PROMISSORY NOTE The first and most common, a **promissory note**, is *a short-term financing instrument, given by a debtor (called the* promisor*) to a creditor (called the* promisee*) as a legal and binding promise to pay a certain sum of money at a future date, usually with interest at a fixed rate.* A note may be *secured* (backed by specific assets that the creditor may claim if the note is not paid when due) or *unsecured* (backed only by the promisor's reputation). Figure 16.1 is an example of an unsecured promissory note.

Although many promissory notes are payable in one year or less, making them short-term instruments, some extend for more than a year. You may have signed a long-term note to finance the car you drive, your stereo, or your furniture.

DRAFT Unlike a promissory note, which is a debtor's promise to pay a debt, a **draft** is *an instrument completed by a creditor ordering a debtor to pay a specific sum of money.* A draft that orders the debtor to pay the amount immediately is called a *sight draft;* one that allows the debtor a certain time to produce the money is a *time draft*. A draft does not become a binding obligation until the debtor writes the word *accepted* on its face and signs it. Figure 16.2 shows an example of a draft.

Drafts are popular for coordinating the exchange of payment for and title to merchandise when the buyer and seller must deal at arm's length. They are often used by automobile dealers who may sell scores of cars to one another in a single transaction while never meeting personally. Figure 16.3 illustrates such a transaction and the way a draft makes it easier to accomplish.

COMMERCIAL PAPER One instrument used to borrow large amounts for short periods is **commercial paper** *(sometimes referred to as* corporate IOUs*), the unsecured promissory notes of large, financially sound corporations.* Usually issued in such even denominations as $50,000, $100,000, and $500,000, commercial paper can raise several million dollars of short-term capital at one time. Maturities on commercial paper range from less than a week to nine months or more.

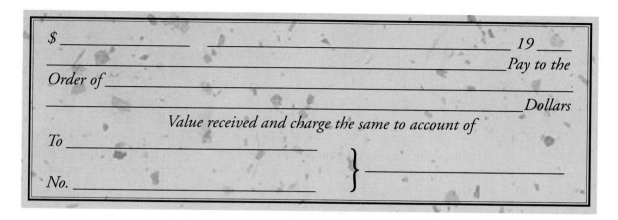

$ _____ _____ 19 ____
_____ Pay to the
Order of _____
_____ Dollars
Value received and charge the same to account of
To _____
                                              } _____
No. _____

Commercial paper houses act as go-betweens, buying these notes from borrowing firms at something less than face value and selling them to organizations with excess cash to lend. The borrowers and lenders rarely meet directly. Commercial paper lenders are often such institutional investors as large corporations, universities, and even hospitals that happen to have large amounts of cash free for short periods of time. Financial sources report that approximately $500 billion worth of these corporate IOUs are outstanding at any given time.

Figure 16.2

Form for a draft.

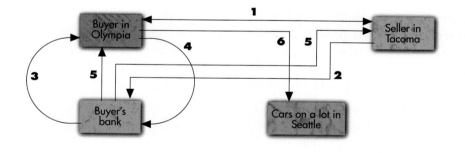

Figure 16.3

A transaction involving a draft.

1. Buyer and seller agree by telephone on the price of fifty cars stored in Seattle.
2. Tacoma seller sends draft to the buyer's bank ordering the Olympia buyer to pay the agreed-upon sum. (Car titles are attached to draft.)
3. Bank officer notifies buyer when draft and titles arrive.
4. The buyer accepts the draft and pays the banker.
5. The banker detaches the titles, delivers them to the buyer, and sends payment to the seller after deducting a fee.
6. The buyer, titles in hand, picks up the cars at the Seattle lot.

CHECKS A check is a kind of draft, because the depositor is the bank's creditor (as you learned in Chapter 15). By writing a check the depositor (creditor) orders the bank (debtor) to pay a certain sum of money to a third party. Business transactions are conducted with two kinds of checks, in addition to those of the company itself.

cashier's check
A check written by a commercial bank against the bank's own money.

The first, a **cashier's check**, is *a check written by a commercial bank against the bank's own money.* It generally is considered the safest kind of check. When a creditor doubts a debtor's ability to pay or has not dealt with that party before, the creditor may require payment by cashier's check. Getting a cashier's check is simple: you go to the proper window on the floor of your commercial bank, give the teller the money (plus a modest fee), and indicate to whom you want the cashier's check written. The bank deposits your money as its own, writes a cashier's check to the designated party, and gives it to you. Depositors who want to transfer funds permanently from one bank to another can do so safely by having their original bank write them a cashier's check for their balance.

certified check
A depositor's personal check that the bank certifies to be good.

The second kind of check, a **certified check,** is uncommon today. It is *a depositor's personal check that the bank certifies to be good,* usually by punching the word *certified* into the face of the check with a machine. The bank customarily sets funds aside in the customer's account so the check will be paid when it returns through the banking system. Most large commercial banks see no reason to both write cashier's checks and certify personal checks, however, so when you ask for a certified check you will probably be sent to the cashier's check window.

Institutions and Methods of Short-Term Financing

Table 16.2

Institutions of short-term financing.

Several institutions provide short-term funds to companies in a variety of ways. Firms normally call on a combination of these institutions and methods, as circumstances and business conditions dictate. It is rare for a business to deal with one alone. The institutions discussed in this section are summarized in Table 16.2.

INSTITUTION	TRANSACTION
Trade credit or open-book accounts offered by suppliers	Obtain merchandise inventory, materials, and supplies on credit
Commercial bank	Borrow on line of credit or revolving credit agreement
Commercial finance company	Borrow using such collateral as inventory, equipment, or trade accounts receivable
Factoring company	Sell business customers' open-book or consumer credit accounts at a discount for cash
Sales finance company	Sell consumers' installment sales contracts at a discount for cash
Consumer finance company	Accept cash that consumers have borrowed from these firms as payment for merchandise

TRADE CREDIT Materials, supplies, and merchandise inventories frequently are purchased on **trade credit** *or* **open-book** accounts. These are *business charge accounts that a selling firm gives buying firms.* The debtor must pay for the items bought within a given time period, usually thirty, sixty, or ninety days.

Trade credit is extended among members of the distribution chain you learned about in Chapter 14 (manufacturers, wholesalers, and retailers). It is not a source of actual money, but it is a way to defer payment until the buyer can resell the merchandise to the next link in the distribution chain.

Sellers who extend trade credit or open-book accounts may give buyers a **cash discount,** which is *a discount given to encourage trade credit debtors to pay their balances before they are due.* It may be quoted, for example, as *2/10, n/30,* meaning that the buyer may deduct 2 percent if the bill is paid within ten days after a specific date (usually the date of the billing). The buyer may, however, choose to pay the net or full amount (the total, less any returns or allowances) within thirty days of the billing date. Buyers typically manage their money so they can pay trade credit accounts within the discount period. The discounts received on an entire year's purchases can add up to impressive savings for most companies.

BORROWING FROM A COMMERCIAL BANK Commercial banks, which you learned about in Chapter 15, are the most popular source of short-term business loans. Companies that obtain working capital from commercial banks usually establish a **line of credit,** which is *a maximum amount that a commercial bank agrees to lend to a business borrower if it has the funds available.* In other words, the amount is assured but not guaranteed.

trade credit *or* open-book accounts
Business charge accounts that a selling firm gives buying firms.

cash discount
A discount given to encourage trade credit debtors to pay their balances before they are due.

line of credit
A maximum amount that a commercial bank agrees to lend to a business borrower if it has the funds available.

Obtaining a line of credit at a commercial bank helps many businesses get through cash-flow problems or take advantage of buying opportunities.

A line of credit is convenient. You can borrow whatever amount you need, making payments as specified. As long as the outstanding debt does not exceed the approved maximum, you still have funds available. Interest is charged only on the amount borrowed. Large corporations may have credit lines of several hundred thousand dollars or more, and credit lines at several banks, to satisfy their short-term cash needs. For example, Chrysler Corporation has obtained a $6.8 billion line of credit from a group of 152 banks. The funds are used mostly to help the company's dealers stock an inventory of cars as well as to finance consumers who buy from the dealers.[1]

revolving credit agreement
A commercial bank's binding promise that the money will be available if the borrowing firm requests it.

Instead of a line of credit, firms may obtain a **revolving credit agreement**, which is *a commercial bank's binding promise that the money will be available if the borrowing firm requests it*. Most banks require business borrowers to keep a compensating balance of from 10 to 20 percent of the borrowed funds on deposit, insisting that borrowers become depositors, too.

YOU DECIDE

How might the bank regulations discussed in Chapter 15 affect a bank's discretion in approving a line of credit?

COMMERCIAL FINANCE COMPANIES An important alternative source of short-term capital is a **commercial finance company,** *a firm that makes cash loans to business borrowers, securing the loans by such assets as trade credit accounts, inventory, or equipment*. Because these companies may take greater lending risks than commercial banks, they may charge higher interest rates. But they are available should a company exhaust its bank line of credit, and they do not require compensating balances as commercial banks do.

commercial finance company
A firm that makes cash loans to business borrowers, securing the loans by such assets as trade credit accounts, inventory, or equipment.

FACTORING COMPANIES Some businesses raise funds from a **factoring company,** *a firm that buys a business's open-book accounts (or sometimes consumer credit accounts) and customarily absorbs all losses if the debtors do not pay*. Usually the factor performs all billing and other bookkeeping activities on the accounts. Originally used in the textile industry, factoring is now common in the container, furniture, and clothing industries as well. Even commercial banks have established factoring departments.

factoring company
A firm that buys a business's open-book accounts (or sometimes consumer credit accounts) and customarily absorbs all losses if the debtors do not pay.

The factor buys the debts at a discount determined by the quality of the accounts being sold. If they are the debts of financially sound companies with good credit ratings, the discount will be lower than if they are slow-paying or otherwise shaky companies.

Debtors may be notified that their original creditor has sold their accounts to a factor and are instructed to make payments to that firm. The selling company may agree, however, to record the payments and relay the money to the factor, who thus escapes a recordkeeping burden. This arrangement is termed a *nonnotification plan*.

Factoring has undergone a facelift in recent years as certain large retailers have sold the balances due from their credit card customers to reduce their bookkeeping load and increase their working capital.

SALES FINANCE COMPANIES Another source of working capital, a **sales finance company,** is *a firm that provides short-term capital to retailers (and sometimes to wholesalers) by purchasing the installment sales contracts (promissory notes) that they have accepted from customers.* Imagine a retailer of furniture or large appliances who accepts customers' promissory notes. When the firm requires additional short-term money, it can convert the notes it holds into cash by selling them to a sales finance company at a discount. Sales finance companies usually buy consumers' promissory notes for one-time purchases, while factoring companies buy the existing balances on open-book accounts owed to businesses, usually by other businesses. The concept is identical, however; the selling firm converts a future obligation into cash on the spot.

Retailers benefit from selling customers' notes to sales finance companies; they avoid keeping records on the customers' monthly payments for the remainder of the notes' lives and they convert the debts to cash, a benefit that is often worth the discount charged by the sales finance company. The sales finance company profits when it collects the full amount owed on a debt that it bought for less than face value.

CONSUMER FINANCE COMPANIES Indirectly involved in a firm's short-term financing activities is a **consumer finance company,** *a company that lends money to final consumers on their promissory notes.* These loans may be secured by the product the consumers intend to buy or by some other valuable item they now own. Merchants who are unwilling to accept a consumer's promissory note may make the sale if the person can borrow from one of these firms (for example, Commercial Credit Corporation or Household Finance Corporation). Consumers with good credit ratings can borrow some cash on unsecured promissory notes.

People who have exhausted their borrowing limits at commercial banks or credit unions may turn to a consumer finance company as a lender of last resort. The same holds true for people with a history of delinquent payments to more conservative lenders. The fact that these firms lend to risky borrowers justifies the relatively high rate of interest they charge on the loans that they grant.

Long-Term Capital

Long-term or fixed capital, you will recall, is money used to buy fixed assets, which are long-lived and (with the exception of land) manufactured items that will be used to produce goods and services for several years. Huge amounts of money are required to buy or build a new plant, purchase new equipment, acquire land for a retail store, or remodel an existing facility that has become inefficient or outmoded. For example, Volkswagen AG, Europe's largest auto manufacturer, announced it will spend a total of $46.7 billion through 1997 to improve plants and equipment.[2] Companies raise money for long-term use with retained earnings and such long-term instruments as securities.

sales finance company
A firm that provides short-term capital to retailers (and sometimes to wholesalers) by purchasing the installment sales contracts (promissory notes) that they have accepted from customers.

consumer finance company
A company that lends money to final consumers on their promissory notes.

MANAGER'S NOTEBOOK

Updating Equipment Versus Placating Stockholders

Top managers in many U.S.-based companies often tend to avoid investing retained earnings in new machinery and equipment. Profits that could have been used for those purposes are often used to increase dividends to stockholders, who expect management to rack up record profits year after year—no matter how outdated the company's equipment has become. This myopic view is now causing major problems for companies that compete against more farsighted firms, such as Toyota, the world's third largest auto maker. Ignoring short-term profitability, Toyota's management has cut costs and streamlined manufacturing operations while increasing production efficiency at a sizzling pace. The company is currently building and upgrading six manufacturing plants world-wide to have a combined production capacity of 1 million vehicles a year.

Although the cost of replacing manufacturing equipment can be staggering (and produce loud complaints from dividend-hungry stockholders), the payoff in productivity and competitiveness can't be disputed. Machines of the 1950s and 1960s that performed a single boring, drilling, or honing operation are museum pieces compared to today's multipurpose CNC (computerized numerical control) machine tools that can perform a full range of machining operations on hundreds of different-sized parts. (Cincinnati Milacron's new Maxim CNC horizontal machining center can juggle up to 180 different drills and metal-cutting attachments at once.) Changeovers can be done in moments by keying in a new command or changing a computer tape.

The price tag for these mechanical magicians is correspondingly high (Milacron's Maxim has a base price of $300,000), but the cost of *not* making such a long-term capital investment will be infinitely worse. For example, United States industries, which claim a modest 15 percent of CNC machine tools, saw manufacturing profits decline from $118 billion in 1988 to $89 billion in 1991. This trend suggests that top management in many manufacturing companies must summon the courage to act in the best interest of the business and channel long-term capital into modernized facilities and equipment without delay. In some cases the company's very survival may be at stake.

(For more on U.S. capital investment, see Edmund Faltermayer, "Invest or Die," *Fortune*, February 22, 1993, p. 42, and Alex Taylor III, "How Toyota Copes with Hard Times," *Fortune*, January 25, 1993, p. 78.)

Retained Earnings

Retained earnings are *profits reinvested in (or plowed back into) a company for improvements and expansion.* Depending on its expected growth rate and long-term capital requirements, a firm will retain some (sometimes all) of its yearly profits for expansion. It is impractical, however—if not impossible—to pay for rapid expansion with a company's profits alone; that would be like saving enough money from your paycheck to pay cash for a home. So, while retained earnings are an important contribution, incorporated firms issue stocks and sometimes bonds to raise most of their long-term capital. Collectively, stocks and bonds are termed *securities.*

Securities

In Chapter 4 you learned that a corporation can raise large sums of money by selling shares of stock to investors who are willing to take an owner's risk. Stocks are *equity securities.* The word *equity* in this sense means ownership; stockholders are the legal owners of their corporations, and *the long-term capital raised by selling stock* is known as **equity capital.**

Corporations may also raise money by selling **bonds,** which are *long-term, interest-bearing promissory notes.* Bonds may not mature for as long as twenty-five years. Bonds, as *debt securities,* represent an obligation to be paid at some future date.

The Law and Securities Sales

Before 1933 only state laws governed how corporations could sell their securities. Potential investors had no federal protection from fraudulent securities marketing schemes. After the stock market crash of 1929, however, the early years of the New Deal saw an array of federal legislation that created the current climate of regulation of corporate financing and protection of investors. Table 16.3 provides a ready reference of the most significant federal controls on the selling of corporate stocks and bonds.

Companies usually must publish a **prospectus** before offering securities for sale. This is *a document that presents a company's financial data for several consecutive years, discusses its position in its industry, describes how it will use the funds raised by a securities sale, and summarizes other information that well-informed investors should have.* The breakup of American Telephone and Telegraph resulted in a prospectus publishing task of truly monumental

---

Long-term capital finances fixed assets.

retained earnings
Profits invested in (or plowed back into) a company for improvements and expansion.

equity capital
Long-term capital raised by selling stock.

bonds
Long-term, interest-bearing promissory notes.

prospectus
A document that presents a company's financial data for several consecutive years, discusses its position in its industry, describes how it will use the funds raised by a securities sale, and summarizes other information that well-informed investors should have.

Table 16.3
Federal laws controlling securities trading.

ACT	PROVISIONS
Securities Act of 1933	Requires a corporation, before it can sell a new issue of securities to the public, to supply information to the federal government in a registration statement and to potential investors in a published prospectus
	Subjects corporations that violate this rule to criminal prosecution and those who willfully misstate information to fine or imprisonment of responsible executives*
Securities Exchange Act of 1934	Created the Securities and Exchange Commission (SEC), a federal government regulatory body that discharges provisions of this law and the 1933 act
	Established specific trading rules to be followed by stock exchanges and by over-the-counter traders to prevent stock manipulation and fraud
	Bans "wash sales"—the simultaneous buying and selling of stock to create the impression of investor interest
	Prohibits the making of misleading statements about a security to encourage others to buy or sell it
	Forbids organized buying or selling of a security to drive its price up or down
	Prohibits trading of securities by corporate employees or other insiders based on information not available to the general public
	Gives the Federal Reserve Board the power to set a *margin requirement,* a minimum payment an investor must make when buying securities (the remainder may be borrowed)
Investment Company Act of 1940	Regulates activities of companies that work primarily in investing and trading in securities and that sell their own securities to the public to register their securities with the SEC
	Requires management to obtain stockholders' approval before substantially changing the nature of the firm's business or investment policies
	Bars persons guilty of securities fraud from being officers or directors
	Prevents underwriters, investment bankers, or brokers from constituting a majority of the board of directors
	Requires that stockholders approve material changes in contracts between the company and its executives
	Prohibits transactions between the companies and their directors, officers, or affiliated companies or individuals unless approved by the SEC
	Bans cross-ownership of securities among such companies
Investment Advisers Act of 1940	Requires persons or companies that are paid for giving securities investment advice to register with the SEC and conform to various laws designed to protect investors
	Requires investment advisers to reveal any financial interest in transactions conducted for clients, to keep records according to SEC rules, and to make those records available to the SEC for inspection

*Registration under these provisions does not imply that the federal government supports or endorses the issue, merely that the issuing corporation has disclosed the information that will allow potential investors to make an informed decision.

proportions. All 2.9 million stockholders in the original company were required to receive a prospectus providing details about the stock of the seven new corporations that were created. The company that printed this 267-page document reported that the job required 1,950 tons of paper, and that all the sheets placed end to end would circle the globe 3.4 times.

In addition to the securities laws outlined in Table 16.3, a 1993 ruling by the Securities and Exchange Commission also requires public corporations to provide more information in the proxy forms (discussed in Chapter 4) that stockholders are sent each year. This information should include:

- A chart that shows how the stock's market price has changed during the past five years
- Tables that clearly summarize executives' total annual compensation from all sources for the past three years
- A statement from the company's compensation committee that explains how the executive compensation program works and why this particular program is used
- Disclosure of potential conflicts of interest among the company's directors (For example, do executives serve as directors of each other's companies or sit on each other's executive compensation committee? Are any members of the compensation committee employed by the parent company or a subsidiary firm?)

Although a prospectus makes the official, or legal, offer, a company typically runs an advertisement called a "tombstone" prospectus in certain magazines or in *The Wall Street Journal* to inform potential investors that the securities are available.

The Mechanics of a Securities Sale

Firms rarely sell securities directly to the general public; it can take months to dispose of the entire issue. Instead they arrange with one or more investment banking firms to purchase the entire issue and retail it to the public. An **investment banking firm,** not to be confused with a commercial bank, is *a firm that purchases an entire issue of new securities from the issuing company as a wholesaler and resells it to the general public.* If a single investment banking firm is unable or unwilling to take the risk of buying and reselling an entire issue, it may form a syndicate of several investment bankers to buy the issue, divide it among themselves, and resell it. After the securities are sold the group is disbanded.

Syndication, by spreading the risk, lets one firm escape the burden of buying and reselling the entire lot of securities. It is also more convenient for the issuing corporation, which receives the money in a lump sum.

Market conditions can have a significant impact on the amount of money a company receives from a new issue of securities. For example, Chase Manhattan Corporation lost an estimated $50 million in new capital when an abrupt

investment banking firm
A firm that purchases an entire issue of new securities from the issuing company as a wholesaler and resells it to the general public.

stock market decline in mid-October 1989 caused the company's investment banker to set the offering price for the new stock at $40.125, some $3.50 lower than the company's existing shares had traded for just before the market dropped.

Registrars and Transfer Agents

Large corporations with thousands of owners find that keeping records on securities is a staggering burden. As a result, companies normally employ large banks to act as their registrars and transfer agents. A **registrar** is *a commercial bank that monitors the number of shares of stock a corporation sells to ensure that it does not sell more than its charter has authorized.* A **transfer agent** is *a commercial bank that records changes in names and addresses for a corporation each time stocks and certain types of bonds are traded.* Earlier certificates must be canceled and current ones issued bearing the new owner's name.

Common Stock

Common stock, which all corporations organized for profit must issue, is *a security held by the corporation's owners.* A document called a **common stock certificate** is *legal evidence of corporate ownership. It gives the owner's name, the number of shares owned, and various data on the corporation itself.* Common stock is bought and held in groups called a **round lot**—*one hundred shares of a stock or multiples thereof*—or an **odd lot**—*less than one hundred shares of a stock.* You saw a sample stock certificate in Chapter 4. Chrysler Corporation recently raised $1.78 billion worth of long-term capital by selling 46 million new shares of common stock. This was the second-largest sale of common stock in history, surpassed only by the May 1992 sale of common shares by General Motors that raised $2.15 billion in long-term capital.[3]

Common stockholders, as the true owners of the corporation, elect its board of directors. These voting rights give stockholders ultimate control over a corporation's affairs.

Dividends

Common stockholders may receive a **dividend,** which is *a portion of company profits paid to stockholders as a return for the risk that they take as owners.* Firms that retain earnings for use as fixed capital, however, may pay a very small dividend, if any. The optional nature of dividends makes common stock a favored security to offer when a firm's financial future is cloudy. It carries no fixed payments, unlike certain other securities. Corporations are not legally required to pay dividends, because they are essentially distributed profits.

Dividends, when paid, are usually paid each quarter. The company or its transfer agent mails a check for the proper amount to the shareholders of record on a specific date. The total dividend that the board of directors approves is divided by the number of shares of common stock outstanding to determine the amount paid on each share.

registrar
A commercial bank that monitors the number of shares of stock a corporation sells to ensure that it does not sell more than its charter has authorized.

transfer agent
A commercial bank that records changes in names and addresses for a corporation each time stocks and certain types of bonds are traded.

common stock
A security held by the corporation's owners.

common stock certificate
Legal evidence of corporate ownership. It gives the owner's name, the number of shares owned, and various data on the corporation itself.

round lot
One hundred shares of a stock or multiples thereof.

odd lot
Less than one hundred shares of a stock.

dividend
A portion of company profits paid to stockholders as a return for the risk that they take as owners.

Firms that want to conserve cash and display concern for investors' welfare may pay a **stock dividend**, which is *a distribution of shares of the company's stock or the stock that it owns in other firms.*

The Preemptive Right

Corporation laws in most states require that corporations give their shareholders a **preemptive right,** which is *a shareholder's right to purchase shares of a company's new stock issues in proportion with the existing shares that he or she owns, before the new shares are offered to the general public.* This law allows you to maintain your current degree of control in the company if you wish. Without this right, your control would be diluted when others bought new shares.

A **warrant** is *a document that conveys the preemptive right to existing stockholders.* It states the number of shares the holder may purchase and the required price per share. Warrants usually have an expiration date after which the company may sell the new lot of shares to anyone. When the warrant price is lower than the market price of shares already outstanding, the warrants acquire a value of their own, and stockholders may sell them.

Stock Splits

A stock's market price is the price negotiated between buyers and sellers. It reflects investor consensus about the firm itself within its industry and the national and world economic and political outlook. If optimistic investors bid a stock's market price extremely high, the company's board of directors, with the approval of existing stockholders, may declare a **stock split.** This is *a subdivision of shares already issued, done to decrease a stock's high market price to an amount that more investors can afford to pay.* Assume, for example, that eager buyers and reluctant sellers have bid the market price for a company's common stock to $350 per share. If the firm declares a five-for-one split and you hold a round lot of 100 shares, you will own 500 shares after the split. The market price per share would be reduced from $350 to $70 ($350 ÷ 5) afterward. Although the total market value of your investment is unchanged, the market price for each share has been reduced to a more affordable level for investors. By reducing the price per share, a stock split enables more investors to buy in round lots instead of odd lots and may bring the price within what some businesses believe is a psychologically attractive trading range—between $20 and $40 per share.

The main difference between a stock dividend and a stock split is that the corporation reduces the stock's *face,* or *par, value* (an arbitrary value per share that the corporation may assign to its stock and print on the front of the stock certificate) in a stock split. The par value is not reduced when a stock dividend is distributed because no new shares have been created.

Stock splits and stock dividends, coupled with a company's sound financial performance, increase not only the number but also the value of investors'

stock dividend
A distribution of shares of the company's stock or the stock that it owns in other firms.

preemptive right
A shareholder's right to purchase shares of a company's new stock issues in proportion with the existing shares that he or she owns, before the new shares are offered to the general public.

warrant
A document that conveys the preemptive right to existing stockholders.

stock split
A subdivision of shares already issued, done to decrease a stock's high market price to an amount that more investors can afford to pay.

shares over the years. For example, one share of Coca-Cola stock, which was worth $40 in 1919, would have grown to 2,304 shares by the end of 1992 as a result of 73 years worth of stock splits and stock dividends. The shares had a total market value of $96,480 at that time.[4] One hundred shares of Home Depot stock purchased in 1981 would have increased to 5,679 shares by mid-1992 as a result of nine stock splits. Splits of 3 for 2, 5 for 4, and 2 for 1 occurred in 1982 alone.[5]

Why Do People Buy Common Stock?

Investors seeking income purchase stock in firms with a record of dividend payments that has been unbroken for several years or, in some cases, several decades. The most intriguing and appealing reason for owning common stock, however, is **capital appreciation,** *an increase in a stock's market price caused by investor optimism.*

If traced from their beginnings, the common stock prices of many well-known companies illustrate this phenomenon. During the early years of McDonald's Corporation, for example, the company's bookkeeper agreed to take some of her pay in common stock instead of cash. When she retired, her shares were worth $70 million. One thousand dollars invested in PepsiCo, Inc. stock in 1965 would have been worth $64,000 at the end of 1992. This company's total return to investors (capital appreciation plus reinvested dividends) grew at a compound annual rate of 30 percent between 1982 and 1992.[6]

Innovative products and services and unexpected events naturally affect how the market price of a company's stock behaves. For example, when shares of Genentech, Inc., one of the original gene-splicing firms, were first offered for sale, optimistic investors bid the price up from $35 to $89 within the first twenty minutes of trading. The day after the 1989 California earthquake, investors quickly purchased shares in certain lumber, cement, and construction engineering firms, as well as companies that regularly built roads and bridges in that state.

Elevators and stock prices, however, have one thing in common: they go down as well as up, and there's no limit to the developments that may alter investors' confidence in a stock. For example, Eastman Kodak's common stock dropped 5⅛ points ($5.125 per share) after a surprise announcement that the company's highly respected chief financial officer had resigned. At the same time, IBM's common stock shot up $1.50 a share due to a rumor that he would take a similar position with that company.[7] The market price of Tenneco Inc.'s stock fell $2 a share after the news that the chairman and CEO was suffering from a brain tumor.[8] During the Great Depression, when investor confidence was shaken to its roots, stocks that sold for lofty amounts in 1929 plummeted to lows that were unthinkable to many investors. American Telephone & Telegraph plunged from 310¼ per share to 69¾, and the New York Central Railroad collapsed from 256½ a share to 8¾. But the greatest fall may have been retailer Montgomery Ward, which fell from 156⅞ a share to a mere 3½. The amounts, like all stock prices, are quoted in dollars per share, in increments of an eighth of a dollar (twelve and one-half cents). When market prices are generally falling, a *bear market* is said to exist; when they are generally rising, a *bull market* is said to be present.

Mutual Funds

A **mutual fund** is *a pool of stocks, bonds, or other securities purchased by a group of investors and professionally managed by an investment company.* People who buy shares in a mutual fund indirectly own a broad range of companies that do business across many industry lines. Mutual fund investors hope to avoid the risks associated with owning stock in only a handful of corporations or those that do business in just one industry, such as aerospace, retailing, or computers. Table 16.4 shows how mutual funds that invest in common stock spread their risk among various industries in recent years.

The company that manages the mutual fund will redeem investors' shares at any time for their net asset value (NAV) per share, which is found by dividing the difference between the fund's debts and total market value by the number of shares outstanding.

Many mutual funds include a sales charge or "load" in the price of their shares to cover management costs and brokers' commissions. The Investment Company Institute states that these sales charges, which vary with the amount invested, may not exceed 8.5 percent of the initial investment. A **front-end load** is *a sales charge applied when mutual fund shares are bought*. A **back-end load** (also known as a contingent deferred sales load) is *a sales charge applied when mutual fund shares are redeemed*. A back-end load may decline with the length of time shares are held. You may also purchase shares in a *no-load mutual fund,* which applies no sales charges whatsoever. Both load- and no-load funds may levy an annual 12b-1 fee (named after a 1980 Securities and Exchange Commission rule) to cover marketing costs and sales commissions. The law requires a fund's prospectus to show all fees and expenses charged to shareholders or to the fund itself, along with various other data, including the fund's annual performance (as compared to the overall securities market), investment strategies and market factors that affected recent performance, and the name of the individual primarily responsible for managing the fund. Figure 16.4 shows the growth in number and type of mutual funds since 1950. Approximately 47 million Americans own stocks or shares of mutual funds that purchase stock.[9]

Preferred Stock

Preferred stock, which some corporations sell with the approval of the common stockholders, is *a class of stock that has a prior or senior claim on assets to that of common stock*. It is still an equity security, but it ranks ahead of common stock in receiving dividend payments and in any cash distributions should a corporation be dissolved.

mutual fund
A pool of stocks, bonds, or other securities purchased by a group of investors and professionally managed by an investment company.

front-end load
A sales charge applied when mutual fund shares are bought.

back-end load
A sales charge applied when mutual fund shares are redeemed.

preferred stock
A class of stock that has a prior or senior claim on assets to that of common stock.

Table 16.4
Diversification of
mutual fund
portfolios
(percentage of
common stock
holdings by
industry).

	1991	1992
Agricultural equipment	0.63%	0.66%
Aircraft manufacturing and aerospace	1.68	1.23
Air transport	0.90	0.95
Auto and accessories (excl. tires)	1.83	2.68
Building materials and equipment	1.84	0.88
Chemicals	4.57	4.70
Communications (TV, radio, motion pictures, telephone)	7.38	7.59
Computer services*	3.37	3.67
Conglomerates	3.30	3.00
Containers	0.13	0.29
Drugs and cosmetics	7.31	6.48
Electric equipment and electronics (excl. TV and radio)	4.67	5.04
Financial (incl. banks and insurance)	16.29	17.65
Foods and beverages	3.20	3.12
Hospital supplies and services	4.19	3.80
Leisure time	1.71	2.64
Machinery	1.59	1.99
Metals and mining	2.53	2.21
Office equipment	2.47	2.00
Oil	8.11	8.02
Paper	1.69	1.59
Printing and publishing	2.02	2.23
Public utilities (incl. natural gas)	5.13	3.83
Railroads and railroad equipment	1.27	1.67
Retail trade	6.10	6.04
Rubber (incl. tires)	0.35	0.37
Steel	0.68	0.61
Textiles	0.92	0.71
Tobacco	1.27	2.26
Trucking and shipping	0.48	0.48
Miscellaneous	2.39	1.61
Total	100.00%	100.00%

Note: Composite industry investments drawn from the portfolios of 60 of the largest investment companies as of the end of the calendar year 1992 whose total net assets represented 37.7 percent of total net assets of all reporting equity companies.

*Includes computer software, consultants, and time sharing.

Source: *1993 Mutual Fund Fact Book*, p. 43. The Investment Company Institute, Washington, D.C. Reprinted with permission.

Figure 16.4
Growth of mutual
funds, 1950–
1992.

Year	Stock, bond, and income funds	Taxable and tax-exempt money market funds	Total
1950	98		
1960	161		
1970	361		
1975	390	36	426
1980	458	106	564
1981	486	179	665
1982	539	318	857
1983	653	373	1026
1984	820	421	1241
1985	1071	457	1528
1986	1355	485	1840
1987	1776	541	2317
1988	2110	605	2715
1989	2253	664	2917
1990	2362	743	3105
1991	2603	820	3423
1992	2984	864	3848

Number of mutual funds

Source: *1993 Mutual Fund Fact Book*, p. 29. The Investment Company Institute, Washington, D.C. Reprinted with permission.

Preferred stock dividends are quoted as a percentage of the face, or par, value. Most pars are $25, $50, or $100. Some companies do not assign a par value to their stocks, however. In these cases the dividend is expressed in terms of dollars per share. Figure 16.5 is a specimen of a preferred stock certificate with a par value of $100 and a dividend rate of $7^3/_8$ percent printed on the certificate. This means that holders will receive an annual dividend of $7.375 per share.

Although preferred stock dividends are assured, they are not guaranteed. The board of directors may decide to pay no dividends at all or to make a partial payment if adverse business conditions impair the company's ability to pay the full amount due. Preferred stock dividends are fixed amounts and will change only if the stock splits.

Preferred Stock Terminology

Preferred stock may also have several features not associated with common stock. These features are stated on the stock certificate itself, or you can confirm them by checking with the company. The primary features that may apply to a given preferred stock issue are:

- *Participating preferred.* This stock can pay an additional dividend beyond

Figure 16.5
Sample preferred
stock certificate.

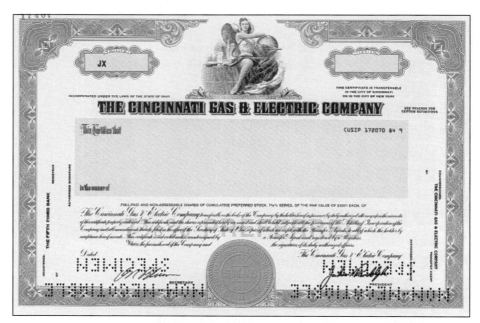

its standard amount, as specified by the corporation. (Most preferred stock
is participating.)

• *Callable preferred.* The issuing company may require the holder to surrender these shares at a call price that is usually slightly higher than the market
price at the time the company exercises its call.

• *Convertible preferred.* This stock may be converted into the company's
common stock if the holder wishes. The conversion ratio (number of
common shares exchanged for one preferred share) is established by the
firm. Because conversion ties the company's preferred stock to its common,
the market price of preferred mirrors any changes in that of the common.

• *Cumulative preferred.* This is preferred stock on which the company must pay
all dividends that are unpaid ("in arrears") before it can pay any dividends to its
common stockholders. (Most preferred stock has this feature.)

• *Noncumulative preferred.* This is preferred stock on which unpaid dividends
do not carry forward to the next year.

• *Adjustable or floating-rate preferred.* This is an innovative form of preferred
first issued in 1982. Unlike traditional preferred, which pays a fixed dividend, the dividend rates on this variation change quarterly according to the
interest rates paid on U.S. Treasury securities (discussed in Chapter 15).
Dividends on most floating rate preferreds range from a minimum of
7.5 percent to a maximum of 16 percent.

The Cincinnati Gas & Electric Company preferred stock shown in Figure 16.5 is cumulative.

Why Do People Buy Preferred Stock?

Investors who buy preferred stock want less risk than those who buy common stock. The fixed but assured dividend, combined with the potential for capital appreciation, makes it an appealing security for conservative individual investors, pension funds, and others with large sums to invest.

Financing with Bonds

When a company sells, or floats, an issue of bonds, it obtains **debt capital,** another name for *the long-term capital raised by selling bonds.* (As you learned, capital raised by selling stocks is called *equity capital.*) Bondholders are actually creditors; the corporation is their borrower or debtor. Bonds are commonly issued with a face, or par, value of $1,000 or multiples thereof, although some have face values as low as $500 or even $100. The face, or par, value is paid to the holder when the bond matures. The **bond indenture** is *a blanket agreement between the corporation and its bondholders that states the bond issue's interest rate, maturity date, and other terms and conditions.*

Interest and Market Price Quotations

As creditors, bondholders have a legal right to collect interest from the corporation. Interest is expressed as a percentage of the bond's face value, which you should assume is $1,000 unless you are informed otherwise. A bond's market price is expressed as a percentage of face value, too. The examples in Table 16.5 illustrate how to convert interest rates and market price quotations into dollars.

You need not hold a bond until maturity once you have bought it. Bonds, like stocks, are often traded between investors, who adjust the market price up or down to compensate for the bond's fixed interest rate in relation to the short-term interest rate available from other investments at the time of sale. Because a bond's interest is fixed for its lifetime but the interest rate it is compared with is constantly changing, it will sell at either a premium or a discount. A **premium** is *the amount by which a bond's market price exceeds its par value;* a **discount** is *the amount by which a bond's par value exceeds its market price.* Bonds rarely sell for exactly their par value.

debt capital
The long-term capital raised by selling bonds.

bond indenture
A blanket agreement between the corporation and its bondholders that states the bond issue's interest rate, maturity date, and other terms and conditions.

premium
The amount by which a bond's market price exceeds its par value.

discount
The amount by which a bond's par value exceeds its market price.

Table 16.5
Interpreting bond interest rate and price quotations.

INTEREST RATE	ANNUAL INTEREST	CURRENT MARKET PRICE QUOTATION	MARKET PRICE OF BOND
8½	$ 85.00	91⅛	$ 911.25
11¼	112.50	119¾	1,197.50
10½	105.00	100	1,000.00
9¾	97.50	87½	875.00

Sinking Funds

By floating a bond issue, a corporation incurs a multimillion-dollar debt payable on a definite future date. To prepare for this day of reckoning, companies usually establish a **sinking fund,** which is *a special fund a company creates and pays money into over the life of a bond issue so dollars will be available to pay off the bonds when they mature.* A bond sinking fund is invested in stocks and bonds of other companies and in United States government securities— the more a sinking fund can earn on its own, the less the company must pay into it.

By ensuring that the company will be able to retire the bonds (pay them off) when they mature, a sinking fund reduces the risk bondholders take in lending money to a corporation, which tends to prop up the market price of the bonds.

Face Value and Format

A bond's face, or par, value, like that of stock, is printed on its face; it has no relationship to market value. If you examine a bond, you will find the company's name, the serial number by which the firm keeps track of the bond, the interest rate, the face, or par, value (sometimes referred to as the *principal*), and the maturity date, on which the corporation will pay the holder the face value.

Bonds had one of two formats before 1982. The first, a **registered bond**, is *one whose owner's name is on record with the company and appears on the bond itself.* If the bond is registered as to principal, it carries a sheet of dated coupons that must be clipped for each interest payment, but its face amount will be paid automatically on maturity to the person whose name appears on the bond and on the company's books. A **fully registered bond** is *one without coupons. The company pays interest automatically to the owner whose name is on record with the firm, and the principal is paid to that person when the bond matures.* The 1982 Tax Equity and Fiscal Responsibility Act requires corporate bonds sold in the United States that mature in one year or more to have a fully registered format. Corporations will thus report the interest paid to those bondholders to the federal government and so reduce the likelihood that the bondholders will fail to declare the interest income on their federal income tax returns.

The second type of bond format, a **coupon *or* bearer bond**, was *one with dated coupons attached, which the bondholder cut off and mailed to the company to collect interest.* When all the coupons were clipped, the bond had matured; the holder sent in the bond itself (the face) to collect the principal from the issuing firm. Bearer bonds carried no owner identification; they were transferred on delivery, meaning the holder was presumed to be the rightful owner. Companies often did not record the names of people who received interest on bearer bonds, which made it possible for bondholders to avoid paying federal income tax on the interest. However, since companies must now issue bonds in

---

sinking fund
A special fund a company creates and pays money into over the life of a bond issue so dollars will be available to pay off the bonds when they mature.

registered bond
One whose owner's name is on record with the company and appears on the bond itself.

fully registered bond
One without coupons. The company pays interest automatically to the owner whose name is on record with the firm, and the principal is paid to that person when the bond matures.

coupon *or* bearer bond
One with dated coupons attached, which the bondholder cuts off and mail to the company to collect interest.

a registered format, bearer bonds will gradually disappear as those that were issued before the 1982 Tax Equity and Fiscal Responsibility Act reach maturity.

All securities should be kept under lock and key—preferably in a safe deposit box at a commercial bank, credit union, or other financial institution.

Bond Yield

Bond yield is *the percentage return that the investor will receive.* A bond bought at 100 (face value) yields its exact interest rate, but because most are bought at a premium or a discount, the return is greater or less than the interest rate stated on the face. The **current yield**—*a bond's annual interest expressed as a percentage of the market or purchase price*—can be calculated, as can the **yield to maturity**—*the percentage return an owner receives if a bond is held until it matures.* Yield formulas and calculations are shown in Figure 16.6.

Types of Bonds

Bonds can be categorized several different ways, based on the assets that secure them and other criteria. The bond certificate itself (as shown in Figure 16.7) states which of these categories the bond fits. The categories are summarized in Table 16.6.

bond yield
The percentage return that the investor will receive.

current yield
A bond's annual interest expressed as a percentage of the market or purchase price.

yield to maturity
The percentage return an owner receives if a bond is held until it matures.

Current Yield

$$\text{Current yield} = \frac{\text{Annual interest}}{\text{Purchase price}}$$

Assume a 9½% bond with a $1,000 face value was bought at 105:

$$\frac{95}{1050} = 0.0905 = 9.05\% \text{ current yield}$$

Assume a 9½% bond with a $1,000 face value was bought at 90:

$$\frac{95}{900} = 0.1056 = 10.56\% \text{ current yield}$$

Yield to Maturity

$$\text{Yield to maturity} = \frac{\text{Annual interest} \left\{ \begin{array}{l} - \text{ annual premium amortization*} \\ or + \text{ annual discount accumulation} \end{array} \right\}}{\text{Average principal (purchase price + face} \div 2)}$$

Assume an 8% bond with a $1,000 face value was bought ten years before maturity at 90:

$$\frac{80 + (100/10)}{1900 \div 2} = \frac{80 + 10}{950} = \frac{90}{950} = 0.0947 = 9.47\% \text{ yield to maturity}$$

Assume an 8% bond with a $1,000 face value was bought ten years before maturity at 110:

$$\frac{80 - (100/10)}{2100 \div 2} = \frac{80 - 10}{1050} = \frac{70}{1050} = 0.0666 = 6.67\% \text{ yield to maturity}$$

*Annual premium amortization and annual discount accumulation are obtained by dividing the premium or discount by the number of years to maturity.

Figure 16.6
Calculating current yield and yield to maturity.

Figure 16.7
Sample pass through trust bond (also known as an equipment trust bond).

Table 16.6
Types of bonds.

TYPE	CHARACTERISTICS
Mortgage bond	A bond secured by a claim against a specific company asset, such as buildings or land. The most secure of all corporate bonds.
Equipment trust bond	Often referred to as an *equipment trust certificate*. A bond issued to finance new equipment, the title to which is held by a trustee for the security of the bondholders. Popular long-term instrument for railroads and airlines (see Figure 16.7).
Income bond	A bond that pays interest only when the company's earnings permit. Unpaid interest may or may not have to be paid in the future, depending on the terms of the bond. A relatively rare type.
Debenture bond	An unsecured bond, backed only by the firm's general reputation. Considered the riskiest bonds of all; usually called, simply, *debentures.*
Callable bond	A bond that the issuing firm may call in and pay off, usually at a premium, permitting the company to remove the debt early if the sinking fund earns greater income than anticipated. Interest payments end on the call date.
Convertible bond	A bond that may be exchanged for the issuing company's common stock. The market price of these bonds rises and falls with that of the company's common stock. Most are debentures. They usually pay a lower interest rate than nonconvertibles.
Serial bond	One from a bond issue that matures in lots or increments, either annually or semiannually, over several years. Essentially the issuing firm pays off a serial bond issue in installments. The bonds with later maturity dates carry a slightly higher interest rate than those with earlier dates.
Zero-coupon bond	A non-interest-bearing bond first marketed in the early 1980s. The bond is sold at a deep discount (perhaps 70 percent of par value or more) and redeemed for face value at maturity. The issuing firm benefits from paying nothing until the bonds mature. Although bondholders bear a greater risk (no money is received until maturity), such bonds have been bought by institutions with a specific need for future cash such as companies that invest employee pension funds.

	SAFETY	GROWTH POTENTIAL	INCOME
Bonds	Greatest	None	Relatively certain
Preferred stock	Good	High	Assured
Common stock	Poor	Highest	Relatively uncertain

Table 16.7
Comparison of
three major types
of security.

Making Decisions About Bonds

Bonds generally are considered safer investments than either class of stock because a bondholder is a creditor rather than an owner of the firm. The company pays interest on the bonds at regular intervals, and they will have a specified value when they mature. As a result, conservative investors may prefer bonds to either kind of stock. Although it is impossible to prescribe a security that is appropriate for everyone's needs, the three major types are compared according to safety, growth, and income in Table 16.7.

As for the issuing company, the decision on whether to issue stocks or bonds is complex. A corporation's long-term financing mix may consist of stocks, bonds, or both. When deciding which security to issue, management compares the fixed costs and other obligations associated with each type against the company's objectives and projected earnings.

A firm that sells common stock typically sacrifices control (through voting rights) in order to raise capital on which there is no fixed cost. A firm is not obliged to pay dividends to common stockholders if profits are low or nonexistent or if the directors choose to reinvest earnings, so common stock is popular with new corporations facing an uncertain future or planning on rapid growth.

Selling preferred stock, however, creates an obligation to pay dividends if at all possible. A firm's financial reputation suffers if it does not pay dividends on preferred stock. On the bright side, preferred stock usually carries no voting rights, so common stockholders may vote to sell it to raise long-term capital without losing control of their firm.

Bonds carry a formidable set of obligations, namely, regular interest payments and a maturity date when the face value, or principal, must be paid. For these reasons, management must be confident that income will be adequate to meet the fixed interest charges on its debt capital and to accumulate enough funds (usually in a sinking fund) to retire the debt at maturity. On the positive side, bond interest payments are business expenses—rent on money borrowed—so they decrease a corporation's taxable income. For example, Time Warner Inc. recently issued $1 billion in debenture bonds and used the funds to call in preferred stock that paid an extremely high dividend. Analysts estimated the move could save the company nearly $300 million a year.[10] Taking advantage of lower interest rates, Phillips Petroleum Company issued bonds with a floating interest rate tied to the going rate in the money market and used the money to call in $1.3 billion worth of bonds issued in 1985 that paid an average annual interest of 14 percent. It is estimated that this decision will save the company $100 million a year in interest.[11]

Leverage

In using **leverage *or* trading on the equity,** *a firm takes advantage of the sound market reputation of its common stock to sell bonds, then uses the capital obtained to improve company operations and earn back a greater return than the interest rate the company pays.* If the bond issue carries a 10 percent interest rate, for example, but the money is spent for new plants, improvements on existing plants, and more efficient new equipment, the firm may earn back, say, 20 percent on the borrowed funds. Leverage is a double-edged sword, however. The annual interest rate is fixed for the life of the bond issue, while the annual return on that borrowed capital varies from one year to the next according to business conditions. Should sales decline or expenses rise, the firm may find that the return earned on borrowed funds is less than their interest rate.

The Securities Market and Personal Investing

Students who want to invest in stocks and bonds need to understand something about the markets where these securities are bought and sold. In addition, they should know how to interpret price information and other relevant data about their securities and appreciate the role that a stockbroker plays in helping them set investment objectives and make other important decisions.

Where to Trade Securities

Securities may be bought and sold either on a stock exchange or in the over-the-counter market, depending on the nature of the company in question.

STOCK EXCHANGES When investors decide to sell their stocks or bonds, they need to contact other potential investors who may be willing to buy. The marketplace where those transactions take place is called a **stock exchange.** This is *a gathering place where the representatives of buyers and sellers of securities meet to make trades.* All but a handful of the exchanges are regulated by the Securities and Exchange Commission, and all have their own boards of governors as well. Both stocks and bonds are traded on exchanges.

Companies may list their securities on an organized stock exchange both for prestige and for the convenience of buyers and sellers. Prestige comes especially from a listing on one of the two national exchanges, the New York Stock Exchange (NYSE) or the American Stock Exchange (ASE or "Amex"). Listing on a national exchange implies size, profitability, and popularity—things a corporation can point to with pride. In addition, a company's investors can buy and sell their securities rapidly and conveniently when they can be traded on one of these centralized auction markets. Stocks of approximately 1,700 companies are listed on the New York exchange and 860 on the American exchange.

There are also regional exchanges in the East (Philadelphia), Midwest (Chicago), and West (San Francisco), and local exchanges in such cities as Honolulu, Pittsburgh, and Salt Lake City. Regional and local exchanges deal primarily in local stocks, but they may also list the stocks of larger national corporations.

Before a stock can be listed on an exchange, exchange officials require the corporation to provide specific operating information and to pay a listing fee plus a few cents for each share of stock outstanding at the time of listing. Qualifications for listing, which vary among the exchanges, are based on the number of publicly held shares, their total market value, the total number of stockholders, and the company's earnings. Brokerage houses that belong to a stock exchange are permitted to make trades there through their representatives who work on the floor of the exchange. Table 16.8 shows the listing requirements of the two national exchanges.

THE OVER-THE-COUNTER MARKET The **over-the-counter market**, which has no central location, is *an informal marketplace made up of brokers who communicate by telephone and computer.* The stocks of approximately 16,000 companies are traded on this market. Price per share and other trading data for OTC stocks are reported by NASDAQ, a computerized quotation system maintained by the National Association of Securities Dealers. These stocks are said to be unlisted because the companies are either unqualified for or unwilling to comply with the listing requirements of an organized exchange. This does not imply that OTC stocks are second-rate. Some nationally known corporations have their shares traded over the counter, including Apple Computer, Adolph Coors Company, Hoover Company, and Pabst Brewing Company.

over-the-counter market
An informal marketplace made up of brokers who communicate by telephone and computer.

	ASE	NYSE
Shares publicly held	500,000	1,100,000
Market value of publicly held shares	$3,000,000	$18,000,000
Number of stockholders	800	2,000 holders of round lots
Pretax income	$750,000 last fiscal year or two of last three fiscal years	Either $2.5 million for the most recent year and $2 million for each of the preceding two years, or a total of $6.5 million for the last three fiscal years, together with a minimum $4.5 million in the most recent fiscal year; all three years must be profitable
Net tangible assets	$4,000,000	$18,000,000

Source: Data from American Stock Exchange, Inc., and New York Stock Exchange, Inc.

Table 16.8

Listing requirements of the two national stock exchanges. (Other conditions may also apply.)

GLOBAL PERSPECTIVE

Although the New York and American stock exchanges are often mentioned in the news, Europe plays host to many stock exchanges where thousands of companies' stocks are traded each business day. Here are Europe's ten largest stock exchanges and the total market value (in billions) of their listed stocks:

1. London ($861.9)
2. Frankfurt ($356.4)
3. Paris ($306.7)
4. Milan ($149.1)
5. Amsterdam ($125.8)

6. Madrid ($123.5)
7. Brussels ($65.7)
8. Copenhagen ($39.1)
9. Athens ($15.4)
10. Luxembourg ($10.5)

European Stock Exchanges

Source: *1993 Business Rankings Annual* (Detroit: Gale Research, Inc., 1993), p. 530.

Learning About Securities

Informed investors know how to interpret the price and related information about their stocks as reported in the financial pages of the newspaper. They should also appreciate how the Dow-Jones Industrial Average acts as a barometer of stock market conditions.

UNDERSTANDING THE FINANCIAL PAGES As a rule, investors can learn certain facts about a company's securities by consulting the financial pages of a daily newspaper or *The Wall Street Journal.* These contain current information on stocks and bonds traded on the New York and American exchanges, at large regional exchanges, and over the counter.

Although they do not provide financial data on the company itself, the financial pages tell how a stock behaved in open trading on a given day and present several other pieces of information. Table 16.9 shows you how to interpret the stock listings on the financial pages.

Dow-Jones Industrial Average
A number that expresses the general trend and condition of the stock market.

THE DOW-JONES INDUSTRIAL AVERAGE The **Dow-Jones Industrial Average,** conceived by Charles Henry Dow, is *a number that expresses the general trend and condition of the stock market.* First published in 1896, it allows us to contrast the state of the present market with that of earlier years, note differences and similarities, and identify reasons for changes. Although there are actually three Dow-Jones averages—for industrial, transportation, and utilities corporations—the industrial average is the one most widely quoted. It is calculated using information such as price-earnings ratios, stock splits, and dividends of thirty firms that are believed to present an accurate sample of American industry. Table 16.10 lists the

Table 16.9
Interpreting stock listings.

1		2	3	4	5	6	7		8	9
52 WEEKS					P-E	SALES				NET
HIGH	LOW	STOCK	DIV	YLD.%	RATIO	100S	HIGH	LOW	CLOSE	CHG.
113¼	65¼	Digital	..	..	16	593	98½	96⅝	98	+⅜
67⅛	41½	Disney	1	1.6	16	354	64¼	63⅞	64	+¾
15¼	10¼	DrPepp	.76	5.7	10	303	13½	13¼	13¼	..
43	28¾	Donnly	1.28	3.2	11	301	41	40¼	40½	+⅜
31	12¾	Dorsey	1	3.7	9	12	27½	27	27	−½
64¾	37⅜	Dover	1.04	1.8	14	66	58½	58¼	58¼	−⅛
39	30¼	DowCh	1.80	5.4	9	1962	34⅜	33½	33½	−½
56	36	duPont	2.40	4.6	12	654	53⅜	52½	52⅝	−⅜
39	30	duPont	pf 3.50	11	..	30	30½	30⅛	30½	−½
50½	38¼	duPont	pf 4.50	11	..	116	41	38⅞	40	..

1. Highest and lowest price per share over the past 52 weeks.
2. The firm's abbreviated name. For example, *Digital* is Digital Equipment Corporation, *Disney* is Walt Disney Productions, and *DowCh* is Dow Chemical Company.
3. Annual dividend (if any) that the company is paying on each share. The abbreviation *pf* in the last two entries identifies preferred stock.
4. Yield or rate of return (as a percentage) that an investor would earn based on the closing price. Determined by dividing the dividend per share by the closing price.
5. Price-earnings ratio, based on the company's most recent earnings. This ratio indicates the level of investors' confidence in the company. It is calculated by dividing the stock's market price by its most recent earnings per share. If a stock now sells for 25¼ and the company reported earnings per share of $2.50, its price-earnings ratio would be 10.10 ($25.25 ÷ $2.50 = 10.10). A high price-earnings ratio indicates that investors are optimistic that the firm will perform well. They are willing to pay a relatively high price to become owners in anticipation of what the firm will earn. A low price-earnings ratio indicates that investors are pessimistic about the company's performance.
6. Number of shares sold today, in hundreds.
7. Highest and lowest price at which shares were traded today.
8. Price at which the last trade was made today.
9. Net change between today's closing price and yesterday's closing price.

To illustrate, let us use du Pont as an example. Shares of this stock have sold for as high as $56 and as low as $36 during the preceding year. The company's most recent annual dividend was $2.40 per share, which represents a 4.6 percent yield based on today's closing price of $52.625 per share. The stock currently has a price-earnings ratio of 12, which suggests that it recently earned $4.385 per share ($52.625 ÷ $4.385 = 12). Investors traded 65,400 shares (654 round lots) today. The highest trade was made at $53.375 per share, the lowest at $52.50. Today's closing price, $52.625, is $.375 lower than yesterday's closing price.

Table 16.10
Stocks used to compute the Dow-Jones Industrial Average.

Allied-Signal, Inc.
Aluminum Co. of America
American Express Company
American Telephone and Telegraph Company
Bethlehem Steel Corporation
Boeing Company
Caterpillar Inc.
Chevron Corporation

Coca-Cola Company
The Walt Disney Company
E. I. du Pont de Nemours & Company
Eastman Kodak Company
Exxon Corporation
General Electric Corporation
General Motors Corporation
Goodyear Tire & Rubber Company
International Business Machines Corporation
International Paper Company
McDonald's Corporation

Merck & Co., Inc.
Minnesota Mining and Manufacturing Company
J. P. Morgan & Co. Inc.
Philip Morris, Inc.
Procter & Gamble Company
Sears, Roebuck & Company
Texaco Inc.
Union Carbide Corporation
United Technologies Corporation
Westinghouse Electric Corporation
F. W. Woolworth Company

firms currently used in computing this average. Calculating the Dow is a major mathematical challenge because of the number of stocks listed, the daily trading volume, and the occasional stock splits that further complicate computations. Still, formulas that adjust for stock dividends and splits over the years allow us to compare today's average to those of earlier years and decades.

Stockbrokers

A **stockbroker** (also called an account executive) is *a person who buys or sells securities for members of the general public.* Many stockbrokers majored in finance in college, and most have earned at least a bachelor's degree.

Brokers must complete an extensive training program run by their companies, and they must also pass licensing examinations administered by the Securities and Exchange Commission, the National Association of Securities Dealers, and the New York Stock Exchange. These examinations verify that they have the knowledge of corporate finance and the securities industry that is necessary to soundly advise investors on which securities to buy and sell.

After completing the necessary training and becoming licensed, brokers buy and sell stocks for clients in the over-the-counter market or on the various exchanges to which their employer, the brokerage firm, belongs. Brokers receive a commission each time they buy or sell securities for their clients, but they are prohibited from **churning,** *advising clients to buy or sell without good reason* merely to generate commissions for themselves.

Just because churning is prohibited doesn't mean it doesn't happen, however. A broker who made trades for the city of Imperial Beach, California reportedly earned $104,000 for himself and his company by making twenty transactions during four months. At the end of that time the city had lost $10,120 as well as its original funds.

The **specialist,** another important figure in the securities industry, is *a person who works at a stock exchange to maintain an orderly market and facilitate trades among brokers.* Specialists work independently of the brokerage firms, either alone or in association with other specialists. Each specialist is assigned exclusive responsibility for a stock or several stocks (only one specialist, for example, handles Home Depot or Disney stock); every stock on the exchange has a specialist assigned to it. Specialists play two main roles.

In one role, specialists preserve the integrity and stability of trading on the exchanges by adjusting the supply of and demand for listed stocks in an orderly way. That is, they must buy their companies' stocks when most investors are selling and sell their accumulated inventory of shares when most investors want to buy. In this way specialists work for the benefit of the exchange and the companies listed thereon by preserving an orderly market. A bear market, a bull market, or mere coincidence may cause the number of buyers and sellers of a company's stock to vary widely at a given time and temporarily imbalance supply or demand.

In the second role, specialists act as brokers' brokers. For example, they may hold a sell order from a particular broker on one of their stocks until approached by another broker who wants to buy the same stock. In this role, they are agents, charging a commission to execute orders for busy brokers who do not have time to wait until another broker with a buy or sell order happens to walk up.

Persons who want to be specialists must be approved by the stock exchange. They must be extremely wealthy because they need to have capital on hand to dampen temporary inequities in supply by buying shares of their assigned stock when necessary.

Investing in Securities

Stockbrokers ask investors to select one of three investment objectives. After opening an account with a stockbroker, investors may also give the broker specific instructions about how they want to purchase and hold their securities.

INVESTMENT OBJECTIVES When you contact a stockbroker and open an account, the broker will meet with you and have you select a main investment objective: growth, safety, or income. Your decision will be influenced by such factors as your age, income level, financial condition, present and desired standard of living, and degree of risk you are willing to take.

If you set growth (or capital appreciation) as a goal, you want the value of your investment to multiply as much as possible. Your broker may recommend that you buy stocks in companies that have the potential to earn high profits if their products or services (which may be in the developmental stages or relatively new on the market) succeed. For example, a $1,000 investment in Wal-Mart stock in 1970 was worth $500,000 in 1989. Four hundred shares of Food Lion stock, which cost several thousand dollars in the early 1970s, were worth more than $3 million in 1988.

If your investment goal is safety, you will want to see your investment dollars used conservatively. The broker may therefore recommend that you buy stock in blue-chip companies—soundly financed industry leaders with prospects for steady, profitable, but not spectacular performance. You also may be advised to buy bonds issued by financially sound corporations or by municipalities, states, or the federal government.

If your investment goal is income, your broker will recommend that you buy stocks of firms whose dividend payments have been uninterrupted for many years or bonds of financially sound companies that will be able to pay the interest when it is due and retire the bonds at maturity. In either case, you want money to be paid to you regularly.

As mentioned earlier, your broker must be trained and licensed to ensure that he or she is qualified to evaluate and suggest securities that conform to your investment objective.

HOW TO BUY SECURITIES After setting your investment objectives with your broker, you instruct him or her to purchase securities accordingly; these instructions can be given over the telephone. You could tell your broker to purchase a round lot (100 shares) of, say, Dow Chemical. She would check the price on a computer on her desk and tell you that it was currently selling at $35 a share. You would then ask her to buy "at market" or make a "limit order."

A **market order** *instructs the stockbroker to buy shares at the best available price*, which would be around the $35 she quoted you. In the end, say she was able to get the shares for $34.50 each—that would cost you $3,450 for the stock, plus the commission for the broker. A **limit order** *instructs the stockbroker to buy shares for no more than a certain price*, say $33 a share. The broker could not purchase any Dow stock for you until she could obtain that price. Limit orders generally are valid only until the end of the day on which they are made, but you can give your broker an *open order*, which keeps the order valid until you cancel it.

Regardless of what kind of order you place, the transaction is accomplished by the broker transmitting your order to a representative of her brokerage firm on the floor of the stock exchange. That representative goes to the trading post for Dow Chemical, a spot where all transactions in Dow stock are made, to look for a representative of someone who wishes to sell the same amount of stock at the price you desire. When the sale is concluded, the representative wires the information back to your broker, who informs you verbally. Shortly afterward, printed confirmation of the transaction is sent to you; you send your broker a check within five business days of the date of the transaction. (This will be reduced to three business days in 1995.) A simple purchase or sale of stock handled through a broker can take less than five minutes from the time the order is placed.

HOW TO HOLD SECURITIES You can have your broker deliver your new securities to you. If so, we recommend that you rent a safe deposit box at a commercial bank or your credit union and keep them under lock and key, because it is extremely difficult to get lost or stolen securities certificates replaced.

To avoid the problems and inconvenience of keeping securities yourself (and having to deliver them yourself to your broker if and when you sell them), we suggest that you set up a **street name account**. This means that *the broker keeps your securities and sends you a statement each quarter for your records*. You will also receive a confirmation slip each time you buy or sell. If you keep securities in street name, the statement you receive reports the shares of stock or number of bonds you own and the price at which each was bought. Dividends or interest may be paid to you or you can have them credited to your account to buy more securities.

Although street name securities could be lost or stolen, the brokerage firm is fully responsible for their safekeeping and must carry insurance to cover such risks. Most active investors prefer the convenience of having an account

market order
Instructs the stockbroker to buy shares at the best available price.

limit order
Instructs the stockbroker to buy shares for no more than a certain price.

street name account
The broker keeps your securities and sends you a statement each quarter for your records.

in street name, and this practice is expected to increase. Some brokerage firms charge an additional fee to investors who insist on having the actual stock certificates, and many large companies have asked stockholders to let them maintain their names, addresses, and number of shares owned on computer files (called "book-entry only" recording) instead of issuing actual certificates.[12] Merrill Lynch has estimated that only 2.1 percent of its customers insist on having stock certificates.

MAKING YOUR OWN INVESTMENT DECISIONS Many investors prefer to rely on the advice of their brokers about which securities to buy and when to sell, and full-service brokerage firms have extensive research departments that provide brokers with detailed financial information of hundreds of companies.

You may prefer, however, to do your own company research and decide for yourself which securities to buy or sell. If so, there are several valuable financial reference publications that you can consult. They contain information about areas such as company sales, profits, dividend payments, projected growth, industry position, acquisitions and mergers, product lines, and projected financial performance. Most college and public libraries subscribe to one or more. You should, of course, add your broker's opinion to the information gathered from these. Be sure, too, to consult the most current issue or edition. Some of the most popular of these sources are:

- *Standard & Poor's Stock Reports*
- *Moody's Handbook of Common Stocks*
- *The Value Line Investment Survey*
- *Moody's Manuals* (organized by category to provide information on industrial, over-the-counter, transportation, utility, and bank and financial stocks)
- *Moody's Dividend Record*
- *Moody's Bond Record*
- *Standard & Poor's Security Owner's Stock Guide*
- *Standard & Poor's Bond Guide*
- *Moody's Handbook of Over-the-Counter Stocks*

> **YOU DECIDE**
>
> How could you reorganize your personal budget to obtain more money to save or invest? What excuses have you used for not doing so? List at least three potential responsibilities and personal goals you could expect to have within the next several years that might make you place a higher priority on a personal investment program.

Investment Strategies

Investors may use two specialized investment strategies: short selling and margin buying. Both of these are highly risky. They should be used only by the most sophisticated investors who are acting on the best possible advice.

SHORT SELLING A **short seller** is *a person who borrows stock from a broker and sells it, hoping to replace the borrowed shares at a lower price if and when the market price declines.* In other words, short sellers hope to make money during a bear market. Most short sales occur because investors believe a stock is overpriced, and they wish to take advantage of the anticipated drop in price. A short sale happens like this:

short seller
A person who borrows stock from a broker and sells it, hoping to replace the borrowed shares at a lower price if and when the market price declines.

Borrow and sell a round lot of XYZ Corporation stock at $32 per share	$3,200
Pay back broker by purchasing a round lot of XYZ stock at $10 per share (assuming market price declines to that point)	1,000
Profit (less broker's commissions)	$2,200

Short sales can be extremely risky. You owe your broker shares of stock, not dollars, and should the stock's market price rise instead of fall, it will cost you more to replace the borrowed shares than you collected when you originally sold them. Because of this, short sales are wise only when you have reliable information that investors will bid a stock's market price down. Such information might be news of an impending lawsuit against the firm for making a hazardous product or a government antitrust action that would break the company up into smaller independent companies or advance information that the firm is about to report heavy financial losses.

You cannot make a short sale with empty pockets. The short seller must place a deposit with the broker equal to the borrowed stock's market price, so that the broker may replace the stock if necessary. The adage "It takes money to make money" is especially true in making a short sale.

To prevent a group of manipulators from selling a firm's stock short to give a false impression of lost investor confidence, each short sale must be identified as such. Stock exchange personnel can then monitor short selling activity on each stock and, if a rash of short sales occur, suspend trading on the target stock to protect small investors who are not privy to special information.

margin buyer
A person who borrows part of a stock's purchase price.

margin
The percentage of the total price that the investor must pay out of pocket.

MARGIN BUYING A **margin buyer** is *a person who borrows part of a stock's purchase price*. The **margin** is *the percentage of the total price that the investor must pay out of pocket*. Margin requirements, which affect inflation rates and investor activity, are set by the Federal Reserve Board. Requirements have been set as low as 40 percent and as high as 100 percent, meaning that investors could enter the market with as much as 60 percent of their funds borrowed. In recent years margin requirements have hovered around 55 percent. Figure 16.8 shows what happens when a stock is bought on margin.

Margin buyers benefit from a bull market. In the example in Figure 16.8, if the market price of the stock rose to $80 per share, the margin buyer could sell 250 shares to pay off the loan (250 × $80 = $20,000) and still hold $60,000 worth of stock at market price. The original investment of $30,000 has doubled in value even though the market price only rose 60 percent because some of the purchase was borrowed as cash and paid back as cash. In addition, if the stock pays dividends, they will offset at least part of the interest on the loan.

As long as the margin stock's market value is greater than the amount of the loan, the lender—which may be a bank or the brokerage firm itself—is satisfied. Should the stock ever become worth less than the loan, however, the broker will place a margin call on the investor, demanding that he or she

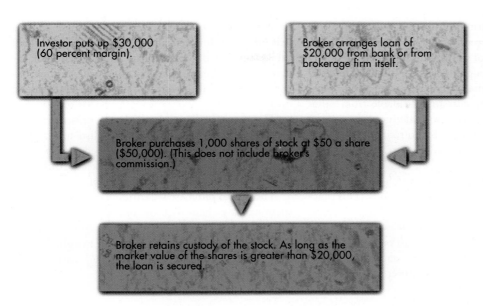

Investor puts up $30,000 (60 percent margin).

Broker arranges loan of $20,000 from bank or from brokerage firm itself.

Broker purchases 1,000 shares of stock at $50 a share ($50,000). (This does not include broker's commission.)

Broker retains custody of the stock. As long as the market value of the shares is greater than $20,000, the loan is secured.

Figure 16.8
How margin buying works (assume a purchase of $50,000 worth of stock when margin requirements are 60 percent).

supply cash or other securities to bring the value of the account up to the value of the loan. If the investor cannot meet this ultimatum, the broker, who has custody of the stock, sells it and the customer must pay any difference between the cash received and the balance of the loan. Investors should expect a broker to place a margin call if the stock's price falls below 75 percent of its original value. Stocks, bonds, and certain United States government securities can be bought on margin.

SUMMARY

Companies must raise money for both the short and the long term to compete successfully in today's business environment. Short-term capital, the money used in day-to-day business operations, is raised to increase a firm's purchasing power, pay debts when cash receipts fall below expectations, and pay unanticipated expenses. In raising short-term capital, a company may use such instruments as promissory notes, drafts, commercial paper, and checks. It may establish trade credit or open-book accounts with several companies, or deal with such institutions as commercial banks, commercial finance companies, factoring companies, sales finance companies, and consumer finance companies.

A company raises long-term or fixed capital to buy assets that produce goods and services for several years. Retained earnings are one source of long-term capital, but few firms can finance major expansion strictly out

of profits. Most will sell equity securities, which are called stocks, and perhaps debt securities, which are called bonds.

Four major federal laws govern sales of securities to the general public. A corporation usually sells a new issue of securities to one or more investment banking firms, which in turn retail them to the general public.

A corporation's common stockholders may receive a cash or stock dividend as a return for their ownership risk if the corporation makes enough profit to pay it. In addition, common stockholders usually receive a preemptive right to purchase shares from new issues of their company's stock in proportion to their current holdings. Corporations sometimes also sell preferred stock, which enjoys a prior claim on the company's dividend payments and assets to that of common stock.

A corporation that finances with bonds borrows

money on its long-term promissory notes. As creditors of the corporation, bondholders have a claim on assets ahead of either class of stockholders. Bondholders may trade their bonds at a premium or a discount to compensate for a bond interest rate that is higher or lower than the interest rate currently available from other investments. Corporations normally create a sinking fund so money will be available to retire a bond issue when it matures.

Companies use leverage when they borrow money through a bond issue hoping to earn a greater rate of return than the interest paid on the bonds. This practice can work against a company, however, if business conditions worsen and the return earned on borrowed funds falls below the interest that must be paid on them.

Investors may trade stocks on one of the stock exchanges or in the over-the-counter market. They should learn how to read the financial pages so they will know certain facts about the securities in which they're interested. Stockbrokers buy and sell stock for investors, but before doing so they will ask their clients to identify an investment goal of growth, safety, or income.

The stock exchanges, which are central auction markets for various stocks, use specialists to maintain stability by selling or buying assigned stocks when necessary. These specialists may also execute orders for busy brokers and receive a commission.

Those who purchase securities may take delivery of them or leave them with the broker in a street name account. Investors who are not overly concerned with safety may become short sellers or margin buyers, depending on market conditions and current economic trends.

KEY TERMS

back-end load p. 515
bond indenture p. 519
bonds p. 509
bond yield p. 521
capital appreciation p. 514
cash discount p. 505
cashier's check p. 504
certified check p. 504
churning p. 528
commercial finance company p. 506
commercial paper p. 502
common stock p. 512
common stock certificate p. 512
consumer finance company p. 507
coupon or bearer bond p. 520
current yield p. 521
debt capital p. 519
discount p. 519
dividend p. 512
Dow-Jones Industrial Average p. 526
draft p. 502
equity capital p. 509
factoring company p. 506
front-end load p. 515
fully registered bond p. 520
investment banking firm p. 511

leverage or trading on the equity p. 524
limit order p. 530
line of credit p. 505
long-term or fixed capital p. 500
margin p. 532
margin buyer p. 532
market order p. 530
mutual fund p. 515
odd lot p. 512
over-the-counter market p. 525
preemptive right p. 513
preferred stock p. 515
premium p. 519
promissory note p. 502
prospectus p. 509
registered bond p. 520
registrar p. 512
retained earnings p. 509
revolving credit agreement p. 506
round lot p. 512
sales finance company p. 507
short seller p. 531
short-term or working capital p. 500
sinking fund p. 520
specialist p. 528
stockbroker p. 528

stock dividend p. 513
stock exchange p. 524
stock split p. 513
street name account p. 530

trade credit *or* open-book accounts p. 505
transfer agent p. 512
warrant p. 513
yield to maturity p. 521

FOR REVIEW AND DISCUSSION

1. How do companies use short-term or working capital? What reasons do firms have for raising such capital regularly?

2. Distinguish among the following instruments used in short-term financing transactions, and describe at least one situation in which each would be used: promissory notes, drafts, commercial paper, checks.

3. List and discuss six sources of short-term financing and the type of transaction that characterizes each.

4. Why do companies raise long-term or fixed capital? What two sources of long-term capital are most popular?

5. Evaluate the following statement: "A well-managed company should be able to pay for expansion strictly from its earnings."

6. Name four laws that govern securities sales. What effect have they had on corporations? How have investors and potential investors benefited?

7. What is the difference between a registrar and a transfer agent? Why do large corporations use both?

8. What benefits and advantages do common stockholders enjoy? What legal right enables them to maintain their proportional control of the company?

9. Why do companies split their stock? Should stockholders view a split as a short-term or a long-term benefit? Why?

10. Describe a mutual fund. Why might someone invest in one of these instead of buying the securities of individual companies?

11. What types of sales charges or other fees may a mutual fund apply? What advice would you offer an investor who is trying to evaluate the costs associated with owning shares in a mutual fund?

12. Contrast preferred stock with common stock. In what ways do the owners of preferred stock receive preferential treatment?

13. Define the following features of some preferred stock: participating, callable, convertible, cumulative, and noncumulative.

14. Compare bonds with promissory notes. What is the major difference? What do they share in common?

15. Express the following bond interest rates and market price quotations in dollars and cents. Then compute the premium or discount on each bond.

Interest	Market Price
8¼	87
11⅛	113
5½	71
9	101

16. Would you advise a corporation that is going to issue bonds to establish a sinking fund? Why or why not?

17. How do registered bonds and coupon bonds differ? How would you distinguish a bond that is registered as to principal from a fully registered bond?

18. Compute the current yield and yield to maturity on a 10%/$1,000 bond purchased at 115 with ten years left until maturity. Compute both yields for the same bond purchased at 90 with ten years to maturity.

19. Summarize the key features of each of the following: mortgage bond, equipment trust bond, income bond, debenture bond, callable bond, convertible bond, serial bond, and zero coupon bond.

20. Compare the three major kinds of securities on the bases of safety, growth potential, and income. Which are best suited for you at this time? Why?

21. What does a firm attempt to do when it uses leverage? Describe the risks and benefits of doing so.

22. What does listing on a major stock exchange imply about a company's stock? What purpose do stock exchanges serve?

23. What is the purpose of the Dow-Jones Industrial Average?

24. What kind of training must stockbrokers usually have? How are they compensated for their work?
25. List three possible investment objectives. Is there one "best" choice? Why or why not?
26. What two roles do specialists play?

27. Which two options do you have for holding the securities you buy? Which is most convenient?
28. Describe the investment strategies of short selling and margin buying and the major points associated with each.

APPLICATIONS

Case 16.1: Stockholder Activism

The eighties were the decade of the corporate takeover. Well-connected entrepreneurs would gather together groups of investors to buy large portions of a corporation's voting stock. When they owned enough, they would push forward with a proxy vote to install their own board of directors. If successful, the new board would restructure the company, sell off holdings, or use other means to turn large profits for the investors.

In the nineties, investors have found new ways of using large stock purchases to influence corporations and to improve returns on investment. Robert Monks is a leader of this movement. His venture, the Lens Fund, targets companies that could be more profitable and buys large chunks of their stock. Using the rights of a shareholder to ensure that he's listened to, Monks then makes recommendations to the corporation's board aimed at making the company more profitable.

Of course, the companies aren't always happy to have Monks involved. In 1990 Monks took aim at his first target: Sears, Roebuck. The company had failed to achieve its goal of a 15 percent return on investment for ten years running. Because of legal maneuvering by the company, Monks lost a run for the board of directors despite receiving more votes than any other director from those who received his proxy card.

Responding to this show of shareholder discontent, Sears made a few executive changes, including stripping some duties from chairman and CEO Edward Brennan. Stockholders, stirred by Monks's influence, didn't feel that this was enough and continued to press the board. In the fall of 1992, yielding to this pressure, Brennan unveiled a massive restructuring of the company. The day of the announcement, over a billion dollars of value was added to the company's stock.

Monks proudly claims that the Lens Fund's successes at Sears and other companies, such as Eastman Kodak, have proved the value of his flavor of shareholder activism. Unfortunately, institutional investors are still wary of his aggressive program. They fear that Monks is too radical, too loud. And for the moment, they prefer to take a more tender approach.

In the long run, the dollars will tell.

Questions

1. Do you think the type of stockholder activism shown by Robert Monks is likely to increase? Why or why not?
2. Aside from having themselves elected to the board of directors, what other means might militant stockholders use to influence how their corporations are managed?
3. List at least three influences on a company's stock price over which top management may have little or no control. What problems might management have when trying to describe the impact of these factors to stockholders?
4. What actions might a company's management and directors take to improve the relationship between themselves and activists such as Robert Monks?

For more information, see Mary Driscoll, "Loaded for Bear," *CFO,* July 1993, p. 27.

Case 16.2: Global Investing

Since the end of the 1980s, the United States dominance of investment markets has declined. This is a direct reflection of the fact that there is a fast-growing world economy where no single country dominates in business—not the United States and not even Japan. Around the world, emerging markets are delivering goods to customers; many of them are doubling and even tripling their growth and gains. As a result, global investing is the hottest game on the planet.

In 1993 the Janus Worldwide Fund, a global mutual fund specializing in return on equity income from hot companies, produced gains that more than doubled those of the U.S. companies that make up the Standard & Poor's 500 stock index. London's Barclays de Zoete Wedd Ltd. investment firm believes that returns for European stock markets are running over 16 percent per year, while U.S. stock markets are showing only 7 percent growth. Japan, in the midst of country-wide corporate restructuring, has begun to recover from its recession and is producing profits of nearly 50 percent per year.

All of this has produced a boom in overseas investing by American businesses. For example, American pension fund managers invested over $18 *billion* in overseas markets in just the first six months of 1993. Consumer investing is up, too: During the same period, they were investing over $1 billion a week in overseas stocks. The net result is that overseas investing by Americans is estimated to increase from $61 billion to $100 billion a year.

Most of the growth in mutual funds is from private enterprise, although bond funds that finance privatization of formerly government enterprises have been hot, too. Foreign autos, beer, computers, telecommunications, and leisure activities are providing the best mutual funds returns. The whole world seems to be booming as individual countries come out of recession and as interest rates remain low.

Questions

1. Investing, especially in the stock market, is always risky. What makes it less so now?

2. What effect does overseas investment have on long-term investments in United States business?

3. How will the emerging democracies of Eastern Europe and the former USSR affect global business and investing?

For more information, see William Glasgall, Larry Holyoke, John Rossant, and Bill Javetski, "The Global Investor," *Business Week*, October 11, 1993, pp. 120–126; and Jeffrey M. Laderman, "Mutual Funds Are Fat—And Investors Are Happy," *Business Week*, October 11, 1993, pp. 128–132.

REFERENCES

1. "Banks Extend Chrysler's Credit Line," *The Orlando Sentinel*, August 19, 1992, p. D-7.
2. Timothy Aeppel, "VW Cuts Sums for Investments in 5-Year Program," *The Wall Street Journal*, January 14, 1993, p. A12.
3. Douglas Lavin, "Chrysler Beats Expectations in Stock Offer," *The Wall Street Journal*, February 3, 1993, p. A3.
4. "Financial Topics." Information prepared in February 1993 by the Financial Division of the Coca-Cola Company for the Industry and Consumer Affairs Department of Coca-Cola USA.
5. Data supplied by Richard A. Clements of Dean Witter Reynolds, Inc. brokerage firm.
6. PepsiCo, Inc. Annual Report, 1992.
7. "Blue-Chip Kodak's Stock Dives After Executive Quits," *The Orlando Sentinel*, April 29, 1993, p. C-5.
8. Amanda Bennett, "CEO's Illness May Endanger Company's Health as Well," *The Wall Street Journal*, January 21, 1993, p. B1; Robert Johnson, "Tenneco's Chairman Has Brain Cancer but Says He'll Stay on Job Indefinitely," *The Wall Street Journal*, January 21, 1993, p. A4.
9. *NYSE: The Capital Market for All Investors*, p. 6. (A publication of New York Stock Exchange, Inc.)
10. Johnnie L. Roberts, "Time Warner Inc. Seeks $1 Billion to Ease Its Debt," *The Wall Street Journal*, January 8, 1993, p. B2.
11. "Refinancing Debt Helps Drive Down Interest Expense," *PhilNews* (a publication of Phillips Petroleum Company), April 1992, p. 1.
12. "Stock Certificates Headed for Extinction," *The Orlando Sentinel*, December 31, 1992, p. C-1.

17

RISK AND INSURANCE

*very business
and every
product has
risks. You can't
get around it.*

LEE IACOCCA

CHAPTER OBJECTIVES
After studying this chapter, you should be able to:

1. Contrast the two kinds of risk that businesses encounter.
2. Outline the risk manager's role in company operations and summarize the methods that he or she can use in dealing with pure risk.
3. Explain how insurable interest, insurable risks, and the law of large numbers affect an insurance company's decision to accept a pure risk.
4. State the difference between a mutual insurance company and a stock insurance company.
5. Discuss how the health of insurance companies is monitored by state regulators and private rating firms.
6. Explain the work of actuaries and loss prevention engineers.
7. Summarize the criteria needed for an insurable risk.
8. Describe the various kinds of insurance that companies may purchase and explain the role of each in protecting firms against pure risk.
9. Discuss the organization and operation of Lloyd's of London and explain its role in providing surplus lines of insurance coverage.

UP FRONT

When Joseph Wells graduated from Texas A&M University with a bachelor's degree in business administration, he took a good, long look at the workplace and determined that the opportunities were in either retail sales or the insurance industry. "Insurance sounded more interesting, and I wasn't sure I'd be good at selling," he says, so he took his first job at USF&G, working in general business insurance. He went on to work at several other insurance companies, gaining experience and developing a sense of what really interested him. "I was trained in casualty underwriting and learned general liability, auto, catastrophic coverage, and workers' compensation. Things became more specialized in workers' comp; we focused less on pricing and more on risk selection. That was more interesting. And there was more of a human element—people instead of autos or intangibles. I liked that, and workers' compensation became my specialty. I was working at an insurer in Texas when I got an offer from Transamerica to go to work for them in San Diego, and I took it."

Workers' compensation is an $11 billion industry in the state of California. Losses as a result of injury on the job run around $8 billion a year. Wells explains that back injuries are the number-one cause of injury, while violence in the workplace has risen to number two in the past few years. "It's also the third most common cause of fatalities, behind construction and auto accidents," he adds.

"Workers' comp used to focus mostly on the physical environment of work—safety guards on machinery, safe scaffold-ing, that sort of thing. Today we are also involved in job descriptions, hiring practices, training, supervision, and in general the way our clients care for their employees. We find there are many more ways to control losses. For example, teaching people how to stretch and exercise, in addition to wearing a waist belt, can alleviate back injuries. We get people to *think* more about what they're doing. Or take personnel issues. If a layoff is properly presented to an employee, and if he or she understands the termination benefits, there may be less chance that the person will come back with a shotgun. People should have access to counseling and should be treated with dignity when they leave a job. How you handle layoffs can affect the employees who stay on the job, too."

Other areas in which workers' compensation has changed include environmental and office work claims. "Asbestos is a top environmental concern, but we also have to deal with toxic chemicals and polluted environments. It's often difficult to evaluate losses in these areas, and it also makes it hard to determine premiums. Carpal tunnel syndrome is a very real disorder that affects the wrists of office workers using a computer keyboard. We often have claims that involve cumulative trauma from working with computers."

Wells supervises a group of eight, which is growing as Transamerica Insurance

JOSEPH WELLS

WORKERS' COMPENSATION UNDERWRITING MANAGER, TRANSAMERICA INSURANCE GROUP

Group's business grows. In fact, business has been so good that TIG split off from Transamerica Corporation into a separate company in 1993. "The insurance industry is often maligned," says Wells. "Customers complain about premiums but often don't see the benefits. Our industry provides a tremendous amount of capital to other companies to create jobs, but more important, *we help save people's lives*. Any time we can prevent a loss, it means that someone didn't get hurt.

"We choose our risks—our customers—very carefully. We don't just look at the type of business they're in, but the quality of their employees. Our loss control department interviews the employer to discuss hiring practices before we issue a policy. If the company is acceptable but needs some help, we provide it. That's a benefit that may cost us some money up front, but in the end it saves money for everyone. We believe that an ounce of prevention is worth a pound of cure."

Wells engages in a variety of activities during a typical workday. In addition to working with his staff of underwriters, he is constantly interacting with the loss prevention and claims departments to keep up to date on various risks. Policies must be regularly assessed, and a decision is made each year on whether or not to renew a particular policy. "There's also a lot of involvement with attorneys, even though we're constantly trying to avoid litigation. I work with our producers—the insurance agents and brokers—who offer new business for us to consider. And I also meet with our policyholders, often in conjunction with loss or claims people, to discuss ways to improve loss control or claims handling. It's not a good thing to learn you weren't doing all you could for a client after you have already lost their business."

Joseph Wells thinks many students misunderstand the nature of the insurance business. "Some people get into it for job stability because it doesn't require prior training or experience. But if you don't recognize how important this work really is, you won't accomplish a lot. This business is about caring for people. You have to find out for yourself if you can feel passionate about this business. There are lots of opportunities if you can motivate yourself and get involved."

Risk, which is the chance of loss, exists in most business decisions and transactions; indeed, it is the hallmark of a capitalistic society. Few business ventures are entirely risk free. In fact, many swashbuckling entrepreneurs embrace potentially profitable risks with verve. Excessive risk, however, can destroy people and companies alike, so managers must be risk conscious as well as profit conscious.

In this chapter we will discuss the kinds of risks that businesspeople face and the measures they can use to deal with them.

Getting Acquainted with Risk

Two kinds of risks are inherent in business activities, and each has its own characteristics and its own implications for business organizations.

Speculative Risk

speculative risk
A situation that may cause loss or gain.

A **speculative risk** is *a situation that may cause loss or gain*. Going into business for yourself is a speculative risk, but you may decide to take that risk, hoping for the reward called profit. Other examples of speculative risk, all of them ultimately taken in the hope of some gain, are:

- Investing time, equipment, money, and human resources to produce a new product
- Investing in the stock market or real estate
- Spending two or four years of your life, labor, and money to earn a college degree

As these examples suggest, people usually take speculative risks voluntarily—they choose to start a business, purchase stocks, or earn a college degree. The decision is up to them.

Pure Risk

Pure risk is *a situation that can only become a loss.* Some examples of pure risk and the losses that result are:

- Destruction of physical property by natural disaster, riot, fire, or vandalism
- Injuries suffered in an automobile accident
- Court awards of damages to customers injured while shopping at a store or to consumers harmed by a product a company makes
- Death of a key business executive
- Medical bills arising from a serious illness

We do not expose ourselves to pure risk voluntarily, but if we lead normal lives we must get out of bed in the morning and go out into the world. Although we may not consider ourselves daredevils, we encounter pure risk constantly in the adventure called living. (Even a golf game can turn deadly, as occurred when one Canadian player was killed when the head of his driver struck a cart and part of its shaft broke off, buried itself in his neck, and severed his carotid artery.[1])

Individuals share many pure risks in common with businesses, although many others are unique to the business situation. In this chapter, we will focus on what businesses can do to remove, reduce, or insure against pure risk.

How Businesses Deal with Pure Risk

Many firms now employ a full-time **risk manager**, *a person hired to identify significant pure risks that a company faces and prescribe effective techniques to deal with them.* The risk manager's responsibility is to recommend one or more of the antirisk actions: avoidance, reduction, transfer, or assumption. The first, avoidance, occurs when a firm elects not to undertake the venture and thus avoids the risk. Let's examine the other three antirisk actions.

pure risk
A situation that can only become a loss.

risk manager
A person hired to identify significant pure risks that a company faces and prescribe effective techniques to deal with them.

Risk Reduction

Under ideal conditions, management can reduce a pure risk so drastically that the likelihood of loss is remote, or—every risk manager's dream—nonexistent. Effective risk reduction programs can save companies thousands of dollars in employee injuries, lost production, and insurance costs. Some examples of risk-reducing activities and efforts are:

- Using flame-retardant or fireproof building materials
- Storing inventory in several warehouses at different locations to minimize potential loss from fire or natural disasters
- Conducting safety programs that teach workers to use machinery properly
- Installing drop safes in retail stores and service stations
- Monitoring customer traffic with closed circuit cameras to discourage shoplifting
- Providing back braces, cranes, hoists, dollies, hand trucks, and conveyors to reduce the likelihood of lower back injury on materials handling jobs

One approach to risk reduction is to require employees to wear safety equipment.

According to Jim Abraham of The St. Paul Companies, the average fire loss for an office building unprotected by sprinkler systems is more than four times greater than one with such a system. Manufacturing plants with sprinkler systems suffer just 20 percent of the fire damage of those without sprinklers. Restaurants are especially vulnerable to fires, so equipping them with sprinklers, quick-response sprinkler heads, fire dampeners in grease ducts, and state-of-the-art smoke and heat detectors may reduce the cost of insurance by as much as 400 percent.

Companies frequently suffer severe losses from risks that could have been anticipated. One tragic example is Texasgulf, which lost seven managers and a pilot—each with an average of seventeen years of service—in a single company plane crash. The managers included the firm's chairman and chief executive officer and three vice presidents. Although such group travel is commonplace, if the executives had traveled on more than one aircraft the loss would have been less serious to the firm.

Large businesses are beginning to appreciate the wisdom of having key executives travel separately. The Trump Organization, which had no such policy, lost three casino executives who perished together in a helicopter crash on the way from New York to Atlantic City. More recently, six top managers of the small Alabama supermarket chain Bruno's Inc., including Chairman Angelo Bruno, died when their corporate plane crashed. Many larger companies, including Quaker Oats and General Motors, have policies that regulate how many directors and top executives may travel on the same plane.[2]

In addition, most large corporations have taken steps to reduce the risk of high-profile executives being kidnapped and held for ransom. Security measures include converting a standard vehicle to an armored car, varying the route traveled to and from the office each day, sending executives and their chauffeurs to defensive driving school, employing bodyguards as receptionists, altering recreational patterns (such as the time and day of weekly golf games), and converting one room in an executive's home into a bulletproof strong room.[3]

Transfer of Risk to a Noninsurer

It is often possible to let another party (not an insurance company) assume certain risks. A firm that leases vehicles, for example, can require the leasing company to insure them. Companies may dispense with risks associated with delivery vehicles altogether by using a delivery service. A business owner who leases a building can require the landlord to insure it, and sellers may require buyers to pay for insurance on products to be shipped to them.

A business usually pays for transferring risk in this way, of course, because the other party often will charge more to enable it to pay for insurance. The business may still benefit, however, because transferring risk to a noninsurer reduces recordkeeping, reporting, and other paperwork expenses that come with insurance agreements and the filing of insurance claims.

Assumption of Risk by Self-Insurance

Large firms sometimes guard against certain kinds of pure risk by creating a **self-insurance fund,** *a special fund of cash and marketable securities that will be used to pay for losses caused by natural disasters such as fire, flood, and earthquake.* This approach is safe and practical only if the risks are very similar (buildings of the same construction housing the same kind and amount of inventory, fixtures, furniture, or equipment) and if the similar risks are scattered over a broad area. With a self-insurance fund, the firm assumes the risk.

The second condition means that self-insurance is appropriate only for firms that are not susceptible to massive localized losses resulting from a single natural disaster. Self-insurance is not recommended for firms with just a

self-insurance fund
A special fund of cash and marketable securities used to pay for losses caused by natural disasters such as fire, flood, and earthquake.

handful of plants or stores or for firms whose facilities are confined to one relatively small geographic area.

Some firms that might find self-insurance practical in certain cases are:

- A retailer with many similar stores (such as Sears)
- A manufacturer or wholesaler with many similar warehouses
- A service firm with many similar offices spread over several states (such as a consumer finance company)

Of course, self-insurance should not be confined to just physical damage. Many firms self-insure for at least part of employees' health care and for workers' compensation claims (which will be discussed later in this chapter).

Self-insurance can be cheaper than going to an insurance company. Consider a chain of 1,000 retail stores that suffered average fire losses of $20,000 a year for the past ten years. Management could assess each store a mere $20 annually, thus accumulating the amount of its average annual loss in a special fund that could be invested in stocks and bonds. Some of these securities could then be sold to pay for fire damage as it occurs. Besides being cheaper than purchasing fire insurance, this system also could stimulate more stringent safety programs and loss-reduction measures than if the firm had transferred the risk to an insurance company.

One problem with self-insurance is the possibility that a loss may occur before the fund is large enough to cover it. This possibility may be dealt with by making a very large initial contribution to the fund or by purchasing insurance to supplement the fund balance until it can be increased by regular contributions to a higher level.

It is somewhat rare for a company to self-insure completely against any risk. More often firms purchase insurance to cover losses that exceed the balance in their self-insurance fund. Generally a company should avoid self-insuring if it is (1) financially unsound, (2) frequently short of cash, or (3) just starting out in business.

Transfer of Risk to an Insurance Company

insurance policy
A legal contract that transfers risk from one party (the *insured*) to another (the *insurer*) for a fee called a *premium*.

law of large numbers *or* law of averages
A mathematical law stating that if a large number of similar objects or persons are exposed to the same risk, a predictable number of losses will occur during a given period of time.

After exploring alternate ways of dealing with risk and using one or more, management may still wish to transfer remaining risks to an insurance company. If that firm agrees to accept the risk, it will issue an **insurance policy**, which is *a legal contract that transfers risk from one party (the* insured*) to another (the* insurer*) for a fee called a* premium. Insurance is a major defense against pure risk. The insurance company will reimburse the insured up to the maximum amount specified in the policy if the loss occurs.

The premium that an insurance company charges for bearing a risk of loss is based on the **law of large numbers,** sometimes called the **law of averages.** This is *a mathematical law stating that if a large number of similar objects or persons are exposed to the same risk, a predictable number of losses will occur* *during a given period of time.* It is the concept that makes insurance work. Once an insurance company accumulates enough data on losses attributable to a certain risk to apply the law of averages, it can forecast the likelihood of loss and the average dollar amount of each loss. Then the company computes the premium it will charge. The premium will be high enough to cover expected claims, to expand and improve its operations, and (for one type of insurance company) to pay dividends to stockholders.

The law of averages reveals, for example, that both of the following are true:

- Those who smoke more than a pack of cigarettes a day double their chances of having heart attacks.
- Approximately half of those suffering second heart attacks will die as a result.

Knowing the statistics, insurers can set life and health insurance rates for smokers that reflect the increased risk involved in insuring them. Figure 17.1 illustrates the effect of the law of averages on auto insurance rates: Because younger men are involved in more accidents, rates for them are higher. As they grow older and the risk of their being in an accident decreases, the rate goes down.

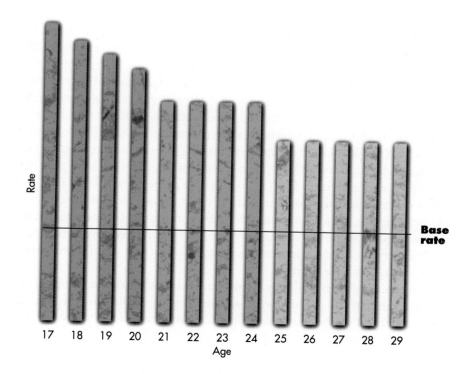

Figure 17.1
Effect of age on auto insurance rates for men.

Source: Courtesy Insurance Information Institute.

insurable interest
The idea that the policyholder (the person who pays the premiums) must stand to suffer a financial loss before he or she will be allowed to purchase insurance on a given risk.

principle of indemnity
The policyholder cannot profit by insurance.

deductible
An amount of a loss that the insured agrees to pay.

Two other principles are essential to an understanding of insurance. The first is **insurable interest**, *the idea that the policyholder (the person who pays the premiums) must stand to suffer a financial loss before he or she will be allowed to purchase insurance on a given risk.* This prevents inappropriate persons from betting that a given risk will become a loss by paying premiums on an insurance policy and winning (by collecting the insurance money) if it does. If insurers did not require an insurable interest, you could buy insurance on anyone's life or property purely for personal gain; some unscrupulous people would be tempted to cause losses when the law of large numbers did not do the trick.

Generally speaking, married couples have an insurable interest in each other's lives, corporations in the lives of key executives, and partnerships in the owners' lives. You cannot buy life insurance on distant relatives, however, or on persons unrelated to you, and you cannot insure buildings, autos, or other property in which you have no financial investment or risk.

The other important insurance principle is the **principle of indemnity**: *the policyholder cannot profit by insurance.* You can buy physical damage insurance on a building to pay the replacement value of the building or the face value of the policy, whichever is less, but you cannot buy insurance for more than the building is worth. If you wanted to insure a building appraised at $300,000 for $600,000, the insurance company would reject your application; you cannot collect twice the value of property that is destroyed. And having that much insurance might encourage you to cause some accident, as the destroyed building would be so much more valuable than the building in operation.

Because the amounts of losses vary, insurance companies find it practical to offer a **deductible**, which is *an amount of a loss that the insured agrees to pay.* The deductible is actually a form of self-insurance that benefits both the insured and the insurer. The insured benefits because a deductible lowers the premium that the insurance company charges. Personal auto insurance policies with a deductible of $500 may cost several hundred dollars less a year than those with a deductible of $100. A deductible, especially a large one, also prompts management to work harder to prevent losses, because the company would have to pay a significant amount before insurance takes over. Insurers benefit because deductibles eliminate costly and irritating investigations, paperwork, and recordkeeping for small nuisance claims and reduce the payout required when losses do occur.

An insurance company will pay an insured loss (less the deductible) only up to the face value of the policy. If you are underinsured, therefore, a financial loss may force you to make up the difference out of your own resources. The seventy-eight-year-old Larraburu Brothers sourdough bakery in San Francisco lost a $2 million lawsuit after one of its delivery trucks injured a child. Because the firm's insurance policy had a face value of only $1.25 million, insufficient to cover the damage award, the company had to make up the difference. The only solution was a drastic one: selling the company.

Insurance Companies and Their Personnel

There are two kinds of insurance companies, classified according to ownership. Both kinds employ two types of specially trained experts who help to make their operations efficient, accurate, and sound.

Mutual Companies and Stock Companies

A **mutual insurance company** is *one owned by its policyholders,* who elect a board of directors to oversee the company's operations. Policyholders act like stockholders in this regard, except that they are also being insured. Several examples of mutual companies are Equitable Life Assurance Society of the United States, Massachusetts Mutual Life Insurance Company, Connecticut Mutual Life Insurance Company, The Mutual Life Insurance Company of New York (MONY), and Prudential Insurance Company of America. As the foregoing company names imply, mutual insurance companies are especially strong in the field of life insurance.

A **stock insurance company** is *one owned by stockholders,* like the traditional corporations you learned about in Chapter 4. Despite their different philosophies, however, the cost of identical coverage from a mutual company and a stock company of similar size is approximately equal.

Reserves

Insurance companies are required by law to keep reserves available to meet loss claims by policyholders, just as commercial banks must keep reserves available to meet depositors' demands. These reserves, like commercial bank deposits, appear as liabilities on the companies' financial statements. The funds not held in reserve are invested, making insurance companies among the largest institutional investors in the nation. They invest millions in such income-producing assets as stocks and bonds, office buildings, apartment complexes, and shopping centers. Table 17.1 presents the total assets and the face value of the policies in force of the top four mutual and stock insurance companies. Figure 17.2 shows how life insurance companies invested money not required for reserves in one recent year.

Investigating an Insurance Company's Health

Some consumers worry about the financial soundness of their insurance company and its ability to withstand the flurry of claims that would follow a

---

YOU DECIDE

Considering the current body of statistics on smoking and health, it seems odd for tobacco companies and insurance companies to fall under the same corporate umbrella. Nevertheless, that's the case with Franklin Life Insurance Company and American Tobacco Company (both owned by American Brands) and several others as well. What rationale may the parent company have for owning two such companies?

mutual insurance company
One owned by its policyholders.

stock insurance company
One owned by stockholders.

Table 17.1
Top four mutual insurance companies and stock insurance companies according to total assets.

	ASSETS (IN BILLIONS)	INSURANCE IN FORCE (IN BILLIONS)
Mutual Companies		
Prudential Insurance Company of America	$148.4	$820.7
Metropolitan Life Insurance Company	110.8	948.0
Equitable Life Assurance Society	50.4	308.2
New York Life Insurance Company	42.7	311.5
Stock Companies		
Teachers Insurance and Annuity Association	55.6	29.8
Aetna Life Insurance Co.	52.4	311.1
Connecticut General Life Insurance Co.	41.7	421.4
Travelers Insurance Company	35.7	214.9

Figure 17.2
Distribution of assets of United States life insurance companies.

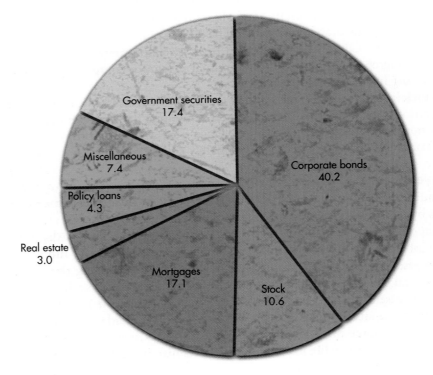

Source: *Life Insurance Fact Book*. American Council of Life Insurance.

major disaster. Regulatory agencies monitor the health of companies that do business in each state, which minimizes the likelihood that an insurer will go bankrupt without warning. If a company fails, however, state regulators will try to sell part or all of the firm to a healthy insurance company in the same fashion that the FDIC (Chapter 15) may try to merge a weak bank with a stronger one. If all efforts fail, however, policyholders would have to rely on emergency payoff programs created by the insurance industry in each state to cover the claims on their policies. Although most state programs have no actual funds available, they can raise money to cover policyholders' claims by making assessments against financially sound insurance companies.

Consumers who want to confirm the financial health of an insurance company may obtain a rating from one of several companies that evaluate an insurer's ability to meet policyholders' claims. These include:

- A. M. Best
- Moody's
- Standard & Poor's
- Duff & Phelps
- The Insurance Forum
- Weiss Research

Actuaries and Loss Prevention Engineers

An **actuary** is *a person who analyzes the likelihood of loss and the average amount of damage involved in pure risks and, applying the law of averages, computes the premium that the insurance company should charge to assume the risk.* Actuaries usually have a college education including extensive course work in mathematics and statistics. Actuaries work with tables like the one in Table 17.2. It is based on statistics about the lives and deaths of policyholders of several large life insurance companies.

A **loss prevention engineer (LPE)** is *an engineer who specializes in removing or reducing risk.* These engineers, who usually have a degree from a four-year college, may be employed by an insurance company or by any firm that faces a wide variety of risks, such as a conglomerate with interests in chemicals, explosives, manufacturing, and mining. Because they know how to use machinery, equipment, materials, and devices to remove or reduce risks, LPEs can significantly reduce the amount of insurance an organization requires in many hazardous operations. They can also construct loss prevention programs that will reduce the premiums on the insurance purchased.

When a company first applies for insurance, an LPE may be called in to examine its operations and recommend accident prevention measures. This procedure is advantageous to the insured, the insurer, and society at large. When Marineland of Florida applied to the Hartford Insurance Group for coverage, Hartford's loss control experts surveyed Marineland's operations for hazards that could be reduced or eliminated. Responding to their recommendations, Marineland redesigned its parking area so pedestrians were better protected from moving automobiles, improved its pedestrian traffic flow, and installed warning signals on the highway separating the attraction from the visitors' parking lot so drivers would watch for pedestrians crossing the road.

actuary
A person who analyzes the likelihood of loss and the average amount of damage involved in pure risks and, applying the law of averages, computes the premium that the insurance company should charge to assume the risk.

loss prevention engineer (LPE)
An engineer who specializes in removing or reducing risk.

Table 17.2
Actuary's mortality table: Number of deaths per 1,000 persons at various ages.

| | COMMISSIONERS' 1980 STANDARD ORDINARY (1970–1975) | | | | UNITED STATES POPULATION (1979–1981) | |
| | MALE | | FEMALE | | | |
AGE	DEATHS PER 1,000	EXPEC-TATION OF LIFE (YEARS)	DEATHS PER 1,000	EXPEC-TATION OF LIFE (YEARS)	DEATHS PER 1,000	EXPEC-TATION OF LIFE (YEARS)
20	1.90	52.37	1.05	57.04	1.20	55.46
22	1.89	50.57	1.09	55.16	1.32	53.60
24	1.82	48.75	1.14	53.28	1.33	51.74
26	1.73	46.93	1.19	51.40	1.31	49.87
28	1.70	45.09	1.26	49.52	1.30	48.00
30	1.73	43.24	1.35	47.65	1.66	46.12
32	1.83	41.38	1.45	45.78	1.37	44.24
34	2.00	39.54	1.58	43.91	1.50	42.36
36	2.24	37.69	1.76	42.05	1.70	40.49
38	2.58	35.87	2.04	40.20	1.97	38.63
40	3.02	34.05	2.42	38.36	2.32	36.79
42	3.56	32.26	2.87	36.55	2.79	34.96
44	4.19	30.50	3.32	34.77	3.35	33.16
46	4.92	28.76	3.80	33.00	4.01	31.39
48	5.74	27.04	4.33	31.25	4.88	29.65
50	6.71	25.36	4.96	29.53	5.89	27.94
52	7.96	23.70	5.70	27.82	6.99	26.28
54	9.56	22.08	6.61	26.14	8.30	24.65
56	11.46	20.51	7.57	24.49	9.78	23.06
58	13.59	18.99	8.47	22.86	11.51	21.52
60	16.08	17.51	9.47	21.25	13.68	20.02
62	19.19	16.08	10.96	19.65	16.28	18.58
64	23.14	14.70	13.25	18.08	19.11	17.19
66	27.85	13.39	16.00	16.57	22.16	15.85
68	33.19	12.14	18.84	15.10	25.85	14.56
70	39.51	10.96	22.11	13.67	30.52	13.32
72	47.65	9.84	26.87	12.28	35.93	12.14
74	58.19	8.79	33.93	10.95	41.84	11.02
76	70.53	7.84	42.97	9.71	48.67	9.95
78	83.90	6.97	53.45	8.55	57.42	8.93
80	98.84	6.18	65.99	7.48	68.82	7.98

Note: Mortality rates contained in the 1980 Commissioners' Standard Ordinary Table were obtained from experience of 1970–1975, but contain an added element designed to generate life insurance reserves of a conservative nature in keeping with the long-term guarantees inherent in life insurance contracts. Premiums for life insurance policies, on the other hand, are based on assumptions that include expected mortality experience.

Source: *1992 Life Insurance Fact Book* (Washington, D.C.: American Council of Life Insurance), 1992, pp. 126–127.

GLOBAL PERSPECTIVE

How does a major insurance company span the globe with its services? The St. Paul Companies does so through The Minet Group, a London-based insurance company, founded in 1929, that became a wholly owned subsidiary of The St. Paul in 1988.

According to The St. Paul, Minet employs some 3,500 people in more than 100 offices in thirty-two countries. The company provides an assortment of complex insurance brokerage services and specializes in selling liabil-ity policies to multinational accounting, legal, architectural, and engineering firms as well as insuring fine arts and jewelry owned by discriminating collectors and museums world-wide.

Insurance Goes World-Wide

Criteria for an Insurable Risk

Insurers are cautious about selecting the risks they insure. Their caution is justified, because an insurance company that neglects to evaluate risks carefully or that issues policies indiscriminately may find itself unable to pay the claims that eventually result. Generally, several conditions must be met before an insurance company assumes a risk. (Companies that do not meet these conditions may still be insured, however, through firms that issue surplus lines coverage or through Lloyd's of London, which will be discussed later in this chapter.) These conditions are:

1. A law of averages must exist.
2. The loss must be expressed in dollars.
3. The risk must be spread over a wide geographic area.
4. The insurance company reserves the right to increase the premium, to cancel the policy, or not to renew it if adverse circumstances arise.
5. The insurance company reserves the right to refuse payment under certain circumstances.

A law of averages must exist because the insurance company must possess enough data on the risk to predict how often losses will occur, the average payout associated with each claim, and other factors necessary to calculate a satisfactory premium. If no law of averages exists on a given type of risk (such as interplanetary space travel), the insurance company would be "flying blind"—it would have to guess at the likelihood of loss.

Commercial satellite-launching companies such as McDonnell Douglas Company and General Dynamics Corporation may charge more than

$100 million to place a satellite in orbit. Because these firms use government facilities at Cape Canaveral Air Force Station, the Department of Transportation requires them to purchase more than $80 million worth of property damage insurance. As experience with space flight has increased, the maximum amount of insurance that companies are willing to provide has increased.

A second condition for an insurable risk is that the loss must be expressed in dollars. As we learned in Chapter 15, money gives us a way to measure the value of countless goods and services. If a loss cannot be expressed in dollars, the insurance company and the would-be policy owner lack a common denominator for expressing the worth of the insured item. Consider, for example, a painting that your great-great-grandmother did in high school. Even though it may have been handed down from one generation to the next and is treasured by members of your family, it has value only to them, not to the person on the street. Therefore insurance against the destruction, loss, or theft of the painting or other property that has only sentimental value may not be available.

A third condition for an insurable risk is that the risk must be spread over a wide geographic area. This concept, which was referred to in our earlier discussion of self-insurance, is equally important to insurance companies. For example, losses caused by certain natural disasters occur regularly in some parts of the country: freezing temperatures in northern states may burst pipes, and buildings may be damaged by the resulting water leakage as well as by the weight of snow and ice on their roofs. Parts of California often experience destructive brush fires and mud slides, property in the midwest may be destroyed by tornadoes, and states on the Gulf and Atlantic coasts may suffer hurricane damage. If the insurance company spreads the risks it insures across the nation, however, a high number of loss claims in some states may be offset by a lower number in others—and this makes the law of averages work.

A fourth condition, that the insurance company must reserve the right to increase the premium, to cancel the policy, or not to renew it if adverse circumstances arise, is reasonable from the insurance company's view. As the character of a risk changes, the company should be able to change its standards for accepting that risk. Consider, for example, someone with a "clean" driving record (no moving violations). If that person commits one or more major offenses (driving while intoxicated, speeding, or careless driving, for example), most insurance companies would raise the premiums significantly, cancel the policy, or refuse to renew it on its anniversary date, depending on the firm's operating policies and the severity of the offense.

A final condition for an insurable risk is that the insurance company must reserve the right to refuse payment under certain circumstances. Situations may arise that can make insurance companies the victims of their own policies or that may require them to pay claims for catastrophes that no insurance company should reasonably be expected to cover. The typical life insurance policy, for example, will not pay benefits if the insured is killed in an act of war. This stipulation is logical because wartime conditions cause more claims than the law of averages for life expectancy (which is based on peacetime conditions) predicts. Similarly, many life insurance policies will not pay if the insured is killed while piloting an aircraft, hang-gliding, driving in an automobile race, or engaging in other high-risk activities as defined in the policy itself. Such policies may not pay in the event of suicide, because self-destruction is considered intentional rather than a fateful occurrence. Health insurance policies customarily exclude preexisting conditions (illnesses that were present before the policy was issued) because such illnesses are no longer risks, they are certainties for that specific person. In addition, life insurance companies may refuse to sell policies to people with health problems that would materially decrease their life expectancy. Such was the case with basketball star Magic Johnson, who was found to have AIDS after undergoing a physical examination in connection with his application for a life insurance policy.

What Insurance Does a Company Need?

Many of the pure risks that companies face may be protected against through insurance. The number and scope of pure risks that a large company must deal with are massive. A manufacturer, for example, may have millions of dollars of machinery, equipment, fixtures, materials, and products destroyed in a single plant fire. Businesses are also exposed to a variety of risks whenever they own and operate motor vehicles. Customers, visiting salespeople, and other nonemployees may file lawsuits to recover damages for injuries incurred on the premises, and legal action may also be brought by consumers who were injured by products the company manufactured, installed, or distributed. These examples are just a few of many potential hazards that companies encounter in the course of doing business, and they help to build a strong argument for carrying a sound and complete program of insurance. This section will provide you with a working knowledge of the types of insurance that companies can purchase against various risks.

Fire insurance

A fire insurance policy covers damage caused to buildings by fire; its language may exclude the building's contents. Although a basic fire insurance policy covers only damage by fire, you may expand it by purchasing **allied lines or extended coverage,** *a feature that can be added to a fire insurance policy to encompass financial loss caused by such hazards as riot and civil commotion, hail, wind, falling objects, land vehicles, water, smoke, and possibly vandalism and malicious mischief.*

One very broad category of physical damage coverage is **all-risk physical damage or multiple-line coverage,** which fire insurance companies have offered for more than thirty years. This is *added fire insurance coverage that embraces all risks except those that the policy specifically excludes.* It may be added to a basic fire

allied lines or extended coverage A feature that can be added to a fire insurance policy to encompass financial loss caused by such hazards as riot and civil commotion, hail, wind, falling objects, land vehicles, water, smoke, and possibly vandalism and malicious mischief.

all-risk physical damage or multiple-line coverage Added fire insurance that embraces all risks except those that the policy specifically excludes.

Fire is the most common cause of physical damage to businesses.

insurance policy, and it is usually more reassuring than so-called named peril policies that cover only specifically stated risks. Damage to the building itself is not usually part of all-risk physical damage coverage (because the building is covered by the basic policy), but this extension reimburses financial loss caused by damage to inventory, materials, supplies, furniture, or fixtures. It is not unusual for chain retailers to supply merchandise to stores in several states from one gigantic regional warehouse. This practice naturally makes these large companies quite vulnerable to fire losses.

History has recorded some enormous losses by fires and earthquakes in the United States:

- The 1906 San Francisco earthquake and subsequent fires destroyed 28,000 buildings and caused approximately $5 billion in damage in current dollars.
- The 1871 Chicago fire destroyed 17,340 buildings and caused some $2 billion in damage in current dollars.
- Insurance companies paid $960 million in claims after the 1989 San Francisco earthquake and $234 million in claims after the Santa Barbara fire.
- Insurance claims associated with a 1991 fire in Oakland, California amounted to approximately $1.5 billion.

Most recently, Hurricane Andrew caused the filing of more than $15.5 billion worth of insurance claims in South Florida in August 1992, including $2.7 billion in claims filed with Allstate Insurance Company and $2.1 billion filed with State Farm. These massive payouts prompted Allstate to drop some 300,000 Florida policyholders, while other companies quickly raised their rates to offset the cost of damages and claims expected to be caused by future hurricanes. The Florida Insurance Department reported that payouts to cover Andrew's destruction equaled the total amount of homeowners' insurance premiums that insurance companies had collected in Florida for the previous twenty years. If the storm had struck 40 miles farther north, however, its destruction would have reached $50 billion.[4]

An insurance policy's language and differing interpretations of that language sometimes can cause confusion. A businessperson must fully understand what assets and losses are protected in a fire insurance policy and its accompanying clauses. Fire policies do not usually cover damage caused by an exploding boiler, for example; a company usually needs a separate boiler and machinery policy.

As a rule, most fire policies contain a **coinsurance clause**, *a stipulation that a company must insure a minimum (usually 80 percent or more) of a property's total value before the business will be fully reimbursed for a partial loss.* Insureds who do not purchase the stipulated amount must bear part of a loss themselves, above and beyond the deductible.

Insurance companies have no difficulty justifying coinsurance clauses. Most fire losses are partial ones; total destruction is rare. Without a coinsurance requirement, business owners would buy only enough insurance to cover the dollar amount of assets most likely to be destroyed according to the law of averages. Insurance companies would have trouble surviving if each policy they sold covered only the typical loss claim.

With coinsurance a firm that bought the required coverage would receive the total amount of the loss (less the deductible) up to the face value of the policy. An underinsured company (one that buys less insurance than the coinsurance clause requires) is reimbursed for a loss in the proportion of the actual amount of insurance to the coinsurance minimum. Figure 17.3 illustrates how this works.

coinsurance clause
A stipulation that a company must insure a minimum (usually 80 percent or more) of a property's total value before the business will be fully reimbursed for a partial loss.

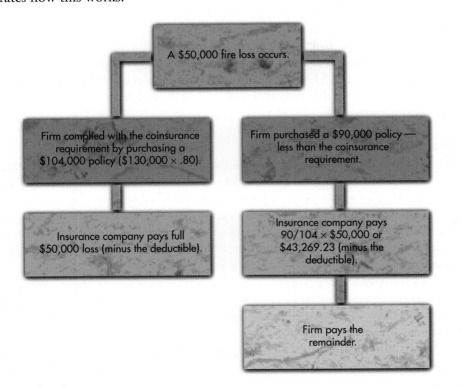

Figure 17.3
How a coinsurance clause works.

business interruption insurance
Coverage that can be added to a basic fire insurance policy. It covers consequential losses, those that result from fire or other perils covered in the fire policy.

Business interruption insurance, like allied lines and multiple-line coverage, is *coverage that can be added to a basic fire insurance policy. It covers consequential losses, those that result from fire or other perils covered in the fire policy.* Consequential loss coverage may, for example, pay employees' salaries or wages, business taxes, loan installments, and other fixed expenses that must be paid even if the business is closed temporarily by fire or other disaster. It may also pay the owner's normal profit while the business is being reconstructed, and pay to lease equipment and rent temporary quarters while the original facilities are being rebuilt. A drive-in theater whose screen was destroyed by a storm closed down for twenty-six days in midsummer. Data from the firm's accounting records showed revenues and expenses before the disaster, allowing the insurer to project them for the future. The company's insurer paid $2,990 in business interruption coverage, the projected net income lost during the shutdown.

One of the worst industrial accidents in history occurred in late 1989, when a fire and explosion at Phillips Petroleum Company's Pasadena, Texas chemical plant injured 125 people and left 19 people either dead or missing. The blast, which created a fireball visible for 15 miles and broke windows a mile away, was estimated to be equivalent to 10 tons of TNT. More than half of the 800-acre facility was destroyed. The company had various types of coverage on the property, including business interruption insurance, but deductibles totaled $70 million. Until this tragedy, Phillips had accumulated the best safety record in the petroleum industry.

contingent business interruption insurance
Insurance that covers a firm's losses when a key supplier's or customer's business is damaged.

A variant called **contingent business interruption insurance** is *insurance that covers a firm's losses when a key supplier's or customer's business is damaged,* something that could financially injure a company even though it suffers no physical damage itself. This coverage is not included in standard business interruption coverage.

Motor Vehicle Insurance

Many states require certain types of motor vehicle insurance (most notably bodily injury liability coverage) and leave other types optional. Businesses and individuals should avoid buying only the minimum required coverage, however, considering the losses that can result from a motor vehicle accident. In this section we will explore the most common types of motor vehicle insurance and describe how they function. A deductible is applied in most of these coverages.

collision and upset
Motor vehicle insurance that pays to repair damages to the insured vehicle up to its actual cash value (ACV) less the deductible if it collides with an object (including another vehicle) or overturns.

Collision and upset is *motor vehicle insurance that pays to repair damages to the insured vehicle up to its actual cash value (ACV) less the deductible if it collides with an object (including another vehicle) or overturns.* Property damage or personal injury done by your car is covered by property damage and bodily injury liability insurance (which will be discussed later in this section). Creditors on an auto loan protect their claim against the value of the car by requiring the borrower to supply proof of collision and upset insurance. This proof ensures that the car will be repaired or its cash value paid to the lender if it is damaged or destroyed in an accident. Because cars now contain highly complex miniature computers under the hood or dashboard that monitor or control the lights, brakes, fuel metering, and other systems, some insurance companies declare a car a total loss if the dashboard gets wet.

Property damage liability is *motor vehicle insurance that pays for damage the insured vehicle does to the property of others,* up to the face value of the policy. An insured vehicle can easily cause more property damage than the policy covers; when that happens, the insured must pay the difference. One hapless driver lost control of his car, which jumped the curb and sideswiped the front ends of a row of new Cadillacs parked on a dealer's lot. Another driver ran into and demolished an antique Packard—appraised at $100,000—that was being driven to a classic auto rally. Neither had enough property damage liability insurance to cover the damage fully.

Bodily injury liability, *sometimes called* PIP (personal injury protection) insurance, is *motor vehicle insurance that pays court-awarded damages for bodily injury, up to the face value of the policy, if the insured person is judged liable for a motor vehicle accident.* If you are held responsible for an accident that permanently handicaps another, that person is sure to sue you. If you lose, and the court judgment against you exceeds the face value of your insurance policy, you may have to pay the injured person a regular sum of money for the rest of your life. Because bodily injury liability suits often result in multimillion-dollar settlements today, businesses and individuals alike should be well insured against this risk.

Until recently, persons involved in an automobile accident had to engage in a lawsuit to determine which one was legally liable before insurance benefits for bodily injury liability could be collected. This process was expensive and typically delayed the payment of insurance benefits for several years. In the early 1970s, however, several states passed laws providing for **no-fault auto insurance,** which is *auto insurance that enables the parties to an accident to collect for bodily injury from their respective insurance companies, regardless of who was at fault.* Such laws were intended to streamline the settlement of bodily injury claims and reduce the backlog of auto accident lawsuits jamming the court system.

The provisions of no-fault insurance laws vary from one state to another. Differences exist primarily in:

- The maximum amount a person may collect for medical or funeral expenses
- The maximum amount a disabled person is allowed to collect to compensate for lost income
- Rights to bring suit (the parties may be legally barred from suing each other except in accidents involving death, permanent disability, disfigurement, or medical bills in excess of a stated amount)

property damage liability
Motor vehicle insurance that pays for damage the insured vehicle does to the property of others.

bodily injury liability
Sometimes called *PIP (personal injury protection) insurance;* motor vehicle insurance that pays court-awarded damages for bodily injury, up to the face value of the policy, if the insured person is judged liable for a motor vehicle accident.

no-fault auto insurance
Auto insurance that enables the parties to an accident to collect for bodily injury from their respective insurance companies, regardless of who was at fault.

Prohibiting or severely limiting each party's right to sue the other would make no-fault insurance cheaper, proponents argued, because insurance companies wouldn't be paying attorneys' fees to defend their insureds in cases to establish fault. Insurance companies would also operate more cheaply assuming that state no-fault laws would limit or prohibit so-called pain and suffering claims by persons injured in accidents. Insurance analysts believed that the cost of insurance would decline under such circumstances despite the fact that both parties would collect for bodily injury from their insurers without a fault-finding suit.

In actual practice, no-fault insurance has not been an outstanding success, because some states have not taken away each party's right to sue for pain and suffering. Other states prohibit these suits unless medical bills reach a certain "threshold for suit," but in several states one party can sue the other for pain and suffering after medical bills exceed just $500. This law provides an incentive for some injured persons to run up medical expenses unnecessarily just to qualify to file a pain-and-suffering suit against the other party.

Medical payments is *a form of motor vehicle insurance that pays the medical bills of the insured and of others the insured has injured while driving a vehicle,* up to the amount stated in the policy. Injured parties may also sue for bodily injury liability, but given escalating health care costs it is wise to be well protected against this particular risk.

Comprehensive physical damage is *motor vehicle insurance that protects the insured vehicle against most damage except that caused by collision and upset.* Some examples of hazards normally covered by comprehensive physical damage insurance are fire, flood, hail and dust storms, theft of the vehicle itself, theft of its contents (with such possible exclusions as tape decks and CB radios), vandalism, and interior damage not caused by normal wear and tear. This coverage excludes such normal deterioration as paint faded by the sun and rusted body panels, however, and it will not cover mechanical damage caused by operator negligence (as when the engine is damaged after being run without adequate oil).

Uninsured motorist protection is *coverage that pays the insured for bodily injuries caused by at-fault but uninsured or underinsured drivers and by hit-and-run drivers.* Damage to the vehicle itself would be covered by collision and upset insurance. If you or others in your car are injured by another driver with no insurance and few or no assets, a court judgment against that person for medical payments may be of little comfort. There are no payments to be had. The "underinsured" feature provides payment in the event that you or other occupants of your car suffer injuries that exceed the dollar limits of the other driver's policy. A summary of motor vehicle coverage appears in Table 17.3.

Workers' Compensation Insurance

Workers' compensation insurance is required of most employers in all fifty states. *It pays part of an employee's wage or salary plus medical expenses, and any necessary rehabilitation, retraining, job placement, or counseling, if a worker is*

---

medical payments
A form of motor vehicle insurance that pays the medical bills of the insured and of others the insured has injured while driving a vehicle.

comprehensive physical damage
Motor vehicle insurance that protects the insured vehicle against most damage except that caused by collision and upset.

uninsured motorist protection
Coverage that pays the insured for bodily injuries caused by at-fault but uninsured or underinsured drivers and by hit-and-run drivers.

workers' compensation insurance
Pays part of an employee's wage or salary plus medical expenses, and any necessary rehabilitation, retraining, job placement, or counseling, if a worker is accidentally injured on the job or contracts a job-related disease.

BODILY INJURY COVERAGE	POLICY-HOLDER COVERED	OTHERS COVERED	PROPERTY DAMAGE COVERAGE	POLICY-HOLDER'S CAR COVERED	PROPERTY OF OTHERS COVERED
Bodily injury liability	✓		Property damage liability		✓
Medical payments	✓	✓	Comprehensive physical damage	✓	
Uninsured motorist protection	✓	✓	Collision and upset	✓	

accidentally injured on the job or contracts a job-related disease. It also pays a lump sum to a spouse or child of a worker killed on the job. This coverage favors both the employer and employees. The employer benefits because workers' compensation laws prohibit employees from suing employers for job-related injuries or illnesses (their relief comes through the filing of an insurance claim). Employees benefit because they receive prompt payment for medical treatment, lost wages, and other claims connected with on-the-job injuries or illnesses without having to prove the employer negligent in a costly lawsuit.

Insured businesses can save themselves a lot of money by adopting stringent risk-reduction measures, especially employee safety programs. Workers' compensation insurance premiums are based on the following statistics:

1. Employer's accident claim rate
2. Degree of hazard or risk inherent in the job
3. Size of employer's payroll

An employer in a hazardous business, such as explosives manufacturing, will pay higher premiums than the operator of, say, a retail clothing store. Rates may vary from one-tenth of 1 percent of a company's payroll to more than 20 percent. According to the Bureau of Labor Statistics, safety and health risks in manufacturing tend to be higher than for most other industries. Injury rates are the highest in companies that produce lumber and wood products, food, and fabricated metal goods.

In recent years workers' compensation rates rose much faster than the inflation rate. This condition is due in part to higher medical costs and also to compensation-related payouts.

In some states workers' compensation laws allow employers to self-insure or join a self-insurance fund maintained by a trade association. Most companies, however, choose to cover this risk by purchasing insurance.

Table 17.3

Summary of motor vehicle insurance coverage.

Public Liability Insurance

Public liability insurance is *insurance that covers financial loss caused by an injury to a nonemployee that results from the business's negligence and that occurs on its premises.* (It is also available to homeowners.) Being found guilty of negligence does not mean that you deliberately caused an injury, only that you did not exercise due care to prevent it.

Public liability claims can arise even from the simplest of accidents. For example, a customer who sued a South Carolina supermarket after he injured his head and back by slipping on a green bean was awarded $50,000 in damages.

Businesspeople assume the responsibility of keeping their premises reasonably safe, but if an injured person sues for public liability, a jury decides what "reasonably safe" means. If it finds the company negligent, the jury also sets the amount of damages to be paid to the injured party. Because juries are holding companies strictly accountable for maintaining safe premises, a judgment may easily exceed the face value of a company's policy, and the firm may be financially strapped or even forced to liquidate its assets to pay the difference.

Product Liability Insurance

Product liability insurance is *coverage that protects a firm against financial loss when persons file suit claiming they were injured by its product.* As in public liability suits, juries decide whether the firm is at fault for the product-related injury and what damages, if any, the injured party will be paid. Juries have held manufacturers liable because products did not perform as advertised, because customers were not warned about the dangers of using them, or because the warnings, though present, were not conspicuous enough.

Given the current trend of court judgments in favor of the plaintiff in product liability suits, premiums have risen astronomically. Manufacturers of such products as aircraft parts, power lawn mowers, and grinding wheels have had difficulty finding an insurer who will assume the risk of product liability. Product liability claims prompted Cessna Aircraft Company to stop making small planes in 1986. Such claims aren't merely confined to machinery, of course. For example, a consumer sued a food processing company when she reportedly found a severed finger and a Band-Aid in a four-ounce can of mushrooms she used to make Easter dinner.[5]

Consumers and juries are rightly outraged at the performance failure of some products that results in unnecessary and avoidable injury. Businesses, on the other hand, are alarmed at the apparently punitive attitude juries are taking, sometimes blaming a manufacturer for a consumer's poor judgment. A homeowner sued a power lawn mower manufacturer because he cut off his fingers while holding the mower and using it to trim his hedge; he won the case. One result of the rise in product liability cases and awards is increased prices, for manufacturers pass their costs along to consumers. For example, the cost of DPT vaccine for diphtheria, pertussis, and tetanus rose from $.15 to $7.69 per dose in just five years, primarily because of some $5 billion worth of product liability lawsuits during that time.

Fidelity Bond

Not a financing instrument, a **fidelity bond** is *an insurance policy that reimburses an employer for financial loss resulting from employee dishonesty.* The insurance company (called the *surety*) bonds or insures the acts of a second party (the employee, or *principal*), who works for the employer (the *obligee*). If the employee has been proved to have committed theft, the insurance company reimburses the employer up to a specified maximum and attempts to recover the value of the stolen property from the employee. There are three kinds of fidelity bonds:

Jack-in-the-Box faced expensive lawsuits when patrons of this outlet in North Seattle were poisoned by meat tainted with *E. coli.*

1. A blanket bond covers all present and future employees.
2. An individual bond covers a specific employee.
3. A schedule bond covers a specific group of people or jobs.

Employers commonly purchase fidelity bonds to cover retail store salespeople, bank tellers, warehouse workers, traveling salespeople who carry expensive samples, and any other workers who have custody of or access to cash or valuable inventory.

Surety Bond

A **surety bond**, *sometimes called a* performance bond, is *insurance that guarantees that a contract will be completed.* It is often used in the construction industry for projects such as buildings, highways, bridges, and even ships. Miscellaneous forms are also available to guarantee the solvency of a bank or guarantee that a self-insured company can in fact pay a certain dollar amount of loss out of its self-insurance fund. A surety bond insures the principal's character, skill, and ability to complete a contract according to its terms. If the contract is not fulfilled satisfactorily, the customer may petition the insurance company that bonded the contractor to set things right. This may be done in at least three ways; the insurance company can (1) provide a loan if the contractor ran out of money, (2) hire another contractor to finish the job, or (3) pay the customer the face amount of the surety bond.

Assume that you hired a bonded construction company to build your home. Later you discover that the company used standard-grade materials instead of the premium ones that you contracted and paid for and that it also failed to follow the blueprints correctly. If the builder does not remedy these defects, you could sue for breach of contract, requesting the firm that posted the surety bond to find another company to do the work properly.

A company that wants to obtain a surety bond must supply extensive information to the bonding company, which then conducts an investigation and decides whether to stand behind that firm's work. A contractor with a history of shoddy work and frequent customer disputes may find it difficult if not impossible to obtain a surety bond.

Life Insurance

life insurance
Insurance that protects against economic loss resulting from death.

beneficiary
One or more persons or organizations that the policyholder designates to receive the cash payment on a life insurance policy.

double indemnity
A feature that guarantees that twice the face value of a life insurance policy will be paid if the insured dies accidentally.

Life insurance is *insurance that protects against economic loss resulting from death.* It is a unique form of insurance because it covers a risk that is certain to become a loss. When the insured person dies, the face value of the policy is paid to the **beneficiary**, *one or more persons or organizations that the policyholder designates to receive the cash payment on a life insurance policy.* Most policies provide for **double indemnity**, *a feature that guarantees that twice the face value of a life insurance policy will be paid if the insured dies accidentally.* Life insurance is a flexible instrument that should be part of everyone's plan for financial security. The belief that "the insurance company is betting you won't die and you're betting that you will" is distorted and inaccurate. There are many variations of life insurance that can be tailored to suit the insured's financial goals and circumstances. In general, life insurance can:

- Provide money to pay the deceased's debts and funeral costs
- Pay an income to survivors after the insured's death
- Guarantee that a certain amount of money will be paid to the insured person some time in the future or to a beneficiary after the insured person dies
- Provide a retirement income to supplement money received from social security, an employer's pension program, or any other sources
- Create a fund that may be borrowed against or converted to cash in an emergency

Table 17.4 summarizes the types of insurance you can buy to accomplish these goals and introduces related terminology.

POLICY	CHARACTERISTICS
Term insurance	Pays only if the insured dies during a specified period of time. Cheapest form of coverage. Policies are often renewable (for a higher premium, as the insured is older) and may also be convertible into whole life or an endowment.
Credit life	A type of term insurance that pays the remainder of a debt if a debtor dies.
Whole life*	Remains in effect for the insured's entire life; pays on death.
Straight life	A type of whole life. Premiums are paid until the insured's death. Payments may be difficult for retirees on fixed incomes.
Limited-payment life	A type of whole life. Distributes over a fixed number of years the total premium the insured would pay until death according to the law of large numbers, meaning policy is paid up after a specified period of time though coverage continues until insured's death.
Universal life	A highly modified form of whole life insurance. Part of the premium buys insurance coverage that will be paid if the insured dies. The rest of the premium is invested in high-yield securities that are intended to increase the policy's cash value more rapidly than that of a traditional whole life policy.
Group life	Available to employees through their employer on a master policy, usually without a medical examination required. A popular fringe benefit.
Adjustable life	Insured may raise or lower the face value, lengthen or shorten the protection period, or change the kind of protection as personal circumstances require.
Annuity	A contract that pays the policyholder (annuitant) a fixed sum at regular intervals for a specified period of time. If the annuitant dies before collecting the face value, a beneficiary receives the remainder. Insurer may guarantee a certain percentage return on payments and may pay more than that if investments earn more than anticipated.
Endowment	Combines the characteristics of savings and insurance; the policyholder collects a stated sum if he or she is living when the policy matures. The beneficiary receives the amount the endowment was intended to accumulate (the face value) if the policyholder dies before the policy is fully paid up.

Table 17.4
Types of life insurance.

*Both types of whole life accumulate a *cash surrender value*, an amount the policyholder may collect in cash if the policy is canceled before death or maturity. Policyholders may also borrow against this amount. Cash surrender values increase over time as more premiums are paid in.

Sometimes endowments (see Table 17.4) are included in higher managers' compensation packages. The firm pays premiums, which are a valid business expense for federal income tax purposes. The policy pays a generous sum to the executive at retirement or to the beneficiary if the executive dies beforehand. Because such endowments are a form of insurance, the amount the company pays as premiums is invested to earn money. Thus the employer avoids paying the full amount that the executive collects. The return, or interest, on endowments and annuities may fall short of the inflation rate, meaning they are less desirable as investments. Nevertheless, the discipline of making regular payments and the guarantee of a set rate of return makes them appealing to some people. See Figure 17.4 for a look at the growth of ordinary life insurance in the United States.

Health Insurance

health insurance
Insurance that covers medical expenses incurred by the insured and perhaps the insured's family.

Health insurance is *insurance that covers medical expenses incurred by the insured and perhaps the insured's family.* It is available to individuals, but it is often provided by employers as a fringe benefit. The insurer issues a master policy establishing the terms and conditions of the insurance and describing the employees eligible for coverage. The law of large numbers makes the cost of a group health insurance plan lower than similar coverage purchased by employees as individuals.

The annual total spent for group health insurance premiums nationwide exceeds $105 billion. In short, health insurance now costs employers more than virtually any other employee benefit.

Figure 17.4
Average size of ordinary life insurance policy purchased in the United States.

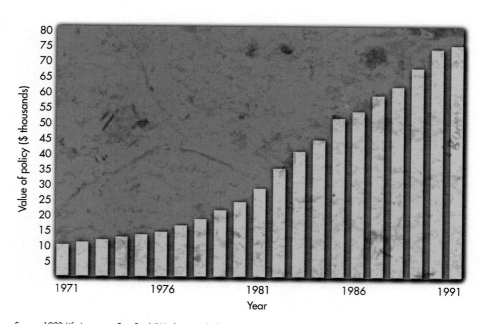

Source: *1992 Life Insurance Fact Book* (Washington, D.C.: American Council of Life Insurance), 1992, p. 11.

Group health insurance usually contains a major medical provision that pays the cost of catastrophic illnesses involving lengthy and expensive treatment and recovery. Some policies set a maximum on this coverage—say, $250,000—but others have no upper limit. The employee usually pays a deductible, after which coverage is provided according to the terms of the master policy. Physician, nurse, hospital, and other fees are paid according to a schedule, and the insured is responsible for the difference. Figure 17.5 shows how public and private health care spending is expected to grow through the year 2000.

Disability Income Insurance

Disability income insurance *pays a sum of money to be spent as the insured chooses if he or she is unable to work because of illness or injury.* This coverage may supplement workers' compensation payments for a job-related illness or injury, and it helps replace income the insured otherwise would have earned. In some cases the definition of *disability* has been expanded to include pregnancy.

Transportation Insurance

Transportation insurance *covers loss of cargo from hazards such as contamination, spoilage, theft, fire, breakage, or collision while in transit.* Such protection is

> ### YOU DECIDE
>
> New York and Vermont have passed regulations that require health insurance companies to sell policies to nearly everyone and charge the same rate to all. This practice, called "community rating," is meant to provide coverage for high-risk individuals such as the chronically ill and the elderly. Opponents say, however, that community rating elevates premiums for everyone and forces healthier people to bear the financial burden for their high-risk neighbors. Do you think community rating may become a trend? Why or why not?

disability income insurance
Pays a sum of money to be spent as the insured chooses if he or she is unable to work because of illness or injury.

transportation insurance
Covers loss of cargo from hazards such as contamination, spoilage, theft, fire, breakage, or collision while in transit.

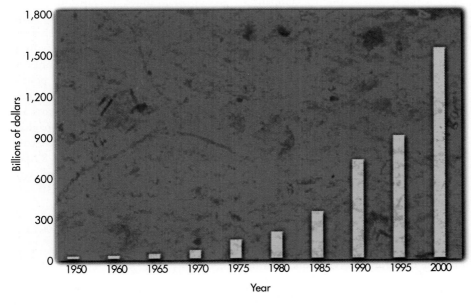

Figure 17.5
The growth of national health costs.

Source: Health Insurance Association of America, *Source Book of Health Insurance Data 1992*, p. 49.

MANAGER'S NOTEBOOK

*Reducing Risks
with Computers*

**HARTFORD STEAM
BOILER INSPECTION
AND INSURANCE
COMPANY**

Insuring steam boilers and machinery may not be a glamorous business, but Hartford Steam Boiler has certainly made it a successful one. This low-profile firm, which has some 35 percent of the market share for boiler and machinery insurance, has carved a successful niche for itself in the competitive world of property and casualty insurance.

Founded in 1866, Hartford's commitment to risk analysis and reduction has made the company a legend in its field. More than 2,500 of its 4,000 employees are engineers, scientists, and technicians. This technical staff, the largest in the boiler and machinery insurance industry, uses state-of-the-art computer modeling (including artificial intelligence) to analyze and reduce the risks of equipment failures because (in the company's words) "customers would rather avoid losses than be paid for them."

Back in the early 1980s Hartford decided to create and maintain a computer database that would record and analyze operating and maintenance problems with turbine generators and other high-speed machinery. This innovative database now contains information on the operating characteristics of some 4,900 machines, 9,000 bearings, 25,000 measurement points, and 100,000 types of operating measurements. Company experts use the information to alert policyholders to potential problems before they occur. The database was complemented more recently by Datalert, a unique monitoring service conceived by Hartford that gathers and reports vibration data on customers' high-speed turbine generators, which may run at more than 20,000 rpm. Operating data on these machines are gathered by hand-held equipment at the customer's plant and transmitted electronically to Hartford's minicomputer. The computer analyzes and compares these data with previously reported vibration data on the customer's generator. If the generator is producing an unnatural vibration pattern, Datalert prints a prioritized list of possible causes and corrective action that may prevent a shutdown. This last service is especially valuable, because a failed turbine generator may cut a manufacturing plant's production capacity by as much as 50 percent, depending on which operations it powers.

Hartford's consultants also recommend preventive maintenance regimens for healthy machinery that take into account the equipment's operating traits, breakdown history, and current condition. This program reduces both insurance premiums and operating losses for customers and the degree of risk assumed by Hartford.

"Our commitment to write only property insurance and prevent accidents and resulting losses is part of our . . . philosophy," said vice president James C. Rowan, Jr. "We will only write policies where we can reduce the risk of accident through our field force of inspectors and engineers." This philosophy has paid off handsomely, indeed. In a field where competitors reportedly pay out 70 to 80 percent of premiums in claims, Hartford's typical payout ranges between 30 and 40 percent.

For more on Hartford Steam Boiler, see Marci Alborghetti, "Steam Boiler Puts on Pressure," *Connecticut Post,* July 28, 1992; Yvette DeBow, "Exploring the Next Reality: Knowledge-Based Systems," *Insurance & Technology,* November 1992, p. 26; *The Hartford Steam Boiler Inspection and Insurance Company 1992 Annual Report;* and William B. Voegtle and Kenneth D. Bever, "Helping to Reduce Turbomachinery Losses Through Advanced Technology and On-Line Expertise," *Turbomachinery International Handbook 1992,* p. 78.

very important to firms such as R. T. French Company, which reportedly ships over $10 million worth of mustard and other products around the world each year. Under the terms of these policies carriers are liable for losses caused by their own negligence, but not for losses caused by floods, earthquakes, or other "acts of God," as the language of most policies has it. Of course, even a carrier who is insured against such risks may lose out if the value of a damaged shipment exceeds the face value of the policy.

There are two kinds of transportation insurance. The first, **ocean marine insurance,** is *insurance that protects a cargo against loss on the high seas.* This insurance is the oldest in existence. Marine insurers have been called on to cover such unusual risks as a sixteen-story floating pulp mill that was moved by water the 15,000 miles from Japan to Brazil. The second, **inland transit insurance,** is *insurance that covers losses caused by catastrophes and acts of God for overland transportation.* It is often issued against such specific risks as collision, wind, lightning, derailment, or hijacking.

Power Plant Insurance

Power plant insurance, *also called* boiler and machinery insurance, *covers losses caused by an exploding steam boiler, furnace, heating plant, or other equipment.* Fire insurance policies usually exclude such hazards, making separate coverage necessary. The insurance company inspects the insured equipment periodically to verify that it is properly maintained and in safe working order.

Credit Insurance

Credit insurance is *insurance that protects a firm against bad debt losses above a maximum amount on trade credit accounts.* A business can buy coverage on specific debtors, but it is more typical to insure all trade credit accounts on the books. The insurer will of course review the quality of the receivables on the books before quoting a premium.

Risk reduction is very practical with credit insurance and can save a lot in premium costs. With perpetual open-book accounts that have high average balances, it is more practical to monitor the debtor's financial health closely. The risk of truly devastating bad debt losses may also be minimized by selling to customers in a wide variety of industries, thereby reducing the risk of loss caused by an abrupt economic decline in a single industry.

Because geographic catastrophes such as hurricanes or droughts may also impair the collection of trade credit accounts, selling to customers over a wide geographic area may be advisable, too. Other ways to reduce the risk of bad debts are to sell on a COD (*cash on d*elivery) basis or to sell to government agencies, which are perhaps the safest class of trade credit customer.

Hazardous Waste Insurance

Hazardous waste insurance is *liability insurance required by the Environmental Protection Agency (EPA) that will provide payment to persons who are awarded*

---

ocean marine insurance
Insurance that protects a cargo against loss on the high seas.

inland transit insurance
Insurance that covers losses caused by catastrophes and acts of God for overland transportation.

power plant insurance
Also called *boiler and machinery insurance,* covers losses caused by an exploding steam boiler, furnace, heating plant, or other equipment.

credit insurance
Insurance that protects a firm against bad debt losses above a maximum amount on trade credit accounts.

hazardous waste insurance
Liability insurance required by the Environmental Protection Agency (EPA) that will provide payment to persons who are awarded compensation for bodily injury and property damage caused by accidents arising from the operation of hazardous waste facilities.

compensation for bodily injury and property damage caused by accidents arising from the operation of hazardous waste facilities. In effect since mid-1982, this regulation applies to owners or operators of some 7,000 facilities that store or dispose of such contaminants. Companies must be insured for at least $1 million per occurrence and $2 million total per year for sudden accidents such as spills, fire, or explosion and $3 million per occurrence and $6 million total per year for nonsudden accidents such as the gradual leakage of carcinogenic or toxic pollutants into the earth or atmosphere. These amounts must be earmarked exclusively for paying claims; they cannot include costs of legal defense.

Because few insurers offered protection against gradual accidents in the past, the EPA requirement to carry that coverage was phased in during a three-year period starting with companies that had the greatest potential for a catastrophe.

Surplus Lines

Surplus lines coverage is *insurance for risks on which no law of large numbers exists.* This type of insurance is bought when there is little or no history on the risk, the likelihood of loss, or the amount of financial damage that the risk taker may incur if it becomes a loss. Some examples are:

- Political risk insurance, which pays if a company's assets in foreign countries are seized by the government. This type of insurance became quite popular after the revolution in Iran.
- Satellite insurance, which covers damage or loss of a satellite. Satellites launched from the space shuttle also must carry $500 million of liability insurance in case they fail to disintegrate on a plunge to earth and cause damage on landing.
- Sexual harassment and sexual discrimination insurance, which pays up to the face of the policy if a company is judged guilty of either offense.

Only a few American insurance companies—Prudential Insurance Company of America, Allstate Insurance Company, INA Corporation, and American International Group—issue this coverage.

Lloyd's of London

Lloyd's of London, a legendary risk-taking institution for nearly 300 years, was born in 1687 in a London coffeehouse owned by Edward Lloyd. The coffeehouse was a gathering place for sailors and sea captains who, thanks to their experience, were able to evaluate shipping risks accurately enough to insure cargoes as a profitable sideline. The organization branched out from its original marine insurance lines to become the most likely insurer in the world for surplus lines.

Technically speaking, a risk is not insured *by* Lloyd's of London; it is insured *through* Lloyd's. The organization has over 19,000 members (called *underwriters* or *Names*) organized into syndicates, who back the risks they insure with their personal wealth. A business wishing to obtain insurance through Lloyd's must contact an authorized agent (there are over 1,200 world-wide) and describe the risk for which insurance is sought. The agent then approaches a broker at Lloyd's headquarters, who in turn approaches underwriters who may be willing to insure part of the risk. These underwriters spread the risk among themselves, agreeing to insure a portion of the total amount desired. Should the risk become a loss, the Names who collectively insured it will pay the proportional amount for which each was committed.

When Prince Charles and Lady Diana Spencer were preparing to marry, British companies produced commemorative medallions and glassware, and American firms ran contests awarding free trips to London. Canadian and Australian businesses also speculated in ventures that depended on the wedding taking place. Lloyd's was asked to underwrite approximately $22 million in insurance to pay the losses suffered by such companies if the wedding were delayed or canceled.

Under its policy of waiting three years to process all claims, Lloyd's recently reported losses of $4.38 billion in 1990 (losses totaled $3.98 billion for 1988 and 1989). These losses resulted not only from claims but also from lawsuits by Names who alleged that management acted irresponsibly in insuring a variety of risks in the late 1980s. The resulting losses left some Names virtually bankrupt.

Lloyd's top managers have responded by cutting staff 27 percent, reducing the operating budget 24 percent, selling the Rolls-Royce that had been provided to the chairman, and changing the policies and procedures used to evaluate applications for insurance. Management hopes that these and other corrective actions will restore both the financial health and the prestige of this institution, which has endured for more than three centuries.[6]

SUMMARY

Businesses deal with two kinds of risks. Speculative risk, such as the risk of doing business, may result in either a gain or a loss. Pure risk can only become a loss. To help deal with pure risk, larger firms usually employ a risk manager, who finds ways to avoid it, transfer it to a noninsurer, or self-insure against it. Risk managers often seek insurance against a given risk if these measures do not neutralize it.

As professional risk takers, insurance companies assume a risk for a fee called a premium. Insurance depends on the law of large numbers to predict the likelihood of loss. Insurance companies are organized as mutual companies, owned entirely by their policy-holders, or as stock companies, owned by stockholders. An insurance company's financial condition is monitored by regulatory agencies in each state where it operates and also by several private rating firms. All insurance companies employ actuaries to analyze the law of large numbers and compute premiums on various pure risks, and they hire loss prevention engineers to advise clients on how to reduce or remove risk. Insurance companies only write a policy if the policy-holder has an insurable interest in the person or object being insured. And insurers only allow coverage up to the replacement value of an object—the policyholder cannot profit from the loss.

The risks that insurance companies accept must meet several conditions. A law of averages must exist on the risk, the loss must be expressible in dollars, and the risk must be spread over a wide geographic area. In addition, the insurance company reserves the right to increase the premium, to cancel the policy, or not to renew it if adverse circumstances arise, and payment may be refused under certain conditions.

Companies require several kinds of insurance, depending on the risks they encounter. Fire insurance covers losses to a building caused by fire, but it can be expanded to include coverage for the building's contents and losses owing to other calamities. Various risks of operating a motor vehicle can be insured against. Laws in all fifty states require employers to purchase workers' compensation insurance, and most firms consider carrying public liability protection. Many businesses—certainly most manufacturers—obtain product liability protection. Many firms whose employees handle money or valuable goods get fidelity bonds, and contractors get surety bonds. Firms in all lines of business offer life and health insurance to employees. Disability income insurance, transportation insurance, and credit insurance are also available. The Environmental Protection Agency now requires owners or operators of hazardous waste facilities to carry insurance that will compensate claimants for bodily injury and property damage caused by both sudden and nonsudden accidents. Companies that face risks for which no law of large numbers exists can purchase surplus lines coverage through such specialized insurance brokers as Lloyd's of London.

KEY TERMS

actuary p. 551
adjustable life insurance p. 565
allied lines *or* extended coverage p. 555
all-risk physical damage *or* multiple-
   line coverage p. 555
annuity p. 565
beneficiary p. 564
bodily injury liability p. 559
business interruption insurance p. 558
coinsurance clause p. 557
collision and upset p. 558
comprehensive physical damage p. 560
contingent business interruption insurance p. 558
credit insurance p. 569
credit life insurance p. 565
deductible p. 548
disability income insurance p. 567
double indemnity p. 564
endowment p. 565
fidelity bond p. 563
group life insurance p. 565
hazardous waste insurance p. 569
health insurance p. 566
inland transit insurance p. 569
insurable interest p. 548
insurance policy p. 546
law of large numbers *or* law of averages p. 546

life insurance p. 564
limited-payment life insurance p. 565
loss prevention engineer (LPE) p. 551
medical payments p. 560
mutual insurance company p. 549
no-fault auto insurance p. 559
ocean marine insurance p. 569
power plant insurance p. 569
principle of indemnity p. 548
product liability insurance p. 562
property damage liability p. 559
public liability insurance p. 562
pure risk p. 543
risk manager p. 543
self-insurance fund p. 545
speculative risk p. 542
stock insurance company p. 549
straight life insurance p. 565
surety bond p. 563
surplus lines coverage p. 570
term insurance p. 565
transportation insurance p. 567
uninsured motorist protection p. 560
universal life insurance p. 565
whole life insurance p. 565
workers' compensation insurance p. 560

FOR REVIEW AND DISCUSSION

1. Why is risk an inherent part of any business venture? What risks do businesspeople accept willingly? What kind must they accept whether they like it or not? Offer examples of each.

2. Describe the risk manager's job and list examples of local companies that have an especially strong need for such a position.

3. Recommend some actions that a firm could take to avoid the risk of loss by the following: fire, employee theft, robbery, explosion, motor vehicle accident, shoplifting, and lawsuits brought by customers injured on the premises.

4. How can you transfer risk to a noninsurer? Who pays the cost in the long run? Why may this still be beneficial?

5. Describe the circumstances under which self-insurance is a reasonable way to deal with risk. List at least two risks that may be dealt with in this way.

6. Explain the following statement: "Most insurance companies will not sell insurance against a risk unless they have enough data to apply the law of large numbers."

7. What is an insurable interest? How does it protect insurance companies and insured persons and property alike?

8. Define the principle of indemnity.

9. How does a deductible benefit both the insurer and the insured?

10. What is the difference between a mutual insurance company and a stock insurance company?

11. Comment on the following statement: "Insurance companies wield considerable economic power in our society."

12. What action may state regulators take on behalf of policyholders if an insurance company goes bankrupt? What else may be done if that effort fails?

13. List at least three firms that rate an insurance company's ability to pay policyholders' claims.

14. Why are actuaries and loss prevention engineers important to an insurance company? How is the insured affected by their work?

15. State the conditions that a risk must meet before a typical insurance company will accept it. What may the insurance company do if adverse circumstances arise? Why is it reasonable for an insurance company to refuse payment under certain conditions?

16. List and discuss the additional coverage that can be added to a fire insurance policy to extend it far beyond its original scope.

17. Why do insurance companies put coinsurance clauses in their policies? What do these clauses do?

18. Construct a table summarizing the various kinds of motor vehicle insurance that are available.

19. Why have several states passed no-fault auto insurance laws? What has impaired the effectiveness of this insurance in some states?

20. Summarize the major features of each of the following kinds of insurance and evaluate the need for each: workers' compensation, public liability, product liability, fidelity bond, surety bond, life insurance (each type), health insurance, disability income insurance, transportation insurance, power plant insurance, credit insurance, and hazardous waste insurance.

21. What kind of life insurance accumulates a cash surrender value? What does that mean for the policyholder?

22. What sets surplus lines coverage apart from the other insurance discussed in this chapter? Give examples of risks that may have to be covered in this way.

23. How does Lloyd's of London spread the risk on insurance that it places? Describe the procedure you would follow if you wanted to insure a risk through Lloyd's.

APPLICATIONS

Case 17.1: A Record Year for Disaster

Crash! Your car slams into the back of that pretty red Ferrari. Sure, your insurance will cover it, but where are your rates going to go? That's right, straight to-ward the sky. In 1992 insurance companies had to pay for Hurricane Andrew, the Los Angeles riots, the Chicago flood, a record number of tornadoes, Hurricane Iniki, and the December nor'easter. Unsurprisingly, property/casualty insurers were hit hard by this series of disasters, but their rates did a surprising thing. They stayed the same.

With insurance stocks buoyed by the expectations of higher rates, investors have been disappointed to find rates unmoved. Some areas of the industry, such as reinsurance, have had skyrocketing prices, but the rates for property/casualty insurance have at most inched upward regionally. The forces that previously had strong effects on the industry haven't taken hold.

Some industry watchers say the "problem" is that the insurance companies have too much capital. With too much money available for insuring people, companies, and property, insurance prices stay low in the same way that gasoline prices drop during an oil glut. This view has, however, not been widely accepted. Using Hurricane Andrew as proof, analysts point out that an industry that can in one incident lose 10 percent of its capital does not have too much capital invested in it. In fact, after 1992 several insurance companies had to supply infusions of capital to their property/casualty subsidiaries.

Therefore, the question remains: Why, after its worst year ever, has the insurance industry failed to raise it rates predictably? On closer analysis, the answer becomes clear. The investment portfolios held by the major companies have helped buoy the capital crunch. Taking advantage of low interest rates, insurers sold over half of their $400 billion bond holdings. This sale had powerful effects. The industry's surplus funds increased 2.7 percent in 1992. Exercising the power of their portfolios, the insurance industry pulled itself out of a crunch. Unfortunately, if more disaster-filled years come their way, insurers may find their resources expended.

Crash! The rates will go up.

Questions

1. Why do insurance rates normally go up when the companies have losses?

2. Do you believe the government should regulate insurance companies' amount of capital? Why or why not?

3. How would you describe an insurance company's ultimate financial goal?

4. Do you think it is wise for insurance companies to allow investment income to offset rate hikes? Why or why not?

For more information, see Suzanne Wooley, "Why Insurance Rates Have Lost Their Old Bounce," *Business Week,* May 10, 1993, p. 52.

Case 17.2: Insuring the Insurers

Reinsurers are companies that take on risks that general insurance companies would like to spread around. They charge healthy rates for insuring insurance. Recent disasters have significantly damaged reinsurance companies, however, and many are exiting the business.

American Reliance Company, a small Florida property insurer, was never a major factor in the insurance industry until 1992. In that year, the insurer collected only $29 million in premiums yet was swamped by $574 million in claims caused by Hurricane Andrew. The company passed along $500 million of the losses to forty-six reinsurers, including Prudential Insurance. Unsurprisingly, like many other companies, Prudential, which suffered $324 million in reinsurance losses in 1992, wants out of the business.

With declining reinsurance offerings from companies such as Prudential and Lloyd's of London, primary insurers are finding it more and more difficult to spread their risks. While capacity is shrinking, demand is increasing, and insurers are paying higher rates for coverage. Furthermore, reinsurers are placing additional constraints on their coverage. Previously they promised a pro rata coverage of all losses, but increasingly reinsurance offerings are stipulating maximum payouts.

Even though reinsurance capacity is currently very limited, primary insurers are scrambling to find coverage. Frightened by the massive losses of several disasters in 1992, primary insurers are altering their policy of avoiding reinsurance in order to maximize profits. Meanwhile, reinsurers are taking advantage of a bull market to raise the capital necessary to take advantage of the primary insurers. Until the reinsurance market grows out of its capacity slump, however, the result is likely to be higher rates for individuals—and businesses—that have something to insure.

Questions

1. How does reinsurance affect the profits of primary insurers?

2. What does it mean when reinsurance rates are rising and coverage is shrinking?

3. Is reinsurance a good idea or one whose time has run out? Justify your answer.

For more information, see Tim Smart and Chris Roush, "Insurers Scramble to Spread the Risks," *Business Week,* April 19, 1993, p. 98.

REFERENCES

1. "Golfer Dies After Club Shaft Breaks, Pierces His Neck," *The Orlando Sentinel,* May 13, 1993, p. D-2.
2. "Corporate Executives Bunch Up on Flights," *The Wall Street Journal,* July 3, 1992, p. B1.
3. Marcy A. Mason, "Don't Become a Kidnap Statistic," *The Wall Street Journal,* May 18, 1992, p. A10; Allanna Sullivan and Caleb Solomon, "Corporate Concern Mounts over Top Officials' Security," *The Wall Street Journal,* June 2, 1992, p. B1; Roger Rowand, "Armored Cars Secure New Favor," *The Orlando Sentinel,* April 29, 1993, p. F-8.
4. Suzy Hagstrom, "Allstate to Stage Stock Offering," *The Orlando Sentinel,* May 20, 1993, p. C-1; Suzy Hagstrom, "Availability of Insurance Dwindles," *The Orlando Sentinel,* May 2, 1993, p. D-1; Greg Steinmetz, "As Insurance Costs from Hurricane Soar, Higher Rates Loom," *The Wall Street Journal,* January 6, 1993, p. A1.
5. "Can of Mushrooms Had a Finger—Woman Sues," *The Orlando Sentinel,* May 14, 1993, p. A-5.
6. Nicholas Bray and Charles Fleming, "Lloyd's Changes Way It Does Business," *The Wall Street Journal,* January 22, 1993, p. A5B; Richard A. Melcher, "Lloyd's Uneasy Rider," *Business Week,* April 26, 1993, p. 84; "Lloyd's of London Loss Tops $4 Billion," *The Orlando Sentinel,* June 23, 1993, p. C-1.

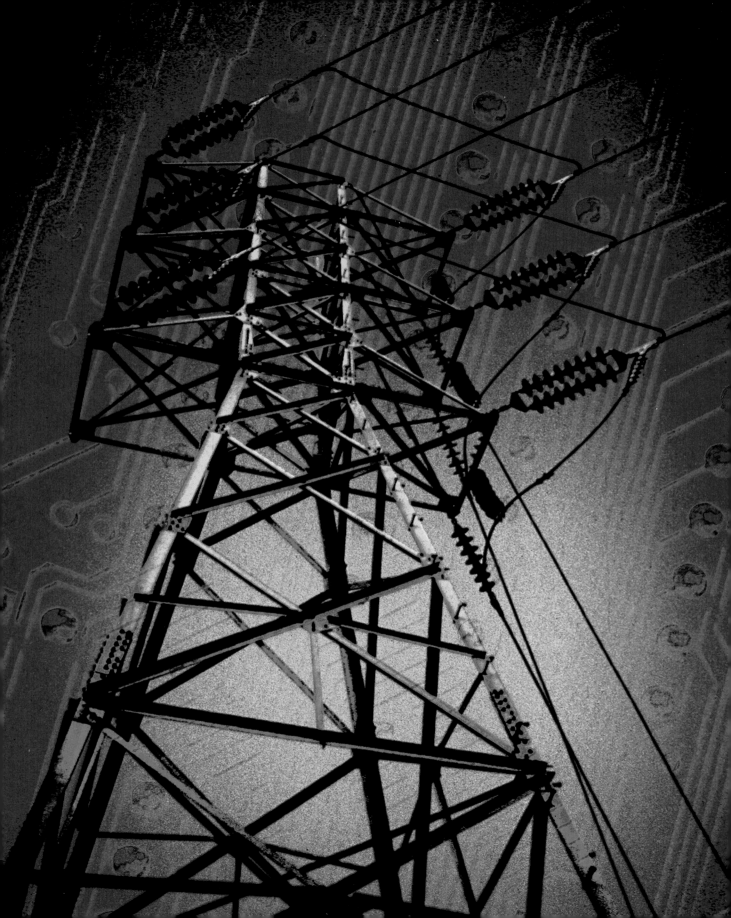

MANAGING INFORMATION

We require both vision and value from information systems . . . a system is visionary if it supports the company's strategic objectives, and it's valuable if it helps us provide higher-quality, lower-cost products and services to customers.

JAMES WOGSLAND
Vice Chairman, Caterpillar Inc.

CHAPTER OBJECTIVES
After studying this chapter, you should be able to:

1. Explain the purpose, development, and use of a formal management information system.
2. Identify the two kinds of data that managers use and describe situations in which both may be necessary.
3. Give examples of data that can be gathered by observation and data that may require a survey.
4. Describe three types of surveys that data collectors may use.
5. Discuss how averages, correlations, and index numbers can be used in summarizing data.
6. Differentiate between analog computers and digital computers.
7. Give examples of computer hardware and software.
8. Summarize the potential of microprocessors and give examples of how they are used today.
9. Propose at least three ways that personal computers may be used by small businesses and individuals and list at least two factors that have caused them to become so popular in recent years.
10. List several popular uses for computers.
11. Describe two major types of computer networks.
12. Compare the advantages and disadvantages of service bureaus, time sharing, and leasing as methods of getting access to a computer

UP FRONT

George Borhegyi is a professional in every aspect of his demeanor, from his well-tailored suit to his telephone manners. As information systems director at Cambridge Technology Partners, he is finding ways for his company to do for itself what it does for its clients: better direct and employ the strategic use of computer technology. CT Partners, an information integration firm in Cambridge, Massachusetts, uses state-of-the-art system development techniques to design and build strategic applications for its clients.

Borhegyi began his career with CT Partners in 1987, shortly after graduating with a degree in electrical engineering from the Massachusetts Institute of Technology. "I wasn't what you'd call a 'technical person,'" he says. "I've always been attracted to technology, but I never had a home computer. In my studies, I always liked business, psychology, *and* technology. The work I do involves all three."

He found use for all three right from the start. His first assignment was as a teaching assistant, helping business executives and salespeople learn how to use computer systems. He also took part in demonstrating the company's ability to quickly develop prototype systems. He worked with office workers and information systems people, writing programs and designing the menus and screens that helped make the prototype work. From there, he began working on system development teams, creating computer systems for customers. "A good computer system is simple, and it gives the customers the kind of information they need when they need it. That should be a primary characteristic of any computer system."

Borhegyi has worked in consulting, on-site demonstrations, rapid prototyping, system design and development, and customer support and empowerment. As his knowledge and skills have grown, he has been given different roles and more responsibilities. "What I'm trying to do now is make it possible for the people who work at CT Partners to do just about anything they want with a computer. We refer to it as the 'open systems, common standards' concept. You see, we have all kinds of different computers—minicomputers, workstations, IBM-compatible PCs, Macintoshes, traveling notebook computers. Our people are encouraged to use whatever computer system works best for them.

"We are a thoroughly networked company as well. All our computers are connected in a company-wide network, which extends to some of our branch offices as well. If employees are traveling with their notebook computer, they can plug into a phone line and call the office to retrieve their electronic mail. A modern company needs to be networked to the world."

Borhegyi believes that the modern definition of management information systems, or MIS, is "to use information technology strategically for the business." This philosophy certainly applies to the types of computer systems CT Partners designs and installs for its customers, but

GEORGE BORHEGYI

INFORMATION SYSTEMS DIRECTOR, CAMBRIDGE TECHNOLOGY PARTNERS

he is ensuring that it is pervasive within the company as well. "In addition to having easy-to-use information technology, we must have easily accessible information as well. A senior vice-president says, 'How many projects are we working on? What are the billables, what are the profit margins, what are the current sales forecasts, which individuals are working on which projects?' and so forth. Management needs to be able to see any kind of information on a computer screen at the touch of one or two keys. We're extending the ability to do this, and to run all aspects of the company this way, from a standardized, easy-to-use technology platform."

Information technology has been a source of continual interest and fascination for George Borhegyi in his work. Perhaps that's why his work continues to be redefined and his responsibilities change and grow. "Technology is so pervasive these days that you can explore interesting business subjects with it," he says. "When you use it to enhance business functions, you can see real rewards. You don't have to be involved in creating computer technology itself, but you can certainly be creative in solving business problems with it."

Gathering and processing data are the foundations of the decision-making process you learned about in Chapter 6. Timely, accurate, understandable data must reach decision makers at all levels if an organization and its people hope to advance and prosper. In this chapter we will learn about the systems and methods that companies use to gather data and convert them into useful information. We will also explore the computer's role in processing large amounts of data swiftly for individuals as well as companies.

The Importance of a Management Information System

management information system (MIS)
An organized approach to gathering data from inside and outside the company and (because of the volume involved) processing it by computer to produce current, accurate, and informative reports for all decision makers.

Large firms answer the challenge of gathering data by constructing a **management information system (MIS)**. This system is *an organized approach to gathering data from inside and outside the company and (because of the volume involved) processing it by computer to produce current, accurate, and informative reports for all decision makers.*

An MIS performs two functions. First, it systematically gathers internal data—such facts about the company as sales, inventory, expenses, prices, rate of production, and numbers of employees—and external data—such facts about the company's environment as competitors' actions, market trends, demographic trends, laws affecting the business, and changes in suppliers. The MIS then processes these data, grouping related facts, analyzing them, and summarizing them in a standard format. The result of these two actions is that data are transformed into information. An MIS appears graphically in Figure 18.1.

In small businesses such as sole proprietorships and partnerships, the owners usually function as their own informal MIS. In huge corporations like General Foods or United Technologies, however, the role and structure of the

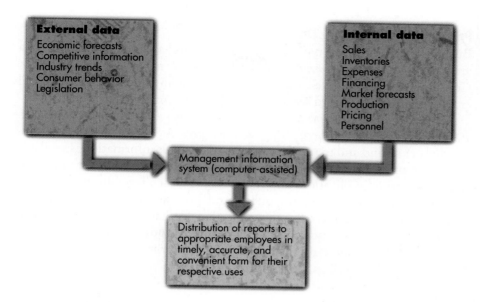

Figure 18.1

A management information system.

MIS are massive. The MIS must accumulate data from every plant and office in the firm and also from relevant external sources such as federal government agencies, trade associations, major consumer groups, and special interest groups. This effort is very important, because employees at all levels must have access to both internal and external information if they are to make intelligent, well-informed decisions. A company's MIS facilitates decision making on literally thousands of matters at every level of the organization each day. For example, Caterpillar Inc., a company with $10 billion in annual sales, sells its products in some 140 countries world-wide. To manage this enormous corporate empire successfully, the company has created a computerized MIS that crosses twenty-three time zones and supports 60,000 terminals and workstations. Caterpillar's employees can exchange data with 900 suppliers and more than 1,000 dealer locations around the globe.[1]

In satisfying employees' information requirements, a large MIS must arrange for essential data to be systematically gathered from all relevant sources and processed promptly and accurately for distribution to the proper persons. A management information system's design, then, must identify sources of relevant data; feed data from those sources to the central clearinghouse (a computer, in large organizations); decide on the formatting and frequency of reports to be issued; convert that data into such reports on a timely and accurate basis; and send them to appropriate recipients.

Gathering, Summarizing, and Presenting Data

To be valuable, data must be collected by the appropriate technique, summarized, and presented clearly and concisely so employees at all levels can understand and apply them in their everyday decision making.

Primary and Secondary Data

Businesses deal with two types of data: primary and secondary. **Primary data** are *data that a company must gather itself or employ some other firm to gather.* Consumer buying motives, the image of a company and its products, and employee attitudes toward work are examples of primary data.

Secondary data are *data that currently exist; they have been recorded somewhere, and management need only go to the source.* As a result, secondary data are cheaper to find and to use than primary data. This information is available from such public sources as federal agencies and from such private sources as trade association publications and magazines. Your college library contains a wealth of secondary data from public and private sources. You will have noticed by this time that we have used a great deal of secondary data in writing this textbook. It has been said, after all, that much of education consists not of learning things, but of learning where to find things out.

YOU DECIDE

Describe how you believe a company's MIS would change and evolve as the firm grows from a small, sole proprietorship with one location to a multinational conglomerate with facilities in several countries.

Businesses, like the rest of us, appreciate the savings and convenience of using secondary data, but often such data cannot answer all of management's questions; some primary data are needed. Before a company selects a location for a distribution center or a manufacturing plant, it may consult data from the U.S. Bureau of the Census on population growth and income in various parts of the country, and it may examine data provided by agencies in several states that offer attractive locations. Typically a firm makes its own study of a potential site to supplement such published data, evaluating each location according to the criteria you learned about in Chapter 11.

Managers follow three steps in dealing with data: (1) they gather data, using whatever devices are appropriate; (2) they analyze or summarize data, following one of several methods; and (3) they draw conclusions from the data and make decisions based on those conclusions. Figure 18.2 illustrates these three steps and their sequence.

Data Collection Techniques

Management has two techniques available for gathering data. The one chosen depends on the circumstances and the questions involved.

OBSERVATION If the information you seek can be readily seen or recorded without asking questions, you can gather it by observation. Wherever possible, you should consider observing with electronic or mechanical devices. They are often cheaper to use than human researchers, and they may be more accurate because they do not suffer fatigue, boredom, and other human frailties. Also, a machine usually does not call attention to itself and thereby potentially influence the behavior being observed. Some everyday examples of mechanical or electronic observers are:

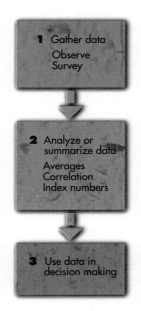

Figure 18.2
The three steps in dealing with data.

- Jukeboxes with counters that tell how many times each record has been played
- Turnstiles with counters that record the number of guests entering and leaving a tourist attraction
- Counters that gather data on traffic flow near an intersection

SURVEYS Companies use surveys to gather data when they need opinions, reactions, or other information that cannot be obtained by simple observation and recording. Surveys would be used to discover:

- Consumer reactions to a package design or a new product flavor
- The average annual income of a family of four in a geographic region
- How employees feel about a firm's training program, promotional opportunities, and pay scale

Management must ask questions to get unobservable data. This can be done with mail surveys, telephone surveys, or personal interviews. With all three methods, questions must be carefully worded, whether on a form or asked by an interviewer, so as not to influence the answer. Prejudicing the respondent invalidates the response.

Although mail surveys are ideal for reaching a farflung group of people, the response may be disappointing, especially if the survey asks for lengthy or detailed responses or for information the respondents must compute or look up. It is always easier to throw the questionnaire away.

To combat this, firms offer incentives that encourage people to answer.

Respondents who do not mind identifying themselves may be offered a gift on returning the completed questionnaire. An alternative is to enclose a gift along with the questions, which makes the person feel obligated to reply. *Fortune*, *Rudder*, and *Aviation Week* have all enclosed cash incentives in their marketing surveys.

A product use card that consumers are required to return to validate a guarantee is one way to gather data from new owners of a product. These cards ask such questions as why you bought the product, in what store, and whether you own anything else made by the manufacturer. As you learned in Chapter 8, these data help a producer identify consumer buying motives, popular marketing outlets, brand loyalty, and other characteristics of a market segment. An example of one such form appears in Figure 18.3.

Figure 18.3

Product use card.

PURCHASE INFORMATION CARD

To better serve you in the future, we would appreciate your filling out and returning this information card to us. Thank you.

1. ☐ Mr.   2. ☐ Mrs.   3. ☐ Ms.   4. ☐ Miss   **39B**

Name (First/Initial/Last)

Street

City   State   Zip

Date of Purchase: ___/___/___ (Mo. Day Yr.)   Model Number ☐☐☐☐

A. Store where purchased:
1. ☐ Drug store
2. ☐ Discount store
3. ☐ Catalog showroom
4. ☐ Department store
5. ☐ Grocery store
6. ☐ Beauty salon
7. ☐ Hardware store
8. ☐ Received as gift
9. ☐ Other

B. If the appliance was a gift, did you request that it be given to you?
1. ☐ Yes   2. ☐ No

C. What brand of this appliance did you previously own?
1. ☐ This is my first one
2. ☐ Conair
3. ☐ Clairol
4. ☐ Gillette
5. ☐ G.E.
6. ☐ Norelco
7. ☐ Pollenex
8. ☐ Schick
9. ☐ Sunbeam
10. ☐ Water Pik
11. ☐ Other: _____

D. How many of this appliance (any type) do you presently have in your household?
1. ☐ This is the only one   4. ☐ 4
2. ☐ 2   5. ☐ 5
3. ☐ 3   6. ☐ More than 5

E. Where did you first learn about Conair appliances?
1. ☐ Magazine advertisements
2. ☐ Recommended by friend
3. ☐ Recommended by store clerk
4. ☐ Newspaper advertisement
5. ☐ T.V. advertisement
6. ☐ Recommended by beauty professional
7. ☐ Other

F. Check the 2 most important factors influencing your selection of this Conair product:
1. ☐ Conair's reputation
2. ☐ Price
3. ☐ Style/ appearance
4. ☐ Lightweight
5. ☐ Durability
6. ☐ Special features
7. ☐ Warranty
8. ☐ Previous experience with Conair's appliances

G. Which of the following have you done in the past 6 months? (check all that apply)
1. ☐ Redeemed a product coupon
2. ☐ Ordered an item from mail order catalog
3. ☐ Sent in product inquiry card from magazine
4. ☐ Bought item from offer received in mail
5. ☐ Entered sweepstakes/contest

H. In which age group are you?
1. ☐ Under 12
2. ☐ 12–17
3. ☐ 18–24
4. ☐ 25–34
5. ☐ 35–44
6. ☐ 45–54
7. ☐ 55–64
8. ☐ 65 & over

I. Marital status
1. ☐ Married   2. ☐ Unmarried

J. Which group best describes your family income?
1. ☐ Under $10,000
2. ☐ $10,000–$14,999
3. ☐ $15,000–$19,999
4. ☐ $20,000–$24,999
5. ☐ $25,000–$29,999
6. ☐ $30,000–$34,999
7. ☐ $35,000–$39,999
8. ☐ $40,000–$44,999
9. ☐ $45,000–$49,999
10. ☐ $50,000 & over

K. Do you have any children in any of the following age groups who are living at home?
1. ☐ Under age 2
2. ☐ Age 2–4
3. ☐ Age 5–7
4. ☐ Age 8–10
5. ☐ Age 11–12
6. ☐ Age 13–15
7. ☐ Age 16–18

L. For you primary residence, do you:
1. ☐ Own a house?
2. ☐ Rent a house?
3. ☐ Own a townhouse/condominium?
4. ☐ Rent an apartment?

M. Which of the following types of credit cards do you use?
1. ☐ Travel/entertainment (American Express, Diners Club, Carte Blanche)
2. ☐ Bank (Master Charge, Visa)
3. ☐ Gas, department store, etc.

N. What is your occupation? (check one)
1. ☐ Professional/technical
2. ☐ Upper mgt./administrator
3. ☐ Sales/service/middle mgt.
4. ☐ Clerical/white collar
5. ☐ Craftsman/blue collar
6. ☐ Student
7. ☐ Housewife
8. ☐ Retired

O. Which of the following interests and hobbies do you and your family enjoy?
1. ☐ Tennis
2. ☐ Golf
3. ☐ Snow skiing
4. ☐ Running/jogging
5. ☐ Camping/hiking
6. ☐ Hunting/shooting
7. ☐ Fishing
8. ☐ Bicycling
9. ☐ Racquetball
10. ☐ Sailing/boating
11. ☐ Stamp/coin collecting
12. ☐ Motorbiking/motorcycling
13. ☐ Home video games
14. ☐ Physical fitness/exercise
15. ☐ Home video recording
16. ☐ Recreational vehicle/4-WD
17. ☐ Photography
18. ☐ CB radio
19. ☐ Home workshop/do-it-yourself
20. ☐ Gardening/plants
21. ☐ Electronics
22. ☐ Automotive work
23. ☐ Sewing/needlework
24. ☐ Crafts
25. ☐ Collectibles/collections
26. ☐ Art & antiques
27. ☐ Stereo music equipment
28. ☐ Foreign travel
29. ☐ Attending cultural/arts events
30. ☐ Gourmet foods/cooking
31. ☐ Health/natural foods
32. ☐ Wines
33. ☐ Fashion clothing
34. ☐ Home furnishings/decorating
35. ☐ Records & tapes
36. ☐ Avid book reading
37. ☐ Science fiction
38. ☐ Astrology/occult
39. ☐ Stock/bond investments
40. ☐ Real estate investments
41. ☐ Self-improvement programs
42. ☐ Community/civic activities

We appreciate your taking the time to complete this card; the information provided will help us serve you better in the future. We participate in a multicompany program whereby you can receive information about new products, developments, trends, etc. related to the interest areas and other information you have indicated above. Please check here if you would prefer not to learn about such products and services. ☐

Other comments and suggestions about our product:

_____

_____

_____

_____

Telephone surveys are more expensive to conduct than mail surveys because researchers must make one-to-one contact, but they can cover as wide a geographic area if a WATS (*Wide Area Telecommunications Service*) line is used. This service is available from the telephone company for a monthly fee.

It is difficult to ask someone to smell a new after-shave lotion over the telephone or to taste a new flavor of Jell-O through the mail. These situations require personal interviews, the most expensive of survey methods. Trained interviewers must contact respondents individually, face to face, and ask them to look, listen, taste, feel, or smell—things that they can only do in person—and give their reaction.

The United States Census was taken by door-to-door personal interviews until 1960, when the Census Bureau switched to mail surveys. By 1980, more than 90 percent of the population was counted that way. The federal government budgeted $2.6 billion—$10.40 per person—for the 1990 census. Postage alone cost approximately $70 million; the bill for printing 81 million fourteen-question forms reached $18 million. (A longer, fifty-nine-question form was sent to one out of every six households.) The Census Bureau hired 480,000 part-time employees to support its regular staff of 9,000 workers and set up 484 local offices outfitted with 6,885 computer terminals, 68,000 cardboard desks, and 75,000 folding chairs. An estimated 38 percent of households that received questionnaires neglected to return them, however, making it necessary to follow up with a personal interview to count them and the 6.5 million households without mail service.

A great deal of market research is conducted through personal interviews.

General Motors reportedly surveys about 100,000 new customers per month in the United States and elsewhere to find out how they feel about having bought a General Motors product and how they were treated by sales and service employees at the GM dealership.[2]

Sampling

It is often impractical, if not impossible, to contact every person or subject in a particular group. Consequently, it becomes necessary to glean data from a **sample,** which is *a cross section of a total group that has the same distribution of characteristics as the larger group (or* universe*) whose characteristics are being explored.* Conclusions about the larger group can be drawn from the data collected about the smaller.

You learned in Chapter 11, for example, that companies test the reliability of various products they buy and make. Depending on the volume involved and the consequences of product failure, however, management may decide to test a sample of products rather than scrutinize every one. If done accurately, this sampling can be as effective as 100 percent inspection, and it is certainly faster and cheaper. It is a particularly valuable method of checking virtually identical products that are mass-produced at rates of hundreds per hour.

Samples fall into two general categories. A firm may take a **random sample,** *one in which every member of the universe has an equal chance of being chosen.* Say the universe chosen was all supermarkets in an area. If a researcher wrote the name of every supermarket on a piece of paper, put the slips of paper in a bowl, and drew out twenty slips, the supermarkets on those twenty slips would be a random sample—the ones not chosen had an equal chance of being chosen.

Researchers generally want to focus their study more closely than that, however, so they use a **stratified random sample,** *one that divides the universe into subcategories, or* strata*, according to one or more characteristics and chooses randomly from within the strata being examined.* A stratified sample may show a market segment that a company wants to learn more about. It may be carefully defined according to such criteria as sex, age, and geographic location. A researcher who needs to understand the habits and preferences of certain drinkers of low-calorie beer, for example, might stratify, or subdivide, the universe of low-calorie beer drinkers to consider females (sex) over twenty-five (age) living in the Northeast (geographic region). Once defined, the stratified sample becomes its own little universe, from which a random sample is then taken.

Management's conclusions and inferences about the universe will be inaccurate if a sample is not representative. Thus, design of the sample itself is one of the most important steps in any data-gathering activity. In one study of American businesses, for example, the researcher drew numerous conclusions about corporate activities and values and the characteristics and work habits of executives. The researcher's approach to gathering data was criticized, how-

sample
A cross section of a total group that has the same distribution of characteristics as the larger group (or *universe*) whose characteristics are being explored.

random sample
One in which every member of the universe has an equal chance of being chosen.

stratified random sample
One that divides the universe into subcategories, or *strata*, according to one or more characteristics and chooses randomly from within the strata being examined.

ever, because he reportedly polled less than 1,100 managers using a sample of just thirteen companies. None of these firms ranked in the top one hundred industrial companies according to annual sales, and only 23 percent of surveyed businesses sold more than $1 billion annually.

Summarizing Data

Once data have been gathered, either by observation or by survey, the next move is to summarize what the data mean. Three summarizing devices can put data into sharp focus: averages, correlations, and index numbers.

AVERAGES Three computations can produce something called an *average*. The usefulness of each computation depends largely on the nature of your data. Each computation begins by looking at an **array** of numbers, which is *a list of numbers ordered from highest to lowest or lowest to highest*.

> **array**
> A list of numbers ordered from highest to lowest or lowest to highest.

The first computation derives an **arithmetic mean**, *an average found by adding the numbers in an array and dividing by the total number of items present.* Say a sales manager is looking at the annual dollar sales that each of her salespeople was responsible for last year: $15,000, $18,000, $23,000, $27,000, $30,000, $48,000, and $56,000. Total sales were $217,000. To find the mean, she simply divides the total by the number of salespeople (seven). The mean is $31,000.

> **arithmetic mean**
> An average found by adding the numbers in an array and dividing by the total number of items present.

An arithmetic mean, however, can be drawn up or down by one or a few extremely high or low numbers in the array. Assume that one salesperson in the example performed superbly and, instead of selling $56,000 worth, sold $91,000 worth. That changes the total to $252,000, making the new mean $36,000—an increase of $5,000. Without seeing the array in question, therefore, it is difficult to judge if an arithmetic mean is reasonably close to the typical figure or not.

> **median**
> The number that appears midway between the highest and the lowest numbers in an array.

The second average avoids this problem; it is not affected by items in the array that are either extremely high or low. The **median** is *the number that appears midway between the highest and the lowest numbers in an array.* In the last example, the array was this:

$15,000
$18,000
$23,000
$27,000
$30,000
$48,000
$91,000

The median is $27,000 because it is midway between the lowest number ($15,000) and the highest ($91,000). The median avoids the pitfall of the mean because it is determined by its position (halfway from either end), regardless of a few extremely high or low numbers. If the number of items in the array is even, add the two in the middle and divide that sum by 2 to compute the median.

The third average, the **mode**, is *the number that appears most often within an array.* Sometimes there is no mode, as in the arrays in the last examples, or there may be multiple modes when several numbers appear an equal number of times. The mode is usually the least useful of the three averages, unless your results can only fall into a few categories or numbers. Imagine, for example, that you are standing in a gambling casino in Atlantic City or Las Vegas (for research purposes only, of course). Observing the roulette wheel for several minutes, you see these numbers come up as winners:

5
17
46
30
11
12
17
38
17

A mean or a median of these results would be meaningless, but the mode (17) indicates that the wheel is out of balance. Your likelihood of winning would be greatest if you bet on that number.

CORRELATION You may be able to identify one or more correlations in your data. A **correlation** is *an if-then connection between two or more elements in a group of data.* This valuable bit of knowledge enables a researcher to forecast the likelihood that the dependent item will change when the controlling item changes. Correlation is at the heart of the law of large numbers you learned about in Chapter 17. If you determine that a correlation exists between two or more variables, you have important predicting power.

In general, a correlation should be logical. It should make sense that a change in item *A* causes a change in item *B*. If you cannot explain the logic behind an apparent correlation, it may be exactly that—an *apparent* one. The elements may only seem related because they changed together and in the same manner each time you happened to record data. Many people are convinced, for example, that there is a correlation between the number of trucks parked outside a restaurant and the quality of the food inside; however, the number of trucks could also be explained by the distance from other restaurants or the fact that the business also sells diesel fuel.

The National Highway Traffic Safety Administration, which studied the repeal of motorcycle helmet laws in four states, found that deaths related to

mode
The number that appears most often within an array.

correlation
An if-then connection between two or more elements in a group of data.

motorcycle accidents rose 23 percent in those states after the laws were taken off the books, while motorcycle registrations increased only 1 percent and total miles traveled by motorcyclists increased very little. In Colorado, where helmet use dropped to 60 percent of motorcyclists after the law was repealed, severe head injuries increased 260 percent and the death rate jumped 57 percent. A correlation seems to exist.

A correlation exists between smoking and lung cancer. Demand for furniture, draperies, and carpeting correlates with the rate of new home construction. Harley-Davidson Motor Company reports a correlation between the unemployment rate of young males and the sale of motorcycles, and retailers have noted a correlation between unemployment and incidents of shoplifting. The volume of help-wanted advertising in major newspapers, which reflects companies' hiring plans, correlates with economic expansion or contraction.

index number
A quantitative device that condenses or summarizes a body of data with several characteristics into a single numerical expression.

INDEX NUMBERS A third summarizing device is the **index number,** *a quantitative device that condenses or summarizes a body of data with several characteristics into a single numerical expression.* The index number allows you to compare a complex situation or condition in the present to an earlier time or to compare several bodies of current data.

Monitoring the rate of inflation, the Bureau of Labor Statistics (BLS) issues two Consumer Price Indexes (CPI-U and CPI-W), which we discussed in Chapter 15. The BLS uses 450 inspectors to gather prices on more than 350 consumer items in a monthly sampling of retail stores and service establishments in eighty-five urban areas nationwide. Using 1982–1984 average prices as the 100 percent or base prices, the bureau then converts current prices into 1982–1984 average dollars. The product of this effort, the CPIs, allows us to see how present consumer prices compare with those of the past and to observe the rate of change. By calculating the CPIs each month, the federal government monitors the inflation rate and can then take appropriate action to try to keep the cost of living under control. A chart showing the behavior of the CPI-U over several years appears in Figure 18.4.

In addition to the Consumer Price Index, the Bureau of Labor Statistics prepares a Producer Price Index (formerly known as the Wholesale Price Index), which expresses the prices wholesalers charge, also expressed in terms of 1982–1984 average dollars. The data for this index are gathered by mail and telephone surveys and a limited number of personal interviews, using a sample of wholesaling firms across the nation. There is a correlation between the behavior of wholesale and consumer prices. When the PPI rises, the CPI usually follows suit within a short time, as manufacturers and retailers pass their increased costs on to consumers.

Presenting Data

Summaries of data should be presented concisely, so users do not have to shuffle, sift, and compare mountains of paperwork to grasp the situation.

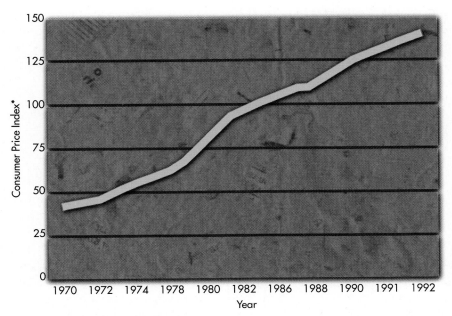

Figure 18.4
The Consumer
Price Index,
1970–1992.

* Consumer Price Index (CPI-U)—urban consumers only.
Source: U.S. Department of Labor, Bureau of Labor Statistics.

There are several popular ways to condense large amounts of data into a compact form, each suitable for particular kinds of data:

- A *pie chart* shows how 100 percent of one unit, such as one dollar, is allocated among various areas. Figure 18.5a shows a pie chart.
- A *horizontal bar chart* (Figure 18.5b) compares different items at the same time.
- A *vertical bar chart* (Figure 18.5c) compares the same item at different times or on different measures.
- A *line graph* indicates the general trend of one or more elements of data over time. Figure 18.4 is a line graph.
- A *statistical map* (Figure 18.5d) compares several geographic regions on the basis of one or more factors.
- A *pictograph* (Figure 18.5e) uses drawings to compare or present data.

Learning About Computers

The most popular and efficient way to process large amounts of data in a management information system is to use a **computer,** *a device that performs large numbers of repetitive calculations automatically and at high speeds, usually with considerable accuracy.* Your electronic calculator can perform many math operations at lightning speeds, but you still have to feed data into it and tell it which operations to perform. Computers, on the other hand, can follow a set of instructions without human intervention until the data processing job is complete. Computers are useful for such jobs as:

computer
A device that per-
forms large numbers
of repetitive calcula-
tions automatically
and at high speeds,
usually with consider-
able accuracy.

Figure 18.5

Some examples
of ways to
display data.

Source: Lawrence J. Gitman
and Carl McDaniel, *The
World of Business* (Cincinnati: South-Western), 1992.

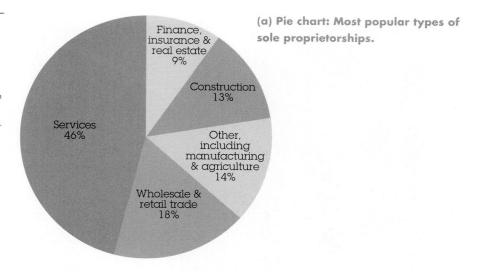

(a) Pie chart: Most popular types of sole proprietorships.

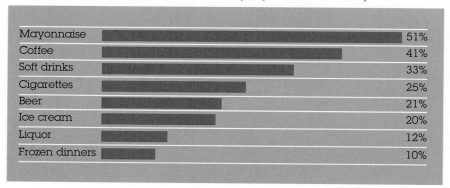

(b) Horizontal bar chart: Where brand loyalty has the most impact.

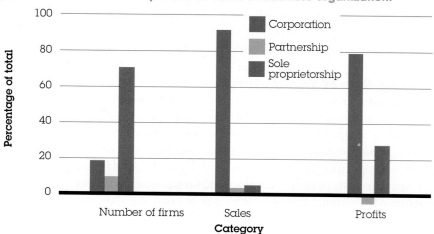

(c) Vertical bar chart: Comparison of forms of business organization.

(d) Statistical map: States with right-to-work laws.

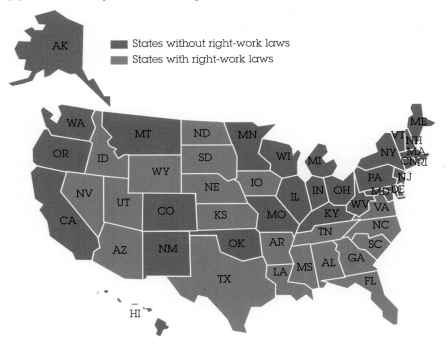

(e) A pictograph: Number of coupons used by households.

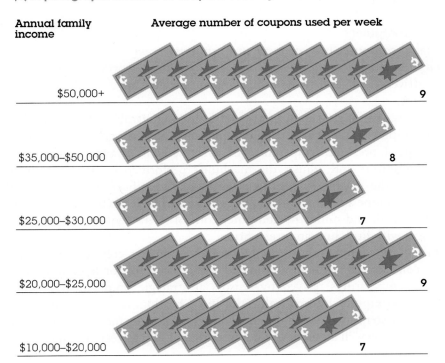

- Adding or subtracting units from inventory and calculating the current balance
- Adding purchases to and deducting payments from a company's trade accounts receivable
- Calculating payroll records, including deductions for such items as taxes, insurance, and union dues

Although computers cannot *think* in the human sense, they can *decide* by remembering, analyzing, and comparing two elements to determine whether one is greater than, less than, or equal to the other.

You do not need a machine to process data. Data can be processed manually, as you probably do when you balance your checkbook every month. Some small businesses employ clerical personnel to maintain payroll and other records with pen and ink. The volume of data that must be handled as an organization grows, however, can make manual processing hopelessly inefficient. The data obtained from the 1880 census (the last one processed without mechanical assistance), for example, took more than seven years to summarize, underscoring the need for more efficient ways to handle the mountain of facts; that census was summarized just two years before the next one began.

Types of Computers

The two main types of computers used in business are analog computers and digital computers.

Analog Computers

analog computer
A computer that takes measurements and processes these data against a model of the problem or situation.

An **analog computer** is *a computer that takes measurements and processes these data against a model of the problem or situation.* A cable-driven speedometer, a spring-driven clock, and cruise control on automobiles are examples of analog computers.

Businesses use analog computers extensively to control complex manufacturing equipment. Once an analog computer has been programmed with the desired speed, pressure, temperature, or other elements of a machine's operation, it monitors and adjusts the machine's performance automatically to ensure that the machine performs according to specifications. In a typical automated engine assembly line, the rough engine block can be bored, honed, drilled, tapped, and milled by computer control to the required engineering tolerances with little human intervention.

One of the more promising applications of analog computers in these energy-conscious times is in automated climate control for large buildings. Reading temperatures relayed by sensors at strategic points throughout a building, a computer automatically adjusts the heating, air conditioning, and ventilation systems. Even with the cheapest system costing more than $20,000, IBM and Honeywell alone have sold more than 2,500 in recent years.

Digital Computers

Unlike an analog computer, which deals with measurements, a **digital computer** is *a computer that processes exact data according to a set of instructions*. It has the potential for 100 percent accuracy, if the following conditions hold:

1. The data are 100 percent accurate.
2. The instructions for processing the data are accurate and complete.
3. The computer's electronic components do not fail (a rare occurrence, but possible).

Digital computers are used more widely because they can do so many repetitive chores in such areas as inventory control and payroll recordkeeping. Their applications are limited only by management's ingenuity.

The first digital computer, built in 1946 at the University of Pennsylvania, was a behemoth called ENIAC (*E*lectronic *N*umerical *I*ntegrator *a*nd *C*alculator). Large enough to fill a two-car garage, this 30-ton monster had 70,000 resistors, 10,000 capacitors, and 6,000 switches. On the average, one of its 18,000 vacuum tubes failed every seven minutes. Compared with today's computers, it was a dinosaur. Transistors developed by Bell Laboratories in the late 1950s made smaller computers possible and reduced computing time to millionths of a second, a remarkable improvement over ENIAC's ponderous speeds. Modern microprocessors (discussed later in this chapter) perform calculations in billionths of a second (*nanoseconds*) and are approaching the trillionth-of-a-second threshold. By comparison, a person performing one calculation per second, twenty-four hours a day for seventy years would do fewer than 2.25 billion. The blinding speed of today's computers is the result of miniaturization. As electronic components are reduced in size, the time they require to perform computing tasks decreases accordingly.

You probably will encounter digital computers in many places, because they are easily applied to so many business operations. The rest of this section focuses on them by describing their components.

HARDWARE When we speak of computer **hardware**, we are referring to *the five tangible parts or units of a digital computer* (Figure 18.6):

- The **input unit**, *the device used to enter data into the computer for processing*
- The **memory unit**, *the computer's electronic warehouse, which stores data as instructed by the program*
- The **arithmetic unit**, *the unit of the computer that performs mathematical computations on data*
- The **control unit**, *the coordinating part of a computer, which directs the other parts to perform their respective functions to complete the data processing job*
- The **output unit**, *the part of a computer that presents the processed data in a form that management can use*

---

digital computer
A computer that processes exact data according to a set of instructions.

hardware
The five tangible parts or units of a digital computer.

input unit
The device used to enter data into the computer for processing.

memory unit
The computer's electronic warehouse, which stores data as instructed by the program.

arithmetic unit
The unit of the computer that performs mathematical computations on data.

control unit
The coordinating part of a computer, which directs the other parts to perform their respective functions to complete the data processing job.

output unit
The part of a computer that presents the processed data in a form that management can use.

Figure 18.6
Parts and terminology of a digital computer system.

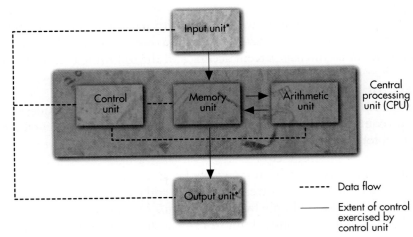

*Peripheral equipment (need not be in the same location as the CPU).

The memory, arithmetic, and control units are located in the computer's central processing unit (CPU). The input and output units, sometimes called *peripheral equipment*, need not be located with the CPU; they often are located elsewhere and connected to the CPU by telephone lines or other electronic means.

Data are usually input to the computer on a keyboard or by an optical scanner that "reads" them directly off a source document. Processed data emerge as information through various output media. Video display terminals (VDTs) display the processed data on cathode ray tubes (CRTs), something like a television screen. Information can also be printed on paper or recorded on disks or tape.

software
All elements of a computerized data processing system other than hardware.

program
A software element stored in the memory unit that feeds step-by-step instructions to the control unit, which then commands one of the other hardware units to perform whatever operation is needed.

SOFTWARE **Software** generally can be defined as *all elements of a computerized data processing system other than hardware.* More specifically, software includes operating manuals and other printed matter, customer training programs, maintenance services, and programming assistance. However, the term is most often used to refer to programs themselves. A **program** is *a software element stored in the memory unit that feeds step-by-step instructions to the control unit, which then commands one of the other hardware units to perform whatever operation is needed.* Each data processing job requires a separate program; without it a computer is useless.

Writing a program is time-consuming and expensive; the programmer must anticipate every conceivable decision or computation that must be made during the job and tell the computer what to do in each case. Some computer manufacturers provide little programming support, which can make a computer seem like a car without a driver: all the hardware is there, but it lacks the key element to set it in motion. Firms that cannot use ready-made programs because their computing requires certain particular operating characteristics or information must either hire software companies or employ their own programmers to write custom programs. For example, Citicorp, which spends an estimated $1.5 billion per year on computer systems, employs 4,000 programmers and managers world-wide to write in-house software for systems that process millions of transactions each day.[3]

COMPUTER LANGUAGES Programs must be written in a language that is compatible with the computer itself and with the type of data it will process, whether commercial or scientific. Such a language is a set of symbols that the machine understands, a communications bridge between person and computer. Some of the most popular computer languages include:

- FORTRAN (short for *formula translation*). This language can be used to write programs for a great many scientific data processing jobs. It is quite simple to learn, but its popularity also stems from the fact that it was developed in 1957 by IBM employees for IBM equipment, some of the most commonly used hardware. It can be used with numerous other brands as well. In addition to its use in scientific applications, FORTRAN is also a popular language for writing many of the animation and video-editing programs that produce computerized special effects in such motion pictures as *Jurassic Park*.[4]
- COBOL (*c*ommon *b*usiness-*o*riented *l*anguage). This language was developed in the late 1950s to meet the needs of the U.S. Department of Defense, the largest computer user in the nation at that time. The department wanted a language that could be used with many different computer brands and models at many locations. COBOL is designed for processing commercial rather than highly scientific data.
- PL/1 (*P*rogramming *L*anguage *O*ne). This language was developed as a bridge between FORTRAN and COBOL, combining the best features of both. An extremely flexible language, it accommodates scientific and commercial data.
- BASIC (*B*eginner's *A*ll-purpose *S*ymbolic *I*nstruction *C*ode). This language is relatively simple to use, making it popular as a fundamental programming language. Its simplicity and technical capabilities make it particularly suitable for sophisticated business data processing applications, including payroll, accounts receivable, and other accounting tasks. It is probably the most popular language today.

Microprocessors

A **microprocessor**, also called a *computer on a chip,* is *a microscopic maze of circuits etched on a layered piece of silicon a fourth of an inch square.* Invented in 1974, these snowflake-sized large-scale integration (LSI) chips contain thousands of electronic components that are almost too small to imagine. Chips used for memory storage in today's desktop computers easily hold more than

microprocessor
A microscopic maze of circuits etched on a layered piece of silicon a fourth of an inch square.

GLOBAL PERSPECTIVE

Computer software has been used to teach languages for many years, but recent improvements in color, sound, and motion have made computerized learning more popular than ever for executives who need a crash course before going abroad.

Current programs can flash pictures on a computer monitor, "speak" the words or phrases students are trying to master, and repeat the student's pronunciation for comparison's sake. Some Apple Macintosh machines are already equipped to run such software, and IBM-compatible PCs can be modified to do so by adding a sound card, microphone, and speakers that cost approximately $300.

The most popular languages taught by computer-assisted learning are Spanish, Japanese, French, and English, but the U.S. Defense Language Institute has applications that are somewhat more exotic. Its staff of 700 instructors use computers to teach every tongue from Arabic to Tagalog.

(For more information on computer language tutors, see William M. Bulkeley, "Language Software Tackles Many Tongues," *The Wall Street Journal,* January 25, 1993, p. B4.)

Computer Language Tutors: Grooming Managers for Jobs Abroad

256,000 (256K) bits of information, the equivalent of a large city's telephone directory, in cells a thirtieth of the width of a human hair. Microprocessors can perform 6 million calculations per minute, compared with ancient ENIAC's 300,000 per minute. This almost incomprehensible speed has decreased the cost of some computer calculations from a dollar to less than a penny in just ten years.

Within the past eight years, refined production methods and better engineering have expanded the reliability and capabilities of microprocessors impressively. These developments, coupled with increased competition among manufacturers, have caused a steady decline in computer prices. In 1983 one researcher summarized the extent and magnitude of these changes in efficiency by claiming that if the trend had occurred in the auto industry, a Rolls-Royce would get 3 million miles to the gallon. At the close of the 1980s, however, microprocessor technology had improved to the point where the same Rolls-Royce would get 30 million miles per gallon.

Manufacturing LSI chips demands fanatical precision and cleanliness. Circuits are usually drawn hundreds of times larger than their actual size and then photographically reduced and transferred to a silicon chip using a complex variation of photoengraving called *photolithography.* Light passing through a glass negative etches each circuit's intricate pattern onto the chip, one at a time, layer on layer, until the complex of circuits is complete. (An even more precise procedure using electron beams has been developed that can inscribe lines visible only with a microscope.) Intel Corporation's model 8088 chip, which contained 30,000 transistors, has been replaced by the model 486 chip, which contains 1.2 million transistors. The 486 may eventually be replaced by the company's superpowerful Pentium chip, which has 3.1 million transistors and can execute more than 100 million instructions per second—a speed equal to that of a mainframe computer. Intel plans to spend $2–$3 billion on research and development and plant modifications to manufacture the Pentium chip, which is exceptionally good at processing video images.[5]

The production environment for these virtually invisible components must be immaculate. A particle of dust will cause a microprocessor circuit to fail and so ruin the entire chip. Assembly takes place in sterile "white rooms," where employees are prohibited from wearing makeup, hair and beards must be covered, and workers dress in sterile garments that reduce the contamination of circuits by debris from street clothing.

Silicon-chip microprocessors are now used in cash registers, microwave ovens, electronic memory typewriters, and traffic-light controls. High tech has even invaded the hand-tool market. Some companies now produce microprocessor-equipped levels that light up and make a sound when level or plumb. Some models can read angles through 360 degrees and give four different digital readouts.

Some cars have microprocessors that report driving miles available at a given speed on the remaining fuel supply and maintain climate control to within 1 degree. Microprocessors regulate a car's ignition, carburation, and pollution control equipment.

Ford Motor Company's Electronics Division has developed an on-board microcomputer that can process more than 1 million control commands per second to regulate such things as fuel metering and spark advance. A microprocessor-based device that is used in many Ford race cars stores data about the car's performance on a particular track. The data can be downloaded (transferred) to a computer for analysis during pit stops. An even more sophisticated telemetry system can beam radio signals from a race car's onboard computer to a computer in the pits, giving the crew instant data on fifteen different engine functions from moment to moment.

The Personal Computer Revolution

Three general categories of computers are in use today. The first group, mainframe computers, may cost several million dollars and form the heart of a large company's management information system. The second group, minicomputers, cost up to $100,000 and are often used by medium-sized companies. The third category, microcomputers, or personal computers (PCs), have prices ranging from several hundred dollars to as much as $30,000. Miniaturization has dramatically decreased the size of PCs in recent years. They're now available in laptop (8 to 15 pounds), notebook (4 to 7 pounds), and hand-

Laptop computers are proving useful for all sorts of businesspeople who need to spend time in the field.

held (8 ounces to 3 pounds) models. United Parcel Service's drivers use hand-held computers to record delivery times and other necessary data right on the customer's doorstep.[6] Microcomputer owners range from computer "hackers" (or hobbyists) to curious consumers, engineers, small-business owners, and authors—including the team that wrote this textbook.

First introduced in 1977, early PCs had only enough memory to store about two pages of data. Today's machines, by comparison, have many times more memory and speed than their pioneer ancestors. Some observers estimate that there is currently one computer terminal for every three white-collar workers.

Powered by microprocessors, PCs have revolutionized the way that millions of us work, play, learn, communicate, make decisions, and otherwise process data. Personal computers are commonplace teaching tools in every course from foreign languages to physics. *Computer literacy*—the ability to use a personal computer in a nontechnical fashion—is a graduation requirement at many educational institutions. Some observers believe that a working knowledge of computers will be essential for future citizens to function effectively in a world that will embrace computers in so many ways.

Beyond educational and game applications, PC owners now put these compact, powerful, and tireless machines to work in areas such as small-business accounting, investment analysis, personal budgeting, complex engineering calculations, and word processing, complete with color graphics. Although declining prices have spurred the growth of PC sales, another significant factor is simplicity. Most machines tend to be *user friendly,* which means that a novice can learn to run them without knowing what really goes on inside and without knowing how to program them. Because technical jargon, baffling codes, and complicated keyboard procedures have been sim-

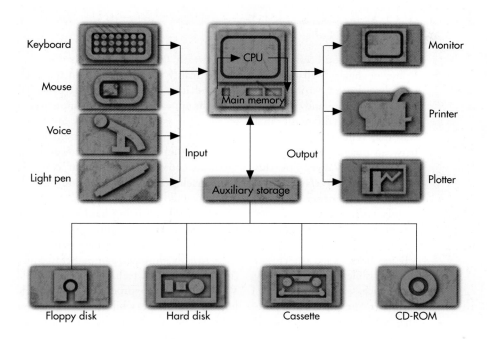

Figure 18.7
Parts of the
personal
computer and
what they do.

Source: Jack B. Rochester and Jon Rochester, *Computers for People: Concepts and Applications*
(Homewood, Ill.: Richard D. Irwin, 1991), p. 40.

plified through user-oriented instruction manuals and programs, microcomputers are less intimidating to the first-time user. In fact, user-friendliness has been taken to the maximum with the development of speech-recognition programs that make computers able to recognize, execute, and answer voice commands. This capability promises to make computers available to everyone, regardless of keyboarding skills.[7] Figure 18.7 presents a user-friendly breakdown of the parts of a personal computer.

Tasks within their capabilities are typically cheaper to perform on microcomputers than on their bigger brothers, mainframe computers, because microcomputers need neither highly trained operators nor special facilities (which may include under-the-floor wiring and additional air conditioning to keep components cool). All reputable microcomputer software companies provide instructional manuals so first-time users can learn to run the programs in a matter of hours with no programming knowledge. One company claimed that graphs of financial forecasts that cost $36 in mainframe computer time were produced for $.06 on a microcomputer.

As you may have guessed, this enormous growth in the PC market has triggered proportional growth in markets for support products and services and markets for items such as PC-related furniture, disk drive head-cleaning kits, dust covers, floppy disk file boxes, printer ribbons, paper, and stands.

MANAGER'S NOTEBOOK

Virtual Reality: With Computers, Seeing Is (Almost) Believing

Strap on a microprocessor-filled helmet or goggles, pull on a high tech glove, hook up to an Amiga 3000 computer, and you can live your personal fantasies in a way that blurs the boundaries between imagination and reality. Look out, Walter Mitty; this head trip is first class all the way. The experience is called *virtual reality,* and it takes anyone on incredible flights of fantasy without leaving the room. VR has been called the closest thing possible to an out-of-body experience.

At the core of VR's phenomenal NASA-based technology is one simple fact: your brain believes what you see. A VR game's Amiga computer (one of the most powerful graphics computers in existence today) processes and sends three-dimensional stereoscopic images to monitors inside each eyepiece, which project the images directly into your eyes—and brain. So, to paraphrase a popular athletic maxim, what your eyes conceive, your brain believes. A VR game becomes especially eerie when novices discover that all their movements (running, hiding, firing an imaginary weapon, etc.) are picked up by a tracking device and fed into the computer, which processes and projects them through the headset's goggles and quadraphonic stereo system into the wearer's eyes and ears. In a virtual reality game, you're no spectator; you're *there,* right in the thick of the action. What goes around comes around, and when it does, you'd better duck! Want to play Arnold Schwartzenneger in *The Terminator?* No problem! Clint Eastwood in a Dirty Harry flick? VR can make your day!

How soon will VR games be available to the general public? Well, don't hold your breath. Right now there's only one virtual reality game machine on the market, and it sells for $55,000. It probably won't be appearing soon at a campus video arcade near you, because there are fewer than 100 of them in the United States. The rental business is brisk, however; an Orlando company that bought two VR game machines leases them to conventions for an average of $10,500 a day.

In addition to being hard to find, VR games are also rather primitive in the graphics department. Players have compared them to early Nintendo games. Before long, though, improved technology will enable VR equipment to produce astonishingly high-quality images while shrinking clumsy helmets and goggles to about the size of a pair of sunglasses.

Virtual reality has many more applications than acting as a travel agent for inventive intellectual illusions, however. In the near future:

- Realtors with VR equipment can take prospects on a tour of every home in their listings—without ever leaving the office.
- Doctors can perform hundreds of procedures using new medical equipment before they ever touch a patient.
- Prospective students can tour the campuses of several colleges from one location.
- Disabled persons can tour the great cities of the world without leaving their homes.

. . . and all because computers make virtual reality the closest thing to being there.

For more on virtual reality see "Virtual Reality Shoots Buyers into Gum Ads," *The Orlando Sentinel,* May 29, 1993, p. D-10; Linda Shrieves, "Eager Players Have Hard Time Finding Games," *The Orlando Sentinel,* April 17, 1993, p. E-1; "The Reality Behind the Technology," *The Orlando Sentinel,* April 17, 1993, P. E-1; and Michael Ryan, "Go Anywhere! But Don't Leave Your Chair," *Parade Magazine,* March 21, 1993, p. 18.

Uses for Computers

Computers can fill several roles within an organization. Their applications are restricted only by management's imagination and willingness to initiate change.

Simulation

Computer simulation, which has grown in step with the complexity of business operations, requires a mathematical model of a particular operation, piece of equipment, or situation. The computer can then reproduce the model electronically. For example, General Motors can duplicate the conditions of an automobile crash test with computer simulation, thus avoiding the cost of demolishing a real automobile. GM also uses simulation to analyze how solar radiation on certain types of glass affects the comfort of the car's interior; identify potential inefficiencies or bottlenecks in manufacturing processes; compare alternative product designs; and predict how productive a manufacturing system may be under various operating conditions.[8]

Computers are also used to train pilots, by controlling the Link flight simulator, to simulate an actual aircraft cockpit under flight conditions. The simulation is so faithful that the Federal Aviation Administration has declared Link trainer experience to be the equivalent of actual flying time. A computer reproduces natural engine and weather sounds, projects pictures of actual airport runways under all weather, light, and speed conditions onto the pilot's windshield, and instructs hydraulic equipment to move the cockpit exactly the way an actual aircraft would respond to the pilot's touch in every situation. Microprocessors perform over 500,000 calculations per second to make the Link accurately reproduce the feeling and reaction of a high-speed aircraft.

Computer simulations are used extensively to train personnel in the armed services.

Applied to the training of railroad engineers, the newest $8 million simulator can faithfully reproduce the feel and behavior of a train pulling various numbers of cars under all track conditions and situations. The line between simulation and reality vanished completely for one trainee who, confronted with an impending collision, leaped from the make-believe cab and fractured his ankle.

Simulation works as well for training boat pilots as it does railroad engineers. The Seamen's Church Institute has an $800,000 computer simulator that can be used to train merchant seamen, members of the Coast Guard, or pleasure-boat owners. The instructor can challenge students by altering simulated wind, weather, or water traffic conditions, causing engine trouble, making navigation systems fail, or calling up a storm front.

The most complex simulations require computers that perform millions of calculations per second to create the hypothetical conditions that engineers or managers want to duplicate. When simulation demands stretch the capabilities of conventional machines, companies must employ so-called supercomputers like those built by Cray Research of Minneapolis, Minnesota. The $11 million Cray X-MP weighs several tons, houses 240,000 silicon chips, and can perform 400 million operations per second (compared with the humble Apple IIe, which has 31 chips and does only half a million operations per second). This and competing machines generate so much heat that they require internal freon gas cooling systems to keep them from self-destructing. Their abilities are as impressive as their statistics, however. Users such as General Motors can simulate solid objects so realistically that they are virtually indistinguishable from actual photographs—including highlights reflected by automobile paint and chrome strips. Automotive engineers can simulate wind tunnel tests on automobiles electronically without leaving their desks, or create and observe the heat and pressures that occur inside the combustion chambers of a running engine—almost as if they were looking through a window. Companies also use supercomputers to determine how forests react to air pollution, research the spread of the AIDS virus, and investigate the cause of irregular heartbeats.

File Maintenance

A more humble but also more universal job that computers do well is maintaining data files on such subjects as accounts receivable and payable, sales, payroll, and inventory. One of the biggest examples of this burdensome task is the Social Security Administration's periodic update of each citizen's personal account during his or her working life. It would require an army of clerks and mountains of handwritten records to do this task manually.

Dun & Bradstreet reportedly makes some 35,000 changes to the company's database of more than 9.7 million businesses each business day. Employees at

D & B's National Business Information Center must perpetually add names of new companies, delete names of those that went out of business, update changes in companies' names, and input new financial information.[9]

Summaries

Computers can be used to summarize data for reports on such subjects as overtime hours worked by a department, actual versus budgeted sales and expenses, and income by division or product. Crompton Company, a textile manufacturer, has a computerized system that summarizes the output of weavers at its Leesburg, Alabama plant. The system has generated lively competition among loom operators, who can check with the computer to compare their output for a given period with that of co-workers.

Automated Control

Another popular computer application, mentioned in our discussion of analog computers, is automated control of machines that perform repetitive operations. Many cities use computers to synchronize traffic lights along busy streets. Electronic sensors suspended above the streets monitor the flow of cars passing underneath at any given time and inform the computer, which automatically adjusts traffic light cycles along the route so traffic can flow freely around the clock. Researchers at Georgia Institute of Technology have adapted computer programs used to train military combat pilots to a traffic control project called Terminus (Traffic Event Response and Management for Intelligent Navigation Utilizing Signals). Tentatively planned for launching in Atlanta in 1996, Terminus would be able not only to change traffic cycles but also perhaps to change the direction of travel on reversible traffic lanes while perpetually monitoring and evaluating the number and flow of vehicles to minimize the effect of traffic jams caused by major sports events or accidents. The potential savings in lost time and wasted fuel are expected to be enormous.[10]

Computerized control systems are essential in complex manufacturing situations, too. Firms such as Honeywell, Leeds & Northrop, and Foxboro produce systems that are tailored to specific customers' needs. For example, A.E. Staley Manufacturing Company controls syrup production with a Foxboro system that feeds operators constant data on liquid flows and other matters connected with making syrup. Employees of Atlantic Richfield Company use Honeywell systems to regulate as many as 3,000 variables during the petroleum-refining process. Exercising perpetual and precise control over operations ensures that the end products of refining conform to quality assurance standards.

Sorting

Many companies use computers to sort data into certain categories. Your college may have computer-sorted lists of students by alphabetical order, zip code, major field of study, and alphabetical order within each zip code and major. Such data can also be sorted according to campus at large state universities with several campuses. Law enforcement agencies have computerized auto registration lists by license number and registered owner, which allow police officers to make a radio check for outstanding warrants and other important information before stopping a vehicle.

Computer Networks

Because state-of-the-art personal computers now boast as much computing power as large mainframes once had, many organizations link them together to form highly flexible networks among hundreds of terminals or locations. Decentralizing from a mainframe computer to a network of PCs can dramatically reduce software and hardware costs. All the PCs in a network may be able to share one copy of an expensive program as well as other costly resources such as plotters, high-capacity storage devices, and laser printers that may cost several thousand dollars.

> ### YOU DECIDE
>
> Some observers speculate that computerized storage and retrieval systems may eventually replace books and other documents. What problems might such a development cause in the future? What benefits might result?

LAN *or* local area network
A computer network that connects the computers and printers at one geographic location.

There are two major types of computer networks. A **LAN *or* local area network** is *a computer network that connects the computers and printers at one geographic location,* such as a large office complex or a manufacturing plant. For example, the Christian Broadcasting Network replaced the Hitachi mainframe computer at its main headquarters in Virginia Beach, Virginia with a LAN of 600 powerful desktop PCs. This move reduced its annual software costs from $450,000 to $80,000 and cut operating staff by 50 percent.[11] The Bank of America uses LANs to link more than 25,000 desktop computers at branches throughout the United States.

Some sources estimate that half of all PCs used by businesses today are part of a LAN.[12] Most LAN computers are physically connected to each other by telephone wiring or coaxial or fiber optic cables, although some transmit data by infrared or radio frequency signals.[13] In addition to sharing expensive software and hardware, LANs also enable employees to access data files that would otherwise be controlled by one person or department.

WAN *or* wide area network
A computer network that connects computers and printers across great distances.

The second type of computer network, a **WAN *or* wide area network,** is *a computer network that connects computers and printers across great distances.* Ignoring physical and geographic boundaries, WANs link computer users at far-flung locations by telephone lines or satellites. For example, a WAN would enable employees at every office of a multinational corporation to communicate and exchange data with colleagues halfway around the world. Figure 18.8 shows an example of a corporate WAN.

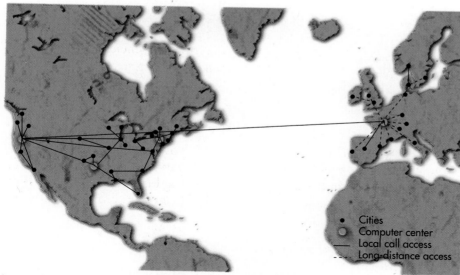

Source: Jack B. Rochester and Jon Rochester, *Computers for People: Concepts and Applications* (Homewood, Ill.: Richard D. Irwin, 1991), p. 363.

Figure 18.8
A corporate WAN.

Service Bureaus, Time Sharing, and Leasing

Not all companies that wish to use a computer must purchase one. Three other ways of gaining access to computers have become popular in recent years, making powerful computing capacity available to smaller firms.

A **service bureau** may be a practical way for small companies to avail themselves of automated data processing. This is *a firm that processes clients' data on its own computer (or one that it has access to) for a fee.* Once the service bureau has written a program to process the customer firm's data, the customer simply delivers its documents to the service bureau, which processes the data as agreed and returns the information or other output. Companies that keep records manually and employ large staffs of clerical personnel may find that a service bureau can do the same work faster and cheaper. A service bureau can write a company's paychecks, maintain its payroll records, update its inventory records, bill its trade credit customers and record payments received from them, write checks to the business's creditors, record and summarize sales and expense data, and produce financial statements that management can use to evaluate the company's financial health. Table 18.1 presents a checklist that small firms can use in deciding whether a service bureau would be worth hiring.

After the customer firm has paid the service bureau's programming fee, or selected a standard program to avoid this initial expense, it is charged for the time the service bureau spends on each data processing job. Firms that hire a service bureau to process their data must comply with the service bureau's schedules, delivering complete and correct data on time. If they fail to do so,

service bureau
A firm that processes clients' data on its own computer (or one that it has access to) for a fee.

HOW MANY OF THESE DO YOU HAVE EACH MONTH?	GIVE YOURSELF THESE POINTS	YOUR POINTS
Number of checks written	10 points for each 100	_____
Number of employees (including salespeople)	1 point per employee	_____
Number of customers' accounts receivable	10 points for each 100	_____
Number of invoices you prepare	10 points for each 100	_____
Number of purchases or purchase orders	10 points for each 100	_____
Number of different items you carry in inventory	10 points for each 1000	_____
Do you have very large items in inventory, such as trucks?	10 points if answer is yes	_____
Do you need help keeping track of your inventory?	10 points if answer is yes	_____
Total points for your business		_____

If you fill in the blanks honestly and your total comes to 100 or more, you would probably benefit from using a service bureau. Even if your total is less than 100, you might be able to benefit. But no simple test such as this can make the decision for you. Look into it carefully. Remember that electronic data processing should reduce costs or increase income enough to repay every dollar you put into it.

Source: John D. Caley, *Computers for Small Business,* Small Business Administration, Small Marketers Aids No. 149, p. 4.

Table 18.1

Checklist to determine whether a business can benefit from using a service bureau.

---

time sharing
A form of computer use in which several firms buy or rent access to a computer that is owned by another firm.

their job may be backed up in the service bureau's work flow, and important information may not reach the customer firm when it is needed.

Large companies with excess computing capacity may also act as service bureaus, a practice that has become a profitable sideline for some. With certain standard programs already written, these firms can process competitors' data for a fee rather than letting their own computer sit idle for a time.

Time sharing is *a form of computer use in which several firms buy or rent access to a computer that is owned by another firm.* Input and output hardware units at the clients' locations are linked by telephone line or other method to the central processing unit on the time-sharing company's premises. Time sharing, like service bureaus, is used commonly for routine data processing operations such as preparing payroll, updating inventory records, and running monthly statements for open-book account holders.

The time-sharing market has been affected by the growth of microcomputers in small-business data processing. Nevertheless, some small-business owners may adopt time sharing before deciding to purchase their own microcomputer, while others have data processing jobs that require greater memory storage than the typical personal computer contains. Software features are another advantage. Most time-sharing companies have programs that process and manipulate data in more ways than the word processing or accounting programs that run on personal computers.

Time sharing offers more flexibility than does a service bureau. Time-sharing customers have direct access to the computer virtually around the clock, and the computer's lightning speed permits it to handle the data processing load of many time-sharing customers simultaneously. Customers usually rent the peripheral equipment and pay a fee for the amount of computer time used during a given period.

Considering the rapid technological advances that are characteristic of the computer industry, many firms choose to lease machines rather than buy them. This lets them avoid being stuck with a new yet technically obsolete computer, because the leasing company often allows its customers to exchange their current computers for newer models after several years. Unlike time sharing and service bureaus, leasing gives a company full control over its own computerized data processing.

Leasing costs vary according to the size and capabilities of the computer. Management should select a machine that can be adapted to changes in the company's data processing requirements and business operations over several years.

SUMMARY

Large companies gather and process internal and external data in a formalized management information system. Such data are classified as primary if they have not been assembled before and secondary if they have. Managers use both types of data when examining a problem or exploring a business opportunity.

Observation is a suitable method of data collection if it is not necessary to ask questions. Firms use mail, telephone, or personal interview surveys, however, when they require opinions, reactions, or other data that cannot be gathered by simple observation.

Averages, correlations, or index numbers may summarize data succinctly and meaningfully. The choice depends on the characteristics of the data. Such visual aids as pie charts, bar charts, statistical maps, and pictographs help to present data in a meaningful, easy-to-understand fashion.

Computers are used to process large quantities of data rapidly because they can perform many repetitive calculations quickly and accurately without human intervention. Analog computers, widely used to control manufacturing equipment, process measurements against a model of the problem or situation. Digital computers, the type that businesses use more often, accommodate such data processing jobs as payroll calculations, inventory recording, and billings for trade accounts receivable. They require programs that feed them step-by-step instructions. Programs must be written in a computer language that is compatible with the computer and the type of data it processes.

Microprocessors, mazes of circuits photographically etched on layers of snowflake-sized silicon chips, have pushed the frontiers of data processing speed far beyond what transistors made possible in the 1950s.

Powered by microprocessors, microcomputers (personal computers) have revolutionized the way that many of us process data. In fact, some educational institutions now require computer literacy as a prerequisite to graduation. Declining prices combined with simplicity of operation have accelerated sales of personal computers to individuals and small businesses. Their popularity naturally has encouraged the growth of support companies that supply floppy disks, software, and accessories.

Businesses have put computers to work in such areas as simulation, file maintenance, information summarizes, control of automated equipment, and information sorting. Larger organizations link personal computers together into networks that join hundreds of terminals or locations world-wide. Many firms gain access to computers through service bureaus, time sharing, and leasing. The choice depends on the company's size, the degree of flexibility it requires in its computerized data processing, and the nature of the data that the computer must process.

FOR REVIEW AND DISCUSSION

1. Describe the differences as you see them between the management information system in a large corporation such as General Foods and the one in a small local company that customizes vans. List three examples of internal and external data that each firm must gather and process.

2. Discuss at least one major personal decision you have made that required you to gather primary data. List one decision you have made using strictly secondary data, and one that involved both.

3. Indicate whether you would use observation or a survey to gather data on each of the following circumstances, and why you would make that choice: traffic flow past a potential retail store location; spendable income of teenage customers in a record and tape shop; the number of drivers who use city streets instead of a new crosstown expressway charging a toll of a quarter per car; peak customer traffic periods at a popular fast-food restaurant; and the most popular breeds of dog and cat purchased from a pet store.

4. Evaluate mail, telephone, and personal interview surveys on each of the following criteria: geographic coverage, cost, need for interviewer training, control over the accuracy of responses, language bias, interviewer bias, and flexibility.

5. Why is a representative sample essential to a reliable observation or survey? Cite one situation in which a

random sample would be desirable and another that would call for a stratified random sample.

6. Calculate the mean, median, and mode of the following array:

12
15
23
34
40
40
56
72
95

7. Under what circumstances can a mean be misleading? What other average may be more representative in such a case, and why? In what situation would a mode be more meaningful than either a mean or a median? Why?

8. Give at least two examples of pieces of information that show a correlation. How do you explain the correlation? Why would knowledge of it be valuable?

9. Under what circumstances would an index number be a useful way to summarize data? Is this a more complex summarizing tool than averages or correlations? Why or why not?

10. List at least one example of data that could be displayed on each of the following visual aids: pie chart, horizontal bar chart, vertical bar chart, line graph, statistical map, and pictograph.

11. What makes a computer different from a hand-held electronic calculator? Why is this difference significant?

12. What is the difference between an analog computer and a digital computer? Which has the greater potential for business use? Why?

13. List and briefly describe the function of each of the five units of a digital computer's hardware.

14. Name some tangible examples of computer software. What is the most important piece of software in actual computer operation? Why?

15. List some potential uses of microprocessors. What products that you own or work with, if any, contain them?

16. What is the difference between mainframe computers, minicomputers, and microcomputers or personal computers?

17. What factors have caused personal computers to become so popular? List at least three ways that personal computers may be used by individuals and by small-business owners.

18. List at least one example of how computers are used in the following: simulation, file maintenance, summaries, automated control, and sorting.

19. Describe the difference between a LAN and a WAN. What benefits do they offer a business and its employees? What impact have they had on the sale and popularity of mainframe computers?

20. What data processing features can service bureaus offer small companies? What restrictions and conditions must customer firms accept in using a service bureau?

21. Contrast time sharing with the use of a service bureau and a microcomputer. Should a company's size be a factor in choosing one over the other? Why or why not?

22. What characteristic of the computer industry can make leasing more attractive than purchasing for a company that needs its own in-house computer? What should management consider when selecting a machine to lease or buy?

APPLICATIONS

Case 18.1: Educating MIS Professionals

While computers have had magical effects on the modern world, the idea of spending one's career as a programmer has had a diminishing appeal. Over the past decade, the number of students interested in a computer career has continually dropped. This lack of interest has left MIS departments searching for new ways to inspire new recruits and to retrain and educate existing personnel.

To provide training for corporate MIS personnel, Washington University formed the Center for the Study of Data Processing (CSDP), a business-education partnership, in 1976.

CSDP has forty member organizations that appreciate its philosophy of lifelong education. Because a university education in computer science does not provide for the continuing changes in technologies and computer applications, membership in an organization such as CSDP provides companies with an efficient way to keep employees current in their spe-cialty. In addition to providing training and recruiting of professionals, CSDP conducts ongoing research on the uses of MIS. By keeping on the leading edge of strategic MIS use, companies can use their investment efficiently rather than buying technology for technology's sake.

Questions

1. Why do you believe employers are having difficulty finding competent MIS employees?

2. How should businesses encourage students to enter computer fields?

3. How does membership in training/research partnerships for MIS departments help a company as a whole?

4. What other efforts should companies make to ensure the long-term efficiency of their MIS services?

For more information, see Jack B. Rochester, "Business and Education: Forming New Partnerships," *IS Analyzer,* April 1989.

Case 18.2: Software Woes

In the last decade, computers have become much less expensive. While many companies still use centralized computers, such as mainframes, to support large groups of employees, most companies have found that it is more efficient to supply their people with desktop personal computers (PCs) instead of, or in addition to, centralized services. These desktop computers, when networked together, provide many of the advantages of centralized computers while allowing people to personalize the way they work.

Unfortunately, all of this power in the hands of workers provides a set of additional headaches for MIS directors. Unlike centralized computers, which run one copy of a program and allow multiple users to have access to it, each personal computer must be supplied with its own copy, and each copy must be paid for. Managing hundreds, even thousands, of copies of a dozen or more programs can be a nightmarish task. Further, because each of these programs is constantly being upgraded by its publisher, an MIS director must evaluate the costs of upgrading against the benefits provided by the new versions.

Luckily, software publishers have found a way to simplify this task. A company can purchase a site license for a software program. A site license is an agreement that allows a company to freely use a piece of software on an agreed upon number of machines for an overall fee. Usually these licenses do not specify an exact number of machines but rather allow usage of a specified maximum number of copies. There are, however, disadvantages to site licensing. The MIS department usually receives only a single set of program disks and manuals. MIS personnel must therefore do most of the program installation and training work rather than delegating it to individual workers.

A final problem facing MIS departments is the random use of software that has not been paid for. Because of the wide compatibility between personal computers, it is easy for users to trade programs or bring them in from home. Since it is illegal for any piece of software to be used on more than one computer unless it is licensed, a company can be sued if employees use unlicensed programs. It is therefore essential that MIS management assures that employees are not working with unlicensed software.

Questions

1. What are the advantages of software site licensing?
2. When should companies buy individual copies of software rather than license it?
3. How can a MIS department ensure that a company's employees are not using unlicensed software?

For more information, see *Communications Week,* July 5, 1993, p. 5.

REFERENCES

1. Jenny McCune, "Vision and Value," *Beyond Computing,* January/February 1993, p. 51.
2. *1992 General Motors Public Interest Report,* p. 8.
3. "When Machines Screw Up," *Forbes,* June 7, 1993, p. 110.
4. Joel Millman, "Artistic Programming," *Forbes,* March 29, 1993, p. 94.
5. "Andy Grove: How Intel Makes Spending Pay Off," *Fortune,* February 22, 1993, p. 56; Belinda Luscombe, "Products That Make Markets," *Fortune,* June 14, 1993, p. 82.
6. Ripley Hotch, "Computers Find Their Voice," *Nation's Business,* May 1992, p. 49.
7. Gene Bylinsky, "At Last! Computers You Can Talk To," *Fortune,* May 3, 1993, p. 88; "More Computers Are Taking Dictation," *The Wall Street Journal,* December 21, 1992, p. B1; "Hands Full? Just Keep Talking and This Computer Types for You," *The Wall Street Journal,* December 21, 1992, p. B1.
8. *1992 General Motors Public Interest Report,* p. 12.
9. *Business Failure Record* (New York: Dun & Bradstreet, 1993), inside front cover.
10. Glenn Ruffenach, "Lab Computes Dead End for Traffic Jams," *The Wall Street Journal,* July 2, 1993, p. B7.
11. Alice LaPlante, "The Big Deal About Thinking Small," *Forbes ASAP,* March 29, 1993, p. 22.
12. Alice LaPlante, "The Big Deal About Thinking Small," p. 22; Tom Inglesby, "Battling Boxes and Technology Knockouts," *Manufacturing Systems,* May 1993, p. 16.
13. John A. Murphy, "Wireless LANs: Networks Unplugged," *Beyond Computing,* May/June 1993, p. 28.

19

ACCOUNTING FOR PROFITS

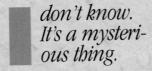

*don't know.
It's a mysteri-
ous thing.*

ROGER SMITH
*Former Chairman, General Motors
(when asked by* Fortune *to explain what
caused GM's financial problems)*

CHAPTER OBJECTIVES

After studying this chapter, you
should be able to:

1. Discuss the history of accounting.
2. Discuss the functions that an accounting system is organized to
   perform.
3. Describe the six groups that need
   accounting data for decision
   making.
4. Contrast the work of a bookkeeper with that of an accountant.
5. Summarize the credentials and
   qualifications that set a CPA apart
   from other accountants.
6. Explain the purpose and significance of the audit function of
   CPAs.
7. Give reasons for choosing a fiscal
   year that is different from the calendar year.
8. Describe an income statement and
   the information this statement
   contains.
9. Describe a balance sheet and the
   information this statement contains.
10. Explain the purpose of a cash
    flow statement.
11. Perform certain financial analyses
    based on the income statement
    and the balance sheet, and one
    that requires data from both
    statements.
12. List several sources of infor-
    mation for comparative financial
    analysis.

UP FRONT

"**P**art accountants, part detectives, we're the fraud busters. We want to wreak vengeance on the forces of evil," says Joseph T. Wells, laughing. "White-collar crime is a problem that has really only begun emerging over the past five to ten years. Yet white-collar crime outstrips street crime, in terms of dollar losses, by a hundred to one," he continues, now totally serious. "Fighting white-collar crime is one of the fastest-growing career fields for the twenty-first century."

Joe Wells ought to know. He heads the Association of Certified Fraud Examiners (ACFE), an Austin, Texas organization of over 10,000 professionals dedicated to training, education, and certification in the field of business fraud detection and deterrence. After graduating from the University of Oklahoma with a bachelor's degree in business administration, Wells went to work as an accountant for Coopers & Lybrand, one of the Big Six U.S. accounting firms. "I learned the nuts and bolts of how businesses operate, and I wouldn't trade that experience for anything. But it was mentally exhausting, and during a casual conversation with a fellow employee I learned that the Federal Bureau of Investigation hired certified public accountants to work on fraud. I kind of kicked back and fantasized about becoming a crime fighter. Then I did it."

Wells worked for the FBI for ten years, often specializing in cases involving political corruption. "I put a lot of politicians in jail for accepting bribes," he recalls. "I was involved in over 200 criminal convictions, including the 1972 Watergate scandal," in which members of President Richard Nixon's reelection committee were arrested in Democratic party headquarters while attempting to tap the telephones. Upon leaving the FBI, Wells opened his own consulting practice in Austin, leading a group of criminologists in business fraud busting.

"The workplace is surprisingly dishonest," says Joe. "Who doesn't know someone who has lied, stolen, or cheated on the job? Our figures say it's about 80 percent. Independent CPAs are supposed to be watchdogs, but they don't have enough clout. The auditing profession is coming under more and more criticism for not uncovering financial fraud and corporate misdeeds at the board room level—for example, the savings and loan debacle of the late 1980s. Some audit firms now have what they call 'SWAT teams' to sniff out fraud, but they may lack the necessary skills. A certified fraud examiner is a specialist who can not only investigate allegations of misdeeds but design prevention programs as well. The ACFE has identified this career specialty and consolidated a set of skills that will become the global authority for white-collar crime into the next century."

No one knows for sure how much white-collar crime costs business, because much of it goes either undetected or unreported. "But if we look at the big picture," says Wells, "and we assume that for every business dollar as much as two cents is lost

JOSEPH T. WELLS

CHAIRMAN, ASSOCIATION OF CERTIFIED FRAUD EXAMINERS

due to corporate wrongdoing or deviant behavior in the workplace, we're talking about 70 percent of pretax profits, or $180 billion a year, lost to white-collar crime." Yet whatever the actual numbers are, white-collar crime puts American business at a disadvantage when competing globally.

Forensic accounting is another name for the work trained CPAs do in white-collar crime, and Joe Wells says it's a very specialized—and valued—profession. "It's a good career path for an accounting major. Most college students don't know that at the federal level alone, there are 100,000 investigation positions to deal with fraud. These jobs require a degree in accounting and, preferably, certification by the ACFE and two years of experience.

"It's an exciting, dynamic, people-oriented field," he continues. "We go beyond the books. It not only produces a good income but provides something intrinsically satisfying, some inner rewards for creating a more honest and ethical workplace."

Joseph Wells's Association of Certified Fraud Examiners is now active not only in the United States but in twenty-three other countries around the world. Wells spends most of his time involved in education, lecturing, researching, and writing about white-collar crime. He has written three books and teaches at several universities. "Over 600 colleges and universities use our ACFE course material, and three major universities have a graduate-level course in fraud examination. It won't be long before all schools of accounting will offer these courses."

Italy, the hub of world trade during the fifteenth century, honed the skills of business to a sharper edge than any other nation at that time. Such business practices as accounting originated and flourished there as a natural result.

A Venetian monk named Luca Paciolo wrote the first book about bookkeeping in 1494, basing it on his work as a tutor to a merchant's son. It clearly reflected the author's background as a mathematician, but this work also outlined most of the bookkeeping practices and procedures that are part of the broader field of accounting today. Paciolo introduced the principles of double-entry bookkeeping, in which each transaction is recorded in at least two accounts. This system, fundamental in today's bookkeeping, provides checks and balances through which bookkeepers may detect and correct errors and verify accuracy. It is sometimes referred to as "the method of Venice." Paciolo's clear, precise, and accurate work became the standard bookkeeping reference of its day, and his ideas have been used throughout the centuries with few changes.[1]

Management has always considered accounting data to be guideposts to profit, but such data took on additional importance when the securities laws that you learned about in Chapter 16 placed larger corporations under federal scrutiny. Today publicly held companies must report their financial standing to federal and state regulatory agencies. This government regulation, combined with the growing sophistication of management techniques and the increasing complexity of corporate operations, has increased the demand for accountants and has accelerated accounting's popularity as a career.

Accounting in Perspective

A firm's **accounting system** is *an organized approach to gathering, recording, analyzing, summarizing, and interpreting financial data to determine a firm's financial condition.* Accounting is a highly specialized part of a company's management information system, which you learned about in Chapter 18. As this definition implies, a company must often employ many people to ensure that its accounting system performs its required functions efficiently and effectively. For a large corporation with many facilities, this usually means making one or more persons responsible for accounting functions at each plant or office. These individuals will gather, record, analyze, summarize, and interpret accounting data for their respective locations and send it to divisional or regional offices, where it may be combined with data from other plants or offices and relayed to headquarters for use by top management.

The tasks performed in an accounting department are summarized in Figure 19.1, which shows the accounting cycle. For small companies, these operations may be performed by hand. As you learned in Chapter 18, for many large corporations the volume of data to be processed is so great that many of these operations must be performed by computer. Either way, the result of the work carried on during the accounting cycle is to produce reports that help management perform the controlling function you learned about in Chapter 6. These reports enable decision makers to compare what is happening to a company financially with what they expected to happen, and to evaluate the causes and effects of the difference.

accounting system
An organized approach to gathering, recording, analyzing, summarizing, and interpreting financial data to determine a firm's financial condition.

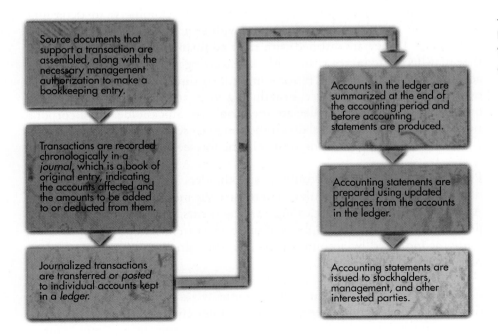

Figure 19.1
The accounting cycle.

Source documents that support a transaction are assembled, along with the necessary management authorization to make a bookkeeping entry.

Transactions are recorded chronologically in a *journal,* which is a book of original entry, indicating the accounts affected and the amounts to be added to or deducted from them.

Journalized transactions are transferred or *posted* to individual accounts kept in a *ledger.*

Accounts in the ledger are summarized at the end of the accounting period and before accounting statements are produced.

Accounting statements are prepared using updated balances from the accounts in the ledger.

Accounting statements are issued to stockholders, management, and other interested parties.

Who Needs Accounting Data?

Accounting data must acknowledge the concerns and needs of many groups and individuals both inside and outside a company. Many decisions that these parties make will be based largely, if not entirely, on information contained in financial reports and other accounting documents.

MANAGEMENT Management at all levels uses accounting data to monitor the success of plans and progress toward objectives. Accounting data reveal, for example, the number of units sold during a given period, revenue received from sales, expenses associated with selling and with the general operation of the business, production costs, inventory levels, and a host of other significant facts. Managers simply could not function without periodic feedback of this sort.

Management is often compelled to take unpleasant but necessary action when accounting data signal declining profits or other dire financial problems. For example, the combined effects of dynamic shifts in foreign competition, marketing practices, management techniques, and manufacturing technology (along with one-time adjustments to comply with changes in accounting procedures for health care benefits) caused General Motors, Sears, Roebuck, and IBM—once considered to be undisputed industry leaders—to report massive financial losses in 1992. These three firms reportedly lost a total of $32.4 billion, more than four times what the 1990–1992 Gulf war cost U.S. taxpayers.[2]

OWNERS Owners use accounting data to evaluate their decision to become owners. By reporting the health of their company, accounting data enable owners (whether sole proprietors, partners, or stockholders) to determine whether the risk they have taken is providing a sufficient return on their investment. If they are satisfied with their company's financial performance, they may decide to increase their risk (by investing more capital or purchasing additional shares of stock). If accounting data disclose financial difficulties, owners may react, for example, by reducing costs, attempting to increase sales, or taking other actions to alleviate the problems. Stockholders of a corporation may decide to sell their shares if the company seems destined to operate at a loss or to earn disappointing profits in the foreseeable future.

POTENTIAL INVESTORS Would-be stockholders also scrutinize accounting data to decide which companies seem to have the most sound financial future. Although a firm may run appealing advertisements, have a highly competitive product, and enjoy high employee morale, its current and potential financial status, as indicated by accounting data, are the ultimate factors on which to base an investment decision.

CREDITORS Potential creditors use a company's accounting data as justification for approving or denying a loan. In Chapter 16, for example, you learned that a commercial bank must have accounting data from an applicant before it can decide whether to grant a line of credit.

UNIONS Unions examine a company's accounting data closely before negotiating a new labor-management agreement. The company's past, present, and anticipated financial condition form the basis for union proposals on wages and fringe benefits.

GOVERNMENT All levels of government require companies to submit accounting data to comply with the law. This applies to the Internal Revenue Service on a federal level and to county and city governments, which base certain taxes on the value of assets reported on a company's books.

Bookkeeping and Accounting

Many persons use the terms *bookkeeping* and *accounting* as synonyms, but business students should realize that they differ significantly. Bookkeeping is a routine clerical function within the field of accounting, and a **bookkeeper** is *a clerical worker who maintains the financial records that an accountant shapes into usable information.* Accounting, on the other hand, has a much broader scope. An **accountant** is *a person who has the education and experience to evaluate the significance of information derived from a company's financial records, interpret its impact on operations, and participate in higher management decisions that are made as a result.*

The CPA

The definition of an accountant states that accountants usually have extensive training. Some people may adopt the label *accountant* with few formal credentials, but a certified public accountant (CPA) is a recognized professional who must receive specific training and meet certain requirements, just like a lawyer or a physician. A CPA achieves this stature by completing required academic study (usually a four-year college degree in accounting) and passing a rigorous three-day examination prepared and administered by the American Institute of Certified Public Accountants (AICPA). After successfully completing this test, which encompasses accounting theory, accounting practice, auditing, and law, the candidate receives a CPA certificate.

Many states require a minimum of two years' work experience in a CPA office, in addition to the certificate, before a person may begin private prac-

bookkeeper
A clerical worker who maintains the financial records that an accountant shapes into usable information.

accountant
A person who has the education and experience to evaluate the significance of information derived from a company's financial records, interpret its impact on operations, and participate in higher management decisions that are made as a result.

Unlike bookkeepers, accountants examine, analyze, and interpret a company's financial records.

tice as a CPA. Beyond this, states have continuing education provisions that require CPAs to attend courses or seminars regularly so they will keep abreast of changes in their profession. State regulations on work experience and continuing education are not uniform, but the state board of accountancy can supply details on becoming a CPA in your state.

The Audit Function

State and federal laws require corporations to have their books audited or examined at least once a year by an independent certified public accounting firm. Before the 1930s audits mostly verified mathematical correctness using a sample of a client's accounts. Then McKesson & Robbins, a major drug company, was found to have reported fictitious inventories in nonexistent warehouses on its financial statements, and auditing took on new significance. A certified public accounting firm's regular audit is not done specifically to detect fraud, however, nor does it vouch for the accuracy of a company's financial reports. It does enable the firm to evaluate the extent to which the client's accountants followed generally accepted accounting practices and to express a professional opinion on how fairly the client's financial statements reflect its financial position. This opinion, which only CPAs are legally qualified to provide, is given considerable weight by lenders, current and potential stockholders, such government regulatory agencies as the Securities and Exchange Commission, labor unions preparing for contract renegotiations, major suppliers, customers, and firms that may wish to acquire the company.

The CPA's responsibility in auditing a client firm acquired greater significance as bankruptcies rose in the late 1970s. Escalating bankruptcies prompted lawsuits by disgruntled creditors and stockholders who claimed that reckless or indifferent auditing by the certified public accounting firm prevented it from uncovering evidence that bankruptcy was imminent. Thus, argued the plaintiffs, the accounting firm should be held liable for their losses. The AICPA's auditing standards now declare that an auditor should be alert to the possibility of fraud and must examine a client's accounting records with "professional skepticism." Although fraud detection remains a lesser audit objective, accountants in the future must be more sensitive to evidence of fraud than ever before.

Despite accountants' increased concern about fraud and their intensified auditing efforts to reveal it, some cases may go undetected for a very long time. For example, Crazy Eddie, Inc., a New Jersey–based discount electronics retailer, closed its doors after almost nineteen years of apparent profitability. The company's stock, which sold for as much as $43.25 per share, plummeted to $0.25 per share as news of the failure spread. An investigation revealed evidence of falsified accounting records, including some $65 million worth of missing inventory. Adjusting the company's books for these missing or "phantom" goods eliminated all the profit that the company, which was the largest

GLOBAL PERSPECTIVE

In Some Countries, Compensation Goes Beyond a Paycheck

Are executives paid about the same amount worldwide? Yes and no. Payroll accounting records would suggest that second-echelon executives in the United States receive considerably more, but numbers don't tell the whole story.

Accounting principles and tradition in countries such as Germany and Japan combine to compensate many managers below the CEO level in ways that don't appear on paychecks. For example, higher-level German and Japanese executives may drive company-owned cars, enjoy company-paid country club memberships, receive pricey gifts from their employers, and even bill some of their vacation expenses to the company. Such practices are all perfectly acceptable and taken for granted.

American executives, on the other hand, may receive more in simple dollars but less in total compensation. *The Wall Street Journal* commissioned the consulting firm of Towers Perrin to do a survey of the value of senior managers' *total* compensation (including benefits and perquisites) that produced the following amounts:

COUNTRY	AVERAGE TOTAL COMPENSATION FOR EXECUTIVES BELOW THE CHIEF EXECUTIVE OFFICER
Italy	$219,573
France	190,354
Japan	185,437
Great Britain	162,190
United States	159,575
Germany	145,627
Canada	132,877

Source: Data from Amanda Bennett, "Managers' Incomes Aren't Worlds Apart," *The Wall Street Journal,* October 12, 1992, p. B1.

---

electronics chain in the Northeast during the 1980s, had reported during its lifetime. President Eddie Antar and his two brothers were accused of receiving $80 million from the sale of overvalued stock. If convicted, Antar may serve up to 100 years in prison and be fined more than $160 million.[3] MiniScribe Corporation, a manufacturer of computer disk drives, came under fire for recording shipments to its own warehouses as sales and falsifying figures in order to give the impression of increasing growth despite an industry decline. In addition, the company was accused of shipping more than twice the number of drives that customer firms had ordered, which inflated its sales by $9 million on one transaction alone. Although overshipped units were returned,

YOU DECIDE

Companies of all sizes now keep their accounting records on computers. What challenges does this practice present for CPAs who must audit a client's computerized records? Do computerized records increase the potential for fraud? Why or why not?

the company had nevertheless recorded the higher figure on its books. Management was also accused of unsuccessfully trying to convince a team of auditors that a load of products on a nonexistent cargo ship should legitimately be considered sold.

The Accountant's Discretion

Although accounting deals with quantifiable data (usually dollars and cents), accountants enjoy some discretion in applying generally accepted accounting principles. Within the limitations of the Internal Revenue Code and the accounting profession's own guidelines, a firm may legitimately apply one set of accounting rules for financial reporting purposes and another set when computing federal and state income taxes. A company may select one of several methods of computing the value of its year-end merchandise inventory and cost of goods sold, for example, or of calculating annual depreciation on assets that it owns. Each approach produces a different net profit figure and alters the other amounts that appear on the business's financial statements.

Generally accepted accounting principles are established, clarified, and modified by the **Financial Accounting Standards Board (FASB),** *a group created in 1973 through the joint efforts of the American Institute of Certified Public Accountants and several other accounting organizations to be the overall rule-making body for the accounting profession.* The FASB's periodic pronouncements significantly affect the decisions of accountants in designing accounting systems, interpreting financial statements, and advising companies on financial matters.

Financial Accounting Standards Board (FASB) A group created in 1973 through the joint efforts of the American Institute of Certified Public Accountants and several other accounting organizations to be the overall rule-making body for the accounting profession.

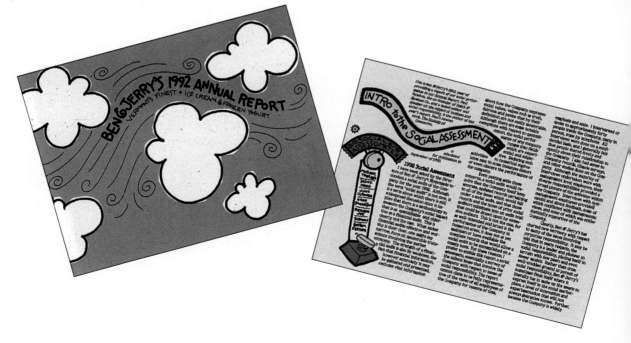

The Fiscal Year

A **fiscal year** (also termed *budget year* or *management year*) is *the twelve-month period that a company adopts for financial accounting purposes.* Although the fiscal year is frequently the same as the calendar year, other beginning and ending months may be chosen to correspond with the business's natural twelve-month cycle if customer behavior (as with tourist attractions) or model or style changes (as with clothes, cars, or lawn and garden equipment) create such a cycle.

By declaring a fiscal year that begins and ends when business activity is slowest, management can summarize financial results when the number of daily accounting transactions to be recorded is lowest. The data processing burden on personnel and equipment thus becomes as light as possible. Automobile dealers may choose a fiscal year of September 1 through August 31, closing the books for financial reporting purposes during the changeover to new models, when sales activity and inventories are minimal. Toy manufacturers and retailers often operate from July 1 to June 30, placing Christmas, their busiest time, at midyear.

Accounting Statements

The document in which businesses summarize their financial condition each year is called an **annual report**. Management needs financial information more often that that, however, to control operations effectively, so certain documents are produced quarterly, too. Stockholders usually receive quarterly or interim financial reports as well as the annual report.

fiscal year
The twelve-month period that a company adopts for financial accounting purposes.

annual report
The document in which businesses summarize their financial condition each year.

Although the main purpose of annual reports is to convey financial information to stockholders, many companies use the opportunity to produce slick or unusual promotional booklets.

This was not always so, however. In the nineteenth century many companies did not issue annual reports. One reason, of course, was that they were not required to do so. The chief reason, though, was that most corporations before the turn of the century were owned by small groups of local stockholders, many of whom were related to or friends of the top managers. Thus it was relatively easy for stockholders of that time to stay abreast of how their company was performing. Only since the early 1900s, when corporate ownership extended to large numbers of widely scattered stockholders, has this formal summary of financial condition become an annual publication, expected by stockholders and required by law.

The terminology and format of the accounting statements found in companies' annual reports vary from one company to another and from industry to industry, so we will depart from our habit of using examples from actual companies and discuss major accounting statements with fictitious firms as examples.

A complete financial report contains three major accounting statements, each with its particular purpose. They are the income statement, the balance sheet, and the cash flow statement.

The Income Statement

The **income statement**, popularly called the *profit and loss,* or *P&L,* statement, is *an accounting statement that summarizes a company's revenues, cost of goods sold (if it sells merchandise), expenses, and net profit or loss over a period of time.* Although an income statement may reflect such time spans as a month or a quarter, the example shown in Figure 19.2 covers one year.

The **revenue** section presents *cash or other items received in exchange for merchandise or services.* In a merchandising firm, customers may return certain items or receive sales allowances for such reasons as buying shopworn goods. As a result, the dollar value of these returns and allowances is subtracted from the gross sales figure to produce net sales for the period.

Under **cost of goods sold**, the statement shows *the cost of obtaining the merchandise that was sold to produce the net sales.* This cost is computed very logically. The merchandise inventory at the beginning of the accounting period is added to net purchases during the period to determine the total value of goods available for sale. The ending inventory is then subtracted from this figure to get the cost of merchandise actually sold during this period.

Gross profit on sales is *the profit that a company made after deducting cost of goods sold from net sales but before subtracting operating expenses.*

The section on **operating expenses** presents *the value of items or services used or consumed in normal company operations during an accounting period.* In our example, expenses are classified into two main categories, *selling* and *general and administrative,* with individual accounts for each. This separation allows management to monitor and control spending in each area and decide whether it should be curtailed or increased. **Net income before taxes** is *the amount a*

income statement
An accounting statement that summarizes a company's revenues, cost of goods sold (if it sells merchandise), expenses, and net profit or loss over a period of time.

revenue
Cash or other items received in exchange for merchandise or services.

cost of goods sold
The cost of obtaining the merchandise that was sold to produce the net sales.

gross profit on sales
The profit that a company made after deducting cost of goods sold from net sales but before subtracting operating expenses.

operating expenses
The value of items or services used or consumed in normal company operations during an accounting period.

net income before taxes
The amount a firm earned from operations before state and federal income taxes are deducted.

PROFIT-MAKING ENTERPRISES, INC.
Income Statement
Year Ended December 31, 199X

Revenue
   Sales $778,918
   Less returns and allowances   14,872
   Net sales $764,046

Cost of goods sold
   Beginning inventory, January 1, 199X $37,258
   Plus net purchases   593,674
   Goods available for sale $630,932
   Less ending inventory, December 31, 199X   41,540
   Cost of goods sold   589,392
Gross profit on sales $174,654

Operating expenses
   Selling expenses
      Sales salaries $56,718
      Advertising expense   7,418
      Sales promotion expense   5,780
      Total selling expenses $69,916
   General and administrative expenses
      Office salaries $14,378
      Administrative salaries   26,612
      Telephone expense   700
      Insurance expense   2,100
      Depreciation expense, building   3,250
      Depreciation expense, furniture
      and fixtures   1,780
      Utilities expense   6,250
      Total general and administrative expenses   55,070
   Total operating expenses $124,986

Net income before taxes $49,668
   Less federal and state income taxes   18,315

Net income $31,353

Figure 19.2
Sample income
statement.

net income
The amount of profit that a company earned during an accounting period.

firm earned from operations before state and federal income taxes are deducted. **Net income** is *the amount of profit that a company earned during an accounting period.* The accountant's discretion that you learned about on page 624 may suggest that companies decrease net income for anticipated as well as documented expenses. This decrease may be justified if a company must make a significant, one-time expenditure in the near future and wants its financial statements to show the effects of that decision.

You can see from studying Figure 19.2 that conditions that affect a company's sales, cost of goods sold, operating expenses, or taxes cannot help but affect its net income somehow. Companies typically announce the impact of these effects as soon as possible to keep stockholders, creditors, and other interested parties fully informed. For example, Anheuser-Busch once announced a decision to decrease prices on its major brands of beer to counter similar action by competitors that would decrease projected profits for two consecutive years. This news caused the company's stock to drop $4.375 per share. Likewise, decreasing automobile sales caused a domino effect that prompted major steel producers to announce an expected 15 percent fewer shipments and an estimated $700 million decline in sales industry-wide.

The Balance Sheet

balance sheet
An accounting statement that shows a firm's status on the last day of an accounting period.

A **balance sheet** is *an accounting statement that shows a firm's status on the last day of an accounting period.* If you compare a company's accounting period to a reel of movie film, with each frame representing a day's operations, the balance sheet is the last frame on the reel. The firm is frozen on that day for reporting purposes.

The balance sheet shows subtotals and totals in three general areas: assets, liabilities, and owners' equity. These relate to one another in the basic accounting equation:

$$\text{Assets} = \text{liabilities} + \text{owners' equity}$$

(Depending on the firm's form of organization, this third element also may be called *capital, net worth, proprietorship, partners' equity,* or *stockholders' equity.* However it is referred to, it reports the owners' claims against the business on the day the balance sheet was prepared.)

The balance sheet presents a detailed view of this equation. Like the income statement, it has various categories of accounts. Figure 19.3 shows an example of a balance sheet for our hypothetical corporation. Familiarize yourself with the important terms that it shows.

assets
Things of value that businesses, government, or individuals own.

current assets
Cash, items that will become cash within one year, and prepaid expenses.

Assets may be defined as *things of value that businesses, government, or individuals own.* Here we focus specifically on things of value that a company owns. They can be classified in several ways. The sample statement presents two common categories of assets. **Current assets** consist of *cash, items that will become cash within one year* (such as inventory and trade accounts receivable),

PROFIT-MAKING ENTERPRISES, INC.
Balance Sheet
December 31, 199X

Figure 19.3
Sample balance sheet.

Assets
Current assets
Cash $17,280
Accounts receivable   84,280
Inventory   41,540
Prepaid expenses   12,368
Total current assets $155,468

Plant and equipment
Building $43,980
Less accumulated depreciation 10,550 $33,430

Furniture and fixtures $19,200
Less accumulated depreciation 5,250   13,950

Land   14,000
Total plant and equipment assets   61,380
Total assets $216,848

Liabilities
Current liabilities
Notes payable $10,000
Trade accounts payable   41,288
Salaries payable   400
Taxes payable   14,000
Total current liabilities $65,688

Long-term liabilities
Mortgage payable $8,000
Bonds payable   3,280
Total long-term liabilities   11,280
Total liabilities $76,968

Stockholders' equity
Common stock, 1,000 shares at $100
par value $100,000
Retained earnings   39,880
Total stockholders' equity   139,880
Total liabilities and stockholders' equity $216,848

Among a company's most important assets are its plant and equipment.

plant and equipment
Sometimes called *fixed assets*, an asset category that includes land and expensive manufactured items that a company will use in its operations for several years.

depreciation
An accounting technique by which management gradually recovers the cost of expensive fixed assets over the course of their expected lives.

liabilities
Debts or creditors' claims that a firm owes on the day the balance sheet is prepared.

current liabilities
Debts that must be paid within one year.

long-term liabilities
Debts that are due in more than one year.

stockholders' equity
The balance sheet section that shows owners' claims against a corporation.

and prepaid expenses (such as insurance premiums, rent, and office supplies). **Plant and equipment,** *sometimes called* fixed assets, is *an asset category that includes land and expensive manufactured items that a company will use in its operations for several years.* The sample balance sheet in Figure 19.3 shows a building and some furniture and fixtures included in this classification.

All plant and equipment assets except land are depreciated. **Depreciation** is *an accounting technique by which management gradually recovers the cost of expensive fixed assets over the course of their expected lives.* In doing so, it acknowledges their decline in value as a result of obsolescence, use, and age. Part of the cost is recorded as an expense on the income statement each year, and that amount is added to a running total in an account called *accumulated depreciation,* which is deducted from the asset's original cost on the balance sheet (as you can see in Figure 19.3). The difference between the original cost and accumulated depreciation is the asset's *book value,* its value to the firm on the day the balance sheet is prepared. A fixed asset's annual depreciation does not necessarily reflect changes in its market value, so book value may not represent what the company would receive if it sold the asset on the balance sheet date.

Liabilities are *debts or creditors' claims that a firm owes on the day the balance sheet is prepared.* Figure 19.3 shows two categories of liabilities. **Current liabilities** are *debts that must be paid within one year.* **Long-term liabilities** are *debts that are due in more than one year.* In the sample, the company has an outstanding mortgage balance of $8,000 and corporate bonds of $3,280, both of which are payable in some future year. These are long-term liabilities.

The balance sheet section that shows owners' claims against a corporation is called **stockholders' equity.** Listed in that section will be the total capital that the firm obtained when it sold shares of common stock—in the sample in Figure 19.3, $100,000 from 1,000 shares at $100 par value. In addition, the retained earnings balance is the cumulative total profit reinvested in the firm as of the balance sheet date. This amount also is considered part of the owners' equity, giving the stockholders in the sample a claim of $139,880 against their company.

Note that the accounting equation balances in Figure 19.3: assets of $216,848 equal combined liabilities and stockholders' equity of $216,848. The accounting equation must always balance. Assets are things of value the business owns, but those things must come from somewhere; they must be supplied by someone in the company or someone outside it. The proportion of assets that comes from inside or outside the company is shown in the other parts of the accounting equation (and of the balance sheet): owners' equity and liabilities. The equation must balance, that is, assets must always equal the total of liabilities and equity, because it must be clear where the total value of assets came from.

YOU DECIDE

Assume that an accountant has misclassified several long-term liabilities as current liabilities on a company's balance sheet. How would such an error affect the company's ability to obtain a line of credit (discussed in Chapter 16) from a commercial bank?

The Cash Flow Statement

A **cash flow statement** is *a document that shows where a company's cash came from during an accounting period and how it was used in operations.* This statement can be especially important in helping management account for the change in a company's net working capital throughout an accounting period. *Working capital* is determined by subtracting the firm's current liabilities from its current assets.

Fluctuations in a company's net working capital and its annual change as a result of operations are important things to know in planning day-to-day operations. Working capital must be adequate to purchase inventory and other needed current assets and to pay debts as they come due. Insufficient working capital can seriously handicap a firm, which may find itself unable to pay its debts as they mature, to take advantage of cash discounts from suppliers, or to purchase enough inventory to receive quantity discounts. Management should monitor changes in working capital from one accounting period to the next to ascertain that it remains high enough to permit sound, economical operations. A sample cash flow statement appears in Figure 19.4.

cash flow statement
A document that shows where a company's cash came from during an accounting period and how it was used in operations.

Financial Analysis

The income statement and balance sheet present summarized totals and account balances, but many valuable facts are obscured by the format of the statements themselves. It is difficult to draw conclusions about certain financial relationships from a cursory reading of these statements. Financial analysis becomes necessary.

Figure 19.4
Sample cash flow statement.

PROFIT-MAKING ENTERPRISES, INC.
Cash Flow Statement
Year Ended December 31, 199X

Cash provided by operations		
Net income	$31,353	
Adjustments to reconcile net income to net cash provided by operations:		
Depreciation, furniture and fixtures	1,780	
Depreciation, building*	3,250	
Net cash provided by operations		$36,383
Cash provided by and used in investing activities		
Purchase of store fixtures	(5,110)	
Addition to building	(18,710)	
Proceeds from sale of property and equipment	1,215	
Net cash used in investing activities		(22,605)
Cash provided by and used in financing activities		
Proceeds from sale of common stock	3,000	
Cash dividends paid	(580)	
Payments on mortgage	(6,000)	
Net cash provided by financing activities		(3,580)
Increase in cash and equivalents		10,198
Cash and cash equivalents at beginning of year		7,082
Cash and cash equivalents at end of year		$17,280

*Depreciation does not cause a physical flow of funds into the firm, but it is an unusual expense in that it does not require an outflow of funds. Proper accounting procedures require that depreciation be added to net income on this statement as shown above.

financial analysis
The use of mathematics to bring important facts and relationships on accounting statements into sharp focus.

ratio
A mathematical statement of the relationship or proportion between two elements, derived by dividing one into the other.

Financial analysis is *the use of mathematics to bring important facts and relationships on accounting statements into sharp focus,* enabling management and other interested parties to determine the firm's financial health with greater precision and clarity. Most such computations are designed to produce a **ratio,** which is *a mathematical statement of the relationship or proportion between two elements, derived by dividing one into the other.* Such ratios and other results are used in making decisions that ultimately affect every segment of the company.

Income Statement Analysis

The following calculations will improve your understanding of the income statement in Figure 19.2. Ratios derived from the income statement frequently use sales as a 100 percent, or base, figure and compare all other elements on the statement to that item.

RATIO OF NET INCOME TO NET SALES

$$\frac{\text{Net income}}{\text{Net sales}} = \frac{31,353}{764,046} = 0.04{:}1 \text{ or } \$0.04{:}\$1$$

The **ratio of net income to net sales** is *a statement of the net income a company earned from each dollar of sales during an accounting period.* Like the results of most financial analysis calculations, it becomes meaningful when compared with the industry standard for a firm of this size. It is a measure of a company's efficiency, answering the question, "How much of each sales dollar ended up as profit?"

A low ratio like the one in the previous calculation is not always a negative sign. Companies that sell a high volume of merchandise at a low profit per unit can survive handsomely, given the proper location, purchasing decisions, and management and marketing techniques.

> **ratio of net income to net sales**
> A statement of the net income a company earned from each dollar of sales during an accounting period.

RATIO OF NET SALES TO NET INCOME

$$\frac{\text{Net sales}}{\text{Net income}} = \frac{764,046}{31,353} = 24.37{:}1 \text{ or } \$24.37{:}\$1$$

The **ratio of net sales to net income**, the inverse of the previous ratio, is *a statement of the amount of sales a firm had to make to earn a dollar of net income.* If competitors are selling less to earn a dollar of net income (or earning more on each dollar of sales), management should reevaluate the firm's purchasing habits, sales efforts, marketing techniques, and expense controls to discover the reasons.

> **ratio of net sales to net income**
> A statement of the amount of sales a firm had to make to earn a dollar of net income.

INVENTORY TURNOVER

$$\frac{\text{Cost of goods}}{\text{Average inventory [(beginning inventory + ending inventory)} \div 2]}$$

$$= \frac{589,392}{(37,258 + 41,540) \div 2}$$

$$= \frac{589,392}{39,399} = 14.96 \text{ times}$$

inventory turnover
A calculation of the number of times a firm sold and re-placed (or turned over) its average stock of goods dur-ing an accounting period.

Inventory turnover is *a calculation of the number of times a firm sold and replaced (or turned over) its average stock of goods during an accounting period.* If the firm's turnover rate is higher or lower than that of competitors, there may be cause for celebration or criticism—it depends on the reason for the difference. Higher turnover may be traced to superior location or marketing efforts; it could also be caused by purchasing inventory hand-to-mouth, which makes the firm lose quantity discounts, process more paperwork than is necessary, and pay progressively higher prices during inflationary times. Inventory turnover is affected by the nature of the merchandise itself as well as by management's purchasing and marketing decisions. Stores that sell jewelry, clocks, or pianos, for example, almost always have lower turnover than stores that sell health food, shoes, or tires and mufflers.

Balance Sheet Analysis

The following calculations are used to analyze balance sheets such as the sample you studied in Figure 19.3.

CURRENT RATIO

$$\frac{\text{Current assets}}{\text{Current liabilities}} = \frac{155{,}468}{65{,}688} = 2.37{:}1 = \$2.37{:}\$1$$

current ratio
An expression of a firm's ability to pay its current debts from its current assets.

The **current ratio** is a measure of safety, *an expression of a firm's ability to pay its current debts from its current assets.* A relatively low current ratio can signal trouble: the company could have difficulty paying current liabilities as they mature. On the other hand, a high current ratio may indicate that a company is keeping unnecessarily large balances of cash, inventory, or other current asset items on hand. If so, management will be criticized for not allocating funds to such long-term uses as buying more efficient equipment or renovating outdated manufacturing facilities. If a large inventory is mainly responsible for a high current ratio, the goods may fall out of style before they are sold. An overstock of seasonal items may have to be marked down drastically to attract buyers before the season ends, or the products will have to be stored until the season starts next year. Many authorities believe that 2:1 is a reasonably safe current ratio.

ACID TEST RATIO

$$\frac{\text{Cash + accounts receivable + marketable securities}}{\text{Current liabilities}}$$

$$\frac{17{,}280 + 84{,}280}{65{,}688} = \frac{101{,}560}{65{,}688} = 1.55{:}1 = \$1.55{:}\$1$$

The **acid test ratio,** more realistic than the current ratio, is *a measure of a firm's ability to pay current debts from its most liquid, or quick, assets—cash and near-cash items.* Such nonliquid items as inventory and prepaid expenses are ignored. Profit-Making Enterprises has $1.55 in quick assets standing behind each $1.00 of current debts on the balance sheet date. It is not unusual for this ratio to approach 1:1, but if it is 1:1 or less, management must quickly determine when the current liabilities mature and confirm that enough cash will be received from sales and accounts receivable collections to pay the debts as they fall due. An extremely low acid test ratio may prompt a firm to borrow against its line of credit at a commercial bank or find some other way to raise short-term cash so it can pay its current debts on time.

acid test ratio
A measure of a firm's ability to pay current debts from its most liquid, or quick, assets—cash and near-cash items.

RATIO OF DEBT TO STOCKHOLDERS' EQUITY

$$\frac{\text{Liabilities}}{\text{Stockholders' equity}} = \frac{76{,}968}{139{,}880} = 0.55{:}1 = \$0.55{:}\$1$$

The **ratio of debt to stockholders' equity** is *the value of claims that creditors have against a firm's assets for each dollar of owners' claims.* This ratio expresses the relative control or claim that different parties have against the business. Highly leveraged companies have a high ratio of debt to stockholders' equity because they have raised so much long-term capital through the sale of bonds. An extremely high ratio of debt to stockholders' equity suggests that the company may have difficulty paying short-term debts, paying interest on bonds, and making contributions to its bond sinking fund, which you learned about in Chapter 16. In our example, however, stockholders' equity is roughly twice creditors' claims.

ratio of debt to stockholders' equity
The value of claims that creditors have against a firm's assets for each dollar of owners' claims.

BOOK VALUE OF COMMON STOCK

$$\frac{\text{Stockholders' equity}}{\text{Common stock shares outstanding}} = \frac{139{,}880}{1{,}000} = \$139.88 \text{ per share}$$

The **book value of common stock** is *the amount per share that stockholders would theoretically receive if a company's assets were sold on the balance sheet date.* During a bear market, when uncertain investors drive a stock's market price down, the book value of some stocks has exceeded the market value. In other words, investors were not willing to pay for shares on the open market the amount that present stockholders would have received (according to balance sheet figures) had the firm's assets been sold. Many investors consider a company's stock a good buy if its book value is greater than its current market value.

book value of common stock
The amount per share that stockholders would theoretically receive if a company's assets were sold on the balance sheet date.

Combined Statement Analysis

Certain analytical computations relate an item on the income statement to another on the balance sheet. One is usually considered most significant: the rate of return on stockholders' equity.

$$\frac{\text{Net income}}{\text{Stockholders' equity}} = \frac{31,353}{139,880} = 0.224 = 22.4\%$$

rate of return on stockholders' equity
The percentage return that the company earned on the owners' investment during the previous accounting period.

The **rate of return on stockholders' equity** is *the percentage return that the company earned on the owners' investment during the previous accounting period.* It is a measure of management's ability to use stockholders' investment effectively. A return that is consistently low suggests that it might be wise for the company's owners to invest their capital in some other venture or to replace certain top managers in the company with ones who would improve leadership and performance. In the sample, the firm earned $0.224 cents on each $1 of owners' investment—a return of 22.4 percent.

It would be convenient if just one calculation revealed a firm's financial condition, but in this case, what would be convenient is not possible. Financial analysis provides ways of looking at a firm from many angles; the typical company will look strong by some measures and weak by others. If financial analysis indicates a current or potential problem, management must act rather than simply react to the situation. This means meeting with various departments, analyzing the problem, and taking action to restore the company to firmer financial ground as soon as possible.

Sources of Comparative Data

Virtually all of the calculations just discussed are most meaningful when compared with a standard in the company's industry or general line of business. In fact, some calculations are practically useless unless the analyst has a yardstick, a typical figure that expresses the condition of competing firms. Knowing how a company stands in relation to competitors can be at least as important as knowing how it stands alone.

Business owners can get comparative data from several sources. Perhaps the best source is a trade association. Such organizations act as clearinghouses of financial information for the businesses they represent. They produce statistics on typical ratios, turnover figures, and other data by sampling member firms of various sizes throughout the country. Figure 19.5 shows a trade association's summary of operating ratios for over 350 profitable hardware stores, using net sales as a base.

Dun & Bradstreet, another popular source, publishes an annual report of key business ratios for 125 lines of business in retailing, wholesaling, manufacturing, and construction. Robert Morris Associates, a national association of bank loan and credit officers, reports ratios for more than 350 kinds of companies. The Accounting Corporation of America and NCR Corporation also publish some industry ratios. Finally, a CPA can recommend additional sources of comparative data to supplement those mentioned here.

Net sales	100.00*
Cost of goods sold	64.92
Margin (gross profit on sales)	35.08
Expenses	
Payroll and other employee expenses	16.23
Occupancy expense	3.23
Office supplies and postage	0.40
Advertising	1.49
Donations	0.08
Telephone	0.24
Bad debts	0.30
Delivery	0.47
Insurance	0.66
Taxes (other than real estate and payroll)	0.46
Interest	0.61
Depreciation (other than real estate)	0.57
Supplies	0.37
Legal and accounting expenses	0.31
Dues and subscriptions	0.08
Travel, buying, and entertainment	0.19
Unclassified expenses	0.64
Total operating expense	26.33
Net operating profit	8.75
Other income	1.65
Net profit before income taxes	10.40

*Numbers expressed as a percentage of sales.
Source: Courtesy National Retail Hardware Association.

Figure 19.5
Sample operating ratios for hardware stores.

MANAGER'S NOTEBOOK

FAS 106 Pinches Bottom Line

The Financial Accounting Standards Board has issued dozens of guidelines that govern accounting procedures, but none have had the impact of the rule known as FAS 106.

Companies used to account for the cost of retirees' health care benefits on a year-to-year basis, which obscured the *total* amount they should eventually expect to pay. For companies like General Motors, Ford Motor Company, and Chrysler Corporation, which have tens of thousands of retirees, this total was staggering. Moreover, escalating health care costs caused the amount to grow by 15 percent per year.

The passage of FAS 106 sent financial executives and retirees alike running for the aspirin. FAS 106 declared that companies must account for the total projected cost of health care benefits by either (1) making a one-time charge against profits (which would produce a multibillion-dollar "paper" loss in one fiscal year), or (2) spreading the projected cost over twenty years. FASB justified this earth-shaking rule on the grounds that companies that would pay out billions in health care benefits in the future should acknowledge that liability in advance, which is basically how pension benefits have been accounted for. If this were not done, financial statements could be misleading.

Many corporate giants bit the bullet and recorded their expected future cost of health care benefits in one year. The result? General Motors took a massive one-time after-tax charge against profits of $22.2 billion in 1992, and Chrysler Corporation (which has three times as many retirees as active workers) took a hit of $4.7 billion. Ford Motor Company's $7.9 billion charge caused the company to report a loss of $7.4 billion for 1992.

Retirees and current employees were naturally drawn into the maelstrom of FAS 106. Companies such as Navistar International Corp, which once paid the medical bills of some 40,000 retirees, have either reduced nonunion retirees' health care benefits or made them pay part of the cost. McDonnell Douglas Corp. opted to give white-collar retirees a lump sum of $18,000 instead of providing health care benefits, which reportedly cut the company's future liability for health care benefits from $1.4 billion to $700 million.

But what about current employees? Observers believe that FAS 106 will cause almost two-thirds of U.S. companies to reduce or eliminate health care benefits for retirees, especially those not covered by labor-management contracts. When today's employees reach retirement, FAS 106 will probably have placed the responsibility for health care costs squarely on their shoulders.

(For more on the impact of FAS 106 see Larry Light (with Kelley Holland and Kevin Kelly), "Honest Balance Sheets, Broken Promises," *Business Week,* November 23, 1992, p. 106, and "GM Charge Reflects Crisis in U.S. Health Care," *The Orlando Sentinel,* February 3, 1993, p. D-1.)

SUMMARY

Management has a fundamental interest in accounting data because such data provide guideposts to profit. Federal securities laws have made accounting even more important as corporations have become legally obligated to report their financial status. Six key groups need accounting data: management, owners, potential investors, creditors, unions, and government.

A firm gathers, records, analyzes, summarizes, and interprets financial data in an organized way through its accounting system. Accounting has a much broader scope than the routine clerical function of bookkeeping: the accountant evaluates financial information, interprets its impact on operations, and participates in higher management decisions that are based on that information.

Certified public accountants (CPAs) are recognized professionals in accounting, having passed a national certifying examination and met state requirements. Only CPAs are legally qualified to evaluate a company's adherence to generally accepted accounting principles and to state how fairly the firm's financial statements reflect its actual financial position. Although accounting deals primarily with quantifiable data, accountants enjoy some discretion in applying generally accepted accounting principles. The Financial Accounting Standards Board (FASB) is the professional rule-making body that approves the application of certain account-

ing principles, and its pronouncements have a considerable effect on the way some transactions will be recorded and referred to in a firm's accounting system.

Companies summarize their financial condition each year in a document called an annual report. This report contains an income statement, a balance sheet, and a cash flow statement. By summarizing a company's revenues, cost of goods sold, and expenses during the accounting period, the income statement reveals the firm's net income or loss for that time. The balance sheet shows the firm's status on the last day of the accounting period by presenting the balances of assets, liabilities, and owners' equity. The cash flow statement accounts for increases and decreases in the company's net working capital throughout the accounting period.

It is difficult to evaluate a company's financial condition simply by reading its accounting statements. To get a true picture one must learn the mathematics of financial analysis. Financial analysis calculations clarify the relationships (usually ratios) between important items in a firm's accounting statements and thus bring a firm's financial health into sharper focus. Current industry-wide data, available from a trade association or other reliable source, can enable a company to determine its relative financial standing in its line of business.

KEY TERMS

accountant p. 621
accounting system p. 619
acid test ratio p. 635
annual report p. 625
assets p. 628
balance sheet p. 628
bookkeeper p. 621
book value of common stock p. 635
cash flow statement p. 631
cost of goods sold p. 626
current assets p. 628
current liabilities p. 630
current ratio p. 634
depreciation p. 630
Financial Accounting Standards
    Board (FASB) p. 624
financial analysis p. 632

fiscal year p. 625
gross profit on sales p. 626
income statement p. 626
inventory turnover p. 634
liabilities p. 630
long-term liabilities p. 630
net income p. 628
net income before taxes p. 626
operating expenses p. 626
plant and equipment p. 630
rate of return on stockholders' equity p. 636
ratio p. 632
ratio of debt to stockholders' equity p. 635
ratio of net income to net sales p. 633
ratio of net sales to net income p. 633
revenue p. 626
stockholders' equity p. 630

FOR REVIEW AND DISCUSSION

1. How does a firm's accounting system relate to its management information system? How does it relate to management's controlling function?

2. Relate each of the following steps to the function of an accounting system after placing them in the correct sequence: summarizing, interpreting, recording, gathering, analyzing.

3. State at least one way in which each of the following groups uses accounting data: management, owners, potential investors, creditors, unions, and government.

4. Distinguish between a bookkeeper and an accountant. Which occupation requires greater preparation? Why?

5. What must one do to become a certified public accountant? How do individual states regulate the practice of CPAs?

6. State the purposes of a certified public accounting firm's regular audit. Why would it be unrealistic to require a CPA to vouch for the accuracy of a firm's financial reports after this audit?

7. What individuals and groups are interested in a CPA's opinion of a firm's financial statements? Give a reason for the interest of each.

8. Explain the following statement: "Accountants are allowed some discretion in applying many generally accepted accounting principles."

9. How does the Financial Accounting Standards Board influence the practice of accounting?

10. State at least one situation or condition that might induce a firm to use a fiscal year that does not coincide with the calendar. Give an example of a business that could justify this choice.

11. What time is usually covered in an income statement? List and discuss the types of information that this statement provides.

12. What time does the balance sheet cover? How does it serve as a detailed expression of the accounting equation (assets = liabilities + owners' equity)?

13. What kinds of assets are depreciated? Why does this treatment make sense?

14. Describe the role of a cash flow statement. What general categories of information appear on it?

15. Evaluate the following statement: "If you can't perform financial analysis and interpret the results, you won't know much about a company's financial condition."

16. The following calculations are used to analyze an income statement. Explain what information must be assembled to calculate them, and what they reveal: ratio of net income to net sales, ratio of net sales to net income, and inventory turnover.

17. The following calculations are used to analyze a balance sheet. Explain what information must be assembled to calculate them, and what they reveal: current ratio, acid test ratio, ratio of debt to stockholders' equity, and book value of common stock.

18. What does the rate of return on stockholders' equity reveal? How is it computed?

19. Why is accurate comparative information essential for accurate and complete financial analysis?

20. Where can a business owner find information for comparative financial analysis? Which source is the most valuable? Why?

APPLICATIONS

Case 19.1: Accounting for Stock Options

Good accounting can mean the difference between a successful business and an unsuccessful one. By keeping track of assets, expenses, debts, and sales, a business finds out where it is succeeding and where it is failing, and, most important, whether it is making a profit. Other than the amount of time spent with the calculator, it sure sounds simple. Unfortunately, as a current issue facing the Financial Accounting Standards Board (FASB) shows, it isn't that easy.

Stock options—rights to purchase shares of a company's stock at a certain price—are a lucrative

form of compensation that many corporations offer their employees and executives. Employees who exercise these options make money when the company's stock goes up. Thus, for employees of growing, successful companies, stock options are a popular type of compensation. Options are also popular among corporate leaders for another reason—they're free.

Unlike the money that goes into paychecks, pension plans, health care, and even company picnics, current accounting practice does not recognize any costs for giving away options. This accounting loophole allows corporations to give valuable nonsalary compensation while maintaining a strong bottom line.

Uproar over astonishing stock option gains by executives, such as the $197 million netted by Disney's CEO Michael Eisner, has caused the FASB to look into creating rules that would charge stock options against corporate earnings. This is a move that almost nobody wants. The change in accounting would bring about billions of dollars of paper losses. It would also make it more difficult for companies to reward their workers for good performance. Stock options also link executives to shareholder interests. Finally, serious problems are faced in finding a model that accurately reflects the value of option packages.

Many in the business world are concerned about the huge payments made in the form of stock options. However, almost all agree that making a change in accounting procedure to account for them is the wrong response. Other controls, such as better reporting requirements, might be the answer.

Questions
1. Why do large companies prefer stock options as a form of compensation?
2. Why should stock options be charged against corporate earnings?
3. What other changes could companies make to quiet the uproar over huge executive compensation packages?

For more information, see John A. Byrne, "Hands Off My Stock Pile," *Business Week,* April 12, 1993, p. 28.

Case 19.2: Control Freaks
Financial controls are bookkeeping tools that allow a company to be certain that its assets and sales are being properly tracked. Maintaining them well is costly in funds and manpower. Maintaining them poorly risks heavy legal penalties.

Between 1984 and 1988, the median fine for corporate crime was $10,000. By 1990 that figure had jumped to $200,000. The mean average had leaped to $825,000 in the same period. Not only did fines increase, but the probability of going to prison and the amount of time spent there also went up. The heftier penalties have encouraged executives to take a stronger stance on controlling their assets.

Efforts to prevent fraud and theft sometimes receive low priority. Concerns about getting the product out the door simply come first.

Even when a company does implement stringent financial controls, they can be difficult to maintain. GE Lighting Systems, a subsidiary of General Electric, has complex, company-wide controls that attempt to monitor the company's assets. Unfortunately, the details change so quickly that GE has found maintaining these internal controls to be prohibitively expensive.

These problems seem to result from the way financial controls are developed. Controls fall to the accounting personnel, who add them as an afterthought to normal business procedures. A report by the Committee of Sponsoring Organizations of the Treadway Commission (COSO) says that this is a backward way of implementing controls. COSO recommends instead that companies integrate controls into every step of their business transactions instead of dumping the duty on the accounting staff. For the time being, however, it will still be accounting's responsibility to teach the rest of the company how to monitor finances.

Questions
1. Why is it important for a company to have financial controls?
2. What other personnel in a company in addition to those in the accounting department could share responsibility for financial controls?
3. Why are many financial controls so expensive?

For more information, see Lori Calabro, "All Eyes on Internal Controls," *CFO Magazine,* August 1993, p. 51.

REFERENCES
1. Richard Brown (ed.), *The History of Accounting and Accountants* (New York: A.M. Kelley, 1968), p. 108; Lee Berton, "Father of Accounting Is a Bit of a Stranger To His Own Progeny," *The Wall Street Journal,* January 29, 1993, p. A1.
2. Carol J. Loomis, "Dinosaurs," *Fortune,* May 3, 1993, p. 36.
3. "Jury Begins Deliberations in Crazy Eddie Antar Trial," *The Orlando Sentinel,* July 17, 1993, p. D-10.

CAREER CAPSULE 4

*Career
Opportunities
with Texaco*

What is it like to work for one of the largest, most widely known petroleum companies in the world? This career capsule will answer part of that question.

Texaco Inc. is generally recognized as a progressive, positive force in the petroleum industry. As one of the original companies created to produce and refine the enormous Texas oil deposits discovered in the early 1900s, this firm has undergone a host of changes in step with global energy production and environmental concerns during the last several decades.

Recent college graduates who choose a career with Texaco are told that the company is theirs to build. They're expected to make meaningful decisions, shoulder major responsibilities, and push the limits of their potential from their earliest days on the job. In keeping with the nature of its business, Texaco offers a variety of career opportunities to graduates with various engineering degrees, but highly qualified grads in nontechnical fields are much in demand as well.

MARKETING
Texaco's marketing representatives may have majored in marketing or several other areas that have prepared them to answer the challenges of large-scale retail and wholesale petroleum and chemicals marketing. In this capacity, they're both managers and salespeople. Those who work in retail marketing provide direction to the owners and managers of Texaco service stations on such subjects as marketing, business services, pricing, promotional strategy, planning, and general merchandising techniques. Wholesale marketing reps work closely with companies that operate chains of service stations as well as with fuel oil distributors, truck stop managers, and corporate accounts.

These representatives act as both business analysts and management consultants, providing the experience and knowledge that will help their clients' businesses prosper. Entry-level positions in marketing may lead to promotions to such areas as credit card marketing, customer service, advertising and sales promotion, and regional sales and marketing management.

INFORMATION TECHNOLOGY
Computer science graduates may work in Texaco's Information Technology Department, which is based in Houston. This department consists of a highly sophisticated management information system that provides the mountains of data management needs to coordinate the company's global business activities. The Information Technology Department designs, develops, and maintains information and communications systems for the entire company and its individual business units to acknowledge the various types of customers that they serve.

ACCOUNTING AND FINANCE
In a company with approximately 450 separate business units, gathering, analyzing, consolidating, and interpreting financial and operating data can present a formidable challenge, indeed. Graduates with a bachelor's or master's degree in accounting or finance may work in the areas of gas and oil accounting or in the accounting department of various units that manufacture petroleum products and chemicals. In addition to more traditional responsibilities, accounting and finance employees may be assigned to special projects, work on creating, maintaining, and improving financial controls, manage the company's short-term investments, or become internal auditors. Regardless of their responsibilities,

they'll work closely with management to enhance Texaco's profitability and efficiency in a highly competitive market.

HUMAN RESOURCES

Texaco's employees are the main ingredient in the company's recipe for success. Management has adopted a company-wide campaign to increase employee participation in decision making and to develop and improve job-related skills that will enhance each person's overall effectiveness. Business graduates with a degree in human resources management or other appropriate areas can become an integral part of these activities by developing and maintaining the appropriate policies and programs to increase interaction between employees at all levels. In addition, they may become responsible for recruiting, training, developing, or retaining employees.

Part Five

Special Challenges and Issues

20

BUSINESS LAW
AND THE LEGAL
ENVIRONMENT OF
BUSINESS

T*he law's final justification is in the good it does or fails to do to the society of a given place and time.*

ALBERT CAMUS

CHAPTER OBJECTIVES

After studying this chapter, you should be able to:

1. Differentiate between common law and statutory law.
2. Distinguish between torts and crimes, and name the two general categories of each.
3. Discuss the organization and operation of the United States court system.
4. Describe the major subdivisions of the Uniform Commercial Code, including laws having to do with contracts, agency, sales, property, negotiable instruments, and bankruptcy. Also discuss the specific characteristics of patents, secrecy, trademarks, and copyrights.
5. Summarize the legal and regulatory environment in which today's business operates.

UP FRONT

"When I was thirteen years old, I decided that I wanted to be like Perry Mason when I grew up," recalls Carolyn Veal-Hunter. "But when I got to law school, I found out that the life of a trial lawyer wasn't for me. Rather than try criminal or civil cases in a courtroom, I wanted to influence policy and make a *real difference* in the world."

In the legal sense, policy applies to activities of the government. "A good lawyer has got to understand the law, and governmental policies have an impact on almost every aspect of society, especially with regard to business," says Veal-Hunter. "Policy has the ability to make a difference in the quality of life. Even the water we drink is subject to regulatory conditions and policies. In our work here at Cordoba Corporation, we have to be knowledgeable about policies that affect our clients and the work we do with them. We must also stay abreast of the policies that affect the way we conduct our own business affairs."

Cordoba Corporation is a diversified consulting firm headquartered in Los Angeles. Started in 1983, it is a minority owned and operated firm that, in Veal-Hunter's words, is "an infrastructure firm. We work with businesses and governmental agencies that build the infrastructure of California: commercial office buildings, federal and state buildings and prisons, roadways, railways, and the like. We assist in three areas. The first is planning, such as urban land use and transportation planning. The second is development, such as construction and program management.

The third is systems, such as software design and development."

Veal-Hunter is in charge of Cordoba's Sacramento office. She came to the company with a strong background in government policy and business law. A native Californian, she earned her undergraduate degree in psychology and sociology from the University of California at San Diego and attended UCLA Law School. She was active in the Black Law Students Association, and that experience, combined with several internships in Washington, D.C., led to her interest in policy. She was an intern at the National Cable Television Association, an advocacy group, where she worked on the 1984 Cable Television Act. That in turn led to a second internship as a staff attorney with the Federal Communications Commission, and studies of common carriers. "Internships taught the best lessons possible. They exposed me to the workplace," Veal-Hunter says. "I was not restricted to library research and writing memos. I was actually affecting policy in the television and telecommunications arena."

She left the FCC to return to California, where she took a job with the California State Assembly Utilities and Commerce Committee, drafting and analyzing legislation. "The committee was concerned with public utilities and public transportation,

CAROLYN VEAL-HUNTER

GENERAL COUNSEL AND REGIONAL MANAGER, CORDOBA CORPORATION

and it gave me an opportunity to continue my telecommunications regulatory work." She was also responsible for helping minority contractors have an equal opportunity to bid on state and public utility contracts; during her four years there she helped raise the minority contracts from 7 percent to 20 percent. "I was able to say that I helped make business grow and created new jobs, and that is very satisfying to me."

Veal-Hunter next took her skills into her own private consulting practice, where she helped assist women- and minority-owned businesses understand state procurement practices. Then Cordoba called, and "instead of a multitude of clients, I had one client with a multitude of business interests for me to help with. The Sacramento office is like my own business. I started it from ground zero and hired the staff, and I'm responsible for it as a profit center. After just two years of operation, we were in the black."

Today she manages the consultants who work out of her office, as well as overseeing the legal aspects of all of Cordoba's contracts with clients. "We're growing, and moving fast," she says. "Sometimes we're the prime contractor and hire subcontractors to work for us. Sometimes we're a subcontractor. I review all our work contracts to assure that Cordoba Corporation's interests are being served. For example, we have contracts to develop computer systems for a client, as well as employment contracts that put our people at the client site to do consulting or other work. The client often initiates the contract, and if we sign it too quickly we may be signing a bad deal. While most of our contracts go smoothly, there are often details that have to be discussed.

"Conducting sound, ethical business practices is enhanced when based on a clear written agreement between the parties," says Veal-Hunter. "It is seldom in anyone's best interests to take a disagreement to litigation. In most cases it will cost more than the amount of money in contention. Most important is maintaining good client relations. We're a small company, and still growing, and have always been able to work things out rather than go to court. A document that has been of great help to us is one we call our contract checklist, that answers all the important questions up front."

Carolyn Veal-Hunter has used her law background and her work experience to become an able business manager. Does she recommend obtaining a law degree to business majors? "The best law schools teach you a thought process that can easily be transferred to the business arena. The analytical process you learn in law school is aimed at achieving an equitable and fair result. Achieving such results is equally important in the business world."

Many legal concerns influence business conduct. In fact, certain points of law were integral parts of material you studied earlier in this book in the areas of forms of business organization, labor relations, marketing, and finance. In this chapter we will not try to give you a comprehensive view of the laws relating to business; rather, we will introduce you to certain basic aspects of the legal system in the United States, summarizing major areas of business law and exploring the legal environment in which business has gained its ever-increasing influence on our society.

The Legal System of the United States

In the democratic form of government found in the United States, regulation of business and personal conduct falls into two general categories: common law and statutory law. **Common law** is *a body of law based on records of early English court decisions settling disputes that involve people and property.* A historical legacy that stands apart from written rules of law, common law has evolved in and influenced court decisions in America since before the Revolutionary War. Common-law cases follow the doctrine of *stare decisis* (Latin for "to stand by the decisions"), which holds that prior court decisions set a precedent for future decisions on cases that have the same elements of controversy or similar relationships among the parties.

Statutory law is *a written body of rules created and approved by a group of persons (generally referred to as a* legislature*), which presumably expresses the will of the citizens it represents.* Statutory law is enforced in the appropriate courts and administered by law enforcement agencies and their duly authorized representatives, including police officers, game wardens, the marine patrol, and sheriff's deputies. Statutory laws require that certain penalties be levied against violators.

Torts and Crimes

A **tort** is *a private or civil wrong or injury committed against a person or property for which a court will award damages if the wronged party (called the* plaintiff*) can submit adequate proof that the accused wrongdoer (called the* defendant*) was guilty, through either negligence or intent, of committing the act in question.* A personal damage tort is wrongful harm to an individual, including damage to the person's reputation or feelings. This can occur, for example, if someone intentionally spreads lies about another person's private life. A property tort is wrongful damage to someone's property, as when a crop duster accidentally sprays a defoliant on a farmer's field of wheat. Most torts involve acts of negligence.

A **crime,** on the other hand, is *a violation of a law passed by a legislative body.* The appropriate government (federal or state) will bring charges in its own name against the offender. (A tort requires a private individual to charge that a wrongful act has been committed.) Criminal laws most often cover crimes against person or property such as robbery or murder. Sometimes, however, businesspersons commit actions that violate criminal statutes, such as arson, fraud, embezzlement, or bribery.

Cases involving crimes are heard in criminal courts. Tort cases are aired in civil courts. Statute law may give certain courts special jurisdiction over such cases as juvenile offenses, probation, and domestic matters between husband and wife. In criminal cases, the plaintiff (which is always a government) must prove the defendant guilty beyond a reasonable doubt. In cases involving torts it is not necessary to prove the injury or damage beyond a reasonable doubt; the plaintiff need only prove by a preponderance of the evidence that a wrong was done. Criminal cases are decided by juries, with judges presiding over the

common law
A body of law based on records of early English court decisions settling disputes that involve people and property.

statutory law
A written body of rules created and approved by a group of persons (generally referred to as a *legislature*), which presumably expresses the will of the citizens it represents.

tort
A private or civil wrong or injury committed against a person or property for which a court will award damages if the wronged party (called the *plaintiff*) can submit adequate proof that the accused wrongdoer (called the *defendant*) was guilty, through either negligence or intent, of committing the act in question.

crime
A violation of a law passed by a legislative body.

In district courts, juries hear trials involving violations of federal law.

proceedings and ruling on technical legal questions. Civil cases can be handled similarly, but if both parties to a civil case agree to do so, the question may be decided by a judge rather than by a jury.

The Federal Court System

Criminal cases that violate federal statutes are heard in the federal court system. (Each state has a similar court system for hearing cases involving violations of state law.) The lowest federal courts, district courts, are those in which juries decide questions or disputes of fact involving violations of federal law. The court, represented by a judge, rules on legal questions and ensures that attorneys for the plaintiff and defendant observe proper legal procedure. Each state has between one and four federal district courts, depending on its size.

Acting as buffers between the district courts and the Supreme Court, the courts of appeals (also called circuit courts) hear appeals based on alleged procedural errors that occurred in district court trials. Cases appealed to the circuit courts and the Supreme Court are heard only by judges. Circuit court decisions are final unless the United States Supreme Court agrees to review a case appealed beyond that level. Decisions of the Supreme Court are final; they can only be overturned by a later Supreme Court decision or a constitutional amendment. The circuit courts also review and enforce orders and rulings of such quasi-legal bodies as the Federal Trade Commission and the National Labor Relations Board. Figure 20.1 illustrates the hierarchy of the

Figure 20.1
Hierarchy of the federal court system.

U.S Supreme Court (1)

U.S Courts of Appeals (11)

U.S District Courts (90)

federal court system. The Supreme Court also may agree to hear appeals from state courts.

Business Law

The **Uniform Commercial Code (UCC)** is *a comprehensive body of business law that encompasses various kinds of transactions.* Drafted by the National Conference of Commissioners on Uniform State Laws, it has been adopted by all states except Louisiana, thus ensuring that business transactions will be handled consistently from state to state. In this section, we will examine several areas of business law covered by the UCC.

The Law of Contracts

A **contract** is *a legally binding agreement between two or more parties obliging them to do or refrain from doing certain acts.* When you sign a contract you voluntarily give up certain legal rights that you would otherwise enjoy. Although some contracts may be wholly or partly oral, the law requires that a contract be written if it involves any of the following:

- A purchase or sale of real estate
- A sale of goods for a price that exceeds $500
- An agreement to pay another's debt
- An obligation that cannot be performed within one year of the date of the agreement

A valid contract must have each of the elements illustrated in Figure 20.2 and described in the following paragraphs.

Uniform Commercial Code (UCC)
A comprehensive body of business law that encompasses various kinds of transactions.

contract
A legally binding agreement between two or more parties obliging them to do or refrain from doing certain acts.

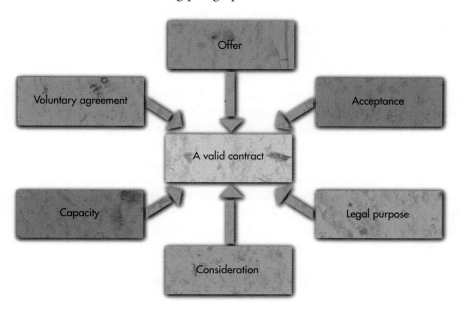

Figure 20.2
The elements of a valid contract.

OFFER Extreme precision is not necessary, but the offer must be clear enough for a reasonable person to understand what the offeror meant. In addition, the offeror must have intended to make the offer and to communicate it to the offeree. Such frivolous offers as jokes or casual remarks or offers that were not intentionally communicated may be declared invalid by a court.

ACCEPTANCE A valid acceptance of the offer requires the same general conditions as a valid offer. Intent to accept, clarity of acceptance, and intentional communication to the offeror must all be present.

LEGAL PURPOSE A contract's purpose or object must comply with the law. One party to a contract cannot bring suit against the other for breach of contract if the act required by the agreement is illegal.

CONSIDERATION A valid contract requires that both parties exchange something of value, which is called consideration, or *quid pro quo* (Latin for "something for something"), as an inducement to enter the agreement. Each party thus establishes an obligation to the other. Consideration may be an act performed or withheld, money, goods, or services rendered, or any combination of such things that lends weight to each party's obligation. In general, it need not be tangible or possess economic value. The law usually does not attempt to weigh the relative worth of each party's consideration.

Walt Disney Company and Coca-Cola Company entered into a contract that will bind both parties until the year 2005. According to the terms of the deal, Disney agreed that Coca-Cola's products would be the only soft drinks sold at Disney attractions, and Coca-Cola would have the right to use current Disney characters, as well as those that might be created in the future, in certain promotional campaigns and advertisements created jointly by Coke and Disney. According to a Disney executive, both companies "have a mutually beneficial relationship."

CAPACITY Capacity is a requirement that the contracting parties be of sound mind, understand what they are agreeing to, and be of legal age to enter into a contract. Persons who can prove that they made a contract while under the influence of alcohol or drugs, or while senile, insane, or not of legal age to make a contract, may successfully avoid their obligations under it.

Although minors may not be required to fulfill most contracts they make before they reach the age of majority (either eighteen or twenty-one in most states), they may be held liable for contracts they made to acquire items essential to their maintenance (rent, food, clothing, medical care) if they are self-supporting.

VOLUNTARY AGREEMENT A final requirement of a legally valid contract is that both parties make the agreement voluntarily, without restraint or influence, acting of their own free will. A person who signed a contract because he or she was threatened or otherwise placed under duress cannot be compelled by a court to perform the agreement.

If all of these requirements are met in a contract that you signed, you are bound to carry out your share of the bargain, whether or not you understood its terms. The law assumes that you understood the contract if you signed it.

The Law of Agency

An **agent** is *one who is authorized to transact business and exercise authority on behalf of another party.* The **principal,** *the person whom an agent represents,* grants the agent authority to act on his or her behalf.

The law of agency exists because it is sometimes necessary or desirable to employ someone who has a special knowledge or skill to act on your behalf. Because you cannot be in two places at the same time, you may also employ an agent to close a deal in a distant location. Agents are used to buy or sell real estate, purchase securities, make travel arrangements, find work for actors and musicians, sell various products, and accomplish many other business transactions.

The Law of Sales

The law of sales, also covered by the Uniform Commercial Code, deals only with the sale of new, tangible personal property. Companies that sell such property often issue a written **warranty,** *a document that states certain facts and conditions about a product's operation and correct use and clarifies the limits of its performance under various circumstances.* A warranty's terms include conditions under which the product or its parts will be repaired or replaced and the kinds of use or abuse that would void the company's obligation to fix or replace the product. The manufacturer's express warranty usually is printed on a piece of paper packed with the product.

The law of sales also holds sellers to certain implied warranties regardless of the terms of their express warranty. Implied warranty under the law of sales falls into four general categories that are described in Table 20.1.

The Law of Property

Another subdivision of the Uniform Commercial Code encompasses the ownership and transfer of *real property,* which is the earth and things firmly attached to it, including crops, buildings, trees, and minerals. Property law also covers certain rights having to do with *personal property,* which is simply defined as objects other than real property and any intangible rights or interests held in such objects. Real property is generally immovable, while personal property consists of transportable objects or rights to them: bonds, furniture, or a sailboat, for example.

agent
One who is authorized to transact business and exercise authority on behalf of another party.

principal
The person whom an agent represents.

warranty
A document that states certain facts and conditions about a product's operation and correct use and clarifies the limits of its performance under various circumstances.

YOU DECIDE

List at least one product that federal or state laws now prohibit companies from manufacturing and selling. What problems did this action pose for the manufacturer? For customers? Do you feel the action was justified? Why or why not?

Table 20.1
Categories and terms of implied warranties.

CATEGORY	TERMS
Implied warranty of title	The seller implies that he or she is the lawful owner and can convey that ownership to the buyer.
Warranty of sale by sample or description	The seller warrants that the merchandise that is delivered will match the sample merchandise or the description used to make the sale. (This term can be important when buying merchandise from a catalog or from such samples as the swatches of material used to sell rugs.)
Warranty of fitness for a particular purpose	The seller is responsible for a product's failure if he or she assumed the role of expert adviser to the buyer.
Warranty of merchantability	Goods must be suitable for ordinary usage. (This is a central issue in many product liability cases.)

One area of property law that has particular importance for businesspeople is intellectual property: patents, trademarks, and copyrights. Because these properties have a significant bearing on a firm's identity in the marketplace and its survival in the world of business, we will explore them in some detail.

PATENTS The Patent and Trademark Office of the United States Department of Commerce grants a **patent,** *a legal right allowing an inventor to exclude others from making, using, or selling an invention, a design, or a plant for a stated length of time.* An invention becomes public property after its patent expires, and anyone may then produce and sell it. Patents are renewable only by act of Congress.

The abbreviation *Reg. U.S. Pat. Off.* followed by a patent number confirms that the product is patented and duly registered in the Patent Office. Labels saying *Patent pending* or *Patent applied for* afford no legal rights; they simply mean that the inventor has applied for a patent and expects to receive it.

Three kinds of patents can be obtained. The choice depends on the nature of the item. A *utility patent* is a patent with a life span of seventeen years awarded to those who invent a new, useful, and unobvious industrial or technical process, machine, or chemical composition or a new, useful, or novel improvement on existing machines, processes, or materials. "Useful" simply means that the invention must perform its intended function.

A *design patent* is a patent awarded on an ornamental device for a period of three-and-half, seven, or fourteen years, whichever the applicant chooses. Such patents may protect designs on floor coverings or styles of automobile bodies.

A *plant patent* provides seventeen years of protection for a new species of plant that is asexually reproduced (grown from cuttings, grafting, or other nonseed methods). A horticulturalist who produces a new variety of rose or

patent
A legal right allowing an inventor to exclude others from making, using, or selling an invention, a design, or a plant for a stated length of time.

apple may obtain the exclusive right to produce and market it by obtaining a plant patent. Figure 20.3 shows the number of U.S. patents granted by nationality of the inventor. Note the increased intensity of foreign competition to U.S. inventors.

OBTAINING A PATENT Patenting is a horse race. The first inventor who files an application stands the best chance of receiving the patent. If two people apply for patents on identical devices almost simultaneously, each may have to establish the date on which the idea was conceived.

The first step is the preliminary search, an examination of existing patents filed in the search room of the Patent Office, to determine whether a similar or identical device has already been patented. Patent records are open to the public, enabling you to make your own search, but it is usually faster and cheaper to employ a patent attorney, who can have a search made within several days.

If a search reveals that no invention like yours has been patented, your attorney will probably advise you to apply for a patent. A patent application includes an oath, a description of your device, a drawing (where possible), and a statement of claims about the unique character of your invention. You must also pay a filing fee.

Figure 20.3
U.S. patents granted, by nationality of inventor.

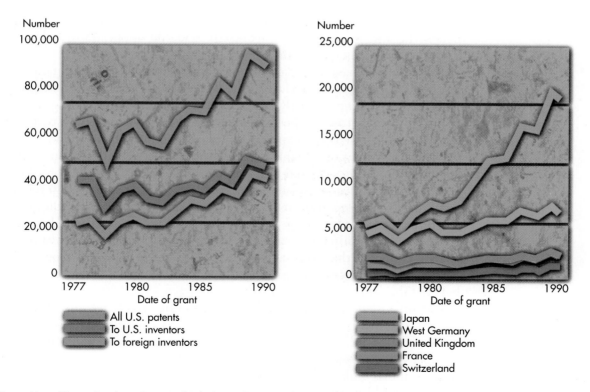

Source: National Science Foundation, *Science and Technology Pocket Data Book, 1992*, NSF 92-331 (Washington, D.C.: NSF, 1992), p. 48.

Because applications are examined in the order in which they are received, several months will pass before your application is reviewed by a patent examiner who is familiar with the category into which the invention falls. If the examiner finds that the device is similar to an already patented one, you will be informed of this and advised to alter the invention in a manner that would make it patentable before reapplying. If the invention is unique, the Patent Office will award you a patent. You must then pay an issue fee. If two or more people work together to create an invention, and each had a share in the ideas that formed it, the patent will be issued to them jointly. But if one person supplied all the ideas for an invention and others merely assembled it or provided financing, the patent will be issued solely to the person who furnished the ideas. Applicants who are denied a patent may appeal the decision to the board of appeals of the Patent Office.

Many inventors have conceived products that had nothing to do with their range of experience or interest. For example, Kodachrome film was invented by a musician, the parking meter by a journalist, and the airplane by two bicycle mechanics. Successful inventors must also have the determination not to give up when they encounter failure. Thomas Edison, for example, tried 50,000 experiments before finally perfecting the storage battery. He took the failures in stride, however, saying, "I have gotten lots of results. I know fifty thousand things that won't work."

The Patent Office takes an average of almost nineteen months to award a patent, because it receives approximately 150,000 applications each year. There are approximately 24 million patents on record.

Patent holders have every right to aggressively defend infringement on their patents. For example, Procter & Gamble received a $125 million settlement from Keebler Company, RJR Nabisco, and Frito-Lay for violating its patented process for making Duncan Hines crisp and chewy cookies. At that time the amount was the largest reported court award in patent litigation.

When the patent on a highly profitable product expires, the company that owned it can expect sales and profits to decline for at least two reasons. First, competitors are usually poised to start making the product and selling it for less as soon as it comes off patent. Second, the company that owned the patent will often lower the product's price in an effort to hold onto the market share it accumulated during the years the patent was in effect. One investment analyst predicted that Monsanto's sales of NutraSweet would drop by 50 percent when the patent expired at the end of 1992, and another analyst believed the company's stock would drop between 15 and 20 percent when its patent on Calan, a popular drug for controlling hypertension, expired in 1993.[1]

One alternative to obtaining a patent, of course, may be to keep certain product information secret. Secrecy may be practical if products are made from formulas with several ingredients that must be measured in exact proportions and blended in a precise sequence. Secrecy also may be applied to a manufacturing process that gives an end product a unique appearance, finish, durability, or other characteristic. Bailey's Original Irish Cream, a liqueur, is made with a secret formula that competitors have been unable to duplicate to date, giving Bailey's sales of 1 million cases per year. The formula somehow prevents the cream from curdling in the bottle for up to two years.

Although secrecy prevents a company's exclusive right to a product from expiring in seventeen years (as it would if it were patented), secrecy requires management to take considerable precautions to safeguard its formulas or processes from accidental or intentional disclosure by employees.

Many companies veil their developmental laboratories in secrecy until new products have been perfected and are ready for marketing. Such is the case at Wendy's International, for example, where doors to the test kitchens have coded locks, and information on new products is distributed on a "need-to-know" basis only.

TRADEMARKS In addition to awarding patents, the Patent and Trademark Office also registers trademarks. A **trademark** is *a brand name, brand mark, or trade character that has legal protection.* A company uses trademarks to identify its products and to distinguish them from competitors. A company's name (also referred to as a *trade name*) may be registered with the Patent and Trademark Office if it appears in or forms part of the trademark that identifies its products.

> **YOU DECIDE**
>
> Assume that a friend would like to conceive an idea for a patentable invention or create an original work of authorship that could be copyrighted. What areas of interest or topics would you suggest that he or she consider? What mental attitude or state of mind would seem to encourage creative thinking in those directions?

trademark
A brand name, brand mark, or trade character that has legal protection.

Trademarks come in a wide variety of forms.

Once a firm's trademark is approved and registered, it receives legal protection for ten years. The company must file an affidavit between the fifth and sixth year after registration stating that the mark is currently in use in commerce, however, and if this is not done the registration will be canceled. Registration may be renewed for ten-year periods thereafter, unless the firm cancels it or surrenders the trademark. If over time the public comes to use a trademark generically to identify a product rather than one company's specific version of it, the courts may strip the firm of its trademark protection. Some former trademarks that have been held to be generic are linoleum, shredded wheat, aspirin, yo-yo, brassiere, kerosene, aerosol, cellophane, harmonica, escalator, and zipper.

Registered trademarks are usually followed by the symbol ® or ™. A firm may also register its **service mark**, which is *a mark or words used in sales or advertising literature to distinguish a firm's services from those of its competitors.*

Companies treasure the financial value and consumer recognition of their trademarks and service marks, and they defend them vigorously to discourage generic use. The word *brand* is stated or printed after the product's name in television and print advertising and on package labels for such products as Sanka decaffeinated coffee, Scotch cellophane tape, and ReaLemon reconstituted lemon juice in the hope that this will reinforce the idea that these are registered trademarks and not generic words. Corporate attorneys for Rollerblade, Inc., which manufactures a highly popular brand of in-line skates, have informed careless writers that the company's registered trademark should not be used as a verb.[2] Table 20.2 presents some trademarks that have been registered for many years, along with the generic products they refer to.

One of the most widely publicized legal battles over trademark protection began in the early 1970s when Parker Brothers threatened to sue an economics professor at San Francisco State University for naming his new board game "Anti-Monopoly." The company contended that his name infringed on its right to use the word *Monopoly* as the registered trademark for its board game ("Monopoly" had been protected by trademark since 1935). After Parker Brothers reportedly declined offers by the professor's lawyers to alter the name of his game, he sued in California district court to have the trademark "Monopoly" declared invalid. Nine years of decisions and appeals followed as Parker Brothers pursued the matter all the way to

service mark
A mark or words used in sales or advertising literature to distinguish a firm's services from those of its competitors.

Table 20.2
Well-known trademarks and the products they refer to.

REGISTERED TRADEMARK	GENERIC PRODUCT
Kleenex®	Paper tissues
Jeep®	Four-wheel drive vehicles
Coke® and Coca-Cola®	Cola-flavored drinks
Xerox®	Photocopying machines
Levi's®	Jeans
Band-aid®	Adhesive bandages
Formica®	Plastic laminate
Q-Tips®	Cotton swabs
Teflon®	Nonstick coating
Vaseline®	Petroleum jelly
Styrofoam®	Foam insulating material
Magic Marker®	Felt-tip marking pen

GLOBAL PERSPECTIVE

Similar Trademarks Cause International Problems

Similar trademarks may be registered in several countries, a fact that sometimes creates problems for companies doing business across borders. For example, firms whose plastic packages bear the triangular "chasing arrows" recycling symbol, which is a U.S. trademark registered by the Society of the Plastics Industry Inc., have encountered trouble in Belgium, the Netherlands, and Luxembourg (the Benelux countries) because a Dutch paper industry trade group has registered a highly similar trademark in those countries.

The dilemma is compounded by the fact that twenty-seven states in the United States require the "chasing arrows" logo on recyclable plastic packages, making use of that trademark even more widespread than it otherwise would be. Consequently, U.S. manufacturers that also want to export their products to the Benelux countries have been threatened with trademark infringement lawsuits there. The controversy is currently frustrating international efforts to make the U.S. trademark an international symbol for recyclable plastics.

(For more information on the recycling symbol, see Don Loepp, "Altered Recycle Symbol Required in Benelux," *Plastics News*, January 27, 1992, p. 1.)

---

the United States Supreme Court. In early 1983 that court let stand a circuit court of appeals ruling that stripped "Monopoly" of trademark protection, thus making it generic.

COPYRIGHTS Registered by the Copyright Office of the Library of Congress, a **copyright** is *a set of legal rights granted to the creator of an original work of authorship, such as an artistic, dramatic, literary, or musical production.* The creator of a copyrighted work may be called an author, artist, or composer, depending on the nature of the work. A copyright owner may do the following with a copyrighted work:

- Reproduce it
- Create works derived from or based on it
- Sell duplicates of it
- Perform it or display it publicly
- Authorize others to do any of the above

copyright
A set of legal rights granted to the creator of an original work of authorship, such as an artistic, dramatic, literary, or musical production.

Examples of works that are copyrighted rather than patented are as follows:

- Books
- Musical scores and lyrics to songs
- Dramatic works (including accompanying music)
- Choreography
- Photographs, sculpture, or works of graphic art
- Motion pictures, slides, filmstrips, videodiscs, videotapes, televised productions, and other audiovisual works
- Phonograph records, tapes, and compact discs

Under the provisions of the Copyright Act of 1976, works created after January 1, 1978 are protected until fifty years after the creator's death. Works originated by more than one person and copyrighted jointly receive protection for fifty years after the last surviving creator's death. The creator receives automatic copyright protection the moment the work is placed in a visual or audible form—written, filmed, or otherwise recorded. Copyrights owned by corporations are protected for seventy-five years.

Notice of copyright on nonsound works usually appears as the symbol © or the abbreviation *Copr.* followed by the owner's name and the year the work was first published or produced.

The issue of copyright protection became especially important to the film industry after videocassette recorders (VCRs) were introduced in the early 1970s. Walt Disney Productions, Universal Studios, and other filmmakers claimed that home taping of movies violated copyrights and caused them financial losses. After a seven-year battle between moviemakers and VCR manufacturers, the U.S. Supreme Court ruled that taping televised movies does not violate copyright laws as long as copies are limited strictly to home viewing and are not used for personal gain.

Copyrightholders, like patentholders, are often quick to defend their legal rights in court. Piracy of copyrighted material is a problem of serious proportions, as many large companies will confirm. For example, the Film and Video Security Office of the Motion Picture Association of America reported seizing 65,512 pirated videocassettes worth $3.3 million in just one year alone. The sale of counterfeit products bearing the unauthorized likeness of Disney characters reportedly costs Walt Disney Company $10 to $20 million per year in royalties. It may surprise some people to know that the song "Happy Birthday To You," which was copyrighted in 1935, earns almost $1 million a year in royalties for the copyright owner, Birchtree Ltd., and is expected to continue to do so until the copyright expires in 2010. Although actual figures are confidential, it has been estimated that the sales of products bearing the likenesses of cartoonist Charles M. Schulz's copyrighted Peanuts comic strip characters may be as high as $1 billion a year.

Negotiable Instruments Law

The Uniform Commercial Code addresses various transactions involving **negotiable instruments,** which are *written promises or requests that certain sums of money be paid to the bearer or to order.* Negotiable instruments include promissory notes, checks, and drafts, all of which you learned about in Chapter 16. To be negotiable, an instrument must be:

1. In writing
2. Signed by the maker
3. An unconditional promise to pay
4. For a specific sum of money
5. Payable on demand or at a definite time
6. Payable *to order* or *to bearer*

negotiable instruments
Written promises or requests that certain sums of money be paid to the bearer or to order.

The UCC also specifies several types of indorsement, each of which has special meaning when used on a negotiable instrument. A *blank indorsement* is a simple signature: "Paul J. Owens." Blank indorsement creates a bearer instrument, one that can be transferred from one subsequent party to the next without further indorsement. Whoever possesses a bearer instrument is presumed to own it and can cash it.

A *special indorsement* is generally the safest kind. An example would be: "Pay to the order of Ellen Johnson, (signed) Paul J. Owens." Johnson must now indorse the instrument before it can be transferred to another party, because Owens's indorsement dictated that it be paid only to Johnson.

A *restrictive indorsement* dictates a specific purpose or use and so restricts future handling: "Pay to the order of National Bank for deposit only, account number 93476-007-8, (signed) Paul J. Owens." In this case, the instrument's future is restricted. It can only be deposited in Owens's bank account. If Owens should lose it, the restrictive indorsement would prevent the finder from forging Owens's name as a blank indorsement and receiving cash for the instrument.

A *qualified indorsement* allows the holder to avoid responsibility for paying the instrument if the maker refuses or fails to pay and causes the instrument to bounce: "Paul J. Owens, without recourse." If you indorse a check this way, however, you may have trouble finding another party who will give you cash for it, because that party cannot bring legal action against you if the maker refuses to pay. On the other hand, a qualified indorsement may be the safest in situations where you doubt that the maker will pay and you want to avoid liability for payment as a subsequent holder of the instrument. Agents sometimes receive instruments payable to them that were written to pay debts owed to their principals. In this case, a principal would not expect the agent to stand behind the instrument merely because it was payable to the agent but should be willing to accept it from the agent with the agent's qualified indorsement.

The Federal Reserve System now has a standard indorsement guideline that is meant to expedite the movement of checks through the banking system. Checks must be indorsed on the back within 1¹/₂ inches of the "trailing edge" (the end of the check that has the accountholder's name and address printed on it). Depositors who ignore this guideline may find that the check is delayed in processing or, in extreme cases, the bank may refuse to accept it for deposit.

The Law of Bankruptcy

bankruptcy or insolvency
The state of being unable to pay one's creditors' claims as they come due.

Bankruptcy *or* insolvency is *the state of being unable to pay one's creditors' claims as they come due.* As you learned in the discussion of accounting in Chapter 19, a firm's assets must equal the sum of its liabilities and its capital. When the firm operates at a loss over several years, capital and assets decline and liabilities may increase to a point where debts outweigh assets, thus destroying the accounting equation, and also the business.

A firm that is besieged by creditors may petition the federal district court to declare it bankrupt, a procedure called *voluntary bankruptcy.* When a group of creditors petitions the court to declare a debtor bankrupt so they may collect at least part of their claims, that is called *involuntary bankruptcy.*

The current federal bankruptcy law, which became effective in 1979, streamlined and simplified bankruptcy procedures. In the absence of fraud or gross mismanagement, a company's current management team is allowed to stay in place and negotiate a reorganization plan that will permit the firm to pay off its creditors over an extended period of time. Further legal actions may be taken if repayment proves to be impossible. The American Bankruptcy Institute reported 971,517 bankruptcies filed in the United States in 1992, 8 percent of which were filed by businesses.[3]

Businesses that are unable to pay their debts often have no choice but to file for bankruptcy.

The Legal Environment of Business

Various state and federal government agencies possess legal or quasi-legal power to regulate business operations. Table 20.3 introduces the most influential federal regulatory agencies. The creation of these agencies began with the Interstate Commerce Commission in 1887. Today at least 116 government agencies and programs control some facet of business activity.

Table 20.3
Principal federal regulatory agencies.

AGENCY, YEAR ESTABLISHED	MAJOR ACTIVITIES
Interstate Commerce Commission (ICC), 1887	Approves rates, routes, and methods of operation for truck, bus, and rail carriers operating in interstate commerce (its scope was reduced somewhat by the Motor Carrier Act of 1980)
Federal Reserve Board, 1913	Regulates the operations of commercial banks belonging to the Federal Reserve System; governs national policy on money and credit
Federal Trade Commission (FTC), 1914	Administers the terms of several laws passed to protect consumers; investigates incidents of alleged monopoly, restraint of trade, or unfair or deceptive trade practices; its goal is to maintain fair and free competition
Food and Drug Administration (FDA), 1931	Sets standards of quality for food and drug products; grants operating licenses to drug manufacturers and distributors
Federal Communications Commission (FCC), 1934	Awards operating licenses to radio and television stations; regulates interstate and international telephone and telegraph operations
Securities and Exchange Commission (SEC), 1934	Regulates the issue of stocks and bonds and the operation of the various stock exchanges
Federal Aviation Administration (FAA), 1948	Sets airport safety standards; monitors aircraft fitness and maintenance; licenses pilots
Equal Employment Opportunity Commission (EEOC), 1964	Monitors and attempts to eliminate discrimination based on race, color, religion, sex, national origin, or age in all places of employment and in labor unions
Environmental Protection Agency (EPA), 1970	Protects and enhances the environment through the control and abatement of air, water, solid waste, noise, radiation, and toxic substance pollution
Occupational Safety and Health Administration (OSHA), 1971	Develops, implements, and enforces job safety and health standards in four categories: general industry, maritime, construction, and agriculture
Consumer Product Safety Commission, 1972	Sets standards for product safety to protect the public against unreasonable risk of injury; has the power to recall defective or hazardous products through their manufacturers
Nuclear Regulatory Commission, 1975	Licenses persons and companies to build and operate nuclear reactors and to own and use nuclear materials; inspects sites to ensure that rules and standards are being observed
Federal Energy Regulatory Commission, 1977	Sets rates and charges for the transportation and sale of natural gas and the transmission and sale of electricity and licensing of hydroelectric projects; sets rates for the transportation of oil by pipeline, as well as the valuation of such pipelines

MANAGER'S NOTEBOOK

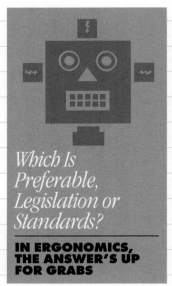

Which Is Preferable, Legislation or Standards?

IN ERGONOMICS, THE ANSWER'S UP FOR GRABS

Equipment should have a user-friendly design. That's the basis of the science of ergonomics, a field that has gained in stature with the widespread use of personal computers and workstations. The trouble is, some groups favor passing legislation that dictates certain ergonomic aspects of computer workstation design and operation, while others favor using voluntary, industrywide standards to achieve the same result.

The debate over laws versus standards came to a head with the passage of a short-lived San Francisco ordinance, which took effect in January 1992 and was repealed the following month. The ordinance mandated ergonomic design specifications for video display terminals (VDTs), workstations, and furniture and the overall office environment. Chair adjustments, the quality and environment of VDTs, workstation dimensions and lighting, rest breaks, alternative assignments for pregnant VDT operators, and employee ergonomic training were all covered in this law. The cost of compliance was estimated to be extremely high, especially for small businesses, and firms that did not comply would be subject to hefty fines.

Business owners and trade groups vigorously objected to the law's detail. They argued that ever-changing computer and workstation technology would make legally prescribed ergonomic guidelines impractical and obsolete. Instead of passing yet another inflexible law, they said, why not encourage employers to adopt scientific standards that serve as guidelines? Many of these standards exist already. In the United States, the American National Standards Institute/Human Factors Society, OSHA, and individual states all have standards for VDTs and operator workstations. The International Standards Organization and the European Community are expected to announce guidelines for VDT users in the near future.

The debate over law versus standards on computer ergonomics hinges on the fact that laws often set specifications far more rigid than medical or scientific research would justify. Laws are also unlikely to acknowledge improvements in equipment design. But standards, although lacking the force of law, are much more flexible. Companies can adapt them to dynamic job settings and computer and workstation technology alike. Employers would tend to embrace ANSI and related standards on workstation ergonomics because it's the smart thing to do. Changes that would reduce operator fatigue or increase productivity would be good for the company as well as its employees. Furthermore, employers point out that much if not most furniture and equipment used by computer operators already has an ergonomic design. It's just a matter of training operators to adjust the height, angle, lighting, and other variables to customize workstations for their personal physiques.

For more on the controversy about legislated ergonomics, see Patricia M. Fernberg, "Laying Down the Law on Ergonomics," *Modern Office Technology,* October 1992, p. 74.

Business Regulation Today

In the past, companies sometimes engaged in questionable business practices that harmed consumers, smaller competitors, or the environment. As some of the more serious abuses came to light, federal and state governments began to mandate social consciousness through intensified regulation. Some observers today, however, feel that overzealous regulators unnecessarily inhibit businesses' efforts to pursue their goals. When Eli Lilly & Company petitioned the Food and Drug Administration for clearance to market a drug for arthritis, the required paperwork reportedly exceeded 100,000 pages.

Under the FDA's system of testing, it takes seven to ten years for a drug company to develop, test, and clear for sale new drugs to combat various diseases and illnesses. Consequently, among nations in the world, the United States ranked:

- 32nd in approving the anticancer drug doxorubicin
- 51st in approving the antituberculosis drug rifampin
- 64th in approving the antiallergenic drug cromolyn
- 106th in approving the antibacterial drug co-trimoxazole

This is *not* to argue that drugs should be allowed on the market without adequate safeguards to confirm their performance and effects. Thalidomide, a tranquilizer whose use by pregnant women caused many birth defects in Europe in the 1950s and early 1960s, was never approved for use in the United States. Nevertheless, the lengthy test procedure can keep helpful drugs off the market for years.

What Price Regulation?

The total cost businesses pay to comply with federal regulations alone is estimated at more than $100 billion per year. A survey by the National Federation of Independent Business (NFIB) disclosed that small-business owners ranked government regulations and red tape their second most important problem after taxes.

Compliance procedures usually apply as stringently to small firms as to large ones. Government report formats are generally identical for both large and small firms; the same data may be required from a 500-employee company as from one with 50,000 workers. The smaller firm, lacking the full-time regulatory compliance staff that many large firms have created, will find the report more costly to complete. As a result, the small-business owner's time and attention is drawn away from management to matters of less value to the business itself. An NFIB poll concerning government surveys disclosed that small-business owners averaged almost nine hours and spent $238 preparing just one large report—the federal government's Annual Survey of Manufacturers. Federal agencies most subject to criticism for burdensome paperwork are the Internal Revenue Service and the Departments of Health and Human Services, Transportation, and Agriculture.

Responses to Regulation

Responses to regulation have ranged from combative to cooperative. Between these two extremes can be found various measures that companies, managers, and regulators alike may adopt in achieving their respective goals constructively. Several of them are explored here.

IMPROVED SELF-POLICING Greater self-policing and voluntary attention to the matters scrutinized by government regulators may minimize the need for future regulations. By keeping their own houses in order and publicizing their voluntary controls, industry leaders can discourage government interference. This has long been the practice within the legal, accounting, and medical professions, and it certainly could be transplanted to business in general. The result might be the demise of various regulatory agencies as legislators agree to let the private sector be its own watchdog. Self-policing might begin with a voluntary code of conduct, stringently enforced industrywide by committees or examining boards composed of executives from the companies involved.

THE POWER OF LOBBYING Individual firms and trade associations can lobby to have lawmakers consolidate overlapping government authority and eliminate agencies' duplication of regulatory activities, so that, for example, one report or inspection would satisfy the needs of several agencies at once. In addition, regulators could be required to justify each form and inspection and to stop gathering unnecessary or irrelevant information.

Some opponents of excessive regulation hope that regulators will someday be required to produce economic impact statements disclosing the effect of new reports and external controls on a business's costs, employee productivity, and other vital matters. This would require a comprehensive law, however, because many large agencies, such as the Consumer Product Safety Commission and the Federal Trade Commission, operate with considerable autonomy. Nevertheless, a law requiring bureaucrats to balance the costs of controls against the expected benefits would help to ensure that future regulations place no greater burden on society than do the conditions they seek to alleviate.

Nearly 400 firms, including Union Carbide, Texaco, Ford, International Paper, and Dow Chemical, have their own lobbyists or other employees in Washington to keep their fingers on the pulse of government and to maintain positive relations with influential lawmakers whose decisions will ultimately affect company operations. Anheuser-Busch has a vice-president of national affairs, Allied Corporation has created a senior vice-presidency in charge of government affairs, and INA Corporation has established a similar position within its corporate structure.

FOCUSING ON RESULTS Regulators (and legislators who make regulatory proposals) might also concentrate on the results they want business to achieve—reduced accidents, healthier working environments—rather than on the way the business community must reach them. Goal-oriented government, like goal-oriented business managers, would establish the results to be achieved, leaving the mechanics of getting there up to the companies involved. At present, a host of specific, prescriptive regulations are in place, at a greater cost than if management were allowed to use its own judgment about ways to reach the ultimate objectives that regulations address.

FINANCIAL PENALTIES AND REWARDS One government report that examines the cost of federal paperwork to American industry suggests that fines be levied on companies that fail to reach mandated results. Financial penalties would decrease as firms aligned their operations with legal guidelines. The government might also consider providing tax incentives to firms that meet legislated goals and levying greater taxes on those that do not. Ultimately, firms that operate within legally acceptable bounds in such areas as workplace and product safety and pollution abatement would pay lower taxes, charge lower prices for their products, and enjoy a competitive advantage over companies that complied with the law less fully or enthusiastically.

Deregulation

Deregulation emerged in Washington on a limited scale in the late 1970s and early 1980s, as Congress and the administrations of presidents Jimmy Carter and Ronald Reagan, spurred by public opinion and aggressive lobbying, began limiting the investigatory powers of many agencies and repealing outdated and ineffective rules. Deregulation has currently expanded to include banks, savings and loan associations, and the telecommunications industry as well as all modes of shipping and public transportation. The intent is to encourage the growth of productivity as marketplace incentives fill the gaps left by decreased government regulations.

Following passage of the Airline Deregulation Act of 1978, twenty-two new national and regional airlines started business, compared with none from 1973 through 1978. Several of these new carriers devised interesting market segment appeals by catering to budget-conscious travelers, wealthy "carriage trade" customers, or (in the case of Muse Air) nonsmokers. Long-distance customers also benefited from the epidemic of fare wars that accompanied increased competition. For a short while at least one airline sold one-way tickets between New York and Los Angeles for $99, but such bargains were offset by higher fares and reduced service to smaller cities. Following the shakeout in route changes, a total of seventy-three small towns had regular air service terminated.

Such dramatic changes in operations affected airline workers too. More than 50,000 were laid off, while others approved pay freezes or wage decreases, fewer fringe benefits, and longer work hours. Some airlines gave workers shares of stock in exchange for these concessions to a new, competitive environment.

The deregulation that eliminated the Interstate Commerce Commission's financial requirements to start a trucking company caused the birth of 11,000 new firms. Unfortunately such increased competition, aided by a recession in the late 1970s (which decreased shipping volume), triggered a price war that cut truckers' income by as much as 30 percent. Consequently, the number of independent truckers declined from almost 300,000 in the late 1970s to 100,000 by the early 1980s. Shippers have realized material gains from trucking deregulation, however, as more companies have been forced to compete on price alone. The traffic manager at one large manufacturing plant estimated that his facility saved $1 million in shipping costs as deregulation caused cheaper rates. Deregulation has brought intensified price cutting among rail carriers, too.

In the financial area, deregulation of banks and savings and loan associations led to a rise in interest rates that benefited thrifty consumers; however, this development had a negative impact on real estate borrowers and the users of bank-sponsored credit cards such as Visa and MasterCard. Deregulation also played a role in the historic crisis that has yet to be resolved in the savings and loan industry (see Chapter 15). The breakup of massive American Telephone and Telegraph was intended to introduce more competition within the communications industry.

All these deregulatory moves, and many more, indicate that the federal bureaucracy is responding to public and business protest against excessive control. There is also congressional support for a dual system of reporting and inspection based on the size of a business.

SUMMARY

The law in the United States consists of common law, based on the evolution of court decisions from the earliest English courts to the present, and statutory law, a written body of legislated rules. Torts (private or civil wrongs) are tried in civil courts, and crimes (public wrongs) are tried in criminal courts. The three-tiered federal court system allows for appeals of court decisions; most states have a similar court system.

Much of business law is covered by the Uniform Commercial Code, which virtually every state has adopted. The UCC law of contracts specifies what contracts must be written and presents the six elements required for a contract to be valid. The law of agency governs the legal relationship of an agent to the principal he or she represents. The law of sales, which pertains only to new, tangible personal property, enumerates several implied warranties that sellers make to buyers.

The UCC's law of property covers both real and personal property. Federal laws govern the ownership and use of intellectual property: patents, trademarks, and copyrights. Inventors apply to the Patent and Trademark Office for a utility patent, a design patent, or a plant patent. Once a patent is awarded, the holder has the right to exclude others from making, selling, or using the item for a fixed length of time. The Patent and Trademark Office also registers trademarks and service marks, which are words, names, symbols, or devices that firms use to identify their products or services and to distinguish them from those of competitors. A copyright, recorded by the Copyright Office of the Library of Congress, guarantees certain rights to persons who create an original work of authorship. The Uniform Commercial Code also deals with the law of negotiable instruments, which affects the transfer of promissory notes, checks, and drafts, and the law of bankruptcy.

Businesses operate within an intricate network of state and federal regulations issued by a variety of regulatory agencies. Regulations are administered by at least 116 different federal agencies and programs. The cost of meeting the reporting requirements of these agencies is eventually paid by the consumer in the form of higher prices. Because living in today's legal environment can be costly, companies are concerned about reducing and streamlining regulatory demands. Companies and individual managers have found that they can respond to excessive regulation by improving self-policing, staying abreast of legislative trends, and lobbying for legislative change. Sympathetic regulators have been able to reduce the burden on businesses by setting regulatory objectives and leaving the choice of methods to business and by creating a system of financial penalties and rewards for affected firms.

KEY TERMS

agent p. 655
bankruptcy *or* insolvency p. 664
common law p. 651
contract p. 653
copyright p. 661
crime p. 651
negotiable instruments p. 663
patent p. 656

principal p. 655
service mark p. 660
statutory law p. 651
tort p. 651
trademark p. 659
Uniform Commercial Code (UCC) p. 653
warranty p. 655

FOR REVIEW AND DISCUSSION

1. Where did our body of common law originate? What is the doctrine on which it is based? How does statutory law differ from common law?
2. What is the difference between a tort and a crime? What is the difference between a personal damage tort and a property tort?
3. Diagram the hierarchy of the federal court system. Which courts conduct jury trials? Which act as buffers? Which concern themselves with procedural errors? Which serves as a last resort for appeals?
4. What advantage does a state receive when it adopts the Uniform Commercial Code?
5. List and define the six elements of a legally binding contract.
6. What four types of contracts must be made in writing? Give the reasons for that requirement in each case.
7. Cite several business transactions that might require the involvement of an agent.
8. Evaluate the following remark about written warranties: "The big print giveth and the small print taketh way." What does it mean? Is it true? If so, what implications does it have for consumers?
9. Discuss the four implied warranties covered in the law of sales. Give examples of business transactions in which each would play an important role.

10. Define the two kinds of property that are covered by the UCC law of property.
11. Discuss the importance of patents, trademarks, and copyrights in a business firm's marketing.
12. What are the principal features of the three kinds of patents? What procedure would an inventor follow to apply for a patent?
13. Do you think the commercial lives of most patents are equal to, less than, or greater than their legal lives? Give reasons for your answer, and cite examples.
14. Under what conditions may secrecy be preferred to patenting? What measures should management take to protect the security of trade secrets?
15. What things can be registered as trademarks? What action can a firm take to prevent its trademark from being used generically?
16. What rights would you enjoy if you copyrighted a commercially valuable work?
17. What three instruments of payment fall under the UCC negotiable instruments law? List the six conditions each such instrument must meet to be negotiable.
18. Describe the conditions under which each of the following indorsements might be used: blank indorsement, special indorsement, restrictive indorsement, and qualified indorsement.

19. Under what circumstances might someone be declared bankrupt?
20. What problems does the federal bureaucracy present for small and large businesses alike? How does regulation inhibit new product development?
21. Recommend several measures that companies and individual managers can take to reduce the regulatory burden. How might sympathetic regulators fulfill their mandate without placing undue demands on businesses?

APPLICATIONS

Case 20.1: Fighting to Keep a Trademark

Sheldon Jacobs is the owner of a restaurant in Minneapolis famed for the way it roasts its chicken. He spent $3 million developing his oven. He compares the twenty-three-function computerized wood burner to a Mercedes-Benz, boasting that "I can make your tennis shoe taste good." He calls his process Woodroast.

Unfortunately, in the years since he introduced his oven, chicken roasted over wood has become very popular among both restaurateurs and diners, and Jacobs has become increasingly concerned with the reputation of his process. Woodroast has been a registered trademark since 1987. In recent years, however, it has become difficult and rather expensive for Jacobs to track down people using his trade name—either inadvertently or on purpose.

Luckily, most restaurants that he confronts don't mind ceasing to use the phrase, but some do resist. One of the resistors is Kenny Rogers Roasters Wood Roasted Chicken. But after being hit with a lawsuit, the chain agreed to phase out the term; instead they now make "Oak Roasted Chicken."

Jacobs feels that it is absolutely essential that his Woodroast trademark be protected, fearing the fate of the thermos, the escalator, and the zipper. Many trademark names have lost their legal protection because the public used them to describe all similar products. Jacobs feels that unless he is vigilant in the protection of this trademark, he will be stripped of legal protection.

Jacobs may face an uphill battle, however. Starting with a product name that is already common usage for a method of cooking meats, Jacobs will find it difficult to convince the courts to uphold his trademark against infringement. Further, even if he succeeds at his current legal efforts, the commonness of his trade name will quite likely cause it to become widely used and bring about the loss of trademark protection in the future.

Questions

1. How can products and companies be stripped of trademark protection?

2. How can companies protect their legal rights to their trademarks?

3. What special challenges does Jacobs face in protecting his Woodroast trademark?

4. Do you think that uses of the term Wood Roasted should be disallowed by Jacobs's trademark? Why or why not?

For more information, see Jyoti Thottam, "So Far, He Hasn't Claimed Credit for Bringing Combustion to Wood," *The Wall Street Journal,* July 7, 1993, p. B1.

Case 20.2: Lending a Helping Hand

Business generally likes to keep government out of the way. Almost universally, the potential of involvement by a government agency is enough to put business leaders into an uproar. Complaints about taxation, regulation, investigations, and many other things are commonplace. In a recent case, however, Pepsi-Cola was able to overcome, and even take advantage of, the traditional adversarial relationship between government and business.

In 1993 the Pepsi-Cola company was faced with a potentially damaging situation. Early in June newspapers in Seattle and New Orleans carried reports of people finding syringes in cans of Pepsi. Over the next two weeks, fifty people came forward with similar stories. A week after the reports broke, Craig Weatherup, CEO of PepsiCo, received a call from David Kessler, the chairman of the Food and Drug Administration (FDA). Weatherup later said, "It was clear we knew the same thing: that for this to be happening defied logic."

Kessler told Weatherup that, despite political pressure, he would not be ordering a recall of Pepsi products. He felt that there would be no public safety advantage to an expensive recall operation. The next day, the TV networks asked whether Pepsi wished to make a statement. Weatherup's prepared a video segment showing how it was nearly impossible for foreign objects to be put in the cans. Over the course of the day, Weatherup appeared on six news programs. Then, that night, he and Kessler both appeared on Nightline. By then, Kessler's agency had an arrest pending. Apparently, a Pennsylvania man had fabricated a tale about Pepsi tampering.

In his television appearances, Weatherup's straightforward, no-nonsense persona appealed to the public. Kessler's presence added legitimacy to what was said. On Nightline, they covered the technical details of a canning operation, and Kessler listed the penalties for fraud. Between them they created a convincing front at a time when the public had become jaded by repeated corporate equivocation on safety issues. Together, business and government squelched a fraudulently created scandal—saving Pepsi's summer sales.

Questions

1. How did the FDA's assistance help Pepsi?

2. What are the advantages of better government-business interaction?

3. What possible harms are there from government-business collusion for businesses? For the country?

4. Do you think the news media help or hurt companies caught in embarrassing situations? Defend your answer.

For more information, see Laura Zinn, "The Right Moves, Baby," *Business Week,* July 5, 1993, p. 30.

REFERENCES

1. Mark D. Fefer, "Stocks to Avoid," *Fortune 1993 Investor's Guide,* Fall 1992, p. 148.
2. *The Wall Street Journal,* January 16, 1992, p. A1.
3. "Bankruptcy Rise Slows," *The Wall Street Journal,* March 18, 1993, p. B6.

21

INTERNATIONAL BUSINESS

*T*he Chinese expression Shang chang ru zhan chang *translates literally as, "The marketplace is a battlefield." That is how the Asian people view the importance of success in the business world. The success of a nation's economy influences the survival and well-being of a nation as surely as does the course of battle.*

CLIN-NING CHU
The Asian Mind Game

CHAPTER OBJECTIVES
After studying this chapter, you should be able to:

1. Describe the scope and importance of international trade.
2. Explain the major concepts involved in international trade: balance of trade, balance of payments, and exchange rate.
3. Explain why a nation and an individual business choose to participate in international business.
4. Summarize the alternative approaches a business firm may use to operate in international business.
5. Describe the development of multinational corporations and the strategies they use.
6. Explain the concept of a global or transnational corporation.
7. Identify and explain the barriers to international trade.
8. Describe the aids to international trade.
9. Identify and describe the conflicts that occur between an international business and the host and home countries.

UP FRONT

David Elder heads one of the most innovative and progressive companies in the world: PSION, Inc., of Concord, Massachusetts, the U.S. subsidiary of PSION Plc, the world's leading manufacturer of personal hand-held computers. It is a position he earned through hard work and by coming up through the ranks. He has the kind of experience that will help him manage a global enterprise in an extremely competitive and fast-changing market.

Since PSION Plc of London, England created the Organiser hand-held computer in 1984, it has grown to a $70 million company with world-wide operations. In 1993 PSION introduced its Series 3 palmtop computer, with all the features and functions of a laptop or desktop computer. The Series 3 was declared "one of the most innovative consumer electronics products of the year" at the annual Consumer Electronics Show. Palmtop computers are expected to grow to a $1.6 billion industry over the next decade.

David Elder embodies the global nature of the computer business. Born in Edinburgh, Scotland, he was educated at Manchester University and is fluent in German, French, and Russian. He worked in the export division of the Gillette Company for six years, during which he learned that export is very much in his blood. "I've done business in over fifty countries during my career," he says. "What's interesting is to learn about different cultures and national characteristics in the way people conduct business. You must learn to be flexible enough and humble enough to adapt to people's idiosyncrasies."

Elder's work at PSION began in England, where he was export director from 1986 to 1990. Under his direction, PSION developed export relationships with over forty-five international partners, accounting for 45 percent of total sales. "PSION competes in the global market with Casio and Sharp, but we take a very different approach; we do not market a commodity product," says Elder. "PSION began as a software company, and so we are very software-oriented. We place a great deal of emphasis on customer service and support. Our sales staff is well trained, and we provide heavy service for our retail stores, helping the sales staff learn about our product. We want them to recommend a PSION product to their retail customers."

In 1991 Elder was promoted to managing director of PSION GmbH, the company's German subsidiary, where he managed a staff of sixteen. "I've found that it's a very good idea to have my people involved in the business process in an individual way. We at PSION give our people a much greater say in how the process works, and I think this gives us a powerful advantage against our competitors." Elder built two distribution channels for PSION products: corporate and retail sales. Among the corporate accounts he helped acquire were Lufthansa, Siemens, IBM, and the Volkswagen-Audi Group. He and his team built relationships with computer whole-

DAVID ELDER

PRESIDENT, PSION, INC.

salers, distributors, computer systems developers, value-added resellers (VARs), and catalog order companies. He also developed retail sales outlets through department stores. During his two-year tenure, PSION increased sales in Germany by 100 percent.

Elder's success in Germany led to his promotion to president of PSION Inc. His mission is to expand operations throughout North America. Currently, over 600 VARs and 300 retailers buy and market PSION products, in such stores as The Wiz, J&R Computer World, Good Guys, and Circuit City Impulse Stores. Elder also plans to expand corporate sales; companies such as Caldor, McGraw-Hill, Martin-Marietta, and Exxon currently use PSION computers.

David Elder believes there are great business opportunities in the emerging global economy. "Telecommunications will produce a global trading environment over the next ten years," he says, "but we must never forget to respect the differences in people and countries. Japan, Europe, and America will form trading blocs, but remember, each does business in different ways, and that difference is what helps each do what it does best.

"If you're planning a career in business, don't be afraid or feel demeaned by selling things," he counsels. "I regard myself as well educated and as a salesperson, and I'm very proud of that. I encourage people to get involved in international sales, for the work is fulfilling and ultimately it will make the world a better place for all of us."

Imagine that all world trade were to cease tomorrow at 11:00 A.M.

- How would you get your morning coffee or the sliced bananas for your corn flakes?
- How would your car get you to work on time without imported oil refined to gasoline?
- What would you wear without your imported clothes from Taiwan, Korea, or Singapore?
- What would you do after dinner with no French or German wine to sip and no Sony television to watch?

Obviously from these examples, the saying that "no man is an island" could apply to the business community. As we have learned, businesses are interrelated; they do business with one another and affect one another's operations. The same observation can be extended to business on an international scale.

The Scope and Importance of International Trade

The world is now like an international department store. Many products whose brand names are household words are produced in other countries. Norelco razors, Volvo automobiles, and Heineken beer are produced abroad and marketed in the United States. Conversely, products produced in the United States are found in the marketing channels of other countries. Gillette razor blades, Jeep four-wheel-drive vehicles, Coca-Cola beverages, and Chris Craft yachts are produced in America and are sold world-wide.

Familiar American logos can be found in countries all over the world.

International business is not an element of the future. It is here now. The clock in the international arena is ticking faster and faster. Communications and transportation have made the world smaller. Political and economic decisions have opened up new business opportunities, new alliances, a new set of problems, and new potential solutions.

In the last five years the international scene has exploded. The eastern European nations of East Germany, Czechoslovakia, Hungary, Poland, Bulgaria, Yugoslavia, Romania, and Albania—with their evolving political and economic systems—have become the new frontier. Eastern Europe is joining western Europe, North America, and the Pacific Rim countries in the world marketplace. The changes in the old Soviet Union have sent western European and American capitalists flocking there to create business partnerships. The changes in the European Community making western Europe one common market have changed the strategies of businesses all over the world.

As noted in previous chapters, everywhere businesses are breaking out of their national borders. Harley-Davidson has its big machines rumbling in Japan, Australia, and Europe; Domino's and Pizza Hut are battling it out in Japan; and Wal-Mart and K mart are setting up shop in Mexico. In addition, Pier 1, the retailer that has helped America's armchair travelers fill their homes with colorful, hand-made knickknacks and furniture from forty-four countries, plans to have 250 stores outside the United States within seven years.[1] The world is becoming smaller and smaller as the borders of international trade expand.

Before we examine the concepts associated with international business, let's take a look at the impact of international trade on other nations as well as on the United States.

The International Picture

The very economic health of some countries is significantly affected by their ability to sell to global markets. Examples include Japan and Germany, which export 17 and 26 percent of their gross domestic product (GDP), respectively.

When looking at the world marketplace, we see that Germany has captured 11 percent of the world trade, Japan has 9 percent, and the Asian Tigers—Hong Kong, Singapore, South Korea, and Taiwan—have 11 percent.

Beyond the economic effects, increased economic interdependence among nations has two other observable results:

- Increasing the variety of goods and services available to people of all nations improves the standard of living everywhere.
- Through trade interactions, nations are encouraged to understand and work with each other. Countries that communicate with one another—and depend on each other—are less likely to go to war with each other.

importing
Buying goods and
services abroad.

exporting
Selling goods and
services abroad.

Table 21.1

Leading United
States export and
import partners
(in billions of
dollars).

The U.S. Picture

The United States is involved in international trade through **importing**, *buying goods and services abroad*, and **exporting**, *selling goods and services abroad*. Although the United States exports less than 8 percent of its GDP, international trade is important both to the nation and to individual domestic companies.[2] American exports continue to rise, now exceeding $425 billion. The United States has moved past Germany as the world's leading exporter, with a 14 percent share of world trade. On the import side, the United States is also the world's largest importer, with 13 percent of the world's imports, equaling over $530 billion. Table 21.1 lists the primary nations the United

LEADING MARKETS FOR U.S. (EXPORTS)			LEADING U.S. SUPPLIERS (IMPORTS)		
RANK	COUNTRY	$ BILLION	RANK	COUNTRY	$ BILLION
1	Canada	77.8	1	Japan	97.2
2	Japan	39.2	2	Canada	89.1
3	Mexico	23.2	3	Germany	33.4
4	United Kingdom	19.1	4	Taiwan	32.4
5	Germany	16.2	5	Mexico	30.6
6	Taiwan	15.1	6	South Korea	27.5
7	South Korea	14.1	7	United Kingdom	24.1
8	France	13.9	8	France	16.1
9	Australia	10.0	9	Hong Kong	15.8
10	Singapore	8.7	10	Singapore	14.2

Source: *United States Department of Commerce News,* January 6, 1993, p. 2.

Figure 21.1
Where U.S.
exports go.

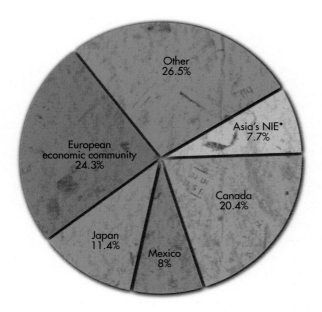

Other
26.5%

Asia's NIE*
7.7%

European
economic community
24.3%

Canada
20.4%

Japan
11.4%

Mexico
8%

*Newly industrialized economies: South Korea, Taiwan, Hong Kong, Singapore.
Source: "U.S. Trade Outlook," *Business America*, April 10, 1993, p. 6.

States markets to (exports) and is supplied by (imports). Figure 21.1 presents a view of United States export "pie."

Not only is international trade big business for the nation, it plays a significant role in the revenue and profitability of many companies. Boeing, General Motors, General Electric, Philip Morris, and Hewlett-Packard are companies for which global sales are important. Another example, Sun Microsystems—a company that did not exist a decade ago—now gets half of its total sales from outside the United States. Table 21.2 shows the leading exporters among United States corporations. Note the significance of the export sales as a percentage of total sales for Boeing, McDonnell Douglas, and Intel.

Major Concepts in International Trade

Business on an international scale has a language all its own. The important terms to know include *balance of trade, balance of payments,* and *exchange rate.*

Balance of Trade

A nation's **balance of trade** is *the difference between the dollar value of a nation's exports and the dollar value of its imports.* If exports exceed imports, a *trade surplus* exists and the country has a favorable balance of trade. If the imports exceed exports, a *trade deficit* exists and the country has an unfavorable balance of trade. In 1992 the United States had an unfavorable balance of trade of $105.1 billion.[3]

balance of trade
The difference between the dollar value of a nation's exports and the dollar value of its imports.

Table 21.2

Leading exporters among U.S. corporations.

RANK/COMPANY	MAJOR EXPORTS	U.S. EXPORTS (IN $ MILLIONS)	AS % OF TOTAL SALES	TOTAL SALES (IN $ MILLIONS)
1 Boeing	Commercial and military aircraft	17,856	58.7	30,414
2 General Motors	Motor vehicles, parts	11,284	8.4	132,774
3 General Electric	Jet engines, turbines, plastics, medical systems	8,614	13.8	62,202
4 IBM	Computers, related equipment	7,668	11.7	65,096
5 Ford Motor Co.	Motor vehicles, parts	7,340	7.2	100,785
6 Chrysler Corp.	Motor vehicles, parts	6,168	16.7	36,897
7 McDonnell Douglas	Aerospace products, electronic systems	6,160	32.9	18,718
8 E. I. Du Pont De Nemours	Specialty chemicals	3,812	10.1	37,386
9 Caterpillar	Heavy machinery, engines, turbines	3,710	36.4	10,182
10 United Technologies	Jet engines, helicopters, cooling equipment	3,587	16.2	22,032
11 Hewlett-Packard	Measurement and computation products and systems	3,223	22.2	14,541
12 Philip Morris	Tobacco, beverages, food products	3,061	6.1	50,157
13 Eastman Kodak	Imaging, chemicals, health products	3,020	14.7	20,577
14 Motorola	Communications equipment, cellular phones	2,928	25.8	11,341
15 Archer-Daniels-Midland	Protein meals, vegetable oils, flour, grain	2,600	30.3	8,567
16 Digital Equipment	Computers, related equipment	2,200	15.7	14,024
17 Intel	Microcomputer components, modules, systems	1,929	40.4	4,778
18 Allied-Signal	Aircraft and automotive parts, chemicals	1,729	14.6	11,882
19 Sun Microsystems	Computers, related equipment	1,606	49.3	3,259
20 Unisys	Computers, related equipment	1,598	18.4	8,696

Source: Bureau of Trade Statistics.

Balance of Payments

A nation's balance of trade determines its **balance of payments,** *the difference between a country's total payments to other countries and its total receipts from other countries.* When a country experiences a trade deficit, there is an unfavorable balance of payments to pay for the goods. When the opposite situation occurs, there is a favorable balance of payments.

Activities that affect the balance of payments include banking, transportation, military transactions, and profits from companies operating in foreign countries. Table 21.3 shows the U.S. balance of payments compared with the balance of payments of other nations throughout the world. Notice Japan's particularly healthy balance of payments.

Country	Outstanding Balance of Payments (in $ millions)
Australia	−9,852
Canada	−25,529
Egypt	+1,903
France	−6,148
Germany	−9,485
Japan	+72,905
Mexico	−13,283
Netherlands	+9,206
Norway	+4,939
People's Republic of China	+13,765
Philippines	+4,208
Saudi Arabia	−25,738
United Kingdom	−9,447
United States	−3,690

Source: *Balance of Payments Statistics Yearbook,* Volume 43, Part 2 (Washington, D.C.: 1992), International Monetary Fund, pp. 6–7.

Table 21.3
Balance of payments throughout the world.

Exchange Rate

Each country has its own currency. When a contract for the sale of goods between countries is made, the price must be converted from one country's currency to the other's. The *rate at which the money of one country is converted or exchanged for the money of another* is known as the **exchange rate.**

The exchange rate can either be *floating*—the rate varies with market conditions—or established by the government—a *controlled* exchange rate.

A country's government can affect the exchange rate in various ways, in turn affecting the attractiveness of its goods. For example, the government can practice **devaluation,** or *increasing the rate of exchange at which foreign currency will be traded for domestic currency.* If the United States were to raise the exchange rate for British pounds from $3.50 for £1 to $5.00 for £1, it would encourage the British to buy more U.S. exports (£1 buys $1.50 more goods after the devaluation) and would increase the cost of British goods to American importers by $1.50 for each £1. As exports to Britain rose and imports from that country declined, the trade deficit with Britain might be eliminated.

Conversely, the government can practice **revaluation,** or *decreasing the rate of exchange at which foreign currency will be traded for domestic currency.* If the United States were to lower the exchange rate for British pounds from $3.50 for £1 to $1.00 for £1, the result would be to discourage the British from buying American exports.

balance of payments
The difference between a country's total payments to other countries and its total receipts from other countries.

exchange rate
The rate at which the money of one country is converted or exchanged for the money of another.

devaluation
Increasing the rate of exchange at which foreign currency will be traded for domestic currency.

The Decision to Engage in International Trade

Both nations and individual businesses make conscious decisions to engage in international trade. The main reason for the decision is a scarcity of resources and products.[4] Let's examine this situation from the perspective of a country and then from that of individual companies.

A Nation's Absolute and Comparative Advantage

No country has every raw material or resource it needs. Nor can every nation produce everything it needs. In adition, there are some things, such as steel, that a country may not be able to produce at the lowest possible cost. The result of these situations is that some countries are good at producing particular goods and choose to exploit this ability—or advantage.

An **absolute advantage** occurs when *a nation has a monopoly on a product or can produce it at the lowest cost.* The country can export the product because the country either controls it or can produce it more efficiently. For example, South Africa has an absolute advantage in the production of diamonds. It not only has the majority of the world's diamond mines but has developed and refined its mining operations to efficiently extract the diamonds.

Situations in which a country has an absolute advantage occur infrequently. Usually more than one country can effectively supply a specific good. As a result, most countries rely on a comparative advantage.

A **comparative advantage** occurs when *a nation is better equipped to produce one product or service than other nations.* Essentially, a nation produces for export whatever it is in the best position to make relative to other nations. This specialization may arise from such characteristics as climate, soil, technological development, labor supply and skills, agricultural products (mahogany or teak, for example), or mineral and petroleum deposits. Table 21.4 lists several nations and the products for which they enjoy a comparative advantage. As an example, the United States has a comparative advantage in the aerospace industry. It leads all American industries in exports by a wide margin and also generates the largest trade surplus. On the other hand, America has no competitive advantage in consumer electronics. Rather, its ability to compete and export products is sinking like a rock. Japan now has a significant competitive advantage.[5]

Why Businesses "Go International"

Rather than operating from a position of absolute or comparative advantage, individual companies have other specific reasons for venturing into international business. These include:

1. *Profit potential.* Just as companies working within the borders of the United States target profitable market segments, internationally oriented companies visualize the world market as their overall target market for profitable operations. An example of a "market seeker" would be Coca-Cola or

---

revaluation
Decreasing the rate of exchange at which foreign currency will be traded for domestic currency.

absolute advantage
A nation has a monopoly on a product or can produce it at the lowest cost.

comparative advantage
A nation is better equipped to produce one product or service than other nations.

Procter & Gamble, which seek to expand the scope of their sales and their profits beyond the borders of the United States.

2. *Profit margin.* Closely related to more profits is profit margin—the potential of obtaining a higher percentage of earnings than can be received from domestic operations. Again Coca-Cola is a prime example. By being able to develop joint ventures and control its operating expenses, Coke has a greater profit margin internationally than from its domestic operations.[6]

3. *Established demand.* Less adventurous companies may enter international trade to take advantage of an established demand for American goods. In effect, a company may not have to pioneer new markets but simply piggyback on the efforts of other American firms. Rather than be a "McDonald's" in Russia or China, Burger King and Wendy's have let the demand for fast food increase and have then taken advantage of it.

4. *Raw material.* In addition to seeking a better profit margin, a company might enter international business because it is a raw material seeker. A company such as Texaco with a need to produce, refine, and market raw materials could begin to conduct operations in Saudi Arabia because of that country's oil reserves.

5. *Technology.* A company that was seeking to match its skills with another might become a technology seeker. As an example, Hewlett-Packard and Swedish telecommunications giant Ericsson Telecom AB sought each other out to develop and market integrated computer network management systems.[7]

6. *Production efficiency.* Companies—such as Haggar and General Motors—that need to lower production costs become production efficiency seekers. They go to Asia, Mexico, or Europe to find less expensive labor.

Besides these reasons, going international or global is a matter of survival for many companies. In certain industries, companies cannot survive on their domestic markets if they are in global industries. Take, for example, the

NATION	PRODUCT
Argentina	Sheep, wool, beef, hides
Australia	Sheep, wool, rutile ore for titanium
Bolivia	Zinc, tin
Brazil	Industrial diamonds, coffee, manganese
Canada	Grain
Colombia	Coffee
France	Wine, cheese
Indonesia, Venezuela	Petroleum
Italy	Glass
Japan	Motorcycles, automobiles, electronics
Norway	Forest products
South Africa	Manganese, platinum, chromium
South Korea	Labor, steel
Surinam, Jamaica	Bauxite
Sweden	Seafood
Switzerland	Chocolate
United States	Aircraft, coal, grain, chemicals
Zambia, Zaire	Cobalt

Table 21.4
Nations that have a comparative advantage in producing certain goods.

GLOBAL PERSPECTIVE

Motorola Commits to China

Taking a cautious approach to expansion into China, Motorola initially put together a makeshift plant in the northern port city of Tianjin to crank out its first made-in-China paging devices. The assumption was that local demand would be small and that Motorola would have to find export markets to make the investment pay off.

Was Motorola ever wrong. It now sells the entire weekly output of 10,000 units in China, where a pager with one year of service retails for $200. Motorola no longer talks of the "potential" Chinese market—that market has arrived.

Convinced the boom is for real, Motorola is laying the groundwork for what will be corporate America's biggest manufacturing venture in China. Motorola will soon complete a $120 million first-phase plant in the Tianjin Economic & Technology Development Area to make pagers, simple integrated circuits, and cellular phones. A second-phase plant, which could include automotive electronics, advanced microprocessing, and walkie-talkie systems, will come on-line in three more years.

The Motorola venture symbolizes a huge leap in commitment to China. It goes well beyond setting up factories to take advantage of low-cost labor or to get a foot in the door of China's vast market. Motorola executives expect that, over time, Chinese technicians will play a big global role in the design and engineering of products, such as locals already do at the company's plants in Singapore and Malaysia.

(For more on Motorola's China commitment, see Pete Engardio, "Motorola In China: A Great Leap Forward," *Business Week*, May 17, 1993, p. 58.)

pharmaceuticals business. Twenty years ago it cost $16 million and took four years to develop a new drug and bring it to market. Now developing a drug costs about $250 million and takes as long as twelve years. Only a global product for a global market can support that much risk. As a result, the major pharmaceutical companies have to operate in all major international markets—North America, western Europe, and the Pacific Rim countries.

According to Howard Perlmulter of the Wharton School of Finance, there are 136 industries, from accounting to zippers, where a company has to play world chess or get out. These industries include auto manufacturing, banking, consumer electronics, entertainment, pharmaceuticals, publishing, travel services, and washing machines.[8] These industries are by necessity the territory of international corporations.

Now we know why companies choose to embark on international operations, but what approaches can they use to participate in the international business arena?

Alternative Approaches in International Business

A company can select from a number of alternative strategies for becoming involved in international trade. These alternatives include exporting, foreign licensing, foreign-operated sales branches, joint ventures, and wholly owned subsidiaries. Each succeeding alternative increases the level of commitment of the organization's resources. As a result, companies normally evolve from one strategy to another as their success increases.

Exporting

The easiest and simplest way to enter the international arena is by exporting—selling the company's products to a foreign country. A business can approach exporting in a number of ways: creating an export department, using a foreign intermediary, or working with an export trading company.

If a company chooses to create an *export department,* it is in essence establishing a contact point in the company to initiate sales material, receive inquiries, and process orders. Although having an export department involves little risk, it does require the commitment of capital and management talent.

Using a **foreign intermediary**—*a wholesaler or agent who performs marketing functions for firms that want to do business in other countries*—is one of the least risky ways for a novice company to venture into foreign markets. It requires little investment of capital, time, or effort. Intermediaries often serve a large number of firms, however, so they might not market products as aggressively or as effectively as some of their clients would wish. For manufacturers of raw materials and high-cost capital goods, agents can be extremely effective. The manufacturer is not committing an inventory nor losing control.[9]

A novice company could also dip into the international market by selling its goods to an *export trading company.* In turn, the trading company resells the goods to other companies overseas. The trading company takes title to the goods and moves them from one country to another, simply adding a markup for itself. Trading companies are a good way to enter a foreign market because they are favored by foreign governments.

foreign intermediary
A wholesaler or agent who performs marketing functions for firms that want to do business in other countries.

Foreign Licensing

As foreign markets expand, or if the company wants to take a more aggressive step in the international arena, it can take the step of **licensing.** This is *an agreement between one company (the* licensor) *and another (the* licensee) *that permits the licensee to manufacture and market a product owned by the licensor.* The licensee pays a royalty to the licensor for each unit sold.

Licensing agreements enable a producer to reach markets that for various reasons might otherwise be impossible to penetrate. As an example, TGI Friday's, the Dallas-based restaurant company, has taken an aggressive step in its "mission to be the premier full-service restaurant world-wide." It recently signed licensing agreements to establish fifteen TGI Friday's in Malaysia, Singapore, Indonesia, and Thailand. This deal was quickly followed with

licensing
An agreement between one company (the *licensor*) and another (the *licensee*) that permits the licensee to manufacture and market a product owned by the licensor.

Japanese banks in the United States provide a good example of foreign-operated sales branches.

another licensing agreement for fifteen more eateries in Australia and New Zealand. On the drawing boards is still another licensing agreement with a German brewer for twenty-five restaurants in Germany.[10]

Foreign-Operated Sales Branch

After licensing, the next most adventurous step is for a company to have an ownership interest in a foreign country. This can be achieved through a **foreign-operated sales branch**—*a firm's wholly owned sales organization in a foreign country.* Branch employees (either foreign nationals or citizens of the home country) are hired to sell the products made in the company's domestic plants. This approach gives the producer control over the marketing effort abroad.

foreign-operated sales branch
A firm's wholly owned sales organization in a foreign country.

Joint Ventures

The next step for involvement in international trade is to create a joint venture. By entering a joint venture, a company creates a new "venture" and shares ownership of this company with foreign nationals—individuals, a company, or the nation's government itself. Examples of recent joint ventures are provided by J. C. Penney, Dresser Industries, and Chevron Corp.

J. C. Penney signed a joint venture with Frisa, one of the largest developers of residential, resort, and retail properties in Mexico City. The deal will allow Penney's to pursue its plans to enter the Mexican market with five stores in the next three years.[11]

Dresser Industries established a manufacturing beachhead in Russia by creating a joint venture with private Russian oil and gas companies. Under the arrangement, oil-field services equipment would be manufactured in Russia for Russian industry.[12]

In a deal four years in the making, Chevron Corp. created a joint venture with the Russian government to develop Tenghiz, the biggest oil field to come up for grabs in more than two decades. By gaining Tenghiz, Chevron will have access to up to 4.5 billion barrels of oil—immediately doubling its world-wide reserves.[13]

Wholly Owned Subsidiaries

A still deeper level of involvement in international business is to control both the foreign production and the foreign marketing facilities. This control is achieved through the formation of a **wholly owned foreign subsidiary**—*a set of manufacturing and distribution facilities located in a foreign country but owned by a parent company located elsewhere.* An example is J. I. Case Company, owned by Tenneco, which makes and sells its own heavy earthmoving equipment overseas. Another example is provided by Hunt Oil's subsidiary in Laos. It follows on the heels of subsidiaries established by Hunt Oil in North Yemen, Chile, and China. Companies that have made this major commitment to international business are referred to as *multinationals.*

wholly owned foreign subsidiary
A set of manufacturing and distribution facilities located in a foreign country but owned by a parent company located elsewhere.

Multinational Corporations: A Total Commitment

Companies that are totally committed to operating world-wide are known as multinationals. A **multinational corporation**, although legally based in a "home country," is *a firm that has assets committed to operations and subsidiaries world-wide.* Multinationals may work in partnership with host-country firms, form joint ventures with host-country firms or governments, or simply establish operations on their own. Whatever the arrangement, they can be found producing sewing machines in England, mining bauxite in Australia, and selling insurance in Thailand. Exxon, Xerox, Ford, and Eastman Kodak are all multinationals. Table 21.5 lists the largest U.S. multinationals.

multinational corporation
A firm that has assets committed to operations and subsidiaries world-wide.

Origins of Multinationals

The impetus for the eventual development of American multinational corporations occurred after World War II when European nations badly needed recovery assistance. The U.S. government could not solve European recovery problems merely by exporting domestic production. The best approach seemed to be for American firms to produce needed products overseas. As a result, corporations were encouraged to invest abroad.

In the majority of instances foreign nations welcomed the involvement of American companies in their industrial recovery. Encouraged by this response, U.S. corporations have steadily increased their foreign investment from approximately $7 billion in 1946 to better than $300 billion today.

The growth of multinationals is a two-way street. Foreign multinationals are also opening operations in the United States or buying existing businesses. Foreign investment in the United States quadrupled between 1971 and 1993. Table 21.6 lists the largest foreign multinationals.

Table 21.5
The twenty largest U.S. multinationals.

RANK/COMPANY	SALES ($ MILLIONS)	PROFITS ($ MILLIONS)	ASSETS ($ MILLIONS)	TOTAL STOCK-HOLDERS' EQUITY ($ MILLIONS)	EMPLOYEES
1 General Motors	132,774	(23,498)	191,012	6,225	750,000
2 Exxon	103,547	4,770	85,030	33,776	95,000
3 Ford Motor Co.	100,785	(7,385)	180,545	14,752	325,333
4 IBM	65,096	(4,965)	86,705	27,624	308,010
5 General Electric	62,202	4,725	192,876	23,459	268,000
6 Mobil	57,389	862	40,561	16,540	63,700
7 Philip Morris	50,157	4,939	50,014	12,563	161,000
8 Chevron	38,523	1,569	33,970	13,728	49,245
9 E. I. Du Pont De Nemours	37,386	(3,927)	38,870	11,765	125,000
10 Texaco	31,130	712	25,992	9,973	37,582
11 Chrysler	36,897	723	40,653	7,538	128,000
12 Boeing	30,414	552	18,147	8,056	143,000
13 Procter & Gamble	29,890	1,872	24,025	9,071	106,200
14 Amoco	25,543	(74)	28,453	12,960	46,994
15 PepsiCo	22,083	374	20,951	5,355	371,000
16 United Technologies	22,032	(287)	15,928	3,370	178,000
17 Conagra	21,219	372	9,758	2,232	80,787
18 Eastman Kodak	20,577	1,146	23,138	6,557	132,600
19 Dow Chemical	19,080	(489)	25,360	8,074	61,353
20 Xerox	18,089	(1,020)	34,051	3,971	99,300

Source: Ani Hadjian and Lorraine Tritto, "Another Year of Pain," *Fortune*, July 26, 1993, pp. 191–193. © 1993 Time Inc. All rights reserved.

Operational Strategies

Multinational corporations are specialists in international business. In attempting to minimize costs and maximize marketing opportunities, they focus on producing the product where it can be done the most economically and target their marketing to focus on growth areas.

One cost-saving strategy available to multinationals is **production sharing**, *a manufacturing process that integrates production operations along international lines.* A company may assemble part of an item in one nation, ship it to another for further processing, and market the finished product in yet another country. To illustrate, let's take a look at hand-held calculators. The microcomputer chips that are the heart of a calculator may be made in America, shipped to a developing nation such as Mexico or South Korea for assembly into an end product, and then marketed in such developed countries as the United States, Canada, and England.

production sharing
A manufacturing process that integrates production operations along international lines.

Table 21.6
The twenty largest foreign multinationals.

RANK/COMPANY	SALES ($ MILLIONS)	PROFITS ($ MILLIONS)	ASSETS ($ MILLIONS)	TOTAL STOCK-HOLDERS EQUITY ($ MILLIONS)	EMPLOYEES
1 Royal Dutch/Shell Group (Britain/Netherlands)	98,935	5,408	100,354	52,935	127,000
2 Toyota (Japan)	79,114	1,812	761,131	37,490	108,167
3 IRI (Italy)	67,547	(3,812)	N.A.	N.A.	400,000
4 Daimler-Benz (Germany)	62,202	4,725	192,876	23,459	
5 Hitachi (Japan)	61,465	619	76,667	25,768	331,505
6 British Petroleum (Britain)	59,215	(808)	52,637	15,098	97,650
7 Matsushita Electric Industrial (Japan)	57,480	307	75,645	30,057	252,057
8 Volkswagen (Germany)	56,734	50	46,480	8,356	274,103
9 Siemens (Germany)	51,401	1,136	50,752	13,505	413,000
10 Nissan Motor (Japan)	50,247	(448)	62,978	15,086	143,754
11 Samsung (South Korea)	49,559	374	48,030	6,430	188,558
12 Fiat (Italy)	47,928	446	58,013	11,609	285,482
13 Unilever (Britain/Netherlands)	43,962	2,278	24,267	6,934	283,000
14 ENI (Italy)	40,365	(767)	54,790	11,008	124,032
15 Elf Aquitaine (France)	39,717	1,166	45,129	15,743	87,900
16 Nestlé (Switzerland)	39,057	1,916	30,336	8,891	218,005
17 Toshiba (Japan)	37,471	164	49,341	10,068	173,000
18 Renault (France)	33,884	1,072	23,897	6,145	146,604
19 Honda Motor (Japan)	33,369	306	26,374	9,085	90,900
20 Sony (Japan)	31,451	290	39,700	12,517	126,000

Source: Ani Hadjian and Lorraine Tritto, "Another Year of Pain," *Fortune*, July 26, 1993, pp. 191–192. © 1993 Time Inc. all rights reserved.

Another element of the operating strategy of some multinationals is the tactic of **dumping**, which is *selling the same product internationally below the price charged in one's home market for the purpose of disposing of excess production and maximizing total profits.* As an example, assume that a multinational company controls most of the output and sales of television sets in its home country. As a result of its dominant domestic market position, it is relatively free to charge a higher price in its home country than it could in other countries where greater competition exists. Also assume that it has excessive productive capacity that enables it to produce more televisions than it can sell domestically. Consequently, the managers decide to dump its excess capacity in other countries, charging a lower price than in its own country.

dumping
Selling the same product internationally below the price charged in one's home market for the purpose of disposing of excess production and maximizing total profits.

A real-world illustration of dumping can be seen in the ongoing trade difficulties between Japan and the United States in both the steel industry and in consumer electronics. The American Steel industry has consistently criticized Japanese steelmakers for dumping their products in the United States. The dumping practices have dramatically resulted in underselling domestic producers. Similarly, Zenith has pursued charges of dumping practices against Japanese TV manufacturers for more than a decade.

The Super-Multinational—The Global Corporation

As in all business undertakings, some companies push the boundaries of their existence to new limits. Such is the case with Royal Dutch Shell, Siemens, and Nestlé, which have become the super-multinationals. Each operates as a **global *or* transnational corporation**—*a corporation that looks at the world as one market.* A global corporation manufactures, conducts research, raises capital, and buys supplies wherever it can do the job best. It keeps in touch with technology and market trends all around the world. National boundaries and regulations tend to be irrelevant—or a mere hindrance. Corporate headquarters might be anywhere.

global *or* transnational corporation
A corporation that looks at the world as one market.

Barriers to International Trade

Companies that decide to enter international business operations are confronted with a variety of barriers that can hamper their operations. Among these barriers are language, customs and cultural differences, currency conversion, and political protectionist practices.

Language

A potential problem on the international business scene is created by language barriers. Language can prove to be a large stumbling block, even with the use of interpreters. In negotiations in Japan, for example, the Japanese often say yes when they mean no. They never say no in public—even if they want to deny a request or express a negative intent. And trying to decipher when yes means no can be frustrating for anyone.[14]

Communication problems also occur with body language, or nonverbal communication. In many Asian cultures, it is not proper to look a superior in the eye too often. A bowed head is a sign of deference to an authority figure. First-time visitors to Japan can find this practice confusing unless they know the custom or are mixing with Japanese accustomed to dealing with Westerners.

Other examples of nonverbal communication are boundless:

- Raise your eyebrows in Tunga and you may have bought something; the gesture means "Yes." But in Peru elevated eyebrows mean "Pay me." In Taiwan, blinking at someone is impolite.
- Nodding your head most anywhere in the world means "Yes"—but not in Bulgaria or Greece, where a nod means "No."

Businesspeople with international dealings need to learn about the customs and protocols of the cultures with which they interact.

- Americans who use the familiar "OK" symbol, the first finger touching the thumb to make a circle, could get themselves in trouble in Brazil. There this gesture is an obscene reference to sexual intercourse. In Russia and Greece, this hand sign is simply considered impolite. In Japan it signifies money, and in southern France it means zero or worthless.[15]

Customs and Culture

Limitations in customs and cultural knowledge may create problems. For example, it is useful to know that:

- In Japan, presenting business cards is done in a prescribed manner, and the methods of approaching and gaining introductions to business contacts are more formalized than in the United States.
- The farther south you go in Europe and Latin America, the closer people want to stand to you and the more physical contact they want. They will pat you, hold you, and touch your shoulder.
- Posture can create problems. Putting your feet up on your desk in front of an Arab is considered an insult. Even crossing your legs is less respectful than keeping both feet on the floor.
- While the European handshake is a standard greeting, it is executed with a much limper squeeze—and minus any arm pumping or whacks on the shoulder.[16]

Knowledge of cultural values can assist in conducting business. In Japan, patience and a long-term view can be helpful. Several face-to-face meetings are often necessary—and it may be some time before a Japanese company will discuss business details with a person who does not come highly recommended by some mutual acquaintance.

In addition, much of the business discussion in Japan takes place during "extended business hours"—anywhere from 7 P.M. to midnight—at a local restaurant or bar, and it sometimes involves lively singing and drinking.

During these informal get-togethers, the Japanese allow themselves to "let their hair down," and it is an important time for building trust and rapport. Normally, until a bond of some kind is established, Japanese are typically leery of doing business.

In many instances, business deals have been slowed or completely voided when a Westerner introduced a lawyer into the relationship at the beginning—a well-accepted Western business practice. The Japanese prefer simple contracts that leave open the possibility of negotiations if problems arise.[17]

Currency Conversion

A third potential barrier to international trade is the problem of currency conversion. A firm transacting business with a company in another country faces the ongoing problem of converting its currency to that of the trade partner's currency. Earlier in the chapter we introduced the concept of the exchange rate and the fact that this exchange rate can "float" based on market forces. Negotiations for the sale of a product are made with the realization that the worth of the money can change from day to day.

Politics and Protectionism

Even though countries ideally support unrestricted free trade between one another, the realities of economics, inflation, and recessions have made international trade a political topic and have helped to create legal barriers—quotas, tariffs, and embargoes—to implement a philosophy of **protectionism**. This is *an international trade philosophy that favors the creation of barriers against imports, to shelter domestic industries from foreign competition*. Protectionist arguments run the gamut, but all focus on limiting foreign imports of products that compete with those produced by home industries. Let's examine some of these arguments.

protectionism
An international trade philosophy that favors the creation of barriers against imports, to shelter domestic industries from foreign competition.

HOME INDUSTRIES PROTECTION ARGUMENT The *home industries protection argument* states that trade with other nations will cause domestic industries to lose their customers to foreign competitors, forcing firms out of business and throwing workers out of jobs. This argument has considerable emotional appeal, especially to laborers.

An example of this argument is the recent plea to protect the jobs of American flat glass makers—mirrors, windshields, and other flat glass products. According to one politician, a decision to eliminate any restrictions on Mexican imported glass "means that thousands of flat glass jobs will be needlessly lost."[18]

INFANT INDUSTRIES PROTECTION ARGUMENT The *infant industries protection argument* states that fledgling domestic industries should be protected from imports until they can become well established. Theoretically, as these infant industries gain strength, the nation would eventually achieve a comparative advantage in providing the products or services in question and the trade barriers would be abandoned.

This argument can be heard emerging from third world countries as they try to establish their own industrial base—protection is needed. The argument has been used historically in the United States. For example, when the U.S. motorcycle industry was in its infancy, a tariff on British import motorcycles was instituted.

DIVERSIFICATION FOR STABILITY ARGUMENT The *diversification for stability argument* states that trade with other nations will reduce or inhibit the development of a variety of domestic industries and thus reduce economic stability. This reasoning is behind the protectionist measures of governments in such one-industry economies as Cuba (reliant on sugar), Honduras (bananas), Brazil (coffee), and Middle Eastern nations (oil). Diversification develops a stable economy. Although the stability argument may be valid for countries with a few industries, it does not apply to already diversified economies.

WAGE PROTECTION ARGUMENT The *wage protection argument* states that trade with other nations depresses domestic wages because domestic producers cannot compete with cheap foreign labor. Although this argument has strong patriotic and humanitarian overtones, applicability to the United States has lessened in recent years. American wages, although higher than those in many nations, are no longer the highest among developed countries. Many northern European workers enjoy higher average pay than their American counterparts.

NATIONAL SECURITY ARGUMENT The *national security argument* states that a nation must strengthen and protect its domestic industries that produce strategic defense materials to be able to maintain its defenses. Otherwise, the country will become dependent on other nations for strategic materials needed during wartime, thus jeopardizing its own military capabilities.

This argument can be difficult to implement. For a nation such as the United States, with many resources and a large production capacity, it is relatively easy to maintain independence in production of military hardware. Problems are still encountered, however, when it comes to maintaining steady supplies of scarce but crucial raw materials. For this reason, the U.S. Department of Defense has established stockpiles of important raw materials essential to the production and maintenance of military equipment.

Now that we have discussed the reasons for protectionism, let's examine the tools of protectionism—tariffs, quotas, and embargoes.

tariff *or* import duty
A tax imposed on imported goods.

TARIFF A **tariff *or* import duty** is *a tax imposed on imported goods.* Its purpose is to raise their market prices, making the cost of competing domestic products attractive by comparison. In turn, the demand for domestic products may then increase, benefiting domestic producers and wage earners. Trade associations, labor organizations, and government agencies have encouraged tariffs against such items as leather jackets from Italy and Spain, steel from Japan, wooden and plastic clothespins from Taiwan and China, and fishing tackle from Japan, France, Mexico, Taiwan, and South Korea.

YOU DECIDE

After reviewing the arguments for protectionism, how valid do you think they are? How much protection do American industries need? What dangers are there of retaliation in the international business community if America adopts a protectionist mentality?

To protect the domestic automobile manufacturing industry, car manufacturers and dealers have lobbied to reclassify minivans and sport-utility vehicles as trucks instead of cars for import purposes. As cars, they are taxed at 2.5 percent of the sticker price. As trucks, the tariff would go to 25 percent. That would add $5,000 to the price of a Toyota Previa.[19]

quota
A limit on the quantity of a foreign product that can be brought into a country for resale.

QUOTA A **quota** is *a limit on the quantity of a foreign product that can be brought into a country for resale.* Quotas are more restrictive and absolute than tariffs. They reduce or eliminate the possibility of purchase by placing a ceiling on the number of units imported.

In the past, quotas have been imposed on foreign steel, televisions, textiles, and petroleum products. More recently, a new concept has emerged: developing a quota for products under a voluntary restraint agreement (VRA). Under such deals, foreign producers agree—voluntarily—that they will supply only a certain percentage of a market. In the steel industry a VRA has been in place since 1984. It limits imports to 20 percent of the U.S. market. The argument supported by protectionists is that these quotas resulted in saving 17,000 steel industry jobs.

embargo
A government order that prohibits firms from importing some or all of the products made in a given country.

EMBARGO An **embargo** is *a government order that prohibits firms from importing some or all of the products made in a given country.* For example, the United States has in the past imposed embargoes on goods from China, and it maintains them against all goods from Cuba and North Korea. After Fidel Castro won control of Cuba, Americans who wanted Havana cigars had to buy them in Canada or Europe and smoke them before returning to the United States.

Most embargoes, like the one against Cuba, are politically motivated; domestic economic concerns are secondary. As an example, economic sanctions were imposed against South Africa as a result of its national apartheid

International representatives meet regularly at GATT talks to discuss such trade policies as tariff reductions.

policy. An embargo was placed not only on imports but on sending American books *to* South Africa.

Aids to International Trade

A number of aids facilitate international trade. These include international agreements, financial support, and economic alliances.

International Agreements

International trade agreements of significance are GATT and NAFTA.

GATT The **General Agreement on Tariffs and Trade (GATT)** is *an international accord setting trade rules.* It is an attempt to have all nations work together to lower trade barriers. The agreement was created with the idea of limiting the possibility of a country's making a unilateral trade policy and having other nations retaliate. All signers of the agreement—currently 108 nations—have agreed to work together to reduce import tariffs and other policies, such as subsidies, that interfere with the flow of trade.

The discussions between the member nations are called "rounds" of negotiations. The rounds may last a number of years. One such round, identified as the Kennedy round (it was initiated by then President John F. Kennedy), lasted three years and resulted in a 40 percent reduction in tariffs. The current round of talks—the Uruguay round—has been underway since 1986. Focused on extending GATT rules to agriculture, services, textiles, and intellectual property, the round has been drawn out and difficult.[20]

Once agreements have been reached, an administrative agency is put in place to oversee the agreements. As an example of how GATT works, during the middle of the pasta boom in the United States, the Italian pasta manufac-

General Agreement on Tariffs and Trade (GATT)
An international accord setting trade rules.

turers' market share, though still relatively small, was growing at a faster pace than the American producers' share. If this growth had occurred through free competition, no one could have objected. But investigations revealed that the Italian pasta makers were getting money from the twelve-nation European Economic Community for every sale they made in the United States.

The U.S. government filed a grievance with the administrators of GATT. Under Article 9 of the agreement, subsidies for processed agricultural products, such as pasta, are expressly forbidden. One year later a GATT panel in Geneva ruled 3 to 1 in favor of the United States.

North American Free Trade Act (NAFTA)
A trade agreement intended to permanently bind the markets of the United States, Mexico, and Canada into a single commercial entity.

NAFTA The **North American Free Trade Act** (**NAFTA**) is *a trade agreement intended to permanently bind the markets of the United States, Mexico, and Canada into a single commercial entity,* stretching from the Yukon to the Yucatan. When fully operational, the primary impact of NAFTA will be on Mexico-U.S. trade. (Most barriers to free trade between the U.S. and Canada have been phased out by the U.S.-Canada Free Trade Agreement.) Under NAFTA, Mexican tariffs on American-made goods, which average 250 percent higher than U.S. tariffs on Mexican goods, will be phased out over fifteen years. (About 50 percent of Mexico's tariffs were targeted to be eliminated the day NAFTA took effect.) Mexican customs user fees will be eliminated by 1999. And, most nontariff barriers—opening the border and interior to American truckers rather than unloading American trucks and reloading onto Mexican trucks—will be eliminated by 2008.

Financial Support

World Bank
An institution established in 1946 to lend money at low interest rates to developing countries.

Financial support to international trade is provided by two sources: the World Bank and the International Monetary Fund. The **World Bank** is *an institution established in 1946 to lend money at low interest rates to developing countries.* The loans are designed to help redevelop roads, factories, hospitals, and power plants. Today the World Bank also provides loans to help developing nations relieve their debt; the price tag for the loans is a pledge from the countries to lower trade barriers and facilitate private enterprise.

International Monetary Fund (IMF)
An institution that provides assistance for foreign exchange by assisting in stabilizing exchange rates in the world economic community.

The **International Monetary Fund** (**IMF**), founded in 1944, is *an institution that provides assistance for foreign exchange by assisting in stabilizing exchange rates in the world economic community.* In addition, it makes short-term loans to countries—those that have a bad balance of trade—to help in conducting international trade.

Economic Alliances

economic alliances
Agreements among independent nations to promote trade.

Economic alliances are *agreements among independent nations to promote trade.* The nations create agreements to allow trading among themselves without tariffs or to develop one set of trade rules. The most famous of these economic alliances is the European Community (EC), previously called the Common Market. Table 21.7 lists the member nations in the EC as well as those in other economic alliances.

ECONOMIC ALLIANCE	MEMBERSHIP
Association of Southcentral Asian Nations	Indonesia, Malaysia, Philippines, Singapore, Thailand
Central American Common Market	Costa Rica, El Salvador, Guatemala, Honduras, Nicaragua
European Community	Belgium, Denmark, the United Kingdom, France, Greece, Ireland, Italy, Luxembourg, the Netherlands, Germany, Spain, Portugal
European Free Trade Association	Austria, Norway, Portugal, Sweden, Switzerland, Iceland, Finland (an associate member)
Latin American Free Trade Association	Argentina, Bolivia, Brazil, Chile, Colombia, Ecuador, Mexico, Paraguay, Peru, Uruguay, Venezuela
Organisation Commune Africaine et Mauricienne	Benin, Central African Republic, Ivory Coast, Mauritius, Niger, Rwanda, Senegal, Togo, Upper Volta
The Nordic Council	Denmark, Finland, Iceland, Norway, Sweden

Table 21.7
Economic alliances.

The EC has had a major impact on international trade through its activities to eliminate barriers between member countries and create a single European domestic market. The initial start date for this single domestic market was 1992, but the unification efforts focusing on building a single market of 340 million free-spending consumers immediately ran into roadblocks. Of the initial set of twelve goals focusing on eliminating barriers to free trade, developing common technical standards, and facilitating movement across national borders for citizens and laborers, only four have been met. Despite this setback, in these twelve countries airlines now have open skies, banks are free to provide services in any member country, insurance can be sold in all countries, and investors in one country can buy and sell shares in any other.[21]

International Business: The Problem of Conflict

Businesses operating in the international arena, especially multinationals, face ongoing conflicts with both their home country (where they originated and are headquartered) and host countries (where they have affiliates). These conflicts arise from questions of economics and power.

Home-Country Conflicts

Conflicts between international businesses and their home country are usually economic. The businesses are subject to the following criticisms:

- Rather than building a plant in another country, a U.S. company, for example, should build another plant in the United States to provide jobs and keep dollars in the country.

IBM is one of many U.S. corporations that have plants in other countries to take advantage of lower labor costs. This factory is in Guadalajara.

- Moving operations to foreign countries to take advantage of lower wages there tends to depress domestic industry and eliminate jobs for domestic workers.
- The profits of foreign-based operations, by staying in foreign countries, are not taxed by the home nation, which reduces government revenues and allows multinationals to escape their duty to support their countries financially.

The businesses offer the following responses to these criticisms:

- Although production may move to another country, income is still entering the home country because company headquarters are based there—a net gain in productive income for the home country.
- Jobs are not lost by these operations except in declining industries. In the long run those jobs will be replaced by the creation of new positions generated by the income the businesses receive.
- Business shouldn't be subjected to double taxation. The profits of the affiliate are taxed by the host country and then, when some profits are returned to the company's headquarters, they are taxed again by the home country. For the investor, profit is the measure, and companies must try to minimize double taxation.

Host-Country Conflicts

Possibly more fierce are the conflicts between host countries and multinationals, particularly between host countries of the developing third world (Asia, Africa, and Latin America) and American companies. Conflict centers on the

MANAGER'S NOTEBOOK

At some time during its life, a successful company will probably decide whether or not to undertake business outside its home country. There might be many valid reasons not to do so, but according to Herbert G. Rammrath, president of GE Plastics Ltd., two that don't count are "It's too hard" and "The competition is too tough."

If and when a company does decide to go global, it can benefit from these guidelines for success:

- *Customers and markets must define the overall strategy.* A company cannot find the right answers by looking at international trends; rather, the market dictates the specifics. The company then builds from the market need.
- *Customer service is equally important around the world.* Sometimes a U.S. company is more responsive to a customer in Chicago than one located in Bombay. This action annoys, rightfully so, that customer in Bombay—whether the home office in Boston believes it or not.
- *Customers should be serviced by local nationals.* The customer is the most important contact to a business. Communication between the business representative and the customer is most effective in the language of the customer. Therefore, local employees should always be used for direct customer contact.
- *Customers should be able to pay in local currencies whenever possible.* The exchange risk must be assumed by either the supplier or the customer. If it is forced on the customers, it may irritate them to the point of seeking another, more accommodating supplier.
- *A world-wide communications network is essential.* To provide optimum customer service, all employees must be kept up to date regarding the latest products and technologies. With current communications technology, this can be done.
- *Regional headquarters are a must.* Decision making should be close to the market being served. Regional managers help avoid the "seagull syndrome," where the Big Boss flies over once a year, drops a load of edicts, and then goes home. With regional managers, this doesn't happen.
- *All employees must have a global attitude.* To help employees adjust to a global view, Rammrath recommends two steps. First, outlaw the use of the word *domestic*—where is *domestic* when the world is the market? Second, change employee forms that ask, "Citizenship—U.S. or other?" to simply read, "Nationality."

Globalization is not easy—and it is not for everyone. Only those with a sense of adventure should apply.

(For more on a strategy for globalization, see Herbert G. Rammrath, "Globalization Isn't for Whiners," *The Wall Street Journal,* April 6, 1993, p. H1.)

A Strategy for Globalization

fact that multinationals have different goals than the government of the society in which they begin operations. Therefore, the conflicts involve a struggle for power and control. These include conflicts over:

- Who controls the nation's business. The government of the host country wants to ensure control over the way its economy develops and resources are used, while the business wants the freedom to pursue its own operations.
- The direction of industrial growth. Governments that see multinationals under the control of their foreign-owned parent company fear that their own plans for economic development can be undercut by decisions made elsewhere.
- The question of possible nationalization of key industries to avoid their control by foreign countries.
- The fact that the government cannot control the companies' ability to take profits made in its country and move them elsewhere rather than reinvest them. The goal of the business is overall profit, which may even be paid to stockholders living in another country, whereas the goal of the government is further economic growth. Obviously the two conflict. The ability of the business to move money from one operation to another can endanger a host country's balance of payments and undermine the value of its currency.
- The problem of who is running the company. Many multinationals send experienced personnel from headquarters to run foreign operations. The result, host countries feel, is a lack of responsiveness to host-country needs and no gain in the business skills of its population. Many host countries are interested in multinationals setting up training programs to prepare host-country nationals to run the affiliate themselves. These governments do not just want the businesses to provide jobs for many individuals, they want the companies to prepare members of its population for greater responsibility.

SUMMARY

International trade has become an increasingly important part of world economic activity. In addition to economic growth, it aids in increasing everyone's standard of living and contributes to world-wide communication and understanding.

International business has its own terminology—balance of trade, balance of payments, and exchange rate. Balance of trade is the difference between the dollar value of a nation's imports and the dollar value of its exports. The balance of payments is the difference between a country's total payments to other countries and its total receipts from other countries. Finally, the exchange rate is the rate at which money of one country is converted or exchanged for another.

Both nations and individual businesses make conscious decisions to engage in international trade. A nation decides to trade internationally to exploit an absolute or comparative advantage. Individual businesses go international because of profit potential, profit margin, established demand, raw material, technology, and production efficiency.

When a business chooses to operate on an international level, it has a number of options, including exporting, foreign licensing, foreign-operated sales branches, joint ventures, and wholly owned subsidiaries. Each succeeding option requires the use of more resources and a greater commitment to international operations.

Multinational corporations, although legally based in a home country, have assets committed to operations and subsidiaries world-wide. Some multinationals have developed into super-multinationals and operate as global or transnational corporations. A global corporation sees the world as its marketplace. It manufactures, conducts research, raises capital, and buys supplies wherever it can do the job best.

When a business tries to conduct international operations, it must overcome such barriers as language, customs, and cultural differences; currency conversion; and political protectionist practices. In the face of these barriers, there are a number of aids to assist a business. These include international agreements, means for financial support, and economic alliances.

Businesses operating on an international level also face conflicts between themselves and the home and host countries. These conflicts usually revolve around economics and power.

KEY TERMS

absolute advantage p. 684
balance of payments p. 683
balance of trade p. 681
comparative advantage p. 684
devaluation p. 683
dumping p. 691
economic alliances p. 698
embargo p. 696
exchange rate p. 683
exporting p. 680
foreign-operated sales branch p. 688
foreign intermediary p. 687
General Agreement on Tariffs and Trade (GATT) p. 697

global *or* transnational corporation p. 692
importing p. 680
International Monetary Fund (IMF) p. 698
licensing p. 687
multinational corporation p. 689
North American Free Trade Act (NAFTA) p. 698
production sharing p. 690
protectionism p. 694
quota p. 696
revaluation p. 683
tariff *or* import duty p. 696
wholly owned foreign subsidiary p. 689
World Bank p. 698

FOR REVIEW AND DISCUSSION

1. "Some countries rely on international trade for their basic survival." Respond to this statement.
2. Relate the concepts of balance of trade and balance of payments.
3. What is the importance of the exchange rate in international business?
4. Distinguish between absolute advantage and comparative advantage.
5. What are three reasons a business might choose to go international?
6. "A firm can select how deeply it wants to wade into international waters by the approach it takes in international business." Explain this statement and provide examples of the different degrees of commitment a company can make to its involvement in international business.
7. What is a multinational corporation? What operational tactics does it focus on? What is meant by production sharing? by dumping?
8. What is a global or transnational corporation? Where does it operate?

9. Why is protectionism considered a barrier to international trade? What are three arguments for protectionism? How is protectionism implemented through tariffs, quotas, and embargoes?

10. Identify and explain three aids that facilitate international business. Which one is most important to an individual business?

11. What types of conflicts can arise between a host country and an international business? How can some of these concerns be resolved?

APPLICATIONS

Case 21.1: Pier 1 Targets the World

Many people dream of touring the globe, but few get the chance. Those who don't can go to Pier 1. For thirty-one years, Pier 1 has helped America's armchair travelers fill their homes with colorful, handmade knickknacks and furniture from forty-four countries. Shoppers can find a carousel horse from Thailand, Italian dinnerware, or rattan chairs from Indonesia. Pier 1 has satisfied the U.S. consumer's wanderlust so well that it is America's largest retailer of home furnishings.

But despite its position as number one in the market, Pier 1 faces a major problem heading into the 90s—its sales growth has fallen dramatically. Rather than the double-digit growth rates of the late 1980s, the company has struggled with growth figures hovering between 3 and 5 percent. On top of this, profits are down dramatically.

Seeking a solution to these two dilemmas, Pier 1 decided to take its know-how overseas. The initial step was to buy a 50 percent interest in a London-based retailer—already conveniently named The Pier. The next element of the plan called for the opening of fifteen stores in Puerto Rico. Farther into the future, Pier 1 will focus on Mexico, Central America, and South America. The last phase of the strategy envisions Pier 1 stores in the Far East.

In undertaking the venture, Pier 1 faces big challenges. Exporting a shopping experience is tough. Few American stores have tried, and most foreign retailers have bombed in the United States.

For Pier 1, figuring out what puts smiles on non-American faces is critical because its success depends more on local whims than local needs. As Pier 1 president Marvin Girouard states, "You can live the rest of your life and never go into a Pier 1 store, because we don't sell anything that you have to have."

Since the stores appeal to shoppers' imaginations, Pier 1 must know what people in different cultures find exotic and clever. If it succeeds, the international stores will do what their counterparts do: satisfy the wanderlust that lurks in us all.

Questions

1. Of the reasons noted in the chapter section titled "Why Businesses 'Go International,'" which apply to Pier 1? Explain your answer.

2. What barriers does Pier 1 need to overcome in going international? Explain your answer.

3. From the list of alternative strategies for becoming involved in international trade, which would you recommend for Pier 1 to consider? Which one(s) should it choose? Explain your answer.

For more information, see Stephanie Anderson Forest, "A Pier 1 in Every Port?" *Business Week,* May 31, 1993, p. 88.

Case 21.2: Marketing Minefields

A DHL: Worldwide Express advertisement that attracted the fury of the Indonesian government underscores the many hidden minefields and cultural sensitivities for companies trying to build their names and sales position in the booming Southeast Asian region. The DHL advertisement featured five photos of Asian political leaders and a sixth photo of a DHL employee over the caption "Who keeps the world's fastest moving economies moving faster?" The answer that followed, of course, was "It's your local DHL man."

When the ad was published in the Asian *Wall Street Journal* and the *International Herald Tribune,* complaints started surfacing. This seemingly clever—by U.S. standards—advertising effort resulted in youth groups claiming the advertising demeaned their country, the government banning the two newspapers that published the ad, and the government news agency saying that the state expected a published apology from the newspapers and DHL.

Not only did DHL apologize, it learned a lesson. Because there are very diverse cultures, you can step on someone's toes without understanding. But DHL is not the only company involved in international marketing that has made mistakes:

- A Japanese tire company was forced to apologize in Brunei for having tire treads that some critics said resembled verse from the Koran.
- U.S. apple, potato, and grape exporters ran into trouble in Malaysia for mentioning the United States in television ads.
- Foreign companies importing drugs in Islamic Malaysia had to dispel a perception that the companies were using pork products to make drug capsules.

Among the topics that marketing executives generally treat warily in Southeast Asia are religious issues, particularly those involving Islam; anything even mildly negative; colonialism; Japan's role during World War II; and government figures. In addition to these broad principles, individual countries have their specific nerves. Anything Chinese must be handled with care in Indonesia, a country where thousands were killed in the early 1970s in anti-Chinese riots.

Questions
1. What advice would you give a company thinking about marketing in Southeast Asia? Explain your answer.
2. What specific topics should be avoided in marketing efforts in Southeast Asia? Cite examples.
3. What specific steps could a company take to become aware of cultural sensitivities and taboos in a foreign country? Explain your answer.

For more information, see Mark Magnier, "U.S. Firms Sometimes Lose It in the Translation," *Dallas Morning News*, November 15, 1993, pp. 1D, 4D.

REFERENCES

1. Stephanie Anderson Forest, "A Pier 1 in Every Port," *Business Week,* May 21, 1992, p. 88.
2. Therese Eiben, "U.S. Exporters on a Global Roll," *Fortune,* June 28, 1993, p. 94.
3. *United States Department of Commerce News,* July 19, 1993, p. 1.
4. Vern Terpstra, *International Dimensions of Marketing,* 2nd ed. (Boston: Kent Publishing Company, 1988), p. 3.
5. Andrew Kupfer, "How American Industry Stacks Up," *Fortune,* March 9, 1993, p. 32.
6. John Huey, "The World's Best Brand," *Fortune,* May 31, 1993, p. 45.
7. John Phelps, "Ericsson, Hewlett-Packard Announce European Venture," *Los Angeles Times,* January 11, 1993, p. H19.
8. Julie Cohen Mason, "Strategic Alliances: Partnering for Success," *Management Review,* May 1993, p. 11.
9. Jeremy M. Davis, "Exporting: The First Step in the Global Marketplace," *Management Review,* May 1993, p. 43.
10. Richard Alm, "TGI Friday's Food Chain: Dallas-Based Restaurants Multiplying in Pacific Rim, Europe," *Dallas Morning News,* March 27, 1993, p. 1D.
11. Maria Halkias, "Penney Details Plans for Mexican Growth," *Dallas Morning News,* January 29, 1993, p. 1D.
12. Gregg Jones, "Dresser Reaches Russian Plant Deal," *Dallas Morning News,* March 19, 1993, p. 13D.
13. Rose Brady, "The Scramble for Oil's Last Frontier," *Business Week,* January 11, 1993, pp. 42–44.
14. Robert Metz, "Business in the Global Marketplace: When in Rome . . .," *The Boston Globe,* April 28, 1992, p. 42.
15. Ibid.
16. Ibid.
17. Ibid.

18. Anne Marie Kilday, "Lawmakers Seek to Protect Jobs of Texas Glass Makers," *Dallas Morning News,* March 12, 1993, p. 5D.

19. Paul Wiseman, "Clinton Is Faced with Tough Test," *USA Today,* February 4, 1993, p. 2B.

20. Larry Reynolds, "Tough Talk: GATT Round Eight," *Management Review,* May 1993, pp. 49–50.

21. Carla Rapoport, "Europe Looks Ahead to Hard Choices," *Fortune,* December 14, 1992, pp. 144–148.

CAREER CAPSULE 5

Career Opportunities with General Electric

Perhaps the greatest challenge for college students who want to work for General Electric is deciding which of the company's key business areas appeals to them most. GE's subsidiaries include aircraft engines, appliances, financial services, lighting, medical systems, industrial power systems, plastics, and locomotives, to name just a few. The company employs graduates with majors ranging from business, accounting, and finance to physics and virtually all engineering degrees.

Recent college graduates may be placed in one of a variety of carefully designed two-year training programs that create the exceptional leadership skills required by this global corporation whose name has been a household word for generations. Training programs motivate members of the GE family to hone and apply the talents essential to their immediate assignments while simultaneously gaining a broad perspective of the entire company's operations. Trainees receive functional and leadership training by rotating through various jobs and by attending seminars at the company's Management Development Institute in Crotonville, New York.

It goes without saying that a company that invests so much in grooming its future leaders recruits graduates who have not only a strong academic record but also a clear history of exceptional leadership in extracurricular activities throughout their college years. More specifically, General Electric employs:

- People with the self-confidence and energy to create an idea and run with it
- Problem solvers who are committed to doing a quality job
- Innovators who can look at existing resources or systems and initiate changes where needed
- Communicators who can inspire trust and influence teams to action

General Electric's competitive advantage comes from combining smart, confident people with state-of-the-art technology. Management expects everyone to demonstrate leadership in both ideas and actions. College graduates who receive a job offer from GE have the opportunity to build exceptional careers with a strong, vibrant corporation that welcomes the challenge of tomorrow by developing the best in its people today.

APPENDIX
THE BUSINESS OF GETTING A JOB

Most of you reading this book will eventually earn a degree and enter the job market. This appendix is designed to give you some basic information on ways to identify a potentially satisfying career, find job openings in that field, clear an employer's selection hurdles, and understand how large corporations—the primary employers of college graduates—recruit on college campuses.

Choosing a Career

You probably have several friends or acquaintances who enjoy their work. They feel challenged by it, enthusiastic about doing it, and rewarded by the experience of going to work each morning. These fortunate people probably selected their career with care. The close mesh between their personal preferences and the work they have come to do is probably no accident. You, too, can identify a satisfying career if you will invest some time and effort.

Explore Your Interests

Perhaps the fundamental step in choosing a career is to get to know yourself well—to define and describe clearly the aspects of jobs that suit you well and the specific work activities you would prefer to avoid.

One way to do this is to complete a personality inventory questionnaire and checklist like the ones in Figure A.1. Your self-knowledge and suitability for a particular career can be further confirmed by taking one or more tests in your college's counseling department or career guidance office. Two of the more popular ones are:

- The Hall Occupational Orientation Inventory, which requires you to rate the strength of your interest in various activities. In doing so, you indicate characteristics a job must have to attract and satisfy you, and you reveal certain job characteristics that you would find unappealing.
- The Strong Vocational Interest Blank, which measures your preference for various kinds of work, school subjects, recreation, and personal characteristics in other people. The interest profile that emerges can be compared with the preferences, interests, and attitudes required in occupations from accountant to zoologist to determine how compatible you would be with each occupation.

Although brief personality inventories and exercises cannot provide a formula for finding an agreeable job, they should enable you to be reasonably certain of the job characteristics you find attractive and the ones you do not want to encounter.

It is no longer sufficient to do something well. To survive, you now need to do something meaningful.

DAVID FAGIANO
President and CEO,
American Management
Association

Figure A.1

A personality inventory questionnaire and checklist.

1. What kinds of hobbies do you like to work with in your spare time? What is it that makes them appealing to you?

2. Which sports, clubs, and other extracurricular activities do you like best? Why do you like them?

3. What jobs have you had that you liked best? Why did you like them?

4. Do you like to work with abstract ideas or tangible objects? Why?

5. Do you keep calm and cool when being rushed? Do you meet deadlines regularly?

6. Would you prefer to work with a large group, in a small group, or by yourself?

7. Do you like to have well-organized and predictable work assignments or would you rather have a dynamic job that changes every day? Why?

8. Are you comfortable supervising others or would you rather let someone else be the boss? List several reasons for your answer.

9. Which high school and college courses did you enjoy the most? What was it about each that appealed to you?

10. What offices or special honors have you held or received? What personal qualities were responsible for this?

11. Without mentioning a type of work, describe yourself ten years from now. What physical living arrangements do you want? What recreational interests and hobbies do you intend to follow? What kind of people do you want to socialize with and work with? How much income would you like to have?

Yes	No	Personal Characteristic
_____	_____	Work successfully under pressure.
_____	_____	Prefer to work with ideas and concepts.
_____	_____	Prefer to work with tangible objects.
_____	_____	Like routine, methodical work.
_____	_____	Like to supervise others.
_____	_____	Meet deadlines promptly.
_____	_____	Enjoy traveling.
_____	_____	Prefer challenging work assignments.
_____	_____	Am comfortable in the company of strangers.
_____	_____	Would rather work alone or with a small group.
_____	_____	Like to be thought of as a "take-charge" person.
_____	_____	Appreciate a regular paycheck.
_____	_____	Like to associate with people who are members of the "upper class."
_____	_____	Enjoy assignments that require persuading others.
_____	_____	Like to speak in front of groups.
_____	_____	Have little trouble communicating with others.
_____	_____	Prefer to make decisions rather than have others make them.
_____	_____	Ask lots of questions.
_____	_____	Willing to try out new ideas.
_____	_____	Like to help others with their problems.
_____	_____	Make friends easily.

Source: Joseph T. Straub, *The Job Hunt: How to Compete and Win*, pp.3–6. © 1981 by Prentice-Hall, Inc. Published by Prentice-Hall, Inc., Englewood Cliffs, New Jersey 07632.

Build a Career Profile

After you have completed the personality inventory and the tests offered by your college counseling department, you will be ready to build a profile of potential careers that seem appealing. Some methods of obtaining career information are illustrated in Figure A.2.

One of the most interesting ways to obtain information about a career is to interview someone who already does that kind of work. The procedure is simple—merely identify several companies or organizations that employ persons in that field, telephone their local offices (consult the Yellow Pages), and ask for the head of the appropriate department. Tell that person your name, request a meeting, and give the reason for your request, and you will probably be able to make an appointment at a mutually convenient time. You may also be able to get names of people to talk to from your college placement office; many colleges and universities maintain lists of alumni who are willing and happy to talk to students about their careers.

Interviewing people who work in the field serves two purposes. First, it gives you an opportunity to ask questions of someone with firsthand, intimate experience in the career. Second, it gives you the opportunity to contact a potential sponsor, someone who might recommend you for a job should you eventually decide to pursue that career. Your initiative in seeking these people out and your candor in approaching them also portrays you as a bright, ambitious, and thoughtful self-starter. Be sure to arrange meetings with several people in each field to obtain a balanced impression of what the work is like.

In addition to meeting with those who are employed in the field, read current reference materials about careers that interest you. One good source of information is the latest edition of the *Occupational Outlook Handbook*, published annually by the United States Department of Labor, which provides data on required training and other qualifications, expected demand, nature of the work, typical job environment, approximate salary ranges, and various other topics for hundreds of jobs. This information can be supplemented from such other sources as the *Handbook of Job Facts* and the

Figure A.2

How to build a career profile.

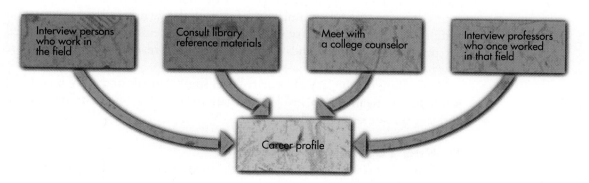

Encyclopedia of Careers and Vocational Guidance to build an even more thorough profile of your particular field. Collectively these sources should provide you with considerable information on a career, including average starting pay, promotional opportunities, and ways to prepare yourself.

Supplement the information you gain from interviewing practitioners and reading reference materials with a visit to your college counseling department or career guidance office, which should have specific information from prospective employers, as well as information about the careers other graduates have pursued.

If you are a student at a large university, you probably will find one or more faculty members who formerly worked in the field you are researching. You can identify them by calling the office of the appropriate department or division or by consulting a faculty directory that presents a brief biography of each professor. Arrange an interview to talk about their experiences and opinions of your potential career.

Choose a Major

The next move is to choose a major field of study that will prepare you for a career that interests you. Colleges offer quite a varied academic menu; if you have not discovered this by now, you soon will. You have so many choices that you may decide to change majors several times between your freshman year and your senior year. You may be able to pursue a certain career by following one of several academic routes. For example, large companies employ marketing trainees with majors in psychology, business administration, and various other areas. Many firms fill their needs for college-educated employees from a host of majors, and certain majors may qualify you to work in several areas.

Fortunately for most of us, the choice of major is not an all-or-nothing commitment. Should you find, after completing several preliminary courses, that the course work is not intellectually gratifying or stimulating, you can change to another field.

Work closely with a college counselor in selecting a major. It is especially important to schedule your courses strategically and in the correct sequence. If possible, balance your schedule so you do not find yourself taking several courses that require large amounts of out-of-class work in the same session (English literature, chemistry, and accounting, for example). Verify the need for prerequisite courses and complete them before enrolling in the more advanced ones.

Depending on the size of your college, some courses may only be offered infrequently. Realizing this will enable you to sign up at the best time for you and to graduate on schedule.

Selling Yourself in a Résumé

Many of the marketing concepts you learned about in Chapter 12 apply to your job search, because getting a job means marketing a unique product—

yourself. You are selling a package of education, attitude, ambition, dedication, and potential that will be developed both on the job and through additional training. You must present yourself clearly and impressively to people who can make or influence a hiring decision. This involves developing a résumé, which demands an understanding of the importance that appearance plays in making a good impression.

A good résumé is the bait that hooks an employer's attention. It should be confined to *one page* and designed so a reader can scan it quickly and easily. It should give your name, address, and telephone number and summarize information about your education, work experience, and any extracurricular activities, hobbies, or interests that are relevant to your desired career. An example of a concise résumé appears in Figure A.3.

The work experience section is especially important. You must show that your responsibilities were meaningful and that you had to exercise maturity, independent judgment, and initiative (see Figure A.3). Action words such as *developed, processed, designed, supervised, submitted,* and *administered* give the impression of meaningful activity and responsibility.

Before writing your résumé, you should make a rough draft listing all the information you want to present, then rewrite and polish it until it is concise and descriptive. You may want to have someone in the counseling center or guidance office or a business or English professor look over your final version.

Several mechanics of résumé preparation deserve your attention.

1. A résumé should always be typewritten or typeset.
2. Grammar, spelling, and punctuation must be flawless.
3. Always give a prospective employer an original or a high-quality copy, never a dot-matrix original or a poor photocopy.

Prospective employers draw many conclusions about applicants from the condition of their résumés. A sloppy appearance (smudges, smeared corrections, overstrikes) implies that the applicant is slipshod, messy, unkempt, and careless. Numerous spelling or grammatical errors imply carelessness or stupidity. Haphazard spacing or an inconsistent format indicates that the person has no concern for consistency or detail. A résumé speaks for you when you may not be present to speak for yourself. Be sure it says what you want it to say.

Finding Out About Job Openings

The most obvious source for finding out about job openings is a newspaper's help wanted listings. But relying on that source alone—or even primarily—can severely limit a student's chances of finding a satisfying job. The fact is, many jobs are never advertised in the newspaper. To find out about those jobs, often the most interesting and rewarding, you must pursue other sources of job information.

Figure A.3

A sample résumé.

RÉSUMÉ

NAME: Paul J. Owens Phone: (904) 672-4359

ADDRESS: 2317 Crest Street
Tallahassee, Florida 23692

CAREER GOAL: Retail Sales Management

EDUCATION: B.S., Marketing, Florida State
University, 1994. G.P.A. 3.40 out of
4.0 possible.

A.A., Business Administration, St.
Petersburg Junior College, June 1992.

WORK
EXPERIENCE: June 1993 to present: Barrows
Department Store, Tallahassee, Florida.
Retail salesperson responsible for cash
and credit sales, inventory control,
merchandise marketing, and producing
various internal reports used by the
store and regional management.

August 1992 to June 1993: Sampson's
Auto Supply, Tallahassee, Florida.
Counter clerk and warehouse worker.
Recorded cash and credit sales,
processed telephone and catalog orders,
gathered items for shipment, received
and processed incoming merchandise.

EXTRA-
CURRICULAR
ACTIVITIES: President and Treasurer, Delta Chi
fraternity; Secretary, F.S.U.
Collegiate Chapter of the American
Marketing Association; President's
list; intramural racquetball, baseball,
and soccer.

HOBBIES,
INTERESTS: Water skiing, racquetball, tennis.

REFERENCES: Furnished upon request.

Source: Joseph T. Straub, *The Job Hunt: How to Compete and Win*, p.21. © 1981 by Prentice-Hall, Inc. Published by Prentice-Hall, Inc., Englewood Cliffs, New Jersey 07632.

Co-ops and Internships

Cooperative employment programs (*co-ops*) permit students to attend college for part of the year and apply their learning to a full-time job for the remainder. Such federal agencies as the Treasury Department and the General Accounting Office have established co-op programs, as have such leading corporations as Deere & Company, General Electric, and General Motors. A sound academic record usually ranks very high in an employer's decision to admit a student to a co-op program.

One appealing aspect of cooperative education is that the organization you work for during part of your academic year has an opportunity to get to know you as a person and as a potential employee. And at the same time, after working for part of three or four years for the same employer, you can come to understand that employer's operations, systems, and philosophy. If the relationship is mutually satisfying, you might be able to step into a full-time position with the employer after graduation. In many cases the step is virtually automatic. Furthermore, several years of co-op training enhances your bargaining power in the job market. Usually, co-op program alumni can negotiate a more responsible position and a higher starting salary than graduates with less meaningful experience who were recruited directly out of the classroom.

The organization and operation of Dow Chemical Company's co-op program provides some interesting insights. Students are given responsibilities related to their major fields of study in areas such as research and development, manufacturing, marketing, and business administration. Dow ensures that they will be considered for full-time employment after graduation. Salaries are based on academic experience, experience in the program, and job performance; responsibility naturally increases with subsequent co-op assignments. The duration of each assignment is tailored to the student's academic year. Dow pays the cost of round-trip transportation from campus to the work location, in addition to group medical insurance and perhaps a paid vacation (depending on how long a work period lasts). Students receive assistance with finding suitable living quarters at each location. Those who take job-related courses while working on a co-op assignment are reimbursed the full amount of their tuition and books. Many other large companies, including Du Pont, Aetna Life & Casualty, and Datapoint Corporation, have summer intern programs.

Although a co-op program might extend your projected graduation date by a year, many co-op alumni swear that the valuable work experience they accumulated and the head start they got in their search for employment after graduation made the delay well worth it. Cooperative education has also been the only way some financially strapped students could afford a college education. By working full time for part of the academic year, they were able to save enough money to pay for the next semester.

You can gain meaningful work experience and valuable personal contacts by participating in a summer co-op program. This arrangement is common in government agencies, where students may work full time or part time. You may also be able to enter a private employer's internship program, earning college credit and perhaps a nominal salary for the time. One-semester internships can earn an average of six credit hours, if the student's work responsibilities are related to his or her major. Internship pay is sometimes meager or nonexistent, but this arrangement, like co-op training, allows you to make valuable personal contacts in an organization while experiencing work that you think might interest you. It also helps you accumulate credit toward your degree. Your counseling office or placement office will be able to supply information on cooperative education or internship programs that are available through your college.

The Placement Office

The placement office is central to every college student's job hunt. Its function is helping students get jobs before they graduate. It does this by performing the following activities and services:

1. Offers data on demand trends in various careers
2. Polls prospective employers on the relative popularity of various fields of study
3. Publishes starting salary surveys tabulated by industry and major field of study
4. Distributes recruiting literature from specific employers that discusses kinds of jobs available, majors and degrees desired, potential work locations, starting salary ranges, the nature of operations, and specific characteristics and qualities that the employer finds most desirable in a prospective employee
5. Provides facilities and procedures for employer representatives to meet and interview graduating seniors
6. Counsels students on how to interview effectively to make a favorable impression on prospective employers

Generally you will not be permitted to interview with prospective employers through the placement office until your senior year. Nevertheless, you should find where it is located and explore the materials and services it offers as soon as possible. Most colleges also have alumni placement programs to help graduates conduct job searches later in their careers.

Professors in Your Major Field

The professors who teach courses in your major are a valuable source of job leads if they maintain regular contact with potential employers. Professors in schools of business and engineering, for example, may have worked with or are consultants to large corporations and so may know influential managers with the authority to hire several outstanding graduates each year. It is not unusual for large firms to have such back-door recruiting arrangements with professors, who recommend students to fill high-paying, top-notch entry jobs. The challenge here is to make sure that your professors know and respect you as a student and as a person. This will take a conscious, discreet effort on your part, but it may pay dividends. Active class participation, volunteering for light research assignments, and other signs of thoughtfulness and diligence should make you stand out.

Networking

Networking requires that you cultivate a system of influential persons who may help you get job interviews. In fact, some network members may be in a position to hire you themselves. Your personal network may include the following:

- Friends, other students, and members of their families
- Professors
- Family friends
- Associates, clients, suppliers, or customers of relatives who are in business
- Members of fraternities or sororities
- Faculty advisers and members of campus clubs related to your major
- Counselors
- Members of your church
- Prominent executives in local companies that you often deal with (such as department stores, restaurants, clothing stores, off-campus bookstores, and supermarkets)

You should become acquainted with these contacts on a personal level and make them aware that you're actively seeking employment. Then follow up periodically and discreetly to remind them that you'd appreciate their assistance.

Other Sources

You may land a job through a private employment agency, but these firms typically deal with experienced people. If you have no meaningful work experience, an agency may not be willing to help you. An employment agency acts as your agent, and you will pay for its services according to a fee schedule and policy discussed at the time you sign a contract with that agency. The fee may be equal to at least a month's salary from the job the agency helps you find. An employer may be willing to pay all or part of the fee on your behalf, but the fee is legally your responsibility. Tax-supported state employment services have jobs available, too, but most of them are nontechnical and nonsupervisory positions, and relatively few require a college background. Most employers with jobs that require a college education fill them from other sources.

Corporate Recruiting

You may not graduate with a major in business, but if you are like most college graduates, you will accept your first career position with a large corporation. This is true whether you majored in anthropology, theology, or zoology, so it is important that you understand the way large companies recruit graduating seniors for entry-level jobs. Figure A.4 illustrates the steps, which are described in the following sections.

The Campus Recruiter

When you investigated the campus placement office, you learned that large employers send representatives called *campus recruiters* to interview graduating seniors there. The placement office periodically announces the names of firms whose recruiters will visit the campus, the dates of those visits, and the specific majors they are looking for. You must then reserve an appointment with any companies you are qualified to interview with and interested in learning about. A recruiter typically spends one or two days on campus, during which time he or she interviews as many as two dozen prospective employees. Because a recruiter may recommend only two or three students for further consideration, qualifying and signing up in time for this campus interview is a major hurdle in a student's job search.

Preparing for the Interview

An interview is a personal sales presentation, and like any effective salesperson you must be prepared to present your most impressive features, make clear the ways they would benefit your prospective employer, and demonstrate your potential to excel in the work for which you have applied. Some contend that the interview is the single greatest challenge facing a job seeker. It is an exchange of information and impressions on which job offers and career decisions hinge.

Interviewing is like anything else—the more you practice, the better you should become. Serious job seekers interview often, getting comfortable with the experience of being scrutinized by strangers who may hold the key to a job offer.

Figure A.4

Typical corporate recruiting procedure.

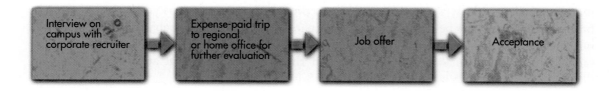

A successful interview starts at the library. You will need facts about such things as your potential employer's major products or services, sales and profit trends, and major markets that the firm sells to. Thorough preliminary research will benefit you in at least two ways. First, you will learn more about the employer's industry position, potential for future success, and scope of operations, so you can make a better-informed decision if you receive a job offer. Second, you gather a body of knowledge that you can use, tactfully, to show the interviewer that you have initiative, foresight, and curiosity (you went to the library on your own and dug it up). Because many students show up for interviews knowing nothing but the employer's name, information from personal research, conveyed during your interview, makes you look more attractive as a potential employee.

Several library sources provide all the information you will probably need. Assuming you are interviewing a company, refer to the list of sources of financial information in Chapter 16. The two best sources for the purpose of job interviews are *Standard & Poor's Stock Reports* and *The Value Line Investment Survey.* Between them they provide a condensed history of a company's financial performance, mention some of its major products, and state any subsidiary firms that the company owns (or the parent company that owns it). These references contain facts that are not common knowledge. An alert interviewer will realize that you did some respectable research if you can refer to such facts during your interview.

It also is equally important to read and make notes from recent magazine articles about the company. These may be found by looking in the *Business Periodicals Index,* which lists articles indexed by company name and gives the title, magazine, date, and page number on which the article appears.

Figure A.5
Questions you may be asked in a job interview.

A genuine interview is a two-way exchange. The employer wants applicants to understand the organization and its job requirements. The employer also wants to assimilate as much information as possible about the applicant's ambitions, plans, background, priorities, and potential for being a solid candidate for the job. Some questions that many employers ask college students who are applying for jobs are presented in Figure A.5. Study them and prepare yourself to offer responsible, intelligible, and interesting answers. But remember: it is impossible to condense the dynamic experience of an interview into a formula. Be prepared for anything.

- What do you have to offer our organization?
- What have you accomplished during your years in college?
- What do you know about our organization?
- What do you expect us to do for you? Why?
- Tell me about yourself.
- What do you expect to be doing in (three, five, ten, fifteen) years?
- If you had your life to live over, what would you do differently? Why?
- If you were to start college over again, what would you do differently? Would you choose the same major? Why or why not?
- How much of your education did you pay for yourself? Why so much (or so little)?
- What kind of training do you expect to receive from our organization?
- What are your plans for future education?

- What responsibility can I expect to have in my starting position? What is the typical career path from that job?
- What kind of training can I expect to receive? Who is responsible for it? How is it provided?
- What is your tuition reimbursement policy for courses taken toward an advanced degree?
- What efforts does your organization make to ensure that new trainees are exposed to meaningful work experience? How will my progress be monitored?
- What is the typical background of a supervisor to whom I would report in my starting position?
- How easy is it to transfer among various departments or divisions within your organization?
- Have there been any recent layoffs of persons in jobs like the one I would have? If so, how did management decide who to retain and who to release?
- Describe the kind of location at which I might be employed. What facilities does it have for education, recreation, housing, and health care?

Figure A.6

Questions you might want to ask in a job interview.

Prospective employers also expect (and are impressed by) inquiring minds, so you should come to an interview prepared to ask as well as answer questions. Figure A.6 presents some questions that many job applicants want to ask during the interview.

In getting ready for an interview, it is helpful if you analyze what you think the employer will require from a prospective employee like yourself. You have an inventory of features—background, education, experience, and skills—and during the interview you must translate these features into benefits you can offer the employer that will satisfy that employer's needs. By role-playing the interview beforehand and anticipating probable questions, you can develop acceptable answers that focus on those things that you alone can offer the employer. Simply put, your goal is to appear to be the most ideal applicant for the available position.

Some additional hints for interviewing effectively include:

1. Be on time. Lateness shows rudeness or indifference.
2. Maintain steady eye contact with the interviewer. Shifty glances imply insecurity or deception.
3. Speak clearly and concisely, avoiding such irritating verbal crutches as "like," "right," "you know," "really," "you're kidding," or other fad words or phrases.
4. Bring a copy of your résumé, an updated copy of your transcript, and any letters of recommendation you have from professors, employers, or influential persons in case the interviewer asks to see them.
5. Do not smoke, even if invited to; it introduces an unnecessary distraction. (One organization admits that its interviewer may offer you a cigarette in a room without ashtrays to test your ability to handle the awkward situation that would arise if you lit up.)
6. Dress conservatively. There is no record of anyone being criticized for presenting a traditional appearance.
7. Do not take notes during the interview. Make a summary of important facts and impressions immediately after leaving.
8. Do not ask questions only about salary. Employers usually reject applicants who put dollars ahead of such job factors as training, promotional opportunity, and meaningful responsibility. Some questions about compensation

are reasonable, however. Asking what criteria are used to determine the actual starting salary within a range (if there is a range), what the potential for salary growth is, and what the company's benefits include are legitimate concerns of potential employees, and interviewers should understand your desire to clarify these matters.

After Your Campus Interview

During the interview, the recruiter should be able to say how long it will be until you have some feedback from the company. If the recruiter does not volunteer this information, it is perfectly reasonable to ask. In addition, it is appropriate for you to write a letter of thanks to the interviewer for the time and information he or she shared with you on campus. This effort, like the preinterview research that was recommended earlier, sets you apart; it is something that less motivated candidates probably will not do.

Soon after the interview, you should receive one of two letters. One will inform you that no vacancies exist for which you are qualified. This could be a polite rejection, but it could also be the truth—the firm may indeed have no current openings. If that is the case, the letter will probably mention that the company will keep your name on file for a specified period of time in the event something opens up. The other letter, however, usually offers an expense-paid trip for further evaluation. Your destination may be a regional office or the company's main headquarters, depending on the firm's size and hiring procedures. As a rule, you can expect to spend a day at the facility being interviewed by a succession of executives who constitute a hiring committee. They may plan to interview quite a number of students like yourself (on different days, of course) and extend job offers to only a select few.

The offer of a trip requires that you arrange an absence from campus with your professors and make travel plans with the company official who contacted you. You will most likely have to plan air transportation, ground transportation, meals, and at least one night's lodging at your destination. Some employers have travel departments that handle most of these details once the date is set; others leave the arrangements to you. If the latter occurs, you may want to use a travel agent. Respect the company's budget by traveling modestly. Fly coach class, eat adequate meals in respectable restaurants, and generally show as much concern for thrift as you would if you were employed by the firm or if you were spending your own money.

The Company Interview

Once you arrive at your destination and check in with the official who helped arrange your trip, you will be told whom you will be meeting during the day and at what times. You will be escorted from one executive's office to the next by a secretary or by the last person you interviewed with.

The managers who interview you may cover a broad spectrum of organizational functions, including labor relations, marketing, manufacturing, finance, and human resources management. Each will be a seasoned executive within his or her area, and their questions will be more extensive and less predictable than those asked by campus recruiters. At lunchtime you will dine with one or more members of this group, giving them an opportunity to evaluate your social skills.

When your day of interviewing is over, the executive who helped arrange your interview should tell you when to expect the final decision on a job offer. Then you will return to campus, submit a statement of travel expenses for reimbursement (supported by receipts), and wait.

Evaluating Job Offers

Job offers are usually made in a letter (perhaps preceded by a telephone call) describing such details as the formal job title and the starting location, date, and salary. The prospective employer should also provide a written description of your duties and responsibilities and be ready to answer all your questions. You will be asked to communicate your decision within a few days. The deadline can be negotiated, of course, if you are awaiting results from other trips to other companies. No reasonable employer will expect you to make a snap decision on such a critical matter.

Many people experience one of the most dramatic transitions in their lives when they leave college and begin work. Going, for example, from being a full-time student who gets money from home to being an independent, self-supporting individual is a radical change. Therefore, in addition to the previously discussed factors, you should evaluate the offer of a starting salary against the budget you have determined you will need to support yourself adequately.

You will have to allow for such items as food, clothing (including, most likely, a more extensive wardrobe than you needed as a student), rent, utilities, and probably the cost of owning and operating an automobile. You also should allocate money for insurance you need that will not be paid by your employer and set aside a sum for savings and for an investment program.

Taking 25 percent off the salary figure offered to you will give the approximate net or take-home pay. If your budget exceeds that figure, you can either recalculate the budget or contact the employer and try to negotiate a higher salary. If you try to do the latter, however, realize that most employers' starting salaries are relatively fixed unless an applicant has meaningful work experience; the amounts do vary, of course, according to the cost of living in a given area of the country. Admittedly, applicants with exceptional qualifications or high-demand degrees may be able to deal for a higher starting salary without meaningful experience; however, many employers adhere to a uniform figure for the sake of fairness.

A job decision is an awesome one. The course you choose will affect you for the rest of your life. Consider the work itself. Does it seem to coincide with the personal and career objectives that you determined? Does the organization appear to be one that you could be comfortable in and satisfied working for? Are its operations stable enough to offer a reasonable degree of job security? Do its demands and those of the job you have been offered reflect the kind of lifestyle you want to pursue after graduation? These and many other questions must be answered as clearly as possible. Remember, however, that no one truly knows what a job or an organization is like until he or she actually goes to work there.

Discuss your job offer with several professors who are knowledgeable about the employer or the work itself. You might also ask the opinion of several of the people whom you interviewed when you were exploring your interests and comparing them with career profiles. Still, regardless of how many outside opinions you seek out, the final decision is yours and it may be the most profound one of your life. We do not mean to imply that you will be locked into this employer or career for the rest of your life. You may change employers several times during your career if competitors offer faster advancement, greater challenge, more responsibility, or (naturally) more money. Furthermore, you may decide to pursue an altogether different career some time in the future, as time and experience change your preferences, interests, and personal priorities. Those things change naturally as part of the adventure called life. Whatever your current or future goals, though, we wish you good luck and good job hunting!

GLOSSARY

absolute advantage Occurs when a nation has a monopoly on a product or can produce it at the lowest cost.

accessory equipment Items that are less expensive than major equipment and are standardized.

accountability Being answerable to others for the results of one's actions.

accountant A person who has the education and experience to evaluate the significance of information derived from a company's financial records, interpret its impact on operations, and participate in higher management decisions that are made as a result.

accounting system An organized approach to gathering, recording, analyzing, summarizing, and interpreting financial data to determine a firm's financial condition.

acid test ratio A measure of a firm's ability to pay current debts from its most liquid, or quick, assets—cash and near-cash items.

acquisition Results when one firm buys a majority interest in another, but both retain their identities.

actuary A person who analyzes the likelihood of loss and the average amount of damage involved in pure risks and, applying the law of averages, computes the premium that the insurance company should charge to assume the risk.

adjustable life insurance A type of life insurance in which the insured may raise or lower the face value, lengthen or shorten the protection period, or change the kind of protection as personal circumstances require.

advertising Any nonpersonal message paid for by an identifiable sponsor to promote goods, services, or ideas.

advertising media The nonpersonal means of sending a promotional message to a target market.

affirmative action Requiring employers to make an extra effort to hire and promote members of protected groups.

agency shop Agreements stipulating that nonunion members must pay union dues.

agent One who is authorized to transact business and exercise authority on behalf of another party.

alien corporation A firm incorporated in a country other than the one in which it operates.

all-risk physical damage *or* multiple-line coverage Added fire insurance that embraces all risks except those that the policy specifically excludes.

allied lines *or* extended coverage A feature that can be added to a fire insurance policy to encompass financial loss caused by such hazards as riot and civil commotion, hail, wind, falling objects, land vehicles, water, smoke, and possibly vandalism and malicious mischief.

amalgamation *or* consolidation Occurs when one firm combines with others to form an entirely new company; former identities are relinquished.

analog computer A computer that takes measurements and processes these data against a model of the problem or situation.

analytic process Production method in which raw materials are broken down to form new products.

annual report The document in which businesses summarize their financial condition each year.

annuity A contract that pays the policyholder (annuitant) a fixed sum at regular intervals for a specified period of time. If the annuitant dies before collecting the face value, a beneficiary receives the remainder.

anticipatory purchasing Occurs when a purchasing agent stockpiles an extremely large supply of an item, well in advance of need, anticipating future problems.

approach The third step in the selling process; the salesperson makes actual contact with the prospect and prepares to deliver a sales presentation.

arbitration A process in which an impartial third party called an arbitrator makes the decision to settle a grievance.

arithmetic mean An average found by adding the numbers in an array and dividing by the total number of items present.

arithmetic unit The unit of the computer that performs mathematical computations on data.

array A list of numbers ordered from highest to lowest or lowest to highest.

articles of partnership A contractual agreement that establishes the legal relationship between partners.

assembly process A variation of synthetic production in which materials or parts are combined without substantial changes.

assets Things of value that businesses, government, or individuals own.

authority The formal, legitimate right of a manager to make decisions, give orders, and allocate resources.

autocratic style A leadership approach in which a manager does not share decision-making authority with subordinates.

back-end load A sales charge applied when mutual fund shares are redeemed.

balance of payments The difference between a country's total payments to other countries and its total receipts from other countries.

balance of trade The difference between the dollar value of a nation's exports and the dollar value of its imports.

balance sheet An accounting statement that shows a firm's status on the last day of an accounting period.

bankruptcy *or* **insolvency** The state of being unable to pay one's creditors' claims as they come due.

barter system An economic system in which two parties trade certain goods and services that each needs to survive.

bearer bond. *See* coupon bond

beneficiary One or more persons or organizations that the policyholder designates to receive the cash payment on a life insurance policy.

benefits Compensation that is not wages, salaries, or bonuses.

bid purchasing A policy of requesting bids from several vendors and selecting the most attractive one.

blacklist The names of pro-union workers circulated among firms to keep the workers from being hired.

bodily injury liability Sometimes called *PIP (personal injury protection) insurance;* motor vehicle insurance that pays court-awarded damages for bodily injury, up to the face value of the policy, if the insured person is judged liable for a motor vehicle accident.

boiler and machinery insurance. *See* power plant insurance

bond indenture A blanket agreement between the corporation and its bondholders that states the bond issue's interest rate, maturity date, and other terms and conditions.

bond yield The percentage return that the investor will receive from a bond.

bonds Long-term, interest-bearing promissory notes.

book value of common stock The amount per share that stockholders would theoretically receive if a company's assets were sold on the balance sheet date.

bookkeeper A clerical worker who maintains the financial records that an accountant shapes into usable information.

boycott A refusal to do business with a given party until certain demands are met.

brand A name, symbol, design, or combination of them that identifies the goods or services of a company.

brand mark A symbol or design used to identify a product and to distinguish it.

brand name A letter, word, or group of letters or words used to identify a product.

break-even analysis A method of determining the number of units that must be sold at a given price to recover costs and make a profit.

break-even point The point at which sales revenue equals total costs.

business An organization engaged in producing and selling, at a profit, goods and services that consumers want.

business format franchise A franchise in which the franchisor gives franchisees a comprehensive, detailed plan for operating the business.

business interruption insurance Coverage that can be added to a basic fire insurance policy. It covers consequential losses, those that result from fire or other perils covered in the fire policy.

business plan A comprehensive summary of the key factors that will affect the operation of the proposed business.

bylaws Internal rules that govern the general operation of a corporation.

capital The total of tools, equipment, machinery, and buildings used to produce goods and services.

capital appreciation An increase in a stock's market price caused by investor optimism.

capitalism An economic system in which both the factors of production and businesses are owned by private individuals.

captive supplier A vendor firm in which the customer firm owns controlling interest or from which it obtains an exclusive supply contract.

cash discount A discount given to encourage trade credit debtors to pay their balances before they are due.

cash flow statement A document that shows where a company's cash came from during an accounting period and how it was used in operations.

cashier's check A check written by a commercial bank against the bank's own money.

catalog stores Stores that send catalogs to customers and also make them available in stores.

centralization A philosophy of organization and management that concentrates authority within an organizational structure.

certificate (articles) of incorporation The application to incorporate that must be filed with the secretary of state, which becomes the corporation's charter after it is approved.

certificates of deposit (CDs) Bank obligations that pay higher interest than regular savings accounts because the depositor agrees to leave the money on deposit for a certain length of time.

certified check A depositor's personal check that the bank certifies to be good.

chain of command The hierarchy of decision-making levels in the company.

chain store One of two or more similar stores owned by the same company.

channel of distribution *or* **marketing channel** A route that goods follow on their journey from manufacturers to consumers.

check *or* **demand deposit** A bank depositor's written order instructing the bank to pay a certain sum to a third party.

churning Advising clients to buy or sell stocks without good reason.

close The point in the selling process when the prospect agrees to buy.

closed corporation A corporation whose stock cannot be purchased by the general public; it is usually owned by a few individuals.

closed shop Agreements stipulating that employees have to be union members at the time they are hired.

code of ethics Formal guidelines for the ethical behavior of individuals in an organization, job, or profession.

coinsurance clause A stipulation that a company must insure a minimum (usually 80 percent or more) of a property's total value before the business will be fully reimbursed for a partial loss.

collective bargaining The process whereby employer and employee representatives jointly negotiate a contract that specifies wages, hours, and other conditions of employment.

collision and upset Motor vehicle insurance that pays to repair damages to the insured vehicle up to its actual cash value (ACV) less the deductible if it collides with an object (including another vehicle) or overturns.

commercial bank A profit-making corporation that accepts customers' deposits and lends them out to businesses and individual borrowers.

commercial finance company A firm that makes cash loans to business borrowers, securing the loans by such assets as trade credit accounts, inventory, or equipment.

commercial paper (Sometimes referred to as *corporate IOUs*), the unsecured promissory notes of large, financially sound corporations.

common law A body of law based on records of early English court decisions settling disputes that involve people and property.

common stock A security held by the corporation's owners.

common stock certificate Legal evidence of corporate ownership. It gives the owner's name, the number of shares owned, and various data on the corporation itself.

communication process The method by which promotional messages travel to reach the consumer.

communism An economic system in which the government controls the factors of production.

comparative advantage Occurs when a nation is better equipped to produce one product or service than other nations.

compensation All forms of financial payments to employees: salaries and wages, benefits, bonuses, profit sharing, and awards of goods or services.

component parts Prefinished items that are put into the final product.

comprehensive physical damage Motor vehicle insurance that protects the insured vehicle against most damage except that caused by collision and upset.

compressed workweek A program that permits employees to fulfill their work obligation in less than the traditional five-day workweek.

computer A device that performs large numbers of repetitive calculations automatically and at high speeds, usually with considerable accuracy.

computer-aided design (CAD) A process that uses highly specialized computer graphics programs to create three-dimensional models of products on a computer screen.

computer-aided manufacturing (CAM) A manufacturing system in which computers direct, control, and monitor production equipment to perform all the steps required to perform a task.

computer-integrated manufacturing (CIM) A system in which all production-related activities, from product design through manufacturing, are controlled by a computer.

conceptual skills The ability to view the organization as a whole and to see how its parts relate to and depend on one another.

conglomerate merger Occurs when one firm buys other firms that make unrelated products.

consolidation. *See* amalgamation

consumer buying motives Factors that cause someone to purchase a product for personal use.

consumer finance company A company that lends money to final consumers on their promissory notes.

consumer market Individuals who buy products for their personal use.

consumer orientation An emphasis on identifying the needs and wants of specific consumer groups, then producing, promoting, pricing, and distributing products that satisfy these needs and earn a profit.

Consumer Price Index (CPI) A figure that measures changes in purchasing power and the rate of inflation by expressing today's prices in 1982–1984 dollars.

consumer products Products intended for the personal use of the consumer.

consumerism Activities undertaken to protect the rights of the consumer.

contingent business interruption insurance Insurance that covers a firm's losses when a key supplier's or customer's business is damaged.

continuous process A production method that uses the same machinery to perform the same operations repeatedly over relatively long periods of time.

contract A legally binding agreement between two or more parties obliging them to do or refrain from doing certain acts.

contract purchasing Occurs when a company and supplier negotiate a contract that defines prices, delivery dates, and other conditions of sale.

control unit The coordinating part of a computer, which directs the other parts to perform their respective functions to complete the data processing job.

controlling The management function of establishing standards, measuring actual performance to see whether the standards have been met, analyzing the results, and taking corrective action if required.

convenience goods Products purchased with a minimum of effort.

convenience store A conveniently located store that carries a wide selection of popular consumer items and stays open long hours.

cooperative An enterprise created and owned jointly by its members and operated for their mutual benefit.

cooperative advertising programs Programs in which the manufacturer agrees to pay part of the advertising costs for the product.

copyright A set of legal rights granted to the creator of an original work of authorship, such as an artistic, dramatic, literary, or musical production.

corporate campaign A tactic designed to influence the opinions of a large corporation's suppliers, customers, creditors, directors, stockholders, and the public to bring pressure on the corporation in bargaining with the union.

corporate charter A document issued by a government that contains all information stated in the original application for a charter plus the powers, rights, and privileges of the corporation as prescribed by law.

corporate IOUs. *See* commercial paper

corporation A legal form of business organization created by a government and considered an entity separate and apart from its owners.

correlation An if-then connection between two or more elements in a group of data.

cost of goods sold The cost of obtaining the merchandise that was sold to produce the net sales.

cost-oriented approach Determining price by focusing on costs of merchandise, accompanying services, and overhead costs, and then adding an amount for desired profit.

cost-push inflation Occurs when producers pass rising labor, materials, and other costs on to consumers by increasing prices.

coupon *or* **bearer bond** One with dated coupons attached, which the bondholder cuts off and mails to the company to collect interest.

craft unions Associations of workers with a specific craft, trade, or skill.

credit insurance Insurance that protects a firm against bad debt losses above a maximum amount on trade credit accounts.

credit life insurance A type of term insurance that pays the remainder of a debt if a debtor dies.

credit union A mutual savings and lending society for people with a common bond.

crime A violation of a law passed by a legislative body.

cultural diversity The fact that minorities—African Americans, Hispanics, and Asians—are collectively becoming the majority in the workplace.

current assets Cash, items that will become cash within one year, and prepaid expenses.

current liabilities Debts that must be paid within one year.

current ratio An expression of a firm's ability to pay its current debts from its current assets.

current yield A bond's annual interest expressed as a percentage of the market or purchase price.

customer departmentalization Grouping activities and responsibilities in departments in response to the needs of specific customer groups.

debt capital The long-term capital raised by selling bonds.

decentralization A philosophy of organizing and management that disperses authority within an organizational structure.

decision making The process of identifying problems and opportunities, developing alternative solutions, choosing an alternative, and implementing it.

deductible An amount of a loss that the insured agrees to pay.

delegation The downward transfer of formal authority from one person to another.

demand The quantity of a product that customers are willing to buy at a particular price.

demand deposit. *See* check

demand-pull inflation Occurs when producers raise prices in response to strong consumer demand.

demographics Statistics on such subjects as age, income, marital status, recreational habits, and ethnic customs for people who live within a given geographic area.

demotion A movement from one position to another that has less pay or responsibility attached to it.

Department of Justice An arm of the federal government; works closely with the FTC to preserve competitive markets through investigations by its Antitrust Division.

department stores Stores organized by departments that provide an extremely wide variety of merchandise.

departmentalization The creation of groups, departments, or subdivisions that will execute and oversee the various tasks that management considers essential.

depreciation An accounting technique by which management gradually recovers the cost of expensive fixed assets over the course of their expected lives.

devaluation Increasing the rate of exchange at which foreign currency will be traded for domestic currency.

development Preparing someone for the new and greater challenges he or she will encounter in another, more demanding job.

digital computer A computer that processes exact data according to a set of instructions.

directing The management function that provides leadership, builds a good working climate, and arranges the opportunity for motivation.

disability income insurance Pays a sum of money to be spent as the insured chooses if he or she is unable to work because of illness or injury.

discount The amount by which a bond's par value exceeds its market price.

discount rate The interest rate that the Fed charges member banks for loans.

discount store A store that has low prices, a broad line of merchandise, and limited or self-service.

discrimination Using illegal criteria in hiring.

disparate impact Any part of the employment process resulting in a significantly higher percentage of a protected group being rejected than the percentage of a nonprotected group.

dispatching The production control step in which a production planner releases a job to the first production department on its route.

dividend A portion of company profits paid to stockholders as a return for the risk that they take as owners.

domestic corporation The term applied to a corporation in the state where it is incorporated.

door-to-door retailer. *See* in-home retailer

double indemnity A feature that guarantees that twice the face value of a life insurance policy will be paid if the insured dies accidentally.

Dow-Jones Industrial Average A number that expresses the general trend and condition of the stock market.

downsizing Elimination of positions, layers of middle management, and entire divisions, in response to competition, the economy, and global changes.

draft An instrument completed by a creditor ordering a debtor to pay a specific sum of money.

dumping Selling the same product internationally below the price charged in one's home market for the purpose of disposing of excess production and maximizing total profits.

economic alliances Agreements among independent nations to promote trade.

economic order quantity (EOQ) The point at which the cost of the item and the cost to store it are equal.

economic system The method a society uses to allocate its resources and meet its needs for goods and services.

embargo A government order that prohibits firms from importing some or all of the products made in a given country.

emotional motives Buying reasons that arise from impulse and psychological needs rather than careful thought and analysis.

employers' association A group that represents several companies in bargaining with a union that has organized their workers.

empowerment Giving individuals in an organization autonomy, authority, and trust and encouraging them to break the rules in order to get the job done.

endowment Combines the characteristics of savings and insurance; the policyholder collects a stated sum if he or she is living when the policy matures. The beneficiary receives the amount the endowment was intended to accumulate (the face value) if the policyholder dies before the policy is fully paid up.

entrepreneur An individual who is willing to take risks in return for profit.

entrepreneurship The skills and risk taking needed to combine with the other three factors of production to produce goods and services.

environmental impact study A report describing how a proposed plant will alter the quality of life in an area.

equal employment opportunity Prohibition of discrimination in employment decisions.

equilibrium price The point at which what the consumers are willing to pay is equal to what producers are willing to accept for a product.

equity capital Long-term capital raised by selling stock.

ethics The standards that govern moral conduct—the difference between right and wrong.

exchange functions Buying and selling—activities that relay products to their intended users.

exchange rate The rate at which the money of one country is converted or exchanged for the money of another.

exclusive distribution Limiting distribution to one retailer or wholesaler in a geographic area.

expectancy theory Vroom's theory that before choosing a behavior, an individual will evaluate various possibilities on the basis of how much work they involve and what the reward is.

exporting Selling goods and services abroad.

extended coverage. *See* allied lines

fabrication process A variation of synthetic production in which new products are created from those already manufactured by changing their form.

facilitating functions Financing, risk bearing, obtaining market information, and standardizing and grading.

factoring company A firm that buys a business's open-book accounts (or sometimes consumer credit accounts) and customarily absorbs all losses if the debtors do not pay.

factors of production Inputs or resources used to produce goods and services.

factory outlets Retail stores set up by manufacturers, where they can sell directly to the retail customer.

Federal Anti-Injunction Act of 1932. *See* Norris-La Guardia Act

Federal Deposit Insurance Corporation (FDIC) A public corporation with a threefold purpose: to build confidence in the nation's banking system, insure depositors' account balances, and promote sound bank management.

Federal Reserve Act of 1913 A law that created the Federal Reserve System, commonly called the Fed, and made it responsible for managing the nation's supply of money and credit.

Federal Trade Commission (FTC) A quasi-judicial body empowered to issue cease-and-desist orders against companies whose combinations would significantly lessen competition.

fidelity bond An insurance policy that reimburses an employer for financial loss resulting from employee dishonesty.

Financial Accounting Standards Board (FASB) A group created in 1973 through the joint efforts of the American Institute of Certified Public Accountants and several other accounting organizations to be the overall rule-making body for the accounting profession.

financial analysis The use of mathematics to bring important facts and relationships on accounting statements into sharp focus.

first-line management *or* **supervisors** Managers at the operating level, the lowest level of management.

fiscal year The twelve-month period that a company adopts for financial accounting purposes.

fixed assets. *See* plant and equipment

fixed capital. *See* long-term capital

fixed costs Costs that remain constant regardless of the number of units produced.

flextime A program that allows employees to decide, within a certain range, when to begin and end each work day.

follow-the-leader pricing Occurs when companies do not set prices but react to others' prices.

follow-up The production control step in which production planners monitor each job's progress along its route and deal with any delays or difficulties that occur; also, the final step in the selling process—it builds and maintains customer loyalty and goodwill.

foreign corporation The term applied to a United States corporation in states other than the one in which it is incorporated.

foreign intermediary A wholesaler or agent who performs marketing functions for firms that want to do business in other countries.

foreign-operated sales branch A firm's wholly owned sales organization in a foreign country.

form utility Value created when a firm's production function manufactures a product.

formal organization The official organization that top management conceives and builds.

forward purchasing A policy of purchasing relatively large quantities to fill needs over longer periods of time.

franchise A license sold by one firm (the *franchisor*) to another (the *franchisee*), allowing it to produce and sell a product or service under specific terms and conditions.

free-rein style A leadership approach in which a manager empowers subordinates to function on their own, without direct involvement from managers to whom they report.

front-end load A sales charge applied when mutual fund shares are bought.

fully registered bond One without coupons. The company pays interest automatically to the owner whose name is on record with the firm, and the principal is paid to that person when the bond matures.

functional authority Authority to make decisions about specific activities undertaken by personnel in other departments.

functional departmentalization The creation of departments on the basis of the specialized activities of the business.

General Agreement on Tariffs and Trade (GATT) An international accord setting trade rules.

general partner A partner who has specific authority to act and bind the business, has operational responsibilities, and has unlimited liability.

general partnership An association of two or more people, each with unlimited liability, who are actively involved in a business.

generic brands Products that carry no brand name.

geographical departmentalization Grouping activities and responsibilities for each department according to territory.

glass ceiling Discrimination that keeps women out of upper-level management jobs.

glass wall Discrimination that prevents women from pursuing fast-track career paths.

global *or* transnational corporation A corporation that looks at the world as one market.

goods Items that have a physical presence.

government corporation A corporation organized by a city, county, state, or federal government to serve a specific segment of the population.

grievance A dispute caused by contract violations or different interpretations of contract language.

grievance procedure A series of steps to be followed by an employee who has a complaint about a contract violation.

gross domestic product (GDP) The total market value of all goods and services that a country produces in one year within its national boundaries.

gross national product (GNP) The total market value of all goods and services that a country produces in one year.

gross profit on sales The profit that a company made after deducting cost of goods sold from net sales but before subtracting operating expenses.

group life insurance Life insurance available to employees through their employer on a master policy, usually without a medical examination required.

hand-to-mouth purchasing Purchasing an item in small quantities, as needed.

hardware The five tangible parts or units of a digital computer.

hazardous waste insurance Liability insurance required by the Environmental Protection Agency (EPA) that will provide payment to persons who are awarded compensation for bodily injury and property damage caused by accidents arising from the operation of hazardous waste facilities.

hazardous wastes Waste materials containing toxic substances.

health insurance Insurance that covers medical expenses incurred by the insured and perhaps the insured's family.

home shopping The use of cable television to merchandise products via telephone orders.

horizontal merger Occurs when one firm purchases other firms that produce similar or competing products.

human resources management The staffing function of an organization.

human resources manager A specialist who handles the more technical human resources matters.

human resources planning The process of forecasting the demand for and supply of personnel for an organization.

human skills The ability to interact and communicate with other people successfully.

hygiene factors. *See* maintenance factors

hypermarket A gigantic discount retail complex that combines the features of supermarkets, department stores, and specialty stores under one roof.

import duty. *See* tariff

importing Buying goods and services abroad.

in-home *or* **door-to-door retailer** A retailer that calls on prospective customers in their homes.

in-house versus out-of-house. *See* make versus buy

income statement An accounting statement that summarizes a company's revenues, cost of goods sold (if it sells merchandise), expenses, and net profit or loss over a period of time.

independent retailer A company that operates only one retail store.

index number A quantitative device that condenses or summarizes a body of data with several characteristics into a single numerical expression.

industrial buying motives Factors that cause an industrial buyer to recognize a need or want and to make a purchase that satisfies it.

industrial market Businesses, government agencies, and other institutions that buy products to use either in their operations or in making other products.

industrial products Goods or services purchased for the production of other goods and services or to be used in the operation of a business.

industrial services Items used to plan or support company operations.

industrial unions Associations of workers employed within a given industry.

inflation A decrease in the value of a society's money.

influence The ability to sway other people to one's will.

informal organization A network of personal and social relationships that arises spontaneously as people associate in the work environment.

injunction A court order prohibiting a party from performing unjust, injurious, or inequitable acts.

inland transit insurance Insurance that covers losses caused by catastrophes and acts of God for overland transportation.

input unit The device used to enter data into the computer for processing.

insolvency. *See* bankruptcy

installations Large, expensive capital items that are the major assets of the business.

institutional advertising Advertising done to enhance a company's public image rather than to sell a product.

insurable interest The idea that the policyholder (the person who pays the premiums) must stand to suffer a financial loss before he or she will be allowed to purchase insurance on a given risk.

insurance counselor An adviser who recommends a comprehensive program to protect a firm against insurable risks and to meet legal or quasi-legal insurance requirements.

insurance policy A legal contract that transfers risk from one party (the *insured*) to another (the *insurer*) for a fee called a *premium.*

intensive distribution Widespread market coverage that utilizes a large number of wholesalers and retailers.

intermittent process A production process that shuts down equipment periodically and readjusts it to make a slightly different product.

International Monetary Fund (IMF) An institution that provides assistance for foreign exchange by assisting in stabilizing exchange rates in the world economic community.

intrapreneurship Entrepreneurship happening within the existing boundaries of a formal organization.

inventory control Balancing the need for adequate stock against the costs of purchasing, handling, storing, and keeping records on it; monitoring of the physical inventory of goods, monitoring inventory levels, and minimizing reorder costs.

inventory turnover A calculation of the number of times a firm sold and replaced (or turned over) its average stock of goods during an accounting period.

investment banking firm A firm that purchases an entire issue of new securities from the issuing company as a wholesaler and resells it to the general public.

job analysis A study that determines the duties associated with a job and the qualities needed to perform it.

job description A written document that outlines a job's title, purpose, major work activities, levels of authority, equipment, machines and materials used, and physical demands or hazardous conditions (if any).

job enlargement Increasing the variety or the number of tasks a job includes, not the quality or the challenge.

job enrichment Designing a job to provide greater responsibility, control, feedback, and authority for decision making.

job evaluation A study that determines the worth of a job to an organization.

job redesign The application of motivational theories to the structure of work for increasing output and satisfaction.

job rotation Assigning people to different jobs or giving different tasks to people on a temporary basis.

job sharing *or* **twinning** A program that permits two part-time workers to divide one full-time job.

job shops Companies that make products to customers' individual specifications.

job specification A written document that lists the human dimensions of a job, including the education, experience, skills, training, and knowledge required for a worker to perform the job successfully.

joint venture A partnership established to carry out a specific project or undertaking.

just-in-time (JIT) inventory system An inventory system that delivers parts to the production line exactly when needed.

labor The total human resources required to turn raw material into goods and services.

Labor-Management Relations Act of 1947. *See* Taft-Hartley Act

Labor-Management Reporting and Disclosure Act of 1959. *See* Landrum-Griffin Act

labor union An organization of workers who have united to negotiate their collective wages, hours, and working conditions with management.

laissez-faire *or* **hands-off approach** Occurs when government does not interfere in the economic system.

LAN *or* **local area network** A computer network that connects the computers and printers at one geographic location.

land The natural resources that can be used to produce goods and services.

Landrum-Griffin Act Also called the Labor-Management Reporting and Disclosure Act of 1959. A federal law that defined the rights of union members in regard to internal union operations and access to union organizational and financial information.

law of large numbers *or* **law of averages** A mathematical law stating that if a large number of similar objects or persons are exposed to the same risk, a predictable number of losses will occur during a given period of time.

lead time The time a supplier requires to process and ship an order.

leader pricing Selling attractive items at lower than normal prices.

leadership The process of influencing individuals and groups to set and achieve goals.

leadership style The approach a manager uses to influence subordinates.

leverage *or* **trading on the equity** Occurs when a firm takes advantage of the sound market reputation of its common stock to sell bonds, then uses the capital obtained to improve company operations and earn back a greater return than the interest rate the company pays.

liabilities Debts or creditors' claims that a firm owes on the day the balance sheet is prepared.

licensing An agreement between one company (the *licensor*) and another (the *licensee*) that permits the licensee to manufacture and market a product owned by the licensor.

life insurance Insurance that protects against economic loss resulting from death.

limit order Instructs the stockbroker to buy shares for no more than a certain price.

limited liability A feature inherent in corporations; stockholders' responsibility for debts is restricted to the amount of their investment in the corporation.

limited partners Partners who are legally barred from participating in the partnership's management but have limited liability for debts incurred by the firm.

limited partnership A partnership arrangement in which the liability of one or more partners is limited to the amount of assets they have invested in the firm.

limited-payment life insurance A type of whole life insurance that distributes over a fixed number of years the total premium the insured would pay until death according to the law of large numbers, meaning policy is paid up after a specified period of time though coverage continues until insured's death.

line-and-staff organization A structure that blends into the line organization staff personnel that advise and serve the line managers.

line authority Direct supervisory authority between a superior and a subordinate.

line of credit A maximum amount that a commercial bank agrees to lend to a business borrower if it has the funds available.

line organization A structure in which a straight line of authority originates from the top manager that connects each successive management level until it reaches the operating level.

lobbying Employing persons to influence state and federal legislators to sponsor laws that further one's own interests or inhibit those of one's opponents.

local area network. *See* LAN

lockout A tactic in which management locks the doors and prevents workers from entering the building.

long-term liabilities Debts that are due in more than one year.

long-term *or* **fixed capital** Money used to buy fixed assets, which are long-lived, and (with the exception of land) manufactured items that will be used to produce goods and services for several years.

loss prevention engineer (LPE) An engineer who specializes in removing or reducing risk.

mail-order retailing Asking buyers to order products from catalogs or brochures sent to their homes or via order blanks placed in newspapers and magazines.

maintenance (hygiene) factors Aspects of a job's environment that must be provided in sufficient quality to avoid employee dissatisfaction.

maintenance shop Agreement stipulating that employees do not have to join a union, but those who do must maintain membership for the length of the contract.

major equipment Machinery and large tools used for production.

make versus buy *or* **in-house versus out-of-house** An either-or question: whether to create one's own supply of an essential item or rely on an outside producer to make it.

management The process of setting and achieving goals through the execution of five basic functions that use human, financial, material, and informational resources.

management by objectives (MBO) A technique designed to improve motivation and commitment by having the manager and employee jointly set objectives, assess progress on the objectives, and evaluate the results.

management functions The five broad activities that managers perform to achieve organizational objectives: planning, organizing, staffing, directing, and controlling.

management hierarchy The various levels of management, usually represented by a pyramid arrangement.

management information system (MIS) An organized approach to gathering data from inside and outside the company and (because of the volume involved) processing it by computer to produce current, accurate, and informative reports for all decision makers.

managers People who direct the activity of others.

manufacturing company A firm that converts raw materials and component parts into consumer and industrial goods.

margin The percentage of the total price that the investor must pay out of pocket when buying stocks on margin.

margin buyer A person who borrows part of a stock's purchase price.

market A group of potential customers with the authority, ability, and willingness to purchase a particular good or service that satisfies their collective demand.

market approach A method of price determination that recognizes that variables in the marketplace influence price.

market order Instructs the stockbroker to buy shares at the best available price.

market segmentation The process of dividing a total market into subgroups with similar characteristics and product needs.

marketing A group of interrelated activities designed to identify consumer needs and to develop, distribute, promote, and price goods and services to satisfy these needs at a profit.

marketing channel. *See* channel of distribution

marketing concept A belief that the firm should adopt a company-wide consumer orientation directed at long-range profitability.

marketing mix The effective meshing of product, price, promotion, and distribution strategies to achieve success.

marketing research The facilitating function of gathering, recording, and analyzing data on customer demands and characteristics so that firms can develop new products and sell existing ones profitably.

marketing strategy An overall plan of marketing activities to meet the needs of a market.

markup pricing Calculating all the costs associated with a product and then determining a markup percentage to cover the costs and expected profit.

materials handling The activities involved in physically handling goods while they are in the warehouse.

matrix organization A structure that temporarily groups together specialists from various departments or divisions to work on special projects.

mean. *See* arithmetic mean

median The number that appears midway between the highest and the lowest numbers in an array.

mediation A process by which an impartial person acceptable to both sides in a labor dispute encourages them to communicate, bargain, and work toward a satisfactory compromise.

medical payments A form of motor vehicle insurance that pays the medical bills of the insured and of others the insured has injured while driving a vehicle.

memory unit The computer's electronic warehouse, which stores data as instructed by the program.

merger Occurs when two or more companies become a single enterprise; the controlling corporation retains its identity and absorbs the others.

microprocessor A microscopic maze of circuits etched on a layered piece of silicon a fourth of an inch square.

middle management All managers below the rank of vice-president but above the supervisory level.

minority enterprise small business investment companies (MESBICS) Venture capital firms designed specifically to provide funds to minority-owned businesses.

mixed capitalism An economic system based on a market economy with limited government involvement.

mixed economies Economies in which there is both private and government ownership and production of goods and services.

mode The number that appears most often within an array.

money Any object that a group of people uses to pay its debts and buy the goods and services that it needs.

morale The attitude or feeling workers have about the organization and their total work life.

motion study A study that identifies the number and kind of movements required to perform a given operation.

motivation The result of the interaction of a person's internalized needs with external influences that determine behavior.

motivation factors Aspects of a job that relate directly to the real nature of the work performed and that are necessary to job satisfaction.

multinational corporation A firm that has assets committed to operations and subsidiaries world-wide.

multiple-line coverage. *See* all-risk physical damage

multiple-unit pricing A practice in which a company offers consumers a lower than unit price if a specific number of units are purchased.

mutual fund A pool of stocks, bonds, or other securities purchased by a group of investors and professionally managed by an investment company.

mutual insurance company One owned by its policyholders.

National Labor Relations Act of 1935. *See* Wagner Act

National Labor Relations Board (NLRB) A federal agency authorized to supervise union certification elections and to investigate complaints of unfair labor practices.

nationalization The change from private ownership of an industry to government ownership.

needs Deficiencies that a person experiences at a particular time, creating a tension (stimulus) that results in wants.

negotiable instruments Written promises or requests that certain sums of money be paid to the bearer or to order.

net income The amount of profit that a company earned during an accounting period.

net income before taxes The amount a firm earned from operations before state and federal income taxes are deducted.

network structure A structure in which a small central organization relies on other organizations to perform manufacturing, marketing, engineering, or other critical functions on a contract basis.

no-fault auto insurance Auto insurance that enables the parties to an accident to collect for bodily injury from their respective insurance companies, regardless of who was at fault.

nonprofit corporations Organizations formed to further the interests and objectives of educational, religious, social, charitable, and cultural groups. No stock is issued, but members enjoy limited liability.

Norris-LaGuardia Act Also known as the Federal Anti-Injunction Act of 1932. A federal law that prohibited courts from issuing injunctions against labor's nonviolent protest activities.

North American Free Trade Act (NAFTA) A trade agreement intended to permanently bind the markets of the United States, Mexico, and Canada into a single commercial entity.

objections A potential customer's verbal or silent forms of resistance to the salesperson's message.

objective performance appraisal Appraisal system in which both the performance criteria and the method of measurement are specifically defined.

ocean marine insurance Insurance that protects a cargo against loss on the high seas.

odd lot Less than one hundred shares of a stock.

odd pricing Selecting as prices amounts that fall just below an even number.

off-price retailer A retailer that buys manufacturer's overruns, odd lots, and closeouts and then sells them at deep discounts.

on-site inspection Occurs when the buyer's inspectors examine purchased items throughout the supplier's manufacturing operations.

open-book accounts. *See* trade credit

open corporation A corporation whose stock can be purchased by anyone who can afford the price.

open market operations The process by which the Fed buys or sells billions of dollars of United States government securities daily through securities dealers in New York City.

open shop Agreement stipulating that workers do not have to join the union or pay dues.

operating expenses The value of items or services used or consumed in normal company operations during an accounting period.

order processing The grouping of products specified by the customer and the accompanying paperwork.

organization A group of two or more persons that exists and operates to achieve clearly stated, commonly held objectives.

organization chart A visual representation of an organization's structure and how its parts fit together.

organizing The management function concerned with (1) assembling and allocating the resources necessary to achieve the organization's objectives, (2) establishing the authority relationships of the organization, and (3) creating the organizational structure.

orientation program A series of activities that give new employees information to help them adapt to the company and their jobs.

output unit The part of a computer that presents the processed data in a form that management can use.

outsourcing. The practice of contracting with outside organizations to provide services normally performed inside a company.

over-the-counter market An informal marketplace made up of brokers who communicate by telephone and computer.

participative style A leadership approach in which a manager shares decision-making authority with subordinates.

partnership An association of two or more people who are co-owners of a business for profit.

patent A legal right allowing an inventor to exclude others from making, using, or selling an invention, a design, or a plant for a stated length of time.

patronage motives Buying reasons based on the characteristics of a specific retail outlet or brand of product.

penetration pricing Introducing a product at a low price intended to capture the mass market for the good or service.

performance appraisal A formal, structured system designed (in line with legal limits) to measure the actual job performance of an employee by comparing it to designated standards.

performance bond. *See* surety bond

personal injury protection insurance. *See* bodily injury liability

personal selling A personal attempt to persuade prospective customers to buy a given good or service.

philosophy of management A manager's attitude about work and the people who perform the work.

physical distribution functions Activities involved in transporting and storing goods.

physical distribution system Activities that take place as goods move through channels.

picketing A tactic in which workers publicly air their complaints against an employer by staging a demonstration outside the building, with protest signs and explanatory leaflets.

place utility Value created when marketing makes a good or service available where the consumer wants it.

planning The management function that involves identifying goals and alternative ways of achieving them.

plant and equipment Sometimes called *fixed assets,* an asset category that includes land and expensive manufactured items that a company will use in its operations for several years.

plant closing A tactic in which management stops operations or sells a plant and moves away rather than surrender to labor's demands.

point-of-purchase displays Promotional devices that are placed where sales transactions occur.

possession utility Value created when ownership (or title) is transferred from buyer to seller.

power The ability to exert influence in an organization.

power plant insurance Also called *boiler and machinery insurance,* covers losses caused by an exploding steam boiler, furnace, heating plant, or other equipment.

preapproach The second step in the selling process, in which the salesperson researches the qualified prospect's background.

preemptive right A shareholder's right to purchase shares of a company's new stock issues in proportion with the existing shares that he or she owns, before the new shares are offered to the general public.

preferred stock A class of stock that has a prior or senior claim on assets to that of common stock.

premium In sales promotion, something of value given free or at a nominal charge as an incentive to buy a product. In securities, the amount by which a bond's market price exceeds its par value.

presentation The fourth step in the selling process, in which the salesperson shows how the prospect can benefit by owning the product.

prestige pricing Setting the price high to convey the image of quality.

price The exchange value of a product expressed in monetary terms.

price discounts Deductions allowed from the established price.

price lining Setting distinct prices for the different models in a product line.

primary boycott Occurs when union members agree not to purchase goods or services from the firm they are in dispute with.

primary data Data that a company must gather itself or employ some other firm to gather.

prime rate of interest A lower rate of interest than that charged to most borrowers.

principal The person whom an agent represents.

principle of indemnity The policyholder cannot profit by insurance.

private enterprise system An economic system in which businesses or enterprises are privately owned.

pro forma financial statements Financial statements that forecast expected sales, expenses, profits, and other financial data for a future accounting period.

processing company A firm that converts natural resources into raw material.

product The basic physical offering and an accompanying set of image and service features that seek to satisfy needs.

product advertising Advertising intended to promote demand for a good or service.

product departmentalization Assembles the activities of creating, producing, and marketing each product into separate departments.

product *or* trade name franchise A franchise in which the franchisor allows the franchisee to sell products bearing the franchisor's trademark or logo.

product liability insurance Coverage that protects a firm against financial loss when persons file suit claiming they were injured by its product.

product life cycle The succession of phases including introduction, growth, maturity, and decline of a product in its market.

production A business activity that uses people and machinery to convert materials and parts into salable products.

production control Coordinating the interaction of people, materials, and machinery so that products are made in the proper amount and at the required times to fill orders.

production management The job of coordinating and controlling all the activities required to make a product.

production orientation Belief that the number-one priority is to produce a good to keep up with demand.

production plan A document that contains a list of materials and equipment needed to manufacture a finished product and also specifies which operations will be performed in-house or out-of-house.

production sharing A manufacturing process that integrates production operations along international lines.

productivity The amount of output for a given amount of input.

professional corporation A corporation formed by licensed professionals such as attorneys, physicians, or accountants.

program A software element stored in the memory unit that feeds step-by-step instructions to the control unit, which then commands one of the other hardware units to perform whatever operation is needed.

promissory note A short-term financing instrument, given by a debtor (called the *promisor*) to a creditor (called the *promisee*) as a legal and binding promise to pay a certain sum of money at a future date, usually with interest at a fixed rate.

promotional mix The correct blending of personal selling, advertising, publicity, and sales promotion.

promotions Job changes that lead to higher pay and greater responsibilities.

property damage liability Motor vehicle insurance that pays for damage the insured vehicle does to the property of others.

prospecting The step in the selling process that identifies potential customers for a product.

prospectus A document that presents a company's financial data for several consecutive years, discusses its position in its industry, describes how it will use the funds raised by a securities sale, and summarizes other information that well-informed investors should have.

protectionism An international trade philosophy that favors the creation of barriers against imports, to shelter domestic industries from foreign competition.

proxy A document that authorizes another party to cast a stockholder's votes at an annual meeting when he or she cannot attend in person.

profit The amount of money remaining from a firm's sales revenue after it deducts its total expenses.

public liability insurance Insurance that covers financial loss caused by an injury to a nonemployee that results from the business's negligence and that occurs on its premises.

publicity Nonpaid, nonpersonal communication to promote the goods, services, or image of a company.

pull strategy A strategy aimed at getting consumers to demand that a product be available in the distribution channel.

purchasing agent A company's in-house expert on where to buy various products.

purchasing procedure A series of steps that a company follows when buying products.

pure capitalism An economic system in which economic decisions are made freely according to the market forces of supply and demand.

pure risk A situation that can only become a loss.

push money A manufacturer's commission paid to salespeople for selling one particular brand over all others.

push strategy A strategy directed at the members of the marketing channel rather than the consumer.

quality assurance The production control step in which the product is inspected at various stages along the route to ensure that it meets standards.

quality of work life (QWL) Management efforts focused on enhancing workers' dignity, improving their physical and emotional well-being, and improving the satisfaction of individual needs in the workplace.

quota A limit on the quantity of a foreign product that can be brought into a country for resale.

random sample One in which every member of the universe has an equal chance of being chosen.

rate of return on stockholders' equity The percentage return that the company earned on the owners' investment during the previous accounting period.

ratio A mathematical statement of the relationship or proportion between two elements, derived by dividing one into the other.

ratio of debt to stockholders' equity The value of claims that creditors have against a firm's assets for each dollar of owners' claims.

ratio of net income to net sales A statement of the net income a company earned from each dollar of sales during an accounting period.

ratio of net sales to net income A statement of the amount of sales a firm had to make to earn a dollar of net income.

rational motives Buying reasons that arise from careful planning and analysis of information.

raw materials Natural and farm products that become part of a final product.

reciprocal buying A practice in which two or more companies become mutual customers, buying each other's goods and services.

recruitment The process of locating and attracting a sufficient number of qualified candidates to apply for the jobs that need filling.

recycling The practice of reclaiming or producing materials from previously manufactured products and using them to make other items.

registered bond One whose owner's name is on record with the company and appears on the bond itself.

registrar A commercial bank that monitors the number of shares of stock a corporation sells to ensure that it does not sell more than its charter has authorized.

relative pricing A decision to set prices above the competition, below the competition, or at the same level as the competition.

reserve requirement A percentage of deposits that member banks must retain on deposit within their own walls or at the Federal Reserve Bank in their district.

responsibility The obligation to carry out one's assigned duties to the best of one's ability.

retailers Those who sell products to the ultimate consumer.

retained earnings Profits invested in (or plowed back into) a company for improvements and expansion.

revaluation Decreasing the rate of exchange at which foreign currency will be traded for domestic currency.

revenue Cash or other items received in exchange for merchandise or services.

revolving credit agreement A commercial bank's binding promise that the money will be available if the borrowing firm requests it.

right-to-work laws State laws that allow workers to obtain and keep jobs without having to join or pay money to a labor union.

risk manager A person hired to identify significant pure risks that a company faces and prescribe effective techniques to deal with them.

robot A reprogrammable, multifunctional manipulator designed to move material, parts, tools, or specialized devices through variable programmed motions to accomplish a variety of tasks.

role A set of expectations for a manager's behavior.

round lot One hundred shares of a stock or multiples thereof.

routing The production control step in which a logical sequence is established for the operations that the product must undergo on its way to completion.

S corporation One that may elect, under Subchapter S of the Internal Revenue Code, to be taxed as a sole proprietorship if owned by one stockholder, or as a partnership if owned by several stockholders.

salary Compensation based on weeks or months worked.

sales orientation One in which the energy of a company is focused on selling the products produced.

sales promotion Those paid marketing activities other than personal selling and advertising.

sales finance company A firm that provides short-term capital to retailers (and sometimes to wholesalers) by purchasing the installment sales contracts (promissory notes) that they have accepted from customers.

sample A cross section of a total group that has the same distribution of characteristics as the larger group (or *universe*) whose characteristics are being explored.

sanctions Penalties such as fines, suspension, or termination.

savings account *or* **time deposit** A sum of money, deposited with a bank, that cannot be withdrawn by writing a check.

savings and loan associations (S&Ls) Thrift institutions that accept time deposits and lend them to a variety of borrowers, especially to buyers of single-family homes.

savings bank A thrift institution that accepts time deposits and lends them for a variety of purposes, but especially for home purchase and construction.

scheduling The production control step that allots time for each operation along the route.

secondary boycott Pressure aimed at businesses that buy from or sell to a firm that is engaged in a labor-management dispute.

secondary data Data that currently exist; they have been recorded somewhere, and management need only go to the source.

selection The process of deciding which candidates out of the pool of applicants have the qualifications for the jobs to be filled.

selective distribution Utilizing a moderate number of retailers and wholesalers.

self-directed work team A work team that sets its own goals, creates its own schedules and budgets, and coordinates work with other departments.

self-insurance fund A special fund of cash and marketable securities used to pay for losses caused by natural disasters such as fire, flood, and earthquake.

selling process A series of seven steps that salespeople follow when persuading prospective customers to make purchases.

separation The departure of an employee from an organization.

service bureau A firm that processes clients' data on its own computer (or one that it has access to) for a fee.

Service Corps of Retired Executives (SCORE) A volunteer organization of over 13,000 active and retired higher managers who advise small-business owners in conjunction with the Small Business Administration.

service mark A mark or words used in sales or advertising literature to distinguish a firm's services from those of its competitors.

services Activities that benefit consumers or other businesses.

sexual harassment Unwelcome sexual advances, requests for sexual favors, or verbal or physical conduct of a sexual nature on the job.

shareholders *or* **stockholders** A corporation's owners, but frequently not the individuals who control and manage the firm day to day.

shopping goods Items purchased after comparative shopping based on quality, design, cost, and performance.

short seller A person who borrows stock from a broker and sells it, hoping to replace the borrowed shares at a lower price if and when the market price declines.

short-term *or* **working capital** Money spent on business operations covering a period of a year or less.

single-source purchasing Buying a product from one company only.

sinking fund A special fund a company creates and pays money into over the life of a bond issue so dollars will be available to pay off the bonds when they mature.

skimming Charging a relatively high price when a product first appears on the market.

Small Business Administration (SBA) A federal government agency started in 1953 to give financial and managerial assistance to owners of small businesses.

social audit A report on the social performance of a business.

social responsibility A belief that business decisions should be made within the confines of both social and economic considerations.

socialism An economic system in which the government controls the operation and direction of basic industries, but there is also private ownership.

software All elements of a computerized data processing system other than hardware.

sole proprietorship A business owned by one individual.

span of control The number of subordinates under the direction of each manager.

specialist A person who works at a stock exchange to maintain an orderly market and facilitate trades among brokers.

specialty advertising Providing "frequent reminder" items that build goodwill and keep a firm's or product's name within the prospect's view.

specialty goods Items that buyers prefer strongly because of their unique characteristics or image.

specialty store A store that offers many models or styles of a specific product.

speculative risk A situation that may cause loss or gain.

staff authority Authority to serve in an advisory capacity.

staffing The management function that attempts to attract good people to an organization and keep them.

stakeholders Those people who have an interest in or are affected by how a business conducts its operations.

standard of living The degree of material wealth in a country.

statutory law A written body of rules created and approved by a group of persons (generally referred to as a *legislature*), which presumably expresses the will of the citizens it represents.

stock certificates Documents that provide legal evidence of ownership of shares in a corporation.

stock dividend A distribution of shares of the company's stock or the stock that it owns in other firms.

stock exchange A gathering place where the representatives of buyers and sellers of securities meet to make trades.

stock insurance company One owned by stockholders.

stock split A subdivision of shares already issued, done to decrease a stock's high market price to an amount that more investors can afford to pay.

stockbroker A person who buys or sells securities for members of the general public.

stockholders. *See* shareholders

stockholders' equity The balance sheet section that shows owners' claims against a corporation.

straight life insurance A type of whole life insurance in which premiums are paid until the insured's death.

stratified random sample One that divides the universe into subcategories, or *strata*, according to one or more characteristics and chooses randomly from within the strata being examined.

street name account A situation in which the broker keeps your securities and sends you a statement each quarter for your records.

strike A temporary work stoppage by employees to bring pressure on management to meet their demands.

strikebreakers Workers who perform jobs until striking workers come to terms with management.

subjective performance appraisal Appraisal system in which the performance criteria and rating scale are not defined.

supermarket A store that provides a wide variety of food items along with a limited amount of household goods in a large, self-service facility.

superstore A giant retail store that sells food and nonfood items but also additional product lines that are purchased routinely.

supervisors. *See* first-line management

supplies Items necessary in the daily operation of a business.

supply The quantity of a product that producers are willing to make available at a given price.

surety bond Sometimes called a *performance bond;* insurance that guarantees that a contract will be completed.

surplus lines coverage Insurance for risks on which no law of large numbers exists.

synthetic process Production method in which materials are combined to form a certain product.

Taft-Hartley Act Also known as the Labor-Management Relations Act of 1947. A federal law that defined specific unfair labor practices by unions, established emergency strike procedures, and prohibited unions from charging excessive or discriminatory fees or dues.

target market The particular customer group at which the company will aim its marketing activities.

tariff *or* **import duty** A tax imposed on imported goods.

team structure A structure that organizes separate functions into a group based on one overall objective.

technical skills Knowledge of and ability to use the processes, practices, techniques, and tools of the specialty area a manager supervises.

term insurance Life insurance that pays only if the insured dies during a specified period of time.

test marketing Introducing a product in strategic geographic locations, rather than everywhere, to assess consumer response.

Theory X A philosophy of management with a negative perception of subordinates' potential for work and attitudes toward work.

Theory Y A philosophy of management with a positive perception of subordinates' potential for and attitudes toward work.

time deposit. *See* savings account

time sharing A form of computer use in which several firms buy or rent access to a computer that is owned by another firm.

time study A study that determines the amount of time an average worker takes to perform a given operation.

time utility Value created when a product is made available when consumers want and need it.

top management The organization's most important manager—the chief executive officer or president—and his or her immediate subordinates, usually called vice-presidents.

tort A private or civil wrong or injury committed against a person or property for which a court will award damages if the wronged party (called the *plaintiff*) can submit adequate proof that the accused wrongdoer (called the *defendant*) was guilty, through either negligence or intent, of committing the act in question.

total costs The total of fixed costs and variable costs.

total quality management (TQM) A comprehensive effort to improve the quality of every department's product or service and achieve increasingly higher levels of customer satisfaction.

total revenue A figure determined by multiplying price times the number of units sold.

trade character A brand mark that has a human quality.

trade credit *or* **open-book accounts** Business charge accounts that a selling firm gives buying firms.

trade name franchise. *See* product franchise

trademark A brand name, brand mark, or trade character that has legal protection.

trading on the equity. *See* leverage

training Supplying the skills, knowledge, and attitudes needed by employees to improve their abilities to perform their jobs.

transfer agent A commercial bank that records changes in names and addresses for a corporation each time stocks and certain types of bonds are traded.

transfers Lateral moves from one position to another having similar pay and a similar responsibility level.

transnational corporation. *See* global corporation

transportation The modes or means of shipping goods.

transportation insurance Covers loss of cargo from hazards such as contamination, spoilage, theft, fire, breakage, or collision while in transit.

unfair labor practices Actions designed to keep workers from joining a union.

Uniform Commercial Code (UCC) A comprehensive body of business law that encompasses various kinds of transactions.

uninsured motorist protection Coverage that pays the insured for bodily injuries caused by at-fault but uninsured or underinsured drivers and by hit-and-run drivers.

union shop Agreements stipulating that a company's new employees must join a union within a certain number of days after being hired in order to keep their jobs.

union steward An employee who has been elected by fellow union members to serve as their representative.

unity of command The requirement that each person in an organization take orders from and report to only one person.

universal life insurance A highly modified form of whole life insurance in which part of the premium buys insurance coverage that will be paid if the insured dies. The rest of the premium is invested in high-yield securities that are intended to increase the policy's cash

value more rapidly than that of a traditional whole life policy.

unlimited liability The fact that a sole proprietor is personally responsible for any debts or damages incurred by the operation of the business.

urban renewal programs Intensive efforts by businesses to refurbish old plants or offices or build new ones in cities, thus providing jobs and improving the city's economic health.

utility The ability of a good or service to satisfy a consumer need.

variable costs Costs that arise when the first unit is produced and that increase with production.

vending-machine retailing Distribution of products to consumers by coin-operated or card-operated machines.

venture capital firm A company that buys stock in new firms that make products or offer services with strong profit potential.

vertical merger Occurs when one firm unites with others that contribute to its product's manufacture or distribution.

wages Compensation based on hours worked.

Wagner Act Also called the National Labor Relations Act of 1935. A federal law that encouraged the formation of unions by prohibiting management from interfering with employees' rights to organize, join, or assist a union.

WAN *or* **wide area network** A computer network that connects computers and printers across great distances.

warehouse clubs Member-only stores that provide a broad range of name-brand merchandise at deeply discounted prices.

warehousing Receiving, identifying, and sorting goods.

warrant A document that conveys the preemptive right to existing stockholders.

warranty A document that states certain facts and conditions about a product's operation and correct use and clarifies the limits of its performance under various circumstances.

whistle-blowers Individuals who take action to inform their bosses, the media, or government agencies about unethical practices within their organizations.

whole life insurance Policy that remains in effect for the insured's entire life; pays on death.

wholesalers Those who sell products to other sellers of goods.

wholly owned foreign subsidiary A set of manufacturing and distribution facilities located in a foreign country but owned by a parent company located elsewhere.

wide area network. *See* WAN

workers' compensation insurance Pays part of an employee's wage or salary plus medical expenses, and any necessary rehabilitation, retraining, job placement, or counseling, if a worker is accidentally injured on the job or contracts a job-related disease.

working capital. *See* short-term capital

World Bank An institution established in 1946 to lend money at low interest rates to developing countries.

yellow dog contract An agreement by workers, as a condition of employment, that they will not join a union.

yield to maturity The percentage return an owner receives if a bond is held until it matures.

zoning ordinances City and county regulations defining the type of business activity that can be conducted at certain locations.

NAME AND COMPANY INDEX

SUBJECT INDEX

PHOTO CREDITS

All chapter-opening photos by Craig McClain.

Chapter 1
7: Courtesy Cambridge Eye Doctors; 9: Gail Meese/Meese Photo Research; 21: Culver Pictures, Inc.; 23: Owen Franken/Stock Boston.

Chapter 2
33: Courtesy U.S. Department of Veterans Affairs; 35: Robert Brenner/Photo Edit; 40: Courtesy Rockwell International; 45: Stephen Frisch/Stock Boston; 49: Courtesy Chemical Manufacturer's Association; 54: Courtesy McDonald's Corporation.

Chapter 3
69: Courtesy Ben & Jerry's Homemade Inc.; 73, 78: Gail Meese/Meese Photo Research.

Chapter 4
91: Courtesy Apple Computer, Inc.; 93: Courtesy Huntington Bancshares Inc.; 100: Catherine Ursillo/Photo Researchers, Inc.; 110: Gail Meese/Meese Photo Research; 112: Bob Daemmrich/Stock Boston.

Chapter 5
119: Courtesy Howda Designz, Inc.; 122: Richard Pasley/Stock Boston; 126, 139; Gail Meese/Meese Photo Research; 135: Blair Seitz/Photo Researchers, Inc.

Chapter 6
155: Courtesy Teknekron Pharmaceutical Systems; 166: Will & Deni McIntyre/Photo Researchers, Inc.; 171: Bill Horsman/Stock Boston.

Chapter 7
185: Courtesy Radius; 196: Peter Menzel/Stock Boston; 204: Blair Seitz/Photo Researchers, Inc.; 206: Michael Newman/Photo Edit.

Chapter 8
219: Courtesy United Communications Group; 228: Kip Brundage/New England Stock Photo; 234: Bob Daemmrich/Stock Boston; 242: Frank Siteman/Stock Boston; 251: Gail Meese/Meese Photo Research.

Chapter 9
259: Courtesy Johnson & Higgins; 265: Seth Resnick/Stock Boston; 286: Jon Riley/Tony Stone Images, Inc.; 291: Lee F. Snyder/Photo Researchers, Inc.

Chapter 10
299: Courtesy Saturn Corporation; 301: Allen Zak/Meese Photo Research; 309: Earl Dotter/Meese Photo Research; 314: AP/Wide World Photos; 323, 325: Jim West/Meese Photo Research; 327: Courtesy AFL-CIO.

Chapter 11
339: Courtesy GE Transportation Systems; 341: Peter Menzel/Stock Boston; 346: Courtesy Volusia County Business Development Corporation; 348: Courtesy Honda of America Mfg., Inc.; 353: David Parker/600-Group/Science Photo Library; 364: Delco/Photo Edit.

Chapter 12
373: Courtesy Salomon North America, Inc.; 375, 390: Gail Meese/Meese Photo Research; 385: Courtesy Stouffer Foods Corporation; 386: Courtesy The Pillsbury Company; 391: Courtesy Mobil Oil Corporation; 394: Courtesy California Avocado Commission.

Chapter 13
405: Courtesy Sarah Rolph Communications; 415: Gail Meese/Meese Photo Research; 418: Courtesy Minolta Corporation; 419: Courtesy Komatsu Company; 421: Culver Pictures, Inc.; 423: Courtesy American Honda Motor Company, Inc.; 426: Courtesy SmithKline Beecham Consumer Brands; 427: Courtesy The Pillsbury Company, "Bake-Off"® is a registered trademark of The Pillsbury Company.

Chapter 14
437: Courtesy Mid Atlantic Cycle Specialties; 448, 449, 462: Gail Meese/Meese Photo Research; 452: Richard Pasley/Stock Boston.

Chapter 15
473: Courtesy New London Trust; 477: Courtesy U.S. Bureau of Engraving and Printing; 481: N. R. Rowan/Stock Boston; 484: Gail Meese/Meese Photo Research; 491: Ellis Herwig/Stock Boston.

Chapter 16
499: Courtesy Black Diamond Equipment, Ltd.; 505: David Young-Wolff/Photo Edit; 509: Charles Gupton/Stock Boston; 518: Courtesy The Cincinnati Gas & Electric Company; 522: Courtesy Federal Express Corporation.

Chapter 17
541: Courtesy Transamerica Insurance Group; 544: John Elk III/Stock Boston; 556: Eric R. Berndt/New England Stock Photo; 563: AP/Wide World Photos.

Chapter 18
579: Courtesy Cambridge Technology Partners, photo by Fredrik D. Bodin; 586: Rhoda Sidney/Photo Edit; 600: Joe Sohm/Chromosohm/Stock Boston; 603: Charles Feil/Stock Boston.

Chapter 19
617: Courtesy Association of Certified Fraud Examiners; 621: John Coletti/Stock Boston; 624–625: Courtesy Ben & Jerry's Homemade, Inc.; 630: Peter Menzel/Stock Boston.

Chapter 20
649: Courtesy Cordoba Corporation; 652: Billy E. Barnes/Tony Stone Worldwide, Ltd.; 659 (clockwise): Courtesy The Pillsbury Company, "Green Giant" is a registered trademark of The Pillsbury Company; Courtesy Microsoft Corporation; Courtesy General Electric Company; Courtesy Ben & Jerry's Homemade, Inc.; 664: Frances M. Roberts/Meese Photo Research.

Chapter 21
677: Courtesy Psion, Inc.; 679: Courtesy Federal Express Corporation; 688: Tony Freeman/Photo Edit; 693: Charles Gupton/Stock Boston; 697: Mark Richards/Photo Edit; 700: Peter Menzel/Stock Boston.